Campus Lodging Guide

B & J Publications

I

Campus Travel Service

Disclaimer

B & J Publications has researched all sources to insure accuracy and completeness of this guide. We cannot however be responsible for last minute college revisions, errors, rate changes, or inaccuracies reported to us by lodging providers and other contributors. On occasion, a few of the YMCA's, colleges or hotels, motels and inns will undergo maintenance and refurbishing projects and will not be available for occupancy.

To Our Readers

Thank you for purchasing our book and we hope your travels are enjoyable and rewarding. In researching this book, the authors have stayed at many colleges, B&B's, and hotels. Overall our experiences were positive, but we would like to hear from our readers about any experiences you have (good, bad, or indifferent) while using facilities listed in our guide.

If you find a facility that is not listed properly, or if your have any suggestions or comments about this book, please call or drop us a note.

19th Edition
Copyright: 1999, Campus Lodging Guide
(Formerly, Budget Lodging Guide & U.S. and Worldwide Travel Accommodations Guide)

B & J Publications
aka
Campus Travel Service
Post Office Box 5486
Fullerton, CA 92838-0486
(714) 525-6683, (800) 525-6633 Fax: (714) 525-6625
Website: www.campus-lodging.com
E-mail: bjpubs@campus-lodging.com

ISBN: 0-945499-10-8
ISSN: 0898-4247
Printed in the United States of America

CONTENTS

TRAVELERS' INFORMATION
CONTENTS

CURRENCY STRATEGIES OVERSEAS

CASH: Dollars are the easiest currency to exchange when traveling overseas, and are practically a necessity if you are traveling to Eastern European Countries. Exchange rates are based on a lower retail rate and can vary widely. Deal only with an "Official" Exchange or Bank. Changing money on a street corner with someone offering you a higher rate is not only foolish, but illegal in many countries. If you must carry large sums of cash, consider a money belt.

CREDIT CARDS: Credit cards are convenient to use, replaceable if lost and can get you a cash advance. When you use credit cards, you get the wholesale exchange rate extended to large international banks. But there are some disadvantages; travelers can never be sure what the exchange rate will be on the charge, and some banks may charge a conversion fee.

AUTOMATIC TELLER MACHINES: Using Automatic Teller Machines will get you the wholesale exchange rates of big bank. Most domestic cards tied into international networks such as Plus, Cirrus and Interlink can be used, and there is usually a service fee. As with credit cards, there is no way of knowing beforehand what exchange rate is being applied. Before you leave home, ask your bank to give you a list of all ATM's available on your network worldwide.. For Cirrus systems call, (800) 424-7787. The PLUS system, call (800) THE-PLUS. Currently PLUS only lists U.S. and Canadian ATM locations.

TRAVELER'S CHECKS: Traveler's checks are nearly as negotiable as cash, and will work in regions where credit cards are virtually unknown and Automatic Teller Machines are non-existent. Unlike cash, they can be replaced if lost or stolen. To exchange U.S. currency into local currency, there's usually a purchase fee, as much as $10.00 whether you change $50 or $500, so it pays to exchange as much as you feel you will need.

TRAVELER'S CHECKS IN FOREIGN CURRENCY: If you buy Traveler's checks in foreign currency before leaving the United States, you can lock in the exchange rate and they have the same safety replaceability as regular traveler's checks. There is no transaction fee to convert them to currency. These are available only before leaving the U.S. and are not available in all currencies. There may also be an initial purchase fee, and the exchange rate is based on retail rates. A transaction fee, plus a lower exchange rate may apply when converting back to dollars.

TIPS: To minimize exchange costs, use ATM cards to obtain cash in foreign currency, or use credit cards for your purchases. Shop around for the best exchange rate when converting dollars and traveler's checks to local currency. The exchange rate may vary widely. Keep some small U.S. bills with you when traveling. They come in handy for tipping tour guides, luggage handlers, hotel personnel, etc. (U.S. currency is welcomed almost everywhere!)

No/Low-Cost Sightseeing
Factory Tours Make a Fun and Educational Addition To Any Vacation

Factory and Company Tours can be a real vacation saver for parents and children who have had enough of museums, monuments, etc.

Planned in advance, these tours can be an exciting low or no-cost addition to your vacation.

Local tourist bureaus and Chamber of Commerces might suggest places you might otherwise miss.

We've listed a few sights to get you started. This is only a sample of what's available across the country. If you are interested in a product or company, call and ask if they offer free tours. (Hint: check AT&T's 800 directory for toll-free numbers)

Dreyer's Ice Cream Factory, 12250 Whiple Road, Union City, CA (Near San Francisco)

Basic Brown Bear Factory, 444 De Haro St., San Francisco, CA. The tour specialty is a chance to Stuff your own teddy bear.

Levi Strauss Factory, 250 Valencia St., San Francisco, CA. Levis made at this factory end up in Japan.

Fortune Cookie Factory, 261 12th St. Oakland, CA

Golden Gate Fortune Cookie Co., 56 Ross Alley, off Washington St., San Francisco, CA. Sample bags of Fortune Cookies are offered to visitors at the end of the tour.

Jelly Belly Jelly Beans, 2400 N. Watney Way, Fairfield, CA, (just north of San Francisco). See large mosaic portraits of famous faces and figures such as Ronald Regan and the Statue of Liberty, each made of 14,000 jelly beans.

Anheuser-Busch, Inc., in Merrimack, NH, Everett Turnpike, exit 10 at 221 Daniel Webster Highway. Tour of the brewery, sampling room, and children will love seeing the Clydesdale Horses

Hershey's Chocolate Factory, 120 S. Sierra, Oakland, CA. Watch Hershey Kisses chocolates being made and wrapped in their foil covers.

On trips to Chicago try; **The Chicago Mercantile Exchange, The Chicago Tribune** newspaper, or the **Chicago Board of Trade**.

Olympia Brewery, in Tumwater Washington, just off Interstate 5 Freeway. Tour of brewing rooms, bottling areas, and sampling room.

Saturn Corp. Visitors Center, 100 Saturn Parkway, MDB 20, Springhill, TN 37174

Toyota Motor Works, 1001 Cherry Blossom, Georgetown, KY 40324. Home of the Toyota Camry and Avalon. Reservations required. Tours on Tuesdays and Thursdays at 8:30, 10:00, 2:00PM and 6:00PM. (502) 868-2000

Cranberry World Visitors Center, 225 Water St. Plymouth, MA. Information on the history, cultivation and uses of the cranberry. Open daily; 9:30-5:00.

Although the following are not companies or factories, the publishers all agree, the best bargain in free sight-seeing can be found in our Nation's Capitol. You might start your visit to Washington D.C. with stops at the **Lincoln Memorial, Jefferson Memoria**l, the **Washington Monument**, the **Vietnam Wall**, and **Arlington National Cemetary**.

Don't forget the **White House**, the **Capitol Building**, **The Supreme Court, National Archives** (Declaration of Independence), **Ford's Theater**, and a favorite with the kids, the **FBI Building**.

The **Smithsonain Museums** have something for everyone in the family and they're all free.
The Air & Space Museum is favorite with kids of all ages.
The National Museum of Natural History/National Museum
National Museum of American History
National Gallery of Art
The National Portrait Gallery
The National Zoo

Going to Boston? Don't forget the **USS Constitution (Old Ironsides)**, the oldest commissioned warship in the US Navy, (open every day except Thanksgiving, Christmas, and New Years Day) guided tours daily 9:30-3:50, self-guided top deck tours 3:50 to sunset, or the **Bunker Hill Monument**, in Bunker Square. The 221 foot granite obelisk has exhibits of the Battle of Bunker Hill at the base, and a spiral staircase to the top. Open daily, 9-4:30

I
N
F
O

AIRFARE SAVINGS

1. Buy your tickets during an airfare sale even if you do not have an exact date you want to travel. Most airlines will let you change the date of travel or the destination for a small or moderate fee. (Ask about the airline's policy before purchasing)

2. Buy tickets 7, 14, 21or 30 days in advance, stay over Saturday night. These tickets are usually non-refundable, but can be 50% cheaper than refundable tickets bought just before traveling.

3. Choose a discount airline if convenient, Reno Air, Southwest or America West, etc.

4. Fly a competitive route, routes traveled by several airlines are cheaper than routes controlled by one airline.

5. The cheapest fares are usually Monday noon through Thursday noon. You have a better chance of finding a lower fare if you begin and end your trip mid-week. Some airlines will often discount flights on Saturdays before 7PM or after 9PM.

6. Discount tickets: Check out consolidators. These are wholesale travel agents that sell cut-rate tickets directly to the public or through certain travel agencies. Check the travel section of your Sunday paper for Consolidator ads. If possible, always pay with a credit card when dealing with Consolidators. On the West Coast, try Sunline Express (800) 786-5463 or (415) 541-0623; Midwest, try Travel Ave. (800) 333-3335, East Coast try, Globe Travel Specialists (800) 969-4562, Fax: (212) 682-8605.

7. Most major U.S. airlines sell senior discount travel coupons, each good for one flight segment within the continental United States. The coupons are valid for one year and are available to travelers over age 62. (two coupons are needed for flights to Alaska and Hawaii) Flights using coupons are eligible for frequent flyer mileage.

8. Lowest rates to Europe are from September 15 to May 14, and there are still low cost summer charter flights available.

I N F O

9. Check out airfares from all the airports close to where you live. Choosing an alternate airport could save you money, even if you have to drive further.

10. Air travellers can hold-down expenses by flying routes involving one or more stops, as opposed to non-stop routes.

11. For up-to-date information on charter flights to Europe, call Caitybird, (888) 248-9247; Condor, (800) 524-6975; Martinair Holland, (800) 366-4655; New Frontiers, (800) 366-6387; Pleasure Break, (800) 777-1566; Travel Charter, (800) 521-5267.

12. Low Cost Flights to 25 Destinations in Europe: UniTravel is a leading tour operator (20 years in business) that purchases thousands of airline seats at low bulk rates. The reservation center operates Monday through Saturday, and delivers tickets by Federal Express. Passengers have the option of staying aboard for as long as a year and can fly to one city and return from another. For a free brochure write to: UniTravel, P.O. Box 12485, St Louis, MO 63132; (800) 325-2222, Fax: (314) 569-2503.

ROUND THE WORLD TICKETS (RTW). Few travelers know about this option and airlines are not aggressive in marketing them. The RTW prices are nothing short of "incredible". The only condition is that you circle the globe in one direction. Fares start at around $2200 for economy, up to around $5000 for first class depending on the miles traveled. Try Delta, (800) 221-1212; United, (800)538-428-4322; Singapore (800) 742-3333; TWA, (800) 892-4141; or Swissair (800) 221-4750. These prices do not include the South Pacific, Africa or South America. Travel to these destinations starts at around $2900 for economy, up to $6200 for first class. **CAUTION:** Your travel agent may be less than enthusiastic about marketing the RTW option. Since the tickets cost less, the agent's commission is reduced, and the work involved is substantial.

AIRLINE TOLL FREE PHONE NUMBERS

Aeroflot	(888) 340-6400
Aerolineas Argentines	(800) 333-0276
AeroMexico	(800) 237-6639
Aeroperu	(800) 777-7717
Air Afrique (Air France)	(800) 456-9192
Air Canada	(800) 776-3000
Air Europa	(888) 238-7672
Air France	(800) 237-2747
Air India	(800) 223-7776
Air Jamaica	(800) 523-5585
Air New Zealand	(800) 262-1234
(ATA) America Transair	(800) 225-2995
Air Tran	(800) 247-8726
Alaska Airlines	(800) 426-0333
ALM Antillean	(800) 327-7230
Alitalia	(800) 223-5730
ANA-All Nippon	(800) 235-9262
Ansett Austrailia	(800) 366-1300
Aloha Airlines.	(800) 367-5250
Alpha Air	(888) 276-1599
American Airlines and American Eagle	(800) 433-7300
American Transair (ATA)	(800) 225-2995
ANA All Nippon Airways	(800) 235-9262
America West	(800) 235-9292
Aspen Mountain Air (formerly Lone star)	(800) 877-3932
Australian	(800) 922-5122
Austrian	(800) 843-0002
Avianca	(800) 327-9832
Bahamasair	(800) 222-4262
British Airways	(800) 247-9297
British Midland Airways	(800) 788-0555
BWIA International	(800) 538-2942
Canadian Airlines	(800) 426-7000
Carnival (now Pan Am)	(800) 437-2110
Cathay Pacific	(800) 233-2742
Cayman Airways	(800) 422-9626
China Airlines	(800) 227-5118
Continental Airlines (Domestic)	(800) 525-0280
Continental Airlines (International)	(800) 231-0856
Canadian	(800) 426-7000
Conquest Airlines	(800) 722-0860
Delta (Domestic)	(800) 221-1212
Delta (International)	(800) 241-4141
Ecuatoriana	(800) 328-2367

Egyptair	(800) 334-6787
El Al Israel	(800) 223-6700
Faucett	(800) 334-3356
Finnair	(800) 950-5000
Hawaiian	(800) 367-5320
Iberia	(800) 772-4642
Iceandair	(800) 223-5500
Japan Airlines	(800) 525-3663
Korean Air	(800) 438-5000
KIWI	(800) 538-5494
KLM	(800) 374-7747
Kuwait	(800) 458-9248
LACSA	(800) 225-2272
Lan Chile	(800) 735-5526
LAP Air Paraguay	(800) 677-7771
LOT Polish	(800) 223-0593
Lufthansa	(800) 645-3880
Malaysian	(800) 552-9264
Malev Hungarian	(800) 262-5380
Mexicana Airlines	(800) 531-7921
Northwest (Domestic)	(800) 225-2525
Northwest (International)	(800) 447-4747
Olympic	(800) 223-1226
Philippine	(800) 435-9725
Qantas	(800) 227-4500
Reno Air	(800) 736-6247
Royal Air Maroco	(800) 344-6726
Royal Jordanian	(213) 233-0470
Saudia	(800) 472-8342
Singapore	(800) 742-3333
South African	(800) 722-9675
Southwest	(800) 435-9792
Swissair	(800) 221-4750
TAP Air Portugal	(800) 221-7370
Thai	(800) 426-5204
Tower Air	(800) 221-2500
TWA (Domestic)	(800) 221-2000
TWA (International)	(800) 892-4141
United (Domestic)	(800) 241-6522
United (International)	(800) 538-2929
US Air (Domestic)	(800) 428-4322
US Air (International).	(800) 622-1015
Varig	(800) 468-2744
Viasa	(800) 468-4272
Virgin Atlantic	(800) 862-8621

I
N
F
O

TRAVEL BARGAINS

MOTORHOME RENTALS - ENGLAND, GERMANY, FRANCE. Rent a motorhome with space for four persons. Comes equipped with kitchen and linens, along with a list of hundreds of campsites. Pop top to full sized campers available. Call Foremost Eurocar, 5658 Sepulveda Blvd. #201 Van Nuys, CA 91411. Toll free: (800) 272-3299.

OVERNIGHT BARGAIN IN THE BIG APPLE: Don't drop $175 or more a night on a skimpy double room at a name hotel. Weekend rates for a comfortable suite in the most desirable and convenient parts of New York start at $65.00 a night per person, double occupancy, subject to availability. The hotels recommended are under one management and in the same general area; the Eastgate Tower, 39th St. between 2nd and 3rd Avenues; the Beekman Tower, 49th St. and 1st Avenue (opposite United Nations); and the Shelburne-Murray Hill at 37th and Lexington. They offer gracious, spacious two and three room apartments on weekends for 60% of their normal weekday rate. Kitchens come equipped with dishwasher, microwave oven and large refrigerator, pots and pans, dishes, glassware, cutlery and coffeemaker with complimentary coffee & tea. Everything is immaculate. For reservations and further information about these three hotels, call (800) 637-8483.

WORK PERMITS FOR OVERSEAS: Information on work permits for Canada, England, France, Ireland, New Zealand, West Germany, Costa Rica, can be obtained from: Council Travel Services, 10904 Lindbrook Dr., Los Angeles, CA 90024. Ph: (213) 463-0655. Student Discounts: Also available from CIT for $16 is an International Student Identity Card which provides discounts up to 50% for air, land, sea transportation, bus tours, movies and merchandise. Students receive a booklet listing all discounts. Important Plus: Purchase of the ID card automatically provides both life and health insurance as long as the ID card is valid.

FIJI ISLANDS: The original "Affordable Fiji" budget accommodations, situated in prime locations: convenient central locations in suva and Lautoka and delightful beach front properties on the west coast and Coral Coast. Accommodation includes city and beach self-contained apartments, hotel accommodations, Youth Hostel rooms, three bed dormitories and sea side bungalows. Prices start from F$8.80 per person per night including Government Tax of 10%. All are close to public transport. For more information, please contact; Affordable Fiji, P. O. Box 2086, Government Buildings, Suva, Fiji Islands. (679) 340-211, FAX: (679) 340-236.

NEW ZEALAND: YHA New Zealand's network of 58 hostels provide clean comfortable and affordable accommodation in fantastic locations throughout New Zealand. Priced from only $NZ10.00/night per person. Hostels offer twin, double or multi-share rooms, modern kitchen and laundry facilities, lounge areas and TV rooms, and can assist you with domestic travel and activity bookings. For further information, contact YHA New Zealand, P. O. Box 436, Christchurch, New Zealand Ph: 64-03-379-9970, FAX: 64-03-365-4476. Email: info@yha.org.nz Website: www.yha.org.nz

NEW YORK CITY: A free 70-page directory containing more than 200 hotel packages in New York City. Programs include museums, sightseeing, dinner. As little as $32 per person per night. Some accommodations with kitchenettes, free parking. Visitors take in Greenwich Village, Harlem, Radio City Music Hall, South Street Seaport, the empire State Building, Rockefeller Center, the U.N., Lincoln Center. Copies of the directory from the New York Convention & Visitors Bureau, Tour Package Directory, 2 Columbus Circle, New York, NY 10019.

I N F O

LOW COST JAPAN: The Welcome Inn Reservation Center, a free service offered by JNTO, will arrange accommodations in Western-Style economy, hotels, ryokan (Japanese-Style Inns), Minshiku (Bed & Breakfast), and pensions. Prices start at about $40 for a single, $80-$100 double. Call or write, Japan National Tourist Office, One Rockefeller Plaza, Suite 1250, New York, NY 10020, (212) 757-5640, to request a directory.

STATE AND NATIONAL PARK CAMPING: Camping in the beautiful ocean front or pine forest state parks of California ranges from $14 to $21 per night. For reservations, call (800) 444-7275. The Colter Bay Village offers overnight tent-rustic camping accommodations for $22.00 a night for two people in Grand Teton National Park, Wyoming. Also available are log cabins with private bath at $55-$77 per night for two people as well as RV hookup facilities at $23 per night. Ph: (307) 543-2855.

WILD WEST DUDE RANCHES: It is still a great horseback riding country, but ranches also now offer a variety: whitewater rafting, float trips, fishing, hiking, sightseeing to ghost towns and places of special interest, and always relaxation amidst western space and beauty. For a copy of the 1996 Dude Ranchers' Association Magazine/Directory that lists & describes 100+ Western dude ranches, located in 13 western states and 2 Canadian Provinces, send $5.00 to: The DRA, P.O. Box C471, La Porte, CO 80535. Ph:(970) 223-8440, Fax: (970) 223-0201

FREE USE OF AUTOMOBILES ANYWHERE IN THE USA OR CANADA: Auto Driveaway Co. delivers cars to cities through out North America. The company wants travelers over age 21 with a valid U.S., Canadian or International drivers license as drivers. When you assist Auto Driveaway in driving one of their late model cars, you benefit with: free use of car, no rental or mileage charges, free tank of gas, maps and routings, and an insured car. Your only expense is part of the fuel. If you take 3 guests, you divide your expenses by 4. See Glacier National Park, the Grand Canyon or the Florida Keys. Auto Driveaway has offices in 33 states, 5 provinces of Canada and 80 metropolitan centers. Write, or phone, or Fax them. They will send you full particulars on this unique opportunity. Auto Driveaway Co., 310 So. Michigan Ave., Chicago, Ill. 60604, Ph: (800) 346-2277, FAX: (312) 341-9100. Other possibilities: Driveaway Service (800) 775-0464.

WHITE HOUSE TOURS: Free tickets for special VIP tours when you're in Washington D.C. can be obtained by writing to your Senator or Representative at the Senate or House of Representative Office Bldg., Washington, D.C. 20510.

SAN MIGUEL de ALLENDE, MEXICO: MI CASA B&B; For comfort loving Americans, rooms at $65 & $85 on a flower-filled roof garden, a couple blocks from the center of town. MI CASA serves a healthy homecooked breakfast and provides shopping, dining and sightseeing tips. Write to: Carmen McDaniel, Canal 58, APDO 496, San Miguel de Allende, Guanajuato, Mexico. Ph: 52-415-2-24-92, Fax: 52-415-2-01-21 Email: tism@mpsnet.com.mx

WORRY-FREE RESERVATIONS IN WASHINGTON D.C.: Free service to book you in a luxury, first class, or budget hotels - will assist in price and location. Recommend calling in advance: Washington D.C. Accommodations, 2201 Wisconsin Ave NW Suite C-110 Washington D.C. 20007. Ph: (800) 554-2220 between 8:30 A.M. and 5:30 P.M. EST., Monday through Friday. Fax: (202) 338-4517 Email: wdca@worldnet.att.net Web: www.dcaccommodations.com

RAILROAD BUFFS: Explore America Fares: Amtrak is offering roundtrip excursion fares for 30 consecutive days of travel with up to 3 stopovers within one region. One region starts at $209.00; two regions $279.00; and three regions $339.00. Sleeping accommodations are extra. Summer fares will be slighty higher. Amtrak offers all travelers age 62 and older a 15% discount on all fares, including sale and All Aboard fares. Many European rail pass issuers also offer senior discounts. Ph: (800) 872-7245.

PARIS APARTMENT RENTALS: Longer stays are less expensive with apartment/house rentals. Sources to contact: PARIS CONNECTION, 301 N. Pine Island Rd., Suite 106, Fort Lauderdale, FL 33324. (305) 475-0615, or in Paris 43-54-64-66. PARIS CONNECTION specializes in central Left Bank locations and includes a two hour orientation to Paris and a transportation pass good for unlimited use of Paris bus & subway with rental of each apartment.

VILLAS IN ITALY: Looking for apartment, villa, farmhouse rentals in Italy? Suzanne Pidduck, Rentals in Italy, represents 1,500 properties in Tuscany (Florence), Umbria (Perugia), the Veneto, (Venice) Rome and Sicily. Most are available for short- term (weekly) rentals; however she also handles several long-term rentals. (monthly) Contact Pidduck at 1742 Calle Corva, Camarillo, CA 93010. Phone toll-free: (800) 726-6702. Fax: (805) 4821-7976.

CONDOMINIUM & HOME RENTALS IN HAWAII: Hundreds of homes and condominiums offered, ranging in price from $50 a night for two persons to an ocean view condo for 4 persons at $80 per night. Daily, weekly, monthly rates available. Hale Hawaiian Apartment Leasing, 479 Ocean Ave., Suite B, Laguna Beach, CA 92651. Free illustrated brochure. Ph: (714) 497-4253; toll-free (800) 854-8843, Fax: (714) 497-4183

CRUISE DISCOUNTS: One of the nation's leading cruise discounters can save you $600 to $2,000 per cabin. Some 2-for-1 cruises on the books. Specializes in Caribbean, Alaska, Mexico, South Seas and Europe. Get a free booklet, The World of Cruising, from The Cruise Line Inc., 150 NW 168th St., North Miami Beach, FL 33169 Ph: (800) 777-0707.

EUROPE ECONOMY CAR RENTALS, LEASING, SELLING: For information on prices, pickup locations, models. Toll free: Europe-by Car, Ph: (800) 223-1516; Auto Europe (includes Eastern Europe Ph: (800) 223-5555; Foremost Eurocar, (800) 272-3299.

NEW LONDON, ENGLAND HOSTEL: A new 320-bed Rotherhithe Hostel, near the Rotherhithe subway stop. Open to all ages. All rooms en-suite, cafeteria, kitchen, currency exchange and sight-seeing service. Cost per person, per night from $27 B&B. Rotherhithe Youth Hostel, Salter Rd., Rotherhithe, London, England SE 16 1PP. Britain/UK, Ph: 44-0171-232-2114, FAX: 44-0171-237-2919.

THE AFFORDABLE TRAVEL CLUB: The Affordable Travel Club for travelers over the age of 40 is an exciting new concept in travel- a private home bed and breakfast. Members stay in other members' homes paying only a gratuity to cover costs. Host members (genuinely friendly people who enjoy offering their extra bedroom and breakfast to fellow travel members) pay a gratuity of $15 single or $20 double to another host member when they travel. Non-hosts pay the host member $25 single or $30 double. Members are located throughout the United States, Canada, and 21 countries overseas. Membership dues are $50 for the Host member and $90 for the Non-host member per year. The Club sends each member a Directory of members and quarterly Supplement/Newsletter updating new memberships. The Club has other advantages. A yearly cruise or tour for members, opportunites to house or house/pet sit are also offered. Members with pets can travel without putting their pet in a kennel by having another Club member come to their home & petsit for them. There is no charge (gratuity) for this service. House & pet sitting listings (stating a need for a sitter or willingness to sit) are printed in Directory and Newsletters. For a free brochure, send a stamped self-addressed envelope to Affordable Travel Club, 6556 Snug Harbor Lane, Gig Harbor, WA 98335.Ph/FAX; (253) 858-2172; Email: atcmiller@Jund.com

HELP IN PLANNING YOUR NEXT VACATION

VISA REQUIREMENTS -FAST SERVICE: To learn what countries require visas, a booklet "Foreign Entry Requirements" tells all. Send 50¢ to: Consumer Information Center, Box 438T, Pueblo, CO 81009. VISA SERVICE. Need a visa, passport photo, or passport renewal in a hurry? Contact Intercontinental Visas, LA World Trade Center, 350 So. Figueroa St., Suite 185, Los Angeles, CA. 90071 Ph: (213) 625-7175. Fax: (213) 714-7170 Service charge varies from $30.00 and up depending on the country.

GIVEAWAY GUIDE: A North American Travel Guide featuring color maps of the 50 states, the Caribbean, Canada and Mexico and an atlas with color maps of 14 European countries are available from Best Western International, P.O. Box 10203, Phoenix, AZ. 85064-0203. Specify whether you want the "North American Travel Guide," the "European Travel Guide"-or both. No postage necessary. Call toll-free (800) 528-1234.

TOLL-FREE TRAVEL NUMBERS: You can easily obtain toll-free number for any airline, hotel, car rental company and some embassy tourist offices by calling AT&T 800 Directory Assistance, 1-800-555-1212, and asking for a particular airline or other office in which you are interested.

DIRECTORY OF ENGLISH SPEAKING PHYSICIANS THROUGHOUT THE WORLD: Information on immunization requirements, tropical diseases, climatic & sanitary conditions are available from IAMAT. Write to International Assn. for Medical Assistance to Travelers (IAMAT) 417 Center St., Lewiston. NY 14092 (716) 754-4883. IAMAT is a non-profit organization that accepts voluntary contributions.

DUTY-FREE SHOPPING: Visitors to Latin America, Africa or Asia can bring back many kinds of products - candy, dishes, jewelry, perfume and more without paying customs duties, under a little-known U.S. program designed to help the economies of developing nations. The program is known as the Generalized System of Preferences, or GSP. Some products, such as ivory and other items made from endangered species of animals and plants may be prohibited from entering the U.S. A free pamphlet, "GSP and the Traveler", explains how the system works. Write U.S. Customs, 1301 Constitution Ave., Washington, D.C., 20229

FOREIGN CURRENCY BY MAIL: Save time and money by purchasing foreign currency in cash & travelers checks before leaving home. Ruesch International offers bank notes from more than 120 countries and commission-free American Express travelers checks in most major currencies. To order call (800) 424-2923, or the office nearest you. (in NY, LA, Washington DC, Chicago, Atlanta, or Boston) Free pocket currency guide with each order.

RAIL TRAVELERS: European railway timetables and Eurail Travelers Guide, along with fold-out map of European rail system with discounts and reduced fare bonuses. Request both from: Eurail Pass, P.O. Box 10383, Stamford, CT 06913.

TO GET YOUR MAIL WHILE YOU'RE TRAVELING: If you're traveling in Europe without advance hotel reservations, it's helpful to make arrangements for having mail or messages sent to you. There are two ways to do it. **American Express** offices in many European cities hold letters for owners of its traveler's checks. A local office can supply you with a booklet that gives addresses of offices handling client mail-look for "full service" listings. **European** post offices will hold mail addressed to you in care of Poste Restante, although some charge a small fee for the service. To make sure your mail doesn't get lost in the shuffle, have correspondents address you by your name as it is written on your passport and underline your last name. And if you're sure you're due a letter and nothing turns up, ask the postal clerk to look under your first name too. Also check the main post office in the city or the one near the main railroad station.

CROSSING BORDERS: Americans who frequently cross the Mexican and Canadian borders can bring home $25 worth of duty-free goods daily. To qualify for the exemption, all items must accompany the traveler and be for personal or household use. Those who travel less often can bring up to $400 worth of goods under the new law, but can only do that once every 30 days. For those returning from a U.S. Possession, the limit is $1,200.

INTERESTED IN FREIGHTER CRUISING? Free booklet, "35 Most Commonly Asked Questions About Freighter Travel" from Cruise and Freighter Travel Assn. Travel Tips Magazine, has features on freighter travel, expeditions and unusual cruises. Published bimontly, $40.00/year. Travel Tips. Flushing, NY 11358. Ph: (800) 872-8584.

US EMBASSY HELP OVERSEAS: Your U.S. Embassy can: (1) replace lost passports in 24 hours: (2) provide a list of English-speaking doctors and dentists, and help secure medical treatment; (3) help you get legal help if you are arrested; (4) assist your return to the USA if you run out of funds.

TELEPHONE CREDIT CARD: When abroad, you can phone the U.S., using a calling card furnished free of charge from your local telephone company. The phone company has a free booklet that shows you how to avoid high surcharges on overseas calls. Ask the operator for a brochure and card application forms.

PROOF OF CITIZENSHIP: A drivers license alone is no longer proof of citizenship in many Caribbean countries, Mexico and the Bahamas. Always carry your passport with you whenever you travel outside U.S. Borders.

OVERSEAS STUDY OPPORTUNITIES

WORK, STUDY, TRAVEL ABROAD: The Whole World Handbook. Compiled by the Council on International Educational Exchange (CIEE) and published by St. Martin's Press. 12th edition, 1994, 605 pages. $13.95. In addition to work and travel information, the handbook includes hundreds of listings for study abroad programs in Africa, Asia, Australia, Europe, and Latin America. **STUDENT TRAVELS** magazine (Free) is a full color magazine providing information on a wide range of topics relating to studying and traveling abroad. To order either of these publications, contact, CIEE, Publications Dept., 205 East 42nd Street, New York, NY 10017, Tel: (800) 349-2433

SPEAK A NEW LANGUAGE: For many Americans, the most rewarding experience of travel is living abroad with a native family and learning the language. Courses and home stays are available in major European countries, Japan and Latin America. Total immersion in a language-speaking the foreign language with the natives after daily course work-promises the best results. The cultural interchange adds more to the value of your visit. The National Registration Center for Study Abroad represents over 100 universities and privately-owned language schools in 30 countries. For a free newsletter, write or call: NRCSA, P.O. Box 1393, Milwaukee, WI 53201. Ph: (414) 278-0631.

FRIENDS OF WORLD TEACHING: More than 1,000 English-language oriented schools and colleges in about 100 countries offer teaching and administrative opportunities to American and Canadian educators. Positions exist in most all fields, on all levels. Salaries vary from school to school, but in most cases they are comparable to those in the U.S. Vacancies occur and are filled throughout the year. Nursing opportunities for registered nurses are also available. Foreign language knowledge is seldom required. Contact Friends of World Teaching, P.O. Box 1049, San Diego, CA 92112. Ph: (619) 299-1010

TRAVEL FOR ACADEMIC GROWTH: A student or working educator can earn 1-6 college credits on an independent basis while studying specific aspects of American or foreign cultures. Your own objectives can be partially met by completing an Academic Log or Project Journal of your journey which emphasizes the events of each day that contributed to teaching enrichment or academic growth. For information, contact: James Galloway, Faculty/Director, Travel for Academic Growth, Goddard College, Plainfield, VT 05667. Ph:(802) 454-7835,(800) 468-4888. He will send you a catalog outlining all the facts about travel for academic enrichment, including sample entries for your journal.

LANGUAGE 2 TRAVEL STUDY PROGRAMS; Learn a Language/Worldwide Locations: An educator or student, can earn 1 - 6 college credits on an independent basis while studying specific aspects of American or foreign cultures & a language.. Your own course objectives can be met by completing an Academic Log or Project Journal of your journey which emphasizes the events of each day that contributed to teaching enrichment or academic growth. Both undergraduate and graduate credit available. Open enrollment all year long. For information, contact: Steven Tash, Travel/Study Program, P.O. Box 16501, Irvine, CA 92623-6501, Ph: (714) 552-8332, 9:00am - 9:00pm. Fax: (714) 552- 0740 Email: travelstudy@jumo.com Website: www.ioc.net/-travelstudy.

4 UNIQUE OPPORTUNITIES TO TEACH OVERSEAS: Current openings in American overseas schools ... also special opportunities in Australia, Japan, England and others. Location of the 12 annual Teacher Recruiting Fairs.Write to: EIS, 4523 Andes Dr., Fairfax, VA 22030

VACATION STUDY ABROAD: More than 1,800 programs for adults are open to Americans interested in international study. Included in the book are costs, housing, dates, locations and deadlines. Price, $36.95+$5.00 handling, IIE Books, Institute of International Education, P. O. Box 371, Annapolis Junction, MD 20701-0371. Fax: (301) 206-9789, Email: iiebooks@pmds.com

INTERNATIONAL UNIVERSITIES, established in 1980, is a private educational organization dedicated to providing the highest quality in foreign language and intercultural studies. Programs are offered in Puebla, Mexico; Nice, France; Slazburg, Austria; Florence, Italy; Quebec, Canada and Albuquerque, New Mexico. Intensive immersion language courses in Spanish, French, Italian, German, and English are primarily scheduled during the summer months, although year round options are available in some countries. International Universities' programs are comprehensively designed to provide participants with travel planning assistance, housing accommodations in the host country, university credit, cultural excursions and weekend tours, plus many special activities in addition to the scheduled classes. International Universities' programs are open to all interested adults. High school students may attend some of the programs with organized school groups. For further details and registration information contact: International Universities, 1101 Tijeras Ave. N.W., Albuquerque, NM 87102, Ph: (800) 547-5678.

HOME STAY LANGUAGE STUDIES: One call and you can be signed up for language studies in Costa Rica, and Mexico. These study programs are tied in with home-stays with families. A four week program starts at $962 and includes tuition, family stays and all meals. Air fare is extra. For a detailed brochure contact: Language Studies Enrollment Center, 13948 Hemlock Dr. Penn Valley, CA 95946. (916) 433-7690, FAX: (916) 432-7615. (Specify the country you wish to visit.)

HOME EXCHANGE PROGRAMS

Now it's popular to choose from an unlimited variety of home-swaps; an apartment on the Left Bank of the Seine in Paris, a cottage in the English Cotswolds, a studio in Tahiti, an Irish farm, a condo in Hawaii, a one-room hunting lodge in Bavaria's Black Forest, or a Swiss chalet. Cars, child-care arrangements, and even maid service are often part of the swap.

An estimated 20,000 travelers will swap homes this year, saving as much as $125 per day on hotels, restaurant meals, and car rentals. A recent home swapper said: "Our four family members had a memorable and educational vacation in Hawaii, and our home was in great shape when we returned. Our estimated savings, $4,000."

The following services charge a small fee for registering your home and sending out an exchange directory. Some agencies charge a fee for putting an exchange match together and providing auxiliary services:

VHR WORLWIDE: Offering luxury villas, apartments, condominiums and private islands throughout The Bahamas, Bermuda, The Caribbean, Central America, Europe, Mexico and the U.S. Call toll-free from U.S. and Canada, (800) NEED-A-VILLA or (800) 633-3284, (201) 767-9393. To fax inquires; (201) 767-5510.

Intervac U.S. Part of the largest & oldest worldwide home-exchange network. It publishes five catalogues a year, containing more than 10,000 homes in more than 50 countries. Members contact each other directly. The $78 cost, plus postage, includes the purchase of two of the company's catalogues (which will be mailed to you), plus the inclusion of your own listing in whichever one of the two catalogs you select. If you want to publish a photograph of your home, it costs $15 extra. The third, fourth & fifth catalogues cost $40, $30 & $30 respectively. Hospitality and rentals are also available. P. O. Box 590504, San Francisco, CA 94159. (415) 435-3497, or toll free in the U.S. (800) 756-HOME. Fax; (415) 435-7440 Email: intervacus@aol.com

Worldwide Home Rental Guide: Hundreds of villas, houses, condos, castles to rent. Caribbean, Bahamas, Europe, USA, Mexico, and Latin America. Photo and profile of property with address and rates. Contact the owners directly. Subscription cost, $18. Worldwide Home Rental Guide, 1112 San Pedro NE Suite 105, Albuquerque, NM 87106 Ph: (505) 255-4271

Worldwide Home Exchange Club - 1,500 homes worldwide with new listings in the U.S., Europe, New Zealand, Australia, Africa, and Eastern Europe. Fee $29. Worldwide Home Exchange: 50 Hans Crescent, London SW1X 0NA , PH: 44-0171-589-6055 or in U.S., 806 Branstford Ave., Silver Spring, MD 20904. PH: (301) 680-8950

Teacher Swap, Inc.- A home swap program exclusively for active, retired, or former teachers. Now entering its 12th year, Teacher Swap had 988 listings from 43 U.S. States, 3 Canadian Provinces, and 36 foreign countries or possessions. A majority of its 610 overseas listings came from France, Spain, England, Germany and Italy. Over 2400 listings in last three years. For **FREE** information, call or fax: (516) 244-2845, or write, Teachers Swap, P.O. Box 454, Oakdale, NY 11769-0454.

Belgium: Taxistop (Jan Klussendorf), Onderbergen 51, B-9000 Ghent, Belgium (32) 91-2232310, Fax: (32) 91-2243144

Great Britain: HomeLink International (Heather Anderson), Linfield House, Gorse Hill Road, Virginia Water, Surrey GU25 4AS, Phone & Fax: (44) 1344.842642,

Canada: HomeLink International (Jack Graber), 1707 Platt Crescent, N.Vancouver, BC V7J IX9, Canada   TEL/FAX: (1) 604-987-3262, E-Mail: jgraber@direct.ca or canada@homelink.org, Web Site www.homelink.org

Czech Republic: HomeLink International (Dr. Alena Klirova), Zitomirski 39, 10 100 Praha I0, Czech Republic, (42) 2-722856

Denmark: Dansk BoligBytte, HomeLink International, (Peter Eberth), Box 53, DK-2900 Hellerup, Denmark (45) 39 61 04 05, Fax: (45) 31 62 0525.   BED & BREAKFAST ALSO AVAILABLE. Email: bed@bbdk.dh

Sweden: Svensk Bostadsbyte, HomeLink International (Peter Eberth), Box 53, DK 2900 Hellerup, Denmark, Ph: 45-3961 0405, FAX: 45-39-610525, E-mail: bed@bbdk.dk. See Internet website for other cheap accommodations in Denamrk. www.bbdk.dk

France: Homelink International- France: (Lilli Engle), C/O American Center, Bel Ormeau 409, Ave.Jean Paul-Coste, 13100 Aix-en-Provence, (33) 42 38 42 38, Fax: (33) 42.38.95.66

Germany: Holiday Service (Manfred Lypold), Seehofstr.50, D-96117, Memmelsdorf 1, Germany (49) 951-43055, Fax: (49) 951-43057, Email: 095143055-0001GT- online.de

Greece: Greece Eurotourism Systems; HomeLink International (Michael Lucas), Mantzarou 5, 106 72 Athens, Greece, (30) 01-3626994, Fax: (30) 01-3626994 & 01-3600389. Family vacations in Greece and the Greek Islands arranged to the specific requirements of clients. Selected hotels, Pensions, B&B's, self-catering studios, apartments, bungalows, & Villas. "Island Hopping Holidays, Inter-Island Excursions, and "Special Interest" Group Holidays- Painting, Rambling, Archaeological, Scuba Diving. Car & bike rentals, yacht charters, luxury crewed yachts and bare boats. (sailing yachts) Charters for 4-12. Transfer Service-All visitors will be met on arrival by one of EuroTourism Guides.

Hungary: Home Exchange International (Laszlo Sovago), 6 Tinodi St., 4200 Hajduszoboszlo, Hungary, (36) 525-2376

Ireland: Homelink International Ireland, (Marie Murphy), 95 Bracken Drive, Port Marnock, Co., Dublin, (353)1-8462598, Fax: (353)1-8460305

Israel: Israel Home Exchange (Fanny Kuhn), 44 Louis Marshall Str., Tel Aviv 62000, Isreal (972) 3-6045407

Italy: Homelink Italia, Casa Vacanze, (di Edoaedo Pujatti),Viale Frassinetti,84 31046 Oderzo, Italy (39) 75-5728662, Fax: (39) 422-815575 Email: casavacanze@oderzo.nettuno.it

Netherlands: They send immediately by airmail their weekly list with extensive up to date domestic listings from Amsterdam and the rest of the Netherlands after receiving your fax or email with creditcard number, month of exp. and subscription amount of $50.00. L. O. V. W. , Postal Box 70.155, NL-9704 AD Groningen, Netherlands, ph: (31) 50-313-2424 FAX: (31)50-313-3177.

New Zealand: HomeLink International (Neil Smith), I Higham Ferrers Pl., Red Beach, Hibiscus Coast, New Zealand (64) 942-64084, Fax: (64) 0-9-4264084, Email: homelink@ihug.co.nz

Portugal: HomeLink Portugal (Julie de Wolff), Chacara dos Lobos-Janes, Malveira de Serra, 2750 Cascais, Portugal, (351) 1 487 2428, Fax: (351) 1 487 2455, E-mail: botzi@ibm.net

Slovakia: HomeLink International (Ing. Dana Drabova), Limbova, 18, 831 01 Bratislava, Slovakia, (42) 7-377103

South Africa: International Home Exchange (Connie Booth), PO Box 23188, Clairemont, Cape Town 7735, South Africa, (27) 21-614334

Switzerland: Holiday Exchange Schweiz, Asylstrasse 24, CH-8810 Horgen, Switzerland, Ph: (41) 1-7251047.

U.S.A.: Homelink, (Karl Costabel), P.O. Box 650, Key West, Fl, 33041, (800) 638-3841, (Toll free, USA & Canada), Ph: (800) 638-3841, International: (305)-294-7766, Fax: (305) 294-1448.

Hotel Discount Reservation Service

Travelers can save up to 30% over corporate rates by using Hotel Reservation Services. These services operate by booking blocks of rooms at a lower price and passing on the savings to the public. Simply call one of the services listed below with your destination, room requirements, price range, etc.

There is no charge for this service.

Travel Planner .... (800) 221-3531
Hotel Reservation Network .... (800) 964-6835
Express Hotel Reservations .... (800) 356-1123
Washington DC Accommodations ..... (800) 554-2220
San Francisco Reservations .... (800) 677-1550
Capitol Reservations .... (800) 847-4832

MAJOR CAR RENTAL AGENCIES

Auto Europe .... (800) 223-5555
Avis Rent a Car .... (800) 331-1084
Budget Rent a Car .... (800) 472-3325
European Car Res. .... (800) 535-3303
EuroDollar (Dollar in U.S.) .... (800) 800-6000
Eurocar (National in U.S.) .... (800) 227-3876
Europe By Car .... (800) 223-1516
  in Los Angeles .... (213) 272-0424
  in New York .... (212) 581-2235
Eurorent .... (800) 521-2235
Foremost Euro-Car .... (800) 272-3299
Hertz .... (800) 654-3001
The Kemwel Group .... (800) 678-0678
Renault Eurodrive .... (800) 221-1052
  West Coast .... (800) 477-7116

COLLEGE LIFE FOR THE YOUNG AT HEART

ELDERHOSTEL: Low-cost adventures in learning can be yours through Elderhostel, a Boston-based organization affiliated with over 2000 different colleges and universities. The programs for those over 55 years old have been expanded to cover five continents: Australia, Asia, Europe, North and South America. (70 countries) Most programs are one week long. The programs start at $320, and include registration, five days of classes, six nights accommodations (dormitory style) extra-curricular activities and meals. Costs for overseas programs vary with each country. Participants may enroll for up to 3 courses per program. No homework or papers are required, just a willingness to learn and enjoy the experience. Elderhostel catalogs are available at each public library and branch facility in the United States. For more information and to get on the mailing list, write to Elderhostel, 75 Federal St., Boston, MA 02110. A catalog of complete offerings is available from: Elderhostel, P. O. Box 1959, Wakefield, MA 01180-5959. Ph: (617) 426-8056, Fax: (617) 426-8351, Email: cady@elderhostel.org   Catalogues are published 8 times yearly. Spaces in popular locations such as New England go quickly, so second and third choices are suggested. Website:www.elderhostel.org

SENIOR VENTURES: Senior Ventures offer one to four week programs for seniors over 50 in six western states, Arizona, California, Colorado, Oregon, Texas, and Washington. You can learn about Shakespeare, art, computers, river rafting, flyfishing, bird watching, bridge, Native American Culture, geology, international travel, and much more. In addition to academic courses, Senior Ventures programs are designed to acquaint you with the area. There is sightseeing, local theatrical productions, lectures, music performances and other activities. All faculty members are experts in the subjects they teach. Program fees include meals, housing, classes and activities. Prices vary with length of program selected and type of accommodations. A deposit of $100.00 per session is required to hold your space in a specific program. Contact: Senior Ventures, 1-(800) 257-0577 for brochure.

SENIOR SUMMER SCHOOL, INC: Senior Summer School is a unique program that was created to offer active Seniors a challenging and satisfying way to avoid the summer heat. Senior Summer School currently has programs in Madison, WI; Santa Barbara, CA; San Diego, and Los angeles, CA; Orono, ME; Odgen, UT; and New Brunswick, Canada. The programs take place in the summer months and range in length from 2,3,4,6,8, or 10 weeks. Over 1500 Seniors are accepted into the program. The participants live in private residence halls which include two-bedroom suites with private baths, private rooms with a community bath, and fully furnished apartments. Participants have the opportunity to take part in university courses, establish new relationships, and explore the area on the many day and weekend trips that are planned. Cooking and housekeeping are included. You'll find the program price is modest when compared to similar programs starting at only $499 for 2 weeks. For more information about a Senior Summer School program, call (800) 847-2466, or write to P.O. Box 4424, Deerfield Beach, FL 33442-4424, or visit website: www.seniorsummerschool.com. Early reservations are recommended as most accommodations are sold out by early spring.

INTERHOSTEL: Interhostel is an educational experience and concentrates on providing interesting and high quality lectures and excursions for intellectually alert and physically active mature adults 50 years or over. Now in its 16th year of operation, Interhostel, developed by the University of New Hampshire Continuing Education department, offers more than 40 travel/study programs in 25 countries. Interhostelers should be prepared to experience the culture of the country they are visiting and not expect to live as they do at home. For information or reservations call: (603) 862-1147, or (800) 733-9753, or write Interhostel, University of New Hampshire, 6 Garrison Ave., Durham, NH 03824-3529.

PASSPORT INFORMATION

All U.S. citizens must have passports for identification while traveling abroad and for re-entry into the United States. No person may have more than one valid U.S. passport of the same type at any one time. Download PDF versions of all applications at www.travel.state.gov/download_applications.html., or write to: National Passport Center, P.O. Box 371971, Pittsburgh, PA 15250-7971

FIRST-TIME PASSPORT APPLICATIONS: When applying for your first U.S. Passport, apply in person at a Clerk of the Court or Post Office which accepts passport applications. You will need the following documents: •Proof of United States citizenship: a certified copy of a birth certificate, a certificate of naturalization or an expired U.S. passport. •Proof of identity (photo ID with signature) •Two recent identical passport photographs. Photographs must be 2x2 inches on a plain white background. Photographs must be front view, full face, regular dress, no hat or dark glasses. •A completed passport application form DSP-11.

PASSPORT RENEWALS: Requirements: If issued within 12 years, applicant was at least 16 yrs. old at the time and if name has not changed. Applicant can apply for a new passport by mail if they can submit their passport, or they may apply in person. Documents required for passport renewals include: U.S. Passport, Two passport photos and a completed passport application (form DSP-82). Previous passport will be returned with new passport.

Mail application and attachments to: National Passport Center, P.O. Box 371971, Pittsburgh, PA 15250-7971

Overnight delivery, send to: Attn: Passport Supervisor, 371971, 3 Mellon Bank Center, Rm. 153-2723, Pittsburgh, PA 15259-0001

FEES: Passport fees for an initial ten-year passport are $60 (over 16 years of age and $40 for a five-year passport if under 16. Passport renewal fees are $40. Make your check or money order payable to Passport Services.

WHEN TO APPLY: Processing time varies, usually three to four weeks, but apply 4-6 weeks before any scheduled international travel. Apply in the fall when workload volume is less.

EMERGENCY PASSPORT: For an emergency trip within five working days: apply in person at the nearest passport agency. Show tickets, travel itenerary and other required items. Or, send application overnight mail and enclose a self-addressed, prepaid envelope for the overnight return of the passport. Include fees payable to passport Services and dates of departure and travel plans. Applications are processed by the departure date indicated on the application form. If you are leaving the country in less than 15 work days, enclose a $35 expediting fee, in addition to the overnight mail fee, and mark the envelope "EXPEDITE."

OBTAINING ADDITIONAL VISA PAGES: Request a 48-page passport at the time of application or send passport with a signed request for more pages to one to the passport agencies.

CHANGING YOUR NAME ON YOUR PASSPORT: To change name, have current, valid passport amended with the new name. Mail passport with Court Order, Adoption Decree or Marriage Certificate showing name change, and a completed passport application form DSP-19 to the nearest Passport Agency. Application must be signed in new name.

INVALID COUNTRIES: Currently, the U.S. passport is not valid for travel to Libya, Lebanon and Iraq.

PASSPORT AGENCIES have limited 24-hour recordings which include basic information. For additional information: U. S Department of State's Passport Information web site: http://travel.state.gov/passport_services.html (click Passport Web button below). Call 900-225-5674 (35cents/minute) for passport information recording, or $1.05/minute to talk to an attendant.

Pre-Trip Planning: Always carry your passport when traveling abroad, even if one is not required to enter the country. Before you leave home, make 2 copies of your passport identification page.

Safeguard Your Passport: Take it out only when you need it for official use.   There are several travel accessories which can help keep your personal items safe.   One person should never carry all the passports for an entire group. Never lend your passport to anyone, use it as collateral, or ask someone to hold it for you. Make two copies of it before you leave home. Leave one copy home with friends. Keep one copy in your handbag or an exposed pocket. If possible have your passport locked in the hotel safe. Waist wallets, neck wallets, leg stashes etc. are available at companies such as Magellan's or Travel Smith.

How to Replace a Lost or Stolen Passport: Immediately contact the nearest police authorities, U.S. embassy or consulate. You will be asked to fill out a DSP-11 form, which is the standard passport application form. You are not required to know the passport number or issuance date to apply for a new passport. If the passport is still valid, you must also complete the DSP-64 form to report the lost or stolen passport. This form must be submitted with the DSP-11 application. Both of these forms can be downloaded and printed from the State Department web site.

Passport Required? A valid passport is required of U.S. citizens departing from the United States for any destination outside of North, South or Central America, and for entering the United States from outside of North, South or Central America. A passport is not required for travel by U.S. Citizens to any territory or waters, subject to the jurisdiction of the United States (Puerto Rico, Guam, American Samoa and the U.S. Virgin Islands.)

FARM-HOME-COTTAGES-CABINS

FRANCE: Do you want to take the family to France, live inexpensively and enjoy French hospitality? This well-kept secret is now revealed to American travelers, Cottages houses, the wing of an inn, or entire floor of a vacation house are available by the week or month, and are located in countryside surroundings. (The French term for these accommodations is gite - pronounced zheet.) All gites have been certified by the Federation Nationale des Gites Ruraux de France. You enjoy the life of a village and still have the urban attraction of the region close by. Average Price: For a family of five for one week: - $175 - average cost per person per day, $5.00. The French Farm and Village Holiday Guide describes each inn/cottage, including location, rooms, amenities such as courtyards, kitchens, sitting rooms, baths, as well as weekly rates. The guide can be obtained from Maison du Tourisme Vert, Gites de France, 35, rue Godot-de-Mauroy, 75009, Paris, France. For price and method of payment, Ph: 33-49-70-75-75.

SWITZERLAND: From the lush valleys to the foothills of the Alps, the farms of Switzerland offer warm, congenial hospitality to the venturesome traveler. Vacation on the farms is more than a holiday, because you establish contact with the family of a working farm. Some lodgings include a kitchen, others offer meals with the inhabitants. Overnight cost: $20 to $50 per person. Ask for the directory, "Swiss Farm Vacation" from the Switzerland Tourism, 608 Fifth Ave., New York, NY 10020. Ph: (212) 757-5944.

TAX DEDUCTIBLE TRAVEL FOR PROFESSIONALS

Teachers, as well as artists, medical, business, science and self-employed professionals, have a golden opportunity to combine travel and study and deduct all of their expenses from their gross income - expenses such as food, lodging, air fares, car expenses, rail tickets, bus fares, passport fees, tips, taxis, laundry, baggage charges, course registration and tuition fees, educational supplies, etc.

In order to qualify for an educational tax deduction, however, the main consequence of the travel must be to develop or improve a specific skill or area of knowledge which is of central importance to accomplishing the taxpayer's job. There must be an identification of the particular job skills that are improved through contact with a particular university. The relationship must be substantial, not simply a stopover. (Reg. Sec. 1. 162-5(d)). For those in business, travel costs away from home are usually a deductible expense when business is transacted - and the employee is not reimbursed by the employer.

INTERNATIONAL CALLING
"COUNTRY CODES"

The Codes listed below are for those most frequently called from the United States. If the country you are calling is not listed below, dial "00" (Operator) for assistance.

The number next to the country is the **"Country Code."**

Australia	61	Jamaica	809
Austria	43	Japan	81
Bahamas	809	Korea	82
Belgium	32	Luxembourg	352
Belize	501	Mexico	52
Brazil	55	Netherlands	31
China	86	New Zealand	64
Costa Rica	506	Norway	47
Denmark	45	Peru	51
Egypt	20	Philippines	63
Finland	358	Poland	48
France	33	Portugal	351
Germany	49	Russia	7
Greece	30	Saudi Arabia	966
Guam	671	Singapore	65
Hong Kong	852	Spain	34
Hungary	36	Sweden	46
Iceland	354	Switzerland	41
India	91	Taiwan	886
Ireland	353	Thailand	66
Israel	972	UK/ Britain	44
Italy	39	Vatican City	39

MONEY SAVINGS-HELPFUL BOOKS, MAGAZINES AND OTHER SERVICES

The following books, magazines and other services have been reviewed and fall within the the criteria of worthwhile and good value for the money. B&J Publications has only expressed it's opinion on the mentioned items and does provide any guarantee of the product or customer satisfaction.

"THE COMPLETE GUIDE TO BED & BREAKFAST, INNS, AND GUESTHOUSE DIRECTORY FOR THE U.S. AND CANADA": Pamela Lanier lists more than 16,000 B & Bs in all 50 states; covers 10 Canadian provinces, Puerto Rico and the U.S. Virgin Islands. Lanier Publishing, Intl., P.O. Box D, Petaluma, CA 94953, (707) 763-0271 (800) 841-2665. In bookstores everywhere!

NEWSLETTER SUBSCRIPTION: Everything you want to know about faraway places with strange sounding names. For a free subscription that describes 90 different travel books, contact Lonely Planet Publications, 112 Linden St., Oakland, CA 94607. Ph: (510) 893-8555.

VACATIONS: An insiders guide to the world's cities, towns, resorts, cruises, tours, romantic inns, singles trips and more! Vacations has great new vacation ideas, tips and insider advice on the best travel deals in the U. S. and abroad. Get the best vacation for the best price. Published quarterly, $9.95 per year. Vacations Publication, 1502 Augusta, Suite 415, Houston, TX 77057 Phone (713) 974-6903.

TRAVEL 50 & BEYOND: Discounts, bargains, tips, advice and new vacation ideas for travelers over 50! There they go again. Just when you thought they were ready for the rocker. Travel 50 & Beyond helps people over 50 find undiscovered spots and hideaways...take advantage of discounts and bargains...maintain health and safety...and more. Published quarterly, $9.95 per year. Vacations Publication, 1502 Augusta, Suite 415, Houston, TX 77057 Phone (713) 974-6903.

INTERNATIONAL LIVING: This newsletter has interesting, helpful and money saving articles on budget travel, international events, shopping, investing, adventure travel, education, real estate & travel safety. Published monthly, $58.00 per year. International Living, published by Agora Inc., 105 West Monument St. Baltimore, MD 21201. Ph: (410) 223-2611

JET SMART: Written by Diana Fairechild, a retired international flight attendant. This 182 page book is a must for frequent, occasional, and once-in-a-lifetime fliers. Offers over 200 tips on how to beat jetlag, sleep soundly in airplane seats, eliminate fear of flying, and much more to make your trip more enjoyable. Check your local bookstore or E-mail: diana@maui.net. World Wide Web address: www.maui.net/diana.

FROMMERS $-A-DAY BUDGET TRAVEL GUIDES: Comprehensive travel guides with information on how to travel on a budget of $45.00 to $60.00 a day. Information includes tips on planning your trip, accommodations and restaurants, tipping, sightseeing, activities, detailed maps, some history of the country, their culture, and recommended books and films for further study. Frommers Guides are available in bookstores nationwide.

LETS GO, INC: Complete guide books for the independent traveler on a budget. The guides include detailed city and regional maps, information on visas, nightlife, food, directions, addresses, phone numbers, opening hours of attractions, budget accommodations, advice on work and study, and much more. Published by Let's Go, Inc., a subsidiary of Harvard Student Agencies, 1 Story Street, Cambridge, MA 02138. Available at bookstores.

GETAWAYS FOR THE WEARY: Retreat Center Guest Houses are oases of beauty and calm where single, couples or families can recharge body and soul. Average price for overnight accommodations **-plus 3 meals daily- are $35.00** per person. **The U.S. and Worldwide Guide to Retreat Center Guest Houses**, lists over 850 centers in the most scenic areas of the world. Send $15.95 to: CTS Publications, P. O. Box 8355, Newport Beach, CA 92660. Postage included in price. Ph: (714) 720-3729

WATCH IT MADE IN THE U.S.A. A VISITOR'S GUIDE TO THE COMPANIES THAT MAKE YOUR FAVORITE PRODUCTS; Bruce Brumberg & Karen Axelrod, $17.95 366 pages. More than 300 companies. Information on how to locate factory tours near your home or while you are on vacation, tour hours, admission, free samples, age and group requirements, gift shops, handicap access and nearby attracations. John Muir Publications
Ref. to page 331 to order.

HELLO FRANCE! AN INSIDER'S GUIDE TO FRENCH HOTELS $50-$90 A NIGHT FOR TWO: Margo Classe; Hotels in Paris and 20 other cities, single, double, or triple occupancies. Hotel discounts and tips on reservations, directions to hotels, what to pack and more. $18.95. Wilson Publishing
Ref. to page 331 to order.

HELLO ITALY! AN INSIDER'S GUIDE TO ITALIAN HOTELS $40-$75 A NIGHT FOR TWO: Margo Classe; Hotels listings for 33 cities, single, double, or triple occupancies, discounts, directions to hotels tips on reservations. what to pack and more. $18.95. Wilson Publishing   Ref. to page 331 to order.

***Hello Spain:* AN INSIDER'S GUIDE TO SPAIN HOTELS $40-$80 A NIGHT FOR TWO:** Margo Classe; Hotel listings for 22 cities: single, double, or triple occupancies, discounts, tips on hotel reservations, directions to hotels, what to pack and more. $18.95; Wilson Publishing   Ref. to page 331 to order.

UNBELIEVABLE GOOD DEALS & GREAT ADVENTURES THAT YOU ABSOLUTELY CAN'T GET UNLESS YOU'RE OVER 50 - This book by Joan Heilman (Contemporary Books) is 300-pages crammed with information about discounts and special opportunities designed specifically for mature people. In other word, perks that 49 and under just don't get. Included are the dctails about discounts on airfares, car rentals, hotels, ski trips shopping, and insurance; a lifetime pass to national parks; over-50 adventure trips; trips for mature singles; free or inexpensive educational opportunities; and membership in clubs that not only take you places but provide peers with whom you can enjoy them. Available from book store for $8.95 or mail or $12.00, (includes S/H) from; Morton Booksellers, 812 Stuart Avenue, Mamaroneck, NY 10543.

IZON'S BACKPACKER JOURNAL: Lucy Izon. This 160-page travel diary with hundreds of tips, helpful quotes, language translations, maps, packing lists, personal & medical information forms & 122 blank pages to record your adventure. Order by credit card from within North America. www.izon.com

IMPORTANT HEALTH TIPS FOR TRAVELERS

To help prevent diarrhea or dysentery when traveling in regions known to be unsafe, follow these rules:

1. Drink boiled or chemically treated water or canned or bottled carbonated beverages. (Be aware that ice can carry bacteria-that brushing your teeth with untreated water creates the same risk) *Water purification tablets, such as Halazone, can be obtained at most drug stores.

2. Eat well-cooked foods that are still hot. Eat only fruit that you have peeled.

3. Try to wash hands frequently. (Carry single package Wash & Dries)

Unfortunately, it's not always possible to confine one's diet to cooked foods and peeled fruit. In the event you contract diarrhea, the following medicines are recommended:

1. For mild cases, try ample amounts of Pepto-Bismol, a non-prescription antacid, or Imodium AD. Minimize food intake - drink fluids.

2. For long-lasting or severe attacks, any of the following doctor-prescribed drugs are recommended: Bactrim, Septra, Doxycycline.

3. To replace lost minerals in the body, drink a sodium/sugar mixture and take potassium pills.

4. A doctor prescribed mild sedative..

5. As a diarrhea preventative, ask your doctor about taking Pepto-Bismol (bismuth subsalicylate). Four tablets a day will reduce your chance of illness by more than 50%. Do not take the medicine for more than three weeks.

6. To find out if inoculations are necessary for the area you're traveling to, call the Center for Disease Control in Atlanta, (404) 639-2572.

If your travels take you to unsafe areas, see your doctor and put together a small medicine kit containing the above drugs. This will provide treatment until you obtain the required medical assistance.

HEALTH INSURANCE WHEN TRAVELING

Before leaving the country, check to see if your health insurance policy will cover you in case of accident or illness.
Please note: Medicare does not cover travelers outside of the United States.
If you need additional coverage, compare policies offered by the following companies:

Travel Assistance International, 1133 15th St. N.W., suite 400, Washington D.C. 20008. (800) 821-2828.
TravMed, P.O.Box 10623, Baltimore, MD 21385, (800) 732-5309
Access America, P.O. Box 90310, Richmond, VA (800) 284-8300
International SOS Assistance, 8 Neshaminy Interplex, Suite 207, Trevose,PA 19053 (800) 523-8930
CIEE: Council on International Educational Exchange, 205 E. 42nd St.,New York, NY 10017 (212) 822-2700

TIPS IF VACATING YOUR HOUSE OR APARTMENT

- ❏ Stop milk, newspaper deliveries.
- ❏ Arrange for mail pickup or forwarding.
- ❏ Make arrangements for plants.
- ❏ Lock all doors and windows.
- ❏ Leave itinerary with friends or relatives in case of emergency.
- ❏ Leave a set of house and car keys with friends/relatives.
- ❏ Request they check your place at frequent intervals.
- ❏ Minor leaks could cause excessive damage.
- ❏ If extended trip, have friend start and idle motors of stored vehicles once a week.
- ❏ Dispose of food susceptible to spoilage.
- ❏ If winter, check pipes for draining, traps winterized, thermostat lowered.
- ❏ Have someone pick up flyers, throwaways, circulars deposited on your property.
- ❏ Leave a small light burning or use an automated unit to put lights on at dusk, turn off at dawn.
- ❏ In some communities, police appreciate notification of extended absence. Will provide extra surveillance of property.
- ❏ Empty trash cans.
- ❏ Tighten all water taps.
- ❏ Safely and securely store all valuable papers and items of worth.
- ❏ If extended trip,have all bills paid up. Check on prepayment of those that come due during your absence.
- ❏ Have lawns mowed and yard work kept up.
- ❏ Don't close blinds or pull down shades.

LAST MINUTE VACATION CHECK-LIST

- ❏ TICKETS
- ❏ TRAVEL ALARM CLOCK
- ❏ READING MATERIAL
- ❏ PASSPORT
- ❏ PHOTOCOPY OF PASSPORT
- ❏ ADDRESS BOOK
- ❏ TRAVELLERS CHECKS
- ❏ CAMERA AND FILM
- ❏ WATCH
- ❏ VACCINATION CERTIFICATE
- ❏ MOTION SICKNESS PILLS
- ❏ FLASHLIGHT
- ❏ LUGGAGE TAGS
- ❏ TRAVEL IRON
- ❏ MEDICINES-PRESCRIPTIONS
- ❏ CHECKBOOK
- ❏ TRAVEL UMBRELLAS
- ❏ MONEY BELT
- ❏ CREDIT CARDS
- ❏ HAIR DRYER
- ❏ MAPS-AUTO CLUB CARD
- ❏ SOME FOREIGN CURRENCY
- ❏ ELECTRIC ADAPTER/CONVERTER
- ❏ FOLD-UP SCISSORS
- ❏ GLASSES/SUN GLASSES
- ❏ GUIDEBOOK
- ❏ KEYS FOR HOUSE/CAR
- ❏ COPY OF PRESCRIPTION
- ❏ DRIVER'S LICENSE
- ❏ FIRST-AID KIT
- ❏ CONFIRMATION OF HOTEL RESERVATIONS
- ❏ TIP CHANGE? $15-$20 IN SINGLE DOLLAR BILLS
- ❏ COMPASS
- ❏ MAGNIFYING GLASS FOR READING MAPS
- ❏ WASH & DRIES FOR QUICK CLEANUPS
- ❏ SMALL PACKAGES OF KLEENEX

TOURIST OFFICES OF USA STATES

To help you plan your vacation, we have listed the addresses and telephone numbers of tourist offices in the United States. Write or call them, and they will provide you with maps, illustrated brochures, special events calendar, scenic areas to visit, historical sites, recreation locales, etc., at no charge.

ALABAMA
Alabama Bureau of Tourism and Travel, Post Office Box 4927, Montgomery, AL 36103-4927, Toll Free: (800) 252-2262, Ph: (334) 242-4169, Fax: (334) 242-4554, E-mail: alabamat@mont.mindspring.com, Web Site: alaweb.asc.edu/ala_tours/tours

ALASKA
Alaska Division of Tourism, Post Office Box 110801, Juneau, AK 99811, Ph: (907) 465-2010, Fax: (907) 465-2287, E-mail: GoNorth@commerce.state.ak.us, Web Site: www.state.ak.us

ARIZONA
Arizona Office of Tourism, 2702 N 3rd Street, Suite 4015, Phoenix, AZ 85004, Toll Free: (888)520-3433, Ph: (602) 248-1480, Web Site: www.arizonaguide.com

ARKANSAS
Arkansas Department of Parks & Tourism Office, 1 Capitol Mall, Little Rock, AR 72201, Toll Free: (800) 628-8725 or (800)-828-8974 , Web Site: www.state.ar.us/html/ark_parks

CALIFORNIA
California Office of Tourism, , Toll Free: (800) 462-2543 or (800)TO-CALIFORNIA, Web Site: www.gocalif.ca.gov

COLORADO
Colorado Travel & Tourism Authority, 3554 N. Academy Blvd., Colorado Springs, CO 80917, Toll Free: (800) 265-6723, Fax: (718) 591-7068, Web Site: www.colorado.com

CONNECTICUT
Connecticut Vacation Center, 505 Hudson St., Hartford, CT 06106, Toll Free: (800) 282-6863, Ph: (860) 258-4355, Fax: (860) 270-8077, Web Site: www.state.ct.us.tourism/

DELAWARE
Delaware Tourism Office, 99 Kings Highway, Box 1401, Dover, DE 19903, Toll Free: (800) 441-8846, Ph: (302) 739-4271, Fax: (302) 739-5749, Web Site: www.state.de.us/

DISTRICT OF COLUMBIA
Washington Convention and Visitors Association, 1212 New York Ave NW, Washington, DC 20005, Ph: (202) 789-7000, Fax: (202) 789-7037, Web Site: www.washington.org

FLORIDA
Florida Division of Tourism, 2129 Ringland Blvd, Sarasota, FL 34230, Toll Free: (888) 735-2872, Fax: (904) 921-9158, Web Site: www.flausa.com/

GEORGIA
Georgia Department of Industry and Trade, Post Office Box 1776, Dept. TIA, Atlanta, GA 30301-1776, Toll Free: (800) 847-4842, Ph: (404) 656-3590, Web Site: www.gomm.com

HAWAII
Hawaii Visitors Bureau, Waikiki Business Plaza, 2270 Kalakaua Ave #801, Honolulu, HI 96815, Ph: (808) 923-1811, Fax: (808) 922-8991, Web Site: www.visit.hawaii.org

IDAHO
Idaho Department of Commerce, 700 West State St, Boise, ID 83720, Toll Free: (800) 635-7820, Ph: (208) 334-2470, Web Site: www.state.idoc.state.id.us/Buttons/buttons

ILLINOIS
Illinois Bureau of Tourism, 100 West Randolph #3-400, Chicago, IL 60601, Toll Free: (800) 223-0121, Ph: (312) 814-4732, Web Site: www.enjoyillinois.com

INDIANA
Indiana Tourism Division, 1 North Capitol Ave #700, Indianapolis, IN 46204, Toll Free: (800) 289-6646, Ph: (317) 232-8860, Web Site: www.ai.org/tourism

IOWA
Iowa Department of Tourism, 200 East Grand Ave., Des Moines, IA 50309, Toll Free: (800) 345-4692, Ph: (515) 242-4705, Web Site: www.state.ia.us/tourism/

KANSAS
Kansas Travel and Tourism Division, 700 SW Harrison St., Suite 1300, Topeka, KS 66603, Toll Free: (800) 252-6727, Ph: (913) 296-2009, Fax: (913) 296-5055, Web Site: www.kansascommerce.com

KENTUCKY
Kentucky Department of Travel Development Visitors Information , 500 Mero St, Frankfort, KY 40601, Toll Free: (800) 225-8747, Ph: (502) 564-4930, Fax: (502) 564-5695, Web Site: www.state.ky.us/tour/tour

LOUISIANA
Louisiana Office of Tourism, Post Office Box 94291, Baton Rouge, LA 70804, Toll Free: (800) 33 GUMBO, (800-334-8626), Ph: (504) 342-8119, Web Site: www.state.louisianatravel.com

MAINE
Maine Publicity Bureau, P.O. Box 2300, Hallowell, ME 04347, Toll Free: (800) 533-9595, Ph: (207) 623-0363, Fax: (207) 623-0388, Web Site: www.visitmaine.com/

MARYLAND
Maryland Office of Tourism Development, 217 East Redwood St., 9th Floor, Baltimore, MD 21202, Toll Free: (800) 543-1036, Ph: (410) 333-6611, Web Site: www.mdisfun.org

MASSACHUSETTS
Massachusetts Office of Travel and Tourism, 100 Cambridge St 13th Floor, Boston, MA 02202 , Toll Free: (800) 447-6277, Ph: (617) 727-3201, Web Site: www.mass-vacation.com/

MICHIGAN
Michigan Travel Bureau, Post Office Box 3393, Livonia, MI 48151, Toll Free: (800) 543-2937, Ph: (517) 373-0670. Web Site: www.travel-michigan.org

MINNESOTA
Minnesota Office of Tourism, 121 7th Place East, St. Paul, MN 55101, Toll Free: (800) 657-3700, Ph: (612) 296-5029, Web Site: www.exploreminnesota.com

MISSISSIPPI
Mississippi Division of Tourism Development, Post Office Box 1705, Ocean Springs, MS 39566, Toll Free: (800) 927-6378, Ph: (800) 873-4780, Web Site: www.mississippi.org

MISSOURI
Missouri Division of Tourism, Post Office Box 1055 , Jefferson City, MO 65102, Toll Free: (800) 877-1234, Ph: (314) 751-4133, Web Site: www.missouritourism.org

TOURIST

MONTANA

Travel Montana, Post Office Box 200533, Helena, MT 59620, Toll Free: (800) 847-4868, Ph: (406) 444-2654, Fax: (406) 844-1800, (406) 444-2808, Web Site: travel.mt.gov

NEBRASKA

Nebraska Travel & Tourism Department, Post Office Box 98913, Lincoln, NE 68509, Toll Free: (800) 228-4307, Ph: (402) 471-3796, Fax: (402) 471-3026, Web Site: www.ded.state.ne.us/tourism

NEVADA

Nevada State Board on Tourism, Capital Complex, Carson City, NV 89710, Toll Free: (800) 638-2328, Ph: (702) 687-4322, Web Site: www.travelnevada.com

NEW HAMPSHIRE

New Hampshire Office of Travel and Tourism, PO Box 1856, Concord, NH 03302-1856, Toll Free: (800) FUN-IN-NH, Ext 162;, Ph: 603-271-2343 Ext 162, Web Site: www.visitnh.gov/

NEW JERSEY

New Jersey Division of Travel and Tourism, 20 West State St CN 826, Trenton, NJ 08628, Toll Free: (800) 537-7397, Ph: (609) 292-2470, Web Site: www.state.nj.us/travel

NEW MEXICO

New Mexico Department of Tourism, 491 Old Santa Fe Trail, Santa Fe, NM 87503, Toll Free: (800) 545-2040, Fax: (505) 827-7402, Web Site: www.newmexico.org

NEW YORK

New York State Travel Info Center, 1 Commerce Plaza, Albany, NY 12245, Toll Free: (800) 225-5697, Ph: (518) 474-4116, Web Site: www.iloveny.state.ny.us

NORTH CAROLINA

North Carolina State Board of Tourism, 430 North Salisbury St., Raleigh, NC 27603, Toll Free: (800) VISIT NC,(800) 847-4862), Ph: (919) 733-4171, Web Site: www.visitnc.com

NORTH DAKOTA

North Dakota Tourism, 604 East Blvd, Bismarck, ND 58505, Toll Free: (800) 435-5663, Ph: (701) 224-2525, Fax: (701) 328-4878, Web Site: www.ndtourism.com

OHIO

Ohio Division of Travel and Tourism, Post Office Box 1001, Columbus, OH 43216, Toll Free: (800) 282-5393, Ph: (614) 466-8844, Fax: (513) 794-0878, Web Site: www.ohiotourism.com

OKLAHOMA

Oklahoma Tourism and Recreation Department, 500 Will Rogers Building, Oklahoma City, OK 73105, Toll Free: (800) 652-6552, Ph: (405) 521-3981, Web Site: www.otrd.state.ok.us

OREGON

Oregon Tourism Commission, 775 Summer St NE, Salem, OR 97310, Toll Free: (800) 547-7842, Ph: (503) 986-0000, Fax: (503) 986-0001, Web Site: www.traveloregon.com

PENNSYLVANIA

Pennsylvania Office of Travel Marketing, Dept. of Commerce, 453 Forum Bldg, Harrisburg, PA 17120, Toll Free: (800) 847-4872, Ph: (717) 787-5453, Web Site: www.state.pa.us

RHODE ISLAND

Rhode Island Tourism Division, 1 West Exchange Street, Providence, RI 02903, Toll Free: (800) U-UNWIND , Ph: (401) 277-2601, Fax: (401) 273-8720

SOUTH CAROLINA

South Carolina Department of Parks, Recreation and Tourism, Post Office Box 71, Columbia, SC 29202, Toll Free: (800) 346-3634, Ph: (803) 734-0122, Fax: (803) 273-8270, Web Site: www.prt.state.sc.us/sc

SOUTH DAKOTA

South Dakota Department of Tourism, 711 East Wells Ave, Pierre, SD 57501, Toll Free: (800) 732-5682, Ph: (605) 773-3301, Fax: (605) 773-3256, E-mail: sdinfo@goed.state.sd.us, Web Site: www.state.sd.us

TENNESSEE

Tennessee Tourism Division, Post Office Box 23170, Nashville, TN 37202, Toll Free: (800) 836-6200, Ph: (615) 741-2158, Fax: (615) 741-7225, Web Site: www.tennessee.net

TEXAS

Texas Department of Tourism, Post Office Box 12728, Austin, TX 78711, Toll Free: (800) 888-8839, Ph: (512) 462-9191, Web Site: www.traveltex.com/RightMain

UTAH

Utah Travel Council , Council Hall, Capitol Hill, Dept. TIA, Salt Lake City, UT 84114, Toll Free: (800) 200-1160, Ph: (801) 538-1030, Web Site: www.utah.com

VERMONT

Vermont Department of Travel and Tourism, 134 State St., Montpelier, VT 05602, Toll Free: (800) 837-6668, Ph: (802) 828-3237, Fax: (802) 828-3367, (802) 828-3233, E-mail: vtinfo@dca.state.vt.us, Web Site: www.travel-vermont.com

VIRGINIA

Virginia Division of Tourism, 1021 E. Cary Street, Richmond, VA 23219, Toll Free: (800) 847-4882, Ph: (804) 786-4484, E-mail: 75143.1111@CompuServe.Com, Web Site: www.virginia.org/cgi-shl/VISITVA/Tourism/Welcome

WASHINGTON

Washington Tourism Development Division, Post Office Box 42500, Olympia, WA 98504, Toll Free: (800) 544-1800, Ph: (360) 586-2012, Web Site: www.tourism.wa.gov

Washington, D.C.

(See District of Columbia),

WEST VIRGINIA

West Virginia Division of Tourism and Parks, 2101 Washington St East, Charleston, WV 25305, Toll Free: (800) 225-5982, Ph: (304) 345-2286, Web Site: www.state.wv.us/tourism

WISCONSIN

Wisconsin Division of Tourism, Post Office Box 7976, Madison, WI 53707, Toll Free: (800) 432-8747, Ph: (608) 266-2161, Web Site: tourism.state.wi.us/agencies/tourism

WYOMING

Wyoming Division of Tourism, I-25 at College Dr., Cheyenne, WY 82002, Toll Free: (800) 225-5996, Ph: (307) 777-7777, Fax: (307) 777-6904, Web Site: www.state.wy.us/state/welcome

TOURIST

FREE TRAVEL INFORMATION FOR YOUR FORTHCOMING TRIP

There are more than 140 national tourist offices throughout the United States that are eager to send you free literature and maps about their country. For the vacationer who wants a calendar of cultural events, festivals, sport tournaments, the tourist bureaus and embassies stand ready to serve. Learning about the places you plan to visit will enhance your understanding and appreciation of them.

While every tourist office has some general literature describing its climate, people, language, currency, you can get information specifically on subjects mentioned on the following lists: Archeology, Architecture, Area Brochures, Arts and Crafts, Camping, City Information, Climate Information, Currency Regulations, Customs Regulations, Educational Opportunities, Excursions, Festivals, Film Festivals, Floklore, Guidebooks, Health Resorts, Hiking and Trekking, History, Local Customs, Local Transportation, Main Tourist Routes, Maps and Charts, Motoring Information, often include maps, National Parks, Forests, Wilderness Areas, Religious Places, Shrines, Churches, Study Abroad and Summer Study Programs.

Be sure to ask for their discount travel booklets. Most countries encourage visits by offering budget rates on food, lodging, bus and rail travel.

FOREIGN TOURIST OFFICES ADDRESSES

ANGUILLA
Anguilla Tourist Information, c/o Medhurst & Associates Inc., 271 Main Street, Northport, NY 11768, Toll Free: (800) 553-4939, Web Site: www.net.ai

ANTIGUA
Antigua & Barbuda Department of Tourism & Trade, 610 Fifth Avenue, #311, New York, NY 10020, Toll Free: (888) 268-4227, Fax: (212) 757-1607, E-mail: antibar@iex.netcom.com, Web Site: www.antiqua.barbuda.org

ARGENTINA
National Tourist Council, 12 West 56th Street, New York, NY 10019, Ph: (212) 603-0443, Fax: 212) 315-5545, Web Site: www.sectur.gov.ar

ARUBA
Aruba Tourism Authority, 1000 Harbor Blvd., Weehawken, NJ 07087, Toll Free: (800) TO-ARUBA, Ph: (201) 330-0800, (212) 246-3030, Fax: (201) 330-8757, E-mail: atanjix@netcom.com, Web Site: www.olmco.com/aruba/

AUSTRALIA (LA Office)
Australian Tourist Commission, Century Plaza Towers, 2049 Century Plaza East, Los Angeles, CA 90067, Ph: (310) 229-4870, (847) 296-4900, Web Site: www.tourism.gov.au/

AUSTRALIA (NY Office)
Australian Tourist Commission, 100 Park Avenue - 25th Floor, New York, NY 10017, Toll Free: (800) 333-0199, Ph: (212) 687-6300, Fax: (212) 661-3340, Web Site: www.tourism.gov.au/

AUSTRIA
Austrian National Tourist Office, P.O. Box 1142, New York, NY 10108, Ph: (212) 944-6880, Web Site: www.anto.com/

AUSTRIA (NY Office)
Austrian National Tourist Office, P.O. Box 1142, New York, NY 10108, Ph: (212) 944-6880, Web Site: www.anto.com

BAHAMAS (LA Office)
Bahamas Tourist Office, 3450 Wilshire Blvd., #208, Los Angeles, CA 90010, Toll Free: (800) 422-4262, Fax: , Web Site: www.interknowledge.com/bahamas/main.html

BAHAMAS (NY Office)
Bahamas Tourist Office, 150 East 52nd Street, New York, NY 10022, Ph: (212) 758-2777, Fax: (212) 753-6531, Web Site: www.interknowledge.com/bahamas/main.html

BARBADOS
Barbados Tourism Authority, 800 Second Avenue, New York, NY 10017, Toll Free: (800) 221-9831, Ph: (212) 986-6516, Fax: (212) 573-9850, Web Site: www.barbados.org/

BELGIUM
Belgian Tourist Office, 780 Third Avenue, New York, NY 10017, Ph: (212) 758-8130, Fax: (212) 355-7675, E-mail: belinfo@nyxfer.blythe.org, Web Site: www.visitbelgium.com/

BERMUDA
Bermuda Department of Tourism, 310 Madison Avenue, New York, NY 10017, Toll Free: (800) 223-6106, Ph: (212) 818-9800, Web Site: www.bermudatourism.com/

BONAIRE
Bonaire Government Tourist Office, 10 Rockefeller Plaza, Suite 900, New York, NY 10020, Toll Free: (800) 826-6247, Ph: (212) 956-5911, Web Site: www.interknowledge.com/bonaire/index.html

BRITISH VIRGIN ISLANDS
British Virgin Islands Tourist Board, 1804Union Street, San Francisco, CA 94123, Ph: (415) 775-0344, Fax: (415) 775-2554, Web Site: www.bvwelcome.com

British Virgin islands
British Virgin Islands Tourist Board, 370 Lexington Ave. , New York, NY 10017, Toll Free: (800) 835-8530, Ph: (212) 696-0400, Fax: (212) 949-8254, Web Site: www.bvwelcome.com

BULGARIA
Bulgarian Tourist Information Center, 2846th Street Suite 1003, New York, NY 10017, Ph: (212) 935-4646, E-mail: balkanusa@aol.com

CANADA
Canadian Consulate General, Tourist Information, 300 S. Grand Ave., 10th Floor, Los Angeles, CA 90071, Ph: (213) 346-2700

CANADA-ALBERTA
Alberta Tourism, City Center, 3rd Floor, 10155 102nd St., Edmonton, ALB T5J 4L6, Toll Free: (800) 661-8888, Ph: (403) 427-4321, Fax: (403) 427-0867 , Web Site: www.discoveralberta.com

CANADA-BRITISH COLUMBIA
Tourism British Columbia, 1117 Wharf St., Victoria, BC V8W 2X2, Toll Free: (800) 663-6000, Fax: (604) 668-3334, Web Site: www.travel.bc.ca

CANADA-MANITOBA
Travel Manitoba, 155 Carlton St, 7th Floor, Dept. 20 , Winnipeg, MAN R3C 3H8, Toll Free: (800) 665-0040, Ph: (204) 945-3777, Fax: (204) 948-2517, Web Site: www.gov.mb.ca/Travel-Manitoba

CANADA-NEW BRUNSWICK
Tourism New Brunswick, Post Office Box 12345 , Fredricton, NB E3B 5C3, Toll Free: (800) 561-0123 , Fax: (506) 789-2044, E-mail: nbtourism@gov.nb.ca, Web Site: www.gov.nb.ca

T
O
U
R
I
S

CANADA-NEWFOUNDLAND &
Newfoundland and Labrador Tourism
Branch, Post Office Box 8730, St.
John's, NF A1B 4K2, Toll Free: (800)
563-6353, Ph: (709) 729-2830, Fax:
(709) 729-1965, E-mail:
info@tourism.gov.nf.ca , Web Site:
www.gov.nf.ca

CANADA-NORTHWEST
TravelArctic, Post Office Box 1320 ,
Yellowknife, NT X1A 2L9, Toll Free:
(800) 661-0788 , Fax: (403) 873
2801, Web Site: www.nwttravel.nt.ca

CANADA-NOVA SCOTIA
Nova Scotia Department of Tourism
and Culture, Post Office Box 130 ,
Halifax, NS B3J 2M7, Toll Free: (800)
341- 6096 , Fax: (902) 420-12286 ,
E-mail: nsvisit@fox.nstn.ca, Web Site:
explore.gov.ns.ca

CANADA-ONTARIO
Ontario Travel, Queen's Park, Toronto,
ONT M7A 2E5, Toll Free: (800)
668-2746, Ph: (416) 314-0944, Fax:
(416) 314-7372, Web Site:
www.travelinx.com/

CANADA-PRINCE EDWARD
Prince Edward Island Dept. of Tourism,
Post Office Box 940, Charlottetown, PEI
C1A 7M5, Toll Free: (800) 565-0267,
Ph: (902) 368-4444, Fax: (902)
629-2428 , E-mail:
mcenter@peinet.pe.ca , Web Site:
www.gov.pe.ca/

CANADA-QUEBEC
Tourisme Quebec, C.P. 979, Quebec,
QUE B3C ZW3, Toll Free: (800)
363-7777 , Fax: (514) 864-3830,
E-mail: info@tourisme.gouv.qc.ca, Web
Site: www.gouv.qc.ca

CANADA-SASKATCHEWAN
Tourism Saskatchewan, 1919
Saskatchewan Dr, Regina, SASK S4P
3V7, Toll Free: (800) 667-7191, Ph:
(306) 787-2300, Fax: (306) 787-5744,
E-mail: travel.info@sasktourim.sk.ca ,
Web Site: www.sasktourism.com

CANADA-YUKON
Tourism Yukon
, Post Office Box 2703, Whitehorse, YK
Canada Y1A2C6, Ph: (403) 667-5340,
Fax: (403) 667-3546, Web Site:
www.touryukon.com/

CARIBBEAN
Caribbean Tourist Association, 20 East
46th Street, New York, NY 10017, Ph:
(212) 682-0435, Fax: (212) 697-4258,
Web Site: www.travelfile.com/get?cto

CAYMAN ISLANDS (FL Office)
Cayman Islands Tourist Office, 6100
Blue Lagoon, Miami, FL 33126, Toll
Free: (800) 327-8777, Fax: (305)
267-2931, Web Site:
www.caymans.com

CAYMAN ISLANDS (LA Office)
Cayman Islands Tourist Office, 3440
Wilshire Blvd., Suite 1202, Los Angeles,
CA 90010, Ph: (213) 738-1968, Fax:
(213) 738-1829, Web Site:
www.caymans.com

CHILE
Chilean National Tourist Board,
Sernatur, Avenue Providencia 1550,
Santiago,Chile, , Toll Free: (800) CHILE
66 (Automated), Fax: Fax:
001-562-251 8459, Web Site:
www.segegob.cl/seratur/inicio.html

CHINA (Glendale Office)
China National Tourist Office, 333 West
Broadway, #3201, Glendale, CA 91204,
Toll Free: (818) 545-7505 (Automated),
(818) 545-7507, Fax: (818) 545 7506,
Web Site:
www.travelfile.com/get?chinanto

CHINA (NY Office)
China National Tourist Office, 350 Fifth
Avenue, Rm #6413, New York, NY
10018, Ph: (212) 760-1710
(Automated), (212) 760-8218, Fax:
(212) 760-8809, Web Site:
www.travelfile.com/get?chinanto

COOK ISLANDS
Cook Islands Tourist Authority, 6033
West Century Blvd #609, Los Angeles,
CA 90045, Ph: (805) 383-1339

COSTA RICA
Costa Rica National Tourist Board, P. O. Box 777-1000, San Jose, Costa Rica , Toll Free: (800) 343-6332, Ph: (506) 222-1090 or 223-1733, ext. 277, Fax: (506) 223-5452 or 555-4997, Web Site: www.tourism-costarica.com

CURACAO
Curacao Tourist Board, 475 Park Ave South, Suite 2000, New York, NY 10016, Toll Free: (800) 270-3350, Ph: (212)683-7660, Fax: (212) 683-9337, E-mail: curacao@ix.netcom.com, Web Site: www.curacao/tourism.com

CYPRUS
Cyprus Tourism, 13 East 40th Street, New York, NY 10016, Ph: (212) 683-5280, Fax: (212) 683-5282, E-mail: gocyprus@aol.com, Web Site: www.wam.umd.edu/~cyprus/tourist.html

CZECH & SLOVAK REPUBLICS
Czech & Slovak Service Center, 1511 K Street NW, Suite 1030, Washington, DC 20005, Ph: (202) 638-5505, Fax: (202) 638-5308, E-mail: cztc@cztc.demon.co.uk, Web Site: www.czech-slovak-tourist.co.uk/index.html

DENMARK
Scandinavian National Tourist Offices , 655 Third Avenue, New York, NY 10017, Ph: (212) 949-2333, Fax: (212) 983-5260, Web Site: www.goscandinavia.com

DOMINICA
Dominica Tourist Office, 820 Second Avenue, New York, NY 10017, Ph: (212) 599-8478, Fax: (212) 808-4975

DOMINICAN REPUBLIC
Dominican Republic Tourist Office, 2355 Falzedo St. Suite 307, Coral Gables, FL 33114, Toll Free: (888) 358-9595, Ph: (305) 444-4592, Fax: (305) 444-4845

EGYPT (Beverly Hills Office)
Egyptian Tourist Authority, 8383 Wilshire Blvd #215, Beverly Hills, CA 90211, Ph: (213) 653-8815, Fax: (213) 653-8961, Web Site: www.touregypt.net

EGYPT (NY Office)
Egyptian Tourist Authority, 630 Fifth Ave #1706, New York, NY 10111, Ph: (212) 332-2570, Fax: (212) 956-6439, Web Site: www.touregypt.net

ENGLAND
(See Great Britian Tourist Authority),

EUROPEAN TRAVEL
, 1 Rockefeller Plaza, Room 214, New York, NY 10020, Ph: (212) 218-1200, Fax: (212) 218-1205, E-mail: DNMCO@aol.com, Web Site: www.visiteurope.com

FIJI
Fiji Visitors Bureau, 5777 Century Blvd #220, Los Angeles, CA 90045, Toll Free: (800) 932-3454, Ph: (310) 568-1616, Fax: (310) 670-2318, E-mail: fiji@primenet.com, Web Site: www.fijifvb.gov.fj

FINLAND
Finnish Tourist Board, 655 Third Avenue , New York, NY 10017, Toll Free: (800) 346-4636, Ph: (212) 949-2333, Fax: (212) 983-5260, Web Site: www.mek.fi/

FRANCE (Chicago Office)
French Government Tourist Office, 676 North Michigan Ave. Ste 3360, Chicago, IL 60611-2819, Ph: (312) 751-7800, Fax: (312) 337-6339, Web Site: www.fgtousa.org/GENINFO.htm

FRANCE (LA Office)
French Government Tourist Office, 9454 Wilshire Blvd. #715, Los Angeles, CA 90212, Ph: (310) 271-2358, Web Site: www.fgtousa.org/GENINFO.htm

FRANCE (NY Office)
French Government Tourist Office, 444 Madison Ave, New York, NY 10022, Ph: (212) 838-7800, (900) 990-0040 ($.95/minute), Web Site: www.fgtousa.org/GENINFO.htm

FRENCH WEST INDIES
(See French Government Tourist Office), (Guadeloupe, St. Barts & St. Martin),

GERMANY (NY Office)
German National Tourist Office, 122 E 42nd St., 52nd Floor, New York, NY 10168, Ph: (212) 661-7200, Fax: (212) 661-7174, E-mail: gntony@aol.com

TOURIST

GREAT BRITAIN
British Tourist Authority, (England, Scotland, Wales, Northern Ireland), 551 5th Ave #701, New York, NY 10176, Toll Free: (800) 462-2748, Ph: (212) 986-2200, Fax: (212) 986-1188, Web Site: www.visitbritain.com

GREECE (LA Office)
Greek National Tourist Organization, 611 W Sixth St #2198, Los Angeles, CA 90017, Ph: (213) 626-6696, Fax: (213) 489-9744, E-mail: gnto@aurora.eexi.gr/eng.htm

GREECE (NY Office)
Greek National Tourist Office, 645 Fifth Ave, New York, NY 10022, Ph: (212) 421-5777, Fax: (212) 826-6940, E-mail: gnto@aurora.eexi.gr/eng.htm

GRENADA
Grenada Board of Tourism, 820 Second Ave, Suite 900D, New York, NY 10017, Toll Free: (800) 927-9554, Ph: (212) 687-9554, Fax: (212) 573-9731, Web Site: www.grenada.org

GUADELOUPE
(See French Government Tourist Information),

GUAM
Guam Visitors Bureau, 1150 Marina Village Parkway, Suite 104, Alameda, CA 94501, Toll Free: (800) 873-4826, Fax: (510) 865-5165

GUATEMALA
Guatemalan Tourist Commission, 299 Alhambra Circle #510, Miami, FL 33134, Ph: (305) 442-0651

HONDURAS
Honduras Tourist Office, P.O. Box 140458, Coral Gables, FL 33114, Toll Free: (800) 410-9608, E-mail: 104202.3433@compuserve.com, Web Site: www.hondurasinfo.hn

HONG KONG (LA Office)
Hong Kong Tourist Association, 10940 Wilshire Blvd #1220, Los Angeles, CA 90024, Ph: (310) 208-4582, Fax: (310) 208-1869, E-mail: hktalax@aol.com, Web Site: www.hkta.org

HONG KONG (NY Office)
Hong Kong Tourist Association, 590 Fifth Ave, New York, NY 10036, Ph: (212) 869-5008, Fax: (212) 730-2605, E-mail: hktanyc@aol.com, Web Site: www.hkta.org

HUNGARY
Hungarian Tourist Board, 150 East 58th Street, New York, NY 10510-0001, Ph: (212) 355-0240, Web Site: www.hungary.com/

ICELAND
Scandinavian National Tourist Offices, 655 Third Ave, New York, NY 10017, Ph: (212) 949-2333, Fax: (212) 983-5260, Web Site: www.goscandinavia.dom

INDIA
India Tourist Office (Los Angeles), 3550 Wilshire Blvd #204, Los Angeles, CA 90010, Ph: (213) 380-8855, Fax: (213) 380-6111, Web Site: www.tourindia.com

INDIA
India Tourist Office (New York), 30 Rockefeller Plaza, North Mezzanine, New York, NY 10112, Toll Free: (800) 953-9399, Ph: (212) 586-4901, Fax: (212) 582-5260, Web Site: www.tourindia.com

INDONESIA
Indonesia Tourist Promotion Office, 3457 Wilshire Blvd #104, Los Angeles, CA 90010, Ph: (213) 387-8309, (213) 387-2078, Fax: (213) 380-4876

IRELAND
Irish Tourist Board, 345 Park Ave, New York, NY 10154, Toll Free: (800) SHAMROCK, (800) 223-6470, Ph: (212) 418-0800, Fax: (212) 371-9052, Web Site: www.ireland.travel.ie/

ISRAEL
Israel Government Tourist Info Center, 800 Second Avenue, New York, NY 10017, Toll Free: (800) 596-1199, Ph: (212) 560-0650, Fax: (212) 499-5645, E-mail: hgolan@imot.org, Web Site: www.infotour.co.il

ISRAEL
Israel Government Tourist Office, 6380 Wilshire Blvd #1700, Los Angeles, CA 90048, Toll Free: (800) 596-1199, Ph: (213) 658-7462, Fax: (213) 658-6543, Web Site: www.infotour.co.il

ITALY (Chicago Office)
Italian Government Tourist Board, 500 North Michigan Ave, Chicago, IL 60611, Ph: (312) 644-0990, Fax: (312) 644-3019

ITALY (LA Office)
Italian Government Tourist Board, 12400 Wilshire Blvd #550, Los Angeles, CA 90025, Ph: (310) 820-0098, Fax: (310) 820-6537

ITALY (NY Office)
Italian Government Tourist Board, Rockefeller Center, 630 Fifth Ave, New York, NY 10111, Ph: (212) 245-4822, Fax: (212) 586-9249

JAMAICA (LA Office)
Jamaica Tourist Board, 3440 Wilshire Blvd, Suite 1207, Los Angeles, CA 90010, Toll Free: (800) 233-4582, Ph: (213) 384-1123, Fax: (213) 384-1780, Web Site: www.jamaicatravel.com/jtboffice.html

JAPAN (New York office)
Japanese National Tourist Organization, 1 Rockefeller Plaza Ste,1250 , New York, NY 10020, Ph: (212) 757-5640, Fax: (212) 307-6754, E-mail: jntonyc@interport.net

JAPAN (San Francisco office)
Japanese National Tourist Organization, 360 Post Street, Suite 601, San Francisco, CA 94108, Ph: (415) 989-7140, Fax: (415) 398-5461, E-mail: sfjnto@aol.com, Web Site: www.into.go.jp

KENYA (Beverly Hills Office)
Kenya Consulate & Tourist Office, 9150 Wilshire Blvd #160, Beverly Hills, CA 90212, Ph: (310) 274-6635, Fax: (310) 859-7010, Web Site: www.embassyofkenya.com

KENYA (NY Office)
Kenya Consulate & Tourist Office, 424 Madison Ave, New York, NY 10017, Ph: (212) 486-1300, Fax: (212) 688-0911, Web Site: www.embassyofkenya.com

KOREA (LA Office)
Korea National Tourism Corporation, 3435 Wilshire Blvd #350, Los Angeles, CA 90010, Ph: (213) 382-3435, Fax: (213) 480-0483, Web Site: www.knto.or.kr

KOREA (NJ Office)
Korea National Tourism Office, 2 Executive Drive 7th Floor, Fort Lee, NJ 07024, Ph: (201) 595-0909, Fax: (201) 585-9041, Web Site: www.knto.or.kr

LUXEMBOURG
Luxembourg National Tourist Office, 17 Beekman Place, New York, NY 10022, Ph: (212) 935-8888, Fax: (212) 935-5896, E-mail: luxnto@aol.com, Web Site: www.visitluxembourg.com/wlcm_mn.htm

MACAU (LA Office)
Macau Tourist Information Bureau, 3133 Lake Hollywood Dr, Los Angeles, CA 90078, Ph: (213) 851-3402, Fax: (213) 851-3684

MALAYSIA (Los Angeles office)
Malaysian Tourist Information Center, 818 W. Seventh St., Los Angeles, CA 90017, Ph: (213) 689-9702, Fax: (213) 689-1530, E-mail: malinfo@aol.com, Web Site: www.interknowledge.com/malaysia

MALAYSIA (New York office)
Malaysia Tourism Promotion board, 595 Madison Ave, Suite 1800 , New York, NY 10022, Toll Free: (800) KLUMPUR, Ph: (212) 754-1113, Fax: (212) 754 1116, E-mail: mtbp@aol.com, Web Site: www.interknowledge.com/malaysia

MALTA
Malta National Tourist Organization, 350 Fifth Avenue, Ste. 4412, New York, NY 10118, Ph: (212) 695-8229, Fax: (212) 695-8229, E-mail: 104452,2005@compuserve.com

T O U R I S T

MARTINIQUE
Martinique Promotion Bureau, A division of the French Government Tourist Office, 444 Madison Ave, New York, NY 10022, Toll Free: (800)-391-4909, E-mail: Martinique@NYO.COM, Web Site: www.martinique.org

MEXICO (LA Office)
Mexico Government Tourist Office, 10100 Santa Monica Blvd #224, Los Angeles, CA 90067, Ph: (310) 203-8191 , Fax: (310) 203-8316, Web Site: www.mexico-travel.com

MEXICO (NY Office)
Mexico Government Tourist Office, 405 Park Ave, Ste. 1401, New York, NY 10022, Toll Free: (800) 446-3942, Ph: (212) 838-2949, Fax: (212) 753-2874, Web Site: www.mexico-travel.com

MONACO
Monaco Government Tourist & Convention Bureau, 845 Third Ave 19th Floor, New York, NY 10022, Toll Free: (800) 753-9696, Ph: (212) 759-5227, Fax: (212) 754-9320, E-mail: mgto.ny@ix.netcom.com, Web Site: www.monaco.mc/usa

MOROCCO
Moroccan Tourist Office, 20 East 46th St #1201, New York, NY 10017, Ph: (212) 557-2520, Fax: (212) 949-8148, Web Site: www.tourism-in-morocco.com

NETHERLANDS
Netherlands Board of Tourism, 225 N Michigan Ave #326, Chicago, IL 60601, Ph: (312) 819-0300, Fax: (312) 819-1740, Web Site: www.nbt.nl/holland

NEW ZEALAND
New Zealand Tourism Board, 501 Santa Monica Blvd #300, Santa Monica, CA 90401, Toll Free: (800) 388-5494, Ph: (310) 395-7480, Fax: (310) 395-5453, Web Site: www/nztb.govt.nz

NORWAY
Norwegian Tourist Board, 655 Third Avenue, New York, NY 10017, Ph: (212) 949-2333, Fax: (212) 983-5260, Web Site: www.norway.org/main.html

PANAMA
IPAT (The Panama Tourist Bureau), P. O. Box 4421, Zone 5, The Republic of Panama, , Ph: (507) 226-7000 (507) 226-3544, Fax: (507) 226-3483 (507) 226-6856, Web Site: www.panamainfo.com/

PHILIPPINES
Philippine Department of Tourism, 447 Sutter St #507, San Francisco, CA 94108, Ph: (415) 956-4060, Fax: (415) 956-2093, E-mail: pdotsf@aol.com

POLAND
Polish National Tourist Office, 275 Madison Ave #1711, New York, NY 10016, Ph: (212) 338-9412, Fax: (212) 338-9283, E-mail: poltrvl@poland.net, Web Site: www.poland.net/polandtravel/

PORTUGAL
Portuguese National Tourist Office, 590 Fifth Ave, New York, NY 10036, Toll Free: (800) PORTUGAL, Ph: (212) 354-4403

PUERTO RICO (Miami office)
Puerto Rico Tourism Company, P.O. Box 5268, Miami, FL 33102, Toll Free: (800) 866-STAR ext 17, Web Site: www.gorp.com/gorp/location/pr.pr.ht m#address

PUERTO RICO (New York office)
Puerto Rican Tourism Company, 575 Fifth Ave., 23rd floor, New York, N.Y., NY 10017, Ph: (212) 818-1886, Fax: (212) 818-1866, Web Site: www.gorp.com/gorp/location/pr.pr.ht m#address

ROMANIA
Romanian Tourist Office, 14 East 38th Street, 12th Floor, NewYork, NY 10016, Ph: (212) 545-8484, Fax: (212) 251-0429

RUSSIA
The Russian National Tourist Office, 800 Third Ave, Suite 3101, New York, NY 10022, Ph: (212) 758-1162, Fax: (212) 758-0933, Web Site: www.russia-travel.com

SABA & ST. EUSTATIUS
Saba & St. Eustatius Tourist Office, c/o Medhurst & Associates, Inc., 271 Main St, Northport, NY 11768, Toll Free: (800) 722-2394

SCANDINAVIA (Iceland, Norway,
Scandinavian National Tourist Offices, 655 Third Ave, New York, NY 10017, Ph: (212) 949-2333, Fax: (2120 983-5260, Web Site: www.goscandinavia.com

Scandinavia(Iceland,
Scandinavian National Tourist offices, 655 Third Ave., New York, NY 10017, Ph: (212) 983-5260, Fax: (212) 983-5260, Web Site: www.goscandinavia.com

SCOTLAND
(See Great Britain),

SINGAPORE (LA Office)
Singapore Tourist Promotion Board, 8484 Wilshire Blvd #510, Beverly Hills, CA 90211, Ph: (213) 852-1901, Web Site: www.travel.com.sg/sog

SINGAPORE (NY Office)
Singapore Tourist Promotion Board, 590 Fifth Ave 12th Floor, New York, NY 10036, Ph: (212) 302-4861, Fax: (212) 302-4801, Web Site: www.travel.com.sg/sog

SINT MAARTEN
Sint Maarten Tourism Office, 675 Third Avenue, Ste. 1806, New York, NY 10017, Toll Free: (800) 786-2278, Ph: (212) 953-2084, Fax: (212) 953-2145

SLOVAK REPUBLIC
(See Czech & Slovak Republics),

SLOVENIA
Slovenia Tourist Office, 122 E. 42nd St, New York, NY 10168, Ph: (212) 682-5896, Fax: (212) 661-246

SOUTH AFRICA (LA Office)
South African Tourism Board, 9841 Airport Blvd #1524, Los Angeles, CA 90045, Ph: (310) 641-8444, Fax: (310) 641-581

SOUTH AFRICA (NY Office)
South African Tourism Board, 500 Fifth Ave, New York, NY 10110, Toll Free: (800) 822-5368, Ph: (212) 730-2929, Fax: (212) 764-1980

SPAIN (Beverly Hills Office)
Tourist Office of Spain, 8383 Wilshire Blvd #960, Beverly Hills, CA 90211, Ph: (213) 658-7188, Fax: (213) 658-1061, Web Site: www.okspain.org

SPAIN (NY Office)
Tourist Office of Spain, 666 Fifth Ave., 35th Floor, New York, NY 10022, Toll Free: (888)-OKSPAIN, Ph: (212) 265-8864, Web Site: www.okspain.org

ST. BARTS
(See French Government Tourist Information),

ST. CROIX
(See U.S. Virgin Islands),

ST. JOHN
(See U.S. Virgin Islands),

ST. KITTS & NEVIS
St. Kitts & Nevis Tourism Office, 414 E. 75th St., 5th Floor, New York, NY 10021, Toll Free: (800) 582-6208, Fax: (212) 734-6511, E-mail: skbnev@ix.netcom.com, Web Site: www.interknowledge.com/stkitts-nevis

ST. LUCIA
St. Lucia Tourist Board, 820 Second Ave, New York, NY 10017, Toll Free: (800) 456-3984, Ph: (212) 867-2950, Fax: (212) 867-2795, Web Site: www.st-lucia.com/

ST. MARTIN
See French Government Tourist Information,

ST. THOMAS
(See U.S. Virgin Islands),

ST. VINCENT & THE
St. Vincent & the Grenadines Tourist Office, 801 Second Ave., 21st Floor, New York, NY 10017, Toll Free: (800) 729-1726, Fax: (212) 949-594

ST.VINCENT & THE GRENADINES
St. Vincent & the Grenadines Tourist office, 810 Second Ave, 21st Floor, New York, NY 10017, Toll Free: (800) 729-1726, Ph: (212) 949-5946, Web Site: www.stvincentandgrenadines.com

SWEDEN (NY Office)
Swedish Tourist Board, 655 Third Avenue, New York, NY 10017, Ph: (212) 949-2333, Fax: (212) 983-5260, Web Site: www.gosweden.org/

Switzerland
Switzerland Tourism, 608 Fifth Ave., New York, NY 10020, Ph: (212) 262-6116, Web Site: www.switzerlandtourism.ch/

SYRIA
Tourist Office of Syria, c/o Syrian Consulate, , Ph: (202) 232-6313, Fax: (202) 265-4585

TAHITI
Tahiti Tourist Promotion Board, 300 N Continental Blvd #180, El Segundo, CA 90245, Toll Free: (800) 365-4949, Ph: (310) 414-8484, Fax: (310) 414-8490, Web Site: www.tahiti-tourisme.com

TAIWAN
Taiwan Visitors Association, 333 N Michigan Ave, Chicago, IL 60601, Ph: (312) 346-1038, Fax: (312) 346-1037, Web Site: www.tbroc.gov.tw

TAIWAN (NY Office)
Taiwan Visitors Association, 1 World Trade Center #7953, New York, NY 10018, Ph: (212) 466-0691, Fax: (212) 432-6436, Web Site: www.tbroc.gov.tw

TAIWAN (SF Office)
Taiwan Visitors Association, 166 Geary St #1605, San Francisco, CA 94108, Ph: (415) 989-8677, Fax: (415) 989-7242, Web Site: www.tbroc.gov.tw

THAILAND (LA Office)
Thailand Tourist Authority, 3440 Wilshire Blvd #1100, Los Angeles, CA 90010, Ph: (213) 461-9814, Fax: (213) 461-9834, E-mail: tatla@ix.netcom.com, Web Site: www.tat.or.th/

THAILAND (NY Office)
Thailand Tourist Authority, 5 World Trade Center, New York, NY 10048, Ph: (212) 432-0433, Fax: (212) 912-0920, E-mail: tatny@aol.com, Web Site: www.tat.or.th/

TONGA
Tonga Consulate General, 360 Post St #604, San Francisco, CA 94108, Ph: (415) 781-0365, Fax: (415) 781-3964

TRINIDAD & TOBAGO
Trinidad & Tobago Tourism Development Authority, 7000 Boulevard East, Guttenberg, NJ 07093, Toll Free: (800) 748-4224, Fax: (201) 869-7628, Web Site: www.visittnt.com/

TURKEY
Turkish Tourism & Information Office, 821 United Nations Plaza, New York, NY 10017, Ph: (212) 687-2194, E-mail: tourney@soho.ios.com, Web Site: www.turkey.org/turkey

TURKS & CAICOS
Turks & Caicos Tourist Board, P. O. Box 128, Grand Turk, Turks & Caicos BWI, Toll Free: (800) 241-0824, Fax: (809) 946-2733

VIRGIN ISLANDS (British) NY
British Virgin Islands Tourist Board, 370 Lexington Avenue, New York, NY 10017, Toll Free: (800) 835-8530, Ph: (212) 696-0400, Fax: (212) 949-8254, Web Site: bviwelcome.com

VIRGIN ISLANDS (British) SF
British Virgin Islands Tourist Board, 1804 Union Street, San Francisco, CA 94123, Ph: (415) 775-0344, Fax: (415) 775-2554, Web Site: bviwelcome.com

VIRGIN ISLANDS (U.S.) LA
U.S. Virgin Islands Division of Tourism, (St. Croix, St. John, St. Thomas), 3460 Wilshire Blvd #412, Los Angeles, CA 90010, Ph: (213) 739-0138, Fax: (213) 739-2096, Web Site: www.usvi.net

VIRGIN ISLANDS (U.S.) NY
U.S. Virgin Islands Division of Tourism, (St. Croix, St. John, St. Thomas), 1270 Avenue of the Americas #2108, New York, NY 10020, Ph: (212) 332-2222, Fax: (212) 332-2223, Web Site: www.usvi.net

WALES
, (See Great Britain),

HOSTELS
ALL AGES WELCOME

Hostels are friendly, comfortable places, filled with people from around the world looking for adventure and excitement on a budget. Just a few dollars a night can get you a bunk in the country or city almost anywhere in the world.

Reservations are suggested during peak travel seasons.

What To Expect When Hosteling:

Accommodations are usually dorm style rooms, one for women, one for men, but many offer private rooms for families, couples or groups which can be reserved in advance.

Bath and toilet facilities are usually communal, with one for men and another for women.

Most hostels also have self-service kitchens or cafeterias, dining areas, secure storage and common rooms for relaxing and laundry facilities.

Bring your own linens, Hostelling International locations require a sleeping sack. (Available from Travel Gear (800) 825-7085. www.walkabouttravelgear.com)

Some hostels are in wonderful historic buildings which have been renovated and adapted for hostel use.

Privacy will be in short supply, but meeting people from around the world more than makes up for most inconveniences.

Hostels are open to all ages, except in Bavaria, Germany, where the age limit is 26 unless you are a youth group leader or head of a family.

Services and hours are limited to keep costs down.
Overnight fees average $8 to $17 per person, per night. Major cities such as Rome, Munich, London and Sydney are less than $20.

Most hostels are handicapped accessible, welcome groups and can provide meeting rooms and catered meals.

Hostelling International-American Youth Hostels (HI-AYH) has 5000 hostels in 70 countries, including 150 in the United States. Yearly membership is $25 for adults, $10 for children under 18, $35 for a family, and senior citzens pay $15. Hostelling International has an international reservation service, discounts on admissions, car rentals, transportation, and much more. A membership card is required to stay at HI-AYH locations. If you do not have a card, you will pay $3.00 more than the price listed.

For a handbook describing American Youth Hostels or to join, contact: Hostelling International-American Youth Hostels, 733 15th Street N.W., Suite 840, Washington, D.C. 20005, Ph. (202) 783-6161, Fax: (202) 783-6171. E-mail: Tpyle@ATTMAIL.COM. or AYH, 1434 2nd St., Santa Monica, CA 90401. Ph. (310) 393-3413.

Hostelling International-American Youth Hostels, publishes two directories listing every HI hostel. Below is a list of available publications and brochures. All prices include postage and handling. (Books will only be shipped to U.S. addresses.) Telephone orders are accepted with a credit card.

International Guide - Americas, Africa, Asia and the Pacific $13.95
International Guide-Europe $13.95
Hostelling North America $2.00
England & Wales Guide $5.50
Scotland Guide $5.50
Australian Guide $5.50
New Zealand Hostels $5.50
Japan Map $1.00
USA Map, Free

American Association of International Hostels (AAIH) is an independent hostel group with 450 locations. The accommodations vary from basic to luxury. Usually a valid passport or student card is all you need to check in.

American Associations of International Hostels, 250 West 77th St., Suite 906, New York, New York 10024. Ph. (212) 769-9039.

NEW ZEALAND, YHA New Zealand, P. O. Box 436, Christchurch, New Zealand Ph: 64-03-379-9970, FAX: 64-03-365-4476. Email: info@yha.org.nz Website: www.yha.org.nz

This only only a partial listing of hostels available in the United States. To find additional hostels in the Unites States, Canada, or worldwide web, check local tourist information offices or Chamber of Commerces.

Check out **www.izon.com**, a good source for information on hostels and backpacking.

Worldwide
Colleges/Universities
CONTENTS

U N I V

COLLEGES & UNIVERSITIES

WELCOME TO COLLEGE RESIDENCE LODGING

A. Save more than 50% over conventional lodging - additional savings on meals at college cafeterias.

B. Sports facilities, course offerings, cultural activities available at campus site.

C. Situated in scenic park-like settings, or in intellectually stimulating urban areas

WHAT TO EXPECT WHEN STAYING IN COLLEGE ROOMS

A. Clean, safe, comfortable sleeping quarters (no bellhops or valet parking tips to pay)

B. Twin bedded rooms, although some colleges have suites, apartments, or single rooms.

C. Three varieties of bathrooms: private baths, attached baths connecting two rooms, shared bath (showers and toilets down the hall).

D. Desks, chairs, closet space, TV/lounge area, air conditioning, linen and towel service (some may charge extra), coin operated laundry machines, pay telephones.

E. Access to sport facilities (in most cases), library, theater productions, workshops, food service, cultural events, parking, mail and telephone services.

COME EQUIPPED

A. Bring sleeping bags for children. Many colleges allow small children to sleep free in their parent's room. Inquire about children accommodations when making reservations.

B. A few colleges do not provide linens and towels - have a set handy just in case. This can save on extra linen charge.

C. Some colleges offer cooking facilities. Cookware and utensils are useful if you intend to stay for an extended period.

D. Bring tennis rackets, golf clubs, swimsuits, cameras, coffee maker, portable radio or TV, snacks, etc.

U
N
I
V

HOW TO BOOK UNIVERSITY ACCOMMODATIONS

I. MAKE ADVANCE RESERVATIONS. In most cases advance reservations are required. However, in the event that you're in the area of one of the Universities listed in the Guide, and have not made a reservation, give the college a call. Often the University can accept you on short notice. Since some colleges host conferences, it's wise to reserve early.

II. SPECIFY DATES YOU WISH TO STAY, NUMBER OF PERSONS IN THE PARTY, AND HOW MUCH OF AN ADVANCE DEPOSIT IS REQUIRED. Try to allow for alternative dates in the event your first choice dates are booked. IMPORTANT: Inquire about the cancellation policy in case your plans change.

III. RECONFIRM PRICES AND TYPE OF ACCOMMODATIONS AVAILABLE. Some prices are subject to change on short notice. Also inquire about any restrictions-such as rules on pets, alcohol in the rooms, check-out times, etc.

IV. REMINDER: If you telephone for reservations, the rates when calling between 11 P.M.. and 8 A.M.. are 60% less than the full day rate. This is a great advantage to Westerners who want to call East and reach someone during business hours.   For Easterners who want to make reservations at Western Schools, the 5 P.M.. to 11 P.M.. rates are 30% cheaper than full day rates.

HOW TO USE THE GUIDE IN FOREIGN COUNTRIES

1. For travelers planning to stay abroad, it is advised to write or call, well before the time you plan your stay. The response to your reservation request, even from non-English speaking countries, will usually be in English, although you may have to brush up on your French in some cases.

2. If reservations have not been made and you arrive on the scene baggage in hand, ask the local tourist office at the air terminal or railroad station to make the necessary calls. Language and foreign phone usage often require supreme patience, even on behalf of the natives.

3. Have ample foreign currency with you to pay for phone courtesies, taxis, busses, baggage handling, tips, etc. ATM's are a smart way to deal with foreign currency - safer than carrying large sums. They are readily available in banks, airports, hotels, etc.

4. Most universities listed can accommodate social, professional, sport, fraternal, etc., groups.

5. Check into purchasing a tourist travel pass for local transportation (bus, subway, train, etc). Most passes can be bought through your local travel agent before leaving USA.

Because of the fluctuating value of the dollar, some prices for overseas lodging may be subject to a 10% to 15% increase. However, most lodging prices will still be less than $30.00 per day, per person.

T= TRAVELERS ACCOMMODATIONS
E= EDUCATION-RELATED INTERESTS
C= CONFERENCE ACCOMMODATION

TRAVELERS ACCOMMODATIONS

MOST OF THE INSTITUTIONS IN THIS CATEGORY ALSO
PROVIDE LODGING, FOOD, MEETING ROOMS, AND
FACILITIES FOR FAMILY REUNIONS, CONFERENCES,
FRATERNAL GROUPS, SOCIAL CLUBS, SPORT
ASSOCIATIONS, SEMINARS, YOUTH CLUBS, ETC.

Universities and Colleges in this section are available to the
general public. Children are welcome unless stated otherwise in
the listing. Resevations are generally required, but if you find
yourself in a city with a listed university, give them a call, they
may be able to accommodate you on short notice.

EDUCATION-RELATED INTERESTS

MOST OF THESE INSTITUTIONS ALSO PROVIDE LODGING,
FOOD, MEETING ROOMS, AND FACILITIES FOR GROUPS,
CONFERENCES, FRATERNAL GROUPS, SOCIAL CLUBS,
SPORT ASSOCIATIONS, SEMINARS, AND YOUTH CLUBS WITH
AN EDUCATIONAL RELATED AGENDA.

The colleges and universities listed provide overnight
accommodations for individuals and families whose visit coincides
with some "educational purpose" of the Institution. College
housing directors are most cooperative and recognize the following
suggestions as tying into their educational objectives:

• Retired Educators
• College Faculty or Graduates on Sabbatical
• Possible enrollment of a child, grandchild, other relative, or
  yourself
• Inquiring about conference facilities for future meetings of your
  group
• Your need to use library resources
• Interviewing staff members on topics of interest

CONFERENCE ACCOMMODATIONS

THE COLLEGES AND UNIVERSITIES LISTED IN THIS CATEGORY PROVIDE OVERNIGHT ACCOMMODATIONS TO MEMBERS OF NON-PROFIT ORGANIZATIONS - SUCH AS, SPORTS, CHURCH, CHARITABLE, EDUCATIONAL, SOCIAL, FRATERNAL, OR NATURE GROUPS. FAMILY REUNION MEETINGS ON COLLEGE CAMPUSES HAVE BECOME A POPULAR AND INEXPENSIVE WAY FOR CELEBRATING SUCH OCCASIONS.

Generally there is no minimum number of members required for classifying yourself as a group. Make up your own group entity and take advantage of comfortable lodging and inexpensive food service offered by more than 85 universities.

When calling a school, make reservations in the name of your group, and state the length of time you wish to stay.

Although B & J Publications has researched all sources to insure the accuracy and completeness of the Campus Lodging Guide, it cannot assume the responsibility for last-minute college revisions, errors, rate changes or inaccuracies reported by University sources. On occasion, a few of the listed colleges undergo maintenance and refurbishing projects and are unavailable for occupancy.

U
N
I
V

KEY to ABBREVIATIONS

PRICING
S=Single Price
D=Double Price

PAYMENT
Per. Ck=Personal Check
Trav. Ck=Travelers Check
M/C=Master Card
Amex=American Express

ROOM TYPE
SR=Student Room
Apt.=Apartment
Suite=Suite

BED TYPE
S=Single Bed
D=Double Bed

BATH TYPE
C=Communal
S=Shared W/Joining Rm
P=Private

FOOD SERVICE
No=No Food Service
Caf.=Cafeteria
SB=Snack Bar
VM=Vending Machines
NR=Nearby Restaurants
OCR=On Campus Rest.

&=Handicapped Accommodations
?=Did Not Respond to Update Requests

SPECIAL NOTE; When utilizing student rooms, please remember most do not provide all the services or amenities of standard Hotels & Motels such as soap, shampoo, etc. When linens are provided, sometimes towels/wash cloths are not include. Be safe, pack your own. Other items to consider bringing: Coffee maker, Portable Radio or TV, Snacks, etc.

COLLEGE & UNIVERSITY ACCOMMODATIONS

AUSTRALIA

Australia Capital Territory

1   Canberra, ACT   ?   &

Australian National Univ. (T)
Burton and Garran Halls, G P O Box 813, Canberra, ACT Ph: 61-62-674700, ASK
FOR: Mr. Hudson, Mrs. Powell
ROOM PRICING: (S) $18.00, $30.00/B&B, $50.00/Full board, • PAYMENT: Cash
Trav. Ck Visa M/C • DATES AVAILABLE: Nov. 1-Feb. 28, • BED TYPE: S •
BEDS: 1 • FOOD: Caf. VM • INFO: Children welcome, families can be
accommodated. • ACTIVITIES: Central point for Aust. tours; National Capital of
Australia; Parliament houses; recreation water sports; wide range of tourist
attractions.

2   Canberra, ACT   &

Australian National Univ. (T)
Ursula College, Daley Rd., Canberra, ACT 2600, Ph: 61-06-279 4300, E-mail:
Therese.May@anv.edu.av, ASK FOR: Conf. Mgr.
ROOM PRICING: (S) $35.00, (D) $50.00, (includes breakfast only), • PAYMENT:
Cash Trav. Ck Visa M/C • DATES AVAILABLE: Apr.16-30, July 2-16,Sept.
17-Oct. 3, Dec.-Feb. 12, • BED TYPE: S • BEDS: 1-2 • FOOD: Caf. SB VM NR
OCR • INFO: Free laundry, Free Parking, Linens provided, Tea/Coffee in room,
Bar, Lounge, games room, quiet gardens • ACTIVITIES: Easy access to all major
attractions in Canberra. Walking distance to Botanic gardens, Lake Burley,
Griffen and city center.

3   Canberra City, ACT   &

Burgmann College (T)
Daley Rd., Acton, Canberra City, ACT 2601, Ph: 61-06-2675202, 61-06-2675222,
E-mail: vicki.guyer@anv.edu.au, ASK FOR: Vicki Guyer, Conf. Manager
ROOM PRICING: (S) $28.00, (D) $43.00, Includes - breakfast, lunch, dinner.
Student rate., • PAYMENT: Cash Per. Ck Visa M/C • DATES AVAILABLE: Nov.
25-Feb. 20, and some year round, • BEDS: 1 • FOOD: Caf. • INFO: Available all
year round - B&B or fully catered. Conference facilities available. • ACTIVITIES:
Billiard room, TV room. Canberra is 2 hrs. from Snowy Mountains and coast. Set
in attractive bush and mountain area; Parliament House; Science and Tech.
Center; sport facilities; Lake Burley Griffin.

New South Wales

4   Armidale, NSW   ?   &

Univ. of New England (T)
Wright College, Armidale, NSW 2351, Ph: 61-067-73-2813, ASK FOR: College
Office
ROOM PRICING: (S) $19.00, (includes breakfast), • PAYMENT: Cash Visa M/C •
DATES AVAILABLE: Year round, Best availability: Apr. 16- May1, June 16 -
Ju;y12.• BEDS: 1 • FOOD: Caf. VM • INFO: Children welcome. • ACTIVITIES:
Folk museums; waterfalls and national parks; historic homesteads; regional art
gallery.

5   Armidale, NSW   &

University of New England (T)
Mary White College, Armidale, NSW 2351, Ph: 61-02-6773-1000,   Fax:
61-02-6773-1010, E-mail: babbey@metz.une.edu.au, ASK FOR: Mr. Abbey-
Principal
ROOM PRICING: (S) $23.00/ B&B, (D) $37.00/ B&B, • PAYMENT: Cash M/C •
DATES AVAILABLE: Year-round, subject to availability., • ROOM TYPE: SR • BED
TYPE: S • BEDS: 1-2 • BATH: C S • FOOD: Caf. • INFO: Free laundry faciliaties
with coin dryers, shared ensuite rooms available, linens included, free parking, TV
lounges, catering for vegetarians available.
 • ACTIVITIES: Armidale (pop. 22,000) is a cosmopolitan & rural city with major
educational facilities & historical interests, incl. art galleries & museums. 2 1/2
hours from coast, ideal for tourists, day trippers, backpackers.

6   Callaghan, NSW   ?   &

University of Newcastle (T)
Halls of Residence, 1980 N. W. Blackmore, Callaghan, NSW 2308, Ph: 61-
049-241004, ASK FOR: Norma Cairns
ROOM PRICING: (S) $60.00, • PAYMENT: Cash Per. Ck • DATES AVAILABLE:
Nov., Dec., Jan., Feb., • BED TYPE: S • BEDS: 1 • FOOD: Caf. • INFO: Coin
washers/dryers, TV lounges, free parking. • ACTIVITIES: Sauna, darkroom, table
tennis, pool, snooker billiards, tennis, squash. Close to beaches; lake; Pokolbin
Vineyard   Area.

7   Chippendale, NSW   ?   &

International House, University of Sydney (T)
96 City Road, Chippendale, NSW 2008, Ph: 61-2- 9950-9800 or 61-2-9950-9804,
ASK FOR: Geoffrey Andrews, Director
ROOM PRICING: (S) $32.00, • PAYMENT: Cash Visa M/C • DATES AVAILABLE:
Dec.-Feb., June-July, • BEDS: 1-2 • FOOD: Caf. VM NR • INFO: Bedding
furnished, Bath, private and shared,3 meals incl. per day. • ACTIVITIES:
Swimming, tennis, theater, films, concerts, lectures, museums.

8   Kensington, NSW   &

University of New South Wales (T)
International House, Anzac Parade, Kensington, NSW 2033, Ph: 61-2- 313 0600,
6-12-313-6346, ASK FOR: Conf. Coordinator
ROOM PRICING: (S) $24.00/B&B, $32.00/Full board, • PAYMENT: Cash Trav.
Ck • DATES AVAILABLE: Nov.25 -Feb.23; July 6-26, • BED TYPE: S • BEDS: 1
• FOOD: Caf. VM NR • INFO: Coin washers/dryers, no alcohol, two TV lounges,
linens included.   B&B only, 3 weeks over Christmas Holiday. No persons under
16 years of age. • ACTIVITIES: 15 min. to city center, beaches, parks, heated
swimming pool, jogging track, golf course, tennis, squash, close to Sydney's Int'l.
Air Terminals. Pool is in gym opposite I.H.
DIRECTIONS: 200 metres from Anzac Parade, Kensington, on Campus of UNSW

9   Kensington, NSW   &

Warrane College (T) Univ. of New South Wales
Corner Anzac Parade & Barker St., P. O. Box 123, Kensington, NSW 2033, Ph:
61-2 662-6199, Fax: 61-2 662-2992, ASK FOR: Bursar
ROOM PRICING: Students: $36.50 night, $185.00 week. (S), Summer 8 weeks,
$155.00, Non-student: $39.00 night, $217.00 week., • PAYMENT: Cash Trav.
Ck Visa M/C • DATES AVAILABLE: Nov-Feb. , • BEDS: 1 • FOOD: Caf. VM •
INFO: Limited to men (men's college) , cleaning service. Washer/dryer, TV lounge,
cleaning service, linens changed weekly. • ACTIVITIES: 5km from city center; close
to beaches; good transportation system.

U
N
I
V

10 Newtown, NSW

Women's College (T) Univ. of Sydney
15 Carillon Ave., Newtown, NSW 2006, Ph: 61-(02) 9517-5000, Fax: 61-(02) 9517-5006, E-mail: office@womensco.usyd.edu.au , Web Site: www.usyd.edu.au/su/womens, ASK FOR: Len Cupitt
ROOM PRICING: (S) $33.00/B&B, $42.00/Full board , (D) $48.00B&B, $62.00/Full board , Discounts for students, • PAYMENT: Cash Per. Ck Trav. Ck • DATES AVAILABLE: July 3-25, Nov. 30-Feb. 20, • BEDS: 1 • FOOD: Caf. • INFO: Children welcome, coin washers/dryers, TV lounge, free parking, coffee bars, linens and towels provided. Open to men and women. • ACTIVITIES: Fishing, surfing, theater, sporting events. 10 min. to center of Sydney - seaport, largest city of Australia.

11 Northryde, NSW   ?

Dunmore Lang College (T)
Macquaire University, 130 Herring Rd., Northryde, NSW 2113, Ph: 61-2-9856-1000, Fax: 61-2-9856-1009, ASK FOR: Business Manager
ROOM PRICING: (S) $55.00-$65.00, (D) $85.00, • PAYMENT: Cash Trav. Ck • DATES AVAILABLE: Mid. Nov.-Mid. Feb Some self-contained apts. avail . year round, Single study rooms• ROOM TYPE: SR Apt. • BED TYPE: S • BEDS: 1-2 • BATH: C P • FOOD: Caf. VM NR • INFO: Children welcome, linens included. • ACTIVITIES: 18 kms from center of Sydney; Koala Park; beaches; metropolitan capital; campus in garden setting; modern rooms.

12 Sydney, NSW   ?   &

St. John's College (T)
8 A Missenden Rd., Camperdown 2050, Sydney, NSW Ph: 61-2-9394-5200, Fax: 61-2-9550-6303, ASK FOR: Rector: Marshall J. McMahon
ROOM PRICING: (S) $65.00, B/B, $280/week, • PAYMENT: Cash Visa M/C • DATES AVAILABLE: Year round, • BED TYPE: S • BEDS: 2 • FOOD: NR • INFO: No children, coin washers/dryers, TV lounge, free parking. • ACTIVITIES: Close to transport, city.

13 Sydney, NSW   &

University of New South Wales (T)
Shalom College, Sydney, NSW 2052, Ph: 61-2-9663-1366, E-mail: shalomcollege.unsw.edu.au, ASK FOR: Beverly Solsky
ROOM PRICING: (S) $31.00, (D) $51.00, (Includes breakfast), • PAYMENT: Cash • DATES AVAILABLE: July 6-24, Dec. 1- Feb. 20, • ROOM TYPE: SR Apt. • BEDS: 2 • BATH: C • FOOD: Caf. • INFO: In addition to single rooms, 2 flats available to accommodate 4 persons in each. • ACTIVITIES: Events and attractions of downtown Sydney-Opera House; natural harbor; cruises.
DIRECTIONS: Barker Street off Anzac Parade. College situated by Pizza Hut. Located 3 minute wald from main bus route into the city which is 20 minutes away from the opera house and waterways of the city. Close to some of the most beautiful beachs on the eastern shore like the famous Bondi Beach.

14 Wollongong, NSW

International House (T) University of Wollongong
Wollongong, NSW 2522, Ph: 61-042-299-711, ASK FOR: Office Manager
ROOM PRICING: (S) $25.00/Full room and board, (D) $42.00(full room and board), • PAYMENT: Cash Trav. Ck • DATES AVAILABLE: Dec., Jan., Feb., • BEDS: 1-2 • FOOD: Caf. SB VM NR • INFO: Linens included, phones in rooms, TV lounge, coin washers/dryers, free parking. • ACTIVITIES: Beaches, scenic coastline bush walking, mtr. hiking, fauna flora reserves, 1 hr. to Sydney by train.

Queensland

15   Brisbane, QLD

Univ. of Queensland (T)
Cromwell College, Walcott St., St. Lucia 4067, Brisbane, QLD Ph:
61-07-33771300, Fax: 61-07-33771499, Web Site: www.uq.edu.au/cromwell,
ASK FOR: Bursar
ROOM PRICING: (S) $20.00, (D) $40.00, (Bed plus 3 meals), • PAYMENT: Cash
Trav. Ck Visa M/C • DATES AVAILABLE: Jan. 1-Feb.7, Mar. 31-Apr. 4,
July7-19, Sept. 22-Oct. 3, Dec. 9-31., • BED TYPE: S • BEDS: 1 • FOOD: Caf. •
INFO: Children welcome. coin washers/dryers, TV lounge, free parking, linens
included.Tennis, basketball, and volleyball courts. Billiard table, chapel for
worship. • ACTIVITIES: Capital city of Brisbane and attractions close by. Campus
gym, pool, cinema, libraries. Close public transport to city and coastal beaches.

16   Brisbane, QLD

Univ. of Queensland, Grace College (T)
Walcott St., St. Lucia, Brisbane, QLD 4067. Ph: 61-7-3842-4003, Fax:
61-7-3842-4180, ASK FOR: Mrs. Hayden, Bursar
ROOM PRICING: Call for rates, • PAYMENT: Cash Trav. Ck • DATES
AVAILABLE: After Nov. 15, See other Info• ROOM TYPE: SR Apt. • BED TYPE: S
D • BEDS: 1 • BATH: C P • FOOD: Caf. NR • INFO: Children welcome.
Additional dates available during June -July , Sept.- Oct. Coin washers/dryers •
ACTIVITIES: Close to city center of Brisbane; native fauna and flora sanctuary;
river trips; botannical gardens; friendly atmosphere and campus garden setting.

17   Brisbane, QLD

Univ. of Queensland, Int'l House (T)
5 Rock St., St. Lucia, Brisbane, QLD 4067, Ph: 61-7-3870-9593, Fax:
61-7-3870-3968, E-mail: ih@mailbox.uq.edu.au, ASK FOR: Office Mgr.
ROOM PRICING: (S) $18.00/B&B, (D) $30.00/B&B, Discount for Students, •
PAYMENT: Cash Per. Ck Visa M/C • DATES AVAILABLE: June 27-July 17,
Sept. 20 - Oct. 3, • BEDS: 1 • FOOD: Caf. • INFO: Children welcome. Additional
dates avail: Nov. 28-Feb. 8. Weekly and monthly rates available. • ACTIVITIES:
University campus sports & recreation facilites; close to city markets; museums;
theatres; cafes; close to transport. Lone Pine Koala Bear Sanctuary; famous
Australian wool market/woolshed; close to Brisbane, city of 1 million.

18   St. Lucia, QLD   ?   ♿

Univ. of Queensland, Emmanuel Clg. (T)
Sir William Mac Gregor Dr., St. Lucia, QLD 4067, Ph: 61-07- 871-9370, ASK
FOR: Supervisor Residential Serv.
ROOM PRICING: (S) $20.00/B&B, $28.00/Full board, (D) $30.00/B&B,
$48.00/Full board, • PAYMENT: Cash Per. Ck • DATES AVAILABLE: July 1-17,
Sept.16- 30, Dec.2 - Feb. 16, • BED TYPE: S • BEDS: 1 • FOOD: Caf. VM NR •
INFO: Some guest rooms and self-catering flats available year round. •
ACTIVITIES: Central bus to Brisbane tourist attractions; City on the bay;
surrounding mtns.; museums; cathedrals; Gov't. bldgs.; Ascot Race Course;
water sport activities.

19   St. Lucia, QLD   ♿

Univ. of Queensland, Women's Clg. (T)
College Rd., St. Lucia, QLD 4067, Ph: 61-7-33774500, 61-07-38712500
, Fax: 61-07-38709511, ASK FOR: House Manager 61-7-33774500
ROOM PRICING: (S) Aus. $48.00/B&B, $58.00/ Full board(Conf. rate) Casual
guests(S) $35 and up Apts. $70 and up., • PAYMENT: Cash Per. Ck Trav. Ck •
DATES AVAILABLE: Dec.1-Feb.1, 2 wks. in July, Sept., • ROOM TYPE: SR Apt.
Suite • BED TYPE: S • BEDS: 1-2 • FOOD: Caf. SB VM NR OCR • INFO: Children
welcome. Conferences, telphones. Coin washers/dryers, linens included, TV
lounge, evening tea. Prices vary with B&B or Full Board. 150 seat tiered
air-conditioned lecture theatre with latest audio-visual equip. • ACTIVITIES: Tennis
court. Lone Pine Koala Sanctuary; Mt. Coot-THA Botanical Gardens; transport
available to city and tourist attractions.

U
N
I
V

20 St. Lucia, QLD   ?

University of Queensland (T)
King's College, St. Lucia, QLD 4067, Ph: 61-07 871-9600, ASK FOR: The Master
ROOM PRICING: (S) $32.00/Full board, $42.00 for large groups., • PAYMENT:
Cash Per. Ck • DATES AVAILABLE: Apr. 17- 22, July 3-15, Sept. 18-30,
Dec.11- Feb.7, Dec.2-Feb.20; Apr.16-May 1• BED TYPE: S • BEDS: 1 • FOOD:
Caf. NR • ACTIVITIES: Capital city of Brisbane; Gold Coast University sports
and cultural facilities.

South Australia

21 No. Adelaide, SA   ♿

Lincoln College, Univ. of Adelaide (T)
45 Brougham Pl.,, No. Adelaide, SA 5006, Ph: 61-8-8290-6005, Fax: 61-8- 8267
2942, E-mail: vince@lincolncollege.adelaide.edu.au, ASK FOR: G.A. Vincent
ROOM PRICING: (S) $32.00/B&B   U.S.-$19.00, • PAYMENT: Cash Trav. Ck
Visa M/C • DATES AVAILABLE: Dec. 1-Feb. 14, Apr. 14-25, July 7-25, Sept.
22-Oct. 3, • BED TYPE: S • BEDS: 1 • FOOD: Caf. VM NR • INFO: Children
welcome by prior arrangement.   TV lounge, 3 laundromats, some parking. •
ACTIVITIES: Festival Theater; casino; overlooks park; buses close by; airport and
railway within easy reach. Airport Bus.

22 No. Adelaide, SA   ? ♿

Univ. of Adelaide, St. Ann's College (T)
187 Brougham Pl.,, No. Adelaide, SA 5006, Ph: 61-08-267-1478,   Fax:
61-08-267-1903, ASK FOR: Chris Irvine
ROOM PRICING: (S) $25.00/B&B, $33.00/ Full board, • PAYMENT: Cash •
DATES AVAILABLE: Some year round, See other Info• ROOM TYPE: SR • BED
TYPE: S • BEDS: 1 • BATH: C • FOOD: Caf. VM NR • INFO: Children welcome.
Dates avail.: April 13-23, Sept. 21-Oct.1, Dec. 21-Feb. 13, 1999. • ACTIVITIES:
Wildlife reserve; Zoological gardens; museums; sports; parks; waterfront activities.

Tasmania

23 So. Hobart, Tasmania

Jane Franklin Hall, Univ. of Tasmania (T)
6 Elboden St., So. Hobart, Tasmania 7004, Ph: 61-3-62-23-2000, Fax:
61-3-62-24-0598, E-mail: throne@tassie.net.au, Web Site:
www.utas.edu.au/jane-franklin, ASK FOR: Dr. John Thorne, Conf. Co-ordinator
ROOM PRICING: (S) $25.00, (D) $35.00, • PAYMENT: Cash Visa • DATES
AVAILABLE: Dec; Jan; & Feb;, • BEDS: 1 • FOOD: VM NR OCR • INFO: Children
welcome, discounts for groups and families staying more than a few days.
Walking distance to central Hobart. • ACTIVITIES: Close to SW.Tasmanian
wilderness area; extensive lake and waterway system; beautiful Hobart Harbour
(world's finest); Aust. oldest architecture; parks; tennis; unpolluted air; situated
in spacious landscaped gardens.

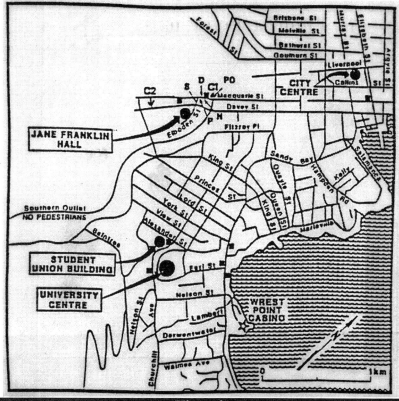

Victoria

24 Bundoora, VIC   ? &

La Trobe University (T)
Menzies College, Bundoora, VIC 3083, Ph: 61-03-9479-1071, Fax:
61-03-9479-3690, ASK FOR: Dennis Campbell, House Manager
ROOM PRICING: (S) $25.00, (D) $30.00, • PAYMENT: Cash Trav. Ck Visa M/C
• DATES AVAILABLE: Year round, • ROOM TYPE: SR • BED TYPE: S • BEDS:
1-3 • BATH: C P • FOOD: Caf. VM NR • INFO: Linens provided. • ACTIVITIES:
Swimming and tennis. Campus located in huge parkland; tram to Melbourne city
center; wildlife reserves.

25 Bundoora, VIC   ?

La Trobe University (T)
Chisholm College, Kingsbury Dr., Bundoora, VIC 3083, Ph: 61-03-9479-2875,
Fax: 61- 03-9479-1211, ASK FOR: Jan Lees
ROOM PRICING: Hostel, (S) $13.50, Backpackers, Conference $26.00, •
PAYMENT: Cash Per. Ck Trav. Ck • DATES AVAILABLE: Nov. 20 - Feb. 21, •
ROOM TYPE: SR • BED TYPE: S • BEDS: 1 • FOOD: Caf. SB VM NR • INFO:
Children $11.50 per night. Free laundry facilities, native & bush setting, TV
lounge. • ACTIVITIES: Billliards & Table tennis.   University campus facilities: bar,
cinema, banks, post office, sports complex. Close to shopping centers; Bus or
tram to city center.

26 Bundoora, VIC   ?   ♿

La Trobe University (T)
Glenn College, Bundoora, VIC 3083, Ph: 61-(03) 9479-5100,   Fax: 61- (03)
9479-5151, ASK FOR: Mr. F. Martin
ROOM PRICING: (S) $AU 25.00, (Includes breakfast & dinner), • PAYMENT: Cash
Trav. Ck Visa M/C • DATES AVAILABLE: Late Nov. - Mid. Feb., • BEDS: 1 •
FOOD: Caf. OCR • INFO: Single rooms, free laundry, telephones and internet
access. • ACTIVITIES: Full university campus facilites; banks; sporting facilites;
theatre; shops; access to city attractions via public transport.

27 Carlton, VIC

University of Melbourne (T)
Medley Hall, 48 Drummond St., Carlton, VIC 3053, Ph: 61-03-9663-5847, ASK
FOR: Carol Butters - Principal
ROOM PRICING: $A30 per person (bed only)
$A35 per person (bed & light breakfast), • PAYMENT: Cash Per. Ck • DATES
AVAILABLE: Nov.20 - Feb. 25, • BED TYPE: S • BEDS: 1 • FOOD: NR • INFO:
Children welcome, use of laundry and kitchen facilities at no extra charge,
Minimum stay, 3 nights. • ACTIVITIES: Medley Hall within easy walking distance of
Melbourne City Center; Shops; Theater; Air Terminals; Rail Station all within 1
mi.; Royal Park; Exhibition Gardens; All sport facilities.

28 Clayton, VIC   ?   ♿

Monash University (T)
Wellington Rd., Clayton, VIC 3168, Ph: 61-03-544-8133, ASK FOR: Admissions
Office
ROOM PRICING: (S) $26.00/B&B, • PAYMENT: Cash Per. Ck • DATES
AVAILABLE: Dec.-Jan, Feb., July, Nov., • BEDS: 1 • FOOD: Caf. NR • INFO:
Children welcome. Monash; Howitt, Deakin, Roberts Farrer, and Richardson
resident halls, provide a total of 860 rooms. • ACTIVITIES: Water sport activities;
easy access to Melbourne; boating to Phillip Island; wildlife sanctuaries; surfing;
beaches.

29 Parkville, VIC   ♿

Ormond College, Univ. of Melbourne (T)
College Crescent, Parkville, VIC 3052, Ph: 61-03-9344-1100,   Fax: 61-03
9344-1111, ASK FOR: Conference Office
ROOM PRICING: (S) $45.00/B&B (Australian Dollars), • PAYMENT: Cash Visa
M/C • DATES AVAILABLE: Nov.28 - Dec. 20, Jan 3 - Feb. 12, June 29-Jul.25,
• BED TYPE: S • BEDS: 1 • FOOD: Caf. NR • INFO: All linens supplied, room
service daily. TV lounge, free parking. Free laundry facilites. • ACTIVITIES:
Sports, tennis and squash courts, jogging tracks, access to Univ. gym facilities.
Melbourne Zoo; Botanical Gardens; Lygon St. with Italian Quarter and
International restaurants; cultural advantages of Melbourne.
DIRECTIONS: Near corner of Royal Parade and Gatehouse Street in Parkville; 10
minutes journey on the #19 tram from the heart of Melbourne.

30 Parkville, VIC   ♿

Univ. of Melbourne, International House (T)
241 Royal Parade, Parkville, VIC 3052, Ph: 61-3-9347 6655, Fax: 61-3-9349 1761, E-mail: c.chia@ihouse.unimelb.edu.au, ASK FOR: john Vernon, Business Manager
ROOM PRICING: (S) $25.00/B&B,$32.00 Full board, (D) $50.00/ B&B, $64.00/Full board, Discount for longer stays, child. half price, • PAYMENT: Cash Per. Ck Trav. Ck Visa • DATES AVAILABLE: Nov. 28- Feb. 20, June 27-July24, some year round, • ROOM TYPE: SR Apt. Suite • BED TYPE: S • BEDS: 1 • BATH: C S P • FOOD: Caf. VM NR • INFO: Friendly staff, all linens included. Laundry facilities, phones in rooms, tea and coffee making facilities, conference facilites avail. Some rooms with private baths. • ACTIVITIES: Tennis, squash courts,BBQ facilities, overlooking parks. Close to zoo; city center; and cultural center. Transport at door, safe, restful environment. International flavour.

31 Parkville, VIC   ?   ♿

Univ. of Melbourne, Trinity College (T)
Royal Parade, Parkville, VIC 3052, Ph: 61-03-349-0025, ASK FOR: Lisa- Maree Jones
ROOM PRICING: (S) $30.00, (D) $60.00, Per person (bed & breakfast), • PAYMENT: Cash • DATES AVAILABLE: June-July; Nov. 20-Feb. 15;, • ROOM TYPE: SR • BATH: C • FOOD: Caf. VM NR • INFO: Children welcome, linen and towels provided. • ACTIVITIES: University set in beautiful gardens; jogging, walking access, Univ. gym facilities, Melbourne zoo; International restaurants. 2 min. tram ride to city centre.

Western Australia

32 Crawley, WA   ?

St. George's College, Univ. WA (T)
Mounts Bay Rd.,, Crawley, WA 6009, Ph: 61-9-449-5555, Fax: 61-9-449-5544, E-mail: stgconf@cygnus.uwa.edu.au
ROOM PRICING: (S) $16.00 -30.00, (D) $40.00, (includes breakfast), • PAYMENT: Cash Visa M/C • DATES AVAILABLE: Dates available upon request, • ROOM TYPE: SR • BED TYPE: S • FOOD: Caf. VM NR • INFO: Children welcome, phone in every room. Tudor architecture and magnificent gardens. • ACTIVITIES: Swan River; King's Park; beautiful beaches; Fremantle; Perth City.

33 Nedlands, WA

St. Catherine's College (T)
Stirling Highway, Nedlands, WA 6009, Ph: 61-8-9386-5847, Fax: 61-8-9386-3844, E-mail: stcats@cygnus.uwa.edu.au, ASK FOR: Tara Holmes
ROOM PRICING: (S) $35.00 B/B, • PAYMENT: Cash Per. Ck Trav. Ck • DATES AVAILABLE: Dates avail. on request., • BED TYPE: S • BEDS: 1-2 • FOOD: Caf. VM NR • INFO: Student rates, self-contained flats available, close to public transport, computer room. Laundry, recreation/TV room, private telephone. • ACTIVITIES: Tennis & squash courts. 10 minutes from city center; close to swan river; Port of Fremantle; King's Park; Rottnest Island; pool.

34 Nedlands, WA   ?   ♿

Univ. of WA, Kingswood College (T)
Hampden Road, Nedlands, WA 6009, Ph: 61-09-4239447, 61-09-4239423, ASK FOR: Conference Office
ROOM PRICING: (D) $68.00, (includes breakfast), • PAYMENT: Cash Trav. Ck Visa M/C • DATES AVAILABLE: Year round, • BEDS: 1-2 • FOOD: Caf. VM NR • INFO: Children welcome, private bath. Phone, air-conditioned student rooms. Price disc. from Nov.-Feb. • ACTIVITIES: Perth City; Fremantle; King's Park; Zoo; surfing beaches; transport.

35 Nedlands, WA   ? &

Univ. of WA, St. Columba College (T)
Stirling Hwy, Nedlands, WA 6009, Ph: 61-9-386-0400, ASK FOR: Rev. Dr. N. Kentich
ROOM PRICING: (S) $16.00, Full Board during June-July period $32.00, •
PAYMENT: Cash Only Visa M/C • DATES AVAILABLE: Dec. 2-Feb. 15; June
15-July 15, • BED TYPE: S • BEDS: 1-2 • FOOD: Caf. SB VM NR • INFO:
Children welcome. Limited access for handicapped. • ACTIVITIES: 10 min. to
Perth; close to ocean beaches; Swan River; King's Park; 30 min. to Fremantle -
all sports; museums, etc. on campus.

AUSTRIA

36 Innsbruck   ? &

Hotel "Rossl Inder Au" (T)
Hottinger AU 34, A-6020 , Innsbruck, Ph: 43-0512-28 68 46, Fax: 43-0512-29
38 50
ROOM PRICING: (S) $52.37/B&B, (D) $83.00/B&B, • PAYMENT: Cash Trav. Ck
Visa M/C Amex • DATES AVAILABLE: July 1 -Sept. 30, • BEDS: 1 • FOOD: NR
• INFO: Children welcome. • ACTIVITIES: Innsbruck is at the base of beautiful
Austrian Alps.

37 Innsbruck   ?

International Student House (T)
Rechengasse 7, A-6020 , Innsbruck, Ph: 43-512-501-0
ROOM PRICING: (S) $30.00- $37.00, (D) $50.00- 65.00, Breakfast, $7.00per
person, • PAYMENT: Cash Trav. Ck • DATES AVAILABLE: July 1- Sept.30, •
BED TYPE: S • FOOD: Caf. • INFO: For every 20 paying guests, one person is
free. • ACTIVITIES: Cultural activities; sports; sightseeing

38 Innsbruck   ?

Jugendherberge Innsbruck (T)
Reichenauerstrasse 147, A-6020, Innsbruck, Ph: 43-512-346179,   Fax:
43-512-34617912, E-mail: yhibktirol.com, ASK FOR: Housing Office
ROOM PRICING: Hostel, price includes breakfast, (S) $35.00, (D) 50.00. 6 bedded
rooms: $14.00; 4 bedded rooms: $17.00., • PAYMENT: Cash Only • DATES
AVAILABLE: Year round, except for Christmas holidays., • BEDS: 2-6 • BATH: C
P • FOOD: VM NR • INFO: Washers/dryers, TV lounge with sat. reception, free
parking, self-catering kitchen, International Youth Hostel Card required. Sheets
and hot showers included. • ACTIVITIES: Rococco churches; panorama paintings;
Olympic Museum; Gothic Museum; Ice Stadium open all year; 14 discotheques;
lakes; mountain hiking; Glacier-Skiing year round in Stubai Valley, 11/2 hours by
bus. Club Innsbruck.

39 Innsbruck   ?

Universitat Innsbruck (T) Techniker Wohnheim
Fischnaler Str. 26, A-6020 , Innsbruck, Ph: 43-512-2821100,   Fax:
43-512-28211017
ROOM PRICING: (S) $22.00, (D) $42.00, Discount rates w/student card, •
PAYMENT: Cash Trav. Ck Visa • DATES AVAILABLE: July 15 -Aug. 31, •
ROOM TYPE: SR • BED TYPE: S • BEDS: 1-3 • BATH: C • FOOD: Caf. SB NR
OCR • INFO: Special prices for groups, TV lounge, free parking, linens included,
children welcome. • ACTIVITIES: Concerts, museums, exhibits, lakes, day trips to
Vienna, Salzburg, Mountains

40 Linz   ? &

Katholische Hochschulgemeinde (T)
Menger Str. 23, 4040 , Linz, Ph: (43) 0732-244011, Fax: (43) 24401 72
ROOM PRICING: (S) $14.00   (D) $22.00 , • PAYMENT: Cash • DATES
AVAILABLE: July 1 -Sept 25, • FOOD: Caf. • INFO: Free parking, coin
washers/dryers, TV lounge, Children welcome. • ACTIVITIES: Jogging route,
swimming, theaters, concerts, sighseeing, mountain climbing.

---

41 Linz ⚐

Studentenwerk/Sommerhaus (T)
Julius Raab Strasse 10, 4040 LINZ, Linz, Ph: 43-0732-2457, ASK FOR: Manager
ROOM PRICING: Breakfast included, (S) $25.00-$50.00, (D) $50.00- $75.00, This
office can inform you of 10 or more, other lodging facilities., • PAYMENT: Cash
Visa M/C • DATES AVAILABLE: Year round, • BED TYPE: S • BEDS: 1-2 •
FOOD: Caf. OCR • INFO: Rooms with TV, telephones.Coin Washer/Dryer, Free
Parking, Linens included. Rooms will be cleaned by house staff. • ACTIVITIES:
Indoor pool, tennis, squash, cultural activities, sightseeing. Gymnastic Hall, Table
Tennis, Solarium.

42 Salzburg

Billroth Hotels (T)
Billrothstrasse 10-18, 5020 , Salzburg, Ph: 43-662-620-596, Fax:
43-662-625963, ASK FOR: Residence Office
ROOM PRICING: (S) $40.00 - $63.00, (D) $65.00 - $95.00, Breakfast included, •
PAYMENT: Cash Trav. Ck Visa M/C Amex • DATES AVAILABLE: July 1- Sept.
24, • BEDS: 1-4 • FOOD: Caf. SB OCR • INFO: Coin washers/dryers, TV lounge,
free parking, outdoor swimming pool, coach parking. • ACTIVITIES: Close by:
Bavarian and Swiss Alps; Mozart festival; thriving market place; cathedrals;
palace; Int'l music center; Salzburg Festival. (end of July to end of Aug.)
DIRECTIONS: From Hwy A 10: Get off at Salzburg - Sud (South) go to Salzburg
Center. At the 4th traffic light (3rd is not running regularly) turn right to Billroth
Str. Follow street to NE ARE on left side.

43 Vienna ?

Jugendgastehaus (T) Hutteldorf-Hacking
Schlossberggasse 8, 1130 , Vienna, Ph: 43-1-877-15-01, Fax: 43-1-877-02-632,
ASK FOR: Housing Office
ROOM PRICING: Hostel, (S) $15.00, (D) $30.00, (Includes breakfast), • PAYMENT:
Cash Visa • DATES AVAILABLE: Year Round, • ROOM TYPE: SR • BED TYPE: S
• BEDS: 2-8 • BATH: C P • FOOD: Caf. VM • INFO: Children welcome, Youth
hostel card required. Coin washers/dryers, TV lounge, (satellite TV) free parking,
Linens included. • ACTIVITIES: Vienna and surroundings.

44 Vienna

Unterstutzungsverein f. Studierende (T)
an der Universitat f. Bodenkultur, Potzleinsdorfer Str. 40, A-1180, Vienna, Ph:
479-29-77 Voice or Fax, ASK FOR: Dir., Studenthouse
ROOM PRICING: Per person, per night, (S) $10.00-$25.00, • PAYMENT: Cash •
DATES AVAILABLE: July 1-Sept. 30, • BED TYPE: S • BEDS: 1-2 • FOOD: No •
INFO: Self-service kitchen. • ACTIVITIES: School in beautiful out-skirts of Vienna,
theater, opera, Ring City tours, museum, world famous art galleries.

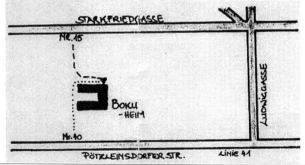

BELGIUM

45 Brussels   ?

Vrije Universiteit Brussell (T)
Triom Flaan 1, Toegang 7, 1050 , Brussels, Ph: 32-02-629 28 31, Fax:
32-02-629 36 19, ASK FOR: W. Emmerechts, Housing Serv.
ROOM PRICING: (S) $12.00, (D) $20.00, 5 days or longer $ 8.00 per night, •
PAYMENT: Cash Only • DATES AVAILABLE: July 15 -Sept. 25, • FOOD: Caf. SB
NR • INFO: Children under 12 years, half price. • ACTIVITIES: Belgian coast;
Wavre Recreation Park; town center; elegant books and antigue market; Parliment
square; palaces; 100 museums.

46 Ghent   ?

Universiteit Gent (RUG) (T)
Stalhof 6, 9000, Ghent, Ph: 32- 91 264 71 00, ASK FOR: Myriam Van Den
Branden
ROOM PRICING: (S) $15.00, Breakfast incl., • PAYMENT: Cash Only • DATES
AVAILABLE: July 15 -Sept. 25, • ROOM TYPE: SR • BED TYPE: S • BEDS: 1 •
BATH: C • FOOD: Caf. SB VM NR • ACTIVITIES: Sightseeing; Cathedrals; fine
art museums; architecture.

BRITAIN/UK

England

47 Birmingham, England

The Univ. of Birmingham, Chamberlain Hall (T)
Church Road, Edgbaston, Birmingham, England B15 3SZ, Ph: 44-0121- 454
6022, Fax: 44- 0121- 456 2415, ASK FOR: Julie Zacaroli, Conference Office
ROOM PRICING: (S) $40.00/B&B, • PAYMENT: Cash Per. Ck Trav. Ck •
DATES AVAILABLE: Easter Vacation
Mid June - Mid Sept., • BED TYPE: S • BEDS: 1-2 • FOOD: Caf. VM NR • INFO:
Coin washers/dryers, TV lounge, free parking. • ACTIVITIES: Sports Centre,
Tennis, Swimming, Licensed Bar.

48 Durham, England   ?   &

Van Mildert College (T) Mill Hill Lane
Box No. Dur/H93, Durham, England DH1 3LH, Ph: 44-0191 374 3967, Fax:
44-0191 374 3974, ASK FOR: Elaine Watson
ROOM PRICING: Bed & Breakfast/ per person, (S) $28.00, (D) $52.70, •
PAYMENT: Cash Per. Ck Trav. Ck • DATES AVAILABLE: Mar. 15 - Apr.16,
June 20 -Sept. 30, • ROOM TYPE: SR • BED TYPE: S • BEDS: 2 • BATH: C S P
• FOOD: Caf. VM • INFO: Coin washers/dryers, linen included, free parking,
children welcome, licensed bar. • ACTIVITIES: Sports Centre, tennis, swimming.
Close to Durham City- world Heritage Site; Cathedral and Castle; Botanical
Gardens; Museums.

49 Exeter, England   ?   &

Univ. of Exeter, Devonshire House (T)
Box No. EX794, Stocker Road, Exeter, England EX4 4PZ, Ph: 44-01392-211500,
Fax: 44-01392-263512 (24 Hrs.), E-mail: conferences@exeter.ac.uk, ASK FOR:
Nicky Brown, Holiday Bkg. Office
ROOM PRICING: (S) $20.00/B&B (D) $46.00/B&B, • PAYMENT: Cash Only •
DATES AVAILABLE: Mar. -Apr., July -Sept. , Dec.-Jan., • ROOM TYPE: SR • BED
TYPE: S • BEDS: 1-2 • BATH: C P • FOOD: Caf. SB VM • INFO: Coin
washer/dryer, TV lounge, free parking. • ACTIVITIES: Sports centre, tennis,
swimming, licensed bar

50 Gloucestershire, England   ?

Royal Agricultural College, Cirencester (T)
Box. No. RA/ H93, Cirencester, Gloucestershire, England GL7 6JS, Ph: 0285
640644, Fax: 0285 650219, ASK FOR: Teresa North, Conf. Office
ROOM PRICING: Bed & Breakfast, (S) $25.00 - $50.00/standard p/p, $40.00 -
$60.00/en-suite p/p, • PAYMENT: Cash Only • DATES AVAILABLE: Aug. 6- Oct.
6, • BED TYPE: S • BEDS: 1-2 • FOOD: Caf. VM NR • INFO: Eight different
lodging facilities. • ACTIVITIES: Sports centre, tennis, licensed bar.

(T) = Travelers Accommodations   (E) = Educational Related   (C) = Groups & Conference Use

51 Guildford, Surrey, England

University of Surrey (T)
Box No. SUR/H93, Guildford, Surrey, England GU2 5XH, Ph: 44-01483-259157, Fax: 44-01483-579266, ASK FOR: Karen Madgwick, Conf. Office
ROOM PRICING: (S) $43.00/B&B, • PAYMENT: Cash Visa M/C • DATES AVAILABLE: June 7 - August 24, • ROOM TYPE: SR Apt. • BED TYPE: S • BEDS: 1 • BATH: C P • FOOD: Caf. VM NR • INFO: Facilities available for groups, self-catering flats & houses, free parking, linens provided. • ACTIVITIES: Sports Centre, tennis, licensed bar. Close to town & station. 35 minutes by rail from London.

U N I V

52 Kent, England

The Univ. of Canterbury, Tanglewood (T)   Univ. Canterbury, Canterbury
Kent, England CT2 7LX, Ph: 44-01227 828000, Fax: 44-01227 828019, E-mail:
ConferenceCaterbury@urc.ac.ur, Web Site: www.urc.ac.uk/hospitality
ROOM PRICING: (S) $29.00/B&B, (D) $48.00/B&B, • PAYMENT: Cash Per. Ck
Trav. Ck Visa M/C • DATES AVAILABLE: Apr. 1 - 25, July - Sept. , • BEDS:
1-2 • FOOD: Caf. SB VM NR OCR • INFO: Laundry, shops, banks, bars, TV
lounge, free parking.   En-suite rooms available. • ACTIVITIES: Nearby:
swimming, water sports. Sports centre, tennis, library, theatre. Vineyard trail;
Day Trips to France & Belgium; close to Canterbury.
DIRECTIONS: From the North or West: M25, M20, M2, A2. Canterbury to the
university: Canterbury Central Ring Road, A290 Nhitstable, St Thomas Hill,
Approx. (1 mile) 1,6 Km along the A 290, University entrance on right (sign
posted) near top of hill.

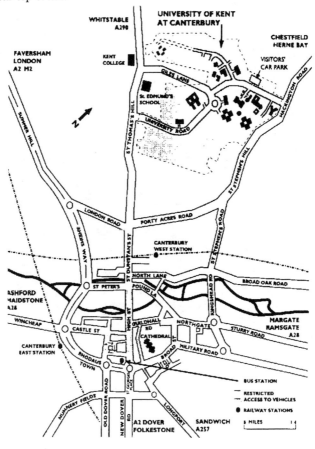

53　Kent, England　　　　　　　　　　　　　　　?

University of London, Wye College (T)
Wye, Ashford, Kent, England TN25 5AH, Ph: 44-0233-812401, Ext: 351, ASK
FOR: General Manager
ROOM PRICING: (S) $25.00/B&B, (D) $52.00/B&B, • PAYMENT: Cash Per. Ck
Trav. Ck • DATES AVAILABLE: April, July 1 -Sept. 30, • BED TYPE: S • FOOD:
Caf. SB VM NR • INFO: Can accommodate conferences up to 190 persons. •
ACTIVITIES: Surrounding countryside of superb beauty; Canterbury Cathedral,
Gateway to the Continent. Agricultural College of University of London.

54　Lancaster, England　　　　　　　　　　　?　♿

Lancaster University (T)
Box No. LA/H93, Bailrigg, Lancaster, England LA1 4YT, Ph: 44-0152- 465201,
Ext: 2176, Fax: 44-0152- 4843695, ASK FOR: Hilary Barraclough, Conf. Off.
ROOM PRICING: (S) $38.00, Bed & Breakfast, • PAYMENT: Cash Only • DATES
AVAILABLE: Mar. 23 - Apr. 15, July 1 - Sept. 25, • ROOM TYPE: SR Apt. • BED
TYPE: S • BATH: C P • FOOD: Caf. • ACTIVITIES: Sports centre, tennis,
swimming, licensed bar.

55　Leeds, England　　　　　　　　　　　　?　♿

University of Leeds (T)
Box No. LE/H93, Leeds, England LS2 9JT, Ph: 44-0113-2336100, Fax:
44-0113-2336107, ASK FOR: Mrs. Susan Lacey
ROOM PRICING: (S) $32.00/B&B, • PAYMENT: Cash • DATES AVAILABLE: Mar.
29-Apr. 22, July 5-Spet. 30,, • BED TYPE: S • FOOD: Caf. • INFO: Flats
available for up to 5 persons. • ACTIVITIES: Sports Centre, Tennis, Licensed Bar.

56　Liverpool, England　　　　　　　　　　　?

Univ. of Liverpool (T) Greenbank House
Greenbank Lane, Liverpool, England L17 1AG, Ph: 44-0151-794-6440, Fax:
44-0151- 794-6520, ASK FOR: Caroline Griffiths, Conf. Officer
ROOM PRICING: (S) $22.00, Bed & Breakfast, • PAYMENT: Cash • DATES
AVAILABLE: Apr. 13- May 1, June 15- Sept. 18 , • ROOM TYPE: SR • BED TYPE:
S • BEDS: 1 • BATH: C • FOOD: Caf. • ACTIVITIES: Sports centre, tennis,
swimming, licensed bar.

57　London, England

Campbell House (T) University College
5-10 Taviton Street, London, England WCIH OBX, Ph: 44-0171-391-1479, Fax:
44-0171-388-0060, ASK FOR: House Manager, V. Griffiths
ROOM PRICING: (S) $30.00, (D) $51.00, • PAYMENT: Cash Only Trav. Ck •
DATES AVAILABLE: June-Sept., • ROOM TYPE: SR • BED TYPE: S • BEDS: 1-2 •
BATH: C • FOOD: VM NR • INFO: Georgian houses in central London with
self-catering accommodations. Reductions on stays of over 7 days. • ACTIVITIES:
London sight-seeing; theaters; cinema; museums; concerts, etc.
DIRECTIONS: Nearest underground Euston Station. From there cross Euston
Road, walk through small garden at the side of "Friends House" , turn right, cross
the street. Taviton St. is on the left and Campbell house is half way down the
street on the left.

58　London, England　　　　　　　　　　　　♿

Goldsmith's College, University of London (T)
Lewisham Way, New Cross, London, England S.E. 146NW, Ph: (0171) 919 -7132,
Fax: 0171 919 -7134, E-mail: S.Bailey-Watts@gold.ac.uk, ASK FOR: Sam
Bailey-Watts, Trading Services Manager
ROOM PRICING: (S) £20/person/night, • PAYMENT: Cash Trav. Ck Visa Amex
• DATES AVAILABLE: Mar.22 -Apr.23, July 4 -Sept.18, • BEDS: 1 • FOOD: Caf.
VM NR OCR • INFO: Children welcome, reserv. required • ACTIVITIES: Tennis
courts, gymnasium, licensed bar. Close to art galleries; theaters; opera; historic
Greenwich; the Thames; near trains; underground buses; Royal Observatory.

U
N
I
V

(T) = Travelers Accommodations　(E) = Educational Related　(C) = Groups & Conference Use

59 **London, England**   ⑆

International House (T)
109 Brookhill Road, Woolwich, London, England SE 18 6RZ, Ph:
44-0181-854-1418, Fax: 44-0181-855-9257, ASK FOR: Director or Deputy
ROOM PRICING: Hostel, (S) $20.00 - 22.90, (D) $15.00-$66.00/person, includes
breakfast, Disc. for longer stays, • PAYMENT: Cash Trav. Ck • DATES
AVAILABLE: Mid.- Dec.- Early Jan., Easter vacation, Late June- Late Sept., •
ROOM TYPE: SR Apt. • BED TYPE: S • BEDS: 1-2 • BATH: C P • FOOD: Caf.
VM NR • INFO: Children welcome, linens provided. Laundry room, telephones in
reception area,   Apartments per day: $39.84 - $47.29. Self catering & B&B. •
ACTIVITIES: TV room, table tennis. Thames Barrier National Maritime muesum;
riverboats; Queens House Greenwich; Millenium Dome; Greenwich Park; London
sightseeing.
DIRECTIONS: From Heathrow - Underground Piccadilly line-change Hammersmith
to District Line to Embankment Station, then a short walk to Charing Cross train
station direct to Woolwich Arsenal station.
From Gatewick Airport train station to London Bridge, NOT Victoria, then change
to train direct to Woolwich Arsenal Station.

60 **London, England**

International Students House (T)
229 Great Portland St., London, England W1N 5HD, Ph: 44-0171-631-8310, Fax:
44-0171-631-8315, E-mail: accom@ish.org.uk, Web Site: www.ish.org.uk, ASK
FOR: Accommodations Officer
ROOM PRICING: Single 29.50, Twin £21.00/person, 3/4 bedded 17.50   ,
Multi-bedded, bed only £9.99, • PAYMENT: Cash Trav. Ck Visa M/C • DATES
AVAILABLE: Year Round, Most at Christmas, Easter,Summer• ROOM TYPE: SR •
BED TYPE: S • BEDS: 1-2 • BATH: C P • FOOD: Caf. SB VM NR OCR • INFO:
No children, student groups welcome, additional housing at 10 York Terrace East,
NW. $16.00 refundable key deposit. Ensuite rooms available.   Coin
washers/dryers. • ACTIVITIES: student accomodations and club conference
center, cyber caje/, fitness Center. Comfortable bar, fitness centre London Zoo;
Regents Park; Madame Tussauds; In the heart of the West End. Includes new
and exciting Cyber Cafe.

61 **London, England**

John Adams Hall (T) University of London
15-23 Endsleigh St., London, England WC1H 0DP, Ph: 44-0171-387-4086, Fax:
44-0171-383-0164, ASK FOR: Carrie Marshall
ROOM PRICING: Approx. Prices: Bed and breakfast, (S) $32.00(stud),
$35.00(indiv), (D) $56.00 (stud), $61.00 (indiv) , • PAYMENT: Cash Trav. Ck Visa
M/C • DATES AVAILABLE: Year round, except Dec.22-Jan.6, • ROOM TYPE: SR
Apt. • BED TYPE: S • BEDS: 1-2 • BATH: C P • FOOD: Caf. VM NR • INFO: Coin
washer/ dryer, children welcome. • ACTIVITIES: Games room, T.V. rooms, study
rooms, music room.   Close to City, Centre of London; Theatreland; British
Museum; major underground and main line train stations.
DIRECTIONS: From Custom Station, about 3 minutes walk. Cross Euston Road
at pedestrian crossing, walk through the small garden near "Friends Meeting
House, turn left then rightf into Endsleigh St.

62 **London, England**

King's Campus Vacation Bureau, King's College London (T)
127 Stamford St., London, England SE1 9NQ, Ph: 44-0171-928-3777, Fax:
44-0171-928-5777, ASK FOR: Conference Administrator
ROOM PRICING: (S) $26.50 - $36.00/B&B, (D) $48.00 - $54.60/B&B, Longstay
discount, • PAYMENT: Cash Trav. Ck Visa M/C • DATES AVAILABLE: Dec.
14-23, 1997, April 3-23, June 9-Sept.16, • ROOM TYPE: SR • BED TYPE: S •
BEDS: 1-2 • BATH: C P • FOOD: Caf. SB VM NR • INFO: Children welcome.
King's College has 8 residence halls within Cen. London, more than 3000 beds
available. Bed linen and towels provided. Car & bus parking on 2 campuses.
Children welcome. • ACTIVITIES: College overlooks park area; quiet locations; all
tourist attractions easily accessible by public transport.All residences have access
to TV Lounges/TV's. All are easily reached by public transport. Good locations for
all tourist attractions.

(T) = Travelers Accommodations   (E) = Educational Related   (C) = Groups & Conference Use

L. S. E. , Rosebery Hall (T)

90 Rosebery Ave., London, England EC1R 4TY, Ph: (071)-278-3251, Fax: (071) 278-2068, ASK FOR: Office Administrator

ROOM PRICING: (S) £24-30, (D) £42-46, Bed & Breakfast, • PAYMENT: Cash Per. Ck Trav. Ck Visa M/C • DATES AVAILABLE: Mar. 20- Apr. 24, June 13-Sept. 24, • BED TYPE: S D • FOOD: Caf. VM NR • INFO: Conference rooms. • ACTIVITIES: Buckingham Palace; St. Paul's Cathedral; Tower of London.

DIRECTIONS: London Transport: Rosebery Avenue is served well by public transport. Both Angel (Northernline) and Farrington (district and Circle lines) underground stations are within a few minutes walk. Bus routes 19 and 38 go down Rosebery to Oxford St., the British Museum, Piccadilly Circus and Knightsbridge; Number 17 goes to Covent Garden and the Strand.

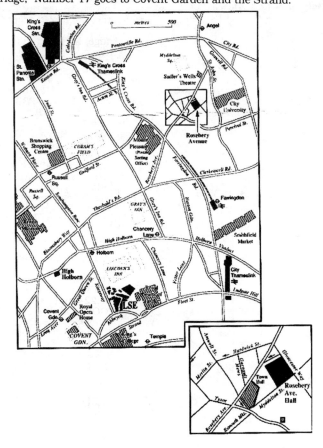

U
N
I
V

64 London, England　　　　　　　　　　　　　　?

London Hospital Medical College (T) Student's Hostel
Philpot St., London, England E.1, Ph: 44-0171-377-7626, ASK FOR: Summer Lodging
ROOM PRICING: Per week, per person, (S) $129.00/B&B, $142.00/B&B + dinner, • PAYMENT: Cash • DATES AVAILABLE: April 1- Sept. 30, • ROOM TYPE: SR • BED TYPE: S • BEDS: 1-2 • BATH: C • FOOD: Caf. • INFO: $450.00 per person, per calender month for bed and breakfast. $476.00 per person, per calender month for dinner, bed, and breakfast. • ACTIVITIES: Lounges with TV, pool and table tennis tables, nearby tennis courts, reading room, squah courts, launderette

65 London, England　　　　　　　　　　　　　　♿

London School of Economics (T)
Houghton St., London, England WC2 2AE, Ph: 44-171-955-7575,　Fax: 44-171-955-7676, E-mail: vacations@lse.ac.uk, ASK FOR: Conference Office
ROOM PRICING: Six residences providing Bed and Breakfast or self catering. singles,pairs, triples; standard and en-suite(S) (D) from 17£/person, • PAYMENT: Cash Per. Ck Trav. Ck Visa M/C Amex • DATES AVAILABLE: Mar. 20- April 24, June17 - Sept. 25, • ROOM TYPE: SR • BED TYPE: S • BEDS: 1-2 • FOOD: Caf. SB VM NR OCR • INFO: Butlers Wharf Residence, (S/C),44- 0171-407-7164. Carr Saunders Hall, (B&B, S/C), 44-0171-323-9712. (B&B), Rosebery Ave. Hall, (B&B), 44-0171-278-3251. Bankside House, (B&B) 44-0171-633-9877. High Holbom 44-171-379-5589, Panhild 44-171-387-7743 • ACTIVITIES: All of London and environment.

66 London, England

London School of Economics (T) Passfield Hall
Endsleight Place, London, England WC1 HOPW, Ph: 44-0171-387-3584,　Fax: 44-0171-387-0419, ASK FOR: Bursar
ROOM PRICING: (S) $35.00/B&B, (D) $70.00/B&B, Triple, $80.00/B&B, • PAYMENT: Cash Trav. Ck Visa M/C • DATES AVAILABLE: July,Aug.,Sept., Mar.-Apr., • ROOM TYPE: SR • BED TYPE: S • BEDS: 1-3 • BATH: C • FOOD: Caf. VM • INFO: Coin washer/dryer, TV lounge. • ACTIVITIES: Central London. Near British Museum; Madame Tussards; Oxford Street; West End.

67 London, England   ?

Middlesex University (T) PLA Halls of Residence
Chancellor Place off Agroorome Rd., London, England N22-6UZ, Ph: (081)--888-4866, ASK FOR: Accomm. Manager
ROOM PRICING: (S) $15.00, apartment for 6 persons, $395., • PAYMENT: Cash Trav. Ck • DATES AVAILABLE: June 27 - Sept. 9, • BEDS: 1 • FOOD: No • INFO: Bed linens provided, fully equipped kitchens. • ACTIVITIES: London only 20 minutes away. 5 minute walk from Colindale Tube Station. (Northern Line) 5 min. walk from Woodgreen Tube Station. (Piccadilly Line)

68 London, England

Queen Mary and Westfield College (T)
Mile End Road, London, England E1 4NS, Ph: 44-0181-983-0146, ASK FOR: Sue Mussett, Conf. Officer
ROOM PRICING: (S) $26.70, (D) $31.00, (includes breakfast), • PAYMENT: Cash Visa • DATES AVAILABLE: Apr. 6- Apr.30, June 13-Sept.17, • ROOM TYPE: SR • BED TYPE: S • BEDS: 1 • BATH: C S • FOOD: Caf. SB VM NR • INFO: Children over 10 years welcome, Educational and travel groups. • ACTIVITIES: Close to underground station and central London.

69 London, England   ?   ♿

Royal Holloway, Univ. Of London (T)
Box No. RH/H93 Royal Holloway, Egham Hill, London, England TW20 0EX, Ph: 44-01784 443045, Fax: 44-01784 437520, ASK FOR: Susan Nicholls
ROOM PRICING: $27.50/B&B, • PAYMENT: Cash • BEDS: 1 • FOOD: Caf. • ACTIVITIES: Tennis, Licensed Bar

U
N
I
V

The London Goodenough Trust (T) London & Wm. Goodenough House
Mecklenburgh Square, London, England WC1N 2AB, Ph: 44-0171-837-8888, ASK
FOR: The Warden
ROOM PRICING: (S) £23.000+vat, (D) £36.00+vat, Suites: £62.00- £82.00, (For
less than 3 months stay) Discounts for 3 months or longer, • PAYMENT: Cash
Visa M/C • DATES AVAILABLE: Year Round-Fellowship House, • ROOM TYPE:
SR Apt. Suite • BED TYPE: S • BATH: C P • FOOD: Caf. VM NR • INFO: 100
1-3 bdrm. flats avail. for 1 to 6 mo. leases. Children's nursery in   Wm.
Goodenough House, 320 singles/men, 101 singles/women. Post-graduate students
only during academic year. • ACTIVITIES: Health club. Easy walking distance to
the British Museum London University. Senate House, Inns of Court and Law
Society - within 1 mile of major London attractions.

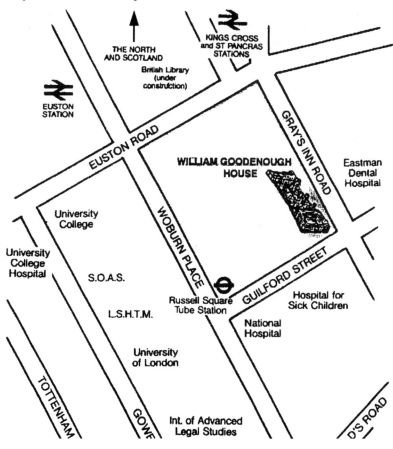

The Univ. of Westminster (T) Commercial Services
Luxborough Suite, 35 Marylebone Road, London, England NW1 5LS, Ph: 44-0171-911-5807, Fax: 44-0171- 911-5141, E-mail: comserv@Westminster.ac.uk
ROOM PRICING: (S) $36.00 - $65.00, • PAYMENT: Cash Trav. Ck Visa •
DATES AVAILABLE: July 5- Sept. 16, • ROOM TYPE: SR Apt. • BEDS: 1-2 •
BATH: C S P • FOOD: Caf. SB VM NR OCR • INFO: Up to 1200 beds, some
ensuite, available in 7 student residences. Coin laundry, TV lounge, 24 hour
access & security.   (car parking available at Harrow Hall) • ACTIVITIES: Central
and north London locations, near Royal parks and public gardens. Very accessible
by public transit and within easy walking distance to main tourist sights and local
attractions. Houses of Parliament; Westminster Abbey; Madam Tussauds.
DIRECTIONS: Marylebone Hall: Baker Street Tube Stop, International House:
Lambeth/North Waterloo Tube Stop, Wigram House: Victoria Tube Stop, Furnival
House: Archway/Highgate Tube Stop, Wells Street: Oxford Circus Tube Stop,
Alexander Fleming: Old Street Tube Stop, Harrow Hall: Northwick Park Tube Stop

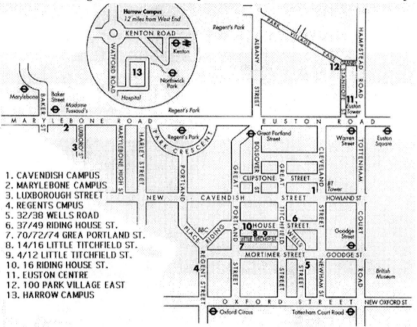

1. CAVENDISH CAMPUS
2. MARYLEBONE CAMPUS
3. LUXBOROUGH STREET
4. REGENTS CMPUS
5. 32/38 WELLS ROAD
6. 37/49 RIDING HOUSE ST.
7. 70/72/74 GREA PORTLAND ST.
8. 14/16 LITTLE TITCHFIELD ST.
9. 4/12 LITTLE TITCHFIELD ST.
10. 16 RIDING HOUSE ST.
11. EUSTON CENTRE
12. 100 PARK VILLAGE EAST
13. HARROW CAMPUS

U
N
I
V

72 London, England

University College, London (T) Residence Office
117 Gower Street, London, England WC1 E 6BT, Ph: 44-0171-380-7077, Fax:
44-0171-383-0407, ASK FOR: Vacation Accommodation
ROOM PRICING: Hostel, (S) £14.50 - £23.00, • PAYMENT: Cash Trav. Ck Visa
• DATES AVAILABLE: Dec.17 - Jan. 6, Mar. 24 - Apr. 20, June 8 - Sept. 23., •
BED TYPE: S • BEDS: 1-2 • FOOD: Caf. SB VM NR • INFO: Laundramat, Bar &
TV Lounge. • ACTIVITIES: Tennis courts, squah courts. Central location - Close to
theaters, shops and restaurants. British Museum and the New British Library
DIRECTIONS: As we have various halls dotted around central London, this may be
difficult. We have a booklet available with a map.

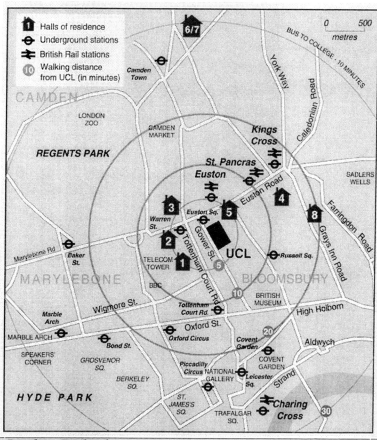

73 London, England   ?

University College London (T) Ramsay Halls
Gower Street., London, England WCIE 6BT, Ph: (071) 387-7966, Fax: (071)
383-0407, ASK FOR: Helen Jenkins, Site Mgr.
ROOM PRICING: (S) $13.00-$28.00, (D) $27.00-$57.00, Bed and breakfast, •
PAYMENT: Cash Trav. Ck • DATES AVAILABLE: Dec. 19-Jan. 8, Mar. 3-Apr. 4,
• FOOD: Caf. SB VM • INFO: Children welcome. Call ahead for reservations, Bar,
Laundry. Additional dates available: June25-Sept. 24. • ACTIVITIES: Central
location near West End Shops; Theaters; good transportation; Regents Park.

74 London, England   ? ♿

University College, London (T)
Max Rayne House/Ivor Evans Hall, 109 Camden Road,, London, England NW1
9HA, Ph: 44-0171- 485-9377, Fax: 44-0171-284-3328, ASK FOR: Residence
Manager, C. Marshall
ROOM PRICING: (S) $31.00, 2-nights plus-$30.00, (D) $53.00, 2-nights
plus-$52.00, • PAYMENT: Cash Per. Ck • DATES AVAILABLE: Mar. 23 - April
18, June 8 - Sept.19, • ROOM TYPE: SR Apt. • BED TYPE: S • BEDS: 1-2 •
BATH: C P • FOOD: Caf. SB NR • INFO: Children welcome,evening meal also
available. 600 beds available in single and two bed rooms. • ACTIVITIES: Tennis
court, clubhouse with juke box, games, etc. London Zoo; Hampstead Heath;
Camden Market; 20 minutes from West End.

75 London, England   ?

University of London (T) 19-26 Cartwright Gardens,
Hughes Parry Hall, London, England WC1 H 9 EF, Ph: 44-0171- 387-1477, Fax:
44-0171- 383-4328, ASK FOR: Bursar
ROOM PRICING: Hostel, (S) $30.83/ B&B, $36.66/B&B, Dinner, • PAYMENT:
Cash Trav. Ck Visa M/C • DATES AVAILABLE: Mid Dec -Early Jan.; Mid
Mar.- Mid April; Mid June -Sept., • BEDS: 1 • FOOD: Caf. VM • INFO: 290
single, 10 twins. • ACTIVITIES: Squash and tennis courts. Close to theaters;
music; museums; sightseeing in London.

76 London, England   ?

University of London (T) Canterbury Hall
Cartwright Gardens, London, England WC1 H 9EE, Ph: 44-0171- 387-5526, Fax:
44-0171-383-7729, ASK FOR: Bursar, Canterbury Hall
ROOM PRICING: (S) £22.00/B&B, (D) £26.00/B&B, • PAYMENT: Cash Trav. Ck
• DATES AVAILABLE: Mar.- April, June- Sept., (During British Univ. vacations)•
ROOM TYPE: SR • BED TYPE: S • BEDS: 1 • BATH: S P • FOOD: Caf. NR •
ACTIVITIES: Tennis, squash, theatre, films, concerts, lectures, museums.
Central London sightseeing; Meeting & Lecture rooms; theaters and cinemas
nearby.

77 London, England   ?

University of London (T) College Hall, Malet Street
London, England WC1 E 7 HZ, Ph: 44-0171- 636-8982 or 44-0171- 580-9131,
Fax: 44-0171-636-6591, ASK FOR: Miss D. C. Cruden, Bursar
ROOM PRICING: Hostel, (S) $20.00/ B&B, $25.00/ B&B& Dinner, (D) $40.00/
B&B, • PAYMENT: Cash Per. Ck Trav. Ck • DATES AVAILABLE: During
University vacations (Easter and Summer), • BED TYPE: S • BEDS: 1-2 • FOOD:
Caf. VM NR OCR • INFO: Must be over 16 yrs. of age. Coin washer/dryer, TV
lounge, no parking. • ACTIVITIES: Central London.

78 London, England   ?

University of London (T) Commonwealth Hall
Cartwright Gardens, London, England WC 1 H 9EB, Ph: 071- 387-0311, ASK
FOR: Miss E.R. Parkin, Bursar
ROOM PRICING: (S) $35.55, Break. & Dinner included, • PAYMENT: Cash Only
Trav. Ck • DATES AVAILABLE: June - Sept., Christmas, Easter, limited dates.•
BED TYPE: S • BEDS: 1 • FOOD: Caf. NR • ACTIVITIES: Tennis, squash in
residence. Cultural activities in London; theater; museums; sightseeing. In
Bloomsbury, good connections to Gatwick and Heathrow airports.

79   London, England

University of London (T)   Connaught Hall
41 Tavistock Square, London, England WC1H 9EX, Ph: 44-0171- 387-6181, Fax 44-0171-383-4109, ASK FOR: Ms. R. Wilson, Bursar
ROOM PRICING: Price in British Pounds, (S) £21.50, (D) £39.00, Includes breakfast, • PAYMENT: Cash Per. Ck Trav. Ck • DATES AVAILABLE: March, April, June- Sept., • BED TYPE: S • BEDS: 1 • FOOD: Caf. NR • INFO: Over 18 yrs.of age.   Bar, TV rooms, and launderette available. • ACTIVITIES: Very attractive central location near to Oxford St.; British Museum and the West End. Ideally situated for mainline railways stations & tube stations.

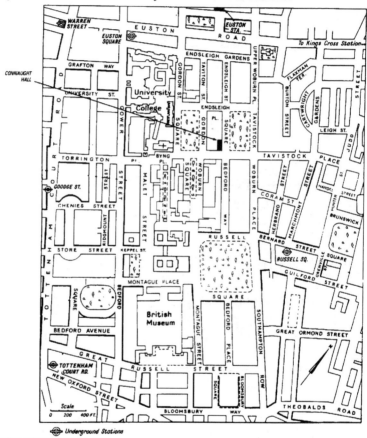

⊕ Underground Stations

80   London, England   ?

University of London (T)   International Hall
Brunswick Square, London, England WC1 N1AS, Ph: 44-0171- 837-0746
• PAYMENT: • ROOM TYPE: • BATH: • FOOD:

81 London, England

University of London (T)
Lillian Penson Hall, Talbot Square, London, England W2 1TT, Ph:
44-0171-685-2500 44-0171-724-1258, ASK FOR: Accommodation Office
ROOM PRICING: (S) $39.00, (D) $58.00, • PAYMENT: Cash Trav. Ck • DATES
AVAILABLE: Year round, Sept.-Oct. Limited availability, • FOOD: Caf. VM NR •
INFO: All rooms have private bathrooms and telephone. Token operated
washers/dryers, TV lounge. Some flats and studios available. No conference
facilities. • ACTIVITIES: Located in Central London.

82 London, England

University of London (T) Nutford House
Brown Street, London, England WIH 6AH, Ph: 44-171- 468-5800, Fax:
44-171-258-1781, ASK FOR: The Bursar
ROOM PRICING: (S) $34.00/ w/breakfast, $41.00/ Full board, (D) $51.00/
w/breakfast, $66.00/ Full board, • PAYMENT: Cash Trav. Ck • DATES
AVAILABLE: Mid-Mar.- Mid-April, Mid- Jun- Mid Sept., During British Univ.
vacations.• ROOM TYPE: SR • BED TYPE: S • BEDS: 1-2 • BATH: C • FOOD:
Caf. • INFO: No smoking, coin washers & dryers, quiet room, privategarden, TV
rooms. Telephones in all rooms • ACTIVITIES: Near Leisure center for swimming
and gym. Studies & Cultural activities in London, minutes away from Oxford
Street for shops and the Royal Parks. Close to Madame Tussauds and
Planetarium.
DIRECTIONS: From Gatwick Airport take the 'Gatwick Express' train to Victoria
Railway station and then a taxi ride to Nutford House.
From Heathrow Airport take the 'Heathrow Express' train to Paddington Station
and then a short taxi ride to Nutford House.

83 London, Uxbridge, England

Brunel University/Conf. Centre (T)
Box No. BU/H93, Uxbridge, London, Uxbridge, England UB8 3PH, Ph:
44-01895-274-000, Fax: 44-01895-203-142
ROOM PRICING: (S) $28.00/ B&B, • PAYMENT: Cash Visa M/C • DATES
AVAILABLE: June18-Sept.18, and some year round, • ROOM TYPE: SR • BED
TYPE: S • BEDS: 1 • BATH: P • FOOD: Caf. SB VM NR • INFO: Located in West
London. Ideal for Central London and Windsor. • ACTIVITIES: Sports centre,
tennis, licensed bar. 40 minutes by tube to Central London; 4 miles from
Heathrow airport.

84 Manchester, England

Manchester/ UMIST Conf. Centre (T)
Box No. UM/H93 P. O. Box 88, Sackville St., Manchester, England M60 1QD, Ph:
44-0161 200 4076, Fax: 44-061 200 4090, ASK FOR: Richard Handscombe -
Sales and Marketing
ROOM PRICING: $29.50, Standard rooms, • PAYMENT: Cash Per. Ck Trav. Ck
Visa M/C • DATES AVAILABLE: June, July,August, • BEDS: 1 • FOOD: Caf. VM
NR • INFO: En-Suite rooms: $50.00, (avail. during vacations) Hotel rooms:
$75.00-$126.00, (avail. year round). • ACTIVITIES: Sports centre, tennis,
squash. City centre site.

85 Manchester, England

University of Manchester (T)
Department C aol, Oxford Road, Manchester, England M13 9PL, Ph:
44-0161-275-2155, Fax: 44-0161-275-2223, ASK FOR: Christine Bolton, Univ.
Conf. Office
• PAYMENT: Cash Per. Ck Trav. Ck • DATES AVAILABLE: Mar. 29 - April 16,
June 14 - Sept. 17, , • ROOM TYPE: SR Apt. • BED TYPE: S • BEDS: 1 • BATH:
C P • FOOD: Caf. NR • INFO: Self-catering flats, 55pounds. Sterling per person
per week in summer. • ACTIVITIES: Close to city centre, shops, pubs. Hour drive
to North Wales. Theatres. Granada Studio Tour, Museum of Science and
Industry, Whitworth Art Gallery and other museums all available locally.
DIRECTIONS: 1-2 Miles South of Manchester City Center. 8 miles north of
Manchester Airport. Follow green "Universities" sign, then local signs.

U
N
I
V

86 Norfolk, England   ♿

University of East Anglia (T)
Norwich NR4 7TJ, Norfolk, England NR4 7TJ, Ph: 44-01603-592941, Fax: 44-01603 -250585, Web Site: www.vea.al.uk, ASK FOR: Jilly Court
ROOM PRICING: (S) $35.00/B&B, (D) $61.25/B&B, • PAYMENT: Cash Per. Ck Trav. Ck Visa Amex • DATES AVAILABLE: Mar. 20 - Apr. 17, June19 - Sept.17, • ROOM TYPE: SR • BEDS: 1-2 • BATH: C P • FOOD: Caf. SB VM NR OCR • INFO: Coin washers/dryers, free parking, fishing on lake. Set in 20 acres of beautiful parkland. Own lake and nature trail. Free parking laundrette. • ACTIVITIES: Sports Centre, Tennis, Licensed Bar. Adjacent to historical city of Norwich.

87 Nottingham, England   ? ♿

University of Nottingham (T)
University Park, Nottingham, England NG7 2RJ, Ph: 44-0115-951-5000, Fax: 44-0115-951-5009, ASK FOR: Conference Officer
ROOM PRICING: $37.00/ B&B, • PAYMENT: Cash • DATES AVAILABLE: Mar. 22 - April. 19, July 6 - Spet. 27, • ROOM TYPE: SR • BED TYPE: S • BEDS: 1 • BATH: C S P • FOOD: Caf. SB VM NR • INFO: 3.000 beds in 13 halls of residence. Full conference facilities available. • ACTIVITIES: Sports Centre, Tennis, Swimming, Licensed Bar. Close to Nottingham City Center tourist attractions; Cinenas; Theaters; Leisure amenities.

88 Sheffield, England   ♿

Univ. of Sheffield, Conf. Services (T)
Box No. SH/H93, Hicks Building, Hounsfeld Rd., Sheffield, England S3 7RH, Ph: 44-0114-222-8822 , Fax: 44-0114- 275-4423, ASK FOR: Louise Barratt, Conf. Mgn.
ROOM PRICING: (S) £ 37-50; (D) £70-100, • PAYMENT: Cash Per. Ck • DATES AVAILABLE: Oct 1- Oct. 15., April 8-May 2, June 10-Sept.16., • ROOM TYPE: SR • BED TYPE: S • BEDS: 1-2 • BATH: C S P • FOOD: Caf. VM NR • INFO: TV lounge, free parking, coin washers/dryers.Linen included • ACTIVITIES: Sports centre, tennis, swimming, licensed bar. Close to sheffield City Center. Close to Peak District National Park.

No. Ireland

89 Belfast, No. Ireland   ♿

The Queen's Univ. of Belfast (T)
78 Malone Road, Belfast, No. Ireland BT9 5BW, Ph: 44-01232-381608, Fax: 44-01232-666680, ASK FOR: Conference Secretary
ROOM PRICING: (S) From £17 approx. Discounts for holders of valid student cards., • PAYMENT: Cash Trav. Ck • DATES AVAILABLE: June 26- Sept.12, • BEDS: 1-2 • FOOD: Caf. SB VM NR • INFO: Bedding furnished, self-catering, coin washers/dryers, TV lounge, free parking. • ACTIVITIES: Tours can be arranged by N. Ireland Tourist Board; Ulster Museum; Botanical Gardens.

90 Londonderry, No. Ireland   ?

University of Ulster (T) Magee University College
The Accommodation Office, Northland Road, Londonderry, No. Ireland BT48 7JL, Ph: 44-0375255, Fax: 44-375629, ASK FOR: I. Murdock, Conference Cord.
ROOM PRICING: (S) $22.00 (D) $44.00, • PAYMENT: Cash Per. Ck • DATES AVAILABLE: July thru Sept. and by arrangement., • FOOD: Caf. • INFO: Children not normally allowed, bedding furnished, bath shared. Free washers/dryers, TV lounge, free parking, all meals by arrangement. • ACTIVITIES: Tennis, billiards, snooker, darts. Occasional concerts and plays; Language study; short courses.

Scotland

91 Aberdeen, Scotland   ♿

University of Aberdeen (T) Conference Offices
Regent Walk, Old Aberdeen, Aberdeen, Scotland AB24 3FX, Ph: 44-01224
272664, Fax: 44-01224 276246, ASK FOR: Conference & Letting Office
ROOM PRICING: Price in British Pounds, (S) £24.20-47.50 single to fully en-suite.,
• PAYMENT: Cash Per. Ck Trav. Ck Visa M/C • DATES AVAILABLE: Mar. 29-
Apr.14, June 14- Sept. 14, Suite avail. year round, • BED TYPE: S • BEDS: 1-2 •
FOOD: Caf. SB VM OCR • INFO: Conference facilities available.   En-suite
accommodations include shower/toilet, TV, Tea/coffee, available year round. Free
parking. All linen supplied. • ACTIVITIES: Sports centre, Tennis, swimming,
licensed bar.
DIRECTIONS: Directions and map available upon request.

92 Dundee, Scotland   ?   ♿

University of Dundee (T) Residence Office
Box No. DUN/H93, Dundee, Scotland DD1 4HN, Ph: 44-01382 344039, Fax:
44-01382 202605, E-mail: g.anderson@dundee.ac.uk, ASK FOR: Graham
Anderson, Bursar of Resi.
ROOM PRICING: Bed & Beakfast, From $30.00, • PAYMENT: Cash Trav. Ck
Visa M/C • DATES AVAILABLE: Mar. 16 - Apri. 17, June 20 - Sept. 20, •
BEDS: 1-2 • FOOD: Caf. SB VM NR OCR • INFO: New en-suite rooms w/TV,
telephones, room safe, and double beds. • ACTIVITIES: Sports Centre, Tennis,
Swimming, Licensed Bar.
DIRECTIONS: University is located in the centre of Dundee City offering historical
and modern attractions.

U
N
I
V

93 Edinburgh, Scotland

Heriot-Watt University (T) Conference Office
Riccarton, Edinburgh, Scotland EH14 AS, Ph: 44-0131-451-3669,　Fax:
44-0131-451-3199, E-mail: ecc@hw.ac.ur, Web Site: www.ccc.scot.net, ASK FOR:
Marketing Executive
ROOM PRICING: (S) $45.00/B&B,
(D) $79.00/B&B, Some year round available, • PAYMENT: Cash Per. Ck Trav.
Ck Visa M/C • DATES AVAILABLE: Year round, • BED TYPE: S • BEDS: 1-2 •
FOOD: Caf. SB VM NR OCR • INFO: Free parking, car or coach, laundry facilities,
shop, bank, hairdresser, bar. Medical center. • ACTIVITIES: Sports centre,
tennis, squash, jogging circut, sunken garden.

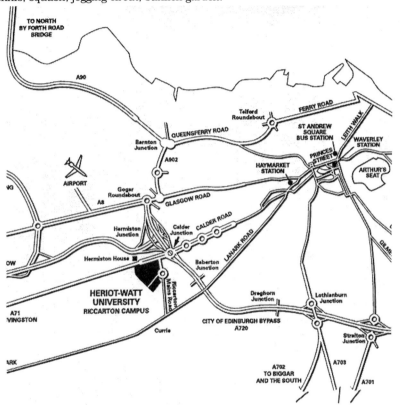

94 Edinburgh, Scotland

Pollock Halls-Edinburgh (T)
Box USC99, 18 Holyrood Park Road, Edinburgh, Scotland EH16 5AY, Ph:
44-031-667-0662, Fax: 44-031-662-9479, E-mail: Hotel.Services@ed.acuk, ASK
FOR: Alan Bruce, Dir.
ROOM PRICING: (S) From $40.00, Includes breakfast (D) From $110.00, including
breakfast, • PAYMENT: Cash Trav. Ck Visa M/C • DATES AVAILABLE: Mar.
24 - Apr.12, June 19 - Sept.25, • FOOD: Caf. SB VM • INFO: Coin
washers/dryers, free parking, linens and full service packages. • ACTIVITIES:
Sports center, tennis, swimming, licensed bar, shop.

95   Glasgow, Scotland   ?

University of Glasgow (T)
Box No. GL/H93, 52 Hillhead Street, Glasgow, Scotland G12 8PZ, Ph: 041 330
5385, Fax: 041 334 5465, ASK FOR: Ishbel Duncan, Conf. & Vacation Off.
ROOM PRICING: Bed & Breakfast, $30.95, • PAYMENT: Cash Per. Ck Trav. Ck
• DATES AVAILABLE: Mar. 21-Apr. 16, June 27-Oct. 4, • FOOD: Caf. VM NR

96   Glasgow, Scotland   ♿

University of Strathclyde (T)
50 Richmond Street, Box No. STR/H93, Glasgow, Scotland G1 1XP, Ph: 44-0141-
553- 4148, Fax: 44-0141- 553 -4149, E-mail: Rescat@mis.strath.ac.uk, Web
Site: www.strath.ac.uk/Departments/RESCAT/Sales, ASK FOR: Linda Brownlie,
Res. & Catering Serv.
ROOM PRICING: (S) $33.00, (D) $53.00, Includes breakfast, • PAYMENT: Cash
Per. Ck Trav. Ck Visa M/C • DATES AVAILABLE: June13 - Sept.12, • ROOM
TYPE: SR Apt. • BED TYPE: S • BEDS: 1-2 • BATH: C S P • FOOD: Caf. NR
OCR • INFO: Self-catering apartments available. Shop. laundry,ensuite rooms
available, bed only rooms also available. • ACTIVITIES: Sports centre, tennis,
swimming, licensed bar.
DIRECTIONS: Glasglow City Centre Location

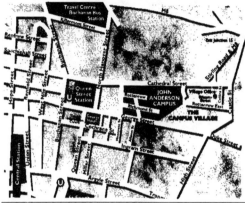

HOW TO GET THERE
By Road
From Edinburgh and the north of England
take Exit 15 off the M8 motorway. At the
second set of traffic lights turn left, then
first right. The Campus Village is on the right.
By Rail
Arrivals from the west and most Intercity
services arrive at Central Station from where
a 10 minute taxi drive will take you to the
Campus Village. Arrivals from Edinburgh
and the east come into Queen Street. This
is a 5 minute walk from the Campus Village.
By Air
A frequent bus service will take guests from
Glasgow Airport to Buchanan Bus Station,
ten minutes walk from the Campus Village.

97   St. Andrews, Scotland

University of St. Andrews (T)
79 North Street, St. Andrews, Scotland Ky16 9AJ, Ph: 44-1334-462000, Fax:
44-1334-462500, E-mail: holidays@St.Andrews.ac.uk, ASK FOR: Linda
Richardson, Conf. & Grp. Serv.
ROOM PRICING: Bed & Breakfast, (S) $40.00-$60.00, (D) $90.00, room
only-$17.00., • PAYMENT: Cash Per. Ck Trav. Ck Visa M/C • DATES
AVAILABLE: June 7- Sept. 16, • ROOM TYPE: SR • BED TYPE: S D • BEDS: 1-2
• BATH: C P • FOOD: Caf. • INFO: Standard rooms with wash basin, superior
rooms-en-suite with double size beds. • ACTIVITIES: Sports Centre, tennis,
running, licensed bar.
DIRECTIONS: Directions provided upon reservation.

U
N
I
V

University of Stirling (T)
Dept. of Commerical Operations, Stirling, Scotland FK9 4LA, Ph:
44-01786-467140, Fax: 44-01786- 467143, ASK FOR: Elaine O'Hare,
Commerical Mgn.
ROOM PRICING: Bed & Breakfast, per person, $40.00- $45.00, • PAYMENT:
Cash Per. Ck Trav. Ck Visa M/C • DATES AVAILABLE: June 4 -Sept. 8, •
ROOM TYPE: SR Apt. • BED TYPE: S • BEDS: 1 • BATH: C S P • FOOD: Caf. SB
VM NR OCR • INFO: Coin operated washers/dryers, TV lounges, free parking,
shops-newstand, chemist, supermarket, post office, bookshop, bank,travel agents;
Bed linen included. • ACTIVITIES: Sports Centre, Tennis, Swimming, Licensed
Bar, Theater/Cinema, Sunbed, Sauna, Squash, 9 hole golf course & Disco. 45
minute drive from campus to Glasgow/Edinburgh/Loch Lomond and Trossachs.

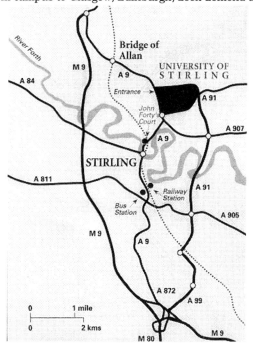

So. Wales

99   Aberystwyth, Dyfed, Wales

University of Wales (T)
Box No. CW/H93, Penglais, Aberystwyth, Dyfed, Wales SY23 3BY, Ph: 44-01970-621960, Fax: 44-01970-622899, E-mail: holidays@aber.ac.uk., ASK FOR: James Wallace, Conf. Office
ROOM PRICING: B&B $28.00/person, en-suite B&B $33.00/person   , • PAYMENT: Cash Per. Ck Trav. Ck • DATES AVAILABLE: Mar. 29-Apr.16, June 17- Sept. 17., • ROOM TYPE: SR Apt. Suite • BED TYPE: S • BEDS: 1-4 • BATH: S P • FOOD: SB VM OCR • INFO: Houses/ apartments available from $385.00 per week. Bed only for individuals (en-suite) at $26.00 Some halls will accept credit cards • ACTIVITIES: Sports centre includes   swmming pool, badminton, Multi-gym, Tennis. On campus theatre and Arts Centre.   Nearby golf courses, walking, beaches.

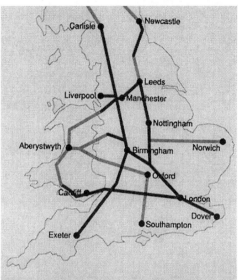

Wales

100 **Cardiff, Wales**   ♿

Cardiff University (T) Southgate House
Bevon Place, Cardiff, Wales CF4 3X2, Ph: 44-01222-874027, Fax: 44-01222-874990, E-mail: HaywardLewis@Cardiff.ac.uk, ASK FOR: Su Hayward-Lewis, Co-ordinator
ROOM PRICING: (S) $20.00, • PAYMENT: Cash Only • DATES AVAILABLE: mid-June to mid-Sept. , • ROOM TYPE: SR • BED TYPE: S • BEDS: 1 • BATH: P • FOOD: Caf. SB VM NR • INFO: Tea & coffee making facilities, self catering kitchen areas. • ACTIVITIES: City Centre Location; Self catering or catered accommodations, en suite facilities. Near Welsh Museum and castles.

CANADA

U
N
I
V

Alberta

101 Banff, ALB   ?

The Banff Center for Conferences (T)
P. O. Box 1020, Banff, ALB T0L 0C0, Ph: (403) 762-6204, ASK FOR: Centre for Conf.
ROOM PRICING: (S) $50.00, (D) $50.00, • PAYMENT: Cash Trav. Ck Visa M/C Amex • DATES AVAILABLE: Year round, • FOOD: Caf. SB VM NR • INFO: No pets, children welcome. • ACTIVITIES: Racquetball, films, art gallery, concerts, swimming, game room, tennis, musuems, TV in public lounge. The Canadian Rockies; Shopping; Whitewater Rafting; Climbing.

102 Calgary, ALB   &

Mount Royal College (T)
#31, Mount Royal Court, Calgary, ALB T3E 7C9, Ph: (403) 240-6275, ASK FOR: Garth Racher, Mgr.
ROOM PRICING: (S) $25.00 - $35.00 +tax S&D, • PAYMENT: Cash Trav. Ck Visa M/C • DATES AVAILABLE: May 15 - Aug. 15, • BEDS: 1 • FOOD: Caf. SB VM NR • INFO: Full kitchens, children welcome, no pets, coin washers/dryers, TV, telephone, free parking. • ACTIVITIES: Swimming pool, fitness center, golf driving range, close to city center. Banff National Park; Rocky Mountains for hiking and camping; Calgary Stampede.

103 Calgary, ALB   &

So. Alberta Institute of Technology (T)
1301 16th Ave., NW, Calgary, ALB T2M 0L4, Ph: (403) 284-8012, Fax: (403) 284-8435, ASK FOR: Linda Lamson
ROOM PRICING: (S) $18.00 Basic Service, $23.00 Full Service, (D) $36.00 Basic Service, $46.00 Full Service, • PAYMENT: Cash Per. Ck Trav. Ck Visa M/C • DATES AVAILABLE: May 1 - Aug. 15, • ROOM TYPE: SR Apt. • BED TYPE: S • BEDS: 1-4 • BATH: P • FOOD: Caf. SB VM NR • INFO: Children welcome with supervision, coin washers/dryers, TV lounge, easy acess to light rail transit, shopping close by. • ACTIVITIES: Campus centre- gymnasium, swimming pool daily pass, $3.50.

104 Calgary, ALB   &

University of Calgary (T)
2500 University Drive, Calgary, ALB T2N 1 N4, Ph: (403) 220-3203, Fax: (403) 220-6760, E-mail: confserv@ucalgary.ca, ASK FOR: Conference Housing
ROOM PRICING: (S)$28.00;$21.00/Student,
(D)$38.00; $30.00/ Student, • PAYMENT: Cash Trav. Ck Visa M/C • DATES AVAILABLE: May 1 - Aug. 31, • ROOM TYPE: SR Apt. • BED TYPE: S • BEDS: 1-2 • BATH: C S P • FOOD: Caf. SB VM NR • INFO: Check in at Kananaskis Hall, open 24 hours. Linens & towels provided • ACTIVITIES: Cultural activities, sports. 1988 Olympic Village.
DIRECTIONS: access from 24th Ave, NW

105 Edmonton, ALB   ?

St. Joseph's College (T) University of Alberta
114 St. & 89 Ave., Edmonton, ALB T6G 2J5, Ph: (403) 492-7681, Fax: (403) 492-8145, ASK FOR: Att: Dir. of Sum. Residence
ROOM PRICING: (S) $20.95 Daily, $130.00/ Wk, $325.00/month, (D) $31.50/Daily, $165.00/Wk, $425.00/month, (Inexpensive meal plans available), • PAYMENT: Cash Per. Ck Trav. Ck • DATES AVAILABLE: May 1 - Aug. 31, • BEDS: 1-2 • FOOD: Caf. VM NR • INFO: Children welcome. Coin washers/dryers, TV lounge, linens included, ironing facilities. Room only rates, B&B, or room + full board available. • ACTIVITIES: Ft. Edmonton Park; Muttart Conservatory; Provincial Museum; West Edmonton Mall; films; concerts; sports; Theatre Festival; Night-life district; 10 mins. from city centre.

106 **Edmonton, ALB**   ? ♿

University of Alberta (T)
116th St. & 87th Avenue, Edmonton, ALB T6G 2H6, Ph: (403) 492-4281, E-mail: conference.service@ualberta.ca, ASK FOR: Dept. of Housing, & Food Service, 44 Lister Hall
ROOM PRICING: (S) $24.00, (D) $32.00, Rates include breakfast, • PAYMENT: Cash Trav. Ck Visa M/C • DATES AVAILABLE: May 1 - Aug. 31, • BEDS: 1-2 • FOOD: Caf. SB VM NR • INFO: Linen and towel services are provided. Economical sleeping bag rates available to youth groups travelling with chaperones. Laundry facilities and dry cleaning on site. • ACTIVITIES: Swimming, tennis, hiking. Close proximity to shopping, cultural & spots facilities.

107 **Fort Mc Murray, ALB**   ♿

Keyano College (T) Clearwater Hall
9809 King Street, Fort Mc Murray, ALB T9H 1L3, Ph: (403) 791-4926, ASK FOR: Clearwater Hall Resdience Office
ROOM PRICING: (S) $25.00, • PAYMENT: Cash Per. Ck Trav. Ck • DATES AVAILABLE: Some year round as space permits. Call ahead., • ROOM TYPE: SR Apt. • BED TYPE: S • BEDS: 1 • BATH: C S • FOOD: Caf. VM NR • INFO: 6 individually-locking private bedrooms in apt. unit. Cable TV in common area, 3 washrooms. Kitchen/Cooking facilities. No children. Coin washers/dryers. • ACTIVITIES: Racquetball, art gallery, concerts, game room, gym, weight room. Oilsands Interpretive Centre; Syncrude & Suncor Plant Tours.

108 **Grande Prairie, ALB**   ?

Grande Prairie Regional College (T)
10726 - 106 Ave., Grande Prairie, ALB T8V 4C4, Ph: (403) 538-0041, Fax: (403) 539-2888, ASK FOR: Housing Office
ROOM PRICING: (S) $19.90, • PAYMENT: Cash Per. Ck Trav. Ck • DATES AVAILABLE: May 1 - Aug. 25, • FOOD: Caf. NR • INFO: Children welcome. • ACTIVITIES: Land of Peace River; Gateway to Alaska Hwy; largest earth-filled dam in N. America.

109 **Lethbridge, ALB**   ♿

Lethbridge Community College (T)
3000 College Dr. So., Lethbridge, ALB T1K 1L5, Ph: (403) 329-7218/Conf. (403) 320-3334, Web Site: www.lethbridgec.ab.ca, ASK FOR: Residence Life Office
ROOM PRICING: (S) $15.00/person/night plus 5% tax, • PAYMENT: Cash Per. Ck Visa M/C • DATES AVAILABLE: May 15 - Aug.15, • BEDS: 1 • FOOD: Caf. SB VM NR OCR • INFO: Self-contained units with kitchens, children welcome. • ACTIVITIES: Tennis, hiking, golf. Waterton National Park; Head Smashed in Buffalo Jump; Remington Carriago Centre. Visit our web page. Alberta Tourism web.

110 **Lethbridge, ALB**   ♿

University of Lethbridge (T)
4401 University Drive, Lethbridge, ALB T1K 3M4, Ph: (403) 329-2244, Fax: (403) 329-5166, E-mail: confserv.ancil@uleth.ca, Web Site: www.uleth.ca/anc--con, ASK FOR: Conference Services
ROOM PRICING: Canadian $: $14.00-$30.00 + Taxes, per person., Discount for students, • PAYMENT: Cash Per. Ck Trav. Ck Visa M/C • DATES AVAILABLE: May 2 - Aug. 29, • BEDS: 1-2 • FOOD: Caf. SB VM NR • INFO: Kitchens available to prepare own food, (no cookware provided), coin laundry, TV lounge, recreation facilities, reservations recommended. • ACTIVITIES: Japanese Gardens; Galt Museum; Waterton Lakes National Park; Whoop Up Days; Remington Carriage Museum; Head Smashed in Buffalo Jump; Birds of Prey Centre.
DIRECTIONS: The University of Lethbridge is located in West Lethbridge, 5 minutes from Highway 2 north and 15 minutes from highway 5 & 4 south and regional airport.

U
N
I
V

111 Medicine Hat, ALB   &

Medicine Hat College (T)
299 College Dr., S.E., Medicine Hat, ALB T1A 3Y6, Ph: (403) 529-3820, ASK FOR: Housing Office
ROOM PRICING: (S) $21.00, $110.25/wk
2-4 people in family $42/night, • PAYMENT: Cash Per. Ck Trav. Ck Visa M/C • DATES AVAILABLE: May 1 - Aug. 15, • ROOM TYPE: SR • BED TYPE: S • BEDS: 1 • BATH: C P • FOOD: Caf. • INFO: No Pets, free washer/dryer in each unit, free parking and linens for conferences. Children welcome. 25 in. TV, extra long single beds. • ACTIVITIES: Echo Dale Park, Elkwater Park, Dinosaur Park, hiking trails, sport facilities.

112 Red Deer, ALB   &

Red Deer College (T)
Box 5111, Red Deer, ALB T4N 6P6, Ph: (403) 342-3257, ASK FOR: Residence Office
ROOM PRICING: Canadian $$, (S) $23.25, • PAYMENT: Cash Per. Ck Trav. Ck Visa M/C • DATES AVAILABLE: May 15-Aug.15, • ROOM TYPE: SR Apt. • BED TYPE: S • BEDS: 1 • BATH: P • FOOD: Caf. VM NR • INFO: Linens included, children welcome, coin washers/dryers, free parkong, TV lounge. • ACTIVITIES: Racquetball, hiking trails, shopping, gym, weight room, bicycle trails.
DIRECTIONS: Off Hwy 2, go east at the 32nd street exit/ Red Deer College is the first right. When on Campus, take the first left and follow the ring road until you see an A-frame building that says Residence Administration.

British Columbia

113 Burnaby, BC   ?   &

Simon Fraser University (T)
Mc Taggart Cowan Hall, Burnaby, BC V5A 1S6, Ph: (604) 291-4503, Fax: (604) 291-5598, ASK FOR: Accommodations Office
ROOM PRICING: (S) $19.00, (D) $42.00, • PAYMENT: Cash Trav. Ck Visa M/C • DATES AVAILABLE: May - Aug., • ROOM TYPE: SR Apt. Suite • BATH: S P • FOOD: Caf. VM NR • INFO: Linens included, children welcome, laundry. • ACTIVITIES: Recreation facilities. Campus 11 miles from downtown Vancouver; mountain and beach sports; golf; museum of Archeology and Ethnology; theaters and park areas.

114 Castlegar, BC   &

Selkirk College/ Kekuli House (T)
Box 1200, 301, Frank Bender Way, Castlegar, BC V1N 3J1, Ph: (250) 365-1227, ASK FOR: Pat Rodrick Res. Mgr.
ROOM PRICING: (S) 20.00 Reduced Service
(S) $35.00 Full Service, • PAYMENT: Cash Visa M/C • DATES AVAILABLE: May 15-Aug.15, • BEDS: 1 • FOOD: VM NR • INFO: Linens incl., 2 wks advance booking recommended, children welcome, laundry facilities available, group rates avail. Cafe service available for groups of 20 or more. • ACTIVITIES: Tennis, hiking, museums, TV in public lounge, game room. Doukhobor Museum; National Exhibition Centre; Zuckerberg's Island; Golf course.

115 Cranbrook, BC   ?

College of the Rockies (T) Purcell House
2700 College Way, Bag 9000, Cranbrook, BC V1C 5L7, Ph: (250) 489-8282, ASK FOR: Pam Catsirelis, Resdence Supervisor
ROOM PRICING: (S) $20.00, (D) $50.00, • PAYMENT: Cash Visa M/C • DATES AVAILABLE: May - Aug. 15, • BED TYPE: S • BEDS: 1 • FOOD: Caf. VM • INFO: Linene Charge: $5.00/day. Children can be accommodated, check first, no pets, groups. Apartments with full kitchens available. • ACTIVITIES: TV in public lounge, track & field. Fort Steele Hertiage Town; numerous lakes; hiking; water park; Railway Museum.

116 **Kelowna, BC**   ♿

Okanagan Univ. College (T) N. Kelowna Campus
3180 College Way, Kelowna, BC V1V 1V8, Ph: (250) 470-6055, Fax: (250)
470-6051, ASK FOR: Dana Webster, Mgr. Conf. Ser.
ROOM PRICING: (S) $25.00, (D) $50.00, $5.00 each addtl. person, • PAYMENT:
Cash Per. Ck Trav. Ck Visa M/C • DATES AVAILABLE: May 1-Aug. 29, •
BEDS: 1-2 • FOOD: Caf. SB VM NR • INFO: 1 and 4 bedroom apartments,
laundry facilities, TV lounge, free parking. Continental breakfast included in
individual tourist rate. • ACTIVITIES: Hiking, rec. centre, aerobics room,
volleyball, tennis. 3 championship golf courses; 80 mile long Okanagan lake;
Scandia Amusement Centre; Grey Monk Winery.
DIRECTIONS: Just off of Highway 97 North, minutes from the Kelowna Airport.

117 **Langley, BC**   ?   ♿

Trinity Western University (T)
7600 Glover Rd., Langley, BC V2Y 1Y1, Ph: (604) 888-7511, ASK FOR: Conf.
Director, Laurie D. Shaw
ROOM PRICING: (S) $22.00-$32.00, (D) $30.00-$40.00, • PAYMENT: Cash Per.
Ck Trav. Ck Visa M/C • DATES AVAILABLE: May 1 - Aug. 15, • BEDS: 2 •
FOOD: Caf. VM NR • INFO: Linen charge: $5.00, no alcohol, no smoking in
campus bldgs. • ACTIVITIES: Gym, tennis.Provincial Park and Lake; nearby
Vancouver; Fort Langley Museum; golf.

118 **Vancouver, BC**   ♿

Carey Theological College, Carey Hall (T)
5920 Iona Dr., Vancouver, BC V6T 1J6, Ph: (604) 224-4308, Fax: (604)
224-5014, E-mail: carey tc@interchange.ubc.ca, ASK FOR: Main Office
ROOM PRICING: (S) $25.00, (D) 50.00 in Canadian $, • PAYMENT: Cash Trav.
Ck • DATES AVAILABLE: May 15-Aug. 8, • ROOM TYPE: SR • BED TYPE: S •
BEDS: 1 • FOOD: Caf. NR • INFO: Linens included, no pets, single dorm rooms
with single bed. Breakfast only • ACTIVITIES: On the U.B.C. campus there are,
films, art gallery, concerts, park, swimming, theaters, tennis, hiking, museums,
TV in public lounge. On the ocean boating; Museum of Anthropology; Japanes
Garden; Science Centre.

119 **Vancouver, BC**   ♿

Saint Andrews Hall (T)
6040 Iona Drive, Vancouver, BC V6T 2E8, Ph: (604) 822-9720, Web Site:
www.standrews.edu, ASK FOR: Summer Housing
ROOM PRICING: (S) $13.00-$36.00, (D) $26.00-$43.00. Family- $54.00(2 singles,
one double), • PAYMENT: Cash Per. Ck Trav. Ck • DATES AVAILABLE:
May1-Aug.26, • ROOM TYPE: SR Apt. Suite • BED TYPE: S • BEDS: 1-2 • BATH:
C S P • FOOD: NR OCR • INFO: Linens provided, children welcome, booking
fee$50.00, applied to account. Bring own towels.Cafeteria available for groups.
Some suites have unequipped kitchens (major appliances only) • ACTIVITIES: Art
gallery, park, swimming, boating, theaters, game room, tennis, hiking, museums,
TV in public lounge. Breathtaking views; Pacific Spirit Park; Use of U. B. C.
facilities.
DIRECTIONS: Located just off of Chancellor Blvd/Southwest Marine Dr. on the
North side of the UBC campus.

U
N
I
V

120 **Vancouver, BC**   ⟨⟩

University of British Columbia (T)
5961 Student Union Blvd., Vancouver, BC V6T 2C9, Ph: (604) 822-1057, Fax:
(604) 822-1069, E-mail: kread@brock.housing.ubc.ca, ASK FOR: UBC Conference
Centre
ROOM PRICING: (S) $18.00- $45.00, May-Aug., (D) $36.00- $65.00, May-Aug.,
$59.00-$65.00, Sept.-April, • PAYMENT: Cash Trav. Ck Visa M/C • DATES
AVAILABLE: Year round, • ROOM TYPE: SR Apt. • BED TYPE: S D • BEDS: 1-3 •
BATH: C P • FOOD: Caf. SB VM NR • INFO: Coin washers/dryers, linens
included, free parking, May-Aug. • ACTIVITIES: 20 min. from city centre and Int'l
Airport; Univ. on summit of Point Grey Peninsula in wooded campus; famous rose
gardens; Museum of Anthropology; golf course; aquatic center; cruises on
Vancouver Bay.
DIRECTIONS: From I-5 or Vancouver Airport, cross Oak St. Bridge. Travel
northbound to 12th Ave., turn left. Follow 12th Ave. 4 miles to Gate One of the
University. Turn left on Westbrook Mall, turn left at Gate 2 of the University onto
Student Union Blvd.

121 **Vancouver, BC**   ?

Vancouver School of Theology (T)
6000 Iona Dr., Vancouver, BC V6T 1L4, Ph: (604) 228-9031, Fax: (604)
822-9031
ROOM PRICING: (S) $15.00-$30.00, $36.00 w/bath, (D) $45.00, $50.00 w/bath,
• PAYMENT: Cash Trav. Ck Visa M/C • DATES AVAILABLE: May 7 - Aug. 25,
suites only, single & twin-year round., • FOOD: Caf. VM NR • INFO: Children
welcome, a few 1 & 2 bedroom suites available for more than 3 night stay. Coin
washers/dryers, free parking. • ACTIVITIES: All of Vancouver; 20 min. from City
Center; ocean view; Rose Gardens; Vancouver Intl. Airport; Museum of
Anthropology; Aquatic Centre.
DIRECTIONS: Located on the campus of University of British Columbia.

122 **Victoria, BC**   ?   ⟨⟩

University of Victoria (T)
P. O. Box 1700, Victoria, BC V8W 2Y2, Ph: (250) 721-8395, Fax: (250)
721-8930, ASK FOR: Housing Service Office
ROOM PRICING: Reservations suggested, (S) $38.00, (D) $50.00, (includes
breakfast), • PAYMENT: Cash Per. Ck Trav. Ck Visa M/C • DATES
AVAILABLE: May 1 - August 28, • ROOM TYPE: SR • BED TYPE: S • BEDS: 1-2 •
BATH: C • FOOD: Caf. SB • INFO: Children welcome, linens incl. Pkg. rate incl.
full rm. & board for stays of 14 days or more. • ACTIVITIES: Lounges w/ cable
TV. Located on beautiful Vancouver Island; Capital of BC; Recreational area for
fishing; boating ; whale watching; home of the 1994 Commonwealth Games.
DIRECTIONS: Enter the university on McKenzie Ave., passing stadium on the right.
Continue through next set of traffic lights (Finnerty). McKenzie Ave. becomes
Sinclair Rd. Take 2nd right into parking lot #5. The reception is located on the
ground floor of the Craigdarroch Office Building, on the right halfway down the
parking lot.

Manitoba

123 **Brandon, MAN**   ?

Brandon University (T) 270 18th Street
Brandon, MAN R7A 6A9, Ph: (204) 727-9799, ASK FOR: M.H. Koschinsky
ROOM PRICING: (S) $20.00, (D) $36.00, Bath shared, • PAYMENT: Cash Per. Ck
Trav. Ck Visa M/C • DATES AVAILABLE: May 15 - Aug. 15, • FOOD: Caf. SB
VM • INFO: Bedding furnished, no pets, no children. • ACTIVITIES: Swimming,
films, art gallery, concerts, game room, museums, TV in public lounge. Golf;
National Park; Waterslides; Conference Center.

124 Winnipeg, MAN   &

Canadian Mennonite Bible College (T)
600 Shaftesbury Blvd., Winnipeg, MAN R3P 0M4, Ph: (204) 888-6781, ASK FOR:
Business Office
ROOM PRICING: (S) $14.50, $12.00, subsequent nights, • PAYMENT: Cash Per.
Ck Trav. Ck • DATES AVAILABLE: May 3 - Aug. 27, • ROOM TYPE: SR • BED
TYPE: S • BEDS: 2 • BATH: C • FOOD: VM • INFO: No smoking or alcohol on
campus, Children welcome, Linen charge: $5.00. • ACTIVITIES: Hiking, game
room. Museum of Man and Nature; Assiniboine Park and Zoo.

125 Winnipeg, MAN

Saint John's College (T)
92 Dysart Road, Winnipeg, MAN R3T 2M5, Ph: (204) 474-8531, (204) 474-9583,
Fax: (204) 474-7610, E-mail: madillj@umanitoba.ca, ASK FOR: Conf. Coordinator
ROOM PRICING: (S) $17.50 Canadian $, • PAYMENT: Cash Per. Ck • DATES
AVAILABLE: May 1-June. 30, • ROOM TYPE: SR • BED TYPE: S • BEDS: 1 •
BATH: C • FOOD: Caf. VM NR • INFO: 2 suites available, 2 two-bedroom. No
smoking.   Coin washers/dryers, TV lounge. • ACTIVITIES: Racquetball,
swimming, tennis. Art gallery; shopping; Riverboat; Museums; city zoo; double
decker bus tours; vintage Steam Locomotive Trip; multi-cultural events.

126 Winnipeg, MAN   ?   &

Univ. College, Univ. of Manitoba (T)
220 Dysart Road, Winnipeg, MAN R3T 2M8, Ph: (204) 474-9751, E-mail:
universitycollege@umanitoba.ca, ASK FOR: Jo-Ann Kubin, General Office
ROOM PRICING: (S) $16.00/ Student, $22.00/ Non-student, • PAYMENT: Cash
Trav. Ck • DATES AVAILABLE: May1-June30, Aug. 15-26, • BEDS: 1 • FOOD:
NR • INFO: Children welcome with supervision, no cribs. • ACTIVITIES:
Racquetball, swimming, tennis, TV in public lounge.   Fort Whyte Nature
Environmental Education Centre; Forks-Shopping & Recreation; River Cruises;
Parks.

New Brunswick

127 Fredericton, NB   ?

Univ. of New Brunswick (T)
P. O. Box 4400, Fredericton, NB E3 B 5A3, Ph: (506) 453-4891,   Fax: (506)
453-3585, E-mail: Rochus@unb.com, ASK FOR: Housing Office
ROOM PRICING: (S) $28.40, (D) $41.50, Discount for Students, • PAYMENT: Cash
Trav. Ck Visa M/C • DATES AVAILABLE: May 15 - Aug. 15, • FOOD: Caf. VM
NR • INFO: Coin washers/dryers, free parking, children welcome. • ACTIVITIES:
Half hour drive to historical King's Landing settlement; Close to city center; hiking
trails; Capital City - province has a 500 mi. long seacoast; river paddleboats.

128 Moncton, NB   &

Atlantic Baptist University (T)
Box 6004 , 333 Gorge Rd., Moncton, NB E1C 9L7, Ph: (506) 858-8970, ASK FOR:
Auxiliary Services Mgr.
ROOM PRICING: (S) $25.00, (D) $35.00, • PAYMENT: Cash Visa M/C • DATES
AVAILABLE: May 15- August15, • BEDS: 1-2 • FOOD: Caf. NR • INFO: No
smoking, children welcome. Coin washers/dryers, free parking.   Cafeteria for
groups.Free Parking. No alcoholic beverages. • ACTIVITIES: Magic Mountain;
Funday National Park; Shedial beaches and water slides; Magnetic Hill Game
Farm.

129 Moncton, NB   ?   &

Univ. de Moncton (T) Centre Universitaire
Moncton, NB E1A 3E9, Ph: (506) 858-4008,   Fax: (506) 858-4585, ASK FOR:
Housing Services
ROOM PRICING: (S) $30.00, (D) $42.00, Discount for students & senior citizens, •
PAYMENT: Cash Per. Ck Trav. Ck Visa M/C • DATES AVAILABLE: May 2 -
Aug. 30, • FOOD: Caf. SB VM NR • INFO: On-campus bookstore, beauty shop,
bank, physical ed. facilities, pool, art gallery, Acadian Museum. • ACTIVITIES:
Close to golf. See: Tidal Bore; Fundy Park; Cape Rocks; Ft. Beausejour; Magnetic
Hill; Magic Mtn.; lobster suppers.

(T) = Travelers Accommodations   (E) = Educational Related   (C) = Groups & Conference Use

130 **Sackville, NB**

Mt. Allison University (T)
Sackville, NB E0A 3C0, Ph: (506) 364-2247, E-mail: dbarrett@mta.ca, Web Site:
www.mta.ca, ASK FOR: Conference Centre
ROOM PRICING: (S) $16.00 + Tax, (D) $28.00 + Tax, Discount for students.
Monthly and weekly rates available, • PAYMENT: Cash Per. Ck Trav. Ck Visa •
DATES AVAILABLE: May 1 - Aug. 30, • ROOM TYPE: SR • BED TYPE: S • BEDS:
1-2 • BATH: C S P • FOOD: Caf. VM NR • INFO: Complete conference services
available. Convention hall on campus. Coin washers/dryers, campus pub, free
parking. • ACTIVITIES: Free use of athletic facilities(including pool). Local shopping
area; one of a kind Waterfowl park; local restaurants famous for maritime
menu; art gallery.
DIRECTIONS: Take Main St. exit to Sackville, New Bruinswick off the trans
Canada highway. Travel approx 1/2 km west to campus

New Foundland

131 **St. Johns, NF**

Memorial University (T)
St. Johns, NF A1B 3P7, Ph: (709) 737-7590, Fax: (709) 737-3520, E-mail:
jvoisey@morgan.ucs.mun.ca, ASK FOR: Jean Voisey, Conference, Residence &
Food Services
ROOM PRICING: (S) $16.00, (D) $25.00, Discount for students, • PAYMENT: Cash
Per. Ck Trav. Ck Visa M/C • DATES AVAILABLE: May 1 - Aug. 31, • FOOD:
Caf. VM NR • INFO: Children welcome. • ACTIVITIES: In the heart of historical
St. John's oldest city in No. America; Center of whale, seal, and cod fisheries;
Island at the entrance of St. Lawrence River.

Nova Scotia

132 **Antigonish, NS**   ?   ♿

St. Francis Xavier University (T)
P. O. Box 5000, Antigonish, NS B2G 2W5, Ph: (902) 867-2473, ASK FOR: Barb
MacDonald, Residence Serv.
ROOM PRICING: (S) $27.60, (D) $37.20, (includes breakfast), • PAYMENT: Cash
Per. Ck Trav. Ck Visa M/C • DATES AVAILABLE: May 15 - Aug. 15, • FOOD:
Caf. • INFO: Coin washers/dryers, free parking. • ACTIVITIES: Visitors have
access to swimming pool, tennis, squash, racquetball courts. Excellent beaches;
side trips to rivers; lakes; beautiful harbors.

133 **Church Point, NS**   ♿

Universite Saint- Anne (T)
Church Point, NS B0W 1M0, Ph: (902) 769-2114, ext. 178, ASK FOR: Charelle
Saulnier, Director of Residences
ROOM PRICING: Canadian $$, (S) $22.75 - $25.75, (D) $45.50 - $51.50,
Discounts for students, • PAYMENT: Cash Per. Ck Trav. Ck Visa • DATES
AVAILABLE: May 3 - Aug. 26, • BEDS: 1-2 • FOOD: Caf. VM NR OCR • INFO:
Cozy home-style residences. Reservations required. Coin washers/dryers, TV
lounge, free parking. • ACTIVITIES: Located on beautiful St. Mary's Bay; Fishing;
whale watching; camping; relatively close to Kejimkuji National Park.

134 **Halifax, NS**   ♿

Dalhousie University (T) Fenwick Place
5599 Fenwick St., Halifax, NS B3H 4J2, Ph: (902) 494-1245, ASK FOR:
Accommodation Office
ROOM PRICING: $19.00 - $72.00 per night, • PAYMENT: Cash Per. Ck Trav.
Ck Visa M/C • DATES AVAILABLE: May - Aug. , • BEDS: 1-5 • FOOD: No VM
NR • INFO: Apartments with kitchen and bath.$51- $72 per night. Parking $4.00
per day, TV lounges, coin washers/dryers. • ACTIVITIES: Beautifull views of
Halifax, close to downtown. Rate includes full usage of Dalplex athletic facility;
Close to all attractions; campus; museums within walking distance.
DIRECTIONS: Follow Hwy 102 to the end where it turns into Bayer's Rd., Right
onto Connaught Ave., Follow to the end, left onto Jubilee Rd., Right onto Oxford St.,
Left onto South St., Right onto South Park St., Left onto Fenwick St., Fenwick
Place is located halfway down the street on the left side.

---

135 Halifax, NS   &

Dalhousie University (T) Conference Services
Room 410, Student Union Bldg., 6136 University Ave., Halifax, NS B3H 4J2, Ph:
(902) 494-8840, Fax: (902) 494-1219, Web Site: www.dal.ca/confserv., ASK FOR:
Housing & Conf. Services
ROOM PRICING: (S) $24.00 - 36.00, (D) $42.00- $54.00, • PAYMENT: Cash Per.
Ck Trav. Ck Visa M/C • DATES AVAILABLE: May-Aug., • ROOM TYPE: SR
Apt. Suite • BED TYPE: S • BEDS: 1-5 • BATH: C S P • FOOD: Caf. SB VM NR
OCR • INFO: Children welcome, parking, linens included, coin washers/dryers, TV
lounge, breakfast, parking, and use of athletic facility included in most rates. •
ACTIVITIES: Racquetball, art gallery, park, swimming, game room, tennis,
museums. Halifax Citadel; Halifax Historical propertites; Point Pleasanat Park.
Close to shopping center and Pleasant Park.
DIRECTIONS: Follow Hwy. 102 to the end where it turns into Bayer's Rd., Right
onto ConnaughtAve., Follow to the end, Left onto Jubilee Rd., Right onto Oxford St.,
Left onto South St., Dalhousie Campus is on the left side of the road.

136 Halifax, NS

Mt. St. Vincent University (T)
166 Bedford Hwy., Halifax, NS B3M 2J6, Ph: (902) 457-6364, Fax: (902)
457-1694, E-mail: collen.forward@msvu.ca, ASK FOR: Colleen Forward
ROOM PRICING: (S) $24.23, (D) $36.96, Discount for students, seniors, and school
groups, • PAYMENT: Cash Trav. Ck Visa M/C • DATES AVAILABLE: April 29 -
Aug. 22, • ROOM TYPE: SR • BED TYPE: S • BEDS: 1-2 • BATH: C • FOOD:
Caf. VM NR OCR • INFO: Coin washers/dryers, linens included, free parking.
Continental Breakfast included. • ACTIVITIES: Located in scenic wooded setting -
overlooks Bedford Basin. Access to gym and game rooms at nominal charge. Art
gallery; fitness trail.
DIRECTIONS: Exit Bedford Highway at Seton Drive

137 Halifax, NS   &

Saint Mary's University (T)
923 Roble St., Halifax, NS B3H 3C3 , Ph: (902) 420-5486 /420-5591 (after 5PM),
Fax: (902) 496-8118, E-mail: conference.office@Stmarys.ca, Web Site:
www.Stmarys.ca/conferences, ASK FOR: Wanda Robinson, Conf. coord.
ROOM PRICING: Canadian$$, (S) $23.00, (D) $33.00, plus taxes, • PAYMENT:
Cash Trav. Ck Visa M/C • DATES AVAILABLE: May - Aug., • ROOM TYPE: SR
Apt. • BED TYPE: S • BEDS: 1- 2 • BATH: C S • FOOD: Caf. SB VM NR • INFO:
Free parking, no pets, all linens and towels included, coin washers/dryers. •
ACTIVITIES: Fitness complex; observatory; laundromats; 24 hour check-in
available; 10 minutes from downtown.
DIRECTIONS: From the Halifax International Airport, take Hwy 102 to Route118
(exit sign indicates Halifax via Bridges). Proceed to the McKay Bridge. Take the
Robie Street exit from the Bridge to 923, Tobie St. - Saint Mary's University. Go to
Loyola building, check in desk (24 hrs.)

138 Halifax, NS   ?

Technical Univ. of Nova Scotia (T)
P. O. Box 1000, Halifax, NS B3J 2X4, Ph: (902) 422-2495, ASK FOR: Suzanne
Kolmer, Dir.Student Services
ROOM PRICING: (S) $32.50, Discount for Students, • PAYMENT: Cash Trav. Ck
Visa M/C • DATES AVAILABLE: May 1 - Aug. 31, • ROOM TYPE: SR • BED
TYPE: S • BEDS: 1-2 • BATH: C • FOOD: Caf. VM NR • INFO: Children welcome
(under 4 yrs. free), free washer/dryer, TV lounge. • ACTIVITIES: 10 min. walk
from downtown Halifax; Close to restaurants; shopping, entertainment and points
of interest; Citadel Museum; historic waterfront; public gardens.

U
N
I
V

139 **Truro, NS**   ?   🔥

Nova Scotia Agricultural College (T)
P.O. Box 550, Truro, NS B2N 5E3, Ph: (902) 893-6671, ASK FOR: Conference Office
ROOM PRICING: (S) $30.00, (D) $40.00, • PAYMENT: Cash Trav. Ck • DATES AVAILABLE: May 1 - Aug. 22, • FOOD: Caf. VM NR • INFO: Farm complex. • ACTIVITIES: Victoria Park and Falls; Scenic shoreline trails; landscaped gardens; Historical Agriculutral Collection;   Nearby: Halifax; Cape Briton Highlands; beaches; Trans Canadian Highway.

140 **Wolfville, NS**   ?   🔥

Acadia University (T)
Wolfville, NS B0P 1X0, Ph: (902) 542-2201, Ext: 317, ASK FOR: Conference Office
ROOM PRICING: (S) $24, (D) $33.10, • PAYMENT: Cash Trav. Ck Visa M/C • DATES AVAILABLE: May 15 - Aug. 15, • FOOD: Caf. • INFO: No pets - children under 12 in same room with parents, No charge. • ACTIVITIES: Grand Pre' Park, Bay of Fundy Tides, local historical museums, 1 hr. from Halifax.

Ontario

141 **Guelph, ONT**   ?   🔥

University of Guelph (T) Conference Office
Drew Hall, Guelph, ONT N1G 2W1, Ph: (519) 824-4120, Ext: 2353, ASK FOR: Cyndy Forsyth
ROOM PRICING: (S) $29.95, (D) $24.95 per person, Discount for students, • PAYMENT: Cash Per. Ck Visa M/C Amex • DATES AVAILABLE: May 1- Aug. 30, • ROOM TYPE: SR • BED TYPE: S • BEDS: 2 • BATH: C • FOOD: Caf. SB VM NR OCR • INFO: Children welcome, no pets, free overnight parking. • ACTIVITIES: Short courses available through Summer Campus program; swimming; squash; tennis.   Close to hiking trails; Niagara Falls; Lion Safari.

142 **Hamilton, ONT**   🔥

Mc Master University (T)
1280 Main St. West, Commons 129B, Hamilton, ONT   L8S 4K1, Ph: (905) 525-9140, Ext: 24781, ASK FOR: Conference Services
ROOM PRICING: (S) $35.00, (D) $55.00, • PAYMENT: Cash Trav. Ck Visa M/C • DATES AVAILABLE: May 15 - Aug. 24, • BED TYPE: S • BEDS: 2 • FOOD: Caf. SB VM NR • INFO: Forty minutes from Toronto. • ACTIVITIES: Swimming, hiking, films, concerts, lectures.Art Museum close to Bontanical Gardens and downtown.
DIRECTIONS: Follow QEW from Toronto directly into Hamilton. Take Main St. West exit from Hwy 403.

143 **Kingston, ONT**   ?   🔥

Queens University at Kingston (T)
Victoria Hall, Kingston, ONT K7L 3N6, Ph: (613) 545-2223, (613) 545-6624, E-mail: Johnsonm@post.queensu.ca, ASK FOR: M. Johnson, Conf. Mgr.
ROOM PRICING: (S) $44.00, (D) $54.00, Breakfast included, • PAYMENT: Cash Per. Ck Trav. Ck Visa M/C • DATES AVAILABLE: May 6 - Aug. 26, • ROOM TYPE: SR • BED TYPE: S • BEDS: 1-2 • BATH: C • FOOD: Caf. SB VM NR • INFO: Campus on shores of Lake Ontario. Free parking, laundry facilities, fair currency exchange, close to U.S. Border. • ACTIVITIES: Guests have access to recreation areas, TV lounges, campus athletic complex. Thousand Island boat cruises; marine museum; Ft. Henry; historical museums; theatre; parkland; swimming.

Canada

College & University Accommodations, continued...

144 Kirkland Lake, ONT

Northern College of (T) Applied Arts &Tech.
140 Government Rd. East, Kirkland Lake, ONT P2N 3L8, Ph: (705) 567-9291,
Ext: 121, Student Housing
ROOM PRICING: (S) $20.00, (D) $20.00, • PAYMENT: Cash Only • DATES
AVAILABLE: June1 - Aug. 26, • BED TYPE: S • BEDS: 1-2 • FOOD: Caf. NR •
INFO: Kitchen facilities, children welcome, bring own linen/towels, gym and fitness
center. College Day Dare Facilities available for a fee from May 1, to August 26.
Coin Washer/Dryer in residence. • ACTIVITIES: Underground mining tours;
wildlife zoo; wood industry tours; museums; sports. Excellent fitness facilities,
great swimming, fishing, hiking, hunting.
DIRECTIONS: From Toranto follow Hwy 400 N to Hwy 11 N. Turn on Hwy 112,
then take Hwy 66 East. (Total mileage is approximately 380 miles)

145 London, ONT ?

Huron College (T)
1349 Western Road, London, ONT N6G 1H3, Ph: (519) 438-7224, Ext: 202, ASK
FOR: Kim Knowles
ROOM PRICING: (S) $20.00/Student, $32.00/Adult, (D) $20.00/Student,
$32.00/Adult, • PAYMENT: Cash Only • DATES AVAILABLE: May1-Aug. 25, •
FOOD: Caf. SB VM NR • INFO: Linens included, children welcome with adult. •
ACTIVITIES: Shopping mall; Main University.

146 London, ONT

Univ. of Western Ontario (T) Room 130, Lambton Hall
1421 Western Road, London, ONT N6G 4W4, Ph: (519) 661-3545, ASK FOR:
Karen Millard, Mgr.
ROOM PRICING: (S) $31.50/B&B, Discount for students & seniors, • PAYMENT:
Cash Trav. Ck Visa M/C • DATES AVAILABLE: May to August, • BEDS: 1 •
FOOD: Caf. VM NR • INFO: Linens included. Monthly and weekly rates available.
• ACTIVITIES: Pay phones, laundry, TV. Theater; movies; museum; city
attractions.
DIRECTIONS: Located in the north end of the city, 20 minutes from Hwy 401 and
just 5 minutes from downtown.

147 North Bay, ONT

Nipissing University/ Canadore College (T)
P. O. Box 5005, North Bay, ONT P1B 8L7, Ph: (705) 474-1550, Fax: (705)
495-2529, ASK FOR: Mr. Chris Lindsay
ROOM PRICING: (S) $25.00, $92.00/Week, • PAYMENT: Cash Per. Ck Trav. Ck
Visa M/C • DATES AVAILABLE: May 24-Aug.19, • ROOM TYPE: Apt. • BED
TYPE: S • BEDS: 1 • BATH: S • FOOD: Caf. VM NR • INFO: 6 single bdrms. in a
furnishd townhome, linens not incl, children welcome w/ adult super., 700 acre
campus with wilderness trails. • ACTIVITIES: Game room, hiking, TV in public
lounge. Gateway to Northern Ontario; Chief Commanda Boat trips; Temagami
Wilderness; Dionne Quints House; park.

148 Ottawa, ONT

Carleton University (T) Tour & Conf. Centre
Ottawa, ONT KIS 5B6, Ph: (613) 520-5611, E-mail: john-tracey@carleton.ca, ASK
FOR: John Tracey, Manager Summer Accommodations
ROOM PRICING: (S) $23.00+ taxes/B&B, (D) $34.00+ taxes/B&B, • PAYMENT:
Cash Visa M/C • DATES AVAILABLE: May 8 - Aug. 24, • BEDS: 1-2 • FOOD:
Caf. SB VM NR OCR • INFO: Children welcome, children under 2 free, linens
included. Unlimited servings in cafeteria, coin washers/dryers, TV lounge, Free
Sat. & Sun. parking. • ACTIVITIES: Campus has athletic centre with Olympic size
pool,($3.00 per swim), pharmacy, post office, convenience stores, game rooms,
pubs. Ottawa; Parliment Hill; Museums; Rodeos; National Arts Centre. All
accessible by #7 bus outside front door.
DIRECTIONS: From West: 401 east to highway 16 to Ottawa. Right on
Meadowlands, left on colonelby Dr., right into Careton University. From West: 417
East to Ottawa, exit Bronson S., right on Sunnyside into University. From South:
16 north and as above.

UNIV

(T) = Travelers Accommodations   (E) = Educational Related   (C) = Groups & Conference Use

B & J Publications   95   *Campus Lodging Guide*

149 **Ottawa, ONT**   ? ♿

University of Ottawa (T)
334-85 University, P.O. Box 450 STN A, Ottawa, ONT K1N 6N5, Ph: (613) 562-5771, Fax: (613) 562-5157
ROOM PRICING: (S) $20.50, (D) $35.00, Discounts for students, • PAYMENT: Cash Trav. Ck Visa M/C • DATES AVAILABLE: May 6-Aug.25, • ROOM TYPE: SR • BED TYPE: S • BEDS: 1-2 • BATH: C • FOOD: Caf. SB VM NR OCR • INFO: Linen included in price, children welcome, coin washers/dryers. • ACTIVITIES: Sports facilities. Language study; walking distance to Parliment Building; Rideau Canal; Museums. Downtown locations.

150 **Peterbrough, ONT**

Trent University (T) Conference Services
Lady Eaton College, Peterbrough, ONT K9J 7B8, Ph: (705) 748-1260, ASK FOR: Jayne Todd, Mgr.
ROOM PRICING: (S) $17.00, (D) $26.00, special conf. rates avail., • PAYMENT: Cash Trav. Ck Visa M/C • DATES AVAILABLE: May1-Aug. 30, • ROOM TYPE: SR • BED TYPE: S • BEDS: 1 • BATH: C • FOOD: Caf. • INFO: Children welcome, free parking, linens included. • ACTIVITIES: Famous canal hydraulic lift locks, Trent-Severn Waterway, Lang-Century village, Whetung Art Gallery, ancient petrogylphs, swimming, boating, tennis, picnic parks,zoo
DIRECTIONS: Hwy 401 East to Hwy 35/115. North to "parkway" Exit at Peterborough. (Approx. 70 miles Northeast of Toronto).

151 Scarborough, ONT

University of Toronto at Scarborough **(T)** Scarborough Campus
1265 Military Trail, Scarborough, ONT M1C 1A4, Ph: (416) 287-7369, Fax: (416) 287-7323, ASK FOR: Summer Visitors Reservations
ROOM PRICING: Family townhouses from: $80.00 per night., • PAYMENT: Cash Trav. Ck Visa M/C • DATES AVAILABLE: May 14 - Aug. 27, Make reservations one week in advance• BEDS: 1 • FOOD: Caf. SB VM NR • INFO: Children welcome, bring own towels, laundry facilities. TV in public lounge. • ACTIVITIES: Park; tennis; hiking;   Metro Toronto, call (800) 363-1990 for free tourist information. Close to Metro Zoo and other attractions.
DIRECTIONS: Highway 401 to Exit 387 Morningside Ave., South to Military Trail. Turn left.

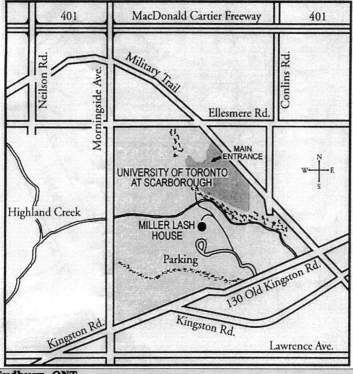

152 Sudbury, ONT

University of Sudbury- Laurentian (T)
Ramsey Lake Road, Sudbury, ONT P3E 2C6, Ph: (705) 673-5661,   Fax: (705)-673-4912, E-mail: rgperron@nickel.laurentian.ca, ASK FOR: Director of Residence
ROOM PRICING: (S) $24.00+ Tax, (D) $35.00+ Tax, • PAYMENT: Cash Per. Ck • DATES AVAILABLE: May 1 - Aug. 25, • BEDS: 1-2 • FOOD: Caf. SB VM NR • INFO: Children welcome with supervision. • ACTIVITIES: 5 min. walk to natural beach;   adjacent to golf course; arboretum;   mining and smelter works;   many lakes for fishing.
DIRECTIONS: Off Paris St., to Ramsey Lak Road.   To Laurentian Universite' Campus. university of Sudbury is off Maniton Rd. on the campus

153 **Thunder Bay, ONT**   ⟨⟩

Confederation College of Applied Arts & Technology, (T)
P. O. Box 398, Thunder Bay, ONT P7C 4W1, Ph: (807) 475-6381, ASK FOR:
Charlie Lalonde
ROOM PRICING: Canadian $$, (S) $25.00, (D) $30.00, • PAYMENT: Cash Trav.
Ck Visa • DATES AVAILABLE: May 20 - Aug. 15, • BEDS: 1-2 • FOOD: Caf. SB
VM NR • INFO: Not suitable for children, coin washers/dryers, TV lounge. •
ACTIVITIES: Tennis, hiking trails, fitness center, basketball, running, biking, art
gallery. Old Fort William; Chippewa Park; Centennial Park.

154 **Thunder Bay, ONT**   ?   ⟨⟩

Lakehead University (T)
955 Oliver Road, Thunder Bay, ONT P7B 5E1, Ph: (807) 343-8779, ASK FOR:
Conf. Office
ROOM PRICING: (S) $19.94, (D) $29.94, • PAYMENT: Cash Trav. Ck Visa M/C
• DATES AVAILABLE: May 1 - Aug. 20, • ROOM TYPE: SR Apt. • BED TYPE: S •
BEDS: 1-2 • BATH: C • FOOD: Caf. VM NR • INFO: Children welcome, TV
lounge, free parking, coin washers/dryers. • ACTIVITIES: Swimming; tennis; golf,
hiking; films, boat cruise; Mt. McKay; Kakabeka Falls; Hillcrest Park; Old Fort
william; Centennial Park; Centennial Conservatory; National Exhibition Centre for
Indian Art; Terry Fox Monument; Quimet Canyon.

155 **Toronto, ONT**   ⟨⟩

Humber College Residences (T)
203 Humber College Blvd., Toronto, ONT M9W 6V3, Ph: (416) 675-3437 or
(888)-548-6327, ASK FOR: Donna Davenport (416) 675-5027
ROOM PRICING: (S) $25.00-$49.00 Bed and Breakfast, • PAYMENT: Cash Per.
Ck Trav. Ck Visa M/C • DATES AVAILABLE: May 8 - Aug. 20, • ROOM TYPE:
SR • BED TYPE: S • BEDS: 1 • BATH: C S • FOOD: Caf. VM NR OCR • INFO: All
rooms air conditioned, children welcome, no pets, coin washers/dryers,shared
washroom and lounge facilities, linens, 24 reception & security, retail services and
meeting spaces. • ACTIVITIES: Racquetball, swimming, hiking, bike paths.
Canada's Wonderland; Black Creek Pioneer Village; Woodbine Mall; Woodbine
Race Track; CN Tower.   Conference and food services,catering, recreation,
swimming, 20,000 square ft. triple gymnasium.   Cardio and weight room,
arboretum
DIRECTIONS: The excitement of the city meets the serenity of the country at
Humber, just 10 minutes from the airport, within 30 minutes of most major
attractions.

156 **Toronto, ONT**

Massey College (T)
4 Devonshire Place, Toronto, ONT M5S 2E1, , Fax: (416) 978 1759, E-mail:
pat.kennedy@utoronot.ca, ASK FOR: Pat Kennedy, (416) 978-2892, or Porter,
(416) 978-2895
ROOM PRICING: (S) $40.00/B&B, (D) $50.00/B&B, Discount for Students &
Seniors.   12% taxes, • PAYMENT: Cash   Trav. Ck Visa M/C • DATES
AVAILABLE: May 1 - August 22, • ROOM TYPE: SR Apt. • BED TYPE: S • BEDS:
1-2 • BATH: C P • FOOD: Caf. • INFO: Linen included, maid service.   Children
welcome, coin washers/dryers, TV lounge. • ACTIVITIES: Quiet, secluded
residence in down town Toronto; Art Gallery;   Royal Ontario Museum; near
subway.

157 **Toronto, ONT**

Neill- Wycik College Hotel (T)
96 Gerrard St. East, Toronto, ONT M5B 1G7, Ph: (416) 977-2320, (800) 268-4358, Fax: (416) 977-2809, E-mail: wycik@inforamp.net, Web Site: www.inforamp.net/~wycik, ASK FOR: Resverations
ROOM PRICING: (S) $24.87, (D) $35.71, 20% Discount for Hostel Members, • PAYMENT: Cash Trav. Ck Visa M/C May 4-Aug.28
• ROOM TYPE: SR • BED TYPE: S • BEDS: 1-2 • BATH: S • FOOD: Caf. VM NR OCR • INFO: Linens included, daily housekeeping service, sauna, rooftop sundeck, TV lounge, laundromat, airport bus to hotel $12.00+tax. Family rooms available, Children welcome. 24 hour front desk and security service. Telephones in room, on site gym. • ACTIVITIES: Located right downtown, minutes away from Maple Leaf Gardens; China Town; CN Tower; Skydome; Eaton's Centre; Royal Ontarion Museum; Entertainment district.
DIRECTIONS: Gardener Expressway East to jarvis, North on Jarvis to Gerrard. Turn left on Gerrard and hotel is on the right side.

158 **Toronto, ON**   &

Ryerson Polytechnical Univ. (T) Pitman Hall Residence, Room 101, 160 Mutual 160 Mutual St., Toronto, ON M5B 2M2, Ph: (416) 979-5296, Fax: (416)-979-5212, Web Site: www.ryerson.ca/conference, ASK FOR: Conference Services
ROOM PRICING: (S) $37.00,$24.00 (for full time student) , • PAYMENT: Cash Trav. Ck Visa M/C • DATES AVAILABLE: mid May- mid Aug., • FOOD: Caf. VM NR • INFO: No Children, linens included, Coin Washer/Dryer , Min. number for Conferences,10. • ACTIVITIES: Game room, Mini Gym, Swimming,TV in public lounge. CN Tower,Skydome Eaton Centre, Pantages Theatre; Royal Ontario Museum; Toronto Center island; park.

159 **Toronto, ONT**   ?

Univ. of St. Michael's College (T)
81 St. Mary St., Toronto, ONT M5S 1J4, Ph: (416) 926-7141, Fax: (416) 926-7139, ASK FOR: Stpehen Fish, Dir. of Conferences
ROOM PRICING: Weekly rates only
(S) $95.00, (D) $80.00, • PAYMENT: Cash Trav. Ck Visa • DATES AVAILABLE: May 18 - Aug. 22, • ROOM TYPE: SR • BED TYPE: S • BEDS: 1-2 • BATH: C • FOOD: Caf. VM NR • INFO: Linens included, weekly maid service. • ACTIVITIES: Heart of downtown Toronto, water sports, planetarium, exclusive shops and restaurants, Sky Dome, zoo, major metropolitan attractions.

160 **Toronto, ONT**   ?

University College (T)
85 Saint George St., Toronto, ONT M5S 2E5, Ph: (416) 978-2532, ASK FOR: Univ. College Summer Business
ROOM PRICING: (S) $29.00, (D) $49.00, • PAYMENT: Cash Trav. Ck Visa M/C • DATES AVAILABLE: May- Aug., • ROOM TYPE: SR • BED TYPE: S • BEDS: 1-2 • BATH: C • FOOD: Caf. NR • INFO: Linens included for daily rates only. • ACTIVITIES: Racquetball, art gallery, concerts, park, swimming, game room, tennis, TV in public lounge. Sky Dome; Eatons Centre; Royal Ontario Museum; Art Gallery of Ontario;

161 **Toronto, ONT**   ?

University of Toronto (T) Conference Services
45 Willcocks Street, Toronto, ONT M5S 1C7, Ph: (416) 978-8735
ROOM PRICING: (Single) Students: $25.00 - $35.00; (Single) Adults: $33.00 - $40.00; (Double) Youth: $22.00 - $28.00; (Double) Adults: $50.00-$56.00. Includes breakfast, maid service, Taxes., • PAYMENT: Cash Trav. Ck Visa M/C • DATES AVAILABLE: Mid-May - Aug.21, May be available sooner• ROOM TYPE: SR Apt. • BED TYPE: S • BEDS: 1-2 • BATH: C S • FOOD: Caf. VM NR • INFO: Children welcome, no pets. Not suitable for infants. • ACTIVITIES: Royal Ontario Museum; Metro Zoo; CN Tower; Sky Dome; Toronto Islands; city cultural events. A variety of residence rooms available across campus.
DIRECTIONS: Main campus is South of Bloor St. between Spadina Ave. & University Ave.

U
N
I
V

(T) = Travelers Accommodations   (E) = Educational Related   (C) = Groups & Conference Use

162 **Toronto, ONT**   ?

University of Toronto (T) University College
85 St. George St., Toronto, ONT M5S 2E5, Ph: (416) 978-2532, (416) 971-2029,
E-mail: UC.residences@utoronto.ca, ASK FOR: Margo Marosy/Whitney Hall
ROOM PRICING: Weekly rates:
(S) $95.00, (D) $150.00, • PAYMENT: Cash Trav. Ck Visa M/C • DATES
AVAILABLE: May 12 - Aug. 24, • BEDS: 1-2 • FOOD: NR • INFO: Children
welcome, linens not included. • ACTIVITIES: University Libraries; University
Athletic Centre; Downtown Toronto; Art Gallery of Ontario; Royal Ontario Museum;
Eaton Centre; Kensington Market.

163 **Toronto, ONT**   ♿

Victoria University (T)
140 Charles St. West, Toronto, ONT M5S 1K9, Ph: (416) 585-4524, Fax: (416)
585-4530, ASK FOR: For reservations
ROOM PRICING: (S) $42.00, (D) $60.00, Discount for students & group rates., •
PAYMENT: Cash Trav. Ck Visa M/C • DATES AVAILABLE: Year round, •
ROOM TYPE: SR Apt. • BED TYPE: S • BEDS: 1-3 • BATH: C S • FOOD: Caf. SB
VM NR • INFO: Children welcome, all prices include breakfast, coin
washers/dryers, TV lounge, linens included. • ACTIVITIES: Tennis, playing field.
All the sights and cultural offerings of Toronto; Center of Toronto.
DIRECTIONS: map enclosed

164 **Toronto, ONT**   ♿

York University (T)
4700 Keele Street, Downsview, Toronto, ONT M3J 1P3, Ph: (416) 736-5020, ASK
FOR: Hospitality York/4 Assiniboine Rd.
ROOM PRICING: (S) $28.00, (D) $42.00, 1,300 Beds available, • PAYMENT: Cash
Trav. Ck Visa M/C • DATES AVAILABLE: May 15 - Aug. 21, • ROOM TYPE: SR
Apt. • BED TYPE: S • BEDS: 1-2 • BATH: C S P • FOOD: Caf. SB VM NR •
INFO: Cultural activities, sports. • ACTIVITIES: Canada's Wonderland Park,
Blackcreek Pioneer Village.

165 **Waterloo, ONT**   ♿

St. Jerome's University (T)
Waterloo, ONT N2L 3G3, Ph: (519) 884-8110 , Web Site: www.sju.uwaterloo.ca,
ASK FOR: Residence/Conference Office
ROOM PRICING: (S) $25.00, (D) $40.00, • PAYMENT: Cash Only • DATES
AVAILABLE: May - mid-Aug. , • FOOD: Caf. VM NR OCR • INFO: Children
welcome. • ACTIVITIES: Campus sports. Stratford Shakesperian Festival;
African Lion Safari; Ontario Place.

166 **Waterloo, ONT**   ?   ♿

University of Waterloo (T) Village 2 Conference Centre
Box 610, Waterloo, ONT N2J 4C1, Ph: (519) 884-5400, ASK FOR: David
Reynolds/Manager
ROOM PRICING: (S) $29.65, (D) $47.25, • PAYMENT: Cash Per. Ck Trav. Ck
Visa M/C Amex • DATES AVAILABLE: May 1-Aug. 31, • FOOD: Caf. VM NR •
INFO: Children welcome. • ACTIVITIES: Racquetball, art gallery, swimming,
tennis, museums, TV in public lounge. Stratford Festival Theater; Mennonite
Country Tours; African Lion Safari; Farmers Markets.

167 **Waterloo, ONT**   ♿

Wilfrid Laurier University (T)
75 University Ave. West, Waterloo, ONT N2L 3C5, Ph: (519) 884-1970, Ext: 3958,
ASK FOR: Glennice Snyder, Conf. Office
ROOM PRICING: (S) $19.00, (D) $37.00, Apts. $35-$80/night + taxes, •
PAYMENT: Cash Per. Ck Trav. Ck Visa • DATES AVAILABLE: May - Aug., •
ROOM TYPE: SR Apt. • BED TYPE: S • BEDS: 1-2 • BATH: C S • FOOD: Caf.
VM NR • INFO: Children under 10, free, A/C residences, Conf.management,
Senior group rates, tours can be arranged. • ACTIVITIES: Racquetball, art
gallery, TV in public lounge, swimming, tennis, concerts, lectures. Mennonite
Country; Woodside Historical Park; Pioneer Village; theater; Stratford Festival;
African Lion Safari.

---

168 **Windsor, ONT**   ?   ♿

University of Windsor (T)
12 Vanier Hall, Windsor, ONT N9B 3P4, Ph: (519) 253 4232, Ext: 3276, ASK
FOR: Elana Findlow
ROOM PRICING: (S) $30.00, (D) $40.00, • PAYMENT: Cash Visa M/C • DATES
AVAILABLE: May 6- Aug. 25, • ROOM TYPE: SR • BED TYPE: S • BEDS: 2 •
BATH: C • FOOD: SB NR • INFO: Children welcome, linens included. •
ACTIVITIES: Swimming, tennis, golf, theater, films, concerts, lectures, museums,
child care available. Language study; Pelee National Park; Walker Historical
Museum.

Prince Edward Island

169 **Charlottetown, PEI**   ♿

University of Prince Edward Island (T)
550 University Ave., Charlottetown, PEI C1A 4P3, Ph: (902) 566-0442, (902)
566-0362, ASK FOR: Residence Mgr., Marc Braithwaite
ROOM PRICING: (S) $36.00, (D) $39.00, includes breakfast-July 1-Aug. 15, •
PAYMENT: Cash Trav. Ck Visa M/C • DATES AVAILABLE: May 15 - Aug. 25, •
ROOM TYPE: SR Apt. • BED TYPE: S • BEDS: 2 • BATH: C P • FOOD: Caf. SB
VM NR • INFO: Children welcome, no pets. Apt. - $65.00 + taxes, per night. •
ACTIVITIES: Tennis, game room., biking trails, close to beaches, short drive to all
tourist facilities. Charlottetown Festival; Confederation Center.
DIRECTIONS: Take bridge connectiong Prince Edward Island to New Brunswick.
$35.00 on return trip. 15 minute crossing. 45 minutes to UPEI from bridge.
Please use Belevedere Ave. entrance.

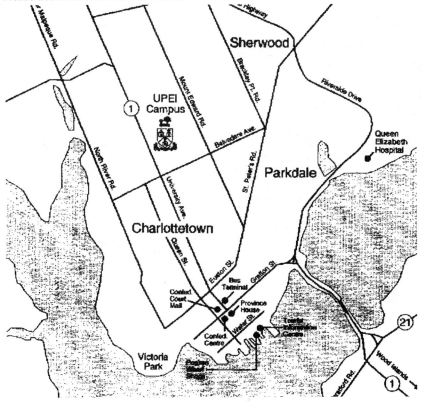

Quebec

170 **Lennoxville, QUE**   ?

Bishop's University (T)
Box 5000, Lennoxville, QUE J1M 1Z7, Ph: (819) 822-9600, Ext:2651, Fax: (819) 822-9615, E-mail: mooisrer@ubishops.ca, ASK FOR: Conf. Office
ROOM PRICING: (S) $25.00 + Taxes, (D) $32.50 + Taxes, Discount for students, • PAYMENT: Cash Per. Ck Trav. Ck Visa M/C • DATES AVAILABLE: May 15 - Aug. 31, • BEDS: 1-2 • FOOD: Caf. VM NR • INFO: No pets, children welcome. Apts. avail. • ACTIVITIES: Bicycle trail; indoor/outdoor swimming pools; sports centre with jogging track, gymnasium, weight room, tennis courts, and golf course. close to may local attractions.

171 **Lennoxville, QUE**   ?

Champlain Regional College (T)
Lennoxville Campus, Lennoxville, QUE J1M 2A1, Ph: (819) 564-3675 or (819) 564-3654, ASK FOR: Residence Services, Fay. Beaudoin
ROOM PRICING: Call for rates, • PAYMENT: Cash Per. Ck Trav. Ck • DATES AVAILABLE: June 25 - Aug. 4, • ROOM TYPE: Apt. • BED TYPE: S • BEDS: 1 • BATH: P • FOOD: NR • INFO: Free parking, coin washers/dryers. Apts. have equip. kitchenette (dishes/pots & pan), dining rm., living rm., full bath, S. beds only. 3 bdrm. apt: $200 per wk., 4 bdrm.: $250 per wk. • ACTIVITIES: Golf course; nearby lakes; Mont Oxford Park; movies in town and on campus.

172 **Matane, QUE**   ?   ♿

College De Matane (T)
616, St.- Redempteur, Matane, QUE G4W 1L1, Ph: (418) 562-1240, Ext: 2525, ASK FOR: Nathalie Arel, Sevice Tourisme
ROOM PRICING: (S) $16.00, (D) $32.00, • PAYMENT: Cash Per. Ck Trav. Ck Visa M/C • DATES AVAILABLE: June 1 - Aug. 8, • ROOM TYPE: SR • BED TYPE: S • BEDS: 1-2 • BATH: C P • FOOD: • INFO: Linens includeed, children welcome. Apts. $49.00 • ACTIVITIES: Interesting city architecture and sculpture; water sports; summer theater; wharf life; shrimp festival; Island Park; golfer's paradise.

173 **Montreal, QUE**   ♿

College Jean-De-Brebeuf (T)
5625 Decelles, Montreal, QUE H3T 1W4, Ph: (514) 342-9342 Ext: 240, Fax: (514) 342-0130, E-mail: Residence@Brebeuf.qc.ca, ASK FOR: Jacques Fournier
ROOM PRICING: (S) $20.00, (D) $30.00, • PAYMENT: Cash Trav. Ck Visa • DATES AVAILABLE: May 20-Aug.15, • ROOM TYPE: SR • BED TYPE: S • BEDS: 1-2 • BATH: C • FOOD: Caf. VM NR • INFO: Children welcome, linens included. • ACTIVITIES: Tennis, gym, TV in public lounge. Downtown Montreal; Museums; Olympic Stadium; Oratory Saint-Joseph.
DIRECTIONS: Take Highway 15; Queen Mary to East until Decelles Ave.

174 **Montreal, QUE**   ?

Concordia University (T) Loyola Campus
7141 Sherbrooke St. West, Montreal, QUE H4B 1R6, Ph: (514) 848-4757, ASK FOR: Jeff Peters, Assistant Dir.
ROOM PRICING: (S) $29.00, (D) $44.50, Sudents & seniors, (S) $21.00 , (D) $42.00, • PAYMENT: Cash Per. Ck Trav. Ck • DATES AVAILABLE: May 15 - Aug. 21, • ROOM TYPE: SR • BED TYPE: S • BEDS: 1-2 • BATH: C • FOOD: Caf. NR • INFO: Children welcome. Coin washer/dryer. • ACTIVITIES: Game room, TV in public lounge. Olympic Stadium (Expos Baseball); Casino Grand Prix; Old Montreal's history & beauty; Outstanding nightlife; International Jazz and Comedy Festival. Botanical Gardens.
DIRECTIONS: See Website for directions. www.concordia.ca/student-centre/services-forstudents/sumrez.H7M

---

175 **Montreal, QUE**

Mc Gill University (T) Summer Accommodation
3935 University St., Montreal, QUE H3A 2B4, Ph: (514) 398-6367, Fax: (514) 398-6770, E-mail: Reserve@residences.Lan.mcgill.ca
ROOM PRICING: (S) $28.00, $22.00/student/seniors ID card, (D) $33.00, • PAYMENT: Cash Per. Ck Trav. Ck Visa M/C • DATES AVAILABLE: May 15 - Aug 15, • BEDS: 1-2 • FOOD: Caf. SB VM NR • INFO: McGill provides up to 700 rooms during the summer months. Coin washers/dryers, TV lounge, parking, linen provided. • ACTIVITIES: Short walk to downtown; Close to summer festivals and parks; daily fee to use swimming pool, tennis courts and gym.

176 **Montreal, QUE**   ?

Montreal Diocesan Theological College (T)
3473 University St., Montreal, QUE H3A 2A8, Ph: (514) 849-4113, ASK FOR: Mary Fox , Cynthia Hawkins
ROOM PRICING: (S) $18.00 - $22.00, • PAYMENT: Cash Per. Ck Trav. Ck • DATES AVAILABLE: May 1 - Aug. 15, • ROOM TYPE: SR • BED TYPE: S • BEDS: 1 • BATH: C • FOOD: VM NR • INFO: Linens included, children welcome, no pets, located downtown near excellent public transportation. Coin washers/dryers. • ACTIVITIES: TV in public lounge. Old Montreal; Museums; Shopping Centers; Cinemas; Restaurants; Fine Arts.

177 **Montreal, QUE**   ?   &

Universite de Montreal (T) Residences
2350 Edouard - Montpetit Blvd., P. O. Box 6128, "Centre-Ville", Montreal, QUE H3C 3J7, Ph: (514) 343-6531, Fax: (514) 343-2353
ROOM PRICING: (S) $17.00 , (D) $24.00, • PAYMENT: Cash Trav. Ck Visa M/C Amex • DATES AVAILABLE: May 12 - Aug. 23, • BED TYPE: S • BEDS: 1-2 • FOOD: Caf. SB VM NR • INFO: Linens included, weekly rates available, lounge on each floor with TV and microwave oven. • ACTIVITIES: Racquetball, films, swimming, tennis, game room. St. Joseph's Shrine; Olympic Stadium & Biodome; Old Montreal; Museums; Casino.

178 **Quebec City, QUE**   ?

Laval University (T) Summer Housing
Parent Residence Hall, Quebec City, QUE G1K 7P4, Ph: (418) 656-5632
ROOM PRICING: (S) $18.00, (D) $25.00, 2,000 rooms available during summer.Disc. for weekly stays, • PAYMENT: Cash Trav. Ck Visa M/C • DATES AVAILABLE: May 10-Aug.20, • ROOM TYPE: SR • BED TYPE: S • BEDS: 2 • BATH: C • FOOD: Caf. SB VM NR • INFO: Children 10 yrs. and older welcome, laundry room, free parking. • ACTIVITIES: French lang., courses, recreation center, Olympic pool, indoor, outdoor tennis, bus service. Aquarium; Citadel; old city; Museum of Civilization.

179 **Riviere-du-loup, QUE**   ?   &

Cegep De Riviere-Du Loup, Resid. (T)
335, Rue St.-Pierre, Riviere-du-loup, QUE G5R 1S8, Ph: (418) 862-6903, (418) 867-2733, ASK FOR: Francine Coeullard, Ser. Logemont
ROOM PRICING: (S) $20.00, (D) $35.00, • PAYMENT: Cash Trav. Ck • DATES AVAILABLE: May 15 - Aug. 15, • FOOD: Caf. SB VM NR • INFO: Children welcome, no pets. • ACTIVITIES: Bowling, swimming, tennis, parks .River cruising; golf; Riviere-du-loup Waterfalls spectacle; museum; theater.

180 **Sherbrook, QUE**   ?   &

University de Sherbrooke (T)
2500 Boul. Universite, Sherbrook, QUE
J1K 2R1, Ph: (819) 821-7663, (819) 821-7616, ASK FOR: Mr. Gelinas, Residence Service
ROOM PRICING: (S) Student: $18.00, Visitor: $27.00, (D) Student: $32.00, Visitor: $38.00, • PAYMENT: Cash Trav. Ck Visa M/C • DATES AVAILABLE: May 5 - Aug. 15, • ROOM TYPE: SR • BED TYPE: S • BEDS: 1-2 • BATH: C • FOOD: Caf. NR • INFO: No children • ACTIVITIES: Located 35 mi. from the Vermont border, known as Queen of Eastern Townships, University is located near beautiful lakes, summer theaters, plentiful outdoor activities.

U
N
I
V

(T) = Travelers Accommodations   (E) = Educational Related   (C) = Groups & Conference Use

181 **Ste Anne De Bellvue, QUE**   ♿

John Abbott College (T)
21275 Lakeshore Rd., Ste Anne De Bellvue, QUE H9X 3L9, Ph: (514) 457-6610, Ext: 234, Fax: (514) 457-4730, ASK FOR: Peder Jacobsen
ROOM PRICING: (D) $44.00, • PAYMENT: Cash Trav. Ck Visa M/C Amex • DATES AVAILABLE: May 30 - Aug. 15, • ROOM TYPE: Apt. • BED TYPE: S • BEDS: 2 • BATH: S • FOOD: Caf. VM NR • INFO: Children welcome, 2 Bdrm Apts. available with furn. kitchen, chambermaid service, laundry room, TV lounge. • ACTIVITIES: Campus sport facilities, fitness center, ecological arboretum. National Wildlife Preserve; short bus trip to Montreal.
DIRECTIONS: On the Trans-Canada Highway, take exit 41 going east on Ste-Marie Road. Take a right at the first stop sign and follow the road past two more stop signs onto the campus. Follow signs to Stewart apartments.

182 **Ste- Therese, QUE**   ?   ♿

College Lionel-Groulx (T)
100 Place Ducharme, Ste- Therese, QUE J7E 3G6, Ph: (514) 430-0008, ASK FOR: Serv. Des Resid., Mr. Ferron
ROOM PRICING: (S) $14.00, • PAYMENT: Cash Only • DATES AVAILABLE: June 1 - Aug. 20, • ROOM TYPE: SR • BED TYPE: S • BEDS: 1 • BATH: S • FOOD: NR • INFO: Fully furnished apts w/kitchen, minimum stay, 5 nights. • ACTIVITIES: Tennis, hiking. swimming. Half hour drive to Montreal, the Laurentian area.

Saskatchewan

183 **Muenster, SASK**   ?   ♿

St. Peter's College (T)
Box 10, Muenster, SASK S0K 2Y0, Ph: (306) 682-1777, ASK FOR: Guest Master
ROOM PRICING: (S) $20.00, (D) $30.00, • PAYMENT: Cash Per. Ck Trav. Ck • DATES AVAILABLE: Year Round, • FOOD: Caf. • INFO: Children welcome, open dorms at $4.00 per nite, (holds 100 persons) bring sleeping bag, no alcohol. • ACTIVITIES: Boating, tennis, raquetball, hiking,park setting. St. Peter's Abbey Church; Monastery; Waldsea Lake; fishing streams.

184 **Saskatoon, Sask**   ?

Lutheran Theological Seminary (T)
114 Seminary Crescent, Saskatoon, Sask S7N 0X3, Ph: (306) 975-7004, ASK FOR: Residence Adm.
ROOM PRICING: (S) $30.00, (D) $52.00, Meals included, • PAYMENT: Cash Per. Ck Trav. Ck Visa • DATES AVAILABLE: May-July, • ROOM TYPE: SR • BED TYPE: S • BEDS: 1-2 • BATH: C • FOOD: Caf. VM NR • INFO: Reservations required. • ACTIVITIES: Jogging trails, art gallery, public parks, museums, tennis, theater.

185 **Saskatoon, SASK**

St. Andrew's College (T)
1121 College Drive, Saskatoon, SASK S7N 0W3, Ph: (306) 966-8970, ASK FOR: Residence Administrator
ROOM PRICING: (S) $18.00, • PAYMENT: Cash Per. Ck Trav. Ck • DATES AVAILABLE: May 1-Aug. 31, • ROOM TYPE: SR • BED TYPE: S • BEDS: 1 • BATH: C • FOOD: NR • INFO: Supply own linens, no smoking, no children. Minimum 1 week accommodation preferred. • ACTIVITIES: Park, swimming, tennis, TV in public lounge. Western Development Museum; Mendel Art Gallery; Wanuskewin Heritage Park; Ukranian Museum of Canada.

186 **Saskatoon, SASK**   ♿

Univer. of Saskatchewan (T) Saskatchewan Hall
131 Sqsk. Hall, 91 Campus Drive, Saskatoon, SASK S7N 0W0, Ph: (306)
966-8600, ASK FOR: Conf. & Catering Serv.
ROOM PRICING: (S) $26.00+Tax, (D) $42.00, • PAYMENT: Cash Trav. Ck Visa
M/C • DATES AVAILABLE: May 1 -Aug. 31, • ROOM TYPE: SR • BED TYPE: S •
BEDS: 1-2 • BATH: C • FOOD: Caf. VM NR • INFO: Linens and towels provided,
resevations required. • ACTIVITIES: Mendel Art Gallery; Meewasin Trail (along
river); Kinsmen Park; Western Development Museum; sport facilities; Kenderline
Art Gallery; Natural Science Muesum.

DENMARK

187 **Copenhagen**   ♿

Copenhagen Danhostel Bellahod (T) Hostel
Herbergvejen 8, Bronshoj, DK-2700, Copenhagen, Ph: 45-38 28 97 15, Fax:
45-38 89 02 10, ASK FOR: Reception
ROOM PRICING: (S) $13.00, Price per person, • PAYMENT: Cash Trav. Ck •
DATES AVAILABLE: Mar. 1- Jan. 15, • BEDS: 4-6 • FOOD: Caf. • INFO:
Breakfast $ 6.00 Dinner $ 10.00. • ACTIVITIES: Only 5 Km from city center;
good bus service; Scandanavia's largest city; Rosenborg Castle; Tivoli, zoo &
gardens; canal boating; sea food cafes; many art galleries; 60 parks; oldest
kingdom in the world founded1167A.D. capital city.

188 **Copenhagen**   ?   ♿

Copenhagen Sleep-In (T)
Blegdamsvej 132, 2100 , Copenhagen, Ph: 45-3526 5059/, Fax: 45-3543 5058,
ASK FOR: Kim Thomsen
ROOM PRICING: Hostel, (S) $13.00, Per person, • PAYMENT: Cash Trav. Ck •
DATES AVAILABLE: July 1 - Aug. 31, • BED TYPE: S • BEDS: 2-6 • FOOD: Caf.
NR • INFO: Blankets and sheets available to rent. Children welcome, tourist
kitchen available. Reception open 24 hours. Hostel card not required. •
ACTIVITIES: Close to bus and trains. Fifteen minutes from the center of
Copenhagen, and The Little Mermaid.

189 **Lyngby**

Lyngby Vanderhjem (T)
Raadvad 1 , DK-2800,, Lyngby, Ph: 45- 4580 30 74, Fax: 45-4580 30 32, ASK
FOR: Youth Hostel Reception open: 8-12 and 4-9
ROOM PRICING: (S) $15.00-19.00, (D) 37.00, • PAYMENT: Cash Only • DATES
AVAILABLE: April 1- Oct. 31, • ROOM TYPE: SR • BED TYPE: S • BEDS: 2-6 •
BATH: S • FOOD: Caf. NR • INFO: 2-6 bed rooms. 21 Family Rooms. Dormitory
rooms available for $15.00. • ACTIVITIES: 15 Km from Copenhagen; 7 Km
from Lyngby; 2 Km to beach; 0.5 Km to golf course. Surrounded by forest.
DIRECTIONS: By car: East on 47 direction Helstngir, take Exit 15
Common: S train to Lyngby. Bus 182 or 183 to Hjortekeer. One hour from
Copenhagen

FINLAND

190 **Turku**   ?

University of Turku (T) Hotel Domus Oboensis
Piispankatu 10 Biskopsgatan, 20500 Turku-ABO 50, Turku, Ph: 921-329-470,
ASK FOR: Hotel Manager
ROOM PRICING: (S) $25.00, (D) $32.00, (for 2), • PAYMENT: Cash • DATES
AVAILABLE: June 1 -Aug. 31, • FOOD: Caf. • ACTIVITIES: Sauna, sightseeing,
cultural activities.

FRANCE

191 **Brest**   ?   ♿

University de Bretagne (T) C.L.O.U.S.
Plateau du Gouguen, 29283 - Brest Cedex, Brest, Ph: (98) 03-38-78, ASK FOR:
Chef du Logement
ROOM PRICING: (S) $12.00, • PAYMENT: Cash • DATES AVAILABLE: July
1-Sept. 30, • BED TYPE: S D • FOOD: Caf. NR • INFO: No animals •
ACTIVITIES: Pleasure boat excursions, beaches, tennis, swimming, hiking, films,
museums, port city.

192 **Caen**   ?

University de Caen (T) C.R.O.U.S.
23, Avenue de Bruxelles, 14034,Cedex, Caen, Ph: (31) 94-73-37, ASK FOR: Chef
du Logement
ROOM PRICING: (S) $10.00, • PAYMENT: Cash • DATES AVAILABLE: June
-Sept., • FOOD: Caf. • ACTIVITIES: Modern city, Rebuilt after WWII. Main
attraction is the D-day landing beaches; seafront war museum; Wm. the
Conqueror's Castle; Normandy Museum.

193 **Chatenay- Malabry**   ?   ♿

Residence de l' Ecole Centrale (T)
Avenue Sully Prud'homme, 92290, Chatenay- Malabry, Ph: 46-60-32-91, ASK
FOR: Mr. Ville, Director
ROOM PRICING: (S) $26.14, (D) $26.14, (includes breakfast), • PAYMENT: Cash
Per. Ck Trav. Ck • DATES AVAILABLE: July-August, • FOOD: VM • INFO: No
alcohol, children welcome with adults. Open during Easter Hollidays, $17.00,
single & double. • ACTIVITIES: All on campus sports facilities, swimming, tennis.
19 miles from Paris; 12 miles from Versailles.

194 **La Garde**   ?

Campus International (T) Universite De Toulon/Var
B. P. 131, 83957 Cedex, La Garde, Ph: 33-494-21-12-82, Fax: 33-494-14-30-52,
ASK FOR: Marie Lavie Ouvieri
ROOM PRICING: (S) $1,420.00/2 weeks, (D) $2,580.00/2 weeks. 1/2 board
available., • PAYMENT: Cash Per. Ck Trav. Ck Visa M/C • DATES
AVAILABLE: June 10 - Sept. 30, summer courses, Jan.20 - Mar.16.
Sept.15-Dec.15., • BEDS: 1-3 • FOOD: SB VM NR OCR • INFO: Price includes all
meals, bike, tuition, afternoon activities, bus shuttles, transfers to & from airport,
trains. Short term French courses, 2-3 wks.(summer) 2-15 wks(winter) •
ACTIVITIES: Recreational activities. Theater; music concerts; movies; local
guided tours; weekend excursions.

195 **Lille**   ?

Maison des Ican (T)
8 Rue Auber, 59000, Lille, Ph: 33-20- 93-58-55, ASK FOR: Michel Bureau
ROOM PRICING: (S) $11.00, • PAYMENT: Cash Per. Ck Trav. Ck • DATES
AVAILABLE: July1-21,Sept1-27, • ROOM TYPE: SR • BED TYPE: S • BEDS: 1 •
BATH: C • FOOD: VM • INFO: Bedding furnished, bath shared. • ACTIVITIES:
Tennis, billiards, ping pong, TV rooms. Cultural activities in area.

196 **Marseilles**   ?

C. R. O. U. S. (T)
42, Rue du 141* R. I. A., 13331 Cedex 3, Marseilles, Ph: 91- 95-90-06, Fax:
91-50-41-19, ASK FOR: Chef des Services
ROOM PRICING: (S) $ 8.00 students, $11.50 non-students, • PAYMENT: Cash •
DATES AVAILABLE: July 1 -Sept. 30 and upon arrangement, • FOOD: NR •
INFO: No children • ACTIVITIES: Language study, sightseeing, cultural activities.
Chief seaport of France, canal barge cruises, castles

197 Paris   ?

Assn. Des Etudiants (T) Protestants de Paris
46 Rue de Vaugirard, 75006, Paris, Ph: 33 (0)143-54-31-49 or 33 (0) 146 332330
, Fax: 33 (0) 1 46-362709 , ASK FOR: Mr.Alan Lortal
ROOM PRICING: (S) $19.00-$21.00, (D) $35.00, (Includes Breakfast) dormitory-
$14.50, • PAYMENT: Cash Per. Ck Trav. Ck • DATES AVAILABLE: July, Aug.
Sept., • ROOM TYPE: SR • BED TYPE: S • BEDS: 4-8 • BATH: C • FOOD: Caf.
VM NR • INFO: No children,18-30 year old students only, dormitoires available
year round, $15.00,single and double only during summer. Reservations taken
for a minimum stay of 1 week. Arrive before 8:45 a.m. to get on waiting list. •
ACTIVITIES: Paris - Eiffel Tower, Notre Dame, Louvre, Luxembourg Gardens,
Pantheon, George Pompidou Art Center, flower and animal markets, the sights
and scenes are endless.
DIRECTIONS: In the sixth district of Paris, near the Senate Bldg. and Luxemborg
Garden.

198 Paris   ?   ♿

FIAP Jean Monnet (T)
30 Rue Cabanis, 75014, Paris, Ph: 33-1-43-13-17-17, Fax: 33-1-45-81-63-91,
E-mail: fiapadmi@fiap.asso.fr, Web Site: www.fiap.asso.fr
ROOM PRICING: (S) $48.00/with Breakfast (D) $31.00 ea. person with breakfast.
Group rates, (S) $53.00, (D) $38.00/person(half board), • PAYMENT: Cash Trav.
Ck • DATES AVAILABLE: Year round, • ROOM TYPE: SR • BED TYPE: S •
BATH: P • FOOD: Caf. SB VM OCR • INFO: B/B bedroom w/ 4 beds; B/B
bedroom w/8 beds; coin washer, tourist information office; Disco , piano bar ,
bar with terrace. Special rates for medium or long stay (medium=14-27 nights),
long= more than 27 nights. • ACTIVITIES: The FIAP Jean Monnet is in Paris, near
all tourist sights.
Paris - Eiffel Tower; Notre Dame; Louvre; Luxembourg Gardens; Pantheon; George
Pompidou Art Center; flower and animal markets.
DIRECTIONS: The FIAP Jean Monnet is on the left bank (south of Paris) close to
Denfert-Rochereau (5Min. walk) and Montparnasse (15 Min. walk). The Metro
(Glaciere or St. Jacques) is 2 minutes from the FIAP.

**U
N
I
V**

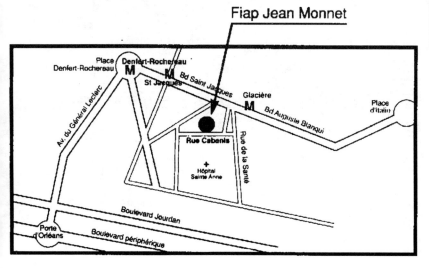

Fiap Jean Monnet

199 **Paris**

Maison Internationale (T)
4 rue Titon, 75011, Paris, Ph: 33-143 71 9921, Fax: 33-143-71-7858
ROOM PRICING: Hostel, 18-30 years of age, (S) $20.00, Register between 8AM & 2AM., • PAYMENT: Cash Trav. Ck • DATES AVAILABLE: Year round, • BEDS: 2-8 • FOOD: Caf. VM NR • INFO: Exceptions can be made on age for groups. Each floor provided with showers and toilets, cafeteria open for breakfast only. Travelers cks must be in French Francs. • ACTIVITIES: All that Paris has to offer; convenient to railroad stations; buses and underground.

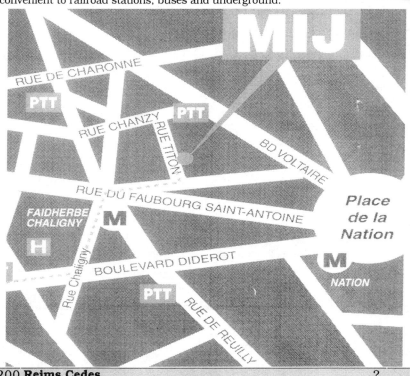

200 **Reims Cedes**   ?

C.R.O.U.S. de Reims (T) BP 2751
34 Blvd. Henri Vasnier, 51063 , Reims Cedes, Ph: 33-0326 50 59 00, Fax: 33-0326 50 59 29
ROOM PRICING: (S) $9.00, students only., • PAYMENT: Cash Only • DATES AVAILABLE: July -Sept., • FOOD: Caf. • INFO: No children, Breakfast-$1.50 fee, studio apt. available. • ACTIVITIES: Vistis to the Champagne Caves; Reims Cathedral; Historic world war battlegrounds.

201 **Rennes**   ?   ♿

University Rennes (T) C.R.O.U.S.
7, Place Hoche, B.P. 115, 35002 - Cedex, Rennes, Ph: (99) 36-46-11, ASK FOR: Msr. Le Directeur
ROOM PRICING: (S) $12.00 per night, shared accommodations for individuals or rooms for couples on arrangement., • PAYMENT: Cash • DATES AVAILABLE: July to Sept. 30, • BED TYPE: S • BEDS: 1 • FOOD: Caf. NR • ACTIVITIES: Cultural activities, sightseeing, capital of Brittany, medieval town, old art museum, Mont Saint-Michael.

202 **Saint Denis**   ?

Academie de Creteil (T) C.R.O.U.S. St. Denis
Place of 8th of May, 1945, 93200 , Saint Denis, Ph: 33-60- 78-14-92, ASK FOR:
Directrice
ROOM PRICING: (S) $12.00, • PAYMENT: Cash • DATES AVAILABLE: June
-Sept., • FOOD: No Caf. • INFO: No children. • ACTIVITIES: 10 min. to the metro
line; All of Paris attractions.

203 **Strasbourg**   ?   ♿

C.R.O.U.S.de Strasbourg (T)
1, Quai du Marie Dietrich, 67084, Strasbourg, Ph: 33-88-36-16-91, ASK FOR:
Chef du Logement, Dos Santos Ferreira
ROOM PRICING: (S) $17.00, • PAYMENT: Cash Only • DATES AVAILABLE: July
1-Aug. 31, • FOOD: NR • INFO: Children over 6 years welcome, no animals •
ACTIVITIES: Boating on the Rhine; enchanting city streets and shops; open
markets; medieval architecture; many cultural events.

204 **Tours**

Univ. D'orleans - Tours (T) C.L.O.U.S.
Boulevard de Tassigny, 37041 - Cedex, Tours, Ph: 33-47- 60-42-42, Fax:
33-47-20-46-33, ASK FOR: Residence Office (Chedes Services)
ROOM PRICING: (S) $9.00, • PAYMENT: Cash Trav. Ck • DATES AVAILABLE:
June 15-Sept 30, • BEDS: 1 • FOOD: Caf. OCR • INFO: Linen charge $2.50, no
children. • ACTIVITIES: Castles on the Loire River; wine growing region; golf
course; gastronomical delights; swimming; museums; concerts.

GERMANY

205 **Berlin**   ?

Jugendgastehaus (T) Youth Hostel
Kluckstrasse 3, 10185 Berlin - Tiergarten, Berlin, Ph: 49-30-261-1097, Fax:
49-30-265-03-83
ROOM PRICING: Per person, (S) $20.00/Junior, $25.00/Senior, (includes
breakfast), • PAYMENT: Cash Trav. Ck • DATES AVAILABLE: Year round, •
BED TYPE: S • BEDS: 4-5 • FOOD: Caf. SB VM NR OCR • INFO: Coin
washer/dryers, free parking, TV room, bed sheets included, children welcome,
very centrally located. Internet Termnial. • ACTIVITIES: Guest lounge with cable
T.V., adjacent to the Gropius Museum and Berlin Wall; East and West Berlin
tours; Lake Wannsee; canal rides; famous Kuferstendam shopping walk; music;
opera; art; concerts - International Flavor Sport Festivals.

206 **Berlin**   ?

Studentenhotel (T) Hubertusallee
Delbruckstrasse 24, D-14193 Berlin, Berlin, Ph: 37-030-8919718, Fax:
37-030-8928698
ROOM PRICING: (S) $43.00, (D) $59.00 , (Includes Breakfast), • PAYMENT: Cash
• DATES AVAILABLE: Mar.-Oct., • FOOD: Caf. VM NR • INFO: Triple $68.00;
Price per room for student-single:$24.00-double:$38.00-3 bedroom:$49.00 •
ACTIVITIES: Guest lounge with cable T.V., adjacent to the Gropius Museum and
Berlin Wall, East and West Berlin tours, Lake Wannsee, canal rides, famous
Kuferstendam shopping walk, music, opera, art, concerts - International Flavor
Sport Festivals.

207 **Berlin**   ?   ♿

Studentenhotel Berlin (T)
Meininger Strasse 10, 10823 , Berlin, Ph: 49-30 784-67-20, Fax: 49- 30 788 15
23, ASK FOR: Mrs. Meier, Mr. Mehlitz, Reser. Off.
ROOM PRICING: (S) $41.00, (D) $62.00, 4 bedded room, $28.00 per person.,
(includes breakfast), • PAYMENT: Cash Only • DATES AVAILABLE: Year Round,
• FOOD: NR • INFO: Children welcome. • ACTIVITIES: City government bldgs;
Europa Center; National Gallery; famous Kurfursten Damm; shopping and dining
district; Lake Wansee Night clubs.

208 **Berlin- Hermsdorf**   ?

Jugendherberge (T) Ernst Reuter, Youth Hostel
Hermsdorfer Damm 48-50, 13467, Berlin- Hermsdorf, Ph: 49-30-404-1610, Fax: 49-30 404 5972
ROOM PRICING: Per person, (S) $15.00, (includes breakfast buffet), members under 27., • PAYMENT: Cash Only • DATES AVAILABLE: Jan-Nov., • BED TYPE: S • BEDS: 6 • FOOD: Caf. VM • INFO: Bus at front door, coin washer/dryer. • ACTIVITIES: Guest lounge with cable T.V. Lake Tegel; canal rides; famous Kurfwerstendamm shopping walk; music; opera; art; concerts; International Flavor Sport Festivals.

209 **Detmold**   ?

Deutsches Jugendherbergwerk (T)
Bismarckstr. 8, 32756 , Detmold, Ph: 49-5231-74010
• PAYMENT: Cash   • FOOD: • INFO: Contact this office for information on 537 low-cost guest houses and youth hostels in Germany.

IRELAND

210 **Belfield, Dublin 4**   ♿

UCD Village (T) c/o Merville Reception
Belfield, Dublin 4, Ph: (353) 1-2697111, Fax: (353) 1-2697704, E-mail: ucdvillage@usit.ie, ASK FOR: Robin Hickey, Mgr.
ROOM PRICING: 24.00£ (Irish Pounds), • PAYMENT: Cash Trav. Ck Visa M/C • DATES AVAILABLE: Jun. 15-Sept.12, • BEDS: 1 • FOOD: Caf. SB NR OCR • INFO: Quality accommodation for individuals, families, and groups in 3-4 bedroom apart.   Ideal for self-catering holidays, children welcome. • ACTIVITIES: Ten minute bus ride from the city center. On campus facilities include restaurant, shop, bar, and sports center.   Conf., sports, and banquet facilities.

211 **Cork**   ? ♿

University College Cork (T)
Castlewhite Apartments, Western Road, Cork, Ph: 353-21-341-473,   Fax: 353-21-902-793, ASK FOR: Pauline Gilheany or Ann Sheehan
ROOM PRICING: (S) $30.00, (D) $47.00, • PAYMENT: Cash Trav. Ck Visa M/C • DATES AVAILABLE: Jun. 16-Sept.16, • BED TYPE: S • BEDS: 1 • FOOD: SB VM NR OCR • INFO: Children welcome, cots on request, no pets, linens included. • ACTIVITIES: Campus is 10 minute walk from city center; the Blarney Stone; Scenic Kinsale Village with seaside restaurants; The ring of Kerry are within easy driving distance.

212 **Dublin**   ♿

Kinlay House Christchurch (T)
2-12 Lord Edward St., Dublin, 2, Ph: 353-1-679-6644, Fax: 353-1-679-7437, E-mail: kindub@usit.ie, ASK FOR: Helen Humphries, Marketing Co-ordinator
ROOM PRICING: 14.00£/person - 4&6 bedded rooms, 17£/person - for two bed rooms , • PAYMENT: Cash Trav. Ck Visa M/C • DATES AVAILABLE: Year Round, • BEDS: 2-6 • FOOD: VM NR • INFO: Self-catering kitchen, children welcome, TV room, free continental breakfast, open 24 hours. • ACTIVITIES: Within walking distance to theaters, museums, shops, and restaurants.

213 **Dublin**   ? ♿

University of Dublin (T) Trinity College
Dublin, 2, Ph: 353-1-608-1177,   Fax: 353-1-671-1267, E-mail: reservations@tcd.ie, ASK FOR: Des O'Connell, Director
ROOM PRICING: (S) $45.00, (D) $90.00, • PAYMENT: Cash Trav. Ck Visa M/C • DATES AVAILABLE: June 1-Sept.30, • BEDS: 1 • FOOD: Caf. OCR • INFO: Linen and full maid service available.   Children welcome. Family apartments available. • ACTIVITIES: Gym, tennis, squash, pool, track. City center location, on a 35 acre campus, home of the world famous Book of Kells.

(T) = Travelers Accommodations   (E) = Educational Related   (C) = Groups & Conference Use

214 **Galway**   ♿

Corrib Village (T)
Newcastle, Galway, Ph: (353) 91 27112, Fax: (353) 91-52241
ROOM PRICING: (S) $33.00, (D) $55.00, approx. cost depending if accomodation is B&B std./en Suite, or self catering., • PAYMENT: Cash Trav. Ck Visa M/C Amex • DATES AVAILABLE: June 12-Sept. 10, • BEDS: 1-2 • FOOD: Caf. OCR • INFO: Self-catering apts. complete with fully fitted kitchen, children welcome, laundry, adventure center, store. Linens included. En-suite apts. have dishwasher, microwave, washer/dryer. Also offer B&B on a nightly basis with self-catering apts. • ACTIVITIES: Located 5 minutes from Galway City center in rural riverside setting. Ideal base from which to explore the spectacular scenery of Galway Bay, Aran Islands, The Burren, Cliffs of Moher, etc. Golf; fishing; water sports; horserioding.
DIRECTIONS: Just off the N 17 on the Newcastle road at the beginning of Clifdon road located outside Galway city. Approx. 5 minute drive.

215 **Galway**   ?   ♿

Kinlay House Egre Square (T)
Merchants Road, Galway, Ph: 353-91-565-244, Fax: 353-91-565-245`, ASK FOR: Jane Colbert, Manager
ROOM PRICING: Hostel Accommodations, (S) $19.55/4 & 6 bedded rooms, (D) $28.00, • PAYMENT: Cash Trav. Ck Visa M/C • DATES AVAILABLE: Year round, • BEDS: 2-6 • FOOD: VM NR • INFO: Self-catering kitchens, open 24 hours. No conference facilities. • ACTIVITIES: Within walking distance to theaters, museums swimming, etc.

U N I V

216 Limerick ♿

University of Limerick (T) Plassey Village & Kilmurry Village
Limerick, Ph: 353-61 202360, Fax: 353-61-330316, ASK FOR: Linda Stevens, Mgr.
ROOM PRICING: (S) $30.00/ B&B, (D) $54.00/ B&B, • PAYMENT: Cash Trav. Ck Visa M/C • DATES AVAILABLE: Jun. 11-Sept.17, • BED TYPE: S D • BEDS: 1 • FOOD: Caf. SB VM NR OCR • INFO: Children welcome, coin washers/dryers, TV lounge, free parking. Linen included • ACTIVITIES: Sports facilities, art galleries, Concert hall. Campus situated on green parkland bordering the river Shannon. Close by: the Burren, Cliffs of Moher, Cork, Kellarney, the ring of Kerry, activity centre at Lough Derg, Bunratty Castle & Folk Park, King Johns Castle. 2 miles from Limerick city
DIRECTIONS: Located 2 miles north of Limerick City off the main N7 route to Dublin.

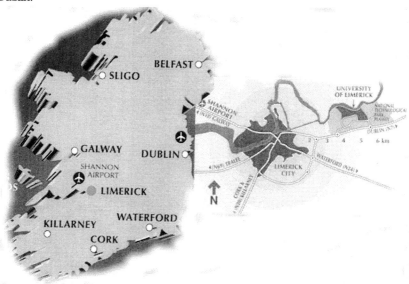

217 Shandon, Cork

Kinlay House Shandon (T)
Bob & Joan Walk, Shandon, Cork, Ph: 353-21-508966, Fax: 353-21-506927, E-mail: lincork@usit.ie, ASK FOR: Hamid Oucherfi, Manager
ROOM PRICING: Hostel Accommodations, (D) $37.40, Twin bedded room, • PAYMENT: Cash Trav. Ck Visa M/C • DATES AVAILABLE: Year round, Open 24 hours• BEDS: 2-12 • FOOD: VM NR • INFO: Children welcome. TV lounge, free parking, laundry facilities, free continental breakfast. • ACTIVITIES: Within walking distance to art galleries, theaters,museums, parks, etc. Central location on bus route to Blarney Castle and within walking distance to other tourist attractions.

ISRAEL

218 **Beer Sheva**   ?

Ben Gurion University (T) Hospitality Dept.
Binyan Ein Gedi 31, P. O. Box 653, 84105, Beer Sheva, Ph: 972-7-6461016,
Fax: 972-7-6472971, ASK FOR: Michael Adam
ROOM PRICING: (S) $40.00, (D) $60.00, • PAYMENT: Cash • DATES AVAILABLE:
Year round-subject to availablitiy., • ROOM TYPE: SR Apt. • BED TYPE: S •
BEDS: 1-2 • BATH: S P • FOOD: NR • INFO: TV in rooms, linens included. No
childrens accommodations. • ACTIVITIES: Dead Sea, Jerusalem 1 hrour 20
minutes away, The entire Negev.

219 **Jerusalem**   ?

Hebrew University / Reznik Dormitory (T)
Mount Scopus, P. O. Box 24011, Jerusalem, 91904, Ph: 02-882672, ASK FOR:
Mrs. Shilla Yaz, Coordinator
ROOM PRICING: (S) $24.00, (D) $32.00, • PAYMENT: Cash • DATES AVAILABLE:
End of July-End of Sept., • FOOD: Caf. • INFO: Children welcome. • ACTIVITIES:
Swimming, tennis, TV in public lounge; The Old City

MALTA

220 **Sliema**   ?

NSTS Hibernia House (T)
Depiro Street, Sliema, Ph: (356) 333859
ROOM PRICING: (S) $9.00-$30.00, (D) $8.00-$30.00, Multi-beds-$5-$8.00, •
PAYMENT: Cash Only • DATES AVAILABLE: Year Round, • FOOD: Caf. • INFO:
No children. Studio apartments, one single bed, shared bath. Also: Apartment
with two single beds, private bath. • ACTIVITIES: Common TV lounge, game room,
sun roof. Centrally located, 20 minutes from Univ.; 5 min. from sea; private
beach club and water sports. English speaking country in the Mediterranean.

NEW ZEALAND

U
N
I
V

221 **Auckland- City Central** ♿

University of Auckland (T) Grafton Hall
40 Seafield View Rd., Auckland- City Central, Ph: 09-3733994, Fax: 09-3779134,
E-mail: graftonhall@auckland.ac.n3, ASK FOR: Manager
ROOM PRICING: Hostel, (S) NZ $39.00, NZ$243.00/weekly, (D) NZ$78.00,
NZ$546/weekly, includes breakfast & dinner, • PAYMENT: Cash Only • DATES
AVAILABLE: Mid. - Nov. - Mid. Feb., • BEDS: 1-2 • FOOD: Caf. VM NR OCR •
INFO: Children welcome, TV lounge. Box lunches available. • ACTIVITIES: Tennis
courts, free laundry, parking, tennis. Superb beaches; close to central city
location; water activities; city cultural attractions. Shopping precincts, main bus
line.

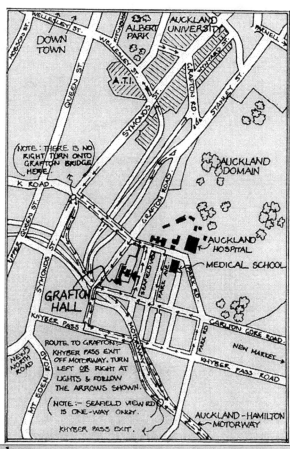

222 **Canterbury** ? ♿

Lincoln University (T)
P. O. Box 84, Canterbury, Ph: 64-03-253-601, ASK FOR: Ms. Faye McGill
ROOM PRICING: Hostel, (S) $40.50, (includes meals), • PAYMENT: Cash • DATES
AVAILABLE: Nov. Mar., April, July- Aug., • BED TYPE: S • BEDS: 1 • FOOD: Caf.
SB VM OCR • INFO: Children welcome. • ACTIVITIES: Boating, farming tours,
natural hot pools, mountains for hiking and skiing, plus all sport facilities on
campus.

223 Christchurch

Canterbury University (T) Ilam Flats
Private Bag 4800, Christchurch, Ph: 64- 3642-656, Fax: 64-3642-923, ASK FOR:
Ms. J. A. Flintoff
ROOM PRICING: (S) $20.00/ Students, $35.00/ Non-students, • PAYMENT: Cash
Per. Ck Visa • DATES AVAILABLE: Nov. 20- Feb. 10, • BEDS: 1 • FOOD: Caf.
VM NR OCR • INFO: Children welcome,   24 flats housing six tenants, free
parking, TV lounge (sky TV),pool room, washer/dryer in flat, linens can be
included on request. • ACTIVITIES: Tennis, boating. Avon River; Southern Alps;
Hagley Park;   Russley Golf Course; Beach recreations center; 5K from city;
Botanical Gardens;
Campus; Several golf courses.

224 Hamilton   ♿

University of Waikato (T)
Private Bag 3105, Hamilton, Ph: 64-838-4084, Fax: 64-838-4058, ASK FOR:
Accommodations and Conference Services Office
ROOM PRICING: (S) $20.00, Bed & Breakfast, • PAYMENT: Cash Trav. Ck Visa
Write or call for dates available• BEDS: 1 • FOOD: SB VM NR OCR • INFO:
Orchard Park Cottages-$89.00 per 4 people.   Laundry facilities, TV rooms,
kitchenettes, free parking, lounges. • ACTIVITIES: Cultural activities, sports,
swimming, tennis, golf, etc.

225 Karori , Wellington

Wellington University (T) Helen Lowry Hall
19 Blakey Ave., Karori , Wellington, 5, Ph: 4767-020, ASK FOR: Warden - C J
Arcus
ROOM PRICING: (S) $25.00 w/breakfast, $20.00/wo breakfast, • PAYMENT:
Cash Only • DATES AVAILABLE: Nov. 10 -Feb. 15, July 1-10., • ROOM TYPE: SR
Apt. • BED TYPE: S • BEDS: 1-3 • BATH: C • FOOD: Caf. NR • INFO: Children
welcome, situated 5 km off campus. $25.00 each additional adult. Free parking,
TV lounge, games room, computer room, 24 coffee, tea, & toast. • ACTIVITIES:
Cruises to southern islands, sailing, cable cars, capital city of Wellington, summer
fishing festivals, public lounge.

226 Kelburn, Wellington   ♿

Victoria Univ. of Wellington (T) Everton Hall
Everton Terrace, Kelburn, Wellington, Ph: 64-4-4720655, Fax: 64-4-4737027,
E-mail: everton@netlink.co.nz, ASK FOR: Clare Young/Silva Slyfield
ROOM PRICING: (S) $50.00/ week, • PAYMENT: Cash Per. Ck Trav. Ck •
DATES AVAILABLE: Nov. 16- Feb. 21 , • BED TYPE: S • BEDS: 1 • FOOD: SB
VM NR • INFO: Individuals or groups. All apartments have their own kitchen,
Communal laundry , washers free and coin operated dryers, TV lounge,   game
aroom. • ACTIVITIES: Close to beaches, Te Papa National Museum, botanical
gardens, sports facilities downtown Wellington, 5 minutes from University and city

227 Kelburn, Wellington   ♿

Victoria University, Weir House (T)
GladstoneTerrace, Kelburn, Wellington, 1, Ph: 64-4-472-1851,   Fax:
64-4-471-1128, E-mail: JaneFulcher@vun.ac.nz, ASK FOR: The Warden
ROOM PRICING: (S) $20.00/B&B, $25.00/Full board, (D) $24.00/B&B,
$36.00/Full board, • PAYMENT: Cash Only Trav. Ck Visa M/C • DATES
AVAILABLE: mid-Nov. - mid-Feb. , • BED TYPE: S • BEDS: 1-2 • FOOD: Caf. VM
NR • INFO: Children welcome, free parking, TV lounges, free laundry facilities,
linens included, conference facilities. • ACTIVITIES: Close to Campus. Attractions
of capital city of Wellington; cable cars; ferry rides to So. Island; botanical
gardens; cathedrals; harbor life; sailing.Te Papa Museum, Theatres, Cable Car.

(T) = Travelers Accommodations   (E) = Educational Related   (C) = Groups & Conference Use

228 Palmerston North   ? ♿

Massey University Residential Services (T)
Palmerston North, Ph: 64-06-3505056,   Fax: 64-06-350-5675, ASK FOR: Halls Administrator
ROOM PRICING: (S) $34.00/B&B, $45.00/B&B and dinner, • PAYMENT: Cash Visa M/C • DATES AVAILABLE: Nov. 13- Feb.19, • ROOM TYPE: SR • BED TYPE: S • BEDS: 1 • FOOD: Caf. SB VM NR • INFO: Childrens rates available. Christmas closedown may affect meal sources. Coin washers/dryers, TV lounge. • ACTIVITIES: 2 hour drive to capital city of Wellington;   close to beaches; mountains; rivers; Agriculture University.

229 Wellington   ♿

Victoria Univ. of Wellington (T) Trinity-Newman Hall
P. O. Box 28-029, Wellington, Ph: 64-04- 475-8471, ASK FOR: Summer Accommodations
ROOM PRICING: Weekly rates, (S) $55.00, (D) $89.50, Min. stay- 4 weeks, • PAYMENT: Cash Per. Ck Visa M/C • DATES AVAILABLE: Nov. 15 - Feb. 20, • ROOM TYPE: Apt. • BED TYPE: S D • BEDS: 1 • BATH: S • FOOD: No NR • INFO: Linens not provided, children welcome, accommodations in separate houses close to university. Cooking & eating utensils not provided. • ACTIVITIES: City beaches; botanical gardens; downtown Wellington with theater, films, art galleries, recreation center.

NORWAY

230 Bergen   ? ♿

Bergen University (T) Fantoft Student Home & Summer Hotel
5036 Fantoft, Bergen, Ph: (55) 276000, Fax: 55-276030
ROOM PRICING: (S) $60.00/B&B, (D) $85.00/B&B, • PAYMENT: Cash Visa • DATES AVAILABLE: May 20-Aug. 8, • BED TYPE: S • BEDS: 1-4 • FOOD: SB VM • INFO: 200 rooms. Various lounges and sitting rooms, fully licensed. Apartments with 3 or 4 beds, $96- $105. • ACTIVITIES: Sightseeing - Fjords, seacoast, lakes, rivers, sports.

231 Trondheim   ? ♿

Singsaker Sommerhotel (T)
Rogertsgt 1, 7016 , Trondheim, Ph: (47) 73 89 31 00, Fax: (47) 73 89 32 00
ROOM PRICING: B&B, (S) $55.00, (D) $85.00, • PAYMENT: Cash Trav. Ck Visa M/C • DATES AVAILABLE: June 8 -Sept. 1, • FOOD: Caf. SB NR • INFO: Children welcome, TV lounge, dogs welcome. • ACTIVITIES: Theater; Museum of Applied Art; Museum of Music; Cathedral Fortress.

RUSSIA

232 Moscow   ?

Moscow Hostel (T) Reservations contact:
409 N. Pacific Coast Hwy., Suite 390, Redondo Beach, CA 90277, USA, Moscow, Ph: (310) 379-4316, Fax: (310) 379-8420
ROOM PRICING: (S) $17.00 , 4 persons per room, • PAYMENT: Cash Per. Ck Visa M/C • DATES AVAILABLE: Year Round, • FOOD: NR • INFO: Visa and travel service available at hostels, Staff are Russian and English speaking. • ACTIVITIES: Sights of Moscow.

233 Moscow   ? ♿

Travelers Guest House (T)
Loc: 50 Bolshaya Perevaslavskaya, 129041 , Moscow, Ph: 7-(095)971-4059, 280-8562, Fax: 7-(095)280-9686
ROOM PRICING: (S) $30.00, (D) $40.00, $15.00 Dorm Rms, 5 persons per room, • PAYMENT: Cash Visa M/C Amex • DATES AVAILABLE: Year Round, • BED TYPE: S • BEDS: 1-5 • FOOD: Caf. SB NR • INFO: Travel & Visa Service, Cafe and Bar in Building, staff speaks fluent English, TV lounge, internation phones, Fax service, kitchen and laundry facilities. • ACTIVITIES: Sights of Moscow; Eco & Adventure Tourism in Siberia and Kirghistan. Trans Siberian & Silk Road Tours; Worldwide Flight reservations.

234 St. Petersburg   ?

St. Petersburg International Hostel (T) Reservations contact:
409 N. Pacific Coast Hwy., Suite 390, Redondo Beach, CA 90277, USA, St.
Petersburg, Ph: (310) 618-2014, Fax: (310) 618-1140
ROOM PRICING: Hostel, (S) $17.00, • PAYMENT: Cash Per. Ck Visa M/C •
DATES AVAILABLE: Year Round, • BEDS: 2-5 • FOOD: NR • INFO: Travel service
available at hostel.   Staff are Russian and English speaking.   For Visa
information, contact our Redondo Beach office. • ACTIVITIES: Located at: 3rd
Sovetskaya Ulitsa 28, 193036.   Phone: 7-812-329-8018, Fax: 7-812-329-8019.
Sights of St. Peterburg; Tours.   Five minute walk to metro. On-Line info;
http://www.sph.su/ryh.

SLOVENIA

235 Ljubljana   ?

Studentski domovi v Ljubljani (T)
Cesta 27 aprila 31, 61000 , Ljubljana, Ph: 061-23735, Fax: (386-61) 218-1567
ROOM PRICING: (S) $8.25, (D) $16.50, 2 bedroom flat w/kitchen & bathroom, •
PAYMENT: Cash Only • DATES AVAILABLE: June 25- Sept. 15, • FOOD: Caf. •
INFO: Accommodations for 350. • ACTIVITIES: Hiking, mountain climbing, Alpine
Lakes, castles, caves, baroque arch.

236 Maribor   ?

Studenski domovi Maribor (T)
Gosposvetska cesta 83, 62000 , Maribor, , Fax: 386-61 29-355
ROOM PRICING: (S) $11.50, • PAYMENT: Cash Only • DATES AVAILABLE: July 1
-Aug. 31, • FOOD: Caf. • ACTIVITIES: Theater, museums, sports, sightseeing.

SPAIN

237 Allicante   ?

Colegio Mayor Universitario (T) Universidad de Alicante
Ctr. San Vicente S/U, San Vicente del Raspeig, 03690, Allicante, Ph: 34-96-566
6611
ROOM PRICING: $480/per month, (S) Meals included, • PAYMENT: Cash •
DATES AVAILABLE: July, • BED TYPE: S • BEDS: 1 • FOOD: Caf. SB VM NR •
ACTIVITIES: Racquetball, swimming, game room, tennis. City of Allicante; (beach)
City of Benidom.

238 Barcelona   ?   &

Colegio Mayor San Raimundo (T)
Avenue Diagonal, 643, 08028, Barcelona, Ph: 330-87-11, ASK FOR: Jose Manuel
Bermudo
ROOM PRICING: (S) $30.00- $40.00, (D) $45.00- $6.00, • PAYMENT: Cash Only
• DATES AVAILABLE: Yearly, except Christmas & Easter, • BED TYPE: S •
FOOD: Caf. NR • INFO: Payment in advance required. • ACTIVITIES: Theater,
museums, sporting events.

239 Barcelona   &

Vila Universitaria (T) Campus De La Universitat Autonoma
De Barcelona, Bellaterra, Cerdanyola Del Valles, 08193 Barcelona, Barcelona, Ph:
34-93-5809355,   Fax: 34-93-5817495, E-mail: etacrod@campus.vab.es, ASK
FOR: Bellaterra Campus Conv. Bureau
ROOM PRICING: (S) $20.00-$30.00, (D) $35.00- $55.00, • PAYMENT: Cash Per.
Ck Trav. Ck Visa Amex • DATES AVAILABLE: Apts. July-Aug. Hotel, year
round., • BEDS: 1-2 • FOOD: Caf. SB VM NR OCR • INFO: 5 different apt styles
accommodating up to 5 persons. Also,50 double rooms in Hotel Campus. Linens
included. Children welcome, no animals. • ACTIVITIES: Racquetball, park,
swimming, game room, tennis, TV in public lounge, medical center, bank,
bookshop.   City of Barcelona(22Km, car, train);   Costa Brava & Catalan
Seashore; Nearby cities of Cerdanyola, Sabadell, Sant Cugat.

U
N
I
V

(T) = Travelers Accommodations   (E) = Educational Related   (C) = Groups & Conference Use

240 **Bilbao** ?

University of Deusto (T) Colegio Mayor Deusto
Apartado 20037, 48048, Vizcaya, Bilbao, Ph: 34-94-435-92-00, ASK FOR:
Dionisia Aranzadi, Mgr.
ROOM PRICING: (S) $32.00, Meals $3.75, • PAYMENT: Cash Only • DATES
AVAILABLE: July 1 - July . 30, • BED TYPE: S • BEDS: 1 • FOOD: Caf. NR •
INFO: No children • ACTIVITIES: Gernika, San Sebastian (Basque Coast),
mountain climbing, swimming, beaches, fascinating port city, museums, parks,
theater.

241 **Cartagena** ?

Universidad De Murcia (T) Univer. Residence Alberto Colao
C/Dr. Perez Espejo, 30203, Cartagena, Ph: 34-07-68-100311, Fax:
34-07-68-100411, ASK FOR: Mrs. Alcia Castro
ROOM PRICING: (S) $15.00, • PAYMENT: Cash Only • DATES AVAILABLE: July -
Sept., • BED TYPE: S • BEDS: 1 • FOOD: Caf. SB VM NR • INFO: Linen charge,
no children. • ACTIVITIES: Racquetball, films, art gallery, bowling, concerts, park,
swimming, game room, tennis, museums, TV in public lounge. Roman Ruins;
The Manga Beach; Golf Club Manga Beach; Mazarron Beach.

242 **Leon** ?

Universidad De Leon (T) Doga Sancha
Campus Universitario de Vegazana, 24071, Leon, Ph: 34-87-20-3414, ASK FOR:
Mrs. Carmen Mesa
ROOM PRICING: (S) $15.00, (D) $30.00, Addit. person $15.00, • PAYMENT: Cash
Only • DATES AVAILABLE: July-Aug., • FOOD: Caf. VM NR • INFO: Linens
included(no towels), no children, only youth hostel assoc. members, $3.00 more per
person over 18 years of age. • ACTIVITIES: Park, swimming, TV in public lounge.
Cathedral; museums.

243 **Santiago De Compostela** ? &

Univer. De Santiago De Compostela (T)
Casa Da Balconada/Rua Nova 6, 15705 , Santiago De Compostela , Ph:
34-81-573906, Fax: 34-81-571310
ROOM PRICING: (S) $24.00, (D) $37.50, • PAYMENT: Cash Only • DATES
AVAILABLE: July 15-Sept. 15, • FOOD: Caf. VM NR • INFO: Linens included. 6
residence halls with 1400 beds. • ACTIVITIES: Racquetball, films, art gallery,
concerts, park, swimming, theaters, game room, tennis, museums, TV in public
lounge.

244 **Zaragoza** ?

Colegio Mayor (T) Universitario Pedro Cerbuna
Ciudad Universitaria, 50009 , Zaragoza, Ph: 34-25-17-50, Fax: 34-56-83-48
ROOM PRICING: (S) $19.25, (with meals), • PAYMENT: Cash Only • DATES
AVAILABLE: July, Aug., Sept., • FOOD: Caf. VM NR • ACTIVITIES: Univeristy
activities, sightseeing, museums, theater, outings.

SWEDEN

245 **Karlstad** ? &

STF:s Vandrarhem Ulleberg (T) Ulleberbsleden
Karlstad, S-653 46, Ph: 46-0541- 56-68-40, Fax: 46-0451-56-60-42
ROOM PRICING: $19.00 -$30.00, per person, Youth Hostel, • PAYMENT: Cash •
DATES AVAILABLE: Year Round, • FOOD: Caf. • INFO: This agency provides an
extended list of hostels for all ages in Central Sweden. Prices start: $19.00 per
night. 3 km from center of Karlstad, includes breakfast.

246 **Linkoping** ? &

Linkoping Univ. /AB Stangastaden (T)
Studerandebostader, Box 10052 (Alsattersg.36), 58010 , Linkoping, Ph:
013-208680, ASK FOR: Housing Office, Kjell Carlgren
ROOM PRICING: (S) $16.50, (D) $28.50, • PAYMENT: Cash • DATES AVAILABLE:
Call for availability, • FOOD: No • INFO: Children welcome. • ACTIVITIES: Blue
Ribbon Gota Canal, Kolmarde Zoo, old towne, sports, films, concerts, museums,
parks, golf.

THE NETHERLANDS

247 Amstelveen   ?

Stichting Hospitum, Guest House (T)
Laan van Kronenburg 9, 1183 AS, Amstelveen, Ph: 31-20- 444-9270, Fax:
31-20-644-6560, E-mail: hospitium@home.vu.nl, ASK FOR: Mrs. S. Bronkhorst
ROOM PRICING: (S) $36.00 - $60.00, (D) $90.00 - $120.00, Prefer some
Educational Interest, • PAYMENT: Cash Trav. Ck Visa M/C • DATES
AVAILABLE: Year Round, • BEDS: 1-4 • FOOD: Caf. NR • INFO: Has fully
furnished apts., with kitchens. Children welcome. Essential to make reservations
far in advance. • ACTIVITIES: Bar, sporting facilities. 20 min. to downtown
Amsterdam; canal tours; world famous art museums (Rembrandt); Diamond
Market of the world; Royal Palace; The Hague; Tulip festival.

248 Wageningen   &

Intern. Conf.Center & Residence (T)
Lawickse Allee II, 6701 AN , Wageningen, Ph: (31) 317 490133, Fax: (31) 317
426243, E-mail: hotel.congres@wicc-wir.nL, ASK FOR: Mr. M. Munsters
ROOM PRICING: (S) $40.00/Conf. center, $70.00/Int. Residence, (D)
$60.00/Conf. center, $100.00/Int. Residence, (includes breakfast), • PAYMENT:
Cash Trav. Ck Visa M/C Amex • DATES AVAILABLE: Year Round, • ROOM
TYPE: SR Apt. • BED TYPE: S • BEDS: 1-2 • BATH: P • FOOD: Caf. VM NR OCR
• INFO: General Public and Conferences or groups. Conference rooms avail.
for10-250. Apartments in International Residence. • ACTIVITIES: Swimming,
films, tennis, parks. Kroller Muller Museum (Van Gogh paintings); boat trips on the
Rhine; zoo.

TURKEY

249 Ankara   ?

Bilkent University (T)
06533 , Ankara, Ph: 90-312-266-4134, ASK FOR: Mr. Erdogan Durn
ROOM PRICING: (S) $10.00, (D) $20.00, • PAYMENT: Cash Only • DATES
AVAILABLE: July 15 - Aug. 30, • BED TYPE: S • BEDS: 2 • FOOD: • INFO: No
children. • ACTIVITIES: Concerts, tennis, TV in public lounge. Cappadochia;
Gordion; Hittite Ruins; Museum of Anarolian Civilzations.

250 Istanbul   ?

Bogazigi University (T) Kennedy Lodge and Guest House
80815 Bebek, Istanbul, Istanbul, Ph: 90-212-26301500, ASK FOR: Gulgin
Atader/ Alexandra Gerrakof
• PAYMENT: • BED TYPE: S • BEDS: 1-2 • FOOD: • ACTIVITIES: View of Mt.
Bosphourus

251 Mugla   ?

Mugla University (T) University Hall
Mugla Universitesi Kotekli Kampusu, 48100 Mugla, Mugla, Ph: 90-
0252-212-4006, ASK FOR: Dir. of Residence Hall
ROOM PRICING: Includes breakfast, (S) $10.00, (D) $17.00, Children over 8,
$4.00,, • PAYMENT: Cash Only • DATES AVAILABLE: June 5- Sept. 9, • BED
TYPE: S • BEDS: 1-2 • FOOD: NR • INFO: Turkish Bath, no linen charge, children
over 8 welcome. • ACTIVITIES: Racquetball, park, TV in public lounge. Mugla
Bazzar; Handcraft exhibition and sales in Yesilyurt village; Ancient Mugla Houses;
Gokova Bay.

USA

U
N
I
V

Alabama

252 Huntsville, AL   ?

University of Alabama/Huntsville (T)
606A South Loop Road, Huntsville, AL 35899, Ph: (205) 890-6108, Fax: (205)
890-6739, E-mail: kamml@email.uah.edu, ASK FOR: Univ. Housing-Leigh Ramm
ROOM PRICING: (S) $14.00 , • PAYMENT: Cash Per. Ck • DATES AVAILABLE:
May 15 - Aug.10, • BEDS: 1 • FOOD: Caf. • INFO: Linen charge: $2.00P/P
children welcome, TVlounge, free parking, coin washers/dryers. • ACTIVITIES
Racquetball, park, swimming, game room, tennis, fitness center. U.S. Space and
Rocket Center.
DIRECTIONS: Interstate 65 to 565 East to Sparkman Drive Exit- 1 mile on right.

253 Montevallo, AL   ♿

Univ. of Montevallo (T)
Station 6280, Montevallo, AL 35115, Ph: (205) 665-6280, ASK FOR: Caron Watts,
Contin. Ed.
ROOM PRICING: (S) $30.00 (D) $30.00, • PAYMENT: Cash Per. Ck Trav. Ck
Visa M/C Discover Amex • DATES AVAILABLE: Year Round, • ROOM TYPE: SR
Apt. • BED TYPE: S • BEDS: 1-2 • BATH: P • FOOD: Caf. SB VM NR • INFO:
Limited areas for alcohol, children welcome with adult supervision, private bath,
linens included, free parking. • ACTIVITIES: Oak Mtn. State Park; Birmingham
35 mi. north; all on campus sports facilities; Tannehill Park; Robert Trent Jones
Golf Trail; Montgomery State Capitol 80 miles South.
DIRECTIONS: I-65 to alabaster exit #238 to Highwat 31 north. Turn left at
highway 119. 12 miles to Montevallo.

Alaska

254 Anchorage, AK   ?

Alaska Pacific University (T)
4101 University Dr., Anchorage, AK 99508, Ph: (907) 564-8238, ASK FOR:
Residence Life
ROOM PRICING: (S) $35.00, (D) $50.00, • PAYMENT: Cash Per. Ck Trav. Ck •
DATES AVAILABLE: May 22- Aug.6, • ROOM TYPE: SR • BED TYPE: S • BEDS: 2
• BATH: C • FOOD: Caf. VM NR • INFO: No alcohol on campus, children welcome
with parents, coin washer/ dryers. Reservations only-no walk -ins. check in only
during office hours, 8:00 AM-5:00 PM. • ACTIVITIES: TV lounge. Portage Glacier;
Alyeska ski resort; Chugach National Forest; ample fishing areas; swimming.

255 Anchorage, AK   ♿

University of Alaska Anchorage (E) Main Apt. Complex
Conferences Services, 3700 Sharon Gagon Ln., Anchorage, AK 99508, Ph: (907) 751-7273 , Fax: (907) 786-4800, E-mail: anjss@uaa.alaska.edu, ASK FOR: Residence Life-Jason Smart
ROOM PRICING: Rates per person, $30-45.00/day, • PAYMENT: Cash Per. Ck Trav. Ck Visa M/C Discover • DATES AVAILABLE: June1-July 31, • BEDS: 1-2 • FOOD: Caf. SB VM NR • INFO: Linens included, free parking, children welcome, TV lounge, coin washers/dryers, no alcohol. 4 bedroom apts., single/double grad suites,suite style res. halls Conference min: 8; must have educational purpose. • ACTIVITIES: Racquetball, art gallery, hiking, bike trails, fitness center. City of Anchorage; Chugach Mountains; Portage Glacier; Anchorage Museum of History and Art; Cook Inlet; Earthquake Park; Flightseeing; World Class Salmon and Halibut fishing; Iditarod Trail.

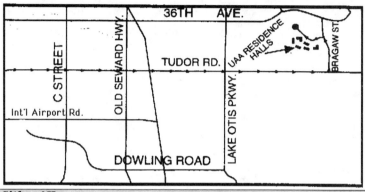

256 Sitka, AK

Sheldon Jackson College (T)
801 Lincoln St., Sitka, AK 99838, Ph: (907) 747-2540, Fax: (907) 747-2212, ASK FOR: Ann Strain
ROOM PRICING: (S) $40.00, (D) $50.00, 3 meals per day $20.00+ 9% tax per person, • PAYMENT: Trav. Ck Visa M/C Discover • DATES AVAILABLE: May 20 - August 15, • BEDS: 2 • FOOD: Caf. • INFO: Child Care Center. Coin Washer and Dryer • ACTIVITIES: All types of boating, Fishing. Totem Park; Music Festival; Russian Bishop's House; old Orthodox Church.

Arizona

257 Prescott, AZ   ?

Embry-Riddle Aero Univ. (C)
3200 Willow Creek Road, Prescott, AZ 86301, Ph: (602) 776-3722, ASK FOR: Business Office
ROOM PRICING: (S) $12.00, (D) $18.00, Min. No. Req. 12, • PAYMENT: Cash Per. Ck • DATES AVAILABLE: Late May - Early Aug., • FOOD: Caf. VM • INFO: Linene Charge: $10 per person, No Children • ACTIVITIES: Racquetball, swimming, game room, tennis, TV in public lounge. Grand Canyon (21/2 hours); Sedona; Painted Desert; Meteor Crater.

U N I V

Arkansas

258 Little Rock, AR   ♿

Univ. of Arkansas/Little Rock (C)
2801 S. University Ave., Little Rock, AR 72204, Ph: (501) 661-1743, ASK FOR: Off. of Student Housing
ROOM PRICING: (S) $21.00, (D) $26.00, • PAYMENT: Cash Per. Ck Trav. Ck Visa M/C • DATES AVAILABLE: May 15-Aug.10, • BEDS: 4 • FOOD: Caf. VM NR • INFO: Linens: $10.00/ wk, no smoking, coin washers/dryers, free parking. • ACTIVITIES: Racquetball, swimming, game room, tennis, TV in public lounge. State Capitol; State Parks; Zoo.

California

259 Belmont, CA   ?

College of Norte Dame (E)
1500 Ralston Ave., Belmont, CA 94002, Ph: (415) 508-3645, ASK FOR: Lisa Dienger, Dir. Conf. & Scheduling
ROOM PRICING: (S) $40.00, (D) $40.00, • PAYMENT: Cash • DATES AVAILABLE: Summer, • ROOM TYPE: SR Apt. • BED TYPE: S • BEDS: 1-3 • BATH: C P • FOOD: Caf. SB VM NR • INFO: Variable linen charge, No smoking or alcohol in lounges. Apartments also available. LIMITED TO GROUPS ONLY. • ACTIVITIES: Art gallery, swimming, tennis, TV in public lounge. San Fracisco; Montery Bay.

260 Berkeley, CA   ?

University of California, Berkeley (T) Conference Services Office
2601 Warring St., Berkeley, CA 94720-2288, Ph: (510) 642-4444, Fax: (510) 642-4888, E-mail: meethere@uclink.berkeley.ed, ASK FOR: Reservations
ROOM PRICING: (S) $36.00, (D) $46.00, Subject to change, • PAYMENT: Cash Trav. Ck Visa M/C • DATES AVAILABLE: June 1- Aug. 11, • ROOM TYPE: SR • BED TYPE: S • BEDS: 2 • BATH: C • FOOD: Caf. VM NR • INFO: Payment collected upon arrival, telephone in room, linens included, coffee served mornings in lobby. • ACTIVITIES: University of Calif. campus, museums, libraries. Sather Tower; Carillon Bell Concerts; Greek Theater; Zellerbach Hall; Recreational sports facility; UC Berkeley Botanical Gardens; close to San Francisco.
DIRECTIONS: Directions provided with reservation confirmation.

261 Burbank, CA   ♿

Woodbury University (T)
7500 Glenoaks Blvd., Burbank, CA 91510, Ph: (818) 767-0888, Ext: 253, ASK FOR: Rosemary E. Ampuero,Coordinator, Special Programs
ROOM PRICING: Call for rates, • PAYMENT: Cash Per. Ck Trav. Ck Visa M/C • DATES AVAILABLE: May 14 - Aug. 13, • BEDS: 2 • FOOD: Caf. VM NR • INFO: Linens available, $10/week, TV lounge, kitchens, food service catering available. • ACTIVITIES: Gym, weight room,basketball court, track, swimming, TV in public lounge. Film studios; Griffith Park 200 acres; equestrian center; Gene Autrey Museum; Hollywood Bowl; 6 Flags Magic Mountain. Within 1 hour drive of every major entertainment attraction in S. California.
DIRECTIONS: From Interstate 5, exit on Buena Vista, go east (toward moun tains), turn left on Glenoaks Blvd. We are two blocks on right side.

262 Carson, CA   ? ♿

California State Univ., Dominguez Hills (T)
1100 E. Victoria, Building X, Carson, CA 90746, Ph: (310) 243-2281, Fax: (310) 516-4275, ASK FOR: Kaveh Razaghi, Housing
ROOM PRICING: (S) $22.00, Standard, $25.00. Deluxe, (D) $32.00, Standard, $44.00, Deluxe, Addtl. person, $16.00, • PAYMENT: Cash Trav. Ck • DATES AVAILABLE: Year round, Reservations required• BEDS: 2 • FOOD: Caf. VM NR • INFO: Linen charge: $3.00 per night, no children, coin washer/ dryers, linens included with standard, kitchens with pots and pans, linens included in deluxe. • ACTIVITIES: Art Gallery, concerts, swimming, recreational sports facilites, game room, tennis, TV in public lounge. Knotts Berry Farm; Disneyland; Magic Mountain; Universal Studios; LA Zoo; LAX; Movieland Wax Museum; Angels and Dodgers Baseball.

---

263 **Chico, CA**   ? &

Calif. State Univ.,Chico (C) University Housing Dept.
Chico, CA 95929-707, Ph: (916) 898-6325, ASK FOR: Tracey Richardson
ROOM PRICING: (S) $35.00, (D) $51.00, • PAYMENT: Cash Per. Ck Trav. Ck
Visa M/C • DATES AVAILABLE: June 11 - Aug. 9, • BED TYPE: S • BEDS: 2 •
FOOD: Caf. VM NR • INFO: Children welcome, coin washers/dryers. •
ACTIVITIES: Beautiful Northern Calif. tree-lined campus; Bidwell Park and
Mansion; Stansbury House; Gateway to Mt. Lassen; Siskiyou Mountains; Lake
Shasta; trout fishing, sports.

264 **Claremont, CA**   ? &

Pitzer College (E)
1050 N. Mills Ave., Claremont, CA 91711, Ph: (909) 621-8104, ASK FOR: Robert
Fossum, Special Prog.
ROOM PRICING: (S) $20.00, (D) $30.00, • PAYMENT: Cash Per. Ck Trav. Ck •
DATES AVAILABLE: May-Aug., • ROOM TYPE: SR Apt. • BED TYPE: S • BEDS:
1-2 • BATH: S P • FOOD: Caf. SB VM NR • INFO: Linens included, Min. no. req.
for conf. 20, children welcome. Suite also available. • ACTIVITIES: Racquetball,
films, art gallery, concerts, swimming, game room, tennis, hiking, museums, TV
in public lounge. Mt. Baldy: Disneyland; Universal Studios; Beaches.

265 **Claremont, CA**   ? &

Scripps College (T)
1030 Columbia Ave., Claremont, CA 91711, Ph: (909) 621-8187, ASK FOR: Gloria
Wright
ROOM PRICING: (S) $22.00, (D) $38.00, • PAYMENT: Cash Trav. Ck • DATES
AVAILABLE: May 231 Aug. 16, • BEDS: 1-2 • FOOD: Caf. VM NR • INFO:
Children welcome with parent. • ACTIVITIES: Disneyland, Knott's Berry Farm,
Queen Mary, beaches, desert, mountains, lakes all within an hour's drive, park,
swimming, tennis.

266 **Eureka, CA**   ? &

College Of The Redwoods (C)
7351 Thompkins Hill Rd., Eureka, CA 95501, Ph: (707) 445-6920, ASK FOR: Bill
Connors, Housing Office
ROOM PRICING: Call for Prices, • PAYMENT: Cash Per. Ck Trav. Ck • DATES
AVAILABLE: Summer, • ROOM TYPE: SR • BED TYPE: S • BEDS: 2 • BATH: S •
FOOD: Caf. SB VM NR • INFO: Children welcome, no alcohol. Prefer groups of
15 or more • ACTIVITIES: All campus sports. Redwoods National Park,;Six Rivers
National Forest; Salmon fishing; Beach-combing; Boating.

267 **Goleta, CA**   ? &

Univ. of Calif. at Santa Barbara (T) Res. Hall, Francisco Torres
6850 El Colegio Road, Goleta, CA 93117, Ph: (805) 968-0711, (800) 426-1067,
Fax: (805) 685-1182, ASK FOR: General Office
ROOM PRICING: (S) $33.00, (D) $44.00, • PAYMENT: Cash Per. Ck Trav. Ck
Visa M/C Discover Amex • DATES AVAILABLE: Res. must be made as avail.
varies., • ROOM TYPE: SR • BED TYPE: S • BEDS: 2 • BATH: S • FOOD: Caf.
VM NR • INFO: Linen charge: $5.00. Children welcome, laundry facilites, free
parking. Call ahead for reservations. TV lounge on each floor. • ACTIVITIES: 25
mter swimming pool, fitness center, tennis courts, sand volleyball, hiking. Blocks
from ocean; resort area; Santa Barbara Mission; Museums; festivals; shopping;
Fiesta.

268 **Hayward, CA**   ?

Calif. State Univ., Hayward (T) Carlos Bee Hall
25400 Carlos Bee Blvd., Hayward, CA 94542, Ph: (510) 582-4747, ASK FOR: Tim
Engestrom, Reception
ROOM PRICING: (S) $25.00, $37.00/with meals, (D) $30.00, $54.00/with
meals, • PAYMENT: Cash Per. Ck Trav. Ck Visa M/C • DATES AVAILABLE:
Year Round, • ROOM TYPE: SR • BED TYPE: S • BEDS: 2 • BATH: S • FOOD:
Caf. • INFO: Children welcome. • ACTIVITIES: Lounge, billiards, laundry facilities.
Nearby: San Francisco; Berkeley, (University of Calif.); Napa Valley Wine Country;
Bay cruises.

269 **Irvine, CA**   ♿

Concordia University (E)
1530 Concordia, Irvine, CA 92612-3299, Ph: (949) 854-8002,ext. 111, Fax: 949-854-6854, Web Site: www.cui.edu, ASK FOR: University Services - Housing
ROOM PRICING: Contact University for prices., • PAYMENT: Cash Per. Ck Trav. Ck • DATES AVAILABLE: May 25 - Aug. 1, • ROOM TYPE: Apt. Suite • BED TYPE: S • BEDS: 2 • BATH: S P • FOOD: Caf. SB VM NR • INFO: No children, unaccompanied by adult. Coin washer/dryer • ACTIVITIES: Nearby: Disneyland, Pacific beaches, Knotts Berry Farm, Performing Arts Center, So. Coast Plaza mall, Univ. of Cal., sporting, cultural events, art festivals.

270 **La Verne, CA**   ?   ♿

University of La Verne (T)
1950 3rd Street, La Verne, CA 91750, Ph: (909) 593-3511, Ext: 4052, ASK FOR: Linda Di Maggio, Housing Off.
ROOM PRICING: (S) $20.00, (D) $30.00, • PAYMENT: Cash Per. Ck Trav. Ck Visa M/C • DATES AVAILABLE: June 4- Aug. 12, • FOOD: Caf. SB VM NR • INFO: Linen charge: $6.00. Children under 2 yr. free, Under 10 yrs., $8.00, no alcohol on campus. • ACTIVITIES: Within an hour from: Disneyland; Universal Studios; Pacific beaches; Hollywood and TV studios; Six Flags Amusement Park. Close to mountains; parks; lakes with boating; 20 min. from Ontario Int'l Airport.

271 **Los Angeles, CA**   ?

Calif. State Univ. Los Angeles (T)
5154 State Univ. Dr., Los Angeles, CA 90032, Ph: (213) 343-2527, ASK FOR: University Conf. - Cheryl Sena
ROOM PRICING: (S) $29.25 Students, $40.50 , (D) $44.50 Students, $57.00, • PAYMENT: Cash Per. Ck Trav. Ck • DATES AVAILABLE: June 15 -Sept. 1, • FOOD: Caf. SB VM NR • INFO: Children welcome. • ACTIVITIES: Sports facilities, theater, concerts, game room, TV in public lounge. Nearby: Disneyland; Knott's Berry Farm; Universal Studios; Hollywood.

272 **Los Angeles, CA**   ?   ♿

Mt. St. Mary's College (C)
12001 Chalon Rd., Los Angeles, CA 90049, Ph: (310) 954-4330, Fax: (310) 954-4339, ASK FOR: Carol Meckler, Facilities Dir.
ROOM PRICING: (S) $54.00, Includes3 meals, Call for room only rate, • PAYMENT: Cash Per. Ck Trav. Ck Visa M/C • DATES AVAILABLE: June 1 - Aug. 15, • ROOM TYPE: SR • BED TYPE: S • BEDS: 1-2 • BATH: C S • FOOD: Caf. VM NR • INFO: 2 campuses -1 downtown L.A.,1 on the west side of L.A. Linens included, coin washers/dryers, free parking. • ACTIVITIES: Santa Monica and Malibu beaches; Hollywood; Universal Studios and City Walk; Movie theaters; shopping malls; Museums; Ethnic and cultural entertainment.

273 **Los Angeles, CA**   ?   ♿

Occidental College (C) Thorne Hall
1600 Campus Road, Los Angeles, CA 90041, Ph: (213) 259-2795, ASK FOR: Pam Bellew
ROOM PRICING: (S) $46.00, (D) $82.00, Includes 3 meals a day, • PAYMENT: Cash Per. Ck Trav. Ck • DATES AVAILABLE: July & Aug., Call for exact dates• ROOM TYPE: SR • BED TYPE: S • BEDS: 2 • BATH: C S • FOOD: Caf. SB VM NR • INFO: Linens included, children welcome. • ACTIVITIES: Films, art gallery, swimming, game room, tennis, Disneyland; Universial Studios.

274 **Los Angeles, CA**   ?   ♿

Univ. of Southern California (T)
620 W. 35th Street, Los Angeles, CA 90089-1332, Ph: (213) 740-0031 or (213) 740-3626, ASK FOR: Sandra Plotin
ROOM PRICING: (S) $35.00, (D) $50.00, • PAYMENT: Cash Per. Ck Trav. Ck Visa M/C • DATES AVAILABLE: May 27- Aug 14, • BEDS: 2 • FOOD: Caf. VM NR OCR • INFO: Children under 5, no charge. 5 yrs. to 12 yrs., half price. Linens included. • ACTIVITIES: All campus sports facilities. Imax Theater; Natural History Museum; All Los Angeles attractions; Disneyland; Knott's Berry Farm; Olvera Street.

(T) = Travelers Accommodations   **(E) = Educational Related**   **(C) = Groups & Conference Use**

275 Northridge, CA   ♿

Cal State, Northridge (T)
17950 Lassen St., Northridge, CA 91330-8286, Ph: (818) 677-2160, Fax: (818) 677- 4888, E-mail: Philip.M.Gin@csun.edu, ASK FOR: Univ. Conf. Srvs, Jeff Miller
ROOM PRICING: (S) $33.00, (D) $44.00, • PAYMENT: Cash Trav. Ck Visa M/C • DATES AVAILABLE: Year Round, • ROOM TYPE: Apt. • BEDS: 2 • FOOD: Caf. SB VM NR • INFO: Children must have adult supervision. Coin washer/dryer, linens included. TV in Public Lounge. • ACTIVITIES: Racquetball, films, art gallery, swimming, theaters, game room, tennis, TV in public lounge. Six Flags Magic Mountain; Universal Studios; Hollywood Bowl; Griffith Observatory.JohnPaul Getty Museum.

276 Oakland, CA   ? ♿

Holy Names College (E)
3500 Mountain Blvd., Oakland, CA 94619, Ph: (510) 436-1508, ASK FOR: Anna Edejer, Special Events & Services
ROOM PRICING: (S) $52.00/day, $410.00/week, (D) $50.00/day p/p, $335.00/week p/p, 19 meals per wkly stay, • PAYMENT: Cash Per. Ck Trav. Ck Visa M/C • DATES AVAILABLE: Year round, • ROOM TYPE: SR • BED TYPE: S • BEDS: 1-2 • BATH: C • FOOD: Caf. SB VM NR • INFO: 400 capacity state of the art theater, 125 capacity studio theater. E-mail: Edejer @ admin.hnc.edu • ACTIVITIES: Spectacular view of San Francisco Bay Area; Jack London Square; Sausalito Waterfront; Fisherman's Wharf; close to San Francisco transport; 10 minutes to Oakland Coliseum. On campus Art Gallery; on campus coffee house.

277 Palos Verdes Peninsula, CA   ?

Marymount College (T)
Palos Verdes Peninsula, CA 90275, Ph: (310) 377-5501, Fax: (310) 265-0642, ASK FOR: Stephanie Hart
ROOM PRICING: Call for Price, • PAYMENT: Cash Visa M/C • DATES AVAILABLE: June 1 -Aug. 15, • ROOM TYPE: Apt. • BED TYPE: S • BEDS: 2 • FOOD: Caf. • INFO: In house laundry facilities, underground parking, telephone. linens extra. • ACTIVITIES: LA Int'l Airport (30 min.); 45 min. to Disneyland; Knotts Berry Farm; Pacific beaches; Univ. Film Studios; beaches nearby. Campus sports.

278 Petaluma, CA   ?

University of Northern California (T)
101 South San Antonio Rd., Petaluma, CA 94952, Ph: (707) 765-6400, Fax: (707) 769-8600, ASK FOR: Donald Haight, Student Services
ROOM PRICING: (S) $20.00, (D) $40.00, • PAYMENT: Cash Per. Ck Trav. Ck • DATES AVAILABLE: Year round-space available basis, • BEDS: 1-2 • FOOD: NR • INFO: Bring your own linens, children welcome with adult supervision, TV lounge. • ACTIVITIES: Park; game room; hiking; daily shuttle bus to nearby cities; San Francisco; Wine Country.

279 Pomona, CA   ♿

Calif. Poly Pomona (T) University Housing Services
59 University Dr., Pomona, CA 91768, Ph: (909) 869-3255, Fax: (909) 869-3985, E-mail: tapearson@csupomona.edu, ASK FOR: Terri Pearson Conference Services Co-ordinator
ROOM PRICING: (S) $28.25, $47.22 (3 meals), (D) $41.00, $78.94 (3 meals), • PAYMENT: Cash Per. Ck Trav. Ck • DATES AVAILABLE: Late June -Labor Day, • BEDS: 2 • FOOD: Caf. SB VM NR • INFO: Coin washer/dryer, TV ounge, game room in each hall, swimming pool, basketball court, volleyball court, staff on call 24 hours. Linens included in price. Fitness center for guests 18 yrs. and older. • ACTIVITIES: Library available M-F and Sunday in summer(closed Sat); Athletic/sports facilities; Raging Waters water Theme park, 5 minutes away; 20 minutes from Ontario Intl. Airport; shopping malls nearby; 30 minutes to Disneyland; Knotts Berry Farm.

280 **Reedley, CA**

Reedley College (T)
995 N. Reed, P. O. Box 586, Reedley, CA 93654, Ph: (209) 638-3641, Ext: 3235 area code chg. 11/98, ASK FOR: Frank Mascola, Res. Superv., Lisa McAndrews, Superv.
ROOM PRICING: Call for Rates, • PAYMENT: Cash Only Visa • DATES AVAILABLE: June 15 -July 31, • BEDS: 2 • FOOD: Caf. VM NR • INFO: No alcohol, provide own linens, coin washers/dryers. • ACTIVITIES: Less than 1 hour to Sequoia National Park; Kings Canyon Nat'l Park; 2 hours to Yosemite; 3 1/2 hr. to San Francisco; 3 hr. to Monterey; Rafting, boating on King's River.

281 **Riverside, CA**   ?   &

Univ. of CA, Riverside (E)
500 West Big Springs Road, Riverside, CA 92507, Ph: (909) 787-5891, Fax: (909) 787-5933, ASK FOR: Conference Office
ROOM PRICING: (S) $38.50, (D) $68.30, Includes 3 meals per day, • PAYMENT: Cash Trav. Ck • DATES AVAILABLE: June 25- Aug. 31, • ROOM TYPE: SR • BEDS: 2 • BATH: C • FOOD: Caf. VM NR • INFO: Linens included. Call in advance for reservation information. • ACTIVITIES: Racquetball, art gallery, concerts, swimming, game room, tennis, hiking, TV in public lounge. 1hour from: Disneyland; Palm Springs; mountains; beaches.

282 **San Francisco, CA**   ?   &

University of San Francisco (E) Summer Guest Housing
2130 fulton St. UC 305, San Francisco, CA 94117-1080, Ph: (415) 422-2824, Fax: (415) 422-2790, E-mail: Ventersg@usfc.edu, ASK FOR: Co-ordinator, Summer Guest Housing
ROOM PRICING: (S) $30.00, (D) $55.00, $25.00 each additional person, • PAYMENT: Cash Per. Ck Trav. Ck Visa M/C Discover Amex • DATES AVAILABLE: June 5 - Aug. 10, • BEDS: 2 • FOOD: Caf. SB VM NR • INFO: Children over 12 welcome, charge for ongoing housekeeping(beds made, clean linen, etc.) • ACTIVITIES: Racquetball, swimming, theaters, game room, tennis, TV lounge. Beaches; Golden Gate Bridge; Downtown; China Town; Golden Gate Park; Fishersman Wharf; Opera; Symphony.

San Jose State University (E)
One Washington Sq., San Jose, CA 95192-0167, Ph: (408) 924-6180, ASK FOR:
Jeri Allen
ROOM PRICING: (S) $25.50, (D) $39.00, • PAYMENT: Cash Per. Ck Visa M/C
• DATES AVAILABLE: June 1-Aug. 9, • FOOD: Caf. VM NR • INFO: Children
welcome. • ACTIVITIES: All campus sports facilities Nearby: Saratoga Springs;
Kelley Park; Happy Hollow Park and Zoo; Mission Santa Clara de Asis; Lick
Observatory; many other attractions.
DIRECTIONS: •From US 101: Take Interstate 280, exit Seventh Street, proceed
North to campus. •From Interstate 880 south: take 101 to Interstate 280, exit
Seventh St. *From Interstate 680 South: Interstate 680 becomes Interstate 280
(at US 101), exit at Seventh St., proceed north to campus.

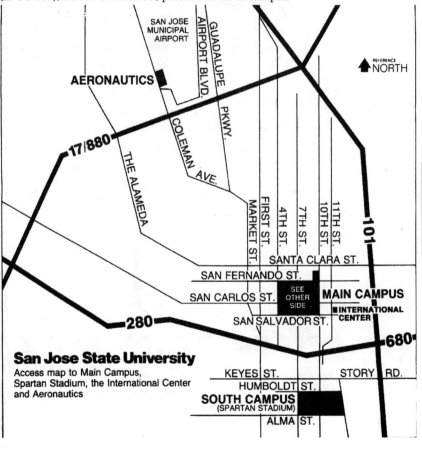

San Jose State University
Access map to Main Campus,
Spartan Stadium, the International Center
and Aeronautics

UNIV

284 **Santa Barbara, CA**   ?   ♿

Univer. of California, Santa Barbara (C)
Santa Barbara, CA 93106, Ph: (805) 893-3072, ASK FOR: Campus Conference
Services
ROOM PRICING: Per Adult, (S) $64.45, (D) $51.25, Includes 3 meals, • PAYMENT
Cash Per. Ck Trav. Ck • DATES AVAILABLE: June 19-Sept. 10, • FOOD: Caf
• INFO: Min. number: 50. Apts. available w/wo meals, linens included, Children
welcome only in apts. • ACTIVITIES: Santa Barbara is a resort town with many
outdoor activities, sailing, windsurfing, hiking, etc., varied entertainment and
shopping opportunities, art gallery, swimming, game room, tennis, TV in public
lounge

285 **Santa Cruz, CA**   ?   ♿

University of California (E) Santa Cruz
Santa Cruz, CA 95084, Ph: (408) 459-2611, ASK FOR: Conf. Office
ROOM PRICING: (S) $50.00-$90.00, (D) $40.00-$80.00, Includes 3 meals
Dormitories and Apts. available, • PAYMENT: Cash Per. Ck Trav. Ck Visa M/C
• DATES AVAILABLE: June 23 -Aug. 31, • ROOM TYPE: SR Apt. • BED TYPE: S
BEDS: 1-2 • BATH: C S • FOOD: Caf. VM NR • INFO: Children over 12 welcome
Coin washer/dryer, Linens included. • ACTIVITIES: One of America's most
beautiful campuses - on Calif. Pacific coast. Close to San Jose Int'l Airport. Near
Carmel and Monterey cultural arts and crafts center; local wineries.

286 **Sonora, CA**   ?   ♿

Columbia College (T) Sonora Hostel
11800 Columbia College Dr., Sonora, CA 95370, Ph: (209) 533-2339, Fax
533-2339, ASK FOR: Call for reservations
ROOM PRICING: Hosteling International Members, $12.00 + Tax, per bed.,
Non-members, $15.00+Tax, per bed., Kitchen Facilities, air-cond. included., •
PAYMENT: Cash Trav. Ck Visa M/C • BEDS: 4-10 • FOOD: Caf. SB VM NF
OCR • INFO: Children OK; BBQ facilities at dorms. Rec. room with big screen
TV. Apt. style units, on site mini mart. • ACTIVITIES: Tennis. Columbia State
Park; Historic Gold Rush Country; White Water Rafting. Snow skiing; water
skiing.

287 **Turlock, CA**   ?   ♿

Calif. State Univ. Stanislaus (E) The Village
801 West Monte Vista, Turlock, CA 95802, Ph: (209) 667-3675, ASK FOR: Housing
Office
ROOM PRICING: (S) $15.00, (D) $26.00, • PAYMENT: Cash Per. Ck Trav. Ck
Visa M/C • DATES AVAILABLE: June-Aug., • ROOM TYPE: SR Apt. • BED
TYPE: S • BEDS: 1 • BATH: C S • FOOD: Caf. SB VM NR • INFO: Linens
included, Children welcome. • ACTIVITIES: Art gallery, concerts, swimming,
game room, tennis, hiking, TV in public lounge. Yosemite National Park; Hershey's
Chocolate Factory; San Francisco.

Colorado

288 **Alamosa, CO**   ?   ♿

Adams State College (E) Coronado & Girault Halls
#1 Pettys Hall, Alamosa, CO 81102, Ph: (719) 589-7232, ASK FOR: Bruce Del
Tondo, Off. of Housing
ROOM PRICING: (S) $12.00, (D) $24.00, • PAYMENT: Cash Per. Ck Trav. Ck •
DATES AVAILABLE: May 20-Aug.5, • ROOM TYPE: SR Apt. • BED TYPE: S •
BEDS: 2 • BATH: C S • FOOD: Caf. SB VM NR • INFO: Linens included, no
alcohol, no pets, children under 12 free, coin washer/dryer, TV lounge, free
parking. • ACTIVITIES: Racquetball, films, swimming, theaters, game room
tennis, TV in public lounge. Great Sand Dunes National Monument; Creede
Repretory Theater; Cumbres Toltec Scenic Railroad; Alligator Farm.

289 **Gunnison, CO**   ? ♿

Western State College of Colorado (C)
Western State College, Gunnison, CO 81231, Ph: (303) 943-2000, (303) 943-7044,
ASK FOR: Joe Winegardner, Conf. Services
ROOM PRICING: (S) $20.75, (D) $31.00, • PAYMENT: Cash Only Per. Ck Trav.
Ck • DATES AVAILABLE: June 19- Aug. 19, • ROOM TYPE: SR • BED TYPE: S •
BEDS: 2 • BATH: C S • FOOD: Caf. SB NR • INFO: Linens included, min. no.
req. for conf., 10. • ACTIVITIES: Racquetball, art gallery, bowling, swimming,
game room, tennis, hiking, TV in public lounge. Black Canyon; Crested Butte;
Blue Mesa Resevoir; Taylor Park.

290 **Lakewood, CO**   ? ♿

Colorado Christian University (T)
180 S. Garrison Street, Lakewood, CO 80226, Ph: (303) 202-0100, Fax: (303)
202-5905, E-mail: jimmccormick@ccu.edu, ASK FOR: Student Life
ROOM PRICING: (S) $15.00 (D) $30.00, • PAYMENT: Cash Per. Ck Trav. Ck
Visa M/C • DATES AVAILABLE: May 3 - Aug. 11, • BEDS: 2 • FOOD: Caf. SB
VM NR • INFO: Linens included, free parking, children welcome, TV lounge, no
pets. • ACTIVITIES: Concerts, parks, game room, bike trails. Mountains;
Professional Sports; Amusement and Water Parks.
DIRECTIONS: From I-25 take 6th Ave. West to Wadsworth exit, south on
Wadsworth to Alameda, west 2 lights to entrance of campus.

Connecticut

291 **Bridgeport, CT**   ? ♿

University of Bridgeport (T)
244 University Ave., Bridgeport, CT 06601, Ph: (203) 576-4228, Fax: (203)
576-4485, ASK FOR: Residential Life Office
ROOM PRICING: (S) $20.00 (D) $40.00 (T) $60.00.   Student, faculty Rate:
$15.00, • PAYMENT: Cash Only • DATES AVAILABLE: May 24 - Aug. 11, •
FOOD: Caf. SB VM NR OCR • INFO: Inquire for children, limited availability for
handicapped.   Coin washers/dryers, TV lounge, cable TV, free parking. •
ACTIVITIES: Tennis courts, pool. ping pong, weight lifting equipment.   Close to
New York City; Barnum Museum; within 1 mile of train station and ferry.

292 **Storrs Mansfield, CT**   ? ♿

University of Connecticut (T)
U-22 DRL, 233 Glenbrrok Road, Storrs Mansfield, CT 06269, Ph: (860) 486-2697,
ASK FOR: Becky Mc Enery
ROOM PRICING: Per person, (S) $18.00-$28.00, (D) $36.00-$56.00, • PAYMENT:
Cash Trav. Ck • DATES AVAILABLE: Year Round, • BEDS: 1-3 • FOOD: Caf.
NR • INFO: Call for availability for children. Some rooms with private bath in
summer. Linens included, free parking. • ACTIVITIES: Films, art gallery,
concerts, swimming, theaters, game room, tennis, hiking, museums, TV in pub.
lounge.   Caprilands Herb Farm; Various Colonial Heritage Sites; 1/2 hr.to
Hartford & Sturbridge Village; Windham Textile Museum.

U
N
I
V

Delaware

293 **Wilmington, DE**   ♿

Goldey - Beacom College (E)
4701 Limestone Road, Wilmington, DE 19808, Ph: (302) 998-8814, ext. 4241
ASK FOR: Michael Carney, Dir. of Housing and Residence Life
ROOM PRICING: (S) $20.00, (D) $40.00, price negotiable., • PAYMENT: Cash Per.
Ck Trav. Ck Visa M/C Discover • DATES AVAILABLE: June 1- Aug. 1, •
ROOM TYPE: Apt. • BEDS: 5-6 • BATH: P • FOOD: VM NR • INFO: Linen charge:
$3.00 per person, Min. stay 3 days. • ACTIVITIES: Racquetball, TV in public
loung, Longwood Gardens; Winterthur Museum; Hagley Museum; Dinner Theater.
DIRECTIONS: •From the North: S on I-95 or I-495, until you are south of
Wilmington. Proceed to Exit 4 (RT 7 N). Turn right on RT 7 at second light, going
North to campus. • From the East: Cross Delaware Memorial Bridge and follow
Baltimore South signs on I-95. Proceed to Exit 4 (Route 7). Turn right on RT 7 as
above •From the South: Proceed North on RT I-95 to Exit 4 (RT 7N) to campus.
•From the West: Follow RT 41 S through Avondale toward Delaware. South of
Avondale, bear right onto RT 7 S to campus.

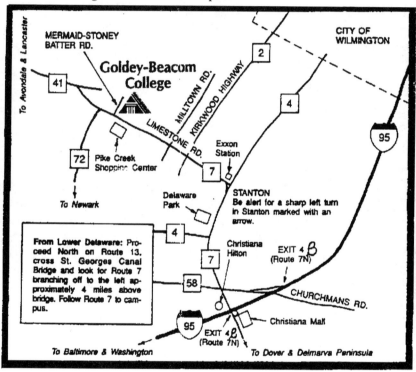

District of Columbia

294 **Washington, DC**   ⛬

Catholic Univ. of America (E)
106 St. Bonaventure Hall, Cardinal Station, Washington, DC 20064, Ph: (202) 319-5277, Fax: (202) 319-6262, Web Site: www.cua.edu, ASK FOR: conf. and summer prgms
ROOM PRICING: (S) $25.00 with A/C, $23.00 no A/C. (D) $46.00 with A/C, 42.00 no A/C. (Reserve and pay in advance) Three day minimum, • PAYMENT: Cash Per. Ck Trav. Ck Visa M/C • DATES AVAILABLE: May 24- Aug. 2, • ROOM TYPE: SR • BED TYPE: S • BEDS: 2 • BATH: C S • FOOD: Caf. SB VM NR • INFO: Children welcome, Refrigerators available for $8.00/week. Meal plans available. Cash accepted in dining halls. Free local telephone service, rooms wired for cable TV, TV lounges • ACTIVITIES: Indoor pool, tennis, racqetball, basketball, weight rooms, tracks, saunas. Nat'l Shrine and monuments; Kennedy Center; Smithsonian Museums; Old Town Alexandria; National Gallery of Art; Congressional offices; Nation's Capital; subway stop on campus.computer acciybts available.
DIRECTIONS: Campus is located at 620 Michigan Ave. NE. Brookland/CUA stop on Metro Red Line.

295 **Washington, DC**   ?   ⛬

George Washington University (E)
2121   I Street N. W. Suite 402, Washington, DC 20052, Ph: (202) 994-6688, ASK FOR: Rebecca Virta, Office of Res. Life
ROOM PRICING: (S) $45.00, (D) $54.00, $25.00/Each addtl. person, • PAYMENT: Cash Per. Ck Trav. Ck • DATES AVAILABLE: May 26 - Aug. 10, • ROOM TYPE: SR • BEDS: 1-6 • BATH: S P • FOOD: Caf. VM NR • INFO: Linens included, children over 12 welcome, air-conditioned, subway station on campus, great location downtown. • ACTIVITIES: Racquetball, films, bowling, swimming, theaters, game room, tennis, museums, TV in public lounge. Nation's Capitol Building; Smithsonian Institution and Zoo; Famous Monuments; Many Art Galleries.

296 **Washington, DC**   ?   ⛬

Georgetown University (E)
Washington, DC 20057-1117, Ph: (202) 687-4560, Fax: (202) 687-4590, ASK FOR: Ms. Rack, Dir. Guest Serv.
ROOM PRICING: (S) $50.00, (D) $50.00, • PAYMENT: Cash Per. Ck Trav. Ck Visa M/C • DATES AVAILABLE: June 3 - Aug. 10, • BEDS: 2 • FOOD: Caf. NR OCR • INFO: Limited facilities for children. Public transportation available. • ACTIVITIES: National Monuments, White House, Smithsonian Museum, Kennedy Center, War Memorials, Georgetown shopping center, tours, cruises of Nation's Capital.

297 **Washington, DC**   ⛬

Howard University (T)
2401 4th St., N.W., Washington, DC 20059, Ph: (202) 806-5661/ 5653/ 9539, (202) 806-4431, ASK FOR: Rev. James Coleman, Res.Life Off.
ROOM PRICING: (S) $18.00, $14.00 (no air cond.), • PAYMENT: Cash Trav. Ck • DATES AVAILABLE: June 1 - July 31, • FOOD: Caf. VM NR OCR • INFO: Linen charge $5.00 per week, per person, no children. Limited handicap accessibility. • ACTIVITIES: National Zoo; Smithsonian Institute; Washington Monument; all of historic Washington D.C.; Old Town Alexandria.

298 **Washington, DC**   ?

Mount Vernon College (C)
2100 Foxhall Road N.W., Washington, DC 20007, Ph: (202) 625-4629, ASK FOR: Office of Special Programs
ROOM PRICING: (S) $55.00, (D) $50.00, • PAYMENT: Cash Per. Ck Trav. Ck • DATES AVAILABLE: May- Aug., • FOOD: Caf. SB NR • INFO: Min. number: 30; linens inckuded, Children welcome. • ACTIVITIES: Swimming, tennis, TV in public lounge. Nations Capital and surrounding areas,

U
N
I
V

299 Washington, DC   ?

The American University (E)
4400 Massachusetts Ave., N.W., Washington, DC 20016-8039, Ph: (202)
885-2599, ASK FOR: Office of Housing Mgmt.
ROOM PRICING: (D) $98.00, (3 wk. min stay), • PAYMENT: Cash Per. Ck Trav.
Ck • DATES AVAILABLE: May 17 -Aug. 8 (3 wk. min stay) Jan.3-May 24 (8 wk.
min. stay), • FOOD: Caf. SB VM NR • INFO: Individual guest must be college
student; Summer conf. housing avail. for non-profit educ. orginzations.; $25.00
-$45.00 day; June1 - Aug.8 • ACTIVITIES: All attractions in the Nation's Capital,
Free shuttle to subway, sports facilities & free parking in summer.

Florida

300 Babson Park, FL   ?

Webber College (T)
P. O. Box 96, Babson Park, FL 33827, Ph: (813) 638-1431, ASK FOR: Linda
Davis
ROOM PRICING: (S) $20.00, (D) $30.00, • PAYMENT: Cash Per. Ck Trav. Ck
Visa M/C • DATES AVAILABLE: May 1- Aug.14, • ROOM TYPE: SR • BED
TYPE: S • BEDS: 2-4 • FOOD: Caf. SB VM NR • INFO: No alchol, no pets,
children welcome with supervision. • ACTIVITIES: One hour drive to Disney World;
Universal Studios; Bok Tower.   Nearby: Sea World; Cypress Gardens; Busch
Gardens; all sports.

301 Daytona Beach, FL   &

Embry Riddle Aeronautical University (T)
600 S. Clyde Morris Blvd., Daytona Beach, FL 32114, Ph: (904) 323-8000, ASK
FOR: Department of Housing
ROOM PRICING: (S) $25.00, (D) $40.00, • PAYMENT: Cash Per. Ck Trav. Ck
Visa M/C Discover Amex • DATES AVAILABLE: May 15- Aug. 4, • ROOM TYPE:
SR Apt. Suite • BED TYPE: S • BEDS: 2 • BATH: C S P • FOOD: Caf. SB VM NR
• INFO: Children welcome, no pets, coin washers/dryers, TV lounge, free parking.
• ACTIVITIES: Three miles from "The world's most famous beach"; sports
facilities; pool; adjacent to airport.   Nearby: Disney World; Space Center; Cypress
Gardens; Sea World.

302 Deland, FL   ?   &

Stetson University (C)
Box 8362, Deland, FL 32720, Ph: (904) 822-8902, ASK FOR: Arlene Smith
ROOM PRICING: (S) $28.00, (D) $28.00, Min. No. Req. 10, • PAYMENT: Cash
Per. Ck • DATES AVAILABLE: June 4-July 31, • ROOM TYPE: SR • BED TYPE: S
• BEDS: 1-2 • BATH: C • FOOD: Caf. SB VM NR • INFO: Bring own linens, no
pets, no alcohol, children welcome w/supervision. Coin washer & dryer, free
parking. • ACTIVITIES: Racquetball, art gallery, swimming,theaters, game room,
tennis, museums, TV in public lounge.   Disney World; Kennedy Space Center;
Daytona Beach; St. Augustine.

303 Fort Lauderdale, FL   ?   &

Nova University (E) Goodwin Hall
3301 College Ave., Fort Lauderdale, FL 33314, Ph: (305) 475-7052, (800)
541-6682 Ext: 7052, ASK FOR: Tommy Jones, Dir. Of Res. Life
ROOM PRICING: (S) $20.00, (D) $28.00, • PAYMENT: Cash Per. Ck Trav. Ck •
DATES AVAILABLE: May 5-Aug.6, • FOOD: Caf. VM NR • INFO: Linens
Charge:$3.00 per person. Can bring your own linens. • ACTIVITIES: Beaches,
boating, fishing, water sports,game room, TV in public lounge, dining hall,
volleyball. Floirda Keys.

304 **Miami, FL**   ?   ♿

Barry University (E)
11300 N.E. 2nd Ave., Miami, FL 33161, Ph: (305) 899-3057, ASK FOR: Theresa Moorehead, Facilities Co-ordinator
ROOM PRICING: (S) $25.00, (D) $30.00, • PAYMENT: Cash Trav. Ck Visa M/C Amex • DATES AVAILABLE: May 15- July 31, • ROOM TYPE: SR Apt. • BED TYPE: S • BEDS: 1-2 • BATH: C S P • FOOD: Caf. SB VM NR • INFO: Children welcome with adults, no cribs, no pets. • ACTIVITIES: Racquetball, swimming, game room, tennis, TV in public lounge. Miami Beach; Everglades National Park; Cocnut Grove; Miami Metro Zoo; Golf; Boating.

305 **Saint Leo, FL**   ?   ♿

St. Leo College (C)
P. O. Box 6665-MC 206B, Saint Leo, FL 33574, Ph: (352) 588-8268, ASK FOR: Summer Conferences
ROOM PRICING: (S) $30.00, (D) $40.00, varied prices, depending on building/room type., • PAYMENT: Cash Trav. Ck Visa M/C • DATES AVAILABLE: Mid-May-Mid-Aug., • ROOM TYPE: SR Apt. • BED TYPE: S • BATH: C S P • FOOD: Caf. SB VM • INFO: Linen charge: $2.25 per person, per day. Chilldren welcome, free parking, TV lounge, coin laundry. • ACTIVITIES: Racquetball, park, swimming, boating, game room, tennis, hiking, golf course. Disney World; Epcot; MGM Studio; Universal Studio; Seaworld; Busch Gardens; West Coast Beaches.

DIRECTIONS: From I-75, go East on SR52 approximately four miles to college. 20 minutes north of Tampa, FL.

306 **Tallahassee, FL**   ?   ♿

Cash Hall Residence (T)
700 N. Woodward Ave., Tallahassee, FL 32304, Ph: (800) 950-2274, ASK FOR: Mary Hartley/Rick Elwood- Sales
ROOM PRICING: (S) $16.00, (D) $23.00, • PAYMENT: Cash Per. Ck Trav. Ck • DATES AVAILABLE: May 7-Aug. 5, • FOOD: Caf. VM NR • INFO: Children welcome. Regular rooms & apartments available. • ACTIVITIES: 2 swimming pools, volleyball courts, computer room, fitness center. More than 1000 acres of public parks and lakes nearby.

U
N
I
V

307 **Tallahassee, FL**

College Park - Osceola Hall (T)
500 Chapel Drive, Tallahassee, FL 32304, Ph: (850) 222-5010,   Fax: (850)
561-0269   or   1-800-553-4255,   Web   Site:
www.rent.net/direct/collegeparkosceolahall
ROOM PRICING: (S) $17.00, (D) $23.00, • PAYMENT: Cash Per. Ck Trav. Ck
Visa M/C Discover • DATES AVAILABLE: May 10-Aug. 8, • ROOM TYPE: SR •
BED TYPE: S • BEDS: 2 • BATH: S • FOOD: Caf. VM NR • INFO: Children
welcome, coin washer/dryer, free parking, TV lounge.Linens optional. •
ACTIVITIES: Pool, recreation room, fitness center, laundry facilities, basketball,
volleyball; 22 miles from Gulf of Mexico, near rolling hills of N.W. Florida; many
golf courses. 5 minute drive to downtown Tallahassee. Walking distance from
Florida State University. Golf courses within 10 miles.
DIRECTIONS: •Traveling East on I-10, take exit 31-A, go east about 7 miles on
Hwy 90. At the light on Call St., veer to the right onto Chapel Dr. "Osceola Hall"
will be on your right. • Traveling West on I-10, take 31-A to US HWY 90, Go
about nine miles and turn left on Woodward Ave.Turn Right at third light,
Pensacola Street. Pass FSU stadium and turn right on Chapel Drive. •Traveling
South on HWY 319 (Thomasville Road), cross I-10. About four miles, it merges into
Monroe St. (US27). Continue South to Tennasee St.(US 90), turn right.Eight blocks
to Woodward Ave., go left. At Penasacola St., turnright. Chapel St. will be on the
right.

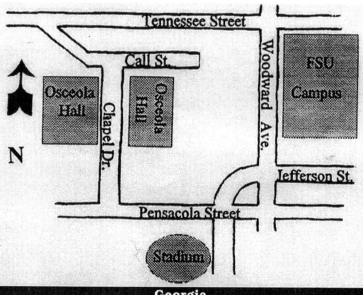

Georgia

308 **Athens, GA**   ?

University of Georgia (T)
Baxter Street, Athens, GA 30602, Ph: (706) 542-1421, ASK FOR: Scott D.
Anderson, Manager of Housing
ROOM PRICING: $30.00, $36.00, • PAYMENT: Cash Per. Ck Trav. Ck • DATES
AVAILABLE: June 20- Aug. 14, • BEDS: 2 • FOOD: Caf. SB VM NR • INFO:
Linens included. • ACTIVITIES: Films, art gallery, concerts, swimming, game
room, tennis, museums, TV in public lounge. Stone Mountain; Six Flaggs; Blue
Ridge Mountains; State Parks.

309 Atlanta, GA ♿

Emory University (E)
University Conference Off., Drawer B, Atlanta, GA 30322, Ph: (404) 727-0427, ASK FOR: Univ. Conf. Office
ROOM PRICING: (S) $27.25, (D) $41.00, • PAYMENT: Cash Per. Ck Trav. Ck Visa M/C • DATES AVAILABLE: May 21 - Aug. 8, • BEDS: 2 • FOOD: Caf. SB VM NR • INFO: Linens available, Sponsorship required, children welcome. • ACTIVITIES: Racquetball, park, swimming, game room, tennis, recreational sports facility, museums, TV in public lounge. Jimmy Carter Presidential Library; MLK Center for Nonviolent Change; Stone Mountain.

310 Dahlonega, GA ?

North Georgia College (C)
Dahlonega, GA 30597, Ph: (706) 864-1918, ASK FOR: Larry Mitchell
ROOM PRICING: Rate varies, call, • PAYMENT: Cash Per. Ck Trav. Ck Visa M/C • DATES AVAILABLE: June 18- Aug. 20, • ROOM TYPE: SR • BED TYPE: S • BEDS: 2 • FOOD: Caf. SB VM NR • INFO: Min. number: 100; Linens not available; no alcohol; no children. • ACTIVITIES: Courthouse Gold Museum, Antique and craft shops, Appalachian Trail, hiking, museums,TV in public lounge

311 Fort Valley, GA ? ♿

Fort Valley State College (T)
805 State College Dr., Fort Valley, GA 31030, Ph: (912) 825-6292, ASK FOR: Dr. Huff, Student Development
ROOM PRICING: (S) $10.00, (D) $16.00, • PAYMENT: Cash Trav. Ck • DATES AVAILABLE: June 15- Aug. 15, • ROOM TYPE: SR Apt. • BED TYPE: S • BEDS: 2 • BATH: C S • FOOD: Caf. SB VM NR • INFO: Linen Chrg.: $2.00 • ACTIVITIES: Confederate Navy Museumm, Springer Opera House (1871); Pine Mountain-Callaway Gardens (12,000 acres); Ft. Benning Infantry Museum, swimming, tennis, park.

312 Oxford, GA ?

Oxford College (C)
100 Hamill St., Oxford, GA 30267, Ph: (404) 784-8393, ASK FOR: Ms. Elam, Campus Life
ROOM PRICING: (S) $32.00 - $35.00, (D) $32.00 - $35.00, (includes food service), • PAYMENT: Cash Only • DATES AVAILABLE: June 1 - July 31, • ROOM TYPE: SR • BED TYPE: S • BEDS: 2 • BATH: C • FOOD: Caf. VM NR • INFO: Children welcome. • ACTIVITIES: Stone Mountain State Park; Lake Oconee; Martin Luther King Center; Atlanta/Carter Center.

Hawaii

313 Honolulu, HI ?

Chaminade University of Honolulu (C)
3140 Waialae Ave., Honolulu, HI 96816, Ph: (808) 735-4760, ASK FOR: Campus Life
ROOM PRICING: (S) $60.00, (D) $85.00, • PAYMENT: Cash Per. Ck Trav. Ck Visa M/C • DATES AVAILABLE: End of May- Aug. 6, • BED TYPE: S • BEDS: 2 • FOOD: Caf. SB VM NR • INFO: Group preferred-Individuals if space available. Price includes 3 meals daily. • ACTIVITIES: Waikiki Beach; Ala Moana; Diamond Head; Honolulu Zoo; Aquarium; surfing; island tours.

314 Honolulu, HI ? ♿

University of Hawaii at Manoa (E)
2555 Dole Street, Honolulu, HI 96822, Ph: (808) 948-8177, ASK FOR: Housing Office
ROOM PRICING: (S) $37.70 (Dorm), (D) $88.40 (2 Bdr. Apt.), $53.40 (1 Bdr. apt), • PAYMENT: Cash Per. Ck Visa M/C • DATES AVAILABLE: May 20- Aug 4, • FOOD: Caf. VM NR • INFO: Linens included, no alcohol. Avail.only if group has 10 members involved in educ.activity . Children welcome. • ACTIVITIES: Art gallery, swimming, boating, tennis, game room, TV in public lounge. Paradise Park; Beaches; Iolani Palace; Foster Gardens.

(T) = Travelers Accommodations   (E) = Educational Related   (C) = Groups & Conference Use

315 **Kaneohe, HI**   ?   &

Hawaii Pacific University (T)
45-045 Kamehameha Highway, Kaneohe, HI 96744, Ph: (808) 236-3574, ASK
FOR: Edward Stephien
ROOM PRICING: (S) $30.00, (D) $40.00, • PAYMENT: Cash Trav. Ck Visa M/C
Discover Amex • DATES AVAILABLE: May 13- Aug. 10, • ROOM TYPE: SR •
BEDS: 2 • FOOD: Caf. SB VM NR • INFO: Coin washer/dryer, TV lounge. •
ACTIVITIES: Art gallery, game room, tennis, hiking, TV in public loung, exercise
and recreation room, on the bus route. Island tours; beaches; surfing; Honolulu
Zoo & Aquarium; Pearl Harbor; Polynesian Culture Center; Diamond Head and
Waikiki Beach.

Idaho

316 **Lewiston, ID**   &

Lewis-Clark State College (T)
500 8th Ave., Lewiston, ID 83501, Ph: (208) 799-2053, Fax: (208) 799-2453,
E-mail: reslife@lcsc.edu, ASK FOR: DeeDee Kanikkeberg, Res. Life
ROOM PRICING: (S) $55.00 (D) $45.00 / weekly rates, • PAYMENT: Cash Trav.
Ck Visa M/C Discover • BEDS: 2 • FOOD: SB VM NR • INFO: TV lounge, coin
washers/dryers, no smoking in facilites, no children. • ACTIVITIES: Game room,
tennis fitness center, golfing, fishing, boat tours, whitewater rafting. Nez Perce
National Historical Park; Lewis & Clark Trail.
DIRECTIONS: Off highway 12.

317 **Rexburg, ID**

Off Campus Housing (T) c/o Rexburg Chamber of Commerce
420 W. 4th South, Rexburg, ID 83440, Ph: (208) 356-5700, Fax: (208) 356-5799
ROOM PRICING: Minimum Stay 1-3 months $300-$550 per month. Approx. 1000
Resident Units, • PAYMENT: Cash • DATES AVAILABLE: May 25- Aug. 25, •
ROOM TYPE: Apt. • BEDS: 2 • BATH: P • FOOD: Caf. NR • INFO: Bring own
bedding and kitchenware. Private Baths-1 and 3 bedroom apts. Call for
descriptive brochure. • ACTIVITIES: Campus Museum, library, gym, walking
track, Botanical gardens, and close to big city. Nearby: Grand Tetons; Jackson
Hole; Yellowstone National Park; Rick's College; International Folk Dance Festival;
golf; fishing.

Illinois

318 **Aurora, IL**   ?

Aurora University (E)
347 S. Gladstone Ave., Aurora, IL 60506, Ph: (603) 844-7595, ASK FOR: Event
Supervisor
ROOM PRICING: (S) $16.00, (D) $29.00, • PAYMENT: Cash Trav. Ck • DATES
AVAILABLE: June 5- Aug. 14, • ROOM TYPE: SR • BED TYPE: S • BEDS: 1-2 •
BATH: C • FOOD: Caf. SB VM NR • INFO: Linen charge:$17.00/week per
person, children welcome with adults or group leader, no alcohol. • ACTIVITIES:
Racquetball, art gallery, hiking, museums, TV in public lounge, computer lb, TV
studio, chapels. Blackberry Historical Farm; City of Chicago (40 min. drive, bus,
train); Hollywood Casion(Riverboat Gaming); Ferilab National Nuclear Accelerator.

319 **Carbondale, IL**   &

Southern Illinois University- Carbondale (C)
Washington Square D, Carbondale, IL 62901, Ph: (618) 453-2301, Fax: (618)
453-2090, ASK FOR: Lisa Schemonia, Univ. Housing
ROOM PRICING: (S) $21.70, (D) $34.30, • PAYMENT: Cash Per. Ck Trav. Ck •
DATES AVAILABLE: May 31 - Aug. 7, • ROOM TYPE: SR • BED TYPE: S • BEDS:
1-2 • BATH: S • FOOD: NR • INFO: Linens included, children welcome, no pets. •
ACTIVITIES: Racquetball, bowling, park, swimming, boating, tennis, hiking,
museum. Giant City Park; Lakes; Bald Knob Cross; Arts & Crafts Marketplace.

---

320 Carlinville, IL ? ♿

Blackburn College (C)
Carlinville, IL 62626, Ph: (217) 854-3231, ASK FOR: Christina Downey
ROOM PRICING: (S) $13.00, (D) $26.00, • PAYMENT: Cash Per. Ck Trav. Ck
Visa M/C Discover • DATES AVAILABLE: June 1- July 14, • ROOM TYPE: SR •
BED TYPE: S • BEDS: 1-2 • BATH: C • FOOD: Caf. NR • INFO: Linen charge:
$3.00 per person. Children welcome. • ACTIVITIES: 350 seats in large
auditorium; small classrooms; 50 seat modern lecture/projection room. Athletic
facilities. 80 acre campus. Beaver Dam State Park; historical sights in Springfield
and Carlinville.

321 Champaign, IL ? ♿

College Park- Illini Tower (T)
409 E. Chalmers, Champaign, IL 61820, Ph: (217) 344-0400, ASK FOR: Jas.
Crossetti - Desk
ROOM PRICING: (S) $30.00, (D) $44.00, • PAYMENT: Cash Per. Ck Trav. Ck
Visa M/C Discover • DATES AVAILABLE: May 28 - Aug. 10, • ROOM TYPE: Apt.
• BED TYPE: S • BEDS: 4 • BATH: P • FOOD: Caf. VM NR • INFO: Children
welcome, Kitchenette and living room. Laundry facilities. • ACTIVITIES: Fitness
center, game room, computer room. Close to all university facilities.

322 Chicago, IL ?

Univ. of Chicago, Int'l House (T)
1414 E. 59th St., Chicago, IL 60637, Ph: (312) 753-2280/ (312) 753-2270, Fax:
(312) 753-1227, ASK FOR: Joyce Penner
ROOM PRICING: (S) $36.00, (D) $60.00, Prices subject to change, • PAYMENT:
Cash Trav. Ck Visa M/C • DATES AVAILABLE: Year Round, • ROOM TYPE:
SR • BED TYPE: S • BEDS: 1 • BATH: C • FOOD: Caf. SB VM NR • INFO: No
children. • ACTIVITIES: Films, museum, game room, TV in public lounge, park.
Museum of Science and Industry; Univ. of Chicago campus; Chicago cultural
attractions.

323 De Kalb, IL ? ♿

Northern Illinois University (T) Holmes Center Guest Rooms
De Kalb, IL 60115, Ph: (815) 753-1444, ASK FOR: Donetta Domina
ROOM PRICING: (S) $38.00, (D) $43.00, • PAYMENT: Cash Per. Ck Trav. Ck
Visa M/C Discover Amex • DATES AVAILABLE: Call for availablity, • ROOM
TYPE: SR • BED TYPE: S D • BEDS: 2 • BATH: P • FOOD: Caf. SB VM NR •
INFO: No charge for children under 16 occupying same room as parents. Some
queen beds available. • ACTIVITIES: Full service type hotel residence. Dinner boat
cruises in nearby Oregon, IL; Frank Lloyd Wright House; Sears Tower;
antique/mining town; museum, sports facilities all nearby. Chicago, 60 miles
east.

324 Edwardsville, IL ? ♿

So. Ill. Univ.-Edwardsville (T)
Box 1256, Edwardsville, IL 62025, Ph: (618) 692-2900, Fax: (618) 692-2833,
E-mail: Cbush@Siue.edu, ASK FOR: Cindy Bush, Asst. Dir. of Housing
ROOM PRICING: (S) $33.00, (D) $46.00, • PAYMENT: Cash Per. Ck Trav. Ck
Visa M/C • DATES AVAILABLE: May 20 - Aug. 1, • BEDS: 2 • FOOD: NR •
INFO: Coin washer/dryers, ample parking, children welcome. • ACTIVITIES: TV
lounge. 25 miles from St. Louis and its attractions. Local attractions as well.

325 Greenville, IL ?

Greenville College (T)
315 East College, Greenville, IL 62246, Ph: (618) 664-2800, Ext: 4540, Fax: (618)
664-1748, E-mail: ggoldsmith@greenville.edu, ASK FOR: Gary Goldsmith,Conf.
Services
ROOM PRICING: (S) $13.00, (D) $22.00, 450 Beds available, • PAYMENT: Cash •
DATES AVAILABLE: June 6 - Aug. 6, Some year round, • BEDS: 1-2 • FOOD:
Caf. NR • INFO: No smoking or alcohol on campus; Linen chg. $2.00;Children OK
• ACTIVITIES: Bock Museum, nearby: Vandalia State House, Carlyle Lake, St.
Louis, tennis, hiking
DIRECTIONS: I-70 to Route 127 north. Turn north at traffic light. Campus is
eight blocks from the traffic light.

U
N
I
V

(T) = Travelers Accommodations (E) = Educational Related (C) = Groups & Conference Use

326 **Lebanon, IL**   ?

McKendree College (E)
701 College Rd., Lebanon, IL 62254, Ph: (618) 537-4481, Ext: 173, ASK FOR: Ed Willett, Operations
ROOM PRICING: (S) $18.00, (D) $30.00, Suites also available, • PAYMENT: Cash • DATES AVAILABLE: May 20 - Aug. 20, • ROOM TYPE: SR Apt. • BED TYPE: S • BEDS: 2 • BATH: C • FOOD: Caf. SB VM NR • INFO: No alcohol on campus • ACTIVITIES: Tennis, game room, new football staduim. St. Louis Art Museum; St. Louis Waterfront Activities; shops; St. Louis Zoo.

327 **Macomb, IL**   ?   ⑆

Western Illinois Univ. (T) Olson Conference Center
400 N. Western Ave., Macomb, IL 61455, Ph: (309) 298-3500, ASK FOR: Olson Conf. Center
ROOM PRICING: (S) $30.00, (D) $35.00, Triple-$42.00/limited availability., • PAYMENT: Cash Per. Ck Trav. Ck Visa M/C Discover • DATES AVAILABLE: Year Round, • ROOM TYPE: SR Apt. • BED TYPE: S • BEDS: 1-2 • BATH: C • FOOD: Caf. VM NR OCR • INFO: Children welcome, under 10 free. Linens included, TV lounge. coin washer/dryer, free parking, open 24 hours, doors locked at 11:00pm. • ACTIVITIES: Bowling, theater, tennis. Nauvoo; Springfield Hannibal, Mo.; Argyle State Park.

328 **Naperville, IL**

North Central College (C)
30 N. Brainard St., Naperville, IL 60540, Ph: (630)637-5858 , ASK FOR: Karl Brooks,or Kris Gustafson Asst. Dir. Residence Life
ROOM PRICING: (S) $17.00, (D) $28.00, • PAYMENT: Cash Per. Ck Trav. Ck • DATES AVAILABLE: Mid- June- Mid- Aug., • ROOM TYPE: SR • BED TYPE: S • BEDS: 1-2 • BATH: C • FOOD: Caf. SB VM NR • INFO: Linen charge: $10.00 per person. Children welcome. • ACTIVITIES: Swimming, Game room, tennis, TV in public lounge, computer labs, 25 yard indoor pool, indoor/outdoor track, weight room. Centennial Beach within walking distance; City of Chicago, short ride away.

329 **Normal, IL**   ⑆

Illinois State University (C)
2600 Office of Residential Life, Normal, IL 61790, Ph: (309) 438-8611, Web Site: www.ORL.iLstu.Edu, ASK FOR: Robert Navarro
ROOM PRICING: (S) $17.00-$24.00, (D) $22.50-$32.00, • PAYMENT: Cash Per. Ck • DATES AVAILABLE: June 1- July 31, • ROOM TYPE: SR • BED TYPE: S • BEDS: 1-2 • BATH: C • FOOD: Caf. SB VM NR OCR • INFO: Linen Charge: $2.00 (W/O full service). Children welcome. TV in lobby. • ACTIVITIES: Art gallery, bowling, park, theaters, game room, tennis, hiking, museums. Comlara Park; Miller Park Zoo; David Davis Mansion; Mitsubishi Motors of America

330 **River Forest, IL**   ?   ⑆

Concordia University (T)
Koehneke Community Center, 7400 Augusta St., River Forest, IL 60305, Ph: (708) 209-3092, ASK FOR: Dir. of Community Events
ROOM PRICING: Includes breakfast, (S) $35.00, (D) $35.00, • PAYMENT: Cash Per. Ck • DATES AVAILABLE: May 25 - Aug. 8, • BED TYPE: S • BEDS: 2 • FOOD: Caf. SB VM NR • INFO: Linens included, no alcohol, no pets. (except for seeing eye dogs) • ACTIVITIES: Nearby movie theater; Frank Lloyd Wright Studio; Chicago Museums; Lake M ichigan.

331 **River Forest, IL**

Dominican University (C)
7900 W. Division, River Forest, IL 60305, Ph: (708) 524-6217, Fax: (708) 524-5990, ASK FOR: Director of Residence Life and University Conference Services
ROOM PRICING: Call for rates, Call for Quotes, • PAYMENT: Cash • DATES AVAILABLE: May 15- Aug. 1, • ROOM TYPE: SR • BED TYPE: S • BEDS: 1-2 • BATH: C • FOOD: Caf. • INFO: No alcohol on campus, no children. • ACTIVITIES: Public transportation is available. Concerts, Theater, Museums. Sports on Campus.Brookfield Zoo; Nearby Chicago.

---

332 **Urbana, IL**   ♿

Hendrick House (T)
904 W. Green St., Urbana, IL 61801, Ph: (217) 365-8000, Fax: (217) 384-4701,
Web Site: www.hendrickhouse.wm, ASK FOR: Rebecca Rowe/ Gen. Man.
ROOM PRICING: Call for prices or check web site. , • PAYMENT: Cash Per. Ck
Trav. Ck Visa M/C • DATES AVAILABLE: May 21 - Aug 19, • ROOM TYPE: SR
• BED TYPE: S • BEDS: 2 • BATH: S • FOOD: Caf. • INFO: Linens included;
Children welcome; Air-conditioned; Parking available for fee; Laundry facilities
available. • ACTIVITIES: All campus sports facilities, game room, bowling, art
gallery, museum, park.

333 **Wheaton, IL**   ?   ♿

Wheaton College (C)
501 College Ave., Wheaton, IL 60187, Ph: (630) 752-5112, Fax: (630) 752-5998,
ASK FOR: Conference Services
ROOM PRICING: Call for quotes, min. required for conf. 20, • PAYMENT: •
DATES AVAILABLE: Call, • BEDS: 1-3 • FOOD: Caf. SB VM NR • INFO: TV
lounge, coin washers/dryers, free parking, children welcome. • ACTIVITIES: Art
gallery; park; swimming; tennis; hiking; museums.

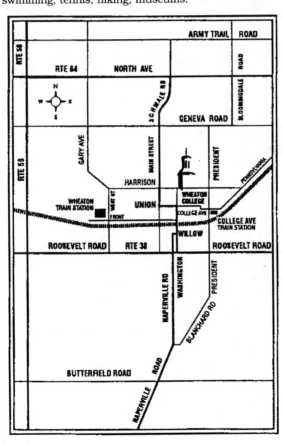

**U
N
I
V**

Indiana

334 **Anderson, IN**   ♿

Anderson University (C)
1100 E. 5th St., Anderson, IN 46012, Ph: (765) 641-4145, Fax: (765) 641-3647, E-mail: Clshank@Kirk.anderson.edu, ASK FOR: Cheryl Shank - Conf. Office
ROOM PRICING: Upon Inquiry, • PAYMENT: Cash Only • DATES AVAILABLE: May 25 - Aug. 9, • BEDS: 2 • FOOD: Caf. SB VM NR • INFO: Linen charge: $6.50. No tobacco or alcohol, children welcome. • ACTIVITIES: Swimming, tennis, bowling, game room, art gallery, TV in public lounge. Nearby: Mounds State Park; Indianapolis, attractions.

335 **Fort Wayne, IN**   ?   ♿

Saint Frances College (E)
2701 Spring St., Fort Wayne, IN 46808, Ph: (800) 729-4732, ASK FOR: Howard Allan, Dir.
ROOM PRICING: (S) $19.00-$25.00, (D) $30.00-$44.00, • PAYMENT: Cash Per. Ck • DATES AVAILABLE: May 15-Aug.1, • FOOD: Caf. VM NR • INFO: Linen Charge: $3 - $5 per person, no alcohol, no pets, no children. Min. No. Req. for conf. 10. Some rms. w/semi-private bath. • ACTIVITIES: Racquetball, art gallery, game room, tennis, TV in public lounge. Zoo; Various Arts Attractions; Foellinger-Freiwnn Botanical Garden; Lincoln Museum.

336 **Hanover, IN**   ♿

Hanover College (T)
Hanover, IN 47243, Ph: (812) 866-7114, ASK FOR: Else Taylor, Brown Campus Ctr.
ROOM PRICING: Only double rooms available (D) $45.00, • PAYMENT: Cash Per. Ck Trav. Ck Visa M/C • DATES AVAILABLE: Year Round, • ROOM TYPE: Suite • BED TYPE: S • BEDS: 2 • BATH: P • FOOD: Caf. SB VM NR • ACTIVITIES: Game room. Clifty Falls State Park; Chautauqua of the Arts; Governor's Cup Regatta; Lanier State Memorial.

337 **Huntington, IN**   ?   ♿

Huntington College (T)
2303 College Ave., Huntington, IN 46750, Ph: (219) 359-4200, ASK FOR: Sharlee Stoner
ROOM PRICING: (S) $12.00- $30.00, (D) $24.00- $30.00, • PAYMENT: Cash Per. Ck Trav. Ck • DATES AVAILABLE: Call for dates available, • ROOM TYPE: SR Apt. • BED TYPE: S • BEDS: 2 • BATH: C P • FOOD: Caf. VM NR • INFO: Conference rate $11.50, linen charge: $3.50, no smoking, no alcohol. • ACTIVITIES: Racquetball, art gallery, concerts, game room, tennis, hiking, TV in public lounge.

338 **Indianapolis, IN**   ?   ♿

Indiana Univ. - Purdue (T) Univ. at Indianapolis
1226 W. Michigan St. at Indianapolis, Indianapolis, IN 46202, Ph: (317) 274-7200, ASK FOR: Assignment Office
ROOM PRICING: (S) $17.90 (D) $31.25, • PAYMENT: Cash Per. Ck Trav. Ck • DATES AVAILABLE: May 31 - July. 1, • BEDS: 1-3 • FOOD: Caf. SB VM NR OCR • INFO: No children under 10 years. Coin washers/dryers, free parking. • ACTIVITIES: Circle Center Mall; Union Station; Monument Circle; Ind. 500 race track; restaurants and nightclubs; campus sports; Hoosier Dome.

339 **Indianapolis, IN**   ?

Marian College (T)
3200 Cold Spring Road, Indianapolis, IN 46222, Ph: (317) 955-6120, ASK FOR: Conference & Events Off.
ROOM PRICING: (S) $12.00, (D) $24.00, • PAYMENT: Cash Per. Ck Trav. Ck Visa M/C • DATES AVAILABLE: May 15-Aug.1, • BEDS: 2 • FOOD: Caf. VM NR • INFO: Bring own linens, no alcohol. • ACTIVITIES: Racquetball, park, game room, tennis, TV in public lounge. Indianapolis Motor Speedway; Lafayette Square Mall; Indianapolis Museum of Art; Velodrome.

---

340 **Marion, IN**　　　　　　　　　　　　　?　♿

Indiana Wesleyan Univ. (T)
4201 S. Washington St., Marion, IN 46953, Ph: (765) 677-2215, Fax: (765) 677-2755, E-mail: confserv@indwes.edu, ASK FOR: Greg Beecher
ROOM PRICING: (S) $15.00- $17.00 (D) $22.00- $26.00, • PAYMENT: Cash Per. Ck Trav. Ck Visa M/C Discover • DATES AVAILABLE: June 8 - Aug. 9, • ROOM TYPE: SR • BED TYPE: S • BEDS: 2 • BATH: S • FOOD: Caf. NR • INFO: Children welcome, no alcohol, no smoking, coin washers/dryers, TV lounge, free parking, morning coffee, linens with request. • ACTIVITIES: Mississippi Reservoir; Salamonie Reservoir; James Dean Historical Museum; Van Buren Popcorn Capitol of the world.

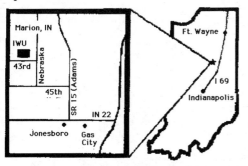

Indiana Wesleyan University is located in Marion, Indiana, just an hour's drive south of Fort Wayne and an hour north of Indianapolis off Interstate 69.

341 **North Manchester, IN**　　　　　　　　　?　♿

Manchester College (T)
North Manchester, IN 46962, Ph: (219) 982-5247, Fax: (219) 982-5088, ASK FOR: Karl F. Merritt, Dir. Conf. Services
ROOM PRICING: Varies; Rates upon request. • PAYMENT: Cash Per. Ck Trav. Ck Visa M/C Discover Amex • DATES AVAILABLE: Summer months and some year round, • ROOM TYPE: SR Apt. Suite • BED TYPE: S • BEDS: 2 • BATH: C S P • FOOD: Caf. SB VM NR • INFO: Children welcome, linen charge. • ACTIVITIES: Tennis, racquetball. Amish Acres, Ft. Wayne Museum, Ft. Wayne Zoo, Wagon Wheel Playhouse, Lincoln Gallery, Ford theater- Honeywell.

342 **Richmond, IN**　　　　　　　　　　　　?

Earlham College (T) Norwich Lodge & Conference Center
920 Earlham Dr., Richmond, IN 47374, Ph: (317) 983-1575, ASK FOR: Kim Mondics, Manager
ROOM PRICING: (S) $25.00- $40.00, (D) $35.00- $45.00, Bed & Breakfast, • PAYMENT: Cash Per. Ck Visa M/C • DATES AVAILABLE: Year Round, • ROOM TYPE: SR • BED TYPE: S D • BEDS: 1-2 • BATH: P • FOOD: • INFO: Children welcome, no alcoholic beverage, no smoking. • ACTIVITIES: Walking trails, tennis. Nearby: many antique shops, Hayes Arboretum, C. Miller Park.

343 **West Lafayette, IN**　　　　　　　　　　?　♿

Purdue University, Residence Halls (E)
105 Smalley Center, West Lafayette, IN 47906, Ph: (317) 494-1023, ASK FOR: Sue Hume Graham/ Housing
ROOM PRICING: (S) $24.65- $45.00, (D) $23.50- 47.50, • PAYMENT: Cash Visa M/C Discover Amex • DATES AVAILABLE: May 15-Aug. 7, • ROOM TYPE: SR Apt. • BED TYPE: S • BEDS: 1-2 • BATH: S P • FOOD: Caf. SB VM NR • INFO: Towels avail. at $1.00/night. Children welcome. Min no. req. for conf: 15, max: 8,000. Conf. complex w/facilities for housing & food service. Dis. rates, for guests over 3000. • ACTIVITIES: Racquetball, films, art gallery, bowling, concerts, swimming, baoting, theaters, game room, tennis, hiking, TV in lounge. Tippecanoe Battlefield; Fort Quiatenon; Greater Lafayette Museum of Art; Columbian Park Wolf Park.

U N I V

(T) = Travelers Accommodations　(E) = Educational Related　(C) = Groups & Conference Use

Iowa

344 Decorah, IA   ♿

Luther College (E)
700 College Dr., Decorah, IA 52101, Ph: (319) 387-1538, ASK FOR: Cindy
Womeldorf, Conference Center
ROOM PRICING: (S) $18.00, (D) $29.00 includes breakfast, • PAYMENT: Cash
Per. Ck • DATES AVAILABLE: Call for dates available, • ROOM TYPE: SR • BED
TYPE: S • BEDS: 2 • BATH: C • FOOD: Caf. SB VM NR • INFO: Children under
10 years,room free. Adult supervision reqired for all student groups. Facility
charge $3.50 per day. • ACTIVITIES: Norwegian Amer. Museum, Amish
community nearby, Upper Iowa River, all sports, films, concerts, theater

345 Dubuque, IA   ?

University of Dubuque (E)
2000 University Ave., Dubuque, IA 52001, Ph: (319) 589-3128, ASK FOR: Nan
Rebholz, Coordinator
ROOM PRICING: Prices negotiable, • PAYMENT: Cash Trav. Ck • DATES
AVAILABLE: June 1 - Aug. 31, • ROOM TYPE: SR • BED TYPE: S • BEDS: 2 •
BATH: C • FOOD: Caf. VM NR • INFO: Small linen charge, children welcome with
supervision. • ACTIVITIES: Tennis, range of campus sports, concerts. Riverboat
dinner cruises; rides; dog racing track; elegant dining locales overlooking the
Mississippi.

346 Indianola, IA   ? ♿

Simpson College (C)
701 North C Street, Indianola, IA 50125, Ph: (515) 961-1428
ROOM PRICING: (S) $12.00-$18.00, (D) $20.00-$26.00, $10.00/additional
person, • PAYMENT: Cash Per. Ck Visa M/C Discover • DATES
AVAILABLE: June 1-July 30, • FOOD: NR • INFO: Linen charge: $3.50 a set,
children welcome, no pets. • ACTIVITIES: Art gallery, park, swimming, game
room, tennis, TV in public lounge. National Balloon Museum; Warren County
Historical Society; Lake Aquabi; 12 miles from Des Moines.

347 Sioux City, IA   ?

Briar Cliff College (T)
3303 Rebecca St., Sioux City, IA 51104, Ph: (712) 279-5494, ASK FOR: Residence
Life -Warren Larson
ROOM PRICING: (S) $15.00, (D) $15.00, • PAYMENT: Cash Only • DATES
AVAILABLE: June 6 - Aug. 15, • ROOM TYPE: SR Apt. • BED TYPE: S • BEDS:
2-4 • BATH: C S • FOOD: Caf. VM NR • INFO: Children welcome. • ACTIVITIES:
Several parks, college sports facilities, boating, swimming, Missouri River. Nearby
Omaha, Nebraska.

348 Storm Lake, IA   ? ♿

Buena Vista University (E)
610 West 4th, Storm Lake, IA 50588, Ph: (712) 749-2403, ASK FOR: Kelly
Farnum Bauer, Box 2974, Siebens Forum
ROOM PRICING: (S) $19.00, (D) $24.00, Guest suites; $25.00- $27.00, •
PAYMENT: Cash Per. Ck Trav. Ck Visa M/C • DATES AVAILABLE: May 25 -
Aug. 15, • ROOM TYPE: SR Suite • BED TYPE: S • BEDS: 2 • BATH: C P •
FOOD: Caf. SB VM NR • INFO: Linen charge: $5.50. Children welcome.
Corporate suites available. • ACTIVITIES: Lake, walking trails, swimming,
canoing, library & Technology Center

Kansas

349 **Leavenworth, KS**   ♿

Saint Mary College (C) Saint Mary Center
4100 S. 4th St. Trafficway, Leavenworth, KS 66048, Ph: (913) 758-6134, Fax: (913) 758-6140, Web Site: www.smcks.edu
ROOM PRICING: (S) $25.00, (D) $36.00, • PAYMENT: Cash Per. Ck Trav. Ck •
DATES AVAILABLE: May 15 - July 31, • ROOM TYPE: SR • BED TYPE: S •
BEDS: 2 • BATH: S • FOOD: Caf. VM NR • INFO: Connferences, groups ,or families,Children welcome, reservations required. Coin washer/dryer, TV lounge, free parking, track, pool, tennis courts, volleyball and raquetball courts •
ACTIVITIES: Nearby: Historic Fort Leavenworth; 30 minutes toKansas City attractions; 40 minutes to worlds of fun and Oceans of Fun; Campus.

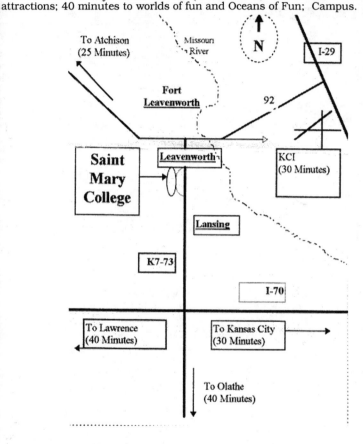

U
N
I
V

350 **Manhattan, KS** ♿

Kansas State Univ. (E)
Manhattan, KS 66506-4601, Ph: (785) 532-6368 or 888-568-5027, ASK FOR
Housing and Dining Services
ROOM PRICING: (S) $22.00, (D) $31.00, • PAYMENT: Cash Per. Ck Trav. Ck
Visa M/C Discover • DATES AVAILABLE: Year round, • ROOM TYPE: SR • BED
TYPE: S • BEDS: 2 • BATH: C • FOOD: Caf. VM NR • INFO: Must be on
university related business. Linens included. • ACTIVITIES: Sports facilities, and
museum, theater. Tuttle Creek; Reservoir; Historical Society; Museum; historic
Fort Riley.
DIRECTIONS: Located 115 miles west of Kansas City and accessible via Interstate
70

351 **North Newton, KS** ?

Bethel College (T)
300 East 27th Street, North Newton, KS 67117, Ph: (316) 283-2500, ASK FOR
Virgil Penner, Office of Conf.
ROOM PRICING: (S) $20.50, (D) $25.00, • PAYMENT: Cash Trav. Ck • DATES
AVAILABLE: June 1-Aug.15, • FOOD: Caf. NR • INFO: Limited number of single
occupancy rooms, linens included, no smoking in rooms or buildings, no alcohol
Children welcome with adult supervision. • ACTIVITIES: Tennis, museums
Kaufman Museum; Warkesten House; Sedgwick County Zoo; Praire People Tours.

352 **Wichita, KS** ♿

Wichita State University (E)
Campus Box 141, Wichita, KS 67260, Ph: (316) 978-3693, ASK FOR: Houusing &
Residence Life
ROOM PRICING: (S) $20.00, (D) $30.00, Discount for groups, • PAYMENT: Cash
Only • DATES AVAILABLE: June 1-Aug.1, • BED TYPE: S • BEDS: 2 • FOOD:
Caf. VM • INFO: Coin washer and dryer, TV lounge. • ACTIVITIES: Campus
sports. Sedgwick County Zoo; Omnisphere; Dinner theater, All-Indian Center
Kansas Cosmosphere.

Kentucky

353 **Berea, KY** ?

Berea College (C)
Berea, KY 40404, Ph: (606) 986-9341, Ext: 6830, ASK FOR: Mary Murray, Dir. of
Spec. Progs.
ROOM PRICING: (S) $18.00, (D) $18.00, • PAYMENT: Cash • DATES AVAILABLE
June 7 - July 31, • ROOM TYPE: SR • BED TYPE: S • BATH: C • FOOD: Caf. •
INFO: Children welcome, with parent superv., no alcohol, limited smoking. Not
air-conditioned. • ACTIVITIES: All campus sports facilities. Nearby: Shakertown -
restored Shaker Village; Kentucky Horse Park; Cumberland Mtns.

354 **Lexington, KY** ?

University of Kentucky (T)
Room 316 Commons, Lexington, KY 40526, Ph: (606) 257-3189, ASK FOR: Bob
Rash
ROOM PRICING: (S) $30.00, (D) $32.00, • PAYMENT: Cash Per. Ck Trav. Ck •
DATES AVAILABLE: May 16-Aug. 7, • FOOD: Caf. VM NR • INFO: No Children. •
ACTIVITIES: Sports Facilities, films, concerts, theater, game room, TV. Kentucky
Horse Park; Red Mile Trotting Track; Lexington Opera House.

355 **Louisville, KY** ?

Spalding University (E) Morrison Hall
947 S. 4th St., Louisville, KY 40203, Ph: (502) 585-9911, ASK FOR: Morrison Hall
ROOM PRICING: (S) $17.00-$21.00, (D) $26.00-$32.00, • PAYMENT: Cash Per.
Ck Trav. Ck • DATES AVAILABLE: Year Round, • BEDS: 2 • FOOD: Caf. SB VM
NR • INFO: Linens included, no alcohol, children welcome, coin washers/dryers. •
ACTIVITIES: Art gallery, game room, TV in public lounge, weight room. Churchill
Downs; Museum of History & Space; T. B. Speed Art Museum.

356 **Louisville, KY**   ?   ♿

University of Louisville (T) Conf. Training Center, Shelby Campus
114 Burhans Hall, Shelbyville Rd., Louisville, KY 40292, Ph: (502) 852-0365, Fax:
(502) 852-8573, E-mail: arsturl@ulkyvm.louisville.edu, ASK FOR: Anita Sturgill
Block
ROOM PRICING: (S) $18.00 (D) $26.00, • PAYMENT: Cash Per. Ck Trav. Ck
Visa M/C • DATES AVAILABLE: Year round, • BEDS: 2 • FOOD: No • INFO:
Linens included, children welcome, no pets, refrigerators & microwaves in dorm
lobbies, TV lounge, coin washers/dryers, free parking. • ACTIVITIES: Churchill
Downs; Belle of Louisville Steamboat; Movie theaters; restaurants; orchestra.
DIRECTIONS: From 264-take Shelbyville Rd. exit; From I-64 West- take
Hurstbourne Lane exit, go straight to Shelbyville Rd.; From I-64 East-take 264
east to Shelbyville Rd.

357 **Morehead, KY**   ?   ♿

Morehead State University (C) Conference Services
UPO 3000, Morehead, KY 40351, Ph: (606) 783-5128
ROOM PRICING: (S) $11.00- $22.00, Private suite $27.50, • PAYMENT: Cash •
DATES AVAILABLE: June 1 - July 31, • ROOM TYPE: SR Apt. • BED TYPE: S •
BEDS: 2-4 • BATH: C P • FOOD: Caf. SB VM NR • INFO: No alcohol •
ACTIVITIES: Cave Run Lake, Daniel Boone National Forest, Carter Caves State
Park, sport and cultural offerings.

358 **Pippa Passes, KY**   ?   ♿

Alice Lloyd College (T)
Lilly Hall, Howard Hall, Berger-AuenHall, Purpose Road, Pippa Passes, KY 41844,
Ph: (606) 368-2101, Ext: 7105, Fax: (606) 368-2125, ASK FOR: Lenore Pollard,
Dir.
ROOM PRICING: (S) $18.00, (D) $24.00, Some triple rooms, Addl. person $10.00,
• PAYMENT: Cash Trav. Ck Visa • DATES AVAILABLE: June 1-July 31, •
BEDS: 2 • FOOD: Caf. VM NR OCR • INFO: Linen charge: $2.00 p/p, no alcohol
or unprescribed drugs, children welcome, washer/dryer available, TV lounge, free
parking. • ACTIVITIES: On campus: racquetball, films, art gallery, bowling,
swimming, game room, tennis, hiking, library, craft shop. Jenny Wiley outdoor
theater; Jenny Wiley Lake; Carr Fork Lake.

359 **Richmond, KY**   ?   ♿

Eastern Kentucky Univ. (T)
Lancaster Ave., Richmond, KY 40475, Ph: (606) 622-1515, ASK FOR: Housing
Office
ROOM PRICING: (S) $14.00, (D) $21.00, • PAYMENT: Cash Per. Ck Trav. Ck
Visa M/C • DATES AVAILABLE: May 15 - Aug. 7, • FOOD: Caf. SB VM NR •
INFO: No alcohol, no pets, children welcome, advance registration and payment
necessary, bring own linens. • ACTIVITIES: White Hall State Shrine; Berea Craft
Areas; Fort Boonesboro; Lexington Horse Park; sport facilities; Valley View Ferry.

Louisiana

360 **New Orleans, LA**   ?   ♿

Loyola University at New Orleans (T)
6363 St. Charles Ave. #001, New Orleans, LA 70118, Ph: (504) 865-3622, ASK
FOR: Priscilla Williams, Coord.
ROOM PRICING: (S) $30.00, (D) $42.00, • PAYMENT: Cash Per. Ck Trav. Ck
Visa M/C • DATES AVAILABLE: June 1- Aug. 1, • FOOD: Caf. VM NR • INFO:
Cooking facilities, central air, computer room. • ACTIVITIES: Tennis, racquetball,
recreation building. French Quarter; Audubon Park & Zoo; Superdome;
Streetcar; Aquarium.

U
N
I
V

Maine

361 Fort Kent, ME   ?

University of Maine (T)
25 Pleasant St., Fort Kent, ME 04743, Ph: (207) 834-7513, ASK FOR: Director of Residence Life
ROOM PRICING: (S) $15.00, (D) $30.00, • PAYMENT: Cash Per. Ck Trav. Ck •
DATES AVAILABLE: May 21- Aug 20, • FOOD: VM NR • INFO: Lower rates for longer stays. Night number: (207) 834-7673 • ACTIVITIES: Canoeing, antiquing, sports, cabarets. Duty-free shopping across Canadian border; Heritage Village (45 min.); Allagash Trail; wilderness area.

362 Portland, ME   ?

Westbrook College (E)
Stevens Ave., Portland, ME 04103, Ph: (207) 797-7261, ASK FOR: Treasurer's Office
ROOM PRICING: Call for rates, • PAYMENT: Cash Per. Ck Trav. Ck Visa M/C
• DATES AVAILABLE: June- August, • ROOM TYPE: SR • BED TYPE: S • BEDS: 1-2 • BATH: C • FOOD: Caf. VM NR • INFO: Extra charge for linens, children welcome with adults. • ACTIVITIES: Park, weight room, hiking, TV in public lounge. Portland Museum of Art; Children's Museum of Maine; L. L. Bean; Oldport.

(T) = Travelers Accommodations   (E) = Educational Related   (C) = Groups & Conference Use

Maryland

363 **Baltimore, MD**   ?

College of Notre Dame of Maryland (T) Mary Meletia Doyle Hall
4701 North Charles St., Baltimore, MD 21210, Ph: (410) 532-6155, Fax: (410)
435-7591, ASK FOR: Frances Bergen
ROOM PRICING: (S) $20.00, (D) $30.00, • PAYMENT: Cash Per. Ck • DATES
AVAILABLE: Mid.- June- Mid.- Aug., • ROOM TYPE: SR • BED TYPE: S • BEDS:
1-2 • BATH: C S P • FOOD: Caf. SB VM NR • INFO: Free parking • ACTIVITIES:
Swimming, art gallery, tennis,game room, TV in public lounge.   Central location;
Inner Harbor; National Aquarium; Campus on main bus line; 10 mins. to train;
numerous restaurants; museums; shopping.

> **By Car:** Take the Baltimore Beltway (Route I-695) to North Charles
> Street (Exit 25). Drive 4.6 miles south on Charles Street to the College
> entrance, on the left, immediately past Homeland Avenue.

> **By Train:** All passenger trains arrive at Pennsylvania Station in down-
> town Baltimore. A taxi from the station to the College of Notre Dame
> takes about 10 minutes.

> **By Plane:** Baltimore-Washington International Airport (BWI) is about
> 45 minutes from Notre Dame. Limousine and shuttle services are
> available to downtown hotels, about 15 minutes from the airport. Most
> hotels are located 15 to 20 minutes from the College. Limousine service
> is also available to the Cross Keys Inn, located only five minutes from
> Notre Dame.

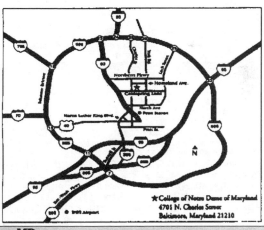

★ College of Notre Dame of Maryland
4701 N. Charles Street
Baltimore, Maryland 21210

U
N
I
V

364 **Baltimore, MD**   ♿

John Hopkins University (E)
3400 North Charles Street, 104 Wolman Hall, Baltimore, MD 21218, Ph: (410)
516-3962, Fax: (410) 516-6444, E-mail: TDecker@jhuhome.res.jhu.edu, ASK
FOR: Toni Decker, Conf. Services
ROOM PRICING: Rates depend on length of stay, • PAYMENT: Cash Per. Ck •
DATES AVAILABLE: June-Mid-Aug., • BED TYPE: S • BEDS: 1-2 • FOOD: Caf.
VM NR • INFO: Linens included, meeting rooms, children welcome w/ adult
supervision. Min. no. req. for conf. 25. • ACTIVITIES: Art gallery, swimming,
theaters, game rm, tennis, excerise rm.,museums, TV in pub. lounge. Baltimore's
Inner Harbor; Ft. McHenry National Shrine; Oriole Park @ Camden Yards;
Washington DC.

---

365 **Baltimore, MD**   ?   &

Loyola College in Maryland (C)
4501 North Charles Street, Baltimore, MD 21210, Ph: (410) 617-5077, Fax: (410) 617-2211, E-mail: wood@loyola.edu, ASK FOR: Joan F. Wood, Special Event Services
ROOM PRICING: (S) $10.00- $25.00, • PAYMENT: Cash • DATES AVAILABLE: Mid.- May- Mid.- Aug., • ROOM TYPE: SR Apt. • BED TYPE: S • BEDS: 1-2 • BATH: C S P • FOOD: Caf. VM NR • INFO: Linen charges vary, children welcome. • ACTIVITIES: Racquetball, art gallery, swimming, tennis, hiking, TV in public lounge. Baltimore Inner Harbor; Baltimore Museum of Art; Oriole Park Camden Yards; Fells Point.

366 **Baltimore, MD**   ?   &

Towson State University (C)
U U 212, Baltimore, MD 21252, Ph: (410) 830-2315, ASK FOR: Event & Conf. Services
ROOM PRICING: (S) $25.00-w/linens, $18.00 -wo/linens $32.00 w/linens, (D) $31.00-w/linens, • PAYMENT: Cash Only Per. Ck Trav. Ck • DATES AVAILABLE: June 10 - Aug. 18, • BEDS: 2 • FOOD: Caf. VM NR • INFO: Available satellite. Free parking, coin washers/dryers. • ACTIVITIES: Gettysburg; Washington D.C.; Chesapeake Bay; attractions of Baltimore - all nearby.

367 **Lanham, MD**

Washington Bible College (T)
6511 Princess Garden Pkwy, Lanham, MD 20706, Ph: (301) 552-1400, Ext: 207, Fax: (301) 522-2775, E-mail: pboswell@bible.edu, ASK FOR: Hostess
ROOM PRICING: (S) $15.00 per person, dorm rooms. Guest Rooms $30.00. Other options available., • PAYMENT: Cash Per. Ck Trav. Ck • DATES AVAILABLE: Year Round (Guest rooms), Summer (Dorms) , • BED TYPE: S • BEDS: 2 • FOOD: Caf. SB NR • INFO: Linen charge: $3.00, Children welcome in guest housing. No smokiing, no alcohol on campus. TV lounge, free parking, washer/dryer. • ACTIVITIES: Sports facilities. Nearby: The White House, Inner Harbor, Smithsonian, Annapolis. 10 miles from Washington DC.

Massachusetts

368 **Amherst, MA**   &

Univ. of Massachusetts at Amherst (T)
918 Campus Center, Amherst, MA 01003, Ph: (413) 545-2591 (413) 549-6000, ASK FOR: University Conf. Housing/Campus Center Hotel
ROOM PRICING: ResidenceHalls, summer only(S) $22.50, (D) $37.00
Campus Center Hotel-(S) $69.00, (D) $79.00, • PAYMENT: Cash Per. Ck Trav. Ck Visa M/C Discover Amex • DATES AVAILABLE: June 1-Aug. 14, Campus Center Hotel - Year round, • BEDS: 2 • FOOD: Caf. SB VM NR • INFO: Children welcome. No charge under 11 yrs. sharing room with parent, child linens not included.Residence hall beds - 2/room. Hotel 1-2/room -private bath. Hotel has 116 rooms, AC, pking garage. • ACTIVITIES: Tennis, films, game room, art gallery. Nearby: Historic Deerfield Village; Old Sturbridge Village; Emily Dickinson House; Basketball Hall of Fame.

369 **Boston, MA**   ?   &

Wentworth Institute of Tech. (E)
550 Huntington Ave., Boston, MA 02115, Ph: (617) 442-9010, Ext: 279, ASK FOR: Joe Muresco
ROOM PRICING: (S) $28.00/no air-conditioning, $32.00/air-conditoning, • PAYMENT: Cash Per. Ck Trav. Ck Visa M/C • DATES AVAILABLE: Mid May-Mid-Aug., • BEDS: 2 • FOOD: Caf. SB VM NR • INFO: Linen charge: $20.00/week, children welcome with chaperons. Min. no. req. for conf. 10. • ACTIVITIES: Theaters, game room, tennis, basketball courts, weight room, indoor-outdoor volleyball, TV in public lounge. Museum of Fine Arts; Isabella Garden Museum; Freedom Trail.

370 **Boston/ Medford, MA**   ?

Tufts University (E)   Boston/ Medford
108 Packard Ave., Boston/ Medford, MA 02155, Ph: (617) 627-3856, Fax: (617) 627-3856, ASK FOR: Conference Bureau
ROOM PRICING: (S) $36.00, (D) $40.00, • PAYMENT: Cash Per. Ck Trav. Ck • DATES AVAILABLE: June 1 - Aug. 10, • BED TYPE: S • BEDS: 2 • FOOD: Caf. SB VM NR • INFO: All campus sports facilities. • ACTIVITIES: Boston Freedom Trail; Cape Cod National Sea Shore; Historic Salem; museums.

371 **Paxton, MA**   ?

Anna Maria College (T)
50 Sunset Lane, Paxton, MA 01612, Ph: (508) 849-3341, ASK FOR: Janet Gemborys
ROOM PRICING: (S) $26.00, (D) $52.00, • PAYMENT: Cash Per. Ck • DATES AVAILABLE: June 15 -Aug. 1, • BEDS: 2 • FOOD: Caf. • INFO: Children welcome, TV lounge, coin washers/dryers. • ACTIVITIES: Old Sturbridge Village, Worcester Art and Science Museum, Higgins Historical Armory, Boston - 1 hour drive.

372 **Salem, MA**   ?   ♿

Salem State College (T)
22 Harrison Road, Salem, MA 01970, Ph: (508) 741-6416, ASK FOR: Lee A. Brossoit
ROOM PRICING: (D) $15.00, Apartment: $20.00, • PAYMENT: Cash Per. Ck Trav. Ck • DATES AVAILABLE: June 1-Aug. 15, • ROOM TYPE: SR Apt. • BED TYPE: S • BEDS: 2 • BATH: C P • FOOD: Caf. SB VM NR • INFO: Linen charge: $5.00/week, children welcome. • ACTIVITIES: Art gallery, tennis, hiking, museums, TV in public lounge. House of the Seven Gables; Salem Witches Museum; Peabody Museum; Pickering Wharf.

---

373 Springfield, MA   ?

Springfield College (E)
263 Alden St., Springfield, MA 01109, Ph: (413) 748-5287, Fax: (413) 748-3534,
ASK FOR: Katherine smith, Conf. Coordinator
ROOM PRICING: (S) $30.00 (D) $44.00, • PAYMENT: Cash Per. Ck Trav. Ck
Visa M/C Discover • DATES AVAILABLE: June 1 - Aug.8, • BEDS: 1-2 • FOOD:
Caf. SB NR • INFO: Linen chg. $5.00. No children, free parking, coin
washers/dryers, advance reservation required. • ACTIVITIES: Basketball Hall of
Fame; Tanglewood; Yankee Candle Factory; Volleyball Hall of Fame.

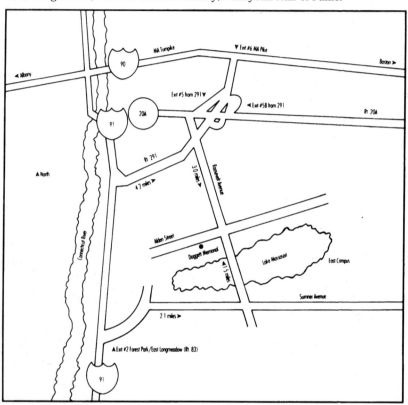

374 Worcester, MA   ?   ♿

Clark University (C)
Housing Office, 950 Main Street, Worcester, MA 01610, Ph: (508) 793-7453, ASK
FOR: Housing & Residential Prog. Office
ROOM PRICING: (S) $16.00-$20.00, (D) $24.00-$32.00, • PAYMENT: Cash Per.
Ck Trav. Ck • DATES AVAILABLE: June 1-Aug.7, • BED TYPE: S • BEDS: 1-2 •
FOOD: SB VM NR • INFO: Linens charge: $4.00 per person/week, children
welcome. Min. required for conf. 25, unless associated with a clark program. •
ACTIVITIES: Worcester Art Museum, Old Sturbridge Village, Higgins Armory
Museum, Spags Shopping Center, racquetball, swimming, TV in public lounge.
Worcester Fashion Outlet Mall.

Michigan

375 Adrian, MI   ?   &

Adrian College (T) Pellowe Hall Conf. Center
110 S. Madison St., Adrian, MI 49221, Ph: (517) 264-3156, ASK FOR: Andrea Wilson, Conf. Dir.
ROOM PRICING: (S) $13.00- $15.00, (D) $22.00- $26.00, Air- conditioned Suites, $34.00- $44.00, • PAYMENT: Cash Per. Ck Trav. Ck • DATES AVAILABLE: Year Round, • ROOM TYPE: SR Suite • BED TYPE: S • BEDS: 2 • BATH: C P • FOOD: Caf. SB VM NR • INFO: Linen charge: $2.00. No alcohol, no smoking, no pets, children welcome(inquire first). TV in public lounge • ACTIVITIES: Racquetball, art gallery, concerts, swimming, game room, tennis.   Irish Hills; Historic Opera House & Theater; Toledo Art Museum; Children's Hands on Museum; Adrian Symphony Orchestra.

376 Albion, MI   &

Albion College (T) Dining & Hospitality Services
611 East Porter, Albion, MI 49224, Ph: (517) 629-0318
ROOM PRICING: (S) $10.00- $32.00, (D) $12.00- $40.00, • PAYMENT: Cash Per. Ck Trav. Ck • DATES AVAILABLE: Summer and some year round, • ROOM TYPE: SR Suite • BEDS: 2 • FOOD: Caf. SB NR • INFO: No alcohol on campus. Campus housing available summer, Bellemont Manor available year round. • ACTIVITIES: Hiking, theater, art gallery. Nearby Jackson Cascades; Space Museum; Kelloggs Cereal tours (25 mi.) at Battle Creek.

377 Allendale, MI   ?   &

Grand Valley State University (T)
Housing Services, 103 Student Services Building, Allendale, MI 49401, Ph: (616) 895-2120, Fax: (616) 895-3790, ASK FOR: Dir. of Conf. Services.
ROOM PRICING: (S) $14.00-$20.00, (D) $17.00-$30.00, • PAYMENT: Cash Per. Ck Trav. Ck Visa M/C Discover Amex • DATES AVAILABLE: May 19 - July 30, • ROOM TYPE: SR Apt. Suite • BED TYPE: S • BEDS: 2 • BATH: C S P • FOOD: Caf. SB VM NR OCR • INFO: Linen charge: $3.00, children welcome w/adult supervision.   Min. no. req. for conf. 2. • ACTIVITIES: Racquetball, swimming, game rm., tennis, TV in public lounge, weight rm., basketball courts, soccer fields. Golf course; Holland Tulip Festival; Grand Rapids Arts Festival; Gerald Ford Museum.

378 Ann Arbor, MI   ?   &

University of Michigan (E) Markley/ Cambridge
541 Thompson, Suite 112, Ann Arbor, MI 48109, Ph: (313) 764-5297, ASK FOR: Housing Divison
ROOM PRICING: (S) $32.00- $62.00, (D) $39.00- $70.00, • PAYMENT: Cash Per. Ck Trav. Ck Visa M/C • DATES AVAILABLE: May 7- Aug.11, • ROOM TYPE: SR • BED TYPE: S • BEDS: 2 • BATH: C • FOOD: Caf. SB VM NR • INFO: Limited A/C, children welcome with supervision, maid service, phones, limited TV. Accomm. primarily for individuals with educ.-related objectives • ACTIVITIES: Museum. U.of M. is a major university with concerts, theater, art galleries, films, all-sports center. Domino Farms; Gerald Ford Library; Gallup Park; close to Greenfield Village; Henry Ford Auto

379 Detroit, MI   &

Wayne State Univ. (E)
5200 Anthony Wayne Dr. NO115, Detroit, MI 48202, Ph: (313) 577-2116, ASK FOR: Ms. Aranki - Marketing
ROOM PRICING: Call for rates, • PAYMENT: Per. Ck Trav. Ck • DATES AVAILABLE: Year Round, • ROOM TYPE: Apt. • BATH: P • FOOD: VM NR OCR • INFO: Children welcome, groups with University affiliation also. • ACTIVITIES: Matthaei Athletic facility; Hilberry and Fisher Theater; Detroit Symphony Orchestra; close to Cultural and Medical Centers. Nearby: Detroit Institute of Arts; African American Museum; Science Center.

---

380 **Grand Rapids, MI**   ⚠

Calvin College (T)
3201 Burton Street S.E., Grand Rapids, MI 49546, Ph: (616) 957-6280, Fax:
616-957-6469, E-mail: stobje@calvin.edu, ASK FOR: Conferences and Campus
Events Office
ROOM PRICING: (S) $18.00, (D) $26.00, • PAYMENT: Cash Per. Ck Trav. Ck •
DATES AVAILABLE: June 1- August 14, • BEDS: 2 • FOOD: Caf. SB VM NR •
INFO: Linenes included, no smoking, no alcohol, children welcome. Min. No. for
Conf. 40. $16.00-$24.00. • ACTIVITIES: Art gallery, swimming, game room,
tennis, hiking, TV in public lounge. Lake Michigan; Gerald Ford Museum.

381 **Grand Rapids, MI**   ?

Grace Bible College (C)
1011 Aldon Street SW, P.O. Box 910, Grand Rapids, MI 49509, Ph: (616)
538-2330, ASK FOR: Jim Molenkamp/ Business Manager
ROOM PRICING: (S) $10.00, (D) $18.00, Min. 20 persons, • PAYMENT: Cash Per.
Ck Trav. Ck Visa M/C Discover • DATES AVAILABLE: May 24-Aug. 12, •
ROOM TYPE: SR • BED TYPE: S • BEDS: 2 • BATH: C • FOOD: VM NR • INFO:
Linens not provided, no smoking, no drinking, children welcome. • ACTIVITIES:
Racquetball, game room, gym. Gerald Ford Museum, Lake Michigan Beaches.
Grand Rapids Arts Festival; West Michigan Whitecaps Baseball.

382 **Hersey, MI**   ⚠

The Adventure Learning Center at Eagle Village (T)
5044 175th Ave., Hersey, MI 49639, Ph: (800) 748-0061, Fax: (616) 832-1468,
ASK FOR: Tamara McLeod
ROOM PRICING: (S) $20.00, (D) $20.00, Child over 10, $10.00
Cabins $10.00-sleeps up to14., • PAYMENT: Cash Per. Ck Trav. Ck • DATES
AVAILABLE: Year round, please call, • FOOD: Caf. NR • INFO: Linen
charage:$2.00 per person, children welcome, no alcohol. • ACTIVITIES:
Swimming; hiking; cross country skiing; snowshoeing; sledding; canoeing; Ferris
State University; extensive snowmobile trail system; borders state forest; 45
minutes to Lake Michigan.

383 **Holland, MI**   ?   ⚠

Hope college (T)
P. O. Box 9000, Holland, MI 49422, Ph: (616) 394-7150, ASK FOR: Barbara
Schipper
ROOM PRICING: (S) $24.00, (D) $28.00, • PAYMENT: Cash Per. Ck Trav. Ck •
DATES AVAILABLE: May 15-Aug.15, • FOOD: Caf. SB VM NR • INFO: Linens
inclued, children welcome, Guest house & Apartments avail. • ACTIVITIES:
Racquetball, swimming, theaters, game room, tennis, TV in public lounge. Lake
Michigan Beaches; Tulip Time Festival; Dutch Heritage Attractions; Shopping;
Outlet Mall.

384 **Kalamazoo, MI**   ?   ⚠

Bernhard Center (T) Western Michigan University
Kalamazoo, MI 49008--3863, Ph: (616) 387-4860, ASK FOR: Asst. Director -
Bern. Ctr.
ROOM PRICING: (S) $18.00 (D) $28.00, • PAYMENT: Cash Per. Ck Trav. Ck •
DATES AVAILABLE: May 15 -Aug. 4, • BED TYPE: S • BEDS: 2 • FOOD: Caf. VM
NR OCR • INFO: Children welcome, youth rates available. • ACTIVITIES: Cultural
center, all sport facilities.Lake Michigan water activities; Nature Center; Air
Museum; Flower, Wine and Harvest Festivals.

385 **Livonia, MI**   ?

Madonna University (T)
14221 Levan, Livonia, MI 48154, Ph: (313) 591-5136, ASK FOR: Residence Hall
Dir.
ROOM PRICING: (S) $20.00, (D) $30.00, • PAYMENT: Cash Trav. Ck Visa M/C
• DATES AVAILABLE: May 8- Aug. 6, • BED TYPE: S • BEDS: 1-2 • BATH: C •
FOOD: NR • INFO: Charge for linens, no smoking, no alcohol, no air conditioning. •
ACTIVITIES: TV in public lounge. Detroit, (Zoo, Museums, Greektown); Ann Arbor,
(Theater, Museums).

(T) = Travelers Accommodations   (E) = Educational Related   (C) = Groups & Conference Use

386 **Marquette, MI**

Northern Michigan University (E) Conference & Guest Housing
Marquette, MI 49855, Ph: (906) 227-2078, E-mail: guest hsg@ NMU.Edu
ROOM PRICING: (S) $20.50, (D) $31.00, • PAYMENT: Cash Per. Ck Trav. Ck
Visa M/C • DATES AVAILABLE: Year Round, • ROOM TYPE: SR • BED TYPE: S
• BEDS: 2-3 • BATH: S P • FOOD: Caf. SB VM NR • INFO: Children welcome, no
pets. • ACTIVITIES: Pictured Rocks National Park; Huron Mtn. Range; Lake
Superior; camping; backpacking; all sports; boating; World's Largest Wooden
Dome; Golf courses; Vegas Style Casinos Nearby.

387 **Marquette, MI**   ?

Northern Michigan University (E) Olympic/Guest Housing
Marquette, MI 49855, Ph: (906) 227-2078, ASK FOR: Conference & Guest housing
ROOM PRICING: (S) $19.75, (D) $29.50, • PAYMENT: Cash Per. Ck Trav. Ck
Visa M/C • DATES AVAILABLE: Year Round, • ROOM TYPE: SR • BED TYPE: S
• BEDS: 2-3 • BATH: S P • FOOD: Caf. SB VM NR • INFO: Children welcome, no
pets. • ACTIVITIES: Pictured Rocks National Park; Huron Mtn. Range; Lake
Superior; camping; backpacking; all sports; boating; World's Largest Wooden
Dome; Golf courses; Vegas Style Casinos Nearby.

388 **Mt. Pleasant, MI**   ♿

Central Michigan University (E)
University Events, 306 Warriner, Mt. Pleasant, MI 48859, Ph: (517) 774-3355,
Fax: (517) 774-7957, ASK FOR: Keith Voeks, Conf. Coordinator
ROOM PRICING: (S) $42.00, (D) $58.00 Groups of 50 or more with one billing, •
PAYMENT: Cash Per. Ck Trav. Ck Visa M/C • DATES AVAILABLE: Mid-May -
Mid August, • BEDS: 4 • FOOD: Caf. SB VM NR • INFO: Children welcome, Linen
charge; $5.00/person. TV in public lounge. • ACTIVITIES: Racquetball, art
gallery, bowling, concerts, swimming, theaters, game room, tennis, hiking,
museums. Golf courses; Casino; 1,000 plus hotel rooms; canoeing; horseback
riding; 60+ restaurants; hockey rink.
DIRECTIONS: just off of US - 27 and M - 20 in the middle of the mitten.

389 **Olivet, MI**   ♿

Olivet College (T) Shipherd Hall, Dole Hall, Blair Hall
Olivet, MI 49076, Ph: (616) 749-7116 or 7197, ASK FOR: Tamyra Walters, Conf.
Dir.
ROOM PRICING: (S) $10.50- $13.75, (D) $16.50- $20.00, • PAYMENT: Cash Per.
Ck • DATES AVAILABLE: June 1- July1, • ROOM TYPE: SR • BED TYPE: S •
BEDS: 1-4 • BATH: C S • FOOD: Caf. SB VM NR • INFO: Linen charge: $6.00,
children welcome, smoking in individually designated rooms only, no smoking in
public buildings. Coin washers/dryers. • ACTIVITIES: Tennis courts, fitness
center, newly remodled swimming pool, T.V. gymnasium facilities, new library,
quiet country atmosphere. Within 25 miles: Lansing; Battle Creek; Historic
Marshall.

390 **Olivet, MI**

Olivet College (T)
Kirk Center, Olivet, MI 49076, Ph: (616) 749-7644, (800) 456-7189
ROOM PRICING: (D) $30.00-$40.00, • PAYMENT: Cash Per. Ck • DATES
AVAILABLE: Call for avail. dates, • FOOD: • INFO: Linens and continental
breakfast included. Small meeting rooms also available. 3 double rooms with
community bath. • ACTIVITIES: Swimming, game room, T.V. gymnasium
facilities, new library, quiet country atmosphere. Within 25 miles:Lansing; Battle
Creek; Historic Marshall.

U
N
I
V

391 **Petoskey, MI**   ♿

North Central Michigan College (T)
1515 Howard, Petoskey, MI 49770, Ph: (616) 348-6611, Fax: (616) 348-6671,
ASK FOR: Bruce Spychalski, Conf./food serv. Dir.
ROOM PRICING: (S) $31.00/person. Groups up to 150 people , • PAYMENT:
Cash Per. Ck Trav. Ck • DATES AVAILABLE: Summer only - May to August, •
ROOM TYPE: SR Apt. • BED TYPE: S • BEDS: 2 • BATH: S • FOOD: Caf. SB VM
NR • INFO: Linens furnished, children welcome. • ACTIVITIES: Tennis, game
room, TV. Golf, fishing; sailing on Lake Michigan; Mackinaw Island; Victorian
homes; fine restaurants.
DIRECTIONS: From US 131, go north. At 1st intersection (Sharon St.) turn
right. Proceed two stop signs, turn right, proceed two blocks, the college is on the
left hand side of the street

392 **Sault Ste Marie, MI**   ?

Lake Superior State Univ. (T)
650 W. Easterday Ave., Sault Ste Marie, MI 49783, Ph: (906) 635-2411, ASK
FOR: Housing Office
ROOM PRICING: Min. stay 1 week, (S) 1 bdr. apt. $200/wk, 2 bdr. apt.
$240/wk, (D) 2 bdr. townhome, (6 beds)$265/wk, • PAYMENT: Cash Visa M/C
• DATES AVAILABLE: June 1- Aug. 1, • ROOM TYPE: Apt. • BEDS: 2 • FOOD:
Caf. VM NR • INFO: Linens included, children welcome, reservations must be
made at least 7 days in advance of stay. Coin washer/dyer. • ACTIVITIES:
Racquetball; tennis; recreation sports center; Sault Ste. Marie Boat Locks; Sault
Ste. Marie, Ontario; Mackinac Island; Tahquamenon Falls.

393 **Traverse City, MI**   ?

Northwestern Michigan College (T)
1701 E. Front, Traverse City, MI 49684, Ph: (616) 922-1408, ASK FOR: East Hall
Desk
ROOM PRICING: (S) $20.00, (D) $30.00, • PAYMENT: Cash Per. Ck Trav. Ck •
DATES AVAILABLE: July 1-Aug. 15, • FOOD: Caf. VM NR • INFO: Children
welcome. • ACTIVITIES: Tennis, TV in public lounge. Interlochen Arts Academy;
Cherry County Playhouse; fishing; golf; national park.

394 **University Center, MI**   ?   ♿

Saginaw Valley State University (E)
7400 Bay Road, University Center, MI 48710-0001, Ph: (517) 790-4255, ASK
FOR: Residential Life
ROOM PRICING: (S) $16.00, (D) $23.00, • PAYMENT: Cash Per. Ck Trav. Ck
Visa M/C Discover Amex • DATES AVAILABLE: May 10 -Aug 15, • ROOM
TYPE: SR Apt. • BED TYPE: S • BEDS: 2 • BATH: S • FOOD: Caf. SB VM NR •
INFO: Children welcome, coin washers/dryers, TV lounge, free parking, linens
included, bunkbeds. • ACTIVITIES: Tennis, hiking, game room, park, art gallery.
Nearby: Saginaw Bay; Frankenmuth Bavarian Village; Japanese Tea House and
Gardens-Saginaw.

Minnesota

395 **Collegeville, MN**   ♿

St. John's University (T) Office of Events and Conferences
Box 2000, Collegeville, MN 56321, Ph: (320) 363-2240, Fax: (320) 363-2658,
E-mail: gdelles@csbsju.edu, Web Site: www.csbsj.edu, ASK FOR: Ginger Delles,
Director
ROOM PRICING: (S) $23.00, (D) $32.50, • PAYMENT: Cash Per. Ck Trav. Ck •
DATES AVAILABLE: June 15 -Aug. 15, • ROOM TYPE: SR • BED TYPE: S •
BEDS: 2 • BATH: C • FOOD: Caf. SB VM NR • INFO: No pets, no RV's, children
welcome. Ideal facilities for meetings, seminars, & workshops, such as
Elderhostels, Etc., Ample housing and meeting spaces for groups up to 1000.
Cafeteria and on site catering. Free parking. • ACTIVITIES: 2,500 acre campus
with lakes and forests,125 year history; Tennis courts; indoor pool; Bookstore; Art
Center; Pottery Shop; Tennis courts, Fitness center, Campus Tours; Benedictine
Monastery; Hill Manuscript Library; Walking Trails; Sinclair Lewis Interp. Center.
DIRECTIONS: Located 80 miles NW of Minneapolis and St. Paul on Interstate 94;
St. Cloud is12 miles east.

(T) = Travelers Accommodations   (E) = Educational Related   (C) = Groups & Conference Use

396 Crookston, MN   ?

Univ. of Minnesota - Crookston (T)
Crookston, MN 56716, Ph: (218) 281-6510, Ext: 351, ASK FOR: Gary Willhite
ROOM PRICING: (S) $14.00, (D) $22.00, • PAYMENT: Cash • DATES AVAILABLE:
June 1-Aug 31, • FOOD: Caf. • INFO: Children welcome, no pets. • ACTIVITIES:
All campus sports facilities, TV in public lounge.

397 Duluth, MN

College of St. Scholastica (T)
1200 Kenwood Ave., Duluth, MN 55811, Ph: (218) 723-6483 or (6084) 723-6483,
Fax: (218) 723-6290, ASK FOR: Housing Director
ROOM PRICING: (S) $28.25, (D) $20.34 - 40.68; includes 13% tax, • PAYMENT:
Cash Only Trav. Ck • DATES AVAILABLE: June 10 -Aug. 10, • ROOM TYPE: SR
Apt. Suite • BED TYPE: S • BEDS: 2-4 • BATH: C P • FOOD: Caf. VM NR •
INFO: Reserv. req., no pets or alcohol, no smoking . • ACTIVITIES: Scenic
Northshore of Lake Superior; 3 museums; heritage and art center; boat tours;
Historic house tours.
DIRECTIONS: 150 miles North of Mpls/St.Paul. follow I 35 N to 21st Ave East
exit. Follow 21st Ave E to Woodland Ave. turn right onto Woodland Ave. Follow
Woodland Ave. to College St. Turn left onto College St. and follow to St. Scholasticia

398 Mankato, MN   ?

Mankato State University (T) Dept. of Residential Life
MSU 30, P.O. Box 8400, Mankato, MN 56002, Ph: (507) 389-1011, ASK FOR:
Dept. of Residential Life
ROOM PRICING: (S) $16.50, (D) $22.00, • PAYMENT: Cash Per. Ck Trav. Ck •
DATES AVAILABLE: June 13-Aug. 18, • BEDS: 2 • FOOD: Caf. VM NR • INFO:
Linens included, no alcohol, no pets. • ACTIVITIES: All campus sports facilities,
Minneopa State Park; area lakes for fishing; Sakata Bike Trail; Blue Earth County
Historical Museum; Minnesota Vikings Training Camp.

399 Marshall, MN   ?

Southwest State University (T)
Marshall, MN 56258, Ph: (507) 537-6136, ASK FOR: Donna Sanders - Housing
ROOM PRICING: (S) $15.00, (D) $20.00, • PAYMENT: Cash Per. Ck Trav. Ck •
DATES AVAILABLE: June 10 -Aug. 15, • FOOD: Caf. SB VM NR • ACTIVITIES:
State parks and lakes; Pipestone Nat'l Monument; sports facilities.

400 Minneapolis, MN   ?

Augsburg College (T)
2211 Riverside Ave., Minneapolis, MN 55454, Ph: (612) 330-1463, ASK FOR: Dan
Taylor, Conf. Coordinator
ROOM PRICING: (S) $15.00-$35.00, (D) $19.00-$45.00, • PAYMENT: Cash Per.
Ck Trav. Ck • DATES AVAILABLE: Year Round, • FOOD: SB VM NR • INFO:
Children welcome. • ACTIVITIES: Beautiful 23 acre campus; 20 min. walk to
downtown Minneapolis; 6 blocks from Mississippi River; 10 min. drive to area
recreational lakes; close to St. Paul; Dome and Mall of America.

401 Moorhead, MN

Concordia College (E)
901 South Eighth Street, Moorhead, MN 56562, Ph: (218) 299-3706, Fax: (218)
299-4409, ASK FOR: Summer Conferences
ROOM PRICING: (S) $14.00, (D) $20.00, • PAYMENT: Cash Trav. Ck • DATES
AVAILABLE: Summer, • ROOM TYPE: SR • BED TYPE: S • BEDS: 1-2 • BATH: C
• FOOD: Caf. SB VM NR • INFO: Linens included, children welcome, no pets, no
RV;s. E-mail: Cadwell@Cord.Edu • ACTIVITIES: TV in public lounge. Heritage
Hjemkomsr Interpretive Center. Close to bike trails.
DIRECTIONS: One and one half miles north of I94 on Mn Hwy 75. Campus is
located at Mn Hwy 75 and 12th Avenue South

U
N
I
V

402 **Saint Cloud, MN**   ?

St. Cloud State University (T)
1st. Ave. South, Saint Cloud, MN 56301, Ph: (612) 255-2166, ASK FOR: Carol Hall, Housing Office
ROOM PRICING: (S) $15.00, (D) $20.00, • PAYMENT: Cash • DATES AVAILABLE: June 1-Aug. 15, • FOOD: • INFO: Linens included, children welcome. • ACTIVITIES: Racquetball, films, bowling, park, game room, tennis, TV in public lounge.

403 **Saint Paul, MN**   &

Concordia University, St. Paul (T)
275 N. Sydicate Ave., Saint Paul, MN 55104, Ph: (651) 641-8201, Fax: (651) 659-0207, ASK FOR: Daniel Taylor
ROOM PRICING: (S) $25.00, (D) $35.00- $40.00, • PAYMENT: Cash Per. Ck Trav. Ck Visa M/C • DATES AVAILABLE: Mid May - Mid August, • ROOM TYPE: SR Suite • BED TYPE: S • BEDS: 2-3 • BATH: C S P • FOOD: Caf. SB VM NR • INFO: Coin washers/dryers, free parking, children welcome, linens included. Advance reservations required • ACTIVITIES: Conveniently located between Minneapolis & St. Paul, close to Mall of America; MN State Capitol; Metrodome; Ordway Theater; MN Zoo.
DIRECTIONS: From Interstate 94, exit on Lexington Ave. 60 South on Lexington one block, turn right on Marshall Ave, Proceed two blocks, turn right on Syndicate Street.

404 **Winona, MN**   ?

Winona State Univ. (T)
8th and Johnson Sts., Winona, MN 55987, Ph: (507) 457-5052, ASK FOR: John Burros, Director of Facilities
ROOM PRICING: Call for rates, • PAYMENT: Cash • DATES AVAILABLE: June 1-Sept 1, • BED TYPE: S • BEDS: 1-2 • FOOD: Caf. • INFO: Children welcome. • ACTIVITIES: Campus sports, game room, bowling, boating, art gallery, park. Nearby: Steamboat Museum, Mississippi River

Mississippi

405 **Columbus, MS**   &

Mississippi University for Women (T)
W Box 1626, Columbus, MS 39703, Ph: (601) 329-7129
ROOM PRICING: (S) $10.00, (D) $16.00, • PAYMENT: Cash • DATES AVAILABLE: Seasonal, call for information, • ROOM TYPE: SR Apt. • BED TYPE: S • BEDS: 2 • BATH: S • FOOD: Caf. SB VM NR • INFO: Children welcome, no pets. Linen charge. • ACTIVITIES: Sports facilities. Nearby: Columbus,historic city sights, antebellum mansions.

406 **Jackson, MS**   ?

Belhaven College (E)
1500 Peachtree St., Jackson, MS 39202, Ph: (601) 968-5904, ASK FOR: Deborah Scott
ROOM PRICING: (S) $15.00- $20.00, (D) $24.00- $30.00, • PAYMENT: Cash Trav. Ck Visa M/C • DATES AVAILABLE: Summer, • ROOM TYPE: SR • BED TYPE: S • BATH: C S P • FOOD: Caf. VM NR • INFO: Children welcome, no alcohol, no smoking in buildings. • ACTIVITIES: Tennis, TV in Public Lounge. Vicksburg National Military Park; MS Museum of Art; Natchez Trace Parkway; Old Capital Museum; MS Museum of Natural Science; Davis Planetarium.

407 **University, MS**   ?

University of Mississippi (T) Miller Hall
University, MS 38677, Ph: (601) 232-7328, ASK FOR: Kathy Tidwell, Assoc. Dir.
ROOM PRICING: (S) $15.00, (D) $20.00, • PAYMENT: Cash • DATES AVAILABLE: May 24 -July 31, • ROOM TYPE: SR • BED TYPE: S • BEDS: 2 • BATH: C • FOOD: Caf. VM • INFO: No linen, children pay as adults • ACTIVITIES: Elvis Presley's birthplace, Sardis Lake, Wm. Faulkner's house, state parks, all campus sports.

Missouri

408 Bolivar, MO   ⅏

Southwest Baptist Univ. (T)
1601 Springfield Rd., Bolivar, MO 65613, Ph: (417) 328-1775, ASK FOR: Ms. R. Watson, Assoc. Dir.
ROOM PRICING: (S) Dorm: $7.75/bed,$15.50/room Lodge:(S) $28.00, (D) $30.00, • PAYMENT: Cash Per. Ck Trav. Ck Visa M/C Discover • DATES AVAILABLE: Summer, • BEDS: 2 • FOOD: Caf. SB • INFO: Linen charge: $5.00, no alcohol, no smoking, no pets, no linen charge for lodge accommodations. • ACTIVITIES: Lake of the Ozarks; Eureka Springs; Jefferson City and Capital, (all nearby); campus sports. Branson

409 Cape Girardeau, MO   ?

Southeast Missouri State University (T)
900 Normal, Cape Girardeau, MO 63701, Ph: (314) 651-2280, ASK FOR: Mary Richards
ROOM PRICING: (S) $24.55, (D) $45.10, (includes 3 meals), • PAYMENT: Cash • DATES AVAILABLE: May 22 -Aug. 6, • FOOD: Caf. SB VM NR • INFO: Linen charge: $6.50 • ACTIVITIES: Trail of Tears Park; Bollinger Mill and covered bridge; Show Me and Recreation Center; St. Louis Iron Mtn. steam train

410 Concordia, MO

Saint Paul's Lutheran High School (T)
205 Main, Box719, Concordia, MO 64020, Ph: (660) 463-2238, ASK FOR: Mrs. Karen Heins, Campus Services
ROOM PRICING: (S) $20.00/first night, $10.00 additional nights., Up to 3 per room, • PAYMENT: Cash • DATES AVAILABLE: Year Round, • ROOM TYPE: SR • BED TYPE: S • BEDS: 3 • BATH: C • FOOD: Caf. NR • INFO: Linen furnished, children welcome, no alcohol, no smoking, free parking, TV lounge. • ACTIVITIES: Tennis, outdoor volleyball. Nearby: Worlds and Oceans of Fun; Arrow Rock; Lake of the Ozarks; Truman Lake; Kansas City Royals and Chiefs; Kansas City Shopping; tennis on campus.
DIRECTIONS: I-70 east of Kansas City at exit 58. Travel south on Main Street, the school is in the middle of the second block on the left. Also visable from I-70 .

411 Fayette, MO   ?

Central Methodist College (E)
411 Central Methodist Square, Fayette, MO 65248, Ph: (816) 248-3392, Ext: 223, ASK FOR: Student Affairs Office
ROOM PRICING: (S) $8.50, $13.00 w/food, (D) $17.00, $26.00 w/food, • PAYMENT: Cash Per. Ck Trav. Ck Visa M/C Discover Amex • DATES AVAILABLE: June, July, Aug., as avialable, remainder of year., • ROOM TYPE: SR • FOOD: Caf. SB VM NR • INFO: Linen Charge: $2.00/day. Children welcome, no alcohol. • ACTIVITIES: Racquetball, art gallery, park, swimming, tennis, museums, TV in public lounge.

412 Fulton, MO   ⅏

Westminster College (T)
501 Westminster Ave., Fulton, MO 65251
, Ph: (573) 642-3361, Fax: (573) 642-2699, E-mail: rueter@micro.wcmo.edu, ASK FOR: Susan Rueter, Dir. of Summer Programs
ROOM PRICING: (S) $18.00, (D) $25.00, Call for specific quotes, • PAYMENT: Cash Per. Ck Trav. Ck Visa M/C Discover Amex • DATES AVAILABLE: MAY 15 - Aug. 1, • BEDS: 1-2 • FOOD: Caf. VM NR • INFO: Children welcome, linens charge: $8.00 per peron. TV lounge. • ACTIVITIES: Racquetball; swimming; game room; tennis; hiking; museums; Winston Churchill Memorial & Library; Berlin Wall Sculpture.

413 **Fulton, MO**   ? ⅃

William Woods College (C)
200 W. 12th St., Fulton, MO 65251, Ph: (314) 642-2251, ASK FOR: Linda Kock,
Bus. Office
ROOM PRICING: (S) $15.00, (D) $15.00, • PAYMENT: Cash Per. Ck Trav. Ck
Visa M/C Discover Amex • DATES AVAILABLE: May 15 - Aug. 15, • FOOD:
Caf. SB VM NR • INFO: Linen charge: $3.00; Children welcome. • ACTIVITIES:
W. Churchill Memorial; Lake of the Ozarks; state parks; many sport facilities.

414 **Kansas City, MO**   ? ⅃

Avila College (E)
11901 Wornall Road, Kansas City, MO 64145, Ph: (816) 942-8400, Ext:
2226/2260, ASK FOR: Jim Branson, Roberta Aguirre
ROOM PRICING: Upon request, • PAYMENT: Cash Per. Ck Trav. Ck Visa M/C
• DATES AVAILABLE: June 1-Aug 15, • ROOM TYPE: SR • BED TYPE: S • BEDS:
2 • BATH: C • FOOD: Caf. SB VM NR • INFO: Children welcome with parents. •
ACTIVITIES: Harry Truman Sports Complex; Worlds of Fun/Oceans of Fun;
Country Club Plaza; Crown Center; Theater; Concerts; Nelson-Atkins Art
Museum; Kansas City Zoo.

415 **Liberty, MO**   ?

William Jewell College (T)
500 College Hill, Liberty, MO 64068, Ph: (816) 781-7700, ASK FOR: Darlene
Atkinson, Assoc. Dir.
ROOM PRICING: (S) $14.00, (D) $28.00, • PAYMENT: Cash Only • DATES
AVAILABLE: May 14- Aug. 13, • ROOM TYPE: SR • BED TYPE: S • BEDS: 2 •
BATH: C S • FOOD: Caf. SB VM • INFO: Linen Charge: $4.75. Children
welcome. • ACTIVITIES: Racquetball, swimming, theaters, tennis. Worlds of
Fun/Oceans of Fun; Harry S. Truman/Library; Woodlands Race Track; Kansas
City royals and Kansas City Chiefs; Crown Center /Plaza; Nelson-Atkins Museum.

416 **Parkville, MO**   ?

Park College (C) Business Manager
8700 N. W. River Park #50, Parkville, MO 64152, Ph: (816) 741-2000, Ext: 382,
ASK FOR: Dr. James Crum, Housing Office
ROOM PRICING: Call for quotes, • PAYMENT: Cash • DATES AVAILABLE:
Summer, • FOOD: Caf. • INFO: Services available and costs will vary according to
negotiations between college and organization. • ACTIVITIES: Within the Kansas
City area, tennis

417 **Saint Louis, MO**   ? ⅃

Fontbonne College (C)
6800 Wydown Blvd., Saint Louis, MO 63105, Ph: (314) 889-1466, ASK FOR:
Facilities Rental
ROOM PRICING: (S) $15.00, (D) $30.00, • PAYMENT: Cash Per. Ck Trav. Ck
Visa M/C • DATES AVAILABLE: June 1- July 31, • BED TYPE: S • FOOD: Caf.
SB VM NR • INFO: Children welcome. • ACTIVITIES: Swimming, concerts. St.
Louis Zoo; City Arch; Bucsh Stadium; many tourist sites; art museum.

418 **Saint Louis, MO**   ? ⅃

Saint Louis University (E)
3630 W. Pine, Saint Louis, MO 63108, Ph: (314) 977-2797, ASK FOR: Conference
Coordinator
ROOM PRICING: (S) $40.00, (D) $50.00, • PAYMENT: Cash Per. Ck Trav. Ck •
DATES AVAILABLE: May 30- July 30, • ROOM TYPE: SR Apt. • BED TYPE: S •
BEDS: 1-2 • BATH: C P • FOOD: Caf. • ACTIVITIES: Fox Theater and
PowellSymmphony. Nearby:Country Club Plaza, Nelson-Atkins Muesum, Worlds of
fun/Oceans of Fun Crown Center, Harry Truman Library, racetrack.

Nebraska

419 Blair, NE

Dana College (T)
Blair, NE 68008, Ph: (402) 426-7250, ASK FOR: Co-ordinator of Conference Services
ROOM PRICING: (S) $23.00, (D) $30.00, • PAYMENT: Cash Only • DATES AVAILABLE: Year Round, • FOOD: Caf. SB VM NR • INFO: Children welcome, no pets, linens included. • ACTIVITIES: All campus sports, TV in public lounge, theater, films. Boys Town; Fort Atkinson; De Soto National Wildlife Refuge; Black Elk - Neihardt Park.

420 Chadron, NE   ?   ♿

Chadron State College (C)
10th & Main St., Chadron, NE 69337, Ph: (308) 432-6380, ASK FOR: Conference Office
ROOM PRICING: (S) $13.00, (D) $20.00, • PAYMENT: Cash Per. Ck Trav. Ck • DATES AVAILABLE: May 9- Aug. 12, • BED TYPE: S • BEDS: 2 • FOOD: Caf. SB VM NR • INFO: Linen charge: $3.00. Children welcome, no alcohol in rooms. • ACTIVITIES: Swimming, tennis. Chadron State Park; the Black Hills; Toadstool Park; Ft. Robinson State Park.

421 Kearney, NE   ?   ♿

Univ. of Nebraska at Kearney (T)
Kearney, NE 68849, Ph: (308) 865-8519, ASK FOR: Sum. Conf. Coordinator
ROOM PRICING: (S) $20.00, (D) $27.00, • PAYMENT: Cash Per. Ck Trav. Ck • DATES AVAILABLE: Year Round, • ROOM TYPE: SR • BED TYPE: S • BEDS: 2 • BATH: C S • FOOD: Caf. SB VM NR • INFO: Children welcome with adult supervision, no alcohol. • ACTIVITIES: Sports facilities, theater. Fort Kearney Museum and Park; Museum of Nebraska Art; Downtown shopping; Pioneer Village.

422 Lincoln, NE   ?

Nebraska Weslegan University (E) Centennial/Plainsman
5000 St. Paul Ave., Lincoln, NE 68504, Ph: (402) 465-2412, ASK FOR: Ann Castner
ROOM PRICING: (S) $12.00-$15.00, (D) $24.00- $30.00, • PAYMENT: Cash Per. Ck • DATES AVAILABLE: June 1-Aug.1, • ROOM TYPE: SR • BED TYPE: S • BEDS: 2 • BATH: C • FOOD: Caf. VM NR • INFO: Linen charge $3.00-$4.00: must be arragned in advance; Children OK with parent • ACTIVITIES: Folsom Zoo, State Capital, University of Nebraska, Omaha, TV in public lounge

423 Lincoln, NE   ?   ♿

Union College (T)
3800 South 48th Street, Lincoln, NE 68506, Ph: (402) 486-2533, call 9:30 a.m.-12:00 noon, ASK FOR: Ron Dodds
ROOM PRICING: (S) $13.00-$20.00, (D) $15.00-$22.00, • PAYMENT: Cash Per. Ck Trav. Ck • DATES AVAILABLE: Year Round, • FOOD: Caf. SB NR • INFO: Conventions welcome. • ACTIVITIES: Swimming, tennis, boating, park, golf. Nebraska State Capitol; Strategic Air Command; Boys Town (Omaha); University of Nebraska State Museum (Lincoln).

424 Lincoln, NE   ?   ♿

University of Nebraska - Lincoln (T)
1100 Seaton Hall, Lincoln, NE 68588-0622, Ph: (402) 472-3561, ASK FOR: Asst. Dir. of Housing
ROOM PRICING: (S) $16.75, (D) $23.00, • PAYMENT: Cash Per. Ck Trav. Ck Visa M/C Discover • DATES AVAILABLE: May 9 -Aug. 14, • ROOM TYPE: SR • BED TYPE: S • BEDS: 2-3 • BATH: C • FOOD: Caf. SB VM NR • INFO: No alcohol on campus, children welcome, linens included. Discount prices avail. for conferences. Conference planning staff available to assist. • ACTIVITIES: Full range of sports, art gallery, museum, bike trails, swimming pool. Children's Zoo; Holmes Park (rental boats); State Capitol bldg.; Close proximity to downtown Lincoln attractions & entertainment.

U
N
I
V

(T) = Travelers Accommodations   (E) = Educational Related   (C) = Groups & Conference Use

425 **Omaha, NE**   ?

College of St. Mary (T)
1901 South 72nd Street, Omaha, NE 68124, Ph: (402) 399-2674, ASK FOR: Mary E. Korbe
ROOM PRICING: (S) $15.00, (D) $30.00, • PAYMENT: Cash Trav. Ck • DATES AVAILABLE: June 1- Aug. 1, • ROOM TYPE: SR • BED TYPE: S • BEDS: 1-2 • BATH: C • FOOD: Caf. VM NR • INFO: Children welcome, no alcohol. • ACTIVITIES: Swimming, museums, TV in public lounge. Boys Town; Shakespeare on The Green, outdoor theater late June to early July; Western Heritage Museum; Royals Baseball; Shopping; Joselyn Museum.

426 **Peru, NE**

Peru State College (C)
Peru, NE 68421, Ph: (402) 872-2246, ASK FOR: Paula Czirr, Assis. Dir. Res. Life
ROOM PRICING: (S) $8.00, (D) $16.00, • PAYMENT: Cash Per. Ck Trav. Ck Visa M/C • DATES AVAILABLE: Summer only, • ROOM TYPE: SR Suite • BED TYPE: S • BEDS: 2 • BATH: C S P • FOOD: Caf. SB VM NR • INFO: Children welcome with supervision. • ACTIVITIES: Sports facilities, films, indoor pool. Lewis and Clark Museum; Boatride - dinner cruise; Indian Cave State Park.

Nevada

427 Incline Village, NV   ?

Sierra Nevada College (T) Campbell Freidman Hall
P.O. Box 4269, Incline Village, NV 89450, Ph: (702) 831-4269, ext. 1614, Fax:
(702) 832-6104, ASK FOR: Erika Nelson
ROOM PRICING: $60.00, • PAYMENT: Cash Per. Ck Trav. Ck Visa M/C •
DATES AVAILABLE: Mid-June - Mid August, • BEDS: 2 • FOOD: Caf. VM NR •
INFO: One time Linen charge, TV lounge, coin washers/dryers, free parking. •
ACTIVITIES: Game room, hiking. Lake Tahoe; Ponerosa Ranch; Championship
Golf Course; Virginia City.

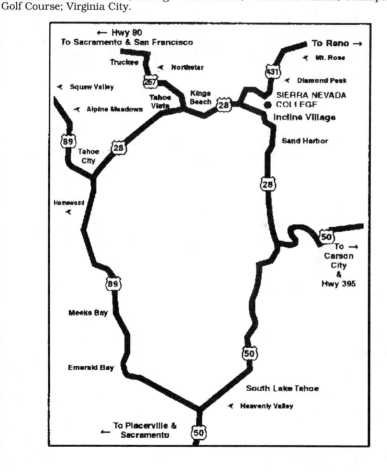

U
N
I
V

428 Las Vegas, NV   ♻

University of Nevada (C) Conference Housing
4505 Maryland Pkwy
Box 452013, Las Vegas, NV 89119, Ph: (702) 895-4211, Fax: (702) 895-4332,
ASK FOR: Residential Life
ROOM PRICING: Varies, based on services requested, • PAYMENT: Cash Per. Ck
Trav. Ck Visa M/C Discover Amex • DATES AVAILABLE: May 23-Aug. 7, •
BEDS: 2 • FOOD: Caf. SB VM NR • INFO: Summer intern housing available also.
Coin operated Washer/Dryer; TV lounges; Volleyball/Basketball courts; computer
connections in room; cable TV.; phone in room; AC in all buildings. • ACTIVITIES:
Campus sports. Mt. Charleston; Lake Mead houseboating and fishing; Hoover
Dam; Las Vegas Strip casinos. Campus Museum-Natural History; desert gardens
- on Campus gym facilities available.

New Hamphsire

429 Center Harbor, NH   ? ♻

Geneva Point Center (T)
HCR 62, Box 469, Center Harbor, NH 03226, Ph: (603) 253-4366, Fax: (603)
253-4883, E-mail: geneva@genevapoint.org, ASK FOR: Tom MacKay
ROOM PRICING: (S&D) $40.00-$70.00, child $20.00. Includes meals., •
PAYMENT: • DATES AVAILABLE: Mid-May-Late Oct., • BEDS: 1-4 • FOOD: Caf.
INFO: Small cabins and lodge rooms. (Conference center-5-300) Linen charge:
$5.00P/P, children welcome, free parking, coin washers/dryers. • ACTIVITIES:
Swimming, tennis, boating, hiking, concerts, bike trails. Nearby: White Mountains;
lakes; tourist sights.
DIRECTIONS: Exit 23 off Interstate 93. East on 104 to Meredith. 25 East to
Mattonboro Neck Road, turn right and follow signs.

---

430 **Rindge, NH**

Franklin Pierce College (E)
College Road, Rindge, NH 03461, Ph: (603) 899-4147, Fax: (603) 899-6448,
E-mail: stella@FPC.edu, ASK FOR: Stella Van Renesse-Walling
ROOM PRICING: (S) $45.00 (D) $90.00, • PAYMENT: Cash Trav. Ck Visa M/C
• DATES AVAILABLE: Mid-May - Mid-August, • BEDS: 2-4 • FOOD: Caf. SB VM
NR • INFO: Linens included, children welcome, free parking, TV lounge, coin
washers/dryers. • ACTIVITIES: Art gallery, park, swimming, boating, theaters,
game room, tennis, hiking, bike trails, fitness center. Numerous art festivals,
including theater and music. Nearby: Skiing, Ingalls Memorial Library,
Peterborough(Our Town)
DIRECTIONS: •From New York City: I-95 N, to I-91 N, to RT10 N (exit 28), to
RT119 E, to the college. •From the east and south of the Mass Pike: Route 2 W,
to 140 N, to RT12 W, to 202 N, to 119 W, to the College. •From Maine and the
Seacoast: I-95, to R101 W, to RT 202 S. to 119 W, to the college. •From New
York/Vermont: Take I-91, exit at Brattleboro, VT (exit 3) and come by way of
Routes 9 E, 12 S, and 119 E to the College. (There is a Franklin Pierce College
campus in Keene with a sign on Route 9 -do not turn off Route 9 until you come to
RT12 South.

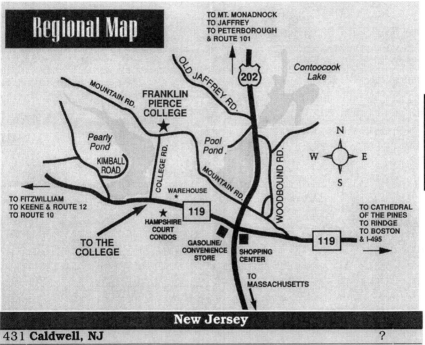

431 **Caldwell, NJ**

Caldwell College (T)
Ryerson Ave., Caldwell, NJ 07006, Ph: (201) 228-4424, Ext: 266, ASK FOR: Mimi
Streleck, Housing
ROOM PRICING: (S) $25.00, $35.00/includes meals, • PAYMENT: Cash • DATES
AVAILABLE: June1- Aug.15, • BEDS: 1-2 • FOOD: Caf. • INFO: Linens included. •
ACTIVITIES: Manhattan, Newark, Jersey City, Trenton

432 **Hoboken, NJ**   ? ♿

Stevens Institute of Tech. (T)
Castle Point on the Hudson, Hoboken, NJ 07030, Ph: (201) 216-5126, ASK FOR:
Ms.Phillips, Dir. Student Housing
ROOM PRICING: (S) $40.00, $155.00/weekly rate, (D) $52.00, $254.00/weekly
rate, • PAYMENT: Cash Per. Ck Trav. Ck • DATES AVAILABLE: June 1-Aug. 8,
• FOOD: SB NR • INFO: All rooms have private bath. Suites with kitchens
avialable, $52.00 single; $64.00 double. • ACTIVITIES: New York City; United
Nations; Rockefeller Center; All attractions of Manhattan; Easy access to bus and
trains.

433 **Newark, NJ**   ? ♿

New Jersey Institute of Technology (T)
180 Bleeker St., Univ. Heights, Newark, NJ 07102, Ph: (201) 596-3039, ASK FOR:
Assis. Director, Residence Life
ROOM PRICING: (S) $40.00, (D) $30.00/per person, (Weekly Rates on request), •
PAYMENT: Cash Per. Ck Trav. Ck Visa M/C • DATES AVAILABLE: June 1
-Aug. 20, • BED TYPE: S • BEDS: 2 • FOOD: Caf. VM NR • INFO: Children
welcome. • ACTIVITIES: All of the cultural; sports; religious; recreational
attractions of New York City , 20 mins. by train.

434 **Newark, NJ**   ? ♿

Rutgers Univ., Newark Campus (T)
350 Dr. M.L. King Blvd., Rm. 203, University Heights, Newark, NJ 07102, Ph:
(201) 648-1037, ASK FOR: Laura Valente, Housing Serv.
ROOM PRICING: (S) $30.00, (D) $40.00, • PAYMENT: Cash • DATES AVAILABLE:
June 1 -Aug. 15, • BED TYPE: S • BEDS: 2 • FOOD: VM NR • INFO: Linens
included, no pets. Preference given to educational/cultural gropus • ACTIVITIES:
Minutes from New York City, Symphony Hall of Newark, International Airport,
Newark Muesum, campus athletic facilities

435 **Trenton, NJ**   ?

Trenton State College (E)
Pennington Rd., Trenton, NJ 08650, Ph: (609) 771-2264, ASK FOR: Kevin
Hourihan - Guest Services
ROOM PRICING: (S) $23.00-$33.00, (D) $40.00-$52.00, • PAYMENT: Cash •
DATES AVAILABLE: June 1-Aug 15, • ROOM TYPE: SR • FOOD: Caf. •
ACTIVITIES: City of Princeton, University town. Nearby: Trenton, Philadelphia,
New Hope, Pesslers Village; sports facilities of campus.

436 **West Long Branch, NJ**   ? ♿

Monmouth College (E)
400 Cedar Ave., West Long Branch, NJ 07764, Ph: (732) 571-3473, Fax: (732)
263-5284, ASK FOR: Conference & Program Services
ROOM PRICING: (S) $22.00 (D) $38.00, • PAYMENT: Cash Per. Ck • DATES
AVAILABLE: Summer, • BEDS: 1-2 • FOOD: Caf. SB VM NR • INFO: Children
welcome, TV lounge, coin washers/dryers, charge for linens. Free parking. •
ACTIVITIES: Art gallery, concerts, swimming, theaters, game room, tennis, fitness
center, beaches, golf courses, fishing, boating, Monmouth Park & Freehold
Racetracks; Shopping malls; PNC Art Center; Sandy Hook; SevenPresidents
Oceanfront Park; Great Adventure Theme Park; Atlantic City.

New Mexico

437 Albuquerque, NM   ♿

The University of New Mexico (C)
201 La Posada Hall, Albuquerque, NM 87131, Ph: (505) 277-5896, ASK FOR:
Conference Supervisor
ROOM PRICING: (S) $16.00, (D) $25.00, • PAYMENT: Cash Per. Ck Trav. Ck •
DATES AVAILABLE: May 21 - Aug. 6, • BEDS: 1-2 • FOOD: Caf. SB VM NR •
INFO: No pets, no alcohol,linens included, convenience store, laundromat. •
ACTIVITIES: Films, art gallery, swimming, tennis, game room, museums, TV in
public lounge. Sandia Tramway; NM Museum of Nat. History; Old Town Hist.
Dist.; Taos Ski Valley; Bandelier Nat. Monument; Rio Grande Zoo; Nat. Atomic
Museum.
DIRECTIONS: I-25 to Lomas Blvd.Then East, across the street from University
Hospital , turn right onto campus.

438 Las Vegas, NM   ?   ♿

New Mexico Highlands Univ. (T)
National Ave., Las Vegas, NM 87701, Ph: (505) 454-3197, ASK FOR: Office of
Housing & Res. Life
ROOM PRICING: (S) $12.00 (D) $24.00, • PAYMENT: Cash • DATES AVAILABLE:
June 1 - Aug. 1, • FOOD: NR • INFO: Bring own linens. • ACTIVITIES: Ft. Union
National Monument; Pecos National Monument; Santa Fe Trail; Santa Fe; Sangre
de Cristo Mountains.
DIRECTIONS: Las Vegas, New Mexico is off I-25 about 1 hour east of Santa Fe,
New Mexico.

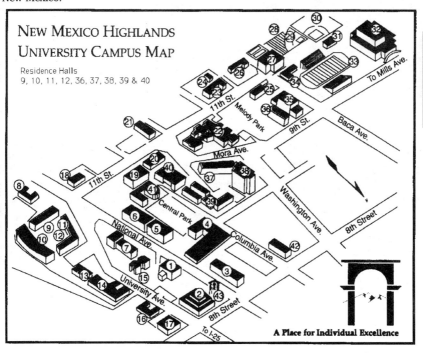

NEW MEXICO HIGHLANDS
UNIVERSITY CAMPUS MAP

Residence Halls
9, 10, 11, 12, 36, 37, 38, 39 & 40

A Place for Individual Excellence

U
N
I
V

---

439 Portales, NM   ♿

Eastern New Mexico Univ. (C) Sta. 39, Campus Union
Portales, NM 88130, Ph: (505) 562-2632, ASK FOR: Stephanie McClary, Housing Co-ordinator
ROOM PRICING: (S) $12.50, (D) $19.00, All buildings air conditioned, • PAYMENT: Cash Per. Ck Trav. Ck • DATES AVAILABLE: May 20 -Aug.1, • ROOM TYPE: SR • BED TYPE: S • BEDS: 2 • BATH: C • FOOD: Caf. SB VM NR • INFO: Children welcome with supervision, no alcohol, additional charge for linens. • ACTIVITIES: Sports, swimming. Carlsbad Caverns;Palo Duro Canyon; Billy The Kid historic area; Blace Water Draw Museum.

440 Santa Fe, NM   ? ♿

College of Santa Fe (C)
1600 St. Michael's Dr., Santa Fe, NM 87501, Ph: (505) 473-6270, Fax: (505) 473-6286, ASK FOR: Conf. & Special Events
ROOM PRICING: (S) $18.00-$20.00, (D) $36.00-$40.00, • PAYMENT: Cash Per. Ck Trav. Ck Visa M/C Discover • DATES AVAILABLE: June 1 -Aug. 12, Groups of 35 or more only, Aug. 12 - May 30.• BEDS: 1-2 • FOOD: Caf. SB VM NR • INFO: Can accept smaller groups during fall, winter & spring. Linens included. Reservations required. Coin washers/dryers, free parking. • ACTIVITIES: Lakes, mtns., camping, swimming. Historic downtown Santa Fe; 8 northern N.M. Indian pueblos in vacinity; Pecos and Bandelier Nat'l Monuments. Santa Fe Opera, July & Aug.; Theater year round.

441 Silver City, NM   ? ♿

Western New Mexico Univ. (T)
Silver City, NM 88061, Ph: (505) 538-6629, ASK FOR: Housing Office
ROOM PRICING: (S) $15.00, (D) $20.00, • PAYMENT: Cash Trav. Ck Visa M/C • DATES AVAILABLE: June 1-Aug 10, • FOOD: SB VM NR • ACTIVITIES: Swimming, tennis, game room, park. Gila National Forest; Gila Cliff Dwellings.

442 Socorro, NM   ?

New Mexico Institute of (C) Mining and Technology
Campus Station Sub 101F, Socorro, NM 87801, Ph: (505) 835-5900, Fax: (505) 835-5907, E-mail: aortiz@admin.nmt.edu, ASK FOR: Anthony Ortiz, Housing coordinator
ROOM PRICING: (S) $16.50, (D) $27.00, Linenes $3.00 per person., • PAYMENT: Cash • DATES AVAILABLE: June 9 - Aug. 4, • BEDS: 2 • FOOD: Caf. • INFO: Children welcome, accommodations depends on availability of space, Conference facilities available. • ACTIVITIES: Two gymnasiums, racquetball & squash courts, weight training equipment, year round swim. pool, gameroom, athletic fields. Champ. 18-hole golf course; Mineral mueseum; Bosque del Apache National wildlife refuge; Indian ruins; Ghost town.

New York

443 Albany, NY   ? ♿

College of Saint Rose (T)
432 Western Ave., Albany, NY 12207, Ph: (518) 454-5171, Fax: (518) 454-5118, ASK FOR: Renee Besanson, Conf. Coordinator
ROOM PRICING: (S) $35.00, (D) $50.00, • PAYMENT: Cash Per. Ck Trav. Ck Visa M/C Discover Amex • DATES AVAILABLE: May 15 -Aug. 15, • FOOD: Caf. SB VM NR • INFO: Children welcome, coin washers/dryers, free parking. • ACTIVITIES: State Capital, located on Hudson River, one of oldest cities in US; race tracks; Performing Arts Center; theater; Summer Festival events.

444 Albany, NY   ? ♿

University of Albany (E) State Quad
1400 Washington Ave., Albany, NY 12222, Ph: (518) 442-5875, ASK FOR: Summer Conf. Housing
ROOM PRICING: (S) $35.00, (D) $44.00, • PAYMENT: Cash Per. Ck Trav. Ck • DATES AVAILABLE: June 5-Aug. 5, • ROOM TYPE: SR Apt. • BED TYPE: S • BEDS: 2 • BATH: S P • FOOD: Caf. SB VM NR • INFO: Linens included, children welcome w/adult supervision. Suites also available • ACTIVITIES: Art gallery, swimming, tennis. State Capitol; Saratoga Race Track; New York City.

445 Alfred, NY ? ♿

Alfred University Saxon Inn (T) One Park Street
Saxon Drive, Alfred, NY 14802, Ph: (607) 871-2600, ASK FOR: Dawn Schirmer
ROOM PRICING: (S) $85.00, (D) $95.00, • PAYMENT: Cash Per. Ck Trav. Ck
Visa M/C Discover Amex • DATES AVAILABLE: Year round, except
Thanksgiving & Christmas holidays., • ROOM TYPE: SR • BED TYPE: S • BEDS: 2
• BATH: P • FOOD: Caf. SB VM NR • INFO: Linens included. Children welcome,
discounts available. Min. no. required for conf. 25. Conf. prices, $40- $60. •
ACTIVITIES: Racquetball, films, art gallery, concerts, swimming, game room,
tennis, museums, TV in public lounge. Swaim Ski Center; Fingerlake Wineries;
Corning Glass Center; Rockwell Museum.

446 Aurora, NY

Wells College (C)
Rt. 90, Main St., Aurora, NY 13026, Ph: (315) 364-3399, ASK FOR: Terry
Martinez, Conf. Services
ROOM PRICING: (S) $32.50, (D) $50.00, • PAYMENT: Cash Per. Ck Trav. Ck •
DATES AVAILABLE: Year Round, • ROOM TYPE: SR Apt. • BED TYPE: S • BEDS:
1-3 • BATH: C • FOOD: Caf. SB VM NR • INFO: Children welcome. Coin
washer/ dryer, free parking. TV lounge, linens included. • ACTIVITIES: Hiking,
golf course on campus, indoor/outdoor tennis, indoor pool, library, gym, winery
tours. Women's Hall of Fame; state wildlife and nature preserve; seasonal lake
swimming.

447 Blaulvet, Ny 10913, NY ♿

Dominican College (T) Hertel Hall
1 Campus Drive, Blaulvet, Ny 10913, NY 10983, Ph: (914) 359-9559 , Fax:
www.dc.edu, ASK FOR: Paul Irish, Dir.Res. Life(914) 359-7800 ext. 305
ROOM PRICING: Conferences and groups. Call for rates, • PAYMENT: Cash Per.
Ck Visa M/C • DATES AVAILABLE: June 1-Aug. 1, • ROOM TYPE: SR Suite •
BED TYPE: S • BEDS: 1-2 • BATH: C P • FOOD: Caf. VM NR • INFO: Linen
charge depends on size of group, Children welcome, no pets. Kitchenette, large
dining room. • ACTIVITIES: Laundry, computer room, TV in public lounge.
Beautiful grounds; Chapel, public transportation to New York City . Historic
Village; Bear Mountain; 15 miles outside NY City; Hudson Park.

448 Brockport, NY ♿

S. U. N. Y. Brockport (T) Conference Co-ordinator
Residence Drive, Brockport, NY 14420, Ph: (716) 395-2285, Fax: (716) 395-2336,
E-mail: Mgardner@brockvma.cc.brockport.edu., Web Site: www.Brockport.edu,
ASK FOR: Mark Gardner
ROOM PRICING: (S) $25.00, (D) $39.00, Suites, $50.00-$70.00, • PAYMENT:
Cash Per. Ck Trav. Ck Visa M/C Discover • DATES AVAILABLE: Year Round,
• ROOM TYPE: SR Suite • BEDS: 2 • BATH: C P • FOOD: Caf. SB VM NR •
INFO: Children Welcome. Handicapped accommdations, $50.00. Coin
washers/dryers, TV lounge. Meeting rooms, fax, copier, audio visual. •
ACTIVITIES: Sports facilities, theater, films. Nearby: Niagara Falls; Rochester
Museum; Art Gallery; Upstate Attractions; Eastman House.

449 Bronxville, NY ?

Concordia College (T) Rippe and Romoser Hall
171 White Plains Road, Bronxville, NY 10708, Ph: (914) 337-9300, Ext: 2128, ASK
FOR: Doris Peko
ROOM PRICING: (S) $30.00, (D) $40.00, • PAYMENT: Cash Per. Ck Trav. Ck •
DATES AVAILABLE: May 20 - Aug.14, • ROOM TYPE: SR • BED TYPE: S • BEDS:
2 • BATH: C • FOOD: Caf. NR • INFO: No linen Charge, No smoking, No alcohol,
Chidren welcome (no cribs). Video conferencing room. Catering available. •
ACTIVITIES: Racquetball, Game room, Tennis, TV in public Lounge. All
attractions of N.Y. City; (30 min. by train) Lower Hudson Valley-West Point; (1
hour by car)

U
N
I
V

450 **Brooklyn, NY**   ♿

Long Island University (T) Conolly Heights Towers
1 University Plaza, Brooklyn, NY 11201, Ph: (718) 488-1046, Fax: (718) 718-488-1548, ASK FOR: Thomas R. Iseley, Director
ROOM PRICING: (S) $35.00, (D) $60.00 , Double apartments, $45.00 per person., • PAYMENT: Cash Trav. Ck • DATES AVAILABLE: June 15-Aug.15, • ROOM TYPE: SR Apt. Suite • BED TYPE: S • BEDS: 1-2 • BATH: C S P • FOOD: Caf. SB VM NR • INFO: Cable TV in Lounge& rooms, low cost laundry facilities, fr telephones available, disc. parking, computer lab,ceiling fan, chlidren allowed. Reg. Rooms, Suites, Apartments available. • ACTIVITIES: Brooklyn Academy of Music; Brooklyn Museum; South Street Seaport; Fulton Shopping Mall- Metrotech Plaza.

451 **Brooklyn, NY**   ♿

Pratt Institute (T)
200 Willoughby Ave., Brooklyn, NY 11205, Ph: (718) 399-5400, Fax: (718) 399-5511, ASK FOR: Christopher Kasik
ROOM PRICING: (S) $28.50, $200 per week, (D) $43.00, $300 per week, • PAYMENT: Cash Trav. Ck • DATES AVAILABLE: June15- Aug.15, • ROOM TYPE: SR • BED TYPE: S • BEDS: 2 • BATH: S • FOOD: Caf. VM NR • INFO: Linens $10.00 per week per person, no pets, children welcome. • ACTIVITIES: Game room, TV in public lounge. Track & weight room, laundry facilities need to be arranged in advance. NY City; Brooklyn Museum; Brooklyn Botanical Gardens; Brooklyn Acad. of Music.

452 **Buffalo, NY**   ?   ♿

Buffalo State College (C)
1300 Elmwood Ave., Buffalo, NY 14222, Ph: (716) 878-6806, ASK FOR: Kristine Nieudorf
ROOM PRICING: (S) $19.00, (D) $38.00, • PAYMENT: Cash Per. Ck • DATES AVAILABLE: All summer, • BEDS: 2 • FOOD: Caf. VM NR • INFO: Children welcome with supervision. • ACTIVITIES: Tennis, swimming, parks. Niagara Falls; Lake Erie; nearby Canadian border and Fort Erie; Darien Lake.

453 **Buffalo, NY**   ?

Canisus College (T)
2001 Main St., Buffalo, NY 14208, Ph: (716) 888-2220, ASK FOR: Kathryn Philliben
ROOM PRICING: (S) $28.00, (D) $40.00, • PAYMENT: Cash • DATES AVAILABLE: June 15-July 15, • FOOD: Caf. • ACTIVITIES: Niagara Falls; Darien Lake Cultural activities in Buffalo.

454 **Farmingdale, NY**   ♿

State Univ. NY Farmingdale (E) Sinclair Hall
Farmingdale, NY 11735, Ph: (516) 420-2010, ASK FOR: Carol Balewski
ROOM PRICING: (D) $25.00, • PAYMENT: Cash Per. Ck Trav. Ck Visa M/C • DATES AVAILABLE: Year Round, • BEDS: 1-2 • FOOD: Caf. SB VM NR • INFO: No alcohol. Group rates available.Year round accomodations. • ACTIVITIES: Robert Moses State Park; Jones Beach State Park; Fire Island Seashore; all attractions of New York City.

455 **Fredonia, NY**   ♿

State Univ. of NY College at Fredonia (E) The Faculty Student Assoc.
Fredonia, NY 14063, Ph: (716) 673-3417, Ext:271, Fax: (716) 673-3339, E-mail: notaro@ait.fredonia.edu, ASK FOR: Paula Szmania, Marketing Manager
ROOM PRICING: Call for quotes, • PAYMENT: • DATES AVAILABLE: Call for dates, • BEDS: 2 • FOOD: Caf. SB VM NR • INFO: TV lounge • ACTIVITIES: Art gallery; game room; tennis; within three miles of Lake Erie; several public golf courses.

---

456 Garden City, NY   ?

Adelphi University (E)
South Ave., Garden City, NY 11530
, Ph: (516) 877-3455, ASK FOR: Amy Harrison, Conf. Coordinator
ROOM PRICING: (S) $18.00-$22.00, (D) $34.00-$40.00, • PAYMENT: Cash Per.
Ck • DATES AVAILABLE: June 15-Aug. 15, • FOOD: Caf. VM NR • INFO: Linen
charge: $1.75/day, no children. • ACTIVITIES: Films, art gallery, concerts,
swimming, theaters, game room, tennis, TV in public lounge. Manhattan: 20 min.
by car, 40 min. by train.

457 Greenvale, NY   ?   &

Long Island University (C) C.W. Post Campus
Greenvale, NY 11548, Ph: (516) 299-2350 or (516) 299-2326, ASK FOR: Ms.
Weiss, Resident Life Office
ROOM PRICING: (S) $31.00, (D) $50.00, • PAYMENT: Cash Per. Ck Trav. Ck •
DATES AVAILABLE: June 1- Aug. 5, • ROOM TYPE: SR • BED TYPE: S • BEDS: 2
• BATH: C S • FOOD: Caf. SB VM NR • INFO: Children welcome, no pets. •
ACTIVITIES: Tennis, swimming, films, concerts. Nearby: New York City;
Sagamore Hill; Old Westbury Gardens; North Shore beaches.

458 Hempstead, NY *FT-13*   ?   &

Hofstra University (T) Student Center, Room 111
Hempstead, NY 11549, Ph: (516) 463-5067, ASK FOR: Andrea Kassel
ROOM PRICING: (S) $25.00, (D) $25.00, • PAYMENT: Cash Trav. Ck • DATES
AVAILABLE: June - Mid-August, • ROOM TYPE: SR Suite • BED TYPE: S • BEDS:
1-2 • BATH: C S • FOOD: Caf. SB VM NR OCR • INFO: Children welcome with
adults, suites available, all air conditioned, linens provided, free parking, coin
washers/dryer. Free bus transportation to & from Hempstead railroad station 24
hours day, 7 days/week. • ACTIVITIES: Parks, sports, theater. New York City, 23
miles; Jones Beach; Westbury Gardens; Westbury Music Fair; Nassau Coliseum.
Roosevelt Field Shopping Center; Mineola and Hempstead Railroad Stations.
DIRECTIONS: Northern State Parkway, Southern State Parkway, or Long Island
Expressway to Meadowbrook Parkway. Exit at Exit M4. Hofstra is 1/4 miles
down Hempstead Turnpike from Meadowbrook Parkway.

459 Keuka Park, NY   ?   &

Keuka College (C)
Keuka Park, NY 14478, Ph: (315) 536-5276, Fax: (315) 536-5216, ASK FOR:
Beth Knaak, Conf. Services
ROOM PRICING: (S) $16.00, (D) $21.00, $5.00 ea. addit. person, • PAYMENT:
Cash Per. Ck Trav. Ck Visa M/C Discover Amex • DATES AVAILABLE:
Various, Call for Dates• ROOM TYPE: SR • BED TYPE: S • BEDS: 2 • BATH: C •
FOOD: Caf. SB VM NR • INFO: Linen Charge: $4.25per person, children welcome.
• ACTIVITIES: Swimming, game room, tennis, TV in public lounge. Several Finger
Lakes Wineries; Scenic Driving Routes; State Parks; Boat Tours.

460 Morrisville, NY *EB-12*   &

S.U.N.Y, Morrisville (T) Conference/catering
P.O. Box 901, Morrisville, NY 13408, Ph: (315) 684-6076, ASK FOR: Diana S.
Johnson
ROOM PRICING: (S) $20.00, (D) $40.00, • PAYMENT: Cash Per. Ck Trav. Ck
Visa • DATES AVAILABLE: May 25 - Aug. 15, • ROOM TYPE: SR • BED TYPE: S
• BEDS: 2 • BATH: C • FOOD: Caf. SB VM NR • INFO: Limited availability
August through May. Children welcome, if supervised, groups up to 1500 people,
numerous classrooms & recreation facilities. • ACTIVITIES: All campus sports
facilities, pool, Ice plex, fitness center, recreation bldg., Chittenango Falls, Earlville
Opera House, Erie Canal State Park. Nearby: Baseball Hall of Fame; Fort
Stanwyck; Farmers Museum; Burnet Park Zoo; located in the heart of historic
Central New York.
DIRECTIONS: SUNY Morrisville is located on Route 20, approximately 35 miles
Southwest of Utica and or 20 minutes South East of Thruway East exit 34.

**U
N
I
V**

(T) = Travelers Accommodations   (E) = Educational Related   (C) = Groups & Conference Use

461 **New York, NY**

Amsterdam Inn (T) Student Hotel
340 Amsterdam Ave.@76th Street, New York, NY 1023, Ph: 212-579-7500, Fax: 212-579-6127, E-mail: INFO@AmsterdamInn.com, ASK FOR: Reservation Dep't
ROOM PRICING: Single $65.00,Double $95.00; rates vary by season., • PAYMENT: Cash Trav. Ck • DATES AVAILABLE: Year round, • FOOD: NR • INFO: Linens, towels included. No children allowed • ACTIVITIES: Central Park, Lincoln Center, Museum of Nat'l History, Beacon Theatre,minutes from 42nd St. Theaters, steps from restaurants

462 **New York, NY**

International House (E)
500 Riverside Dr., New York, NY 10027, Ph: (212) 316-8473, Fax: (212) 316-7182or (212)316-7182, ASK FOR: Contact: Phyliss Burnett
ROOM PRICING: (S) $40.00 & Up (summer only), Guest room or Suites, $100.00 and up year round., • PAYMENT: Cash Visa M/C • DATES AVAILABLE: Year Round, • ROOM TYPE: SR Suite • BED TYPE: S • BEDS: 1-3 • BATH: C P • FOOD: Caf. VM NR • INFO: Most rooms are single occupancy, usually no children, residents under 21 not permtted in the pub., laundry, TV room, AC. Daily telephone service and housekeeping available. • ACTIVITIES: Close proximity to Columbia University, theater sports events, tennis courts, lectures, Riverside Church and Grant's Tomb a 5- minute walk away, all of the myraid attractions of New York City easily reached by subway.

463 **New York, NY**

Murray Hill Inn (T)
143 E. 30th St. (Between 3rd & Lex.), New York, NY 10016, Ph: (212) 683-6900, (888) 996-6376 (toll free), Fax: (212) 545-0103, ASK FOR: Reservation Dept.
ROOM PRICING: Sgl. rm, (private/shared bath, $65.00; Dbl, $47.50 p/p, shared bath. Sgl/dbl; $115 Priv/bath. addtl. person, $15, • PAYMENT: Cash Trav. Ck • DATES AVAILABLE: Year round, rates may vary, • FOOD: NR • INFO: Children welcome, 24 hour consierge, maid service, color TV, fax and copy machine. • ACTIVITIES: Walk to Empire State Building, Macy's, U.N. Penn Station, Grand Central station, Broadway Theaters; Various resturants; minutes from Greenwich Village and SOHO; short ride to Columbia and NYU.

464 **New York, NY**   ?   &

New York University (T)
14A Washington Place, New York, NY 10003, Ph: (212) 998-4621, ASK FOR: Summer Housing
ROOM PRICING: Weekly rates, (S) $152.00-$210.00, With/without meals, (D) $152.00-$210.00, With/without meals, Min. stay 3 weeks, • PAYMENT: Cash Per. Ck Trav. Ck Visa M/C • DATES AVAILABLE: May 18 - Aug. 9, • BEDS: 1-3 • FOOD: Caf. NR OCR • INFO: Must be over 17 years, 24 hour security, air conditioned & non-air conditioned rooms, kitchens avail. • ACTIVITIES: Easy access to restaurants, theaters. Museums; Wall Street; Madison Ave.

465 **New York, NY**   ?   &

New York University (T) School of Law
110 W. Third St. Room 207, New York, NY 10012, Ph: (212) 998-6512, ASK FOR: Dir., Law Housing
ROOM PRICING: (S) $200.00 per wk, (D) $340.00 per wk, Min. 1 week stay, • PAYMENT: Cash Visa M/C • DATES AVAILABLE: Mid-May to Mid.Aug., • FOOD: NR • INFO: Fully A/C, 24 hour doorman bldgs., adults/families, 1 room to 3 bedroom suites, each w/shared kitchen & bath. • ACTIVITIES: Modern residencehalls in heart of Greenwich Village; near WashingtonSq. Park; art galleries; Chinatown; Little Italy; area has small cafes, restaurants; jazz clubs; close to public transportation.

466 New York, NY ?

The Cooper Union (E)
29 Third AVe., New York, NY 10003, Ph: (212) 353-4047, ASK FOR: Residence Manager's Office
ROOM PRICING: Per week, (S) $250.00, (D) $400.00, 2 or 3 bedroom suites, • PAYMENT: Cash Visa M/C • DATES AVAILABLE: June 1- Aug. 1, • ROOM TYPE: Suite • BATH: S • FOOD: VM NR • INFO: Provide own linens and towels, children welcome, no pets, fully A/C, 24 hour doorman. • ACTIVITIES: TV in pubic lounge. Greenwich Village/SOHO; Statue of Liberty; Wall Street; Chinatown.

467 Nyack, NY ?

Nyack College (C)
1 South Blvd., Nyack, NY 10960, Ph: (914) 358-1710, Ext: 380, ASK FOR: John Spaschak, Conf. Director
ROOM PRICING: (S) $24.00, (D) $48.00, • PAYMENT: Cash Per. Ck Trav. Ck • DATES AVAILABLE: May 15 -Aug. 15, • ROOM TYPE: SR • BED TYPE: S • BEDS: 2 • BATH: C • FOOD: Caf. SB VM NR • INFO: No smoking or alcohol. • ACTIVITIES: Close to New York City; West Point; Sleepy Hollow; Bear Mtn. State Park; athletic field.

468 Ogdensburg, NY ?

Mater Dei College (C)
5428 State Highway 37, Ogdensburg, NY 13669, Ph: (315) 393-5930, Ext: 302, ASK FOR: Mr. J. Ward, Aux. Services
ROOM PRICING: (S) $22.00, (D) $26.00, • PAYMENT: Cash Per. Ck Trav. Ck • DATES AVAILABLE: May 17 -Aug. 16, • ROOM TYPE: SR Apt. • BED TYPE: S • BEDS: 2 • BATH: C P • FOOD: Caf. VM NR • INFO: Children welcome, linen charge minimal, coin washers/dryers, TV lounge, free parking. I ndoor excerise/ weight rooms, sauna, fitness equipment, pool, video arcade. • ACTIVITIES: Outdoor basketball, tennis, sand volleyball courts. Nearby: Ottawa, Canadian capital; 1000 Island Tourist area; St. Lawrence Seaway; Fred. Remington Art Museum; Lake Placid; park and golf course within walking distance.

469 Oswego, NY

State Univ. of N.Y. at Oswego (E)
Oswego, NY 13126, Ph: (315) 341-2246, ASK FOR: Residence Life - 303 Culkin Hall
ROOM PRICING: (S) $35.00, 1st night, (D) $46.00, 1st night, ($18.00-$24.00 each addl. night, • PAYMENT: Cash • DATES AVAILABLE: May 20 -Aug. 5, • ROOM TYPE: SR • BED TYPE: S • BEDS: 2 • BATH: C • FOOD: Caf. SB VM • INFO: Children welcome, coin washers/dryers, TV lounge. • ACTIVITIES: Historic Fort Ontario, Erie Canal Museum, 1000 Island Resort Region, films, sports, weekly farmers market, fishing; boating.

470 Purchase, NY ?

Purchase College/SUNY (C)
735 Anderson Hill Road, Purchase, NY 10577, Ph: (914) 251-6320, ASK FOR: Office of Res. Life
ROOM PRICING: (S) $30.00 - $35.00, (D) $50.00 - $60.00, Refundable key deposit $5.00, • PAYMENT: Cash Per. Ck • DATES AVAILABLE: June 1 - Aug. 9, • BEDS: 1-2 • FOOD: Caf. SB VM NR • INFO: Linens included. • ACTIVITIES: Newberger Museum; Four theater performing arts center on campus; 35 min. north of Manhatttan; Sculpture Gardens at nearby Pepsico; some recreational sports facilities available.

U
N
I
V

471 Rochester, NY

Roberts Wesleyan College (T)
2301 Westside Dr., Rochester, NY 14624, Ph: (716) 594-6026, Fax: (716) 594-6059, Web Site: www.rwc.edu/develop/conference, ASK FOR: Richard MacLaren, Conferences
ROOM PRICING: (S) $15.00, (D) $30.00, Addl. person, $7.50, • PAYMENT: Cash Per. Ck Trav. Ck Visa M/C Discover • DATES AVAILABLE: May 23 - Aug.4, • BEDS: 2 • FOOD: Caf. VM NR • INFO: Linen charge: $2.50 per day, children 1/2 price, no smoking or alcohol, AC rooms avail. at higher rate. • ACTIVITIES: Art gallery; swimming; tennis; game room; softball field; excerise room; Fax/copy services; college bookstore; Niagara Falls; Rochester, NY; museums; Lake Ontario;Finger lakes region.
DIRECTIONS: NYS Interstate 90 to exit 46, Route 390 N to Route 490 W, Exit 76, go west 5 miles, campus on right

472 Staten Island, NY

Wagner College (C)
631 Howard Ave., Staten Island, NY 10301, Ph: (718) 390-3221/390-3296, ASK FOR: Conf. Office
ROOM PRICING: (S) $40.00, (D) $55.00, VIP rooms, $55.00 - $70.00, • PAYMENT: Cash Per. Ck Trav. Ck Visa M/C Discover Amex • DATES AVAILABLE: May- August, • BED TYPE: S • BEDS: 1-2 • FOOD: Caf. SB VM NR • INFO: Children welcome with chaperones, groups of 10 or more only. • ACTIVITIES: Manhattan, view of skyline; Staten Island Ferry.

473 Tarrytown, NY

Marymount College (T) St. John's Hall, Gailhac Hall
100 Marymount Ave., Tarrytown, NY 10591, Ph: (914) 332-8209, Fax: (914) 332-4956, E-mail: bishop@mmc.marymt.edu, ASK FOR: Shenna Bishop, Office of conf.
ROOM PRICING: (S) $30.00 (D) $60.00, • PAYMENT: Cash Per. Ck Trav. Ck Visa M/C • BED TYPE: S • BEDS: 1-3 • FOOD: Caf. VM NR • INFO: Linens included, children welcome(supervised), no pets, free parking, TV lounge, coin washers/dryers. • ACTIVITIES: Swimming, tennis, bike trails. Philipsburg Manor; Lyndhurst Gothic Mansion; Sunnyside(home of Washington Irving); Kybuit(once home to the Rockerfellers); Patriot's Park; Tarrytown Music Hall; ethnic restaurants; seasonal fairs.

474 Troy, NY

Rensselaer Polytechnic Institute (C)
Vistors Info. Center, Troy, NY 12180, Ph: (518) 276-6694, Fax: (518) 276-2833, E-mail: Millec3@rpi.edu, ASK FOR: Office of Conference Services, Corey Miller, Dir.
ROOM PRICING: (S) $32.00, (D) $42.00, • PAYMENT: Cash Per. Ck Trav. Ck Visa M/C • DATES AVAILABLE: June 1 - Aug.9, • ROOM TYPE: SR • BED TYPE: S • BEDS: 1-2 • BATH: S P • FOOD: Caf. SB VM NR • INFO: Linens included, air-conditioned, children welcome. • ACTIVITIES: Racquetball, films, art gallery, bowling, concerts, swimming, theaters, game room, tennis, TV in public room. Lake George, NY; Saratoga Springs, NY; Albany(Capital of NY).

475 Utica, NY

Mohawk Valley Community College (T) Dorm Corp.
1101 Sherman Dr., Utica, NY 13501, Ph: (315) 792-5371 or 792-5361, ASK FOR: Summer housing office, Julie Wasson
ROOM PRICING: (S) $12.00, (D) $24.00, $55.00/Weekly, • PAYMENT: Cash Trav. Ck M/C • DATES AVAILABLE: June 2-Aug 2, • ROOM TYPE: SR Suite • BED TYPE: S • BEDS: 2-3 • BATH: C • FOOD: Caf. SB NR • INFO: Optional linen chg: $8.50. Children welcome with supervision. Group rates available, banquet facilities. • ACTIVITIES: TV in public lounge, basement kitchen, walking track. Munson-Williams Art Museum; Utica Zoo; Sangertown Mall; Riverside Mall; 45 min. from Cooperstown Baseball Hall of Fame; 1 hr. to Old Forge & Adirondack Park.
DIRECTIONS: Take exit 31 off NYS Thruway. Follow signs for South Genesee St. Follow South Genesee St. to Memorial Parkway. Take a left on Memorial Parkway and watch for signs directing you to Mohawk Valley Community College.

(T) = Travelers Accommodations   (E) = Educational Related   (C) = Groups & Conference Use

North Carolina

476 Chapel Hill, NC   ?   ⌖

Granville Towers Residence (T)
University Square, Chapel Hill, NC 27514, Ph: (919) 929-7143, (800) 332-3113, Fax: (919) 929-7948, ASK FOR: Marilee Haithcock, Summer Conf.
ROOM PRICING: More than one nights stay, (S) $45.00 , (D) $45.00, • PAYMENT: Cash Visa M/C • DATES AVAILABLE: May 12 -Aug. 8, • ROOM TYPE: SR • BED TYPE: S • BEDS: 2 • BATH: S • FOOD: Caf. VM NR • INFO: Linens available. Children welcome, coin washers/dryers. • ACTIVITIES: Swimming pool, computer room, fitness centers, weight room, basketball court, TV lounge. Location adjacent to UNC Chapel Hill Campus and downtown business district.

477 Chapel Hill, NC   ?

University of North Carolina (E) at Chapel Hill
Teague Hall, CB#5510, Chapel Hill, NC 27599, Ph: (800) UNC-STAY, ASK FOR: Conference Manager
ROOM PRICING: (S) $25.00 - $30.00, (D) $25.00-$30.00, • PAYMENT: Cash Per. Ck Trav. Ck Visa M/C • DATES AVAILABLE: May 17 - Aug 4, • BEDS: 2 • FOOD: Caf. VM NR • INFO: Only older children, no pets, TV lounge, linens available upon request. • ACTIVITIES: Morehead Planetarium; Dean E. Smith Center; Burlington Outlet Mall; parks; sports; theater; galleries; concerts.

478 Cullowhee, NC   ?   ⌖

Western Carolina Univ. (E)
Cullowhee, NC 28723, Ph: (704) 227-7397, ASK FOR: Sue Deitz, Summer School
ROOM PRICING: Varies - according to requirements, • PAYMENT: Cash Per. Ck Trav. Ck • DATES AVAILABLE: May 27 - Aug. 2, • BEDS: 2 • FOOD: Caf. SB VM • INFO: Children welcome. • ACTIVITIES: Cherokee Indian Reservation; whitewater rafting; Smoky Mtns.; Blue Ridge Parkway.

479 Greensboro, NC   ?   ⌖

Greensboro College (T)
815 West Market Street, Greensboro, NC 27401, Ph: (910) 272-7102, ASK FOR: Cindy Cambron, CMP
ROOM PRICING: Please call for rates, • PAYMENT: Cash Per. Ck Trav. Ck Visa M/C • DATES AVAILABLE: May 14- Aug. 5, • ROOM TYPE: SR • BED TYPE: S • BEDS: 1-2 • BATH: C S P • FOOD: Caf. SB VM NR • INFO: Children welcome, 24 hour security and conference assistance, A/C and non-A/C rooms available. • ACTIVITIES: Swimming, tennis, TV in public lounge, computer room, outdoor volleyball. Emerald Pointe Water Park; North Carolina Zoological Park; Historical Attractions; art galleries; shopping; golf.

480 Greensboro, NC   ?   ⌖

Guilford College (C)
5800 West Friendly Ave., Greensboro, NC 27410, Ph: (910) 316-2401, E-mail: watkinsda@rascal.guilford.edu, ASK FOR: Dawn Watkins
ROOM PRICING: (S) $45.00 (D) $35.00, • PAYMENT: Cash Per. Ck Trav. Ck • DATES AVAILABLE: June 1-July 31, • BEDS: 2 • FOOD: Caf. NR • INFO: Conference charge includes meals and linens. Min. No. Req. for conferences, 25. Limited handicap accessibility. Coin washers/dryers, free parking, TV lounges, children welcome. • ACTIVITIES: Racquetball, art gallery, swimming, tennis, hiking/fitness trails on campus, library. 340 acre wooded campus. Battleground National Park; within 30 minutes of winston-Salem with historic Old Salem and High Point, known nationally as the furniture capital of the U.S.

481 Misenheimer, NC   ?

Pffeifer College (C)
P. O. Box 930, Misenheimer, NC 28109, Ph: (704) 463-1360, Ext: 2419, ASK FOR: Julian Domench, Dir. of Summer Camps
ROOM PRICING: (S) $20.00, (D) $20.00, • PAYMENT: Cash Per. Ck Trav. Ck • DATES AVAILABLE: May-July, • ROOM TYPE: SR • BATH: C • FOOD: Caf. SB VM • INFO: No pets; groups only • ACTIVITIES: Morrow Mtn. State Park, Baden Lake, Charlotte attractions, sports, films, High Rock Lakes

---

(T) = Travelers Accommodations   (E) = Educational Related   (C) = Groups & Conference Use

482 Raleigh, NC   ?   ♿

Univ. Towers Residence (T)
111 Friendly Drive, Raleigh, NC 27607, Ph: (919) 755-1943, ASK FOR: Dennis Enry, Housing
ROOM PRICING: (S) $35.00, (D) $36.00, • PAYMENT: Cash Trav. Ck Visa M/C • DATES AVAILABLE: May 22- Aug. 1, • ROOM TYPE: SR • BED TYPE: S • BEDS: 2 • BATH: S • FOOD: Caf. VM NR • INFO: Children welcome. • ACTIVITIES: Pool, fitness center, computer room, state capitol buildings, abundance of summer entertainment, Pulstar Nuclear Reactor, historic district of Oakwood.

483 Salisbury, NC   ♿

Catawba College (C) Barger-Zartman Hall
2300 West Innes Street, Salisbury, NC 28144, Ph: (704) 637-4200, Fax: (704) 637-4211, E-mail: ccurent@crtawba.ed, ASK FOR: J. Clark - Conference Dir.
ROOM PRICING: (S) $25.00, (D) $35.00, • PAYMENT: Cash Per. Ck Trav. Ck • DATES AVAILABLE: May 15 - Auust 10, • ROOM TYPE: SR Apt. Suite • BED TYPE: S • BEDS: 2 • BATH: S • FOOD: VM NR • INFO: Linen charge: $4.00. Children welcome, Min. no. req. for conf.50, if food service is desired. Family suites available. • ACTIVITIES: Racquetball, swimming, game room, tennis, TV in public lounge, outdoor volleyball courts.   Spencer Shops,(Railroad Museum); Salisbury Historic District; 6 nearby public golf courses; High Rock Lake.

484 Salisbury, NC   ?

Livingstone College (T)
701 W. Monroe Street, Salisbury, NC 28144, Ph: (704) 638-5569, ASK FOR: Kim Cannon, Dir. Student Activities
ROOM PRICING: Call for rates, • PAYMENT: Cash Trav. Ck Visa M/C Discover • DATES AVAILABLE: June 1-Aug.1, • FOOD: VM NR • INFO: Linens not included, children welcome. • ACTIVITIES: Game room, tennis, TV in public lounge. Old Salem/ Winston -Salem Historical District; Discovery Place/Charlotte, NC; R.J. Reynolds Tobacco Factory; park; theaters.

485 Wilmington, NC   ?

University of North Carolina- Wilmington (T)
601 College Road, Wilmington, NC 28401, Ph: (919) 395-3241, ASK FOR: Housing and Residence Life
ROOM PRICING: Call for rates, • PAYMENT: Cash Per. Ck • DATES AVAILABLE: May 16-Aug. 1, • FOOD: Caf. VM NR • INFO: Apts. also avail, children welcome, all spaces are air-conditioned. • ACTIVITIES: Park, swimming, boating, tennis, hiking, museums, TV in public room. Excellent golf courses in area; Beach is 4 miles from campus; State Aquarium; Battleship North Carolina; Camp LeJuene.

North Dakota

486 Bismarck, ND   ?   ♿

University of Mary (E)
7500 University Dr., Bismarck, ND 58504, Ph: (701) 255-7500, Ext: 353, ASK FOR: Special Events Coordinator
ROOM PRICING: (S) $19.00, (D) $38.00, • PAYMENT: Cash Only • DATES AVAILABLE: May 10 - July 31, • ROOM TYPE: SR Apt. • BED TYPE: S • BEDS: 2 • BATH: C P • FOOD: Caf. VM NR • INFO: Children welcome with supervision, no alcohol, no pets. Free parking, linens included. • ACTIVITIES: Swimming, tennis, track, racquetball. State Capitol Building; parks; boating; museum.

487 **Grand Forks, ND**   ?   ♿

University of North Dakota (T)
Box 9029, Grand Forks, ND 58202, Ph: (701) 777-4251, ASK FOR: Debi Melby , Assistant Dir.
ROOM PRICING: (S) $21.00, (D) $23.00, • PAYMENT: Cash Per. Ck Trav. Ck Visa M/C Discover • DATES AVAILABLE: Year Round, • FOOD: Caf. SB VM NR • INFO: Linens included, no pets, no alcohol, children welcome. A few apartments available. • ACTIVITIES: Racquetball, art gallery, bowling, swimming, game room, museums, TV in public lounge. Canada; Dakota Queen Riverboat; Center for Aerospace Science.

488 **Jamestown, ND**   ?   ♿

Jamestown College (E)
Jamestown, ND 58405, Ph: 701-252-3467 Ext: 2453, ASK FOR: Director of Student Activities
ROOM PRICING: (S) $10.00, (D) $20.00, Addtl. person $5.00, • PAYMENT: Cash Per. Ck Trav. Ck • DATES AVAILABLE: May 16- July 31, • BED TYPE: S • FOOD: Caf. NR • INFO: Linen charge: $2.00/ week, no alcohol or smoking, children welcome. • ACTIVITIES: Tennis, TV in public lounge, YMCA on campus. National Buffalo Museum; National Wildlife Resource Center.

Ohio

489 **Bluffton, OH**   ♿

Bluffton college (C)
280 West College Ave., Bluffton, OH 45817, Ph: (419) 358-3217, E-mail: bourassam@bluffton.edu, ASK FOR: Mark Bourassa, Conf. Dir.
ROOM PRICING: Depends of Group Size, • PAYMENT: Cash Per. Ck • DATES AVAILABLE: Early June-Mid.Aug., • ROOM TYPE: SR • BED TYPE: S • BEDS: 2 • BATH: C • FOOD: Caf. • INFO: Linen charge: $3.50 (sheets & towels), Children welcome. • ACTIVITIES: Racquetball, game room, tennis, hiking, TV in public lounge. Bowling alley; Movie theater; Swimming Pool; City park.
DIRECTIONS: Located just minutes off I-75 at exits 140 or 142.

490 **Cincinnati, OH**   ?   ♿

Univ. of Cincinnati (T)
P. O. Box 210015, Cincinnati, OH 45221-0015, Ph: (513) 556-2442, ASK FOR: Campus Scheduling & Conf.
ROOM PRICING: (S) $28.00, (D) $28.00, Addtl. person $6.00, • PAYMENT: Cash Per. Ck Trav. Ck • DATES AVAILABLE: Mid-June-Aug.31, • ROOM TYPE: SR Apt. • BED TYPE: S • BEDS: 2-4 • BATH: C P • FOOD: Caf. SB VM NR • INFO: Linens included, children welcome. • ACTIVITIES: Racquetball, bowling, concerts, park, theaters, game room, tennis, TV in public lounge. King's Island Amusement Park; Cincinnati Zoo; Cincinnati Reds Baseball; Union Terminal & Omnimax Theater.

U N I V

---

491 Cleveland, OH   ? ♿

Norte Dame College of Ohio (T) Office of Student Life
4545 College Road, Cleveland, OH 44121, Ph: (216) 381-1680, Fax: (216)
381-3802, ASK FOR: Claudine Grunewald
ROOM PRICING: $20.00 per room, • PAYMENT: Cash Only • DATES AVAILABLE:
May 25 - Aug. 7, • BEDS: 2 • FOOD: Caf. VM NR • INFO: Linen charge: $5.00
per room, per night, children welcome, free parking, TV lounge, coin
washers/dryers, no alcohol, no inside smoking, no pre-marital co-habitation. •
ACTIVITIES: Swimming, tennis, fitness center, spacious well maintained grounds.
Sea World Park; Rock & Roll Hall of Fame & Museum; Great Lakes Science
Center; Downtown Cleveland; Aurora Premium Outlet Shopping; Cedar Point Lake;
Jacobs Field.
DIRECTIONS: Notre Dame is minutes from I-271. Take the Cedar/Brainard exit
and proceed west on Cedar Road. Turn right at Green Road and drive north four
blocks. Turn right on College Road, the entrace is ahead on the left.

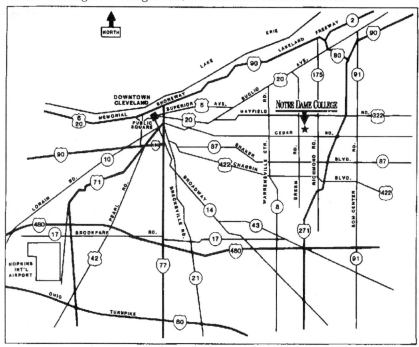

492 Columbus, OH   ? ♿

Capital University (C)
2199 East Main St., Columbus, OH 43209, Ph: (614) 236-6200, ASK FOR: Office
of Prog.Ser.,Christina Baker
ROOM PRICING: ., (S) $16.00, (D) $26.00, • PAYMENT: Cash   • DATES
AVAILABLE: May 22- Aug 1, • ROOM TYPE: SR • BED TYPE: S • BEDS: 2 •
BATH: C • FOOD: Caf. • INFO: Linen charge; Charge for all meals if desired,
facility charge. • ACTIVITIES: Nearby: City Center; Columbus Metroplitan Museum
of Art; Palace Theater; Newport Music Hall; Columbus Zoo; State Capitol Bldg.

493 **Dayton, OH**   ? ♿

Guest Housing, Residence Services (T) Wright State University
Dayton, OH 45435, Ph: (937) 775-4219
ROOM PRICING: (S) $20.00, (D) $20.00, • PAYMENT: Cash Per. Ck Trav. Ck
Visa M/C Discover • DATES AVAILABLE: June 16-Aug. 25, • BEDS: 1-4 •
FOOD: SB VM NR • INFO: Linen charge. • ACTIVITIES: Wright Patterson Air
Force Museum; Carillon Historical Park; Clifton Gorge; Aviation Train; Blue
Jacket; sports.

494 **Defiance, OH**   ? ♿

The Defiance College (T)
701 N. Clinton St., Defiance, OH 43512, Ph: (419) 784-4010, Ext: 585, ASK FOR:
Facility Rentals
ROOM PRICING: (S) $11.00, (D) $11.00, • PAYMENT: Cash • DATES AVAILABLE:
May 8-Aug 10, • ROOM TYPE: SR • BED TYPE: S • BEDS: 1-2 • FOOD: Caf. VM
NR • INFO: $2.25 for linen packet, children pay regular rate, coin
washers/dryers, TV lounge. • ACTIVITIES: Oxbow Lake State Park; Saunder's
Village and Museum; historic Ft. Defiance; Auglaize Village; films; art gallery.

495 **Kent, OH**   ? ♿

Kent State University (E) Korb Guest Hall
P. O. Box 5190, Kent, OH 44242, Ph: (216) 672-6999, ASK FOR: Dept. of
Residencw Services
ROOM PRICING: (S) $15.00, (D) $25.00, • PAYMENT: Cash Per. Ck Trav. Ck
Visa M/C Discover • DATES AVAILABLE: June 1-Aug.12, • ROOM TYPE: SR •
BED TYPE: S • BATH: C • FOOD: Caf. SB VM NR • INFO: Linens included, no
pets, no cooking facilities, children welcome at regular rate. • ACTIVITIES:
Racquetball, films, art gallery, swimming, theaters, game room, tennis, museums,
TV in public lounge, fitness center, golf course. Sea World; City of Akron; Geauga
Lake Amusement Park; Football Hall of Fame.

496 **Oberlin, OH**   ? ♿

Oberlin College (C) Student Union Conference Center
107 Wilder Hall, 135 W. Lorain St., Oberlin, OH 44074, Ph: (216) 775-8730, Fax:
(216) 775-8480
ROOM PRICING: (D) $36.79- $49.06, • PAYMENT: Cash Per. Ck Trav. Ck •
DATES AVAILABLE: Mid June-Mid Aug, • ROOM TYPE: SR • BED TYPE: S •
BEDS: 1-4 • BATH: C • FOOD: Caf. VM NR • INFO: Children welcome. •
ACTIVITIES: Campus sports and recreational facilities. Cleveland; Sea World;
Cedar Point; Amish Country Tours.

497 **Oxford, OH**   ? ♿

Miami University (E) Havighurst Hall
Cook Place, Oxford, OH 45056, Ph: (513) 529-4949, ASK FOR: Conference
Services
ROOM PRICING: (S) $20.00, (D) $32.00, • PAYMENT: Cash Per. Ck Trav. Ck •
DATES AVAILABLE: May 15- Aug. 4, • ROOM TYPE: SR • BED TYPE: S • BEDS:
1-2 • BATH: C • FOOD: Caf. SB VM NR • INFO: Linens included, children
welcome. • ACTIVITIES: Racquetball, art gallery, park, swimming, game room,
tennis, hiking, TV in public lounge. Hueston Woods State Par; Kings Island.

498 **Portsmouth, OH**   ? ♿

Shawnee State University (E)
940 Second Street, Portsmouth, OH 45662, Ph: (614) 355-2217, Fax: (614)
355-2643, ASK FOR: Office of Residence Life
ROOM PRICING: (S) $12.00 (D) $24.00, additional person, $12.00, • PAYMENT:
Cash Per. Ck Visa M/C • DATES AVAILABLE: June - August, • BEDS: 2-3 •
FOOD: Caf. NR • INFO: TVlounge, coin washers/dryers. • ACTIVITIES:
Racquetball, swimming, game room, tennis, fitness center. Shawnee Forest;
Floodwall Murals.

U
N
I
V

(T) = Travelers Accommodations   (E) = Educational Related   (C) = Groups & Conference Use

499 **Westerville, OH**   ?   ♿

Otterbein College (C) Student Affairs Office
Westerville, OH 43081, Ph: (614) 823-1250, ASK FOR: Sue Long
ROOM PRICING: (S) $13.00, (D) $25.00, • PAYMENT: Cash Per. Ck Visa M/C
Discover • DATES AVAILABLE: Mid-June-Mid-Aug., • ROOM TYPE: SR • BED
TYPE: S • BEDS: 2 • BATH: C • FOOD: Caf. VM NR • INFO: No air-condtioning in
residence halls. Min. number for conferences: 50. • ACTIVITIES: Concerts, park,
theaters, tennis, TV in public lounge in res. halls. State Capital; OSU; Columbus
Zoo.

Oklahoma

500 **Lawton, OK**   ?

Cameron College (T)
2800 W. Gore Blvd., Lawton, OK 73505, Ph: (405) 581-2392, ASK FOR: Residence
Life Office
ROOM PRICING: (S) $15.00, (D) $24.00, • PAYMENT: Cash Per. Ck Trav. Ck
Visa M/C • DATES AVAILABLE: Year Round, • ROOM TYPE: SR • BED TYPE: S
• BEDS: 1-2 • BATH: C • FOOD: Caf. SB VM NR • INFO: Linens included, coin
washers/dryers, TV lounge, free parking, linens included. • ACTIVITIES:
Racquetball, concerts, park, swimming, tennis, hiking,
TV in public lounge. Wichita Mountains Wildlife Refuge; Ft. Sill Military
Reservation; Museum of the Great Plains.

501 **Norman, OK**   ♿

Sooner Hotel & Suites (T) University of Oklahoma
300 Kellogg Dr., Norman, OK 73072, Ph: (405) 329-2270, ASK FOR: Housing
Prog. Office
ROOM PRICING: Varies, call for rates, • PAYMENT: Cash Per. Ck Trav. Ck
Visa M/C Discover Amex • DATES AVAILABLE: Year Round, • BED TYPE: S •
BEDS: 2 • FOOD: Caf. SB VM NR OCR • INFO: Children welcome, no pets, no
alcohol. Telephones, TV with cable/HBO, computer jacks, and small refrigerators
in hotel rooms. Suites have 2 bedrooms with queen beds. Continental breakfast,
TV lounge, game room lobby, free parking, passes to fitness ctr. and pool. •
ACTIVITIES: Nat'l Cowboy Hall of Fame, Lake Thunderbird Remington Park,
Racetrack, OK City Zoo, Planetarium, and Omniplex. Museum of Natural History
on Campus.

502 **Norman, OK**   ♿

University of Oklahoma (T) Housing and Food Services
300 Kellogg Dr., Norman, OK 73072, Ph: (405) 329-2270, Fax: (405) 325-7530,
E-mail: psullivan@ou.edu, ASK FOR: Pam Sullivan
ROOM PRICING: Rates based on group size and length of stay, • PAYMENT: Cash
Per. Ck Trav. Ck • DATES AVAILABLE: Year Round, • BED TYPE: S • BEDS:
1-2 • FOOD: Caf. SB VM NR OCR • INFO: coin washer/dryer, TV Lounge, Free
Parking, Linens available, extra charge. • ACTIVITIES: Nat'l Cowboy Hall of
Fame, Lake Thunderbird Remington Park, Racetrack, OK City Zoo, Planetarium,
and Omniplex. Museum of Natural History on Campus.

503 **Stillwater, OK**   ♿

Oklahoma State University (T)
Reside. Life Office, 1st Floor, Scott Hall, Stillwater, OK 74078, Ph: (405) 744-6956,
ASK FOR: Linda Hyman, Conf Mgr.
ROOM PRICING: (S) $22.00, (D) $29.00, • PAYMENT: Cash Per. Ck Trav. Ck •
DATES AVAILABLE: Year Round, • ROOM TYPE: SR • BED TYPE: S • BEDS: 2 •
BATH: C • FOOD: Caf. VM NR • INFO: Children welcome. • ACTIVITIES:
Theater, films, concerts, sports programs, game room open space, rangeland.
Cowboy Hall of Fame.

Oregon

504 **Marylhurst, OR**   ?   &

Marylhurst College (C)
P. O. Box 261, Marylhurst, OR 97036, Ph: (503) 636-8141, Ext: 385, ASK FOR:
Conf. Office
ROOM PRICING: (S) $20.00, (D) $30.00, • PAYMENT: Cash Trav. Ck Visa M/C
• DATES AVAILABLE: Year round, • BEDS: 1-2 • FOOD: Caf. VM NR • INFO:
Accommodations for retreat groups and conference clients only. NO
ACCOMMODATIONS FOR GENERAL PUBLIC. • ACTIVITIES: Near downtown
Portland with it's art Museum, historical museum, Museum of Science & Industry.
Nearby: Ocean beaches; Columbia Gorge; Cascade Mountains; wine country; Mt.
Saint Helens.

505 **Portland, OR**

Linfield College (T) Loveridge Hall
Portland Campus, 2215 N.W. Northrup, Portland, OR 97210, Ph: (503)
413-7212, ASK FOR: Janette Vlahos, Mgr.
ROOM PRICING: (S) $25.00, (D) $50.00, • PAYMENT: Cash Per. Ck Trav. Ck •
DATES AVAILABLE: June 12 -Aug. 13, • ROOM TYPE: SR Apt. • BED TYPE: S •
BEDS: 2 • BATH: C P • FOOD: Caf. VM NR • INFO: Call for children's
accommodation.Coin Washer/Dryer,TV Lounge, Free Parking, Linens. •
ACTIVITIES: WA. Park and Zoo; Famous Japanese Garden; World Forestry
Center; Rose Festival; Museum of Science and Industry; Sat. market for local
artists; salmon fishing Columbia River; One hour to beaches or mountains.

506 **Portland, OR**   ?

Warner Pacific College (T)
2219 S.E. 68th Ave., Portland, OR 97215, Ph: (503) 778-7482, ASK FOR: Housing
Office
ROOM PRICING: (S) $17.00, • PAYMENT: Cash Per. Ck Trav. Ck • DATES
AVAILABLE: Year Round, • BEDS: 2 • FOOD: Caf. VM NR • INFO: Linens
included, non-smokers only, no alcohol, children welcome with adult supervision,
Christian Liberal Arts College. • ACTIVITIES: Park, game room, tennis, hiking, TV
in public lounge. City of Portland; Oregon Coast; Mt. Hood.

507 **Salem, OR**   ?   &

Williamette University (C)
900 State Street, Salem, OR 97301, Ph: (503) 370-6162, ASK FOR: Alice
Sorensen, Summer conf.
ROOM PRICING: (S) $40.50, (D) $79.00, (includes 3 meals), • PAYMENT: Cash
Per. Ck • DATES AVAILABLE: May15 - Aug. 15, • FOOD: Caf. SB VM NR •
INFO: Children under 5 half price, no pets. • ACTIVITIES: State Capitol;
Santiam River; park and sports facilities; boating; 72 mi. to Pacific beaches.

Pennsylvania

508 **Allentown, PA**   ?

Cedar Crest College (E)
100 College Drive, Allentown, PA 18104, Ph: (610) 740-3792 Ext: 3431, ASK FOR:
Dir. of conferences, Jan Firestone
ROOM PRICING: (S) $14.00, (D) $18.00, Add $2.00 for   A/ C, • PAYMENT: Cash
Per. Ck • DATES AVAILABLE: May 25-Aug. 15, • BEDS: 2 • FOOD: Caf. SB VM
NR • INFO: Linens included, no pets, children welcome w/ supervision, Min. No.
for conf. 50. • ACTIVITIES: Art gallery, concerts, park, game room, tennis, TV in
public lounge, arboretum & nature trail. Dorney Park & wildwater Kingdom; 11/2
hr. to NY City; 1 hr. to Philadelphia.

U
N
I
V

509 Allentown, PA   ?   ♿

Muhlenberg College (E)
2301 W. Chew St., Allentown, PA 18104, Ph: (215) 821-3485, ASK FOR: Housing & Conference office
ROOM PRICING: (S) $20.00, (D) $30.00, • PAYMENT: Cash Per. Ck Trav. Ck •
DATES AVAILABLE: May22-Aug.13, • FOOD: Caf. SB VM NR • INFO: Linens included, children welcome w/supervision. • ACTIVITIES: Racquetball, art gallery, concerts, swimming, boating, game room, tennis, museums. Historic Bethleham; Pocono Mtn.; Wildwater Kingdom.

510 Bethlehem, PA   ?   ♿

Lehigh University (T)
63 University Dr., Bethlehem, PA 18015, Ph: (215) 758-4567, ASK FOR: Conf. Services
ROOM PRICING: (S) $23.00- $29.00, • PAYMENT: Cash Per. Ck Trav. Ck •
DATES AVAILABLE: Year Round, • FOOD: Caf. SB VM NR • INFO: Children welcome with supervision, no alcohol, no pets, 550 air-conditioned spaces. •
ACTIVITIES: Lost River Caverns; Dorney Park Wildwater Kingdom; Christmas City year round festival; Historic Bethleham.

511 Bradford, PA   ?   ♿

University of Pittsburgh (E)
300 Campus Drive, Bradford, PA 16701, Ph: (814) 362-0990, Fax: (814) 362-0991, ASK FOR: Dianne Austin, conf. mgr.
ROOM PRICING: (S) $25.00, • PAYMENT: Cash Visa M/C Discover • DATES AVAILABLE: May 10-Aug.18, • ROOM TYPE: Apt. • BED TYPE: S • BEDS: 1-2 •
BATH: S P • FOOD: Caf. SB VM NR • INFO: Linen Charge: $3.00-$7.00. Apt. style housing, all apts.have kitchenettes, children welcome, guests subj. to approv. in accordance w/ Univ. reg. • ACTIVITIES: Tennis, hiking, TV in public lounge. Cafeteria with pool table; Allegheny National Forest; Kinzua Dam and Allegheny Reservoir; Seneca Nation of Indians reservation and National Museum; Historic Kinzua Bridge State Park.
DIRECTIONS: 20 min. from Bradford Regional airport with shuttle service.
Bradford is easily accessible from Interstate 79, Interstate 80, Interstate 90 (NY Thruway), U.S. Route 219, US Route 6, and New York route 17.

512 Bryn Mawr, PA   ?

Bryn Mawr College (E)
Bryn Mawr, PA 19010, Ph: (610) 526-5058, ASK FOR: Conference Office, Lisa Zernicke
ROOM PRICING: (S) $25.00, • PAYMENT: Cash Trav. Ck Visa M/C • DATES AVAILABLE: June 1 - Aug. 15, • FOOD: Caf. SB VM NR • INFO: No children. •
ACTIVITIES: Swimming, tennis. Valley Forge; Philadelphia Museum of Art; Independence National Park; Brandywine River area.

513 **California, PA**   ♿

California University of PA (T)
250 University Ave., Box 39, California, PA 15419, Ph: (724) 938-4444, Fax: (724) 938-5959, ASK FOR: Richard Dulaney, Conf. Services
ROOM PRICING: group-rates
$26-$30/person includes 3 meals/day. , • PAYMENT: Cash Per. Ck • DATES AVAILABLE: May 15-Aug.20, • BEDS: 2 • FOOD: Caf. SB VM NR • INFO: Children welcome, coin washers/dryers, free parking. • ACTIVITIES: Racquetball, art gallery, concerts, swimming, theaters, game room, tennis, TV in public lounge. 1 hr . south of Pittsburgh; Many Historical Landmarks; Antique & Novelty Shops; Frank Lloyd Wright's Falling Water.

514 **Center Valley, PA**   ?   ♿

Allentown College (T) St. Francis de Sales
2755 Station Ave., Center Valley, PA 18034, Ph: (210) 282-3798, E-mail: gjjo@ms1.allencol.edu, ASK FOR: Jerry Joyce, Conf. Office
ROOM PRICING: (S) $14.50, (D) $20.00, • PAYMENT: Cash Only • DATES AVAILABLE: May 19-Aug. 10, • BEDS: 2 • FOOD: Caf. SB VM NR • INFO: Children welcome. All buildings have air-conditioning, townhouses available. Coin washers/dryers, free parking, linens. • ACTIVITIES: All campus sports facilities available, outdoor pool. Dorney Park; Wildwater Kingdom.

U
N
I
V

515 Chambersburg, PA

Wilson College (T)

1015 Philadelphia, Chambersburg, PA 17201, Ph: (717) 262-2003, Fax: (717)-264-1578, E-mail: conferences@wilson.edu, Web Site: www.wilson.edu, ASK FOR: Kathy Lehman, Conf. Dept.

ROOM PRICING: (S) $17.00, (D) $30.00, • PAYMENT: Cash Per. Ck Trav. Ck Visa M/C • DATES AVAILABLE: Year Round, • ROOM TYPE: SR Apt. • BED TYPE: S • BEDS: 2 • BATH: C S • FOOD: Caf. • INFO: Linens included, children welcome, no pets. 2 week advance reservation required. • ACTIVITIES: All campus sports facilities. Nearby: Gettysburg Battle Field; Hershey Park; Harpers Ferry; Baltimore and Washington D.C.

DIRECTIONS: Interstate 81 passes east of town. If approaching from the north, take Chambersburg Exit 6 from Interstate 81, go west on Route 30 (Lincoln Way) to the intersection of Route 30 & North Second St. Turn right and proceed north on Second St (Rt.11 North) which merges into Philadelphia Ave. Main entrance to college is at intersection of Philadelphia and college Ave. From the south, take Exit 5 & turn right onto Wayne Ave. Proceed west on Wayne until it joins with North Second St.

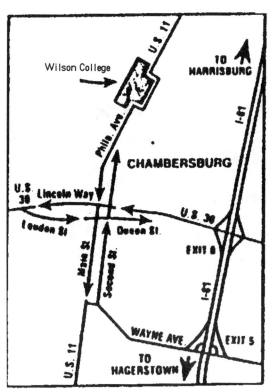

516 Greensburg, PA   ?

Seton Hill College (T) Brownlee & Harvy Halls
College Drive, Greensburg, PA 15601, Ph: (412) 838-4213, ASK FOR: Barbara
Aupperla, Activities Dir.
ROOM PRICING: (S) $10.00 per person, • PAYMENT: Cash Per. Ck • DATES
AVAILABLE: May 15-Aug. 10, • FOOD: Caf. NR • INFO: Conference min. 10;
Linen charge: $5.00 per week, children welcome, groups must provide chaperone
for group members under 18. • ACTIVITIES: Swimming, game room, tennis,
hiking, TV in public lounge. 35 min. from downtown Pittsburgh; 15 min. to Laurel
Highlands Tourist Area; Art museums in Greensburg.

517 Johnstown, PA   &

University of Pittsburgh at Johnstown (E)
450 Schoolhouse Road, Johnstown, PA 15904, Ph: (814) 269-1900, Fax: (814)
269-7500, E-mail: salem+@pitt.edu, ASK FOR: Charles Salem, Conf. Center
ROOM PRICING: (S) $22.10-$35.00, (D) $34.00- $48.00, • PAYMENT: Cash Per.
Ck Trav. Ck Visa M/C Discover Amex • DATES AVAILABLE: May 1 thru
August 25, • ROOM TYPE: SR Apt. • BED TYPE: S • BEDS: 2 • BATH: C S P •
FOOD: Caf. SB VM NR • INFO: Coin washers/dryers, fitness center, sauna, TV
lounge, free parking. Linen charge: $4.75 per person per night. Children
welcome, conference use only, 10 persons minimum required. Groups only. •
ACTIVITIES: Art Gallery, concerts, swimming, Theater, game room, hiking. (650
acres of woodlands) Johnstown Flood Museum; Incline Plane; Flood Memorial;
Galleria Mall; Horizon Outlets.

518 Lewisburg, PA   ?   &

Bucknell University (C)
Reservation, Information & Conf. Services, Lewisburg, PA 17837, Ph: (717)
524-3095, ASK FOR: Judy Mickanis, Conf. & Prog. Serv.
ROOM PRICING: (S) $27.00, (D) $44.00, • PAYMENT: Cash Per. Ck • DATES
AVAILABLE: Mid-June-Mid Aug., • BEDS: 2 • FOOD: Caf. SB • INFO: Children
welcome, linens included • ACTIVITIES: Slifer House Museum, Williamsfort Little
league Museum, racquetball, art gallery, swimming, game room, tennis, hiking, TV
in public lounge

519 Loretto, PA   ?

Saint Francis College of PA (C)
Loretto, PA 15940, Ph: (814) 472-3029, ASK FOR: Office of Residence Life
ROOM PRICING: (S) $38.95, (includes all meals, linens use of facilities), •
PAYMENT: Cash Per. Ck • DATES AVAILABLE: June 1-Aug. 1, • BEDS: 2 •
FOOD: Caf. VM • INFO: Children welcome, coin washers/dryers, TV lounge. •
ACTIVITIES: Swimming, sports. Penn. Railroad Museum; Schwab Estate on
Campus; Gallitzin State Park; Johnston Flood Memorial; Southern Alleghneys
Museum of Art on Campus.

520 Meadville, PA   ?   &

Allegheny College (C)
520 North Main, Meadville, PA 16335, Ph: (814) 332-2749, Fax: (814) 724-8619,
ASK FOR: Mitzi Greene, Conf. Coordinator
ROOM PRICING: Sliding scale. Call for rates., Single & Double Rooms, Minimum
Group Size 5, • PAYMENT: Cash Per. Ck Trav. Ck Visa M/C Discover •
DATES AVAILABLE: Mid May- Mid August, • ROOM TYPE: SR • BED TYPE: S •
BEDS: 2 • BATH: C • FOOD: Caf. SB VM NR • INFO: Linen charge: $6.00 per
week, children welcome with parent. • ACTIVITIES: Campus facilities,
Racquetball, Art Gallery, Park, Swimming, Game Room, Tennis, Hiking, TV in
public lounge.

U
N
I
V

---

521 **Philadelphia, PA**   ? ⚊

Drexel University (E)
101 North 34th St., Philadelphia, PA 19104, Ph: (215) 590-8707, Fax: (215) 590-8788, E-mail: Booneca @ Post.Drexel. Edu, ASK FOR: Mr. Charles Boone, Summer Conf.
ROOM PRICING: (S) $37.00, (D) $33.00, • PAYMENT: Cash Per. Ck Trav. Ck • DATES AVAILABLE: June 24 - Sept. 2, • BEDS: 2 • FOOD: Caf. SB VM NR • INFO: Linens avail. at extra charge, children welcome with supervision, air conditioned halls with kitchens. • ACTIVITIES: Philadelphia zoo; University City Area; 30 min. to Valley Forge; Penn's Landing; sports; Historical Center; Liberty Bell, Independence Hall; 15 min. from airport.

522 **Philadelphia, PA**   ? ⚊

International House of Philidelphia (E)
3701 Chestnut St., Philadelphia, PA 19104, Ph: (215) 387-5125, ASK FOR: Housing Office
ROOM PRICING: (S) $54.00, $435.00- $485.00/ month, for single room Larger units at varied prices, • PAYMENT: Cash Trav. Ck Visa M/C • DATES AVAILABLE: Year Round, • FOOD: VM NR • INFO: Residents must be full-time student, academic affiliate, intern, or professional trainee. Applications upon request. • ACTIVITIES: 24 hour security, activity center, laundry and housekeeping services, linen exchange, parking, access to U of PA athletic facilities, gourmet restaurant. and bar. Travel agency; Centrally located - 5 min. from city center.

523 **Philadelphia, PA**   ?

Moore College of Art (T)
20th at Parkway, Philadelphia, PA 19103, Ph: (215) 568-4515, Ext: 1129, ASK FOR: Katie Davis, Dir. of Residence Life
ROOM PRICING: (S) $20.00, (D) $30.00, Discount for longer stays, • PAYMENT: Cash Per. Ck Trav. Ck Visa M/C • DATES AVAILABLE: May- Aug., • ROOM TYPE: SR • BED TYPE: S • BEDS: 1-2 • BATH: C S • FOOD: Caf. VM NR • INFO: Linens included, children welcome, no pets, no alcohol. • ACTIVITIES: Art gallery, park, museums, TV in public lounge. Philadelphia Museum of Art; Academy of Natural Science; Franklin Institute.

524 **Philadelphia, PA**   ? ⚊

Temple University (T)
1755 N. 13th Street 405 SAC, Philadelphia, PA 19122, Ph: (215) 204-3279, Fax: (215) 204-3261, ASK FOR: Jeff Thompkins, Off. for Summer Programs
ROOM PRICING: (S) $19.00 - $27.00, (D) $18.00- $25.00, • PAYMENT: Cash Per. Ck Trav. Ck • DATES AVAILABLE: Mid-May- Mid-Aug. , • ROOM TYPE: SR Apt. Suite • BED TYPE: S • BEDS: 2 • BATH: C S P • FOOD: Caf. SB VM NR • INFO: Small linen charge Children under 5 free, 5-12 half price. Coin washers/dryers, TV lounge, fitness rooms. • ACTIVITIES: Philadelphia Art Museum, Independence Mall, Valley Forge, Philadelphia Zoo, campus sports facilities.

525 **Pittsburgh, PA**   ? ⚊

Carlow College (T)
3333 Fifth Ave., Pittsburgh, PA 15213, Ph: (412) 578-6319, ASK FOR: Josette Skobieranda, Resid. Life
ROOM PRICING: (S) $20.00, (D) $30.00, • PAYMENT: Cash Per. Ck Trav. Ck • DATES AVAILABLE: May 20 - July 20, (SomeYear round)• ROOM TYPE: SR • BED TYPE: S • BEDS: 1-2 • BATH: C • FOOD: Caf. SB VM NR • INFO: No children, no air-conditioning. • ACTIVITIES: Carnegie Museum; zoo; Scaife Art Gallery; Cathedral of Learning; Phipps Conservatory; Three Rivers Stadium; ballet theater.

---

526 **Pittsburgh, PA**   ? ♿

La Roche College (T)
9000 Babcock Blvd., Pittsburgh, PA 15237-5898, Ph: (412) 367-9300, Ext: 215,
ASK FOR: Anita Carruthers, Dir. of Community & Outreach Servc.
ROOM PRICING: (S) $20.00, (D) $20.00, • PAYMENT: Cash Per. Ck • DATES
AVAILABLE: May 15-Aug 15, • FOOD: SB VM NR • INFO: No children •
ACTIVITIES: Jogging trail, downtown Pittsburgh, theater, movies, fitness center,
sports center on campus. Three Rivers Stadium; North Park.

527 **Pittsburgh, PA**   ?

Point Park College (T)
201 Wood St., Pittsburgh, PA 15222, Ph: (412) 392-3824, ASK FOR: Housing
Office
ROOM PRICING: (D) $15.00, • PAYMENT: Cash Per. Ck Trav. Ck • DATES
AVAILABLE: May 15 -August 15, • FOOD: Caf. VM NR • INFO: All individuals
must be members of the American Youth Hostel, Rooms have private baths. •
ACTIVITIES: TV in public lounge. Nearby: Pittsburgh cultural attractions.

528 **Reading, PA**   ?

Albright College (T)
13th & Bern Steets, P. O. Box 15234, Reading, PA 19612-5234, Ph: (610)
921-7612, Fax: (610) 921-7769, E-mail: Kulpk@albsun.alb.edu, ASK FOR:
Confernce Office
ROOM PRICING: (S) $18.00 - $24.00, Apt. for up to 4 persons. $80-$90/night., •
PAYMENT: Cash Per. Ck Trav. Ck Visa M/C • DATES AVAILABLE: 2nd week
in June-2nd week in Aug., • BEDS: 2 • FOOD: Caf. SB VM NR • INFO: Children
welcome, linen charge $5-$7 per set. TV lounge. Apts. have bath, kitchen, living
area. • ACTIVITIES: Racquetball; art gallery; bowling; swimming; concerts; game
room; tennis; Reading Outlets; Lancaster; Philadelphia; Hershey Park; Crystal
Cave; Hopewell Furnace; Blue Marsh Lake; Roadside America.

529 **Wilkes Barre, PA**   ? ♿

Education Conf. Center at King's College (E)
Kings College, Wilkes Barre, PA 18711, Ph: (717) 826-5807, Fax: (717) 821-5332,
ASK FOR: Brother Herman E. Zaccarelli, C.S.C.
ROOM PRICING: (S) $26.00, (D) $36.00, • PAYMENT: Cash Per. Ck Trav. Ck
Visa M/C Discover • DATES AVAILABLE: May 20 - Aug. 15, • ROOM TYPE: SR
Apt. • BED TYPE: S • BEDS: 2-4 • BATH: C P • FOOD: Caf. SB VM NR • INFO:
Linens included, children welcome, coin washer/dryers. 24 security, conference
facilities for up to 3,000. Also available: 67 apartments with four private
bedrooms in each. • ACTIVITIES: Racquetball, films, art gallery, concerts,
swimming, theaters, game room, tennis, hiking, museums, TV lounge. 2 Blocks
from Downtown Area; Near Pocono Mtn.; Lackawanna Coal Mine Tour; Steamtown
National Historical Site; AAA Baseball Stadium.

530 **Williamsport, PA**   ? ♿

Lycoming College (T)
700 College Place, Williamsport, PA 17701, Ph: (717) 321-4148, ASK FOR:
Director - Summer Conf.
ROOM PRICING: (S) $15.00, (D) $20.00, • PAYMENT: Cash Only • DATES
AVAILABLE: May 11-Aug. 15, • ROOM TYPE: SR • FOOD: Caf. VM NR •
ACTIVITIES: College sports facilities.Penn Grand Canyon; Little League Museum;
Hiawatha Paddlewheeler; Millionaire's Row Mansion tours.

U N I V

Puerto Rico

531 **Mayaguez** ?   &

University of Puerto Rico (T) Hotel Colegial
High #2, Post Street, P O Box 5000   , Mayaguez, 00680, Ph: (809)
265-3891, Fax: (809) 833-2715, ASK FOR: Ana D. Ramirez
ROOM PRICING: (S) $15.00, (D) $25.00, Additioal person $10.00, • PAYMENT:
Cash Per. Ck Trav. Ck Visa M/C Amex • DATES AVAILABLE: Year Round, •
ROOM TYPE: SR • BED TYPE: S • BEDS: 2-3 • BATH: C P • FOOD: VM NR •
INFO: No extra charge for A/C, swimming pool, tennis court, kitchen facilities
available (free), smoking restriced, children welcome. • ACTIVITIES: Beaches; Zoo;
Museums and National Monuments; Shopping Malls.
DIRECTIONS: Fly direct to Mayaguez Eugenio Maria de Hostos Airport. Driving
from San Juan, south route take highway Luis Ferre through Ponce and then
westbound from Ponce take highway #2 to Mayaguez. Driving from San Juan,
north route, take highway #2 to Mayaguez.

532 **San German** ?   &

Interamerican University (T) San German Campus
Call Box 5100, San German, 00683, Ph: (809) 264-1912, Ext: 315/387, ASK
FOR: Res. Hall Mgr.
ROOM PRICING: (S) $37.45, (D) $48.15, (Rooms for 3 or 4 guests available), •
PAYMENT: Cash Per. Ck • DATES AVAILABLE: Dates vary, Inquiry necessary •
FOOD: Caf. VM NR • INFO: Children welcome, air conditioning and linens
provided. Some rooms at discount prices. • ACTIVITIES: Game room, concerts,
museum, art gallery. Nearby: beaches; fishing; Biolominiscent Bay; snorkeling;
diving.

Rhode Island

533 **Smithfield, RI** ?   &

Bryant College (E)
1150 Douglas Pike, Smithfield, RI 02917, Ph: (401) 232-6324, ASK FOR: Shelia
Guay, Conf. Office
ROOM PRICING: Per person, (S) $17.00- $54.00, • PAYMENT: Cash Visa •
DATES AVAILABLE: Year round, • ROOM TYPE: SR • BED TYPE: S • BEDS: 2 •
BATH: S • FOOD: Caf. SB VM • INFO: Linens included, children welcome, no
pets. • ACTIVITIES: Racquetball, swimming, gme room, tennis, TV in public
lounge. Newport, RI,(beaches, shopping); Boston, MA, (Museums, shopping).

South Carolina

534 **Charleston, SC** ?   &

The College of Charleston (E)
40 Coming Street, Charleston, SC 29424, Ph: (803) 953-5523, ASK FOR: Terry
Eby, Dir. Special Groups
ROOM PRICING: (S) $24.00, (D) $26.00, 5 Residence Halls, • PAYMENT: Per. Ck
M/C Discover • DATES AVAILABLE: May 18- Aug. 1, • BED TYPE: S • FOOD:
Caf. SB VM NR • INFO: No linens available, children welcome, some residence
halls have kitchens. • ACTIVITIES: Racquetball, swimming, game room, tennis,
gym facilities, extra charge for gym, pool. Nearby: Historical tours/parks;
Historical Gardens; Museums; Festivals; Beaches; Fishing; Shopping; Dining;
Night-Entertainment.

535 **Clemson, SC** ?   &

Clemson University (E) The Clemson House
Suite 532 Box 345472, Clemson, SC 29634-5472, Ph: (803) 656-0594, ASK FOR:
Conference Services
ROOM PRICING: (S) $13.50-$18.00, (D) $20.00-$38.00, • PAYMENT: Cash Per.
Ck Trav. Ck Visa M/C • DATES AVAILABLE: May 16-Aug. 7, • ROOM TYPE:
SR Apt. • BED TYPE: S • BEDS: 2-4 • BATH: C P • FOOD: Caf. SB VM NR •
INFO: Linens charge: $5.00 per packet; Children welcome, Must have min. of 25
participants for educational function. • ACTIVITIES: Racquetball, films, art
gallery, bowling, concerts, park, swimming, tennis, game rm, museums. Hartwell
& Keowee Lakes; White water rafting-Chattooga River; Historic towns; plantation
tours; Apparal Research Facility tour/ outlet shopping.

(T) = Travelers Accommodations   (E) = Educational Related   (C) = Groups & Conference Use

536 **Conway, SC**   ?   ♿

Coastal Carolina University (E) Office of Residence Life
P. O. Box 29520, Conway, SC 29526, Ph: (803) 347-2406, ASK FOR: Mr. Kim
Montague/Mr. Chris Shaffer
ROOM PRICING: Apt. Units-4 bedroom & One bedroom, (S) $40.00, (D) $40.00, •
PAYMENT: Cash Per. Ck Trav. Ck • DATES AVAILABLE: May 15-Aug.15, •
FOOD: Caf. NR • INFO: Linens charge: $3.00 per day, children welcome, no pets.
Preference given to larger groups. • ACTIVITIES: Myrtle Beach-8 miles; Brookgreen
Gardens-14 miles; Historic Charleston-70 miles; Outlet Malls- Waccamaw; park.

South Dakota

537 **Rapid City, SD**   ?

National American University (T) College Inn
121 Kansas City Street, Rapid City, SD 57701, Ph: (605) 394-4870, Fax: (605)
394-4869, ASK FOR: Diane Lang
ROOM PRICING: (S) $25.00-$38.00 (D) up to $55.00. Private & dorm style rooms.
Group rates available., • PAYMENT: Cash Per. Ck Trav. Ck Visa M/C Amex •
DATES AVAILABLE: June 1 - Mid-Aug., • BEDS: 1-6 • FOOD: • INFO: Linens and
towels included, no pets, children under 16, free, TV lounge, free parking, coin
washers/dryers. • ACTIVITIES: Swimming; Mount Rushmore; Custer State Park;
Keystone, SD; Crazy Horse Memorial ; Badlands; Bear Country; Wind Cave; Jewell
Cave; Deadwood Gaming.

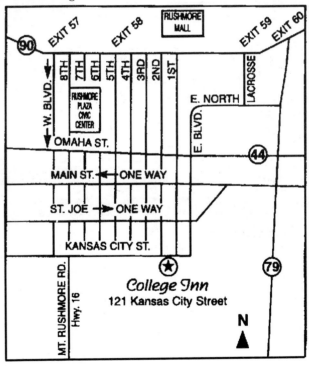

U
N
I
V

Tennessee

538 Harrogate, TN   ? ♿

Lincoln Memorial University (T)
Harrogate, TN 37752, Ph: (615) 869-3611, Ext: 212, ASK FOR: Student
Development Office
ROOM PRICING: (S) $20.00, (D) $36.00, • PAYMENT: Cash Per. Ck Trav. Ck
Visa M/C • DATES AVAILABLE: May- Aug., • ROOM TYPE: SR • BED TYPE: S •
BEDS: 2 • BATH: C P • FOOD: Caf. SB VM NR • INFO: Provide own linens, no
alcohol. • ACTIVITIES: Indoor swimming, tennis, hiking trails.Cumberland Gap
National Park; Lincoln Museum; many lakes and recreation areas nearby.

539 Jackson, TN   ? ♿

Lambuth University (T)
705 Lambuth Blvd., Jackson, TN 38301, Ph: (901) 425-3211, Fax: (901)
988-4700, ASK FOR: Rodney Cook
ROOM PRICING: Room rates negotiable!, • PAYMENT: Cash Per. Ck • DATES
AVAILABLE: Call for dates available, • BEDS: 2-4 • FOOD: Caf. VM NR • INFO:
Free parking, coin washers/dryers, TV lounge. • ACTIVITIES: Swimming, game
room, tennis. Nashville and Memphis are nearby; The Casey Jones Museum is
located in Jackson.
DIRECTIONS: Take I-40 from Memphis, TN toward Nashville. Jackson is approx.
75 miles from Memphis-130 miles to Nashville.

540 Memphis, TN   ? ♿

Rhodes College (C)
2000 N. Parkway, Memphis, TN 38112, Ph: (901) 843-3967, ASK FOR: Ms.
Nelson, Conf. Service
ROOM PRICING: (S) $32.00, (D) $47.00, • PAYMENT: Cash Visa M/C • DATES
AVAILABLE: June-July, • FOOD: Caf. VM NR • INFO: No children, groups of 25
or more only. • ACTIVITIES: Aart gallery, tennis, swimming, hiking. Overton Park
and Zoo; Overton Square - restaurants and shops; Memphis attractions.

541 Nashville, TN   ? ♿

Vanderbilt University (C)
Box 1677, Station B, Nashville, TN 37235, Ph: (615) 343-8699, ASK FOR: Libby
Magill, Conf. Director
ROOM PRICING: (S) $30.00 - $40.00, (D) $30.00 - $40.00, (meals included), •
PAYMENT: Cash • DATES AVAILABLE: Summer, • FOOD: Caf. SB VM NR •
INFO: Non-profit groups only. • ACTIVITIES: Andrew Jackson's Hermitage Home;
Parthenon; Opryland Amusement Park; State Capital and museum; sport
facilities.

Texas

542 Austin, TX   ? ♿

The Castilian Residence Hall (T)
2323 San Antonio St., Austin, TX 78705, Ph: (512) 478-9811, ASK FOR: R.M.
Vanscoy, Director
ROOM PRICING: (S) $28.00, (D) $30.00, • PAYMENT: Cash Per. Ck Trav. Ck
Visa M/C • DATES AVAILABLE: June 1 -Aug. 10, • ROOM TYPE: SR • BED
TYPE: S • BEDS: 2 • BATH: S • FOOD: Caf. VM NR • INFO: Children welcome. •
ACTIVITIES: Exercise and recreation room, indoor pool. Situated in heart of Univ.
of Texas Academic Community; LBJ Library; Lake Travis; capitol buildings.

543 Beaumont, TX   ?

Lamar University - Beaumont (T)
P. O. Box 10041, Beaumont, TX 77710, Ph: (409) 880-8111, ASK FOR: Housing
Office
ROOM PRICING: (S) $10.00, (D) $16.00, • PAYMENT: Cash Trav. Ck Visa M/C
Discover • DATES AVAILABLE: May 15 -Aug. 15, Call for addl. availability• ROOM
TYPE: SR • BED TYPE: S • BEDS: 2 • BATH: C • FOOD: Caf. SB VM NR • INFO:
Children welcome, no pets. • ACTIVITIES: Southeast Texas Energy Museum;
Pleasure Island; Riverfront Park; Gladys City Boomtown; campus sports.

---

544 Belton, TX   ? &

Univ. Of Mary Hardin-Baylor (E)
UMHB Box 426, Belton, TX 76513, Ph: (817) 939-5811, Ext: 232, ASK FOR: Jeff Van Auken, Housing Office
ROOM PRICING: (S) $23.00, (D) $23.00, • PAYMENT: Cash Per. Ck Trav. Ck Visa M/C • DATES AVAILABLE: June 1 -Aug. 20, • ROOM TYPE: SR • BED TYPE: S • BEDS: 2 • BATH: C S P • FOOD: Caf. SB VM NR • INFO: Linen chg. $5.00 per wk, no smoking or alcohol. • ACTIVITIES: Salado-historic city of Old West; fishing lakes; Ft. Hood; sports facilities on campus.

545 Dallas, TX   ?

Dallas Christian College (T)
2700 Christian Parkway, Dallas, TX 75234, Ph: (214) 241-3371, ASK FOR: Carl Burns
ROOM PRICING: (S) $14.00, (D) $14.00, • PAYMENT: Cash Only • DATES AVAILABLE: Year Round, • FOOD: Caf. VM NR • INFO: No linens furished. • ACTIVITIES: TV in public lounge. Rangers Baseball Stadium; 6 Flags Over Texas; Cowboy Football Stadium.

546 Denton, TX

Texas Woman's University (C)
Box 425380, Denton, TX 76204, Ph: (817) 898-3676, Fax: (817) 898-3638, ASK FOR: Dir. of Conf. Events, Brian Dohe
ROOM PRICING: (S) $21.00, (D) $31.50 Minimum of 10 people, • PAYMENT: Cash Per. Ck Trav. Ck • DATES AVAILABLE: Year round, • ROOM TYPE: SR • BEDS: 1 • BATH: S • FOOD: Caf. SB VM NR • INFO: Coin washers/dryers, TV in room, free parking, linens, in room coffee/atea pots, in room refridgerators. • ACTIVITIES: All campus sports facilities; tennis courts; sand volleyball courts; fitness center; art gallery; TV in public lounge; theater; films; concerts; museum; park. Dallas (35 min.); beautiful lakes; golf course.

547 El Paso, TX   ?

University of Texas at El Paso (E)
105 Kelly Hall, El Paso, TX 79968, Ph: (915) 747-5352, Fax: (915) 747-5289, or (915) 747-5651, ASK FOR: Karen Knight, Housing Office
ROOM PRICING: (S) $11.75-$15.75, (D) $17.50-$25.50, $5.00 Each addit. per., • PAYMENT: Cash Trav. Ck • DATES AVAILABLE: Year round, Closed X-mas break• BEDS: 2 • FOOD: Caf. SB VM NR • INFO: Linen chg. $3.00 per day. Limited handicapped availability. Payment must be paid upon arrival. Coin washer/dyer. • ACTIVITIES: Racquetball, game room, art gallery, tennis,TV in public lounge. Nearby: Juarez, Mexico, Carlsbad Caverns.

548 Huntsville, TX

Sam Houston State University (T)
P. O. Box 2416 SHSU Stn., Huntsville, TX 77341, Ph: (409) 294-1816, ASK FOR: Joellen Tipton
ROOM PRICING: (S) $18.00, (D) $24.00, • PAYMENT: Cash Per. Ck Trav. Ck Visa M/C • DATES AVAILABLE: May 31 - July , • BEDS: 2 • FOOD: Caf. VM NR • INFO: Children welcome, no pets, coin washer/dryer. • ACTIVITIES: Campus sports, theater, films. Near Houston; Lake Livingston; Huntsville State Park.

549 Irving, TX   ?

University of Dallas (C)
1845 E. Northgate, Irving, TX 75062, Ph: (972) 721-5378, ASK FOR: Summer Conference Coordinator
ROOM PRICING: (S) $20.00, (D) $32.00, • PAYMENT: Cash Per. Ck Trav. Ck • DATES AVAILABLE: June 1- Aug. 10, • BED TYPE: S • BEDS: 2 • FOOD: Caf. VM • INFO: Linen charge: $10.00, air conditioned, coin washers/dryers, TV lounge, free parking. • ACTIVITIES: Recreational sports facility available on campus. Dallas/Fort Worth Metroplex; Museums; shopping; dining; convenient to Dallas/Fort Worth Airport.

550 **Plainview, TX**   ?

Wayland Baptist University (T) Brotherhood Hall
1900 W. 7th Street, Plainview, TX 79072, Ph: (806) 296-4725, ASK FOR: Pau┃
McGinnis, Student Serv. Office
ROOM PRICING: Rates per person, (S) $5.00, (D) $5.00, • PAYMENT: Cash Per
Ck • DATES AVAILABLE: Call for availablity, • FOOD: Caf. SB VM NR • INFO┃
Linens not provided. • ACTIVITIES: Racquetball, game room, museums, TV ir┃
public lounge. Palo Duro Canyon; "Texas" Musical.

551 **Stephenville, TX**   ?   ♿

Tarleton State University (E)
Box T-280 , Stephenville, TX 76402, Ph: (254) 968-9083, Fax: (254) 968-9954
ASK FOR: Housing & Residence Life, Assistant Dir. of Housing
ROOM PRICING: (S) $10.00 (D) $20.00, • PAYMENT: Cash Per. Ck • DATES
AVAILABLE: June 1 - August 1, • FOOD: Caf. VM NR • INFO: Linens no┃
provided, TV lounge, coin washers/dryers. • ACTIVITIES: Theaters, game room.
DIRECTIONS: Interstate 20 West from Ft. Worth, south on highway 281.

552 **Waco, TX**   ?   ♿

Baylor University (T)
P. O. Box 97033, Waco, TX 76798, Ph: (817) 755-1921, ASK FOR: Jack
Thornton, Univ. Host
ROOM PRICING: (S) $14.00, (D) $14.00, • PAYMENT: Cash Only • DATES
AVAILABLE: May 22 -July 13, • FOOD: Caf. SB VM • INFO: Linen charge:
$10.50(5 days) No smoking or alcohol in dorms. • ACTIVITIES: Many college
workshops, theater presentations.Texas Safari; Strecker Museum; Texas Range┃
Hall of Fame; Armstrong-Browning Library.

Utah

553 **Ogden, UT**   ?

Weber State University (E)
3750 Harrison Blvd., Ogden, UT 84408, Ph: (801) 626-7218, ASK FOR: Briar┃
Stecklein
ROOM PRICING: (S) $17.25, (D) $20.00, Min. No. Req. 50, • PAYMENT: Cash
Trav. Ck Visa M/C • DATES AVAILABLE: August only, • FOOD: Caf. VM NR •┃
INFO: Linene charges incl., no alcohol, no smoking, Children welcome
w/supervision. • ACTIVITIES: Racquetball, bowling, swimming, game room,
tennis, TV in public lounge. The Great Salt Lake; Salt Lake City; Temple Square.

Vermont

554 Burlington, VT   ?   ♿

Trinity College of Vermont (E)
208 Colchester Ave., Burlington, VT 05401, Ph: (802) 658-0337,   Fax: (802)
658-5446, E-mail: charity.trintyvt.edu, ASK FOR: Gil Wood
ROOM PRICING: (S) $32.00 (D) $47.00, • PAYMENT: Cash Per. Ck Trav. Ck •
BEDS: 2 • FOOD: Caf. SB VM NR • INFO: Linen charge: $5.00, children welcome,
TV lounge, coin washers/dryers, no pets, must follow campus regulations. •
ACTIVITIES: Tennis, fitness center. Church St. Marketplace; Melbourne Museum;
Teddy Bear Factory; Lake champlain Ferry.
DIRECTIONS: From south: Take I-87 to exit 20, follow signs to Fort Anne, join
route 4 north, take route 22A north.
From east: Take route2 or 302 to Montpelier, VT-then I-89 north.

555 Plainfield, VT   ?   ♿

Goddard College (T)
Plainfield, VT 05667, Ph: (802) 454-8311, ASK FOR: Ms. Malgeri, Conf.
Coordinator
ROOM PRICING: (S) $22.00, (D) $32.00, • PAYMENT: Cash Per. Ck Trav. Ck
Visa M/C • DATES AVAILABLE: Summer months and some year round, •
ROOM TYPE: SR Apt. Suite • BED TYPE: S • BEDS: 2 • BATH: C P • FOOD: Caf.
SB • INFO: No Pets, children welcome, coin washer/dryer, free parking. •
ACTIVITIES: Hiking, cross country ski trails on property, tennis court, volleyball.
Goddard College on a historic 250 acre estate. Trapp Family Lodge: Granite
quarries at Barre; State Capital at Montpelier; parks.

Virginia

556 Blacksburg, VA

Virginia Polytechnic State University (C)
109 East Eggleston Hall, Blacksburg, VA 24061-0428, Ph: (540) 231-6204 , ASM
FOR: Tom Deuch, Shannon Dove
ROOM PRICING: (S) $17.00, (D) $28.00 - no AC (S) 24.00 (D) 38 - with AC
Discount for youths, • PAYMENT: Cash Per. Ck Trav. Ck • DATES AVAILABLE
May 23- August 14, • ROOM TYPE: SR Suite • BED TYPE: S • BEDS: 1-2 • BATH
C S • FOOD: Caf. SB VM NR • INFO: Linens included, children welcome, no pets
• ACTIVITIES: Racquetball, films, art gallery, bowling, park, swimming, boating
theaters, game room, tennis, hiking, museums, TV in public lounge. Claytor Lake
State Park; Cascades; Jefferson National Forest; Blue Ridge Parkway.
DIRECTIONS: From Interstate 81; take exit 118 (Chrisisansgurg) onto U.S. Rt.460
West, remain on 460 West to Virginia Tech. Take Virginia Tech exit (314 East) of
U.S. 460

557 Charlottesville, VA   ?

University of Virginia (T) Conference Services
Pagehouse Station #1, Charlottesville, VA 22904, Ph: (804) 924-4479, Fax: (804
924-1027, E-mail: SNS8C@Virginia, ASK FOR: UVA Housing Division
ROOM PRICING: (S) $15.00 - $30.00, (D) $20.00 - $40.00, • PAYMENT: Cash
Per. Ck Trav. Ck Visa M/C • DATES AVAILABLE: June 1 - August 15, •
BEDS: 1-2 • FOOD: Caf. SB VM NR • INFO: Children welcome, linens included in
some rates. Arrangements can be made for child care. TV in public lounge. 10
large complexes, 6200 beds. • ACTIVITIES: Racquetball, films, art gallery
concerts, swimming, theaters, game room, tennis, hiking, museums. Discovery
Museum; Wineries, Monticello, home of Thomas Jefferson; Blue Ridge Mountains
Montpelier, Home of James Madison; lakes; parks.

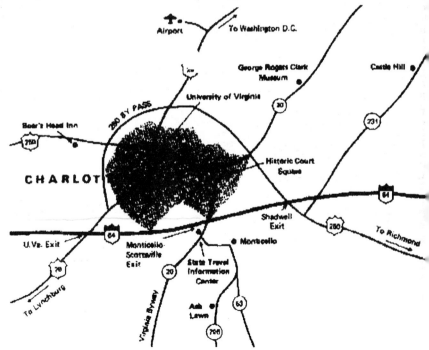

558 Lynchburg, VA　　　　　　　　　　　　　　　? ♿

Randolph- Macon Woman's College (C)
2500 Rivermont Ave., Lynchburg, VA 24503, Ph: (804) 947-8146, ASK FOR: Ruth Anne Oertle, Summer Prog.
ROOM PRICING: (S) $14.00/no air-cond, $18.00/air-cond., (D) $24.00/no air-cond, $30.00/air-cond, • PAYMENT: Cash Per. Ck Trav. Ck • DATES AVAILABLE: June - early Aug., • ROOM TYPE: SR • BED TYPE: S • BEDS: 1-3 • BATH: C • FOOD: Caf. SB VM NR • INFO: Linens included, no pets, children welcome, coin washers/dryers, TV lounge, free parking, phones in each room. • ACTIVITIES: Art gallery, basektball, softball, soccer, weight room, aerobics room, swimming, tennis, baseball, museums.　　Poplar Forrest- Jefferson's Little Monticello; Smith Mountain Lake; Appomattox; Blue Ridge Parkway.

559 Norfolk, VA　　　　　　　　　　　　　　　? ♿

Norfolk State University (T)
2401 Corprew Ave., Norfolk, VA 23504, Ph: (804) 683-8876, ASK FOR: Mrs. Joyce Coker, Aux. Services
ROOM PRICING: (S) $18.00, (D) $24.00, • PAYMENT: Cash Trav. Ck • DATES AVAILABLE: May 20 -July 31, • ROOM TYPE: SR • BED TYPE: S • BEDS: 1-3 • BATH: C S P • FOOD: Caf. SB VM NR • INFO: Linen charge, $3.50. Children welcome with supervision. • ACTIVITIES: Swimming, tennis, films, bowling, game room. Historic Williamsburg; Virginia beach; Busch Gardens; Old Fort Monroe.

560 Radford, VA　　　　　　　　　　　　　　　　　♿

Radford University (E)
Extended Education, Box 6917, Radford, VA 24142, Ph: (540) 831-6512, Fax: 540-831-6119, E-mail: exted@r net.edu, ASK FOR: Greg A. Beecher Dir. of Ext. Ed.
ROOM PRICING: (S) $16.00- $35.00, (D) $24.00- $50.00, • PAYMENT: Cash Per. Ck Trav. Ck • DATES AVAILABLE: May 25- July 30, • ROOM TYPE: SR • BED TYPE: S • BEDS: 1-2 • BATH: S P • FOOD: Caf. SB VM NR • INFO: Linens included in air-conditioned rooms., children welcome, no pets. • ACTIVITIES: Racquetball, art gallery, bowling, swimming, game room, tennis, TV in public lounge. Blue Ridge Parkway; The New River; Jefferson National Forest; Explore Park- Roanoke.
DIRECTIONS: Interstate 81 South to Exit 109 - 5 miles into Radford on Tyler Avenue

U
N
I
V

561 Salem, VA　　　　　　　　　　　　　　　　　?

Roanoke College (C)
c/o Summer Conference Manager, Salem, VA 24153, Ph: (703) 375-2373, ASK FOR: Summer Conf. Manager
ROOM PRICING: (S) $17.00 no air-cond, $20.00 air-cond., (D) $28.00 no air-cond., $32.00 air-cond., • PAYMENT: Cash • DATES AVAILABLE: May 30 - July31, • BEDS: 2 • FOOD: Caf. • INFO: Min. number: 50, Linens included, must use our food service. • ACTIVITIES: Blue Ridge Parkway, Virginia Transportation Museum, Smith Mountain Lake, Center in the Square (arts center), art gallery, park, game room, tennis, TV in public lounge

Washington

562 Bellingham, WA　　　　　　　　　　　　　　　?

International House Bellingham (T)
505 N. Forest St. at Cedar St., Bellingham, WA 92225, Ph: (604) 689-0905
ROOM PRICING: (S) $125.00 (D) $150.00, 2 week min. stay summer, • PAYMENT: Cash Trav. Ck • DATES AVAILABLE: Jun. 15-Sept. 15, • BEDS: 1 • FOOD: Caf. NR OCR • INFO: No smoking, 4 persons per bathroom, 6 persons per kitchen, trees, lawn, veranda, sea 2 blocks away. • ACTIVITIES: Near Vancouver, BC; Alaska Ferry; Near Fairhaven Heritage Village.

563 **Cheney, WA**   ?

Eastern Washington Univ. (T)
EWU Event Planning MS-180, Cheney, WA 99004, Ph: (509) 359-2518, Fax: (509
359-4829, ASK FOR: Jan Ittner
ROOM PRICING: (S) $15.00 (D) $30.00, • PAYMENT: Cash Per. Ck Visa M/C •
DATES AVAILABLE: Varies-call, • FOOD: Caf. SB VM NR • INFO: Linen charge
$5.00P/P, TV lounge, coin washers/dryers, children welcome w/supervision. Cal
for reservations. • ACTIVITIES: Racquetball, art gallery, park, swimming
theaters, game room, tennis, bike trails, fitness center. Near Spokane.

564 **Spokane, WA**   &

Gonzaga University (C)
East 500 Boone Ave., Spokane, WA 99258, Ph: (509) 323-6851, ASK FOR
Conference Services, Scott Murray
ROOM PRICING: (S) $17.00, (D) $30.00. • PAYMENT: Cash Per. Ck Trav. Ck •
DATES AVAILABLE: June 1 -Aug. 10 (12 room hall all year), • ROOM TYPE: SI
Apt. • BED TYPE: S • BEDS: 2 • BATH: S P • FOOD: SB VM NR • INFO:
Children welcome. Groups of15 or more only. • ACTIVITIES: All campus sports
facilities, films, game room, art gallery, museum. Nearby: Spokane River Park
downtown shopping; 75 lakes in a 50 mile radius; tours of historical mansions
Lake Coeur D'Alene tours.
DIRECTIONS: Take I - 90 North to Sharp Ave - West. Go to Pearl St. Then
South to Schovenberg Ctr.

565 **Walla Walla, WA**   &

Whitman College (C)
345 Boyer Ave., Walla Walla, WA 99362, Ph: (509) 527-5251, Fax: (509)
527-5859, E-mail: dohe@whitman.edu, ASK FOR: Brian Dohe/ Dir. Conf. &
events
ROOM PRICING: (S) 21.00, (D) $31.50
Minimum 10 persons, • PAYMENT: Cash • DATES AVAILABLE: June 1-Aug. 14,
• FOOD: Caf. VM NR • INFO: Children welcome, linens included. Member,
ACED-1; open to conferences only. Internet: Dohe@Whitman. EDU • ACTIVITIES
Racquetball, art gallery, park, swimming, game room, tennis, hiking, TV in public
lounge. Whitman Mission; Blue Mountains; Fort Walla Walla Park & Museum:
Winery tours.

566 **Yakima, WA**   &

Yakima Valley Comm. College (T)
1113 So. 14th Ave., Yakima, WA 98902, Ph: (509) 574-4884, Fax: (509) 574-
4747, ASK FOR: SRC manager
ROOM PRICING: Per person, per night, (S) $20.00, • PAYMENT: Cash Per. Ck
Trav. Ck Visa • DATES AVAILABLE: Year Round, • ROOM TYPE: SR • BED
TYPE: S • BEDS: 1-2 • BATH: C • FOOD: Caf. • INFO: Minors must have adult
supervision. Linens included; Coinwashers/dryers; Free parking; rec. room with
pool tables, TV.etc. No miners. • ACTIVITIES: Parks, tennis, TV lounge. Wine
fair, historic shopping area; Indian museum; Yakima Bears Baseball; Yakima
Sunkings Basketball; White Pass Skiing; Capitol Theater.

West Virginia

567 **Athens, WV**   ?   &

Concord College (T)
Athens, WV 24712, Ph: (304) 384-5311, ASK FOR: College Center, Bill Skeat
ROOM PRICING: (S) $15.00 plus tax, (D) $22.00 plus tax, • PAYMENT: Cash
Per. Ck Trav. Ck • DATES AVAILABLE: Mid May - Mid August, • FOOD: Caf.
SB VM NR • INFO: Linen charge $7.50 / 5 days 2 week notice; Children welcome;
No alcohol; No pets. • ACTIVITIES: Racquetball, Swimming, Game Room , Tennis,
TV in Public Lounge, Track and Library. Pipestem State Park, Blue Stone State
Park, Bluestone Lake and numerous outdoor recreation areas. Area rich in
history of coal minning and coal wars.

568 **Buckhannon, WV** ?   ♿

West Virginia Wesleyan College (E)
Buckhannon, WV 26201, Ph: (304) 473-8000, Ext: 8441, ASK FOR: Summer
Conf. Office, Ms. Lively
ROOM PRICING: (S) $15.00, (D) $25.00, • PAYMENT: Cash Per. Ck Trav. Ck •
DATES AVAILABLE: May 20 - Aug. 8, • BEDS: 2 • FOOD: Caf. SB VM NR • INFO:
Linen available, extra charge. Children welcome. • ACTIVITIES: All campus sports
facilities. Blackwater Falls; Audra State Park; State Wildlife Ctr.; Canaan Valley.

569 **Elkins, WV** ♿

Davis and Elkins College (E)
100 Campus Drive, Elkins, WV 26241, Ph: (304) 637-1354, ASK FOR: Conf.
Services
ROOM PRICING: (S) $19.22 & Up, • PAYMENT: Cash Per. Ck Trav. Ck Visa
M/C • DATES AVAILABLE: May 15- July 15, • BEDS: 2 • FOOD: Caf. NR •
INFO: Linens extra charge, children welcome. • ACTIVITIES: Art gallery, concerts,
swimming, game room, tennis, hiking. Cass Scenic Railroad; Augusta Heritage
Arts Festival-July; several caverns nearby; Canaan Valley Resort-Snowshoe
Resort.

570 **Huntington, WV** ?

Marshall University (E)
400 Hal Greer Blvd., Huntington, WV 25755, Ph: (304) 696-3125, ASK FOR:
Facilities Scheduling
ROOM PRICING: (S) $14.00, (D) $24.00, • PAYMENT: Cash • DATES AVAILABLE:
Mid May - Mid Aug., • FOOD: Caf. SB VM NR • INFO: Children welcome, no
alcoholic beverages. Coin washers/dryers, TV lounge. • ACTIVITIES: Sports
facilities, films, art gallery. Nearby: David Harris River Park, Huntington Museum
of Art, glass factories, Greyhound Park.

571 **Montgomery, WV** ♿

West Virginia University Institute of Technology (E)
P. O. Box 30, Old Main, Montgomery, WV 25136, Ph: (304) 442-3183, Fax: (304)
442-1043, E-mail: dr.lord@wvit.wvnet.edu, ASK FOR: Residence Life Dir.
ROOM PRICING: (S) $15.00, (D) $30.00, • PAYMENT: Cash Per. Ck Trav. Ck
Visa M/C Discover Amex • DATES AVAILABLE: May 30 -Aug. 1, • ROOM TYPE:
SR • BED TYPE: S • BEDS: 2 • BATH: C • FOOD: Caf. SB VM NR • INFO:
Pillows and blankets not supplied, children welcome. Coin washers/dryers, TV
lounge. • ACTIVITIES: All campus sports facilities, game room, park. State
Parks; Whitewater rafting; professional baseball; state capitol.
DIRECTIONS: Route 60 to smithers, go across bridge to Route 61, turn left.

U N I V

572 **Morgantown, WV**   ♿

Pierpont Apartments (T)
445 Oakland St, Morgantown, WV 26505, Ph: (304) 598-0092 or 1-800-262-3041,
ASK FOR: Heather Berardi, sales Director
ROOM PRICING: (S) $40.00, (D) $40.00, • PAYMENT: Cash Per. Ck Trav. Ck
Visa M/C Discover • DATES AVAILABLE: Year Round, • BEDS: 1-2 • FOOD:
VM NR • INFO: Children welcome, complete kitchen with microwave. Fully
furnished with w/w carpet. Free parking.Linen rentals. • ACTIVITIES: Cable TV to
all rooms, picnic tables, fitness center, recreation room, volleyball, basketball,
laundry facilities. In rolling hills of WV; UNU Campus; hospitals and Coliseum,
and stadium within walking distance. 45 minutes from Pittsburgh,Pa.

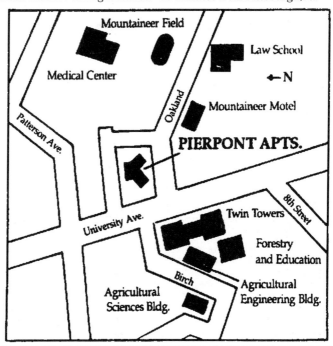

573 **Morgantown, WV**   ?

Summit Hall Residence (T)
211 Grant Ave., Morgantown, WV 26505, Ph: (800) 237-1879, ASK FOR: Frank
Witt, Manager
ROOM PRICING: (S) $25.00 w/linens, $20.00 w/o linens, (D) $36.50 w/linens,
$29.00 w/o linens, • PAYMENT: Cash Per. Ck Trav. Ck Visa M/C • DATES
AVAILABLE: May 15-Aug. 15, • ROOM TYPE: SR • BED TYPE: S • BEDS: 2 •
BATH: S P • FOOD: Caf. VM NR • INFO: Children welcome. • ACTIVITIES: Cable
TV, fitness room, computer room,hiking, swimming. Modern quality
accommodations; finest food service in area; recreational activities; West Virginia
University located on east bank of Monongahela River; Cheat Lake.

574 Morgantown, WV   ? &

West Virginia University (E)
P. O. Box 6430, Morgantown, WV 26506, Ph: (304) 293-2790, ASK FOR:
University Conf. center
ROOM PRICING: (S) $23.50, (D) $31.00, • PAYMENT: Cash Per. Ck Trav. Ck
Visa M/C • DATES AVAILABLE: May 15 - Aug 15, • BEDS: 2 • FOOD: Caf. SB
VM NR • INFO: Rollaway beds, $3.50, coin washers/dryers, TV lounges, free
parking, linens included, children welcome. • ACTIVITIES: Cheat Lake; Whitewater
River rafting; Cooper's State Forest; all campus sports.

575 Salem, WV   &

Salem-Teikyo University (T)
223 West Main Street, Salem, WV 26426, Ph: (304) 782-5301, Fax: (304)
782-5592, E-mail: studev@salem.wvnet.edu, ASK FOR: Depat. of Residence Life
ROOM PRICING: (S) $10.00 (D) $20.00, • PAYMENT: Cash Per. Ck • DATES
AVAILABLE: May 15 - Aug. 15, • BEDS: 2 • FOOD: Caf. SB VM NR • INFO: Linen
charge: $3.00, children welcome, free parking, TV lounge, coin washers/dryers,
advance reservations required. • ACTIVITIES: Racquetball, swimming, game
room, tennis, hiking, museum, bike trails, fitness center. Fort New Salem.
DIRECTIONS: When traveling on I-79, take exit 119 to route 50W for
approximately 16 miles. Follow on route 50 to the Salem-Teikyo University exit
located at the caution lights. Make a left and follow signs to the University.

576 Wheeling, WV   ? &

Wheeling Jesuit College (T)
316 Washington Ave., Wheeling, WV 26003, Ph: (304) 243-2301, ASK FOR:
Student Development/Christohper Smitherman
ROOM PRICING: (S) $33.00, (D) $46.00, • PAYMENT: Cash Per. Ck Trav. Ck •
DATES AVAILABLE: May 19- Aug. 15, • BED TYPE: S • FOOD: Caf. VM •
ACTIVITIES: Racquetball, swimming, game room, TV in public lounge. Olsebaz
Park.

Wisconsin

577 Fond Du Lac, WI   ? &

Marian College (T)
45 South National Ave., Fond Du Lac, WI 54935, Ph: (414) 923-7642, ASK FOR:
Donna Roggentine
ROOM PRICING: Price varies, please call, • PAYMENT: Cash Per. Ck Trav. Ck
Visa M/C • DATES AVAILABLE: June 1- Aug. 12, • ROOM TYPE: SR Apt. • BED
TYPE: S • BEDS: 1-2 • BATH: C • FOOD: Caf. VM NR • INFO: Linens included,
children welcome, coin washer/dryer, free parking, TV lounge. • ACTIVITIES:
Senior programming. Game room; tennis; TV in public lounge. Golfing; Historical
Village.

578 Kenosha, WI   ? &

University of Wisconsin-Parkside (C)
4019 Outer Loop Road, Kenosha, WI 53144, Ph: (414) 595-2027, ASK FOR: Bill
Niebuhr/ Dir. of Res. Life
ROOM PRICING: (S) $18.00, (D) $30.00, • PAYMENT: Cash • DATES AVAILABLE:
June 10-Aug.1, • ROOM TYPE: Apt. • BED TYPE: S • BEDS: 2 • BATH: S •
FOOD: Caf. • INFO: Includes maid & Towel service, apt. stlye setting with singles
and doubles within the apts. • ACTIVITIES: Racquetball, bowling, park,
swimming, game room, tennis, TV in public lounge. Great America Amusement
Park; Chicago Metro area; Milwaukee Metro area.

U
N
I
V

579 La Crosse, WI   ? ♿

Viterbo College (T)
815 S. 15th St., La Crosse, WI 54601, Ph: (608) 796-3841, ASK FOR: Director of
Residence
ROOM PRICING: (S) $20.00, (D) $30.00, • PAYMENT: Cash Per. Ck Trav. Ck
Visa M/C • DATES AVAILABLE: May 20 -Aug. 1, • FOOD: Caf. SB VM NR •
INFO: Children welcome with supervision, no alcohol. Also "apartment" style living
units-weekly rates. • ACTIVITIES: All campus sports facilites, theater, film,
concert, art gallery, park. Near by: Mississippi River; River cruises; boating;
hiking; biking trails; Riverfest; St. Rose's Convent.

580 Ladysmith, WI   ?

Mount Senario College (T)
1500 College Ave. West, Ladysmith, WI 54848, Ph: (715) 532-5511, ASK FOR:
Victor Macaruso
ROOM PRICING: (S) $11.50, (D) $11.50, • PAYMENT: Cash • DATES AVAILABLE:
June 7 -Aug. 11, • FOOD: Caf. SB VM NR • ACTIVITIES: Norhtland Mardis
Gras. Nearby: golf course, lake and river boating, fishing, hiking, tennis.

581 Madison, WI   ?

The Langdon Residence Hall (C)
126 Langdon St., Madison, WI 53703, Ph: (800) 634-1460, (608) 257-6949, ASK
FOR: Front Office
ROOM PRICING: (S) $25.00, (D) $25.00, • PAYMENT: Cash Per. Ck Trav. Ck
Visa M/C • DATES AVAILABLE: May 25 - Aug.15, • ROOM TYPE: SR Apt. •
BED TYPE: S • BEDS: 2 • BATH: C • FOOD: Caf. VM NR • INFO: Children
welcome, coin washers/dryers, TV lounge, morning coffee, linens. • ACTIVITIES:
Sport fields, zoo; fitness center.   Recently remodeled facilties; Circus World
Museum; House On The Rock; located near lakes; Univ. Wisconsin. State Capitol;
State Street shopping and restaurants.

582 Madison, WI

The Towers Residence Hall (T)
502 Frances St., Madison, WI 53703, Ph: (800) 458-1876, ASK FOR: Wm. J.
Levy, Gen. Manager
ROOM PRICING: (S) $52.00, (D) $72.00 group discounts available, • PAYMENT:
Cash Per. Ck Visa M/C • DATES AVAILABLE: Year Round, • ROOM TYPE: SR
• BED TYPE: S • BEDS: 2-4 • BATH: S • FOOD: Caf. VM NR • INFO: Children
welcome, Kitchenettes,meals available,coin washer/dryer. private rooms available.
• ACTIVITIES: 1 block from Univ. of Wis. Campus and Lake Mendota. Directly
located on State Street Mall.

583 Madison, WI   ?

University of Wisconsin - Madison (T)
The Regent, 1402 Regent St., Madison, WI 53711, Ph: (608) 258-4900, ASK FOR:
William Levy, Gen. Manager
ROOM PRICING: (S) $38.00, plus 12% tax, (D) $38.00, plus 12% tax, • PAYMENT:
Cash • DATES AVAILABLE: May 20 -Aug. 20, • FOOD: No • INFO: Children
accommodated 24 hr. reception desk. (Air Conditioned 2 bedroom furn. apts.
available) • ACTIVITIES: Swimming, tennis, theater, films, concerts, hiking,
bowling, boating, Lake Mendota, art gallery, park. Nearby: state capitol, Vilas
Park Zoo, arboretum

584 Milwaukee, WI

Alverno College (T)
4300 South 43th St., P.O. Box 343922, Milwaukee, WI 53234-3922, Ph: (414)
382-6162, Web Site: www.alverno.edu, ASK FOR: Auxiliary Services, Judith S.
Banzhaf
ROOM PRICING: (S) $25.00, (D) $40.00, • PAYMENT: Cash Per. Ck Trav. Ck
Visa M/C • DATES AVAILABLE: June 15 -Aug. 15, • ROOM TYPE: SR • BED
TYPE: S • BEDS: 1-2 • BATH: C P • FOOD: Caf. SB VM NR • INFO: No children,
free parking, T.V. lounge • ACTIVITIES: Theater, hiking, art gallery, park.
Downtown Milwaukee; The Milwaukee Domes; zoo; brewery tours.

585 Milwaukee, WI   ?

Gray's Conference Center (T)
6618 North Teutonia Ave., Milwaukee, WI 53209, Ph: (414) 228-6020, ASK FOR:
Felicia Pennington
ROOM PRICING: (S) $25.00, (D) $50.00, • PAYMENT: Cash Trav. Ck • DATES
AVAILABLE: Varied, call for availability, advance reservations required., • BED
TYPE: S • BEDS: 1-2 • FOOD: VM NR • INFO: No smoking, no alcohol, free
parking. • ACTIVITIES: Tennis, TV in public lounge. Brown Deer Golf Course;
Lake Michigan; Schlitz Audubon Society; Milwaukee County Zoo.

586 Milwaukee, WI   ?

Marquette University (T) Special Events & Conferences
P. O. Box 1881, Milwaukee, WI 53201-1881, Ph: (414) 288-5795
ROOM PRICING: (S) $35.00, (D) $50.00, • PAYMENT: Cash Per. Ck Visa M/C
Amex • DATES AVAILABLE: Year Round, • BEDS: 2 • FOOD: Caf. NR OCR •
INFO: Young children welcome in parents room. Coin washer/dryer, linens
included, parking $2.00. • ACTIVITIES: Milwaukee Public Museum; Pabst
Mansion; Mitchell Conservatory; Old World Wisconsin Center; all sports.

587 Milwaukee, WI   ?   &

Mount Mary College (E) Caroline Hall
2900 N. Menomonee River Parkway, Milwaukee, WI 53222, Ph: (414) 258-4810,
ASK FOR: Sharon Crees
ROOM PRICING: (S) $15.00, (D) $15.00, • PAYMENT: Cash Per. Ck Trav. Ck •
DATES AVAILABLE: June 1 - Aug.1, • BEDS: 1-2 • FOOD: Caf. SB VM NR •
INFO: Min. no. req. for conf.10, linens provided-no towels, no smoking, no
children. Food service $12/day. Free parking, coin washers/dryers, TV lounge. •
ACTIVITIES: Swimming, gym/w. equipment, sand volleyball. Milwaukee County
Zoo; Milwaukee Summer Fest; Milwaukee County Museum; Milwaukee Breweries.

588 Milwaukee, WI

Univ. of Wisconsin - Milwaukee (C)
3400 N. Maryland Ave., Milwaukee, WI 53211, Ph: (414) 229-4065, Fax: (414)
229-4127, ASK FOR: K.R. Busch, Asst. Dir. Housing
ROOM PRICING: (S) $27.00, (D) $37.00, • PAYMENT: Cash Per. Ck Trav. Ck •
DATES AVAILABLE: June 1 -Aug. 1, • ROOM TYPE: SR Apt. • BED TYPE: S •
BEDS: 1-4 • BATH: S P • FOOD: Caf. SB VM NR • INFO: Children welcome with
supervision, ticket operated washer/dryer, TV lounge with cable, cash machine,
stamp machines. • ACTIVITIES: Tennis, swimming, requetball,
parks.Summerfest; water activities on Lake Michigan lakefront; entertainment
festivals; Major Leauge Baseball.

589 Ripon, WI

Ripon College (C)
P. O. Box 248, Ripon, WI 54971, Ph: (920) 748-8164, Fax: (920) 748-7243,
E-mail: Stoncl@Ripon.edu, ASK FOR: Lisa Stone
ROOM PRICING: Call for rates, • PAYMENT: Cash Trav. Ck • DATES
AVAILABLE: June 1- Aug. 10, • ROOM TYPE: SR • BED TYPE: S • BEDS: 1-2 •
BATH: C • FOOD: Caf. VM NR • INFO: Children welcome, no pets, free
washer/dryer, TV lounge,linens, free parking. • ACTIVITIES: Racquetball,
swimming, game room, tennis, TV in public lounge, Libraries, biking trails and
hiking trails, boating, bowling. Antique Shops; Outlet Stores.
Near resort community; watersports and golfing

590 Sheboygan, WI   ?   &

Lakeland College (C)
Box 359, Sheboygan, WI 53082, Ph: (414) 565-1228, ASK FOR: Director of Conf.
and Housing
ROOM PRICING: (S) $9.75 w/o linens, $18.00 w/linens, (D) $15.00 w/o linens,
$27.90 w/linens, • PAYMENT: Cash Per. Ck Trav. Ck • DATES AVAILABLE:
June 1-Aug. 15, • BED TYPE: S • BEDS: 2 • FOOD: Caf. VM NR • INFO: Children
welcome with supervision, conference classroom available, Chapel, Physical ed.
Building, coin laundry, TV lounge, free parking. • ACTIVITIES: Swimming, tennis.
Road America Auto Races; Lake Michigan; fishing; golf courses; Milwaukee and
Green Bay close by.

(T) = Travelers Accommodations   (E) = Educational Related   (C) = Groups & Conference Use

U
N
I
V

591 **Whitewater, WI**

University of Wisconsin-Whitewater (E)
800 West Main St., Whitewater, WI 53190, Ph: (414) 472-3165, Web Site:
www.uww.edu, ASK FOR: Lou Zahn-Office of Continuing Ed.
ROOM PRICING: (S) $12.00, (D) $16.00, • PAYMENT: Cash Per. Ck Trav. Ck
Visa M/C • DATES AVAILABLE: Early Jun-Mid- Aug, • ROOM TYPE: SR Suite •
BED TYPE: S • BEDS: 2 • BATH: C • FOOD: Caf. SB VM NR OCR • INFO: Linen
charge: $8.00. No infants, 13 residence halls. coin washers/dryers; large screen
TV in lounges; lounges on each floor. • ACTIVITIES: Art gallery, bowling, tennis,
game room, hiking, park, swimming. Close to Milwaukee and Madison; Lake
Geneva-tourist spot (lakes, boating, dog track, entertainment); Kettle Moraine
Forest Preserve; local shopping and entertainment.

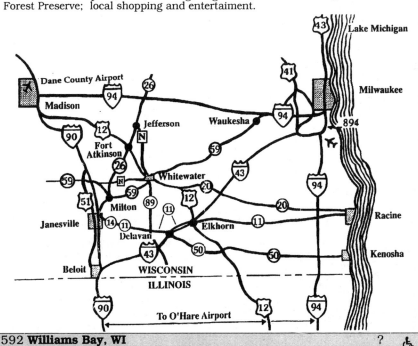

592 **Williams Bay, WI**   ?

George Williams College (T)
P. O. Box 210, Williams Bay, WI 53191, Ph: (414) 245-5531, ASK FOR:
Conference Center
ROOM PRICING: Rates vary according to season & Accommodations, (D) $37.00 to
$65.50, (includes meals & meeting rooms), • PAYMENT: Cash Per. Ck Trav. Ck
• DATES AVAILABLE: Upon arrangement, • BED TYPE: S D • BEDS: 2-4 • FOOD:
Caf. SB VM NR • INFO: Children welcome, Advance Reservations necessary, no
alcohol outside of buildings. Some cottages with kitchens, available. •
ACTIVITIES: Campus sports, game room, boating. Old World Wisconsin; Yerkes
Observatory.

Wyoming

593 Cody, WY   ? ♿

Northwest College (E) A.L. Mickelson Field Station
Painter Route, Cody, WY 82414, Ph: (307) 754-6737, ASK FOR: Ed Stratman,
Supervisor
ROOM PRICING: (S) $8.00, • PAYMENT: Cash Per. Ck Trav. Ck • DATES
AVAILABLE: Year roud, • ROOM TYPE: SR • BED TYPE: S • BEDS: 4 • BATH: C
• FOOD: Caf. • INFO: Lodging for up to 72, plus tenting, cabins with wood stoves,
children welcome, no pets, no alcohol. • ACTIVITIES: Games, hiking, trail rides,
cross country sking, ropes course. Easily accessible mountain retreat surrounded
by National forest.

594 Laramie, WY   ? ♿

University of Wyoming (E)
P. O. Box 3433, Laramie, WY 82070, Ph: (307) 766-3175, ASK FOR: Residence
Office
ROOM PRICING: (S) $15.00+tax, (D) $20.00+tax, • PAYMENT: Cash Per. Ck
Trav. Ck Visa M/C • DATES AVAILABLE: June 1 - Aug. 7, • FOOD: Caf. SB
VM NR • INFO: No children under 10 years, Senior citizen program established. •
ACTIVITIES: Snowy Range Mtns.; Frontier Day in Cheyenne; Jubilee Day in July;
Territorial Prison; sport facilities; fishing.

595 Powell, WY   ♿

Northwest College (E)
231 W. 6th St., Powell, WY 82435, Ph: (307) 754-6660, ASK FOR: Kristie Sullivan,
Hous. & Conf. Coord.
ROOM PRICING: (S) $13.00, (D) $20.00, • PAYMENT: Cash Per. Ck Trav. Ck
Visa M/C • DATES AVAILABLE: June & July, • ROOM TYPE: SR • BED TYPE: S
• BEDS: 2 • BATH: C • FOOD: Caf. VM NR • INFO: Linen charge : $4.00. No
alcohol, no pets, free local calls. • ACTIVITIES: Cable TV in lounges. Nearby are
Yellowstone National Park; Cody's Buffalo Bill Museum; Big Horn National
Reservation area; Shoshone National Forest; 30 minutes from Cody; 1 1/2
hours from Billings, MT.

596 Rock Springs, WY   ? ♿

Western Wyoming Community College (E)
P. O. Box 428, Rock Springs, WY 82901, Ph: (307) 382-1655 or 1644, ASK FOR:
Debi Monroe, Jon Schrade
ROOM PRICING: (S) $10.00, (D) $10.00, • PAYMENT: Cash Per. Ck Trav. Ck •
DATES AVAILABLE: June 1- July 31, • ROOM TYPE: SR Apt. • BED TYPE: S •
BEDS: 2-4 • BATH: S P • FOOD: Caf. SB VM NR • INFO: Linen charge: $3.50.
Children welcome. • ACTIVITIES: Campus is 6,300 ft. above sea level; Dinosaur
exhibit on campus; Fossil Butte; Flaming Gorge Reservoir; Butch Cassidy history;
camping; fishing.

597 Sheridan, WY   ? ♿

Sheridan College (C)
P. O. Box 1500, Sheridan, WY 82801, Ph: (307) 674-6446, Ext: 6157, (800)
913-9139, Ext: 6157, ASK FOR: Ginny Racette
ROOM PRICING: (S) $10.00, (D) $14.00, Weekly rates available, • PAYMENT:
Cash Per. Ck Trav. Ck • DATES AVAILABLE: June 1 -Aug. 10, • ROOM TYPE:
SR • BED TYPE: S • BEDS: 2 • BATH: C • FOOD: Caf. NR • INFO: Alcohol only in
individual rooms, extra charge for linen, free laundry facilities, TV lounge, free
parking. Not available to general public, conferences or small groups using other
college facilities only. • ACTIVITIES: Campus sports, recreational facilities. Custer
Battlefield; Bradford Brinton Memorial Museum; (Western Ranch and Art); fishing;
hunting in the Big Horns.

U N I V

(T) = Travelers Accommodations   (E) = Educational Related   (C) = Groups & Conference Use

Year Round Availability
Accommodations

No	Name		Country	State	City
3	Burgmann College	**(T)**	Australia •	ACT •	Canberra City
4	Univ. of New England	**(T)**	Australia •	NSW •	Armidale
11	Dunmore Lang College	**(T)**	Australia •	NSW •	Northryde
12	St. John's College	**(T)**	Australia •	NSW •	Sydney
22	Univ. of Adelaide, St. Ann's College	**(T)**	Australia •	SA •	No. Adelaide
24	La Trobe University	**(T)**	Australia •	VIC •	Bundoora
30	Univ. of Melbourne, International	**(T)**	Australia •	VIC •	Parkville
34	Univ. of WA, Kingswood College	**(T)**	Australia •	WA •	Nedlands
38	Jugendherberge Innsbruck	**(T)**	Austria •	Innsbruck	
41	Studentenwerk/Sommerhaus	**(T)**	Austria •	Linz	
43	Jugendgastehaus	**(T)**	Austria •	Vienna	
60	International Students House	**(T)**	Britain/UK •	England •	London
61	John Adams Hall	**(T)**	Britain/UK •	England •	London
70	The London Goodenough Trust	**(T)**	Britain/UK •	England •	London
81	University of London	**(T)**	Britain/UK •	England •	London
83	Brunel University/Conf. Centre	**(T)**	Britain/UK •	England •	London,
91	University of Aberdeen	**(T)**	Britain/UK •	Scotland •	Aberdeen
93	Heriot-Watt University	**(T)**	Britain/UK •	Scotland •	
101	The Banff Center for Conferences	**(T)**	Canada •	ALB •	Banff
107	Keyano College	**(T)**	Canada •	ALB •	Fort Mc Murray
120	University of British Columbia	**(T)**	Canada •	BC •	Vancouver
163	Victoria University	**(T)**	Canada •	ONT •	Toronto
183	St. Peter's College	**(T)**	Canada •	SASK •	Muenster
198	FIAP Jean Monnet	**(T)**	France •	Paris	
199	Maison Internationale	**(T)**	France •	Paris	
205	Jugendgastehaus	**(T)**	Germany •	Berlin	
207	Studentenhotel Berlin	**(T)**	Germany •	Berlin	
212	Kinlay House Christchurch	**(T)**	Ireland •	Dublin	
215	Kinlay House Egre Square	**(T)**	Ireland •	Galway	
217	Kinlay House Shandon	**(T)**	Ireland •	Shandon, Cork	
218	Ben Gurion University	**(T)**	Israel •	Beer Sheva	
220	NSTS Hibernia House	**(T)**	Malta •	Sliema	
232	Moscow Hostel	**(T)**	Russia •	Moscow	
233	Travelers Guest House	**(T)**	Russia •	Moscow	
234	St. Petersburg International Hostel	**(T)**	Russia •	St. Petersburg	
239	Vila Universitaria	**(T)**	Spain •	Barcelona	
245	STF:s Vandrarhem Ulleberg	**(T)**	Sweden •	Karlstad	
247	Stichting Hospitum, Guest House	**(T)**	The Netherlands •	Amstelveen	
248	Intern. Conf.Center & Residence	**(T)**	The Netherlands •	Wageningen	
253	Univ. of Montevallo	**(T)**	USA •	AL •	Montevallo
262	California State Univ., Dominguez	**(T)**	USA •	CA •	Carson
268	Calif. State Univ., Hayward	**(T)**	USA •	CA •	Hayward
275	Cal State, Northridge	**(T)**	USA •	CA •	Northridge
276	Holy Names College	**(E)**	USA •	CA •	Oakland
278	University of Northern California	**(T)**	USA •	CA •	Petaluma
292	University of Connecticut	**(T)**	USA •	CT •	Storrs Mansfield
322	Univ. of Chicago, Int'l House	**(T)**	USA •	IL •	Chicago

(T) = Travelers Accommodations **(E) = Educational Related** **(C) = Groups & Conference Use**

No	Name	Country	State	City
325	Greenville College	**(T)** USA •	IL •	Greenville
327	Western Illinois Univ.	**(T)** USA •	IL •	Macomb
336	Hanover College	**(T)** USA •	IN •	Hanover
341	Manchester College	**(T)** USA •	IN •	North Manchester
342	Earlham College	**(T)** USA •	IN •	Richmond
350	Kansas State Univ.	**(E)** USA •	KS •	Manhattan
355	Spalding University	**(E)** USA •	KY •	Louisville
356	University of Louisville	**(T)** USA •	KY •	Louisville
367	Washington Bible College	**(T)** USA •	MD •	Lanham
368	Univ. of Massachusetts at Amherst	**(T)** USA •	MA •	Amherst
375	Adrian College	**(T)** USA •	MI •	Adrian
376	Albion College	**(T)** USA •	MI •	Albion
379	Wayne State Univ.	**(E)** USA •	MI •	Detroit
382	The Adventure Learning Center at	**(T)** USA •	MI •	Hersey
386	Northern Michigan University	**(E)** USA •	MI •	Marquette
387	Northern Michigan University	**(E)** USA •	MI •	Marquette
400	Augsburg College	**(T)** USA •	MN •	Minneapolis
410	Saint Paul's Lutheran High School	**(T)** USA •	MO •	Concordia
419	Dana College	**(T)** USA •	NE •	Blair
421	Univ. of Nebraska at Kearney	**(T)** USA •	NE •	Kearney
423	Union College	**(T)** USA •	NE •	Lincoln
445	Alfred University Saxon Inn	**(T)** USA •	NY •	Alfred
446	Wells College	**(C)** USA •	NY •	Aurora
448	S. U. N. Y. Brockport	**(T)** USA •	NY •	Brockport
454	State Univ. NY Farmingdale	**(E)** USA •	NY •	Farmingdale
461	Amsterdam Inn	**(T)** USA •	NY •	New York
462	International House	**(E)** USA •	NY •	New York
463	Murray Hill Inn	**(T)** USA •	NY •	New York
487	University of North Dakota	**(T)** USA •	ND •	Grand Forks
500	Cameron College	**(T)** USA •	OK •	Lawton
501	Sooner Hotel & Suites	**(T)** USA •	OK •	Norman
502	University of Oklahoma	**(T)** USA •	OK •	Norman
503	Oklahoma State University	**(T)** USA •	OK •	Stillwater
504	Marylhurst College	**(C)** USA •	OR •	Marylhurst
506	Warner Pacific College	**(T)** USA •	OR •	Portland
510	Lehigh University	**(T)** USA •	PA •	Bethlehem
515	Wilson College	**(T)** USA •	PA •	Chambersburg
522	International House of Philidelphia	**(E)** USA •	PA •	Philadelphia
531	University of Puerto Rico	**(T)** USA •	Mayaguez	
533	Bryant College	**(E)** USA •	RI •	Smithfield
545	Dallas Christian College	**(T)** USA •	TX •	Dallas
546	Texas Woman's University	**(C)** USA •	TX •	Denton
547	University of Texas at El Paso	**(E)** USA •	TX •	El Paso
555	Goddard College	**(T)** USA •	VT •	Plainfield
566	Yakima Valley Comm. College	**(T)** USA •	WA •	Yakima
572	Pierpont Apartments	**(T)** USA •	WV •	Morgantown
582	The Towers Residence Hall	**(T)** USA •	WI •	Madison
586	Marquette University	**(T)** USA •	WI •	Milwaukee

U
N
I
V

(T) = Travelers Accommodations   (E) = Educational Related   (C) = Groups & Conference Use

YMCA'S
USA, CANADA & WORLDWIDE
CONTENTS

Y
M
C
A

YMCA's
USA, CANADA and WORLDWIDE

YMCA's are an excellent way of getting the most out of your travel dollars.

Average Room Price:
Single; one night, $12.00-$36.00, Weekly $52.00-$161.00
Double; one night, $20.00-$40.00, Weekly $88.00-$188.00

<u>ALWAYS</u> call and confirm room pricing and availability. Prices vary with location, time of year desired, type of beds, number of people, etc.

Locations may have or provide some or all of the following:
• Private Bath
• Breakfast Included in Room Price
• On site Cafeteria
• Nearby Restaurants
• Swimming Pool
• Sports and Fitness Center
• Advance Reservation by Credit Card
• Sightseeing & Tourist Packages

Inquire about discounts for AAA, AARP, Seniors, Student, Military, etc.

YMCA's
USA, CANADA and WORLDWIDE

Argentina

BUENOS AIRES

Asociacion Christiana de Jovenes **
Reconquista 439, 1003, Buenos Aires, , Argentina • Ph: 54-1-311-4785 Fax: 54-1-313-7738

Australia

ADELAIDE   SA

YMCA **
76 Flinders St., Adelaide, SA 5000, Australia • Ph: 61-8-223-1611 Fax: 61-8-232-2920 • AUS$ 11-30

DARWIN   NT

YMCA, The Espanade **
Doctor's Gully, P. O. Box 1451, Darwin, NT 0800, Australia • Ph: 61-89-818-377 Fax: 61-89-410-288 • AUS$ 30-40

PERTH   W.A.

YMCA JEWELL HOUSE **
180 Goderich St., Perth, W.A. 6000, Australia • Ph: 61-08 9325 8488 Fax: 61-08- 9221 4694 • AUS$ 38-54

Austria

KLOSTERNEUBURG/GU

CVJF/Evangelisches Jugend und
Hutersteig 88, 3400, Klosterneuburg/Gugging, , Austria • Ph: 43-2243-83-501

LINZ

CVJM (YMCA) **
Starhembergstrasse 39, 4020, Linz, , Austria • Ph: 43-732-23 99 09

VIENNA

CVJM (YMCA) **
Kenyongasse 15, 1070, Vienna, , Austria • Ph: 43-1-523-13-04

Bangladesh

BARISAL

YMCA **
Iswar Bose Road, P. O. Box 36, Barisal, 8200, Bangladesh • Ph: 880-431-3952

BOGRA

YMCA • Bhai Pagla **
Majar Lane, P. O. Box 70, Bogra, 5800, Bangladesh • Ph: 880-51-5242

DHAKA

YMCA **
46 New Eskaton Road, G.P.O. Box 2041, Dhaka, 1000, Bangladesh • Ph: 880-2-408-204/880-2-41 8-939

Barbados

BRIDGETOWN

YMCA of Barbados **
Pinfold St., Bridgetown, 3, Barbados • Ph: 809-426-3910 Fax: 809-435-2230 • BOS$ 24-35

Belgium

ANTWEPEN

YMCA *
Kapucinessenstraat 17, B-2000, Antwepen, , Belgium • Ph: 32-3-234-0931 • US$ 12-15

BARVAUX

YMCA **
Le Pre Ligne 10, 6940, Barvaux, , Belgium • Ph: 32-84-466-577 • US$ 12-15

BRUSSELS

Centre Vincent Van Gogh.CHAB YMCA ***
Rue Traversiere 8, B-1030 , Brussels, 1210, Belgium • Att: Jean Yves Hulet • Ph: (32) 2-217-0158 Fax: (32) 2-219-7995 • US$ 15-18

Canada

ALBERTA

EDMONTON   ALB

YMCA of Edmonton **
10030-102 A Avenue, Edmonton, ALB T5J 0G5, Canada • Ph: (403) 421-9622 Fax: (403) 428-9469

YMCA **
10030-102A Avenue, Edmonton, ALB T5J 0G5, Canada • Ph: (403) 425-9622 Fax: (403) 428-9469

BRITISH COLUMBIA

VANCOUVER   BC

YMCA **
404-1045 Howe St., Vancouver, BC V6Z 2A9, Canada • Ph: (604) 681-9622 Fax: (604) 688-0220

VICTORIA   BC

YM-YWCA Victoria
*Female only
880 Courtney St., Victoria, BC V8W 1C4, Canada • Ph: (250) 386-7511 Fax: (250)380-1933

NEW BRUNSWICK

SAINT JOHN   NB

YMCA-YWCA **
19-25 Hazen Ave., Saint John, NB E2L 3G6, Canada • Ph: (506) 634-7720 Fax: (506) 634-0783

NOVA SCOTIA

HALIFAX   NS

YMCA **
1565 South Park St., Halifax, NS B3S 2L2, Canada • Ph: (902) 423-9622 Fax: (902) 425-0155

ONTARIO

BRANTFORD   ONT

YMCA-YWCA **
40 Queen St., Brantford, ONT N3T 3B2, Canada • Ph: (519) 752-6568 Fax: (519) 759-8431

HAMILTON   ONT

YMCA *
79 James St. South, Hamilton, ONT L8P 2Z1, Canada • Ph: (905) 529-7102 Fax: (905) 529-6682

Y
M
C
A

KINGSTON   ONT

YMCA * Female only
100 Wright Crescent,
Kingston, ONT K7L 4T9,
Canada • Ph: (613)
546-2647 Fax: (613)
549-0654

OTTAWA   ONT

Ottawa YM-YW *
180 Argyle Avenue,
Ottawa, ONT K2P 1B7,
Canada • Ph: (613)
237-1320 Fax: (613)
233-3096

YMCA-YWCA *
180 Argyle Ave., Ottawa,
ONT K2P 1B7, Canada •
Ph: (613) 788-5050 Fax:
(613) 788-5036

QUEBEC

MONTREAL   QUE

Montreal YMCA **
1450 Stanley Street,
Montreal, QUE H3A
2W6, Canada • Ph: (514)
849-8393 Fax: (514)
849-8017 • Rms 350

YMCA **/**
1441 rue Stanley,
Montreal, QUE H3A
2W6, Canada • Ph: (514)
849-8393 Fax: (514)
849-8017

SASKATCHEWAN

REGINA   SASK

YMCA *
2400 13th Ave., Regina,
SASK S4P 0V9, Canada
• Ph: (306) 757-9622
Fax: (306) 525-5508

China

SHANGHAI

YMCA **
123 Xi Zang Nan Lu,
Shanghai, 200021, China
• Ph: 86-21-373-2367 •
US $46-136

Cuba

HAVANNA

**Association Cristiana de
Jovenes de Cuba ****
Salud #222, entre
Campanario y Lealtad,
Havanna, 10200, Cuba •
Ph: 53-7-621-239,
53-7-621-219 Fax:
53-7-338-819

Egypt

AZARITA, ALEXANDRIA

YMCA **
18 Dr. Abdel Hamid
Badawy, Azarita,
Alexandria, , Egypt • Ph:
20-3-482-3370

England

BATH

YMCA **
Broad Street, Bath, BA1
5LN, England • Ph: (1225)
460 471 Fax: (1225) 462
465E-mail:
Info@ymcabath.u-net.com

BIRCHWOOD

YMCA **
46 Hamnett Court,
Ainscough Rd.,
Birchwood, WA3 7PL,
England • Ph: (1925) 821
996

BIRKENHEAD,

YMCA **
56 Whetstone Lane,
Birkenhead, Merseyside,
L41 2TJ, England • Ph:
(151) 647 8123 Fax:
(151) 650 1944E-mail:
sam.larmour@birkenhead
.ymca.org.uk

BOURNEMOUTH

YMCA **
56 Westover Road,
Bournemouth, BH1 2BS,
England • Ph: (1202)
|290 451 Fax: (1202)
314 219

BRIGHTON

YMCA **
38 East Street, Brighton,
BN1 1HL, England • Ph:
(1273) 220 900 Fax:
(1273) 220 999

CAMBRIDGE

**YMCA, Queen Anne
House ****
Gonville Place,
Cambridge, CB1 1LY,
England • Ph: 44-(1223)
356 998 Fax: 44-(1223)
312748 • Rms 132

CASTLEFIELD,

YMCA **
Liverpool Road,
Castlefield, Manchester,
M3 4JR, England • Ph:
(161) 839 2567 Fax:
(161) 839 0326

CHELTENHAM

YMCA **
Vittoria Walk,
Cheltenham, GL50 1TP,
England • Ph: (01242)
524 024 Fax: (01242)
232 635

COVENTRY

YMCA **
11 The Quadrant,
Warwick Road, Coventry,
CV1 2EJ, England • Ph:
(1203) 257 312 Fax:
(1203) 632 587

CREWE

YMCA **
Gresty Road, Crewe,
CW2 6EL, England • Ph:
(1270) 257 673

CROYDON

YMCA **
1 Lansdowne Road,
Croydon, CR0 2BX,
England • Ph: (181) 681
3381 Fax: (181) 686
9461

CUMBRIA

YMCA, Lakeside **
Ulverston, Cumbria,
LA12 8BD, England • Ph:
(1539) 531 758 Fax:
(1539) 530 015

DOVER

YMCA **
4 Leyburne Rd., Dover,
CT16 1SN, England • Ph:
(1304) 206 138

DUNFORD, MIDHURST

YMCA **
Dunford House, Dunford,
Midhurst, GU29 OD9,
England • Att: Pauline Dey
• Ph: (1730) 812 381
Fax: (1730) 817 042

EASTBOURNE

YMCA **
23-25 Vicarage Drive,
Eastbourne, BN20 8AR,
England • Ph: (1323) 649
759

GRIMSBY

YMCA **
Peaks Lane, Grimsby,
DN32 9ET, England • Ph:
(1472) 359 621

GUILDFORD

YMCA **
Bridge Street, Guildford,
GU1 4SB, England • Ph:
(1483) 532555 Fax:
(1483) 537161

HALTON, RUNCORN

YMCA, Halton Lodge **
Halton Lodge Avenue.,
Halton, Runcorn, WA7
4LY, England • Ph: (1928)
591 680

HANLEY,

YMCA **
Harding Road, Hanley,
Stoke on Trent, ST1
3AE, England • Ph: (1782)
202 460 Fax: (1782) 206
319

IPSWICH

YMCA **
2 Wellington Street,
Ipswich, LP1 2NU,
England • Ph: (1553) 769
496

KING S LYNN

YMCA **
Columbia Way, King s
Lynn, PE30 2LA,
England • Ph: (1553) 769
496

LEICESTER

YMCA **
7 East Street, Leicester,
LE1 6EY, England • Ph:
(116) 255 6507 Fax:
(116) 255 6509

LINCOLN

YMCA **
St. Rumbold Street.,
Lincoln, LN2 5AR,
England • Ph: (1522) 511
811 Fax: (1S22) 528 154

LIVERPOOL

YMCA **
56/60 Mount Pleasant,
Liverpool, L3 5SH,
England • Ph: (151) 709
9516

LONDON

Barbican YMCA **
Fann Street., London,
EC2Y 8BR, England • Att:
101,651.64compuserve.co
m • Ph: (171) 628 0697
Fax: (171) 638 2420

Ealing YMCA **
25 St. Mary's Road,
London, W5 5RE,
England • Ph: (181) 579
6946 Fax: (181) 579
1129

Ensor House YMCA **
6 Parsons Green,
London, SW6, England •
Ph: (181) 399 5427

German YMCA ***
35 Craven Terrace,
London, W2 3EL,
England • Ph: (171) 723
9276 Fax: (171) 706
2870 • Rms 240

Hornsey YMCA **
184 Tottenham Lane,
London, N8 8SG,
England • Ph: (181) 340
2345 Fax: (181) 340
2345E-mail:
ben.ymca@dial.pipet.com

Indian Student YMCA **
41 Fitzroy Square,
London, W1 P 6AO,
England • Ph: Tel (171)
387 0411 Fax: (171) 383
7651

Lambeth YMCA **
40 Stockwell Road,
London, SW9 9ES,
England • Ph: (0171)
501-9795 Fax: (0171)
501-8005

London City YMCA **
Luwum House, 8 Errol
Street, London, EC1Y
8SE, England • Ph: (0171)
628 8832 Fax: (0171)
628 4080

Polska YMCA **
46 47 Kensington
Gardens Square, London,
W2 4BO, England • Ph:
(171) 229 4678, Hostel
(171) 229 4295

Wimbledon YMCA **
200 The Broadway,
London, SW19 1 RY,
England • Ph: (181) 542
9055 Fax: (181) 542
1086

MILTON KEYNES

YMCA **
402 North Row, Milton
Keynes, MK9 2NL,
England • Ph: (1908) 605
084

NORWICH

YMCA **
48-52 St. Giles Street,
Norwich, NR2 1LP,
England • Ph: (1603) 620
269 Fax: (1603) 768 382

NOTTINGHAM

YMCA **
4 Shakespeare Street.,
Nottingham, NG1 4FG,
England • Ph: (0115)
956-7600 Fax: (0115)
956-7601E-mail:
admin@nottingham.ymca.
org.uk

PENZANCE

YMCA, The Orchard **
Alverton, Penzance,
TR18 4TE, England • Ph:
(01736) 365016 Fax:
(01736) 365016

PETERBOROUGH

YMCA, Tait House **
Eastfield Road,
Peterborough, PE1 40H,
England • Ph: (1733) 896
01

PORTSMOUTH

YMCA **
Penny Street,
Portsmouth, PO1 2NN,
England • Ph: (1705) 864
341 Fax: (1705) 864 341

READING

**YMCA, Marlborough
House** **
Parkside Road, Reading,
RG3 2DD, England • Ph:
(1734) 575 746 Fax:
(1734) 588 584

REDDITCH

YMCA **
Church Hill, Redditch,
B98 9JG, England • Ph:
(1527) 61643

RIPON

YMCA **
5 Water Skellgate, Ripon,
HG4 1BQ, England • Ph:
(1765) 607 609

ROMFORD

YMCA **
Rush Green Road,
Romford, RM7 OPH,
England • Ph: (1708) 766
211 Fax: (1708) 754 211

SHEFFIELD

YMCA **
11-15 Broomhall Road,
Sheffield, S102DQ,
England • Ph: (114) 268
4807 Fax: (114) 268
3472

SOUTH HAMPTON

**YMCA, Fairthorne
Manor** **
Curdridge,
South Hampton, S03
2GH, England • Ph:
(1489) 785228 Fax:
(1489) 798936

ST. HELENS

YMCA **
North Road, St. Helens,
WA10 2TJ, England • Ph:
(1744) 22 529 Fax:
(1744) 29112

Y
M
C
A

SURBITON,

YMCA **
49 Victoria Road,
Surbiton,
Kingston upon Thames,
KT6 4NG, England • Ph:
(181) 399 5427 Fax:
(181) 390 9427

WAFFORD

YMCA, Charter House
**
Charter Place, Wafford,
WD1 2RT, England • Ph:
(1923) 233 034 Fax:
(1923) 226 299

WALTHAMSTOW,

Waltham Forest YMCA
**
642 Forest Road,
Walthamstow, London,
E17 3EF, England • Ph:
(181) 520 0931 Fax:
(181) 521 8581

WELWYN GARDEN CITY

YMCA, Maynard House
**
Peartree Lane, Welwyn
Garden City, AL7 3UL,
England • Ph: (1707) 327
930 Fax: (1707) 377 993

WEST BROMWICH

YMCA **
38 Carters Green, West
Bromwich, B70 9LG,
England • Ph: (121) 553
4211

WILMORTON, DERBY

Derby YMCA, Inc. **
London Road, Wilmorton,
Derby, DE24 8UT,
England • Att: Tony
Gratton • Ph: (1332) 572
076 Fax: (1332) 572
596E-mail:
tony@derbyymca.demon.c
o.uk

WORCESTER

YMCA **
Henwick Road,
Worcester, WR2 5NS,
England • Ph: (1905) 423
197

Finland

HELSINKI

**National Training
Centre • Ranta-Vaahala**
16600 Jarvela,
FIN-00171 , Helsinki, ,
Finland • Ph:
358-18-765-1216 Fax:
358-18-765-5183

NMKY (YMCA) ***
Vourikatu 17, Helsinki, ,
Finland • Ph:
358-0-173-441 Fax:
358-0-179-781 • US$
35-100

KUOPIO

NMKY (YMCA) **
Kauppakatu 40-42,
70100, Kuopio, , Finland
• Ph: 358-71-112-570

OULU

NMKY (YMCA) **
Albertinkatu 2, 90100,
Oulu, , Finland • Ph:
358-81-375-566 Fax:
358-81-311-0376

TAMPERE

NMKY (YMCA) **
Hameenpuisto 14 F,
33210, Tampere, ,
Finland • Ph:
358-31-212-5046 Fax:
358-31-212-5046

TURKU

NMKY (YMCA) **
Sirkkalankatu 27,
20700, Turku, , Finland
• Ph: 358-21-273-1000
Fax: 358-21-232-9461

France

LE HAVRE

Espace UCJG du Havre
**
153 Boulevard de
Strasbourg, 76600, Le
Havre, , France • Ph:
33-35-42-47-86 Fax:
33-35-41-34-65

LORIENT

UCJG, Fort de Gavre
**(In Summer)
23 Boulevard de l'Eau
Courante, 56100,
Lorient, , France • Ph:
33-97-65-94-14

MELUN

**Le Rocheton: Centre
International UCJG La**
rue de la Foret, 77008,
Melun, , France • Ph:
33-1-64-37-12-32 Fax:
33-1-64-37-15-12

SANARY

**UCJG Sanary Centre
Azur** **
Avenue du Nid, BP 75,
83110, Sanary, , France
• Ph: 33-94-74-18-87
Fax: 33-94-34-79-10

STRASBOURG

Ciarus **/***C
7 rue Finkmatt, 67000,
Strasbourg, , France •
Ph: (33)03-88-15-27-88
Fax:
(33)03-88-15-27-89E-mail
: Liarus@media-net.fr •
Rms 101

VILLENEUVE-LES-AVIGN

UCJG
Villeneuve-les-Avignon
7 bis. chemin de la
Justice, 30400,
Villeneuve-Les-Avignon,
France • Ph: (33) 04 90
25 46 20 Fax: (33)
-90-25-30-64

Germany

BERLIN

YMCA **
Einemstrasse 10, 10787,
Berlin, , Germany • Ph:
49-30-26 49 10-0 Fax:
49-30-2-61-43-08E-mail:
cvjm-berlin@pilgrims.life.d
e • DM 40

BRAUNSCHWEIG

YMCA ***
Wollmarkt 9-12
, 38100, Braunschweig,
, Germany • Ph:
49-531-4-61-38 Fax:
49-531-12-50-39 • DM
55-145

DUSSELDORF

YMCA
Graf-Adolf-Strasse 102,
40210, Dusseldorf, ,
Germany • Ph: (49)
211-17285-0 Fax:
(49)211-17285-44 • DM
50-80

HANNOVER

YMCA ***
Limburgstrasse 3,
30159, Hannover, ,
Germany • Ph:
49-511-36-07-1-15 Fax:
49-511-32-27-12 • DM
100-115

LUBECK

YMCA **
Große Petersgrube 11,
23552, Lubeck, ,
Germany • Ph:
49-451-7-89-82 Fax:
49-451-7-89-97 • DM
20-30

MUNICH

**YMCA-CVJM ** **
Landwehrstr. 13, 80336,
Munich, 80336, Germany
• Att: Dietmar Borgards
• Ph: 49-89-55-21-41-0
Fax:
49-89-5-50-42-82E-mail:
muenchen@cvjm.org.de •
DM 40-55

SCHONEBECK

**YMCA ** **
Immermannstrasse 12,
39218 , Schonebeck, ,
Germany • • DM 20-30

Ghana

ACCRA

**YMCA- Greater Accra
Region ***
Castle Road, P. O. Box
738, Accra, , Ghana •
Ph: 233-21-224-700

APEDWA

**YMCA Vocational
School/Hostel ***
P. O. Box 23, Apedwa, ,
Ghana •

HO - VOLTA REGION

**YMCA - Volta Region ** **
Government Transport
Yard Square, P. O. Box
93, Ho - Volta Region, ,
Ghana • Ph: 233-91-374

KOFORIDUA

**YMCA - Eastern Region
** **
Nkubem Villa, P. O. Box
978, Koforidua, , Ghana
• Ph: 233-81-3005

Guyana

GEORGETOWN

**Thomas Lands YMCA ** **
Thomas & Camp Roads,
P. O. Box 10112,
Georgetown, , Guyana •
Att: Mr. Claude
Blackmore, Executive
Secretary • Ph:
592-2-62-087 Fax:
592-2-61881

MACKENZIE, LINDEN

**Mackenzie YMCA ** **
627 Independence Ave., P.
O. Box 10, Mackenzie,
Linden, , Guyana • Ph:
592-4-2275 Fax:
592-4-2275

Hong Kong

KOWLOON

**YMCA International
House *****
23 Waterloo Road,
Kowloon, , Hong Kong •
Ph: 852-2771-9111 Fax:
852-2388-5926 • Rms
227 • US$ 17-104

TSIMSHATSUI,

**"The Salisbury"-YMCA
of Hong Kong ** /***C**
41 Salisbury Road,
Tsimshatsui, Kowloon, ,
Hong Kong • Att: Ms.
Grace Luk, Sales &
Marketing Manager • Ph:
(852)-2311-5809 Fax:
(852)-2739-9315E-mail:
room@ymcahk.org.hk •
Rms 380 • US$ 21-175 •
Conveniently located by
the waterfront of Victoria
Harbour and in business
and shopping district -
Tsimshatsui. All 380
rooms and suites are
equipped with remote
control color television with
satellite and cable
channels, in-house free
movies, IDD telephone,
room safe, card key
security, refrigerator and
in room tea/coffee making
facilities.

WANCHAI

**Harbour View
International House *****
4 Harbour Road,
Wanchai, , Hong Kong •
Ph: 852-2802-0111 Fax:
852-2802-9063 • Rms
320 • US$ 85-140

India

ALLAHABAD

YMCA *
13 Sarojini Naidu Marg,
Allahabad, 211 011,
India • Ph: (532) 624 028

BALMATTA.

YMCA *
Fainir Road, Balmatta.
Mangalore, 575 002,
India • Ph: (824) 25496

BANGALORE

**YMCA ** **
Nrupathunga Road,
Bangalore, 560 002,
India • Ph: (80) 221 1848
Fax: (80) 224 043

BOMBAY

**YMCA ** **
18 YMCA Road, Bombay,
400 008, India • Ph: (22)
309 1191, 307 0601/2/3
Fax: (22) 307 1567

CALCUTTA

**YMCA ** **
25 Jawaharlal Nehru
Road, Calcutta, 700
087, India • Ph: (33) 249
2192, 249 2111 Fax: (33)
249 2234

CALICUT

**YMCA ** **
Calicut, 673 001, India •
Ph: (495) 55740

CANTONMENT.

**YMCA ** **
2 Queen's Road,
Cantonment. Jabalpur,
482 001, India • Ph: (761)
320 530

CHANDIGARH

**YMCA ** **
Sector 11-C, Chandigarh,
160 011, India • Ph: (172)
546 732/540151

COCHIN

**YMCA ** **
YMCA Road, Cochin,
682 001, India • Ph: (484)
225 288

COIMBATORE

YMCA ** /***
Head Post Office Road,
Coimbatore, 641 001,
India • Ph: (91) 0422
39608

CUTTACK

**YMCA ** **
Old Secretariat Road,
Cuttack, 753 001, India
• Ph: (671) 238

ERNAKULAM

**YMCA International
House ** /***C**
Chittoor Road,
Ernakulam, 682 035,
India • Ph: (91) 361 656/
353479/365479/355620
Fax: (91) 0484-364641

ESPLANADE. MADRAS

**YMCA ** **
N.S.C. Bose Road,
Esplanade. Madras, 600
001, India • Ph: (44) 583
941, 583 981 Fax: (44)
583 168

Y
M
C
A

HYDERABAD

YMCA **
Narayanguda,
Hyderabad, 500 029,
India • Ph: (40) 664 670
Fax: (40) 665 023

KOTTAYAM

YMCA **
Kottayam, 686 001,
India • Ph: (481) 560 591

LUCKNOW

YMCA **
13 Rana Pratap Marg,
Lucknow, 226 001, India
• Ph: (522) 283 506

MADURAI

YMCA **
Main Guard Square,
Madurai, 625 001, India
• Ph: Tel. (452) 33469

NEW DELHI

YMCA Tourist Hostel
***
Jai Singh Road, P.B. 612,
New Delhi, 110 001,
India • Ph: (11) 311 915,
312 595 Fax: (11) 374
6035

NILGIRIS, COONOOR

YMCA **
Mount Road, Nilgiris,
Coonoor, 643 102, India
•

OOTACAMUND

YMCA **
58 Commercial Road,
Ootacamund, 643 001,
India • Ph: Nilgiris, 3008

PUNE

YMCA **
6 Arjun Marg, Pune, 411
001, India • Ph: (212) 665
504, 665 509

PUTHUR,

YMCA **
1F. EVR Road, Puthur,
TiruchirapalH, 620017,
India • Ph: (431) 23764

RANCHI

YMCA **
Old Hazaribagh Road,
Ranchi, 834 001, India •
Ph: (651) 304 895 Fax:
(651) 304 895

SALEM

YMCA **
123 Bretts Road, Salem,
636 001, India • Ph: (427)
64342, 66097

SHILLONG

YMCA **
Shillong, 793 003, India •

SHIMLA

YMCA **
The Ridge, Shimla, 171
001, India • Ph: 204 085
252375 Fax:
0091-177-211016

TRIVANDRUM

YMCA **
Trivandrum, 695 001,
India • Ph: (471) 330 059

VISAKHAPATNAM

YMCA ***
Kirlampudi Layout, Beach
road, Visakhapatnam,
530 017, India • Ph:
(891) 555 826 Fax:
(891)565439

Ireland

NEWCASTLE, CO.

**Glen River National
Centre** **
Donard Park, Newcastle,
Co. Down, BT33 0GR,
Ireland • Ph:
353-13967-23172 Fax:
353-13967-26230 • £ 21

Glenada YWCA/YMCA
**
29 South Promenade,
Newcastle, Co. Down,
BT33 0AX, Ireland • Ph:
353-13967-22402 Fax:
353-13967-26229 • £
16-18

Israel

EAST JERUSALEM

East Jerusalem YMCA
/*C
29 Nablus Road, P. O.
Box 19023, East
Jersualem, , Israel • Att:
Capitolina Hotel • Ph:
(972)-2-628-6888 Fax:
(972)-2-627-6301 • Rms
57 • $30-45

JERUSALEM

**Jerusalem International
YMCA** ***
26 King David St., P. O.
Box 294, 91002,
Jerusalem, , Israel • Ph:
972-2-257-111 Fax:
972-2-253-438 • Rms
106 • US$ 95-110

JERUSALEM 294

**Jerusalem Int'l,
YMCA/3-Arches Hotel**
King David Street #26,
Jerusalem 294, , Israel •
Ph: 972-02 25711 Fax:
972-02-235192 • Rms 52

TIBERIAS

**Peniel-by-Galilee •
Guest**
Tiberias, , Israel • Ph:
972-2-257-111 • US$
60-80

Italy

BARDONECCHIA

YMCA ***C
Viale Vittoria, 10052,
Bardonecchia, , Italy •
Ph: 39-122-901273 Fax:
39-122-96192

Jamaica

MONTEGO BAY

MONTEGO BAY YMCA
**
28 Humber Ave., Montego
Bay, , Jamaica • Ph:
876-952-5368

Japan

GOTEMBA, SHIZOUKA

**Tozanso International
Conference Centre** ***
1052 Higashiyama,
Gotemba, Shizouka ,
412, Japan • Ph:
81-550-831-133 Fax:
81-550-831-138 • Rms
500 • US$ 61-125

KOBE

Kobe YMCA Hotel ***
2-7-15 Kano-Cho,
Chuo-Ku, Kobe,
650-0001, Japan • Ph:
81-78-241-7205 Fax:
81-78-231-1031 • Rms
30 • US$ 62-150

TOYOKO

YMCA Hotel **
7 Kanda-Mitoshiro,
Chiyoda-Ku, Toyoko ,
101, Japan • Ph:
81-3-3293-1911 Fax:
81-3-3293-1926 • Rms
40 • US$ 100-170

**Asia Youth Centre •
Korean YMCA in Japan**
2-5-5 Sarugaku-Cho,
Chiyoda-Ku, 101,
Toyoko, , Japan • Ph:
81-3-3233-0611 Fax:
81-3-3233-0633 • Rms
85 • US$ 65-168

Kenya

KISUMU

YMCA **
P. O. Box 1848, Kisumu,
, Kenya • Ph:
254-35-45-183 • Rms
11 • US$ 5010

Lodging for: * = Men only,   ** = Men / Women,   *** = Family,   C = Conference

Kenya

NAIROBI

Nairobi Central YMCA
**
P. O. Box 63063,
Nairobi, , Kenya • Ph:
254-2-726-398,
254-2-726-399 • Rms
87 • US$ 25-55

Nairobi Souath YMCA
**
P. O. Box 59260,
Nairobi, , Kenya • Ph:
254-2-504-896,
254-2-504-296 • Rms
32 • US$ 10-20

YMCA **
Shaauri Moyo, P. O. Box
17073, Nairobi, , Kenya
• Ph: 254-2-553-132,
254-2-556-844 • Rms
100 • US$ 10-15

Korea

SEOUL

YMCA **
9 Chongro- 2 KA,
Chongro-Ku, Seoul,
110-122, Korea • Ph:
82-2-732-8291 Fax:
82-2-733-8009 • US$
39-76

Malaysia

IPOH

YMCA **
211 Jalan Musa Aziz,
30300, Ipoh, , Malaysia
• Ph: 60-5-254-0809,
60-5-253-9464 • Rms
49 • US$ 18-35

KUALA LUMPUR

YMCA **
95 Jalan Padang Belia,
50470, Kuala Lumpur,
, Malaysia • Ph:
60-3-274-1439,
60-3-274-2349 Fax:
60-3-274-0559 • Rms 60
• US$ 13-37

PENANG

YMCA **
211 Jalan Macalister,
10450, Penang, ,
Malaysia • Ph:
60-4-228-8211 Fax:
60-4-229-5869E-mail:
ymcapg@po.jaring.my •
US$ 14-32

Myanmar

MYITKYINA

YMCA **
10 Myothit Quarter,
Myitkyina, , Myanmar •
Ph: 95-101-21536 • US$
10-30

YANGON

YMCA **
263 Maha Bandoola St.,
Yangon, , Myanmar • Ph:
95-1-94128, 95-1-94109
Fax: 95-1-96848 • US$
10-40

New Zealand

AUCKLAND

YMCA ***
Corner Pitt Street and
Greys Ave., Auckland, ,
New Zealand • Att:
Accommodation Officer •
Ph: (64)-9-303-2068 Fax:
(64)-9-303-2068 • Rms
126 • NZ$ 35

CHRISTCHURCH

YMCA Accommodation
/*C
12 Herford St., P. O. Box
2004, Christchurch, ,
New Zealand • Ph: (64)-3
365 0502 Fax: (64) -3
365 1386E-mail:
chchymca@ymca.org.nz

Nigeria

KADUNA

YMCA **
P. O. Box 354, Kaduna,
, Nigeria • Ph:
234-62-210-085

LAGOS

YMCA • Ebute Meta **
111 Borno Way, G.P. O.
Box 2106, Lagos, ,
Nigeria • Ph:
234-1-860-583

YMCA **
77 Awolowo Road, P. O.
Box 2106, Lagos, ,
Nigeria • Ph:
234-1-680-516

Pakistan

KARACHI

YMCA **
Aiwan-e-Saddar Road,
Karachi, , Pakistan • Ph:
92-21-513-022

Papua New

LAE

YMCA Training Centre
and Buablung Haus
P. O. Box 1055, Lae, ,
Papua New Guinea • Ph:
675-472-2764 Fax:
675-472-2654 • Rms 96 •
US$ 12

Philippines

BAGUIO CITY

YMCA **
Baguio City, , Philippines
• Ph: 63-74-4766

CEBU CITY

YMCA **
Jones Ave., Cebu City, ,
Philippines • Ph:
63-32-215-217

DUMAGUETTE CITY

YMCA **
North road, 6200,
Dumaguette City , ,
Philippines • Ph:
63-35-2251-519 Fax:
63-35-2253-633

LAGUNA

YMCA of Los Banos,
Inc. • UPLB Campus,
4030, Laguna, 4031,
Philippines • Att: Mr.
Carolito E. Celon, General
Sec. • Ph: (63)
049-536-2840 Fax: (63)
049-536-4214

METRO MANILA

YMCA of Makati, Inc.
***
7 Sacred Heart Plaza St.,
San Antonio Village,
1200, Metro Manila , ,
Philippines • Ph:
63-2-817-1229,
63-2-817-1244 Fax:
63-2-817-1225 • Rms 72

PANGASINAN

YMCA, Tapuac District
**
Dagupan City 2400,
Pangasinan, , Philippines
•

Poland

GDYNIA

ZMC-YMCA **
ul. Zermoskiego 26,
PL-81346 , Gdynia, ,
Poland • Ph:
48-58-203-115 Fax:
48-58-217-842 • US$ 5

Scotland

GLASGOW

YMCA • David Naismith
Court Aparthotel **
33 Petershill Dr.,
Glasgow, G21 4QQ,
Scotland • Ph:
44-141-558-6166 Fax:
44-141-558-2036

Y
M
C
A

LANARKSHIRE

Wiston Lodge • Biggar
**
Lanarkshire, ML12 6HT,
Scotland • Ph:
44-18995-228 Fax:
44-18995-693

PERTHSHIRE

Bonskeid House •
**Pitlochry **
Perthshire, PH16 5NP,
Scotland • Ph: 44-179647
Fax: 44-179647-3310

Singapore

SINGAPORE

YMCA Tanglin Centre
***
60 Stevens Road,
Singapore, 1025,
Singapore • Ph:
65-737-7755 Fax:
65-737-2297 • Rms 103 •
US$ 43-101

YMCA International
Centre *
70 Palmer Road,
Singapore, 0207,
Singapore • Ph:
65-222-4666 • Rms 50
• US$ 20-47

YMCA International
House *
1 Orchard Road,
Singapore, 0923,
Singapore • Ph:
65-336-6000 Fax:
65-337-3140 • Rms 109 •
US$ 60-80

South Africa

BRIDGETOWN

Andy M. Richards YMCA
*
Box 38241, Bridgetown,
7746, South Africa • Ph:
27-21-637-5150 Fax:
27-21-637-1993

JOHANNESBURG

YMCA *
104 Rissik St.,
Johannesburg, 2001,
South Africa • Ph:
27-11-403-3426 Fax:
27-11-339-4720 • R43

KWA MASHU

Kwa Mashu YMCA *
Private Bag X 019, Kwa
Mashu , 4360, South
Africa • Ph:
27-31-503-5989

OBSERVATORY

**YMCA - Cape Town **
P. O. Box 57,
Observatory, 7935, South
Africa • Att: Heather
Jensen • Ph:
27-21-47-6217 Fax:
27-21-47-6275 • Rms 50

PIETERMARITZBURG

YMCA *
1 Durban road,
Pietermaritzburg, 3201,
South Africa • Ph:
27-331-422-469 Fax:
27-331-450-313 • R47.50

PORT ELIZABETH

YMCA *
31 Havelock St., Port
Elizabeth , 6001, South
Africa • Ph:
27-41-559-792 Fax:
27-41-553-0206

RICHARDS BAY

YMCA **/*C**
P. O. Box 203, Richards
Bay , 3900, South Africa
• Ph: (27)-351-534086/7
Fax:
(27)-351-32243E-mail:
rbymca@iafrica.com

Sri Lanka

COLOMBO

YMCA **/*C**
39 Bristol St., Colombo,
, Sri Lanka • Ph:
94-1-325252 or 325253
Fax: 94-1-423099

KANDY

YMCA *
116 Kotugodella Vidiya,
Kandy, , Sri Lanka • Ph:
94-8-223529 Fax:
94-8-32343

LAVINIA

YMCA *
55 Hotel Road, Lavinia, ,
Sri Lanka • Ph:
94-71-3786

WELIMADA

Welimada YMCA Camp
& Conference Centre *
Nuwara-Eliya road,
Welimada, , Sri Lanka •
Ph: 94-57-5097

Sweden

STOCKHOLM

Hotel KOM •
KFUK-KFUM *
Dobeinsgatan 17-19,
11140, Stockholm, ,
Sweden • Ph:
46-8-235-630 Fax:
46-8-241-143 • Rms 60

SUNDSVALL

KFUK-KFUM *
Box 143, 85103,
Sundsvall, , Sweden • Ph:
46-60-113-5353 Fax:
46-60-176-722

VASTERAS

KFUK-KFUM Lovudden
**
72591, Vasteras, ,
Sweden • Ph:
46-21-185-230

VISBY

KFUK-KFUM • Fridheim
**
Box 1183, 62122, Visby,
, Sweden • Ph:
46-498-64220

Switzerland

GENEVE

Hotel "Le Grenil" **/**
7 Av. Ste Clotilkde, 1205,
Geneve, , Switzerland •
Ph: 41-22-328-30-55
Fax: 41-22-321-60-10 •
Rms 48 • Sfr. 90-190

HASLIBERG-HOHFLUH

CVJM-Jugendzentrum
Hasliberg *
6083, Hasliberg-Hohfluh,
, Switzerland • Ph:
41-36-71-29-35 Fax:
41-35-71-18-39

ST. GALLEN

Stiftung
CVJM-Ferienheim La
Seitzstrasse 3, 9000,
St. Gallen, , Switzerland
• Ph: 41-71-27-89-24 •
Rms 90 • Sfr. 15-65

VAUMARCUE

Camp romand des UCJG
***
2028, Vaumarcue, ,
Switzerland • Ph:
41-38-55-22-44 • Rms
330

WENGEN

Hotel Jungfraublick
YMCA/YWCA *
3823, Wengen, ,
Switzerland • Ph:
41-33-855-27-55 Fax:
41-33-855-27-26 • Rms
45 • Sfr. 70-150

ZURICH

Hotel Gleckenhof YMCA
***
Sihlstrasse 33, 8021,
Zurich, , Switzerland •
Ph: 41-1-211-56-50 Fax:
41-1-211-56-60 • Rms
170 • Sfr. 180-290

Lodging for: * = Men only, ** = Men / Women, *** = Family, C = Conference

Taiwan

TAIPEI

YMCA International Guest House **
Taipei, , Taiwan • Ph: 886-2-311-3201 Fax: 886-2-311-3209 • US$ 52-88

Tanzania

ARUSHA

YMCA Hostel **
India Street, P. O. Box 658, Arusha, , Tanzania • Ph: 255-57-6907 • US$ 10-20

DAR-ES-SALAAM

YMCA Hostel **
Ali Hassan Mwinyi Road, P. O. Box 676, Dar-es-Salaam, , Tanzania • Ph: 255-51-26726 • US$ 10-13

MOSHI

YMCA Hostel **
Kilimanjaro Road, P. O. Box 865, Moshi, , Tanzania • Ph: 255-55-51734 • US$ 10-13

PANGANI

YMCA Hostel & Holiday Resort • Nkoma Bay
P. O. Box 84, Pangani, , Tanzania • • US$ 10-13

Thailand

BANGKOK

YMCA, Collins International House ***
27 south Sathorn road, Bangkok, 10120, Thailand • Ph: 66-2-287-1900 Fax: 66-2-287-1996 • Rms 354 • US$ 30-34

CHIANGRAI

YMCA • (Golden Triangle International
70 Phaholyothin Road, Chiangrai, 57000, Thailand • Ph: 66-53-713-785 Fax: 66-53-714-336 • Rms 48 • US$ 3-20

MENGRAIRASMI,

YMCA International Hotel ***
11 Sermsuk Road, Mengrairasmi, Chiangmai, 50300, Thailand • Ph: 66-53-221-819 Fax: 66-53-215-523 • Rms 120 • US$ 4-65

Ukraine

DUBNO, RIVNENSKA

YMCA **
Kotsyubinskoho 4a, Dubno, Rivnenska oblast, 265100, Ukraine • Ph: 7-03656-43814 • US$ 5-10

KIEV

YMCA **
Flat 171, Balzaka 26A, 253225, Kiev, , Ukraine • • US$ 110-115

TERNOPIL

YMCA **
Vishnivetskogo 2-100, Ternopil, 282016, Ukraine • Ph: (038) 0352 280232 Fax: (038) 0352 227633 or 254533E-mail: din@alisa.ternopil.ua • US$ 12-15

USA

ALABAMA

HUNTSVILLE   AL

Central Branch YMCA *
203 South Greene Street, Huntsville, AL 35801, USA • Ph: (205) 534-6452 • Rms 25

TUSCALOOSA   AL

Central Branch YMCA **
2405 Paul Bryant Drive, P. O. Box 1129, Tuscaloosa, AL 35401, USA • Ph: (205) 758-5503 • Rms 48

ARIZONA

PHOENIX   AZ

Phoenix Downtown YMCA **
350 North First Avenue, Phoenix, AZ 85003, USA • Ph: (602) 253-6181 Fax: (602) 257-5136 • Rms 141

CALIFORNIA

BERKELEY   CA

Downtown Berkeley Branch YMCA *
2001 Allston Way, Berkeley, CA 94704, USA • Ph: (510) 848-9622 • Rms 86

GLENDALE   CA

Glendale Family YMCA *
140 North Louise Street, Glendale, CA 91206, USA • Ph: (818) 240-4130 Fax: (818) 500-1737 • Rms 83

LOS ANGELES   CA

28th Street / Crenshaw Branch YMCA *
1006 East 28th Street, Los Angeles, CA 90011, USA • Ph: (213) 232-7193 Fax: (213) 292-6821 • Rms 50

Hollywood Wilshire Branch YMCA **
1553 North Hudson Avenue, Los Angeles, CA 90028, USA • Ph: (213)467-4161 Fax: (213) 467-3026 • Rms 56

POMONA   CA

Central Branch YMCA *
350 North Garey Avenue, Pomona, CA 91767, USA • Ph: (909) 623-6433 Fax: (909) 622-6192 • Rms 51

SAN DIEGO   CA

San Diego Armed Services YMCA ***
500 West Broadway, San Diego, CA 92101, USA • Ph: (619) 232-1133 Fax: (619) 237-0330 • Rms 271

SAN FRANCISCO   CA

Central Branch YMCA ***
220 Golden Gate Avenue, San Francisco, CA 94102, USA • Ph: (415) 885-0460 Fax: (415) 885-5439 • Rms 105

Chinatown Branch YMCA *
855 Sacramento Street, San Francisco, CA 94108, USA • Ph: (415) 982-4412 Fax: (415) 982-0117 • Rms 50

COLORADO

Y M C A

DENVER CO	**MIDDLETOWN** CT	**WINSTED** CT

Central Branch YMCA
/*
25 East 16th Avenue,
Denver, CO 80202, USA
• Ph: (303) 861-8300
Fax: (303) 830-7391 •
Rms 198

Northern Middlesex
County YMCA *
99 Union Street,
Middletown, CT 06457,
USA • Ph: (203) 347-6907
Fax: (203) 343-6254 •
Rms 62

Winsted Area Branch
YMCA **
480 Main Street,
Winsted, CT 06098, USA
• Ph: (203) 379-0708
Fax: (203) 738-0653 •
Rms 33

ESTES PARK CO

Estes Park Center
YMCA ***C
2515 Tunnel Road, P. O.
Box 20500, Estes Park,
CO 80511, USA • Ph:
(303) 586-3341 Fax:
(303) 586-6087 • Rms
3635

NAUGATUCK CT

Naugatuck YMCA *
284 Church Street,
Naugatuck, CT 06770,
USA • Ph: (203) 729-8239
• Rms 52

DELAWARE

WILMINGTON DE

Walnut Street Branch
YMCA *
10th & Walnut Streets,
Wilmington, DE 19801,
USA • Ph: (302) 571-6935
Fax: (302) 571-6949 •
Rms 18

WINTER PARK CO

Snow Mountain Ranch/
YMCA ***C
P. O. Box 169, Winter
Park, CO 80482, USA •
Ph: (970) 887-2152 •
Rms 305

NEW BRITAIN CT

New Britain-Berlin
YMCA *
50 High Street, New
Britain, CT 06051, USA
• Ph: (203) 229-3787
Fax: (203) 225-8063 •
Rms 90

Central Branch YMCA *
501 West 11th Street,
Wilmington, DE 19801,
USA • Ph: (302) 571-6900
Fax: (302) 656-5035 •
Rms 141

CONNECTICUT

ANSONIA CT

Valley YMCA *
12 State Street, Ansonia,
CT 06401, USA • Ph:
(203) 736-9975 Fax:
(203) 736-9974 • Rms 29

NEW HAVEN CT

Downtown Youth Center
Branch YMCA **
52 Howe Street, New
Haven, CT 06511, USA •
Ph: (203) 865-3161 Fax:
(203) 777-4331 • Rms
150

GEORGIA

ATLANTA GA

East Central Branch
YMCA *
22 Butler Street N.w.,
Atlanta, GA 30303, USA
• Ph: (404) 659-8085
Fax: (404) 659-6026 •
Rms 50

BRIDGEPORT CT

Bridgeport Branch
YMCA *
651 State Street,
Bridgeport, CT 06604,
USA • Ph: (203) 334-5551
Fax: (203) 334-2847 •
Rms 165

NORWICH CT

Southeastern
Connecticut YMCA *
337 Main Street,
Norwich, CT 06360, USA
• Ph: (203) 889-7349
Fax: (203) 889-9658(•
Rms 22

HAWAII

HONOLULU HI

Central Branch YMCA *
401 Atkinson Drive,
Honolulu, HI 96814, USA
• Ph: (808) 941-3344
Fax: (808) 941-8821 •
Rms 114

GREENWICH CT

Greenwich YMCA *
50 East Putnam Avenue,
Greenwich, CT 06830,
USA • Ph: (203) 869-1630
Fax: (203) 869-7252 •
Rms 50

STAMFORD CT

Stamford YMCA **
909 Washington Blvd.,
Stamford, CT 06901,
USA • Ph: (203) 357-7000
Fax: (203) 425-8060 •
Rms 132

Nuuanu Branch YMCA *
1441 Pali Highway,
Honolulu, HI 96813, USA
• Ph: (808) 536-3556
Fax: (808) 533-1286 •
Rms 70

HARTFORD CT

Downtown Branch YMCA
**
160 Jewell Street,
Hartford, CT 06103,
USA • Ph: (203) 522-4183
• Rms 22

TORRINGTON CT

Torrington Area Branch
YMCA **
259 Prospect Street,
Torrington, CT 06790,
USA • Ph: (203) 489-3133
Fax: (203) 482-4853 •
Rms 51

Atherton YMCA **
1810 University Avenue,
Honolulu, HI 96822, USA
• Ph: (808) 946-0253
Fax: (808) 941-7802

ILLINOIS

CHAMPAIGN IL

MERIDEN CT

Meriden YMCA **
500 South Broad Street,
Meriden, CT 06450, USA
• Ph: (203) 235-6386
Fax: (203) 634-6517 •
Rms 92

WILLIMANTIC CT

Willimantic YMCA **
P. O. Box 56,
Willimantic, CT
06226-0056, USA • Ph:
(203) 423-2531 • Rms
13

University of Illinois
YMCA *
1001 South Wright Street,
Champaign, IL 61820,
USA • Ph: (217) 337-1500
• Rms 13

CHICAGO	IL

Austin Branch YMCA **
501 North Central
Avenue, Chicago, IL
60644, USA • Ph: (773)
287-9120 Fax: (773)
287-3661 • Rms 262

**Irving Park Branch
YMCA** *
4251 West Irving Park
Road, Chicago, IL
60641, USA • Ph: (312)
777-7500 Fax: (312)
777-8892 • Rms 220

**Lincoln-Belmont Branch
YMCA** *
3333 North Marshfield
Avenue, Chicago, IL
60657, USA • Ph: (312)
248-3333 Fax: (312)
248-3374 • Rms 224

YMCA Lawson House **
30 West Chicago Avenue,
Chicago, IL 60610, USA
• Ph: (312) 944-6211
Fax: (312) 944-7267 •
Rms 638

**111th Street Branch
YMCA** *
4 East 111th Street,
Chicago, IL 60628, USA
• Ph: (312) 785-9210
Fax: (312) 785-9407 •
Rms 149

**Washington Park Branch
YMCA** **
5000 South Indiana
Avenue, Chicago, IL
60615, USA • Ph: (312)
538-5200 Fax: (312)
538-7857 • Rms 254

EVANSTON	IL

**McGaw YMCA In
Evanston** *
1000 Grove Street,
Evanston, IL 60201,
USA • Ph: (847) 475-7400
Fax: (847) 475-7959 •
Rms 173

LA GRANGE	IL

Rich Port Branch YMCA
**
31 East Ogden Avenue,
La Grange, IL 60525,
USA • Ph: (708) 352-7600
Fax: (708) 352-7635 •
Rms 242

NAPERVILLE	IL

YMCA of Naperville *
34 South Washington
Street, Naperville, IL
60540, USA • Ph: (708)
420-6270 Fax: (708)
420-8677 • Rms 14

NILES	IL

**Leaning Tower Branch
YMCA** **
6300 West Touhy, Niles,
IL 60648, USA • Ph:
(708) 647-8222 Fax:
(708) 647-7736 • Rms
200

OAK PARK	IL

**Oak Park Center Branch
YMCA** *
255 South Marion Street,
Oak Park, IL 60302,
USA • Ph: (708) 383-5200
• Rms 127

INDIANA	
INDIANAPOLIS	IN

**Fall Creek Parkway
Branch YMCA** ***
860 West Ioth Street,
Indianapolis, IN 46202,
USA • Ph: (317) 634-2478
• Rms 97

IOWA	
CLINTON	IA

Clinton YMCA *
300 Fifth Avenue South,
Clinton, IA 52732, USA •
Ph: (319) 243-1364 •
Rms 22

DES MOINES	IA

**Riverfront Branch
YMCA** *
101 Locust Street, Des
Moines, IA 50309, USA •
Ph: (515) 288-0131 Fax:
(515) 288-242 • Rms 167

MASON CITY	IA

Mason City YMCA *
15 North Pennsylvania
Avenue, Mason City, IA
50401, USA • Ph: (515)
423-5526 • Rms 37

SIOUX CITY	IA

Siouxland YMCA *
722 Nebpaska Street,
Sioux City, IA 51101,
USA • Ph: (712) 252-3276
• Rms 47

KANSAS	
KANSAS CITY	KS

Central Branch YMCA *
900 North Eighth Street,
Kansas City, KS 66101,
USA • Ph: (913) 371-4400
• Rms 77

KENTUCKY	

LEXINGTON	KY

**High Street Branch
YMCA** *
239 East High Street,
Lexington, KY 40507,
USA • Ph: (606) 254-9622
Fax: (606) 255-5653 •
Rms 24

LOUISVILLE	KY

**Center For Youth
Alternatives** **
1410 South First Street,
Louisville, KY 40208,
USA • Ph: (502) 635-5233
Fax: (502) 635-1443 •
Rms 20

**Chestnut Street Branch
YMCA** *
930 West Chestnut,
Louisville, KY 40203,
USA • Ph: (502) 587-7405
Fax: (502) 587-2399 •
Rms 41

LOUISIANA	
NEW ORLEANS	LA

**Lee Circle Branch
YMCA** ***
920 St. Charles Avenue,
New Orleans, LA 70130,
USA • Ph: (504) 568-9622
Fax: (504) 568-9622 •
Rms 50

MAINE	
AUBURN	ME

Auburn-Lewiston YMCA
*
62 Turner Street,
Auburn, ME 04210, USA
• Ph: (207) 795-4095 •
Rms 40

PORTLAND	ME

Portland YMCA *
70 Forest Avenue, P. O.
Box 1078, Portland, ME
04101, USA • Ph: (207)
874-1111 • Rms 86

MARYLAND	
CUMBERLAND	MD

**Cumberland Central
YMCA** *
205 Baltimore Avenue,
Cumberland, MD
21502, USA • Ph: (301)
724-5445 Fax: (301)
724-0642 • Rms 47

HAGERSTOWN	MD

Hagerstown YMCA *
149 North Potomac
Street, Hagerstown, MD
21740, USA • Ph: (301)
739-3990 Fax: (301)
739-3992 • Rms 63

MASSACHUSETTS	

Y M C A

ATHOL   MA

Athol YMCA *
545 Main Street, Athol,
MA 01331, USA • Ph:
(617) 249-3305 • Rms
20

ATTLEBORO   MA

Attleboro YMCA *
63 North Main Street,
Attleboro, MA 02703,
USA • Ph: (508) 222-7422
• Rms 14

BEVERLY   MA

Cabot Street Facility *
245 Cabot Street,
Beverly, MA 01915, USA
• Ph: (508) 922-0990 •
Rms 45

BOSTON   MA

Central Branch ***
316 Huntington Avenue,
Boston, MA 02115, USA
• Ph: (617) 536-7800
Fax: (617) 536-3240 •
Rms 333

BROCKTON   MA

**Central Division Branch
YMCA** *
320 Main Street,
Brockton, MA 02401,
USA • Ph: (508) 583-2155
Fax: (508) 588-6730 •
Rms 49

CAMBRIDGE   MA

**Cambridge Family
YMCA** *
820 Massachusetts
Avenue, Cambridge, MA
02139, USA • Ph: (617)
661-9622 Fax: (617)
864-0996 • Rms 136

CHARLESTOWN   MA

**Boston Armed Services
YMCA** ***
150 Second Avenue,
Charlestown, MA 02129,
USA • Ph: (617) 241-8400
Fax: (617) 241-2856 •
Rms 135

CHELSEA   MA

**Chelsea Community
YMCA** *
207 Shurtleff Street,
Chelsea, MA 02150, USA
• Ph: (617) 884-8776 •
Rms 36

HAVERHILL   MA

**Greater Haverhill
YMCA** *
81 Winter Street,
Haverhill, MA 01830,
USA • Ph: (508) 374-0506
Fax: (508) 373-0710 •
Rms 34

LAWRENCE   MA

Lawrence Branch YMCA
*
40 Lawrence Street,
Lawrence, MA 01840,
USA • Ph: (508) 686-6191
Fax: (508) 681-1126 •
Rms 89

LYNN   MA

**Lynn Central Branch
YMCA** *
20 Neptune Boulevard,
Lynn, MA 01902, USA •
Att: Elaine Kurkul • Ph:
(617) 581-3105 Fax:
(617) 581-7397 • Rms 56

MALDEN   MA

Malden YMCA *
83 Pleasant Street,
Malden, MA 02148, USA
• Ph: (617) 324-7680
Fax: (617) 397-8643 •
Rms 42

NEWTON   MA

West Suburban YMCA *
276 Church Street,
Newton, MA 02158, USA
• Ph: (617) 244-6050
Fax: (617) 964-8472 •
Rms 32

PITTSFIELD   MA

Pittsfield YMCA ***
292 North Street,
Pittsfield, MA 01201,
USA • Ph: (413) 499-7650
Fax: (413) 443-6791 •
Rms 80

SOMERVILLE   MA

Somerville YMCA *
101 Highland Avenue,
Somerville, MA 02143,
USA • Ph: (617) 625-5050
Fax: (617) 625-3480 •
Rms 43

MICHIGAN

ANN ARBOR   MI

Ann Arbor YMCA **
350 South 5th Avenue,
Ann Arbor, MI 48104,
USA • Ph: (313) 663-0536
Fax: (313) 663-8232 •
Rms 54

BAY CITY   MI

Bay Area Family YMCA
*
Ill North Madison, Bay
City, MI 48708, USA •
Ph: (517) 895-8596 •
Rms 25

DETROIT   MI

Western Branch YMCA
*
1601 Clark Street,
Detroit, MI 48209, USA
• Ph: (313) 554-2136
Fax: (313) 554-3570 •
Rms 147

FLINT   MI

Flint YMCA **
411 East Third Street,
Flint, MI 48503, USA •
Ph: (313) 232-9622 Fax:
(313) 232-9329 • Rms
147

GRAND RAPIDS   MI

Downtown Branch YMCA
*
33 Library Street N.e,
Grand Rapids, MI
49503, USA • Ph: (616)
458-1141 Fax: (616)
454-8707 • Rms 134

LANSING   MI

Central Branch *
301 West Lenawee Street,
Lansing, MI 48933, USA
• Ph: (517) 484-4000
Fax: (517) 484-6744 •
Rms 70

PORT HURON   MI

Blue Water Area YMCA
*
700 Fort Street, Port
Huron, MI 48060, USA •
Ph: (810) 987-6400 •
Rms 17

SAGINAW   MI

Saginaw YMCA *
1915 Fordney, Saginaw,
MI 48601, USA • Ph:
(517) 753-7721 Fax:
(517) 755-9329 • Rms 99

MISSOURI

POTOSI   MO

YMCA of the Ozarks
***C
Route 2, Potosi, MO
63664, USA • Ph: (314)
438-2154 Fax: (314)
436-1901 • Rms 244

NEBRASKA

NORFOLK   NE

**Camping Services
Branch YMCA** ***
430 south 20th St.,
Norfolk, NE 68102, USA
• Ph: (402) 341-4730

Lodging for: * = Men only,   ** = Men / Women,   *** = Family,   C = Conference

OMAHA NE	**PASSAIC** NJ	**North Brooklyn**

Downtown Branch YMCA
**
430 South 20th Street,
Omaha, NE 68102, USA
• Ph: (402) 341-1600 •
Rms 88

NEW JERSEY

BAYONNE NJ

Bayonne YMCA *
259 Avenue E, Bayonne,
NJ 07002, USA • Ph:
(201) 339-2330 Fax:
(201) 339-3316 • Rms 75

ELIZABETH NJ

Elizabeth Branch YMCA
*
135 Madison Avenue,
Elizabeth, NJ 07201,
USA • Ph: (908) 355-9622
Fax: (908) 355-3572 •
Rms 70

HACKENSACK NJ

Greater Bergen County
YMCA *
360 Main Street,
Hackensack, NJ 07601,
USA • Ph: (201) 487-6600
Fax: (201) 487-4539 •
Rms 53

HOBOKEN NJ

Hoboken- North Hudson
YMCA *
1301 Washington Street,
Hoboken, NJ 07030,
USA • Ph: (201) 963-4100
Fax: (201) 963-5010 •
Rms 96

JERSEY CITY NJ

Jersey City YMCA **
654 Bergen Avenue,
Jersey City, NJ 07305,
USA • Ph: (201) 434-3211
Fax: (201) 333-9129 •
Rms 210

MONTCLAIR NJ

Montclair YMCA *
25 Park Street,
Montclair, NJ 07042,
USA • Ph: (201) 744-3400
Fax: (201) 744-1917 •
Rms 120

NEWARK NJ

Central Branch YMCA
***
600 Broad Street,
Newark, NJ 07102, USA
• Ph: (201) 624-8900
Fax: (201) 624-3024 •
Rms 390

YMCA of Passaic-
Clifton *
45 River Drive, Passaic,
NJ 07055, USA • Ph:
(201) 777-0123 • Rms
122

PATERSON NJ

Paterson YMCA **
128 Ward Street,
Paterson, NJ 07505,
USA • Ph: (201) 684-2320
• Rms 212

PERTH AMBOY NJ

Perth Amboy Program
Center *
182 Jefferson Street,
Perth Amboy, NJ 08861,
USA • Ph: (908) 442-3632
Fax: (908) 324-6359 •
Rms 79

PLAINFIELD NJ

Plainfield Area YMCA *
518 Watchung Avenue,
Plainfield, NJ 07060,
USA • Ph: (908) 756-6060
Fax: (908) 769-5341 •
Rms 62

WESTFIELD NJ

Westfield YMCA *
220 Clark Street,
Westfield, NJ 07090,
USA • Ph: (908)233-2700
Fax: (908) 232-3306 •
Rms 24

NEW YORK

BINGHAMTON NY

Downtown Branch YMCA
*
61 Susquehanna Street,
Binghamton, NY 13901,
USA • Ph: (607) 772-0560
Fax: (607) 772-0563 •
Rms 80

BROOKLYN NY

Prospect Park-Bayridge
YMCA *
357 Ninth Street,
Brooklyn, NY 11215,
USA • Ph: (718) 768-7100
Fax: (718) 499-0425 •
Rms 258

Greenpoint Branch
YMCA *
99 Meserole Avenue,
Brooklyn, NY 11222,
USA • Ph: (718) 389-3700
Fax: (718) 349-214 • Rms
101

YMCA-Twelve Town
570 Jamaica Avenue,
Brooklyn, NY 11208,
USA • Ph: (718) 277-1600
Fax: (718) 277-2081 •
Rms 94

BUFFALO NY

Humboldt Family
Branch YMCA *
347 East Ferry Street,
Buffalo, NY 14208, USA
• Ph: (716) 883-9622
Fax: (716) 875-9195 •
Rms 19

CLARYVILLE NY

Frost Valley YMCA ***C
2000 Frost Valley Road,
Claryville, NY 12725,
USA • Ph: (914) 985-2291
Fax: (914) 985-0056 •
Rms 500

FLUSHING NY

Flushing Branch YMCA
*
38 46 Northern Blvd.,
Flushing, NY 11354,
USA • Ph: (718) 961-6880
Fax: (718) 461-4691 •
Rms 162

Flushing Branch YMCA
*
138 46 Northern Blvd.,
Flushing, NY 11354,
USA • Ph: (718) 961-6880
Fax: (718) 461-4691

GLOVERSVILLE NY

Gloversville YMCA *
19 East Fulton Street,
Gloversville, NY 12078,
USA • Ph: (518) 725-0627
• Rms 19

JAMAICA NY

Central Queens Branch
YMCA *
89-25 Parsons Blvd.,
Jamaica, NY 11432,
USA • Ph: (718) 739-6600
Fax: (718)658-9568 •
Rms 282

Central Queens Branch
YMCA *
89-25 Paarsons Blvd.,
Jamaica, NY 11432,
USA • Ph: (718) 739-6600
Fax: (718) 658-9568

KINGSTON NY

Kingston & Ulster
County YMCA *
507 Broadway, Kingston,
NY 12401, USA • Ph:
(914) 338-3810 Fax:
(914) 338-0423 • Rms 24

Y
M
C
A

LITTLE FALLS   NY

Little Falls YMCA **
15 Jackson, Little Falls,
NY 13365, USA • Ph:
(315) 823-1740 • Rms
16

MOUNT VERNON   NY

**Mount Vernon Family
Center ***
20 South Second Avenue,
Mount Vernon, NY
10550, USA • Ph: (914)
668-4041 Fax: (914)
668-5407 • Rms 38

NEW YORK   NY

**Harlem Branch YMCA
****
180 West 135th Street,
New York, NY 10030,
USA • Ph: (212) 281-4100
Fax: (212) 491-3178 •
Rms 248

**West Side Branch YMCA
****
5 West 63rd Street, New
York, NY 10023, USA •
Ph: (212) 787-4400 Fax:
(212) 580-0441 • Rms
526

**Mcburney Branch YMCA
****
215 West 23rd Street,
New York, NY 10011,
USA • Ph: (212) 741-9210
Fax: (212) 741-0012 •
Rms 278

**Vanderbilt Branch
YMCA ****
224 East 47th Street,
New York, NY 10017,
USA • Ph: (212) 756-9600
Fax: (212) 755-7579 •
Rms 430 • $47-$59

NEWBURGH   NY

Newburgh YMCA *
54 Grand Street, P. O.
Box 428, Newburgh, NY
12550, USA • Ph: (914)
561-4060 Fax: (914)
565-3228 • Rms 9

NIAGARA FALLS   NY

**Niagara Falls Family
YMCA ***
1317 Portage Road,
Niagara Falls, NY
14301, USA • Ph: (716)
285-8491 Fax: (716)
285-1030 • Rms 58

OLEAN   NY

Olean YMCA *
130 South Union Street,
Olean, NY 14760, USA •
Ph: (716) 373-2400 •
Rms 30

PAWLING   NY

**Holiday Hills YMCA
***C**
2 Lakeside Drive,
Pawling, NY 12564, USA
• Ph: (914) 855-1550
Fax: (914) 855-9535 •
Rms 85

PORT CHESTER   NY

**Port Chester/rye Brook
Family Center ***
400 Westchester Avenue,
Port Chester, NY 10573,
USA • Ph: (914) 939-7800
Fax: (914) 939-7200 •
Rms 38

**Port Chester/Rye Brook
Family Center ***
400 Westchester Ave.,
Port Chester, NY 10573,
USA • Ph: (914) 939-7800
Fax: (914) 939-7200

SCHENECTADY   NY

**Schenectady Branch
YMCA ***
13 State Street,
Schenectady, NY 12305,
USA • Ph: (518) 374-9136
Fax: (518) 370-5526 •
Rms 16

SILVER BAY   NY

**Silver Bay Association
***C**
Silver Bay, NY 12874,
USA • Ph: (518) 543-8833
Fax: (518) 543-6733 •
Rms 180

SYRACUSE   NY

**Downtown Branch YMCA
***
340 Montgomery Street,
Syracuse, NY 13202,
USA • Ph: (315) 474-6851
Fax: (315) 474-6857 •
Rms 91

TARRYTOWN   NY

**Tarrytown & North
Tarrytown YMCA ***
62 Main Street,
Tarrytown, NY 10591,
USA • Ph: (914) 631-4807
Fax: (914) 631-4841 •
Rms 53

UTICA   NY

Utica YMCA **
726 Washington Street,
Utica, NY 13502, USA •
Ph: (315) 735-8581 •
Rms 84

WHITE PLAINS   NY

**White Plains Family
Center ***
250 Mamaroneck Avenue,
White Plains, NY 10605,
USA • Ph: (914) 949-8030
Fax: (914) 949-8419 •
Rms 167

YONKERS   NY

Yonkers YMCA *
17 Riverdale Avenue,
Yonkers, NY 10701, USA
• Ph: (914) 963-0183
Fax: (914) 965-5036 •
Rms 75

NORTH CAROLINA

BLACK MOUNTAIN   NC

**Blue Ridge Assembly
YMCA ***C**
84 Blue Ridge Circle,
Black Mountain, NC
28711, USA • Ph: (704)
669-8422 Fax: (704)
669-8497 • Rms 893

CHARLOTTE   NC

Central Branch YMCA *
400 East Morehead
Street, Charlotte, NC
28202, USA • Ph: (704)
333-7771 Fax:
(704)333-9505 • Rms 108

RALEIGH   NC

Capital Area YMCA *
1601 Hillsborough Street,
P. O. Box 10976,
Raleigh, NC 27605, USA
• Ph: (919) 832-6601 •
Rms 25

ROCKY MOUNT   NC

**Rocky Mount Family
YMCA ***
P. O. Box 4063, Rocky
Mount, NC 27803, USA
• Ph: (919) 972-9622 •
Rms 30

OHIO

CANTON   OH

**Downtown Center
Branch YMCA ***
405 Second Street N.w.,
Canton, OH 44702, USA
• Ph: (216) 456-7141
Fax: (216) 456-0513 •
Rms 93

CINCINNATI   OH

**Williams Branch YMCA
***
1228 East Mcmillan
Street, Cincinnati, OH
45206, USA • Ph: (513)
961-7552 • Rms 25

CLEVELAND OH	BETHLEHEM PA	STROUDSBURG PA

Brooklyn Branch YMCA
*
3881 Pearl Road,
Cleveland, OH 44109,
USA • Ph: (216) 749-2355
• Rms 5

Bethlehem YMCA *
430 East Broad Street,
Bethlehem, PA 18018,
USA • Ph: (215) 867-7588
Fax: (215) 867-8295 •
Rms 62

Pocono Family YMCA *
809 Kain Street,
Stroudsburg, PA 18360,
USA • Ph: (717) 421-2525
Fax: (717) 421-2640 •
Rms 17

COLUMBUS OH	CONNELLSVILLE PA	TYRONE PA

Central Branch YMCA *
40 West Long Street,
Columbus, OH 43215,
USA • Ph: (614) 224-1131
Fax: (614) 224-7608 •
Rms 360

Connellsville YMCA **
1100 South Pittsburgh
Street, Connellsville, PA
15425, USA • Ph: (412)
628-0570 • Rms 30

Tyrone Area YMCA *
1062 Logan Avenue,
Tyrone, PA 16686, USA
• Ph: (814) 684-2740 •
Rms 11

EAST LIVERPOOL OH	HARRISBURG PA	YORK PA

East Liverpool YMCA *
134 East Fourth Street,
East Liverpool, OH
43920, USA • Ph: (216)
385-0663 • Rms 17

**East Shore Branch
YMCA** *
Front & Nortn Streets,
Harrisburg, PA 17101,
USA • Ph: (717) 232-9622
Fax: (717) 234-5859 •
Rms 86

**York & York County
YMCA** *
90 North Newberry Street,
York, PA 17401, USA •
Ph: (717) 843-7884 Fax:
(717) 854-1857 • Rms
133

MANSFIELD OH	MC KEESPORT PA	RHODE ISLAND

Mansfield YMCA *
455 Park Avenue West,
Mansfield, OH 44906,
USA • Ph: (419) 522-3511
• Rms 71

Mckeesport YMCA **
523 Sinclair Street, Mc
Keesport, PA 15132,
USA • Ph: (412) 664-9168
Fax: (412) 664-9312 •
Rms 84

		PROVIDENCE RI

**Intown Providence
Branch YMCA** **
164 Broad St.,
Providence, RI 02903,
USA • Ph: (401) 456-0100
Fax: (401) 274-0828 •
Rms 177

MASSILLON OH	NAZARETH PA	

Massillon YMCA *
131 Tremont Avenue S.e.,
Massillon, OH 44646,
USA • Ph: (216) 837-5116
• Rms 50

Nazareth YMCA *
33 South Main Street,
Nazareth, PA 18064,
USA • Ph: (215) 759-3440
• Rms 18

TENNESSEE

MEMPHIS TN

Mason Branch YMCA *
3458 Walker Avenue,
Memphis, TN 38111,
USA • Ph: (901) 323-4505
Fax: (901) 327-7545 •
Rms 45

PAINESVILLE OH	PHILADELPHIA PA

Central Branch YMCA *
933 Mentor Avenue,
Painesville, OH 44077,
USA • Ph: (216) 352-3303
Fax: (216) 354-2076 •
Rms 22

Germantown YMCA *
5722 Greene Street,
Philadelphia, PA 19144,
USA • Ph: (215) 844-3281
Fax: (215) 849-6990 •
Rms 125

TEXAS

EL PASO TX

**El Paso Central Branch
YMCA** **
701 Montana Ave., El
Paso, TX 79902, USA •
Ph: (915) 533-3941 Fax:
(915) 544-8729 • Rms
115

WILLARD OH	PITTSBURGH PA

Willard YMCA **
302 Woodland Avenue P.
O. Box 59, Willard, OH
44890, USA • Ph: (419)
933-6501 Fax: (419)
933-280 • Rms 80

**Centre Avenue YMCA
Branch** *
2621 Centre Avenue,
Pittsburgh, PA 15219,
USA • Ph: (412) 621-1762
• Rms 80

**El Paso Armed Services
YMCA** ***
7060 Comington Street,
El Paso, TX 79930, USA
• Ph: (915) 562-8461
Fax: (915) 565-0306 •
Rms 89

OKLAHOMA

TULSA OK

Downtown Branch YMCA
*
515 South Denver, Tulsa,
OK 74103, USA • Ph:
(918) 583-6201 Fax:
(918) 584-0674 • Rms
121

Allegheny YMCA Branch
*
600 West North Avenue,
Pittsburgh, PA 15212,
USA • Ph: (412) 321-8594
• Rms 70

HOUSTON TX

Downtown Branch YMCA
**
1600 Louisiana Street,
Houston, TX 77002, USA
• Ph: (713) 659-8501
Fax: (713) 659-4314 •
Rms 137

OREGON

SALEM OR	READING PA

Salem Family YMCA *
685 Court Street N.e.,
Salem, OR 97301, USA
• Ph: (503) 581-9622
Fax: (503) 581-9626 •
Rms 16

Central Branch YMCA
**
Reed & Washington
Streets, P. O. Box 1622,
Reading, PA 19603, USA
• Att: Kim Corbit • Ph:
(215) 378-4700 Fax:
(215) 378-4780 • Rms
120

PENNSYLVANIA

Y
M
C
A

Cossaboom Branch YMCA *
7903 South Loop East, Houston, TX 77012, USA • Ph: (713) 643-4396 Fax: (713) 643-9038 • Rms 102

South Central Branch YMCA *
3531 Wheeler Avenue, Houston, TX 77004, USA • Ph: (713) 748-5405 Fax: (713) 748-5415 • Rms 68

VIRGINIA

NORFOLK   VA

Downtown Norfolk Branch YMCA ***
312 West Bute Street, Norfolk, VA 23510, USA • Ph: (804) 622-9622 Fax: (804) 627-4824 • Rms 80

PORTSMOUTH   VA

Portsmouth Armed Services YMCA ***
1504 A Norfolk Naval Shipyard, Portsmouth, VA 23709, USA • Ph: (804) 363-1884 Fax: (804) 363-1953 • Rms 50

WASHINGTON

SEATTLE   WA

Central District YMCA ***
909 Fourth Avenue, Seattle, WA 98104, USA • Ph: (206)382-5000 Fax: (206) 382-7283 • Rms 262

WEST VIRGINIA

WHEELING   WV

Wheeling YMCA *
32 20th Street, Wheeling, WV 26003, USA • Ph: (304) 233-3560 • Rms 62

WISCONSIN

RACINE   WI

Racine YMCA **
725 Lake Avenue, Racine, WI 53403, USA • Ph: (414) 634-1994 Fax: (414) 634-0401 • Rms 100

WAUKESHA   WI

Waukesha YMCA *
320 East Broadway, Waukesha, WI 53186, USA • Ph: (414) 542-2557 Fax: (414) 542-1178 • Rms 33

Wales

ABERPORTH

YMCA Hostel **
Cambrian Way, Aberporth, , Wales • Ph: 44-1239-810-205, ext: 383

CARDIFF

YMCA **
The Walk, Cardiff, , Wales • Ph: 44-1222-497-044

MOUNTAIN ASH

YMCA **
Dyffryn Road, Mountain Ash, , Wales • Ph: 44-1443-473-334

PORT TALBOT

YMCA **
Talbot road, Port Talbot, , Wales • Ph: 44-1639-887-034

RHAYADER

YMCA **
Greenfields, South Street, Rhayader, , Wales • Ph: 44-1597-810-792

SWANSEA

YMCA **
1 Kingsway, Swansea, , Wales • Ph: 44-1792-652-032

Zambia

KITWE

Norfield House Hostel **
P. O. Box 20879, Kitwe, , Zambia • Ph: 260-2-215-495 • Rms 48

BED AND BREAKFAST ALTERNATIVE

ECONOMY MINDED VACATIONERS STRIKE IT RICH
SAVE UP TO $30 PER NIGHT

Budget travelers who like the comfort of a family home, and a start-up morning breakfast with plenty of hot coffee, can cut overnight lodging costs by 50%. The comfort and hospitality of thousands of bed and breakfast accommodations in the U.S. can be found at rates ranging from $45 single, to an average of $75 per double room. Families always enjoy the warm atmosphere and friendly welcome they feel from the host owner.

Bed and breakfast accommodations have had a long and popular following for Britishers who venture forth. B&B's, now a popular alternative to expensive motels in the U.S., come in all shapes and sizes.

Here at your fingertips is information on where you can find bed and breakfast accommodations anywhere in the U.S., Australia, Canada, England, France, Germany, Sweden, and New Zealand.

Practically all of the agencies listed provide free information about their services. To receive a speedy response when writing them, it is suggested that you enclose a self-addressed stamped envelope.

BED AND BREAKFAST RESERVATION SERVICES

Listed below is a small sample of B&B reservation services. Some represent a single city or state, others cover wide sections of the country. Some require a small membership fee. Others sell a list of host homes. They will try to match you with the type of accommodation you're looking for.

Bed and Breakfast Australia, P. O. Box 408, Gordon, NSW, Australia 2072. Can offer homestays and farmstays with Australian families-throughout Australia. Send for free brochure. Ph: Ph: 61-2-498-5344, (from July 1996; 61-2-9498-5344) Fax: 61-2-498-6438, (from July 1996; 61-2-9498-6438)

A B & C Bed & Breakfast Agency, 4390 Frances St., Vancouver, B. C. Canada V5C 2R3. Ph: (604) 298-8815,(800) 488-1941,Fax: (604) 298-5917. E-mail: handcar@direct.ca Modest to luxurious honeymoon accommodations. Good Breakfast, 15-20 min. to downtown Vancouver. also service Victoria & throughout BC. Visa, Mastercard accepted.

B
&
B

Town & Country Bed & Breakfast Reservation Service: Bo: 74542, 2803 West 4th Ave., Vancouver, BC V6K 1K2, Canada. Tel (604) 731-5942. Fax: (604) 731-5942. We offer select homes ir residential areas, usually within 15-20 min. drive to city center. / few guest houses (4- 8) are closer to downtown. The homes hav either shared or private baths, with rates accordingly. The home: vary from one to four guest rooms, modest to luxurious contemporary townhouses to heritage style homes. Rates from $7! - $150 in smaller towns, and $80 - $190 in Vancouver anc Victoria. Please note, we do not have, or mail a list of homes Book early for best choice.

Greater Victoria Visitor Information Centre, 812 Wharf Street Victoria, British Columbia V8W IT3 (250) 953-2033. Information or B & B's and accommodations. For reservations call (800) 663-3883 For information call (250) 953-2033. mpvance@travel.victoria.bc.ca

Toronto Bed and Breakfast, Box 269-235 College St.., Toronto. Ont. M5T 1R5 Canada (416) 927-0354 or (416) 588-8800, FAX (416) 927-0838. Email: beds@torontobandb.can Some with colorec TVs. Comfortable and affordable.

B & B Downtown Network, 3458 Laval Ave., Montreal, Que., Canada H2X 3C8 (514) 289-9749, (800) 267-5180. A network of 8(homes that specialize in the city center, and Old Montreal. Alsc speak Japanese.

Casas Americas, Casas Americas offers B & Bs and selected smal hotels in Honduras, Guatemala, El Salvador and Nicaragua. Accommodations are available in captial cities, towns, (Antigua, Guatemala, Copan, Honduras) beaches including Roatan. Honduras, and numcrous additional locations. Most hosts are English-speaking, a few also speak German. Many Hosts conduci local or ecological tours, provide airport pick-ups, additional meals and other services. For a free directory of axxommodations and rates, write Casa Americas, 613 S. Circle Dr. Barrington, IL 60010-1042. Fax: (706) 516-9079. We also provide information or Spanish-Language schools in each counrty.

Guarlford Grange: Geoff and Wendy Davies, 11 Guarlford Road, Malvern Worcestershire, England WR14 3QW. 44-1684-575996 Rates from £19 English breakfast £29.

French Country Welcome Guide: The guide is available at the federation office: 35 Rue Godot-deMauroy, 75009 Paris (Metro station Madeleine), for $16.00, or $21.00 air mail to the United States. (VISA cards accepted) Visitors to France who are looking for a more personalized place to stay can take advantage of a 6200 member national network of private homes offering bed and breakfast a la Francaise. Grouped under the government-subsidized National Federation of Rural French Lodgings. Participating families live exclusively in the countryside, in small villages and mainly on farms. The federation charter, signed by each family, promises a comfortable room, breakfast croissants or breads, reasonable prices and a friendly welcome. It is a promise that is catching on.

Bed and Breakfast in Germany: Rates as low as $14 per night in thousands of B & B' s in Germany. For the free brochure "Bed and Breakfast in Germany," contact the German National Tourist Office, 11766 Wilshire Blvd. Suite 750, Los Angeles, CA 90025 Ph: (310) 575-9799, Fax: (310) 575-1565

The London Bed and Breakfast: (800) 852-2632.

Wakefield's Great Britain, P. O. Box 3291, Newport, RI   02840, Ph: (401) 849-1298.

New Zealand: Bed & Breakfast HomeLink International; Self-contained apartment, 800 Sq. ft with all modern conveniences. Can accommodate 2 adults comfortably. Equivient to a top motel with full washing facilites. B&B $65.00/night. Longer terms available. (Neil Smith), I Higham Ferrers Pl., Red Beach, Hibiscus Coast, New Zealand (64) 942-64084, Fax: (64) 0-9-4264084, Email: homelink@ihug.co.nz

Russian Bed & Breakfast: Host Families Association (HOFA), 5-25 Tavricheskaya, 193015 St. Petersburg, Russia. Bed & Breakfast At $15-$30 a night and full service at $45-$95 a day per person in 19 cities of the ex-USSR. The rate depends on the number of guests, duration and location of their stay as well as the hosts' English skills. Services available include: Visa invitations, English speaking hosts, matching pet and smoking preferences, meeting at the airport/train, walking guides, car trips. Flexible itinerary, professional Russian Tutor, suggestions for cultural programs and timetables, booking theater tickets. Payment after one day stay. Fax/phone: 011-7-812-275-1992. E-mail: alexei@hofak.hop.stu.neva.ru   U.S. contact: Henry Townsend, (202) 333-9343, Fax: (202) 337-6090

B
&
B

Karlstad: Tourist Office in Karlsted. Carlstad Conference Center 65184 Karlstad, Sweden.   Phone: 46-54-149055, FAX 46-54-149059. This agency provides travelers with names and addresses of clean, certified bed and breakfast accommodations in Karlstad and Vicinity. Hotels from $56.00 per person per night During weekends and in the summer-time, the prices are usually half of the prices quoted.

BED & BREAKFAST PROGRAM: CARETAKERLINK INT'l: They send immediately by airmail their BED & BREAKFAST GUIDE With up to date listings from Amsterdam and the rest of the Netherlands after receiving your fax or email with creditcard number and month of exp. The price inc. amiling is only f.25. (about $13.00). HOLIDAY LINK, Postal Box 70.155, NL-9704 AD Groningen, The Netherlands ph: (31) 50-313-2424 FAX: (31)50-313-3177,   Email bed@holidaylink.com

Alaska Private Lodgings/Stay With A Friend, Mercy Dennis, P O. Box 200047, 1010 West Tenth Ave, Anchorage, AK 99520-0047. Ph: (907) 258-1717, Fax: (907) 258-6613. Directory: $5.00

Mi Casa Su Casa B & B Reservation Service, P.O. Box 950 Tempe, AZ 85281 (602) 990-0682. (800) 456-0682 Fax: (602) 990-3390. Bed & breakfasts in Arizona, New Mexico, Utah, & Nevada. We list over 200 B & B's.

Old Pueblo Homestays,William Janssen, 5644 East 6th St. Tucson, AZ 85711, Ph: (800) 333-9776, Fax: (602) 790-2399 E-mail: JAWS1926@AOL.COM. Brochure; directory; $2.00.

Eye Openers B & B Reservations Throughout California, Bed & Breakfast of Southern California, P.O. Box 694, Altadena, CA 91003   (626) 398-0528, Fax: (626)-296-0183, E-Mail: eobb@Loop.com. Specializes in B&B accommodations from San Diego to San Francisco. A Reservation Service that strives to match travelers requests with a wide range of Bed & Breakfast Homes at affordable prices.

Bed & Breakfast California, P.O. Box 282910, San Francisco, CA 94128-2910 (650) 696-1690   Fax: (650) 696-1699 E-mail: info@bbintl.com (serving CA & NV) For reservations call: (800) 872-4500

Bed & Breakfast Santa Barbara, Marcella Young, P. O. Box 41234, Santa Barbara, CA 93140. Ph: (805) 687-7898, Ph: & Fax: (805) 687-1659, E-mail: CALCOASTBB@AOL.COM. Free Brochure.

B & B Innkeepers of Colorado, P. O. Box 38416, Colorado Springs, C0 80937-8416 Tel: (800) 83-BOOKS ($3.00 for Directory)

Bed & Breakfast Central Information, P. O. Box 38279, Dept. BJ98, Colorado Springs, CO 80937-8279. "The traveler's information source to State Bed & Breakfast Associations across the nation." Send self-addressed stamped envelope for free order form.

B & B Reservations Colorado, Narda & Beverly Reigel/Miller, 2488 Garmisch Dr., Vail, CO 81657. Ph: (800) 748-2666, (207) 476-0792, Fax: (970) 476-0711. Directory; $2.00.

Four Seasons Int'l., B & B Service, 11 Bridlepath Rd., West Simsbury, CT 06092 (203) 658-2181. 20-25 homes. Each home is unique with helpful and friendly hosts.

Bed and Breakfast League, Ltd.,/ Sweet Dreams and Toast, P.O. Box 9490, Washington, D.C. 20016 (202) 363-7767. Fax: (202) 363-8396, Email: bedandbreakfast-washington@erols.com

Bed & Breakfast Accommodations, Ltd. P.O. Box 12011, Washington, D.C. 20005 (202) 328-3510, Fax: (202) 332-3885 E-Mail: BNB Accom @ AOL.COM

B & B of Delaware, Millie Alford, 3650 Silverside Road, Box 177, Wilmington, DE 19810-2211. Ph: (302) 479-9500, Fax: (302) 998-7642. Listings in the states of Delaware, Maryland, and Virginia. Brochure $1.00, send SASE.

Bed and Breakfast Co.- Tropical Florida, P. O. Box 262, S. Miami, FL 33243, (305) 661-3270. (Ph. or Fax)

A & A Bed and Breakfast of Florida, P.O. Box 1316, Winter Park, FL 32790 (407) 628-0322

Georgia: R. S. V. P. Grits (Great Reservations in the South), Marty Barnes, 541 Londonberry Road N. W., Atlanta, GA 30327. Ph: Atlanta, GA 30327 (800) 823-7787, Fax: (404) 252-8886. E-mail: INNFO@AOL.COM Reservations in Alabama & Georgia. Brochure, send SASE.

B & B Inns, 117 West Gordon St. at Chatham Square, Savannah, GA 31401 (912) 238-0518, Fax: (912) 233-2537. Nice accommodations in historic homes, all with full breakfasts. Some private cottages and suites, some single rooms, all have private baths. $65.00-$95.00. An B&B is also available at this sight.

B
&
B

Bed & Breakfast Honolulu (Statewide), 3242 Kaohinani Dr. Honolulu, HI 96817 (800) 288-4666, Fax: (808) 595-2030, Local 595-7533. Our homestays and studios are a pleasant low-cos alternative to hotels! We're Hawaii's largest B&B reservation: service with places on all Islands, including tiny Lanai and Molokai. We also offer rental cars and inter-island air at "resident rates. Rooms/Studios from $45 to $175. Call, fax, email, or write for our free brochure. One call does it all! Email Bnbshi@aloha.net(800) 288-4666

All Islands B & B, 463 Iliwahi Loop, Kailua, HI 96734. U. S. & Canada Toll Free: (800) 542-0344, Local: (808) 263-2342, FAX (808) 263-0308. Over 700 private guest accommodation: through-out all islands. Call and we will customize your lodging, car, and interisland air travel. There are three styles of Bed & Breakfast accommodations ranging from $45.00-$260.00 per night Most have <u>three night minimum</u> stay. Rooms in private home: average $55.00-$75.00 per night for two people, including island style continental breakfast. Many hosts have converted a section of their homes into a studio apartment with private entrances, private baths and tea kitchen (small refrigerator, microwave, coffee maker, etc.) Studios average $65.00-$85.00 per night for two people. Ohana cottages are separate and apart from the main house families. Average price $75.00-$95.00 per night for first two people; additional charge for extra people. Email: cac@aloha.net

Bed and Breakfast Hawaii, P.O. Box 449, Kapaa, HI 96746 (800) 733-1632, Fax: (808) 822-2723, Email: bandb@aloha.net

Louisiana: Bed & Breakfast Travel, Judy Young, 8211 Goodwood Blvd., Suite F, Baton Rouge, LA 70808. Ph: (504) 923-2337, (800) 926-4320, Fax: (504) 926-4320, E-Mail: BNBTRAVEL@AOL.COM. Brochure, send SASE. Listings in Lousiana and Mississippi.

New Orleans Bed and Breakfast, P.O. Box 8163, New Orleans, LA 70182 (504) 838-0071 or 838-0072, Fax: (504) 838-0140

B & B Marblehead & North Shore/Greater Boston & Cape Cod,(N. E.), New England Area; Suzanne Ross & Sheryl Fellmann, P. O. Box 35, Newtonville, MA 02160 Ph: (800) 832-2632, (617) 964-1606, Fax: (617) 332-8572, E-Mail: BNBINC@AOL.COM Free sampling.

House Guests Cape Cod, Box 1881, Orleans, MA 02653 (617) 896-7053, 1-(800) 666-HOST (USA only).

Folkstone B & B Reservation Service, Abigail Miller, 51 Sears Road, Southboro, MA 01772 Ph: (800) 762-2751, (508) 480-0380. Listings in Massachusetts & Connecticut. Brochure, send SASE.

B & B Cape Cod, Nantucket & Martha's Vineyard, Clark Diehl, P.O. Box 341, West Hyannisport, MA 02672-0341   Ph: (508) 775-2772, Fax: (508) 775-2884. Free Brochure.

Berkshire Bed & Breakfast, Eleanor Hebert, P. O. Box 211, Williamsbuarg, MA 01096 Ph: (413) 268-7244, (413) 268-7925, Fax: (413) 268-7243. Brochure, send SASE.

Traveller in Maryland, P.O. Box 2277, Annapolis, MD 21404 (410) 269-6232.

Amanda's B & B Reservation Service, Betsy Grater, 1428 Park Ave., Baltimore, MD 21217-4230. Ph: (410) 225-0001, Fax: (410) 728-8957, E-Mail: PGGT83@PRODIGY.COM Discriptive Listing; $5.00.

Bed & Breakfast Adventures, 2310 Central Ave., Suite 132, North Wildwood, NJ 08260 (800) 992-2632, (609) 522-4000, FAX: (609) 522-6125.

Urban Ventures Inc., P.O. Box 426, New York, NY 10024 (212) 594-5650. FAX: (212) 947-9320

All Around the Town, 150 5th Ave., # 711, New York, NY 10011 (800) 443-3800, Fax: (212) 675-6366. 150 clean, safe, inspected comfortable Manhattan Accommodations. Guest rooms $60-$90; fully furnished, self-catering apartments $80-$120 a night. Discounts for 2 or more weeks.

Bed and Breakfast Network of New York, 134 W. 32nd St., Suite 602, New York, NY 10001 (212) 645-8134.

N.W. Bed & Breakfast Reservation Services: 1067 Hanover Court South, Salem, OR, 97302-6002. Ph: (503) 370-9033 Salem, or (503) 243-7616 Portland. Fax: (503) 316-9118. Areas covered: Oregon, Washington, British Columbia/Vancouver Island, California. Other areas on request. Over 400 B&B's.

New England Hospitality Network, P. O. Box 3291, Newport, RI 02840, Ph: (401) 849-1298.

Bed and Breakfast Texas Style, 4224 W. Red Bird L., Dallas, TX 75237 (214)298-8586, FAX: (214) 298-7118

Guesthouses, Inc., P.O. Box 5737, Charlottesville, VA 22905 (804) 979-7264.

A Pacific Reservation Service, 701 N.W. 60th, Seattle, WA 98107 (206) 782-0539, FAX: (206) 784-0539

B
&
B

HOTELS, MOTEL & INNS
CONTENTS

HOTELS, MOTELS and INNS

Getting the most out of your travel dollar is a concern of most travelers. The following is an extensive list of Hotels, Motels and Inns catering to the needs of budget minded travelers. Classified into two groups, Group 1 identified by **$**, have the lowest price range starting around $30.00 and up for a single room, $35.00 and up for double. Group 2 identified by **$$**, are slightly higher in price, but will still fall within many travelers' budget. Pricing starts around $45.00 and up for single, $52.00 and up for double.

<u>ALWAYS</u> call and confirm room pricing and availability. The pricing will VARY with location, time of year desired, type of beds, number of people, etc.

Locations may have or provide some or all of the following:
• At-door parking
• Cable color TV, with HBO
• Non-smoking rooms
• Direct dial phones, free local calls.
• Tub & shower combinations
• King, queen & double beds, roll away beds & cribs.
• Children under certain ages stay free.
• Family Room
• Kitchenette
• Continental Breakfast
• Swimming pool/spa
• On site or nearby restaurants
• Coin laundry

Check on amenities and services when inquiring about room price and availability.

Inquire about discounts for AAA, AARP, Seniors, Student, Military, etc.

M O T E L

MAIN OFFICE
HOTELS, MOTELS and INNS

Budget Host Inns, P.O. Box 14341, Arlington, TX 76094, Reserv. Ph: (800) 283-4678, Main Office (817) 861-6088, Fax: (817) 861-6089. www.budgethost.com $

Choice Hotels Int., 10750 Columbia Pike, Silver Springs, MD 20901, Main Office (310) 593-5600,
• **Encono Lodge**, Reserv. (800) 424-4777 www.econolodge.com $-$$

Economy Inns of America, 755 Raintree Dr., Suite 200, Carlsbad, CA 92008, Reserv. Ph: (800) 826-0778, Main Office (619) 438-6661, Fax: (619) 431-9212, www. innsamerica.com $-$$

E-Z 8 Motels, 2484 Hotel Circle Place, San Diego, CA 92108 Ph: (619) 291-4824, (800) 326-6835 $

Motel 6, 14651 Dallas Parkway, Suite 500, Dallas, TX 75240 Ph: (214) 386-6161, Reserv. Ph: (800) 466-8356, Fax: (505) 892-8667, www.motel6.com $

Red Carpet, Scottish & Passport, 1726 Montreal Circle, Tucker, GA 30084 Reserv. Ph: (800) 251-1962 $-$$

Shoney's Inns, 217 West Main Street, Gallatin, TN 37066 Ph: (615) 452-7200, Res: (800) 222-2222 www.shoneysinn.com $$

Super 8 Motels Inc., 1910 Eith Ave. NE, Aberdeen, SD 57401-3207, Reserv. Ph: (800) 800-8000, Main Office (605) 533-6634, Fax: (605) 225-5018. www.super8motels.com $-$$

Thriftlodge (Forte Hotels Inc.), 1973 Friendship Dr., El Cajon, CA 92020, Main Office Ph: (619) 448-1884, Fax: (619) 562-0901
• **Thriftlodge**, Reserv. Ph: (800) 525-9055 www.travelodge.com $

Villager Lodge, 339 Jefferson Road, Parsittany, NJ 07054. Reserv. Ph: (800) 328-7829 www.villager.com $

ADDITIONAL RESOURCES
HOTELS, MOTELS and INNS

The following Hotels, Motels and Inns are excellent resource for number of economy lodging providers. Most will provide a free directory of their locations. Call the reserveration number, stop by a nearby location or checkout their Website.

Best Inns of America, P. O. Box 1719, Marion, IL 62959
Ph: (618) 997-5454, Res: (800) 237-8466 www.bestinn.com
Best Western Inc., P. O. Box 10203, Phoenix, AZ 85064-0203
Ph: (602) 957-4200, Res: (800) 528-1234 www.bestwestern.com
Budgetel Inns, 250 E. Wisconsin Ave. Suite 1750, Milwaukee, WI 53202-4221 Ph: (414) 272-8484, Res: (800) 428-3438
www.budgetel.com
Choice Hotels Int., 10750 Columbia Pike, Silver Springs, MD 20901, Main Office (310) 593-5600, Res. (800) 228-2000
www.hotelchoice.com
• **Friendship Inns**,
• **Rodeway Inns**,   www.rodeway.com
Reserverations for the following: (800) 221-2222
• **Clarion Inns & Hotels**,
• **Comfort Inns**, www.comfortinn.com
• **Quality Inns**, www.qualityinn.com
• **Sleep Inns**, www.sleepinn.com
Cross Country Inns, 6077 Frantz Road, Dublin, OH, 43017
Ph: (614) 766-0037, Res: (800) 621-1429
Days Inn, P.O. Box 29004, Phoenix, AZ 85038-5539, Res: (800) 329-7466, Main Office (602) 389-5539 www.daysinn.com
Exel Inns of America, 4706 E. Washington Ave., Madison, WI 53704
Ph: (608) 241-5271, Res: (800) 367-3935
Hampton Inns, 303 Madison Ave., Memphis, TN 38103
Ph: (901) 758-3100, Res: (800) 426-7866
www.hamptoninn-suites.com
Hospitality International, Inc., 1726 Montreal Circle, Tucker, GA 30084 Ph: (404) 270-1180, Res: (800) 251-1962,
www.reserveration.com
Howard Johnson, 3838 Van Buren, Phoenix, AZ 85038, Res: (800) 446-4656, Main Office (800) 247-6350, Fax: (602)389-3960.
www.hojo.com
Independent Motels of America, P. O. Box 202, Winner, SD 57580 Ph: (605) 842-3416, Res: (800) 341-8000, www.imalodging.com
Knights Lodging, 26650 Emery Parkway, Cleveland, OH 44128 Ph: (216) 464-5055, Res: (800) 843-5644   www.knightsinn.com
McIntosh Motor Inns, 440 Feheley Drive, King Of Prussia, PA 19406
Ph: (215) 279-6000, Res: (800) 444-2775
Microtel, One Airport Way, Suite 200, Rochester, NY 14624
Ph: (716) 436-6000, Res: (888) 771-7171 www.microtelinn.com
Red Roof Inns, Inc., 4355 Davidson Road, Hilliard, OH 43026
Ph: (614) 876-3200, Res: (800) 843-7663 www.redroof.com
Susse Chalet Savers, One Chalet Drive, Wilton, NH 03086
Ph: (603) 654-2000, Res: (800) 524-2538 www.sussechalet.com
Travelodge (Forte Hotels Inc.), 1973 Friendship Dr., El Cajon, CA 92020, Main Office (619) 448-1884, Fax: (619) 562-0901 www. travelodge.com • **Travelodge,** Res: (800) 578-7878

M
O
T
E
L

USA
Hotels, Motels & Inns

ALABAMA

ALEXANDER CITY   AL

Super 8 Motel $-$$
1104 US 280 Bypass,
Alexander City, AL 35010,
Res. (800) 800-8000 Ph: (205)
329-8858 Fax: (205) 329-8858

ANNISTON   AL

Super 8 Motel $-$$
6220 McClellan Blvd.,
Anniston, AL 36206, Res.
(800) 800-1000 Fax: (205)
820-1000

Villager $-$$
1015 Hwy 431 N, Anniston,
AL 36206, Res. (800)
328-7829 Ph: (205) 237-2525
Fax: (205) 237-4805

ATTALLA   AL

Econo Lodge $-$$
507 Cherry St.., Attalla, AL
35954, Res. (800) 424-4777
Ph: (205) 538-9925 Fax: (205)
538-5000

BESSEMER   AL

Econo Lodge $-$$
1021 9th Ave. S.W.,
Bessemer, AL 35023, Res.
(800) 424-4777 Ph: (205)
424-9780 Fax: (205) 424-9780

Motel 6 $
1000 Shiloh Ln, Bessemer,
AL 35020, Res. (800)
466-8356 Ph: 205 426-9646
Fax: 205 426-9305

BIRMINGHAM   AL

Super 8 Motel $-$$
1813 Crestwood Blvd.,
Birmingham, AL 35210,
Res. (800) 800-8000 Ph: (205)
956-3650

Villager $-$$
1313 Third Avenue,
Birmingham, AL 35203,
Res. (800) 328-7829 Ph: (205)
323-8806 Fax: (205) 323-5591

Villager $-$$
103 Green Springs Hwy,
Birmingham, AL 35209,
Res. (800) 328-7829 Ph: (205)
942-1265 Fax: (205) 942-1219

CULLMAN   AL

Super 8 Motel $-$$
"I-65 & Hwy 157, Exit 310",
Cullman, AL 35055, Res.
(800) 800-8000 Ph: (205)
734-8854 Fax: (205) 739-9284

DALEVILLE   AL

Econo Lodge Fort Rucker $-$$
241 Daleville Ave., Daleville,
AL 36322, Res. (800)
424-4777 Ph: (205) 598-6304

DOTHAN   AL

Motel 6 $
2907 Ross Clark Cir SW,
Dothan, AL 36301, Res.
(800) 466-8356 Ph: 334
793-6013 Fax: 334 793-2377

Super 8 Motel $-$$
Hwy 231 S. & Ross Clark
Circle, Dothan, AL 36301,
Res. (800) 800-8000

EVERGREEN   AL

Econo Lodge $-$$
Bates Rd., Evergreen, AL
36401, Res. (800) 424-4777
Ph: (205) 578-4701

FAIRFIELD   AL

Villager $-$$
5601 E.J. Oliver Boulevard,
Fairfield, AL 35064, Res.
(800) 328-7829 Ph: (205)
786-5577 Fax: (205) 781-1040

FLAGSTAFF   AL

Master Hosts Inns $$
2610 East Route 66,
Flagstaff, AL 86004, Res.
(800) 251-1962 Ph: (520)
526-1399 Fax: (520) 527-8626

FLORENCE   AL

Super 8 Motel $-$$
Highway 72 & 43 East,
Florence, AL 35631, Res.
(800) 800-8000 Ph: (205)
757-2167 Fax: (205) 757-1282

FULTONDALE   AL

Super 8 Motel $-$$
624 Decatur Highway,
Fultondale, AL 35068, Res.
(800) 800-8000 Ph: (205)
841-2200 Fax: (205) 841-2200

GREENVILLE   AL

Econo Lodge $-$$
946 Fort Dale Rd., Greenville,
AL 36037-1102, Res. (800)
424-4777 Ph: (205) 382-3118
Fax: (205) 382-9200

GULF SHORES   AL

Super 8 Motel $-$$
533 West Beach Blvd., P.O.
Box 4429, Gulf Shores, AL
36547, Res. (800) 800-8000
Ph: (334) 948-4888 Fax: (334)
948-4888

HOMEWOOD   AL

Super 8 Motel $-$$
140 Vulcan Rd, Homewood,
AL 35209, Res. (800)
800-8000 Ph: (205) 945-9888
Fax: (205) 945-9928

HUNTSVILLE   AL

Econo Lodge University $-$$
3772 University Dr.,
Huntsville, AL 35816, Res.
(800) 424-4777 Ph: (205)
534-7061 Fax: (000) 002-0534

Motel 6 $
3200 W University Dr,
Huntsville, AL 35816, Res.
(800) 466-8356 Ph: 205
539-8448 Fax: 205 539-6015

Super 8 Motel $-$$
3803 University Dr.,
Huntsville, AL 35805, Res.
(800) 800-8000 Ph: (205)
539-8881 Fax: (205) 533-5322

Villager $-$$
3100 University Drive,
Huntsville, AL 35816, Res.
(800) 328-7829 Ph: (205)
533-0610 Fax: (205) 533-9849

LANETT   AL

Econo Lodge $-$$
12 E. 22nd St., Lanett, AL
36863, Res. (800) 424-4777
Ph: (205) 768-3500

MADISON   AL

Motel 6 $
8995 Hwy 20, Madison, AL
35758, Res. (800) 466-8356
Ph: 205 772-7479 Fax: 205
772-9771

MOBILE   AL

Econo Lodge Midtown $-$$
1 S. Beltline Hwy., Mobile,
AL 36606, Res. (800)
424-4777 Ph: (205) 479-5333
Fax: (205) 471-4937

Motel 6 $
400 S Beltline Hwy, Mobile,
AL 36608, Res. (800)
466-8356 Ph: 334 343-8448
Fax: 334 343-7502

Motel 6 $
1520 Matzenger Dr, Mobile,
AL 36605, Res. (800)
466-8356 Ph: 334 473-1603
Fax: 334 473-4682

Motel 6 $
5488 Inn Rd/I-10 Service Rd,
Mobile, AL 36619, Res. (800)
466-8356 Ph: 334 660-1483
Fax: 334 660-7832

Scottish Inns $
3939 Government Blvd.,
Mobile, AL 36693, Res. (800)
251-1962 Ph: (334) 661-0070
Fax: (334) 661-5563

Super 8 Motel $-$$
Tillman's Corner, Mobile, AL
36693, Res. (800) 800-8000
Ph: (334) 666-0003 Fax: (334)
661-0800

MONROEVILLE   AL

Econo Lodge $-$$
1750 S. Alabama Ave.,
Monroeville, AL 36460, Res.
(800) 424-4777 Ph: (205)
575-3312 Fax: (205) 575-7780

Scottish Inns $
3236 South Alabama Avenue,
Monroeville, AL 36460, Res.
(800) 251-1962 Ph: (334)
575-3177 Fax: (334) 474-3177

MONTGOMERY   AL

Econo Lodge $-$$
4135 Troy Hwy.,
Montgomery, AL 36116,
Res. (800) 424-4777 Ph: (205)
284-3400 Fax: (205) 284-3400

Motel 6 $
1051 Eastern Bypass,
Montgomery, AL 36117,
Res. (800) 466-8356 Ph: 334
277-6748 Fax: 334 277-9195

Scottish Inns $
520 East South Blvd.,
Montgomery, AL 361116,
Res. (800) 251-1962 Ph: (334)
288-1501 Fax: (334) 281-3629

Super 8 Motel $-$$
1288 West South Blvd.,
Montgomery, AL 36105,
Res. (800) 800-8000 Ph: (205)
284-1700 Fax: (205) 288-0610

Villager $-$$
2750 Chestnut Street,
Montgomery, AL 36107,
Res. (800) 328-7829 Ph: (334)
834-4055 Fax: (334) 263-6703

MOODY   AL

Super 8 Motel $-$$
2451 Moody Parkway, Moody,
AL 35004, Res. (800)
800-8000 Ph: (205) 640-7091
Fax: (205) 640-7466

OPELIKA   AL

Econo Lodge $-$$
1105 Columbus Pkwy.,
Opelika, AL 36801, Res.
(800) 424-4777 Ph: (205)
749-8377 Fax: (205) 745-1700

Motel 6 $
1015 Columbus Pkwy,
Opelika, AL 36804, Res.
(800) 466-8356 Ph: 334
745-0988 Fax: 334 745-2589

OXFORD   AL

Motel 6 $
202 Grace St, Oxford, AL
36203, Res. (800) 466-8356
Ph: 205 831-5463 Fax: 205
831-5628

Red Carpet Inn $
1007 Highway 21 South,
Oxford, AL 36203, Res. (800)
251-1962 Ph: (205) 831-6082

PIKE ROAD   AL

Scottish Inns $
7237 Troy Highway, Pike
Road, AL 36064, Res. (800)
251-1962 Ph: (334) 281-3629
Fax: (334) 281-3629

SCOTTSBORO   AL

Scottish Inns $
902 E Willow St, Scottsboro,
AL 35768, Res. (800)
251-1962 Ph: (205) 574-1730
Fax: (205) 259-1140

SELMA   AL

Passport Inn $
601 Highland Ave, Selma,
AL 36701, Res. (800)
251-1962 Ph: (334) 872-3451
Fax: (334) 872-3451

SHEFFIELD   AL

Econo Lodge $-$$
2807 Woodward Ave.,
Sheffield, AL 35661, Res.
(800) 424-4777 Ph: (205)
381-0236 Fax: (205) 381-0236

SYLACAUGA   AL

Super 8 Motel $-$$
40770 U.S. Highway 280,
Sylacauga, AL 35150, Res.
(800) 800-8000 Ph: (205)
245-7476 Fax: (205) 245-7478

TROY   AL

Econo Lodge Troy State Univ. $-$$
1013 US 231, Troy, AL
36081, Res. (800) 424-4777
Ph: (205) 566-4960 Fax: (205)
566-5858

Scottish Inns $
186 Highway 231 North, Troy,
AL 36081, Res. (800)
251-1962 Ph: (334) 566-4090
Fax: (334) 566-3133

TUSCALOOSA   AL

Motel 6 $
4700 McFarland Blvd E (Hwy
82E) , Tuscaloosa, AL
35405, Res. (800) 466-8356
Ph: 205 759-4942 Fax: 205
759-1093

Super 8 Motel $-$$
4125 McFarland Blvd. East,
Tuscaloosa, AL 35405, Res.
(800) 800-8000 Ph: (205)
758-8878 Fax: (205) 758-2602

ALASKA

ANCHORAGE   AK

Super 8 Motel $-$$
3501 Minnesota Drive,
Anchorage, AK 99503, Res.
(800) 800-8000 Ph: (907)
276-8884 Fax: (206) 956-1418

FAIRBANKS   AK

Super 8 Motel $-$$
1909 Airport Way, Fairbanks,
AK 99701, Res. (800)
800-8000 Ph: (907) 451-8888
Fax: (907) 451-6690

JUNEAU   AK

Super 8 Motel $-$$
2295 Trout Street, Juneau,
AK 99801, Res. (800)
800-8000 Ph: (907) 789-4858
Fax: (907) 789-5819

KETCHIKAN   AK

Super 8 Motel $-$$
2151 Sea Level Drive,
Ketchikan, AK 99901, Res.
(800) 800-8000 Ph: (907)
225-9088 Fax: (907) 225-1072

SITKA   AK

Super 8 Motel $-$$
404 Sawmill Creek Rd, Sitka,
AK 99835, Res. (800)
800-8000 Ph: (907) 747-8804
Fax: (208) 734-7556

ARIZONA

BULLHEAD CITY   AZ

Motel 6 $
1616 Hwy 95, Bullhead City,
AZ 86442, Res. (800)
466-8356 Ph: 520 763-1002
Fax: 520 763-3868

CAMP VERDE   AZ

Super 8 Motel $-$$
1550 West Highway 260, PO
Box 2838, Camp Verde, AZ
86322, Res. (800) 800-8000
Ph: (602) 567-2623

CASA GRANDE   AZ

Motel 6 $
4965 N Sunland Gin Rd,
Casa Grande, AZ 85222,
Res. (800) 466-8356 Ph: 520
836-3323 Fax: 520 421-3094

CHANDLER   AZ

Super 8 Motel $-$$
7171 W. Chandler Blvd.,
Chandler, AZ 85226, Res.
(800) 800-8000 Ph: (602)
961-3888 Fax: (602) 961-3888

DOUGLAS   AZ

Motel 6 $
111 16th St, Douglas, AZ
85607, Res. (800) 466-8356
Ph: 520 364-2457 Fax: 520
364-9332

Thriftlodge $-$$
1030 19th St., Douglas, AZ
85607, Res. (800) 525-9055
Ph: (602) 364-8434 Fax: (602)
364-5687

M O T E L

ELOY   AZ

Super 8 Motel $-$$
3945 W. Houser Rd., Eloy,
AZ 85231, Res. (800)
800-8000 Ph: (602) 466-7804
Fax: (602) 622-3481

FLAGSTAFF   AZ

Budget Host Saga Motel $-$$
820 W Hwy 66, Flagstaff, AZ
86001, Res. (800) 283-4678
Ph: (602) 779-3631

Econo Lodge East $-$$
Lockett & Santa Fe,
Flagstaff, AZ 86004, Res.
(800) 424-4777 Ph: (602)
527-1477 Fax: (602) 527-0228

Econo Lodge Lucky Lane $-$$
2480 E. Lucky Lane,
Flagstaff, AZ 86001, Res.
(800) 424-4777 Ph: (602)
774-7701 Fax: (602) 774-7855

Econo Lodge West $-$$
2355 S. Beulah Blvd.,
Flagstaff, AZ 86001, Res.
(800) 424-4777 Ph: (602)
774-2225 Fax: (602) 774-2225

Motel 6 $
2010 E Butler Ave, Flagstaff,
AZ 86004, Res. (800)
466-8356 Ph: 520 774-1801
Fax: 520 774-1987

Motel 6 $
2500 E Lucky Ln, Flagstaff,
AZ 86004, Res. (800)
466-8356 Ph: 520 779-6184
Fax: 520 774-2249

Motel 6 $
2440 E Lucky Ln, Flagstaff,
AZ 86004, Res. (800)
466-8356 Ph: 520 774-8756
Fax: 520 774-2067

Motel 6 $
2745 S Woodlands Village,
Flagstaff, AZ 86001, Res.
(800) 466-8356 Ph: 520
779-3757 Fax: 520 774-2137

Super 8 Motel $-$$
3725 Kasper Avenue,
Flagstaff, AZ 86004, Res.
(800) 800-8000 Ph: (602)
526-0818 Fax: (602) 526-8786

GILA BEND   AZ

Super 8 Motel $-$$
Hwy 85 & I-8, Gila Bend, AZ
85337, Res. (800) 800-8000
Ph: (602) 683-6311 Fax: (602)
683-2120

GOODYEAR   AZ

Super 8 Motel $-$$
1710 N. Dysart Road,
Goodyear, AZ 85338-1111,
Res. (800) 800-8000 Ph: (602)
932-9622 Fax: (602) 932-4685

HOLBROOK   AZ

Budget Host Holbrook Inn $-$$
235 W Hopi Dr, Holbrook, AZ
86025, Res. (800) 283-4678
Ph: (602) 524-3809 Fax: (602)
524-3072

Econo Lodge $-$$
2596 Navajo Blvd., Holbrook,
AZ 86025, Res. (800)
424-4777 Ph: (602) 524-1448
Fax: (602) 524-2281

Motel 6 $
2514 Navajo Blvd, Holbrook,
AZ 86025, Res. (800)
466-8356 Ph: 520 524-6101
Fax: 520 524-1806

Super 8 Motel $-$$
1989 Navajo Blvd., Holbrook,
AZ 86025, Res. (800)
800-8000 Ph: (602) 524-2871
Fax: (602) 524-3514

KINGMAN   AZ

Motel 6 $
3351 E Andy Devine Ave,
Kingman, AZ 86401, Res.
(800) 466-8356 Ph: 520
757-7151 Fax: 520 757-2438

Motel 6 $
424 W Beale St, Kingman,
AZ 86401, Res. (800)
466-8356 Ph: 520 753-9222
Fax: 520 753-4791

Super 8 Motel $-$$
3401 E. Andy Devine Ave.,
Kingman, AZ 86401, Res.
(800) 800-8000 Ph: (520)
757-4808 Fax: (520) 757-4808

LAKE HAVASU   AZ

Super 8 Motel $-$$
305 London Bridge Rd., Lake
Havasu, AZ 86403, Res.
(800) 800-8000 Ph: (602)
855-8844 Fax: (602) 855-7132

LAKE HAVASU CITY   AZ

E-z 8 Motel $
41 S. Acoma Blvd., Lake
Havasu City, AZ 86403, Res.
800-326-6835 Ext. 17 Ph:
520-855-4023

MESA   AZ

Motel 6 $
336 W Hampton Ave, Mesa,
AZ 85210, Res. (800)
466-8356 Ph: 602 844-8899
Fax: 602 969-6749

Motel 6 $
1511 S Country Club Dr,
Mesa, AZ 85210, Res. (800)
466-8356 Ph: 602 834-0066
Fax: 602 969-6313

Motel 6 $
630 W Main St, Mesa, AZ
85201, Res. (800) 466-8356
Ph: 602 969-8111 Fax: 602
655-0747

Super 8 Motel $-$$
6733 East Main Street, Mesa,
AZ 85205, Res. (800)
800-8000 Ph: (602) 981-6181
Fax: (602) 981-6181

Super 8 Motel $-$$
3 East Main St., Mesa, AZ
85201, Res. (800) 800-8000
Ph: (602) 834-6060

Super 8 Motel $-$$
1550 S. Gilbert Rd., Mesa, AZ
85204, Res. (800) 800-8000
Ph: (602) 545-0888 Fax: (602)
545-0888

NOGALES   AZ

Motel 6 $
141 W Mariposa Rd, Nogales,
AZ 85621, Res. (800)
466-8356 Ph: 520 281-2951
Fax: 520 281-9592

Super 8 Motel $-$$
547 W. Mariposa Rd.,
Nogales, AZ 85621, Res.
(800) 800-8000 Ph: (602)
281-2242 Fax: (602) 281-2242

PAGE   AZ

Econo Lodge $-$$
121 S. Lake Powell Blvd.,
Page, AZ 86040, Res. (800)
424-4777 Ph: (602) 645-2488
Fax: (602) 645-9472

Super 8 Motel $-$$
75 South 7th Avenue, Page,
AZ 86040, Res. (800)
800-8000 Ph: (602) 645-2858

PHOENIX   AZ

E-z 8 Motel $
1820 S. 7th Street, Phoenix,
AZ 85034, Res. 800-326-6835
Ext. 66 Ph: 602-254-9787
Fax: 602-256-0766

Motel 6 $
214 S 24th St, Phoenix, AZ
85034, Res. (800) 466-8356
Ph: 602 244-1155 Fax: 602
231-0043

Motel 6 $
4130 N Black Canyon Hwy,
Phoenix, AZ 85017, Res.
(800) 466-8356 Ph: 602
277-5501 Fax: 602 274-9724

Motel 6 $
2323 E Van Buren St,
Phoenix, AZ 85006, Res.
(800) 466-8356 Ph: 602
267-7511 Fax: 602 231-8701

Motel 6 $
5315 E Van Buren St,
Phoenix, AZ 85008, Res.
(800) 466-8356 Ph: 602
267-8555 Fax: 602 231-9115

Motel 6 $
2548 W Indian School Rd,
Phoenix, AZ 85017, Res.
(800) 466-8356 Ph: 602
248-8881 Fax: 602 230-2371

Motel 6 $
3152 N Black Canyon Hwy,
Phoenix, AZ 85051, Res.
(800) 466-8356 Ph: 602
995-7592 Fax: 602 995-9592

Motel 6 $
2330 W Bell Rd, Phoenix, AZ
85023, Res. (800) 466-8356
Ph: 602 993-2353 Fax: 602
548-3461

Motel 6 $
2735 W Sweetwater Ave,
Phoenix, AZ 85029, Res.
(800) 466-8356 Ph: 602
942-5030 Fax: 602 548-3483

Motel 6 $
1530 N 52nd Dr, Phoenix, AZ
85043, Res. (800) 466-8356
Ph: 602 272-0220 Fax: 602
278-4210

Premier Inn $
10402 Black Canyon Fwy.,
Phoenix, AZ 85051, Res.
800-326-6835 Ext. 67 Ph:
602-943-2371 Fax:
602-943-5847

Super 8 Motel $-$$
4021 N. 27th Ave., Phoenix,
AZ 85017, Res. (800)
800-8000 Ph: (602) 248-8880
Fax: (602) 241-0234

PINETOP   AZ

Econo Lodge $-$$
458 White Mountain Blvd.,
Pinetop, AZ 85935, Res.
(800) 424-4777 Ph: (602)
367-3636 Fax: (602) 367-1543

PRESCOTT   AZ

Motel 6 $
1111 E Sheldon St, Prescott,
AZ 86301, Res. (800)
466-8356 Ph: 520 776-0160
Fax: 520 445-4188

Super 8 Motel $-$$
1105 E. Sheldon, Prescott,
AZ 86301, Res. (800)
800-8000 Ph: (602) 776-1282

PRESCOTT VALLEY   AZ

Motel 6 $
8383 E US 69, Prescott
Valley, AZ 86301, Res. (800)
466-8356 Ph: 520 772-2200
Fax: 520 772-7293

RIVIERA   AZ

Econo Lodge Riverside $-$$
1717 SR 95, Riviera, AZ
86442, Res. (800) 424-4777
Ph: (602) 758-8080 Fax: (602)
758-8283

SCOTTSDALE   AZ

Motel 6 $
6848 E Camelback Rd,
Scottsdale, AZ 85251, Res.
(800) 466-8356 Ph: 602
946-2280 Fax: 602 949-7583

SHOW LOW   AZ

Super 8 Motel $-$$
1941 East Deuce of Clubs,
Show Low, AZ 85901, Res.
(800) 800-8000 Ph: (602)
537-7694 Fax: (602) 537-1373

SIERRA VISTA   AZ

Motel 6 $
1551 E Fry Blvd, Sierra Vista,
AZ 85635, Res. (800)
466-8356 Ph: 520 459-5035
Fax: 520 458-4046

Super 8 Motel $-$$
100 Fab Avenue, Sierra
Vista, AZ 85635, Res. (800)
800-8000 Ph: (602) 459-5380

SPRINGERVILLE   AZ

Super 8 Motel $-$$
Box 1568, Springerville, AZ
85938, Res. (800) 800-8000
Ph: (602) 333-2655 Fax: (602)
333-5149

TEMPE   AZ

Econo Lodge Az State Univ $-$$
2101 E. Apache Blvd., Tempe,
AZ 85281, Res. (800)
424-4777 Ph: (602) 966-5832
Fax: (602) 996-5832

Motel 6 $
513 W Broadway Rd, Tempe,
AZ 85282, Res. (800)
466-8356 Ph: 602 967-8696
Fax: 602 929-0814

Motel 6 $
1720 S Priest Dr, Tempe, AZ
85281, Res. (800) 466-8356
Ph: 602 968-4401 Fax: 602
929-0810

Motel 6 $
1612 N Scottsdale Rd/Rural
Rd, Tempe, AZ 85281, Res.
(800) 466-8356 Ph: 602
945-9506 Fax: 602 970-4763

Super 8 Motel $-$$
1020 E. Apache Blvd., Tempe,
AZ 85281, Res. (800)
800-8000 Ph: (602) 967-8891
Fax: (602) 968-7868

TOLLESON   AZ

Econo Lodge $-$$
1520 N. 84th Dr., Tolleson,
AZ 85353, Res. (800)
424-4777 Ph: (602) 936-4667
Fax: (602) 936-3173

TUCSON   AZ

Econo Lodge $-$$
3020 S. 6th Ave., Tucson, AZ
85713, Res. (800) 424-4777
Ph: (602) 623-5881 Fax: (602)
624-2889

Econo Lodge $-$$
1165 N. Stone Ave., Tucson,
AZ 85705, Res. (800)
424-4777 Ph: (602) 622-7763
Fax: (602) 792-0776

Motel 6 $
755 E Benson Hwy, Tucson,
AZ 85713, Res. (800)
466-8356 Ph: 520 622-4614
Fax: 520 624-1584

Motel 6 $
1031 E Benson Hwy, Tucson,
AZ 85713, Res. (800)
466-8356 Ph: 520 628-1264
Fax: 520 624-1731

Motel 6 $
960 S Frwy, Tucson, AZ
85745, Res. (800) 466-8356
Ph: 520 628-1339 Fax: 520
624-1848

Motel 6 $
4950 S Outlet Center Dr,
Tucson, AZ 85706, Res.
(800) 466-8356 Ph: 520
746-0030 Fax: 520 741-7403

Motel 6 $
4630 W Ina Rd, Tucson, AZ
85741, Res. (800) 466-8356
Ph: 520 744-9300 Fax: 520
744-2439

Motel 6 $
1222 S Frwy, Tucson, AZ
85713, Res. (800) 466-8356
Ph: 520 624-2516 Fax: 520
624-1697

Super 8 Motel $-$$
1248 N. Stone St., Tucson,
AZ 85705, Res. (800)
800-8000 Ph: (602) 622-6446
Fax: (602) 622-6446

Super 8 Motel $-$$
1990 S. Craucroft Road,
Tucson, AZ 85711, Res.
(800) 800-8000 Ph: (602)
790-6021 Fax: (602) 790-6074

WILLCOX   AZ

Econo Lodge $-$$
724 N. Bisbee Ave., Willcox,
AZ 85643, Res. (800)
424-4777 Ph: (602) 384-4222
Fax: (602) 384-3785

Motel 6 $
921 N Bisbee Ave, Willcox,
AZ 85643, Res. (800)
466-8356 Ph: 520 384-2201
Fax: 520 384-0192

WILLIAMS   AZ

Budget Host Inn $-$$
620 Bill Williams Ave,
Williams, AZ 86046, Res.
(800) 283-4678 Ph: (602) 635-
4415

Econo Lodge $-$$
302 E. Bill Williams Ave.,
Williams, AZ 86046, Res.
(800) 424-4777 Ph: (602)
635-4085 Fax: (602) 635-2702

Motel 6 $
831 W Bill Williams Ave ,
Williams, AZ 86046, Res.
(800) 466-8356 Ph: 520
635-9000 Fax: 520 635-2300

**M
O
T
E
L**

Super 8 Motel S-$$
2001 E. Bill Williams Ave.,
Williams, AZ 86046, Res.
(800) 800-8000 Ph: (602)
635-4700

WINSLOW AZ

Econo Lodge S-$$
1706 N. Park Dr., Winslow,
AZ 86047, Res. (800)
424-4777 Ph: (602) 289-4687
Fax: (602) 289-9377

Super 8 Motel S-$$
1916 W 3rd Street, Winslow,
AZ 86047, Res. (800)
800-8000 Ph: (602) 289-4606

YOUNGTOWN AZ

Motel 6 S
11133 Grand Ave,
Youngtown, AZ 85363, Res.
(800) 466-8356 Ph: 602
977-1318 Fax: 602 977-7749

YUMA AZ

Motel 6 S
1640 S Arizona Ave, Yuma,
AZ 85364, Res. (800)
466-8356 Ph: 520 782-6561
Fax: 520 343-4923

Motel 6 S
1445 E 16th St, Yuma, AZ
85365, Res. (800) 466-8356
Ph: 520 782-9521 Fax: 520
343-4941

ARKANSAS

ARKADELPHIA AR

Econo Lodge S-$$
106 Crystal Palace Dr.,
Arkadelphia, AR 71923, Res.
(800) 424-4777 Ph: (501)
246-8026

Super 8 Motel S-$$
118 Valley, Arkadelphia, AR
71923, Res. (800) 800-8000
Ph: (501) 246-8285 Fax: (501)
246-8585

BATESVILLE AR

Super 8 Motel S-$$
1287 North St. Louis Street,
Batesville, AR 72501, Res.
(800) 800-8000 Ph: (501)
793-5888 Fax: (501) 793-5888

BENTON AR

Econo Lodge S-$$
1221 Hot Springs Rd.,
Benton, AR 72015, Res.
(800) 424-4777 Ph: (501)
776-1515 Fax: (501) 776-0247

Scottish Inns S
17900 Highway I-30, Benton,
AR 72015, Res. (800)
251-1962 Ph: (501) 778-4591
Fax: (501) 778-8075

BRINKLEY AR

Econo Lodge S-$$
I-40 & SR 49 N.E., Brinkley,
AR 72021, Res. (800)
424-4777 Ph: (501) 734-2035

Super 8 Motel S-$$
"PO Box 828, I-40 & 49
North", Brinkley, AR 72021,
Res. (800) 800-8000 Ph: (501)
734-3623 Fax: (501) 734-3623

BRYANT AR

Super 8 Motel S-$$
Dell Drive, Bryant, AR
72022, Res. (800) 800-8000
Ph: (501) 847-7888

CLARKSVILLE AR

Super 8 Motel S-$$
1238 S. Rogers Ave.,
Clarksville, AR 72830, Res.
(800) 800-8000 Ph: (501)
754-8800 Fax: (501) 754-2294

CONWAY AR

Motel 6 S
1105 Hwy 65 N, Conway, AR
72032, Res. (800) 466-8356
Ph: 501 327-6623 Fax: 501
327-2749

DEQUEEN AR

Scottish Inns S
1314 US Highway 71 North,
DeQueen, AR 71832, Res.
(800) 251-1962 Ph: (501)
642-2721 Fax: (501) 642-5329

EUREKA SPRINGS AR

Econo Lodge S-$$
US 62 E., Eureka Springs,
AR 72632, Res. (800)
424-4777 Ph: (501) 253-7111

Red Carpet Inn S$
Highway 62 East, Eureka
Springs, AR 72632, Res.
(800) 251-1962 Ph: (501)
253-6665 Fax: 501-253-6973

FAYETTEVILLE AR

Motel 6 S
2980 N College Ave,
Fayetteville, AR 72703, Res.
(800) 466-8356 Ph: 501
443-4351 Fax: 501 444-8034

Super 8 Motel S-$$
1075 S. Shiloh Drive,
Fayetteville, AR 72701, Res.
(800) 800-8000 Ph: (501)
521-8866 Fax: (501) 521-8866

FORT SMITH AR

Motel 6 S
6001 Rogers Ave, Fort Smith,
AR 72903, Res. (800)
466-8356 Ph: 501 484-0576
Fax: 501 484-9054

FT. SMITH AR

Super 8 Motel S-$$
3810 Towson Ave., Ft. Smith,
AR 72901, Res. (800)
800-8000 Ph: (501) 646-3411

HARRISON AR

Super 8 Motel S-$
1330 Hwy. 62/65 North,
Harrison, AR 72601, Res.
(800) 800-8000 Ph: (501)
741-1741 Fax: (501) 741-8858

HAZEN AR

Super 8 Motel S-$$
I-40 and State Road 11,
Hazen, AR 72064, Res. (800)
800-8000 Ph: (501) 255-3563

HOPE AR

Super 8 Motel S-$$
I-30 & Hwy 4, 148 Holiday
Dr., Hope, AR 71801, Res.
(800) 800-8000 Ph: (501)
777-8601 Fax: (501) 777-3142

HOT SPRINGS AR

Downtowner Motor Inn S$
135 Central Avenue, Hot
Springs, AR 71901, Res.
(800) 251-1962 Ph: (501)
624-5521 Fax: (501) 624-4635

Super 8 Motel S-$$
4726 Central Avenue, Hot
Springs, AR 71913, Res.
(800) 800-8000 Ph: (501)
525-0188 Fax: (501) 525-7449

HOT SPRINGS NATION. AR

Econo Lodge S-$$
4319 Central Ave., Hot
Springs National Park, AR
71913, Res. (800) 424-4777
Ph: (501) 525-1660 Fax: (501)
525-7260

JONESBORO AR

Motel 6 S
2300 S Caraway Rd,
Jonesboro, AR 72401, Res.
(800) 466-8356 Ph: 501
932-1050 Fax: 501 935-3421

Scottish Inns S
3116 Mead Drive, Jonesboro,
AR 72401, Res. (800)
251-1962 Ph: (501) 972-8300
Fax: (501) 972-0055

Super 8 Motel S-$$
2500 S. Caraway Rd.,
Jonesboro, AR 72401, Res.
(800) 800-8000 Ph: (501)
972-0849 Fax: (501) 972-0469

LITTLE ROCK AR

Motel 6 S
7501 Interstate 30, Little
Rock, AR 72209, Res. (800)
466-8356 Ph: 501 568-8888
Fax: 501 568-8355

Motel 6 S
10524 West Markham St,
Little Rock, AR 72205, Res.
(800) 466-8356 Ph: 501
225-7366 Fax: 501 227-7426

Arkansas

MALVERN   AR

Super 8 Motel $-$$
"Route 8, Box 719-6",
Malvern, AR 72104, Res.
(800) 800-8000 Ph: (501)
332-5755 Fax: (501) 332-5755

MARION   AR

Scottish Inns $
I-55 North, Exit 10, Marion,
AR 72364, Res. (800)
251-1962 Ph: (501) 739-4467
Fax: (501) 739-4813

MORRILTON   AR

Econo Lodge $-$$
1506 N. SR 95, Morrilton, AR
72110, Res. (800) 424-4777
Ph: (501) 354-5101 Fax: (501)
354-8539

Super 8 Motel $-$$
Hwy 9 Bypass - Business
Jct., Morrilton, AR 72110,
Res. (800) 800-8000 Ph: (501)
354-8188 Fax: (501) 354-6474

MOUNTAIN HOME   AR

Super 8 Motel $-$$
865 Highway 62E, Mountain
Home, AR 72653, Res. (800)
800-8000 Ph: (501) 424-5600
Fax: (501) 424-5600

N LITTLE ROCK   AR

Motel 6 $
400 W 29th St, N Little Rock,
AR 72114, Res. (800)
466-8356 Ph: 501 758-5100
Fax: 501 758-2634

Super 8 Motel $-$$
1 Gray Road, N. Little Rock,
AR 72117, Res. (800)
800-8000 Ph: (501) 945-0141
Fax: (501) 945-7224

PINE BLUFF   AR

Econo Lodge $-$$
321 W. 5th Ave., Pine Bluff,
AR 71601, Res. (800)
424-4777 Ph: (501) 536-6100
Fax: (501) 536-6965

Super 8 Motel $-$$
4101 W. Barraque Street,
Pine Bluff, AR 71602, Res.
(800) 800-8000 Ph: (501)
534-7400

POCAHONTAS   AR

Scottish Inns $
1501 Highway 67 North,
Pocahontas, AR 72455, Res.
(800) 251-1962 Ph: (501)
892-4527 Fax: (501) 892-4592

RUSSELLVILLE   AR

Motel 6 $
215 W Birch St, Russellville,
AR 72801, Res. (800)
466-8356 Ph: 501 968-3666
Fax: 501 890-5207

Super 8 Motel $-$$
P.O. Box 2436, 2404 N.
Arkansas Ave., Russellville,
AR 72801-2204, Res. (800)
800-8000 Ph: (501) 968-8898
Fax: (501) 968-8898

SILOAM SPRINGS   AR

Super 8 Motel $-$$
1800 Hwy 412 West, Siloam
Springs, AR 72761, Res.
(800) 800-8000 Ph: (501)
524-8898 Fax: (501) 524-5989

SPRINGDALE   AR

Econo Lodge $-$$
2001 S. Thompson Ave.,
Springdale, AR 72764, Res.
(800) 424-4777 Ph: (501)
756-1900 Fax: (501) 751-1145

Scottish Inns $
1219 South Thompson,
Springdale, AR 72764, Res.
(800) 251-1962 Ph: (501)
751-4874 Fax: (501) 751-4875

TEXARKANA   AR

Motel 6 $
900 Realtor Ave, Texarkana,
AR 71854, Res. (800)
466-8356 Ph: 501 772-0678
Fax: 501 773-2359

Motel 6 $
900 Realtor Ave, Texarkana,
AR 71854, Res. (800)
466-8356 Ph: 501 772-0678
Fax: 501 773-2359

Super 8 Motel $-$$
325 E. 51st Street,
Texarkana, AR 75502, Res.
(800) 800-8000 Ph: (501)
774-8888 Fax: (501) 773-4653

VAN BUREN   AR

Motel 6 $
1716 Fayetteville Rd, Van
Buren, AR 72956, Res. (800)
466-8356 Ph: 501 474-8001
Fax: 501 474-8294

Super 8 Motel $-$$
106 N. Plaza Court, Van
Buren, AR 72956, Res. (800)
800-8000 Ph: (501) 471-8888
Fax: (501) 471-8728

W. MEMPHIS   AR

Motel 6 $
2501 S Service Rd, W.
Memphis, AR 72301, Res.
(800) 466-8356 Ph: 501
735-0100 Fax: 501 735-4661

WEST MEMPHIS   AR

Econo Lodge $-$$
2315 S. Service Rd., West
Memphis, AR 72301, Res.
(800) 424-4777 Ph: (501)
732-2830 Fax: (501) 732-2830

Super 8 Motel $-$$
901 Club Road, West
Memphis, AR 72301, Res.
(800) 800-8000 Ph: (501)
735-8818 Fax: (501) 735-2133

CALIFORNIA

ALTURAS   CA

Super 8 Motel $-$$
511 N. Main Street, Alturas,
CA 96101, Res. (800)
800-8000 Ph: (916) 257-4213
Fax: (916) 233-3305

ANAHEIM   CA

Econo Lodge Maingate $-$$
1570 S. Harbor Blvd.,
Anaheim, CA 92802, Res.
(800) 424-4777 Ph: (714)
772-5721 Fax: (714) 635-0964

Econo Lodge West $-$$
837 S. Beach Blvd.,
Anaheim, CA 92804, Res.
(800) 424-4777 Ph: (714)
952-0898

Motel 6 $
100 W Freedman Way,
Anaheim, CA 92802, Res.
(800) 466-8356 Ph: 714
520-9696 Fax: 714 533-7539

Motel 6 $
1440 N State College,
Anaheim, CA 92806, Res.
(800) 466-8356 Ph: 714
956-9690 Fax: 714 956-5106

Super 8 Motel $-$$
915 S. West St., Anaheim,
CA 92802, Res. (800)
800-8000 Ph: (714) 778-0350
Fax: (714) 778-3878

Super 8 Motel $-$$
415 West Katella Avenue,
Anaheim, CA 92802, Res.
(800) 800-8000 Ph: (714)
778-6900

Villager $-$$
921 S. Beach Blvd, Anaheim,
CA 92804, Res. (800)
328-7829 Ph: (714) 220-2882
Fax: (714) 828-2668

ARCADIA   CA

Motel 6 $
225 Colorado Pl, Arcadia, CA
91007, Res. (800) 466-8356
Ph: 818 446-2660 Fax: 818
821-1060

ARCATA   CA

Motel 6 $
4755 Valley W Blvd, Arcata,
CA 95521, Res. (800)
466-8356 Ph: 707 822-7061
Fax: 707 822-4827

Super 8 Motel $-$$
4887 Valley W. Blvd., Arcata,
CA 95521, Res. (800)
800-8000 Ph: (707) 822-8888
Fax: (707) 822-2513

ARROYO GRANDE   CA

E-z 8 Motel $
555 Camino Mercado, Arroyo
Grande, CA 93420, Res.
800-326-6835 Ext. 54 Ph:
805-481-4774 Fax:
805-481-9023

M O T E L

Econo Lodge $-$$
611 El Camino Real, Arroyo
Grande, CA 93420, Res.
(800) 424-4777 Ph: (805)
489-9300 Fax: (805) 473-8318

Motel 6 $
9400 El Camino Real,
Atascadero, CA 93422, Res.
(800) 466-8356 Ph: 805
466-6701 Fax: 805 466-5836

Super 8 Motel $-$$
6505 Morro Road (Hwy. 41 W.),
Atascadero, CA 93422, Res.
(800) 800-8000 Ph: (805)
466-6835

Super 8 Motel $-$$
1501 Sycamore Ave.,
Atwater, CA 95301, Res.
(800) 800-8000 Ph: (209)
357-0202

Super 8 Motel $-$$
140 E. Hillcrest Dr., Auburn,
CA 95603, Res. (800)
800-8000 Ph: (916) 888-8808
Fax: (916) 885-3588

E-z 8 Motel $
2604 Pierce Road,
Bakersfield, CA 93308, Res.
800-326-6835 Ext. 47 Ph:
805-322-1901

E-z 8 Motel $
5200 Olive Tree Court,
Bakersfield, CA 93308, Res.
800-326-6835 Ext. 52 Ph:
805-392-1511 Fax:
805-393-0970

Econo Lodge $-$$
200 Trask St. / I-5 &
Stockdale Hwy., Bakersfield,
CA 93312, Res. (800)
424-4777 Ph: (805) 764-5221
Fax: (805) 764-5570

Economy Motels Of America
6501 Colony St., Bakersfield,
CA 93307, Res. (800)
826-0778 Ph: (805) 831-9200

Economy Motels Of America
6100 Knudsen Dr.,
Bakersfield, CA 93308, Res.
(800) 826-0778 Ph: (805)
392-1800

Motel 6 $
1350 Easton Dr, Bakersfield,
CA 93309, Res. (800)
466-8356 Ph: 805 327-1686
Fax: 805 327-2337

Motel 6 $
8223 E Brundage Ln,
Bakersfield, CA 93307, Res.
(800) 466-8356 Ph: 805
366-7231 Fax: 805 366-8834

Motel 6 $
5241 Olive Tree Ct,
Bakersfield, CA 93308, Res.
(800) 466-8356 Ph: 805
392-9700 Fax: 805 392-0223

Motel 6 $
2727 White Ln., Bakersfield,
CA 93304, Res. (800)
466-8356 Ph: 805 834-2828
Fax: 805 834-3923

Super 8 Motel $-$$
901 Real Road, Bakersfield,
CA 93309-1003, Res. (800)
800-8000 Ph: (805) 322-1012
Fax: (805) 322-7636

Motel 6 $
14510 Garvey Ave, Baldwin
Park, CA 91706, Res. (800)
466-8356 Ph: 818 960-5011
Fax: 818 813-0334

Super 8 Motel $-$$
1690 W. Ramsey St.,
Banning, CA 92220, Res.
(800) 800-8000 Ph: (714)
849-6887 Fax: (909) 922-9157

Econo Lodge $-$$
1230 E. Main St., Barstow,
CA 92311, Res. (800)
424-4777 Ph: (619) 256-2133
Fax: (619) 256-7999

Economy Motels Of America
1590 Coolwater Lane,
Barstow, CA 92311, Res.
(800) 826-0778 Ph: (619)
256-1737

Motel 6 $
150 N Yucca Ave, Barstow,
CA 92311, Res. (800)
466-8356 Ph: 619 256-1752
Fax: 619 256-9110

Super 8 Motel $-$$
170 Coolwater Lane, Barstow,
CA 92311, Res. (800)
800-8000 Ph: (619) 256-8443
Fax: (619) 256-0997

Budget Host Golden West $-$$
625 E 5th St, Beaumont, CA
92223, Res. (800) 283-4678
Ph: (909) 845-2185

Motel 6 $
17220 Downey Ave,
Bellflower, CA 90706, Res.
(800) 466-8356 Ph: 562
531-3933 Fax: 562 531-8571

Econo Lodge $-$$
630 El Camino Real,
Belmont, CA 94002, Res.
(800) 424-4777 Ph: (415)
593-5883

Motel 6 $
1101 Shoreway Rd, Belmont,
CA 94002, Res. (800)
466-8356 Ph: 415 591-1471
Fax: 415 593-6415

Econo Lodge $-$$
9733 SR 9, Ben Lomond, CA
95005, Res. (800) 424-4777
Ph: (408) 336-2292

Motel 6 $
42899 Big Bear Blvd, Big
Bear, CA 92315, Res. (800)
466-8356 Ph: 909 585-6666
Fax: 909 585-6685

Super 8 Motel $-$$
1005 N. Main St., Bishop, CA
93514, Res. (800) 800-8000
Ph: (619) 873-8426

E-z 8 Motel $
900 W. Rice Street, Blythe,
CA 92225, Res. 800-326-6835
Ext. 24 Ph: 760-922-9191

Econo Lodge $-$$
1020 W. Hobson Way,
Blythe, CA 92225, Res. (800)
424-4777 Ph: (619) 922-3161
Fax: (000) 006-1922

Motel 6 $
500 W Donlon St, Blythe,
CA 92225, Res. (800)
466-8356 Ph: 619 922-6666
Fax: 619 921-8469

Super 8 Motel $-$$
550 W. Donlon Street,
Blythe, CA 92225, Res. (800)
800-8000 Ph: (619) 922-8881
Fax: (619) 922-8881

Econo Lodge $-$$
630 Ave. of Flags, Buellton,
CA 93427, Res. (800)
424-4777 Ph: (805) 688-0022
Fax: (805) 688-7448

Motel 6 $
333 McMurray Rd, Buellton,
CA 93427, Res. (800)
466-8356 Ph: 805 688-7797
Fax: 805 686-0297

Motel 6 $
7051 Valley View, Buena
Park, CA 90620, Res. (800)
466-8356 Ph: 714 522-1200
Fax: 714 562-8978

Super 8 Motel $-$$
7930 Beach Boulevard,
Buena Park, CA 90620, Res.
(800) 800-8000 Ph: (714)
994-6480 Fax: (714) 994-3874

BUTTONWILLOW   CA

Motel 6 $
20638 Tracy Ave,
Buttonwillow, CA 93206,
Res. (800) 466-8356 Ph: 805
764-5153 Fax: 805 764-6876

Super 8 Motel $-$$
20681 Tracy Ave.,
Buttonwillow, CA 93206,
Res. (800) 800-8000 Ph: (805)
764-5117

CAMARILLO   CA

Motel 6 $
1641 E Daily Dr, Camarillo,
CA 93010, Res. (800)
466-8356 Ph: 805 388-3467
Fax: 805 388-8037

CAMPBELL   CA

Motel 6 $
1240 Camden Ave, Campbell,
CA 95008, Res. (800)
466-8356 Ph: 408 371-8870
Fax: 408 879-0236

CANOGA PARK   CA

Super 8 Motel $-$$
7631 Topanga Canyon Blvd.,
Canoga Park, CA 91304,
Res. (800) 800-8000 Ph: (818)
883-8888 Fax: (818) 703-6799

CARLSBAD   CA

Inns Of America $
751 Raintree Dr., Carlsbad,
CA 92009, Res. (800)
826-0778 Ph: (619) 931-1185

Motel 6 $
1006 Carlsbad Village Dr,
Carlsbad, CA 92008, Res.
(800) 466-8356 Ph: 619
434-7135 Fax: 619 730-0159

Motel 6 $
6117 Paseo del Norte,
Carlsbad, CA 92009, Res.
(800) 466-8356 Ph: 619
438-1242 Fax: 619 931-7958

Motel 6 $
750 Raintree Dr, Carlsbad,
CA 92009, Res. (800)
466-8356 Ph: 619 431-0745
Fax: 619 431-9207

CARPINTERIA   CA

Motel 6 $
4200 Via Real, Carpinteria,
CA 93013, Res. (800)
466-8356 Ph: 805 684-6921
Fax: 805 566-0387

Motel 6 $
5550 Carpinteria Ave,
Carpinteria, CA 93013, Res.
(800) 466-8356 Ph: 805
684-8602 Fax: 805 566-9097

CASTAIC   CA

Econo Lodge $-$$
31410 Castaic Rd., Castaic,
CA 91384, Res. (800)
424-4777 Ph: (805) 295-1070
Fax: (805) 295-9775

CASTRO VALLEY   CA

Econo Lodge $-$$
3928 E. Castro Valley, Castro
Valley, CA 94546, Res. (800)
424-4777 Ph: (510) 537-8833
Fax: (510) 538-9584

CHICO   CA

Econo Lodge Downtown $-$$
630 Main St., Chico, CA
95928, Res. (800) 424-4777
Ph: (916) 895-1323 Fax: (916)
343-2719

Motel 6 $
665 Manzanita Ct, Chico, CA
95926, Res. (800) 466-8356
Ph: 916 345-5500 Fax: 916
894-2846

CHINO   CA

Motel 6 $
12266 Central Ave, Chino,
CA 91710, Res. (800)
466-8356 Ph: 909 591-3877
Fax: 909 590-8319

CHULA VISTA   CA

Motel 6 $
745 iEi St, Chula Vista, CA
91910, Res. (800) 466-8356
Ph: 619 422-4200 Fax: 619
585-8944

COALINGA   CA

Motel 6 $
25278 W Dorris Ave,
Coalinga, CA 93210, Res.
(800) 466-8356 Ph: 209
935-2063 Fax: 209 934-0813

Motel 6 $
25008 W Dorris Ave,
Coalinga, CA 93210, Res.
(800) 466-8356 Ph: 209
935-1536 Fax: 209 934-0814

COLTON   CA

Thriftlodge $-$$
225 E. Valley Blvd., Colton,
CA 92324, Res. (800)
525-9055 Ph: (909) 824-1520
Fax: (909) 825-3502

COMMERCE   CA

Super 8 Motel $-$$
7810 Telegraph Rd.,
Commerce, CA 90040, Res.
(800) 800-8000 Ph: (310)
806-3791

CONCORD   CA

E-z 8 Motel $
1581 Concord Avenue,
Concord, CA 94520, Res.
800-326-6835 Ext. 51 Ph:
510-674-0888 Fax:
510-798-8277

CORONA   CA

Motel 6 $
200 N Lincoln Ave, Corona,
CA 91720, Res. (800)
466-8356 Ph: 909 735-6408
Fax: 909 340-2123

COSTA MESA   CA

Motel 6 $
1441 Gisler Ave, Costa Mesa,
CA 92626, Res. (800)
466-8356 Ph: 714 957-3063
Fax: 714 979-8257

Super 8 Motel $-$$
2645 Harbor Blvd., Costa
Mesa, CA 92626, Res. (800)
800-8000 Ph: (714) 545-9471
Fax: (714) 432-8129

CRESCENT CITY   CA

Econo Lodge $-$$
119 L St., Crescent City,
CA 95531, Res. (800)
424-4777 Ph: (707) 464-2181
Fax: (000) 007-0764

Super 8 Motel $-$$
685 Highway 101, Crescent
City, CA 95531, Res. (800)
800-8000 Ph: (707) 464-4111
Fax: (707) 677-0744

DANVILLE   CA

Econo Lodge $-$$
803 Camino Ramon,
Danville, CA 94526, Res.
(800) 424-4777 Ph: (510)
838-8080

DAVIS   CA

Econo Lodge $-$$
221 D St., Davis, CA 95616,
Res. (800) 424-4777 Ph: (916)
756-1040 Fax: (916) 756-2842

Motel 6 $
4835 Chiles Rd, Davis, CA
95616, Res. (800) 466-8356
Ph: 916 753-3777 Fax: 916
753-0569

EL CAJON   CA

Motel 6 $
550 Montrose Ct, El Cajon,
CA 92020, Res. (800)
466-8356 Ph: 619 588-6100
Fax: 619 588-1973

Super 8 Motel $-$$
588 N. Mollison Avenue, El
Cajon, CA 92021, Res. (800)
800-8000 Ph: (619) 579-1144
Fax: (619) 579-1144

Thriftlodge $-$$
1220 West Main St., El
Cajon, CA 92020, Res. (800)
525-9055 Ph: (619) 442-2576
Fax: (619) 579-7562

EL CENTRO   CA

E-z 8 Motel $
455 Wake Avenue, El Centro,
CA 92243, Res. 800-326-6835
Ext. 18 Ph: 760-352-6620

Motel 6 $
395 Smoketree Dr, El
Centro, CA 92243, Res. (800)
466-8356 Ph: 619 353-6766
Fax: 619 337-1123

EL MONTE   CA

Motel 6 $
3429 Peck Rd, El Monte, CA
91731, Res. (800) 466-8356
Ph: 818 448-6660 Fax: 818
279-5664

ESCONDIDO   CA

Motel 6 $
900 N Quince St, Escondido,
CA 92025, Res. (800)
466-8356 Ph: 619 745-9252
Fax: 619 745-4203

Super 8 Motel $-$$
528 W. Washington Avenue,
Escondido, CA 92025, Res.
(800) 800-8000 Ph: (619)
747-3711 Fax: (619) 747-8385

Villager $-$$
1107 S. Escondido Blvd,
Escondido, CA 92025, Res.
(800) 328-7829 Ph: (619)
737-3538 Fax: (000) 000-0000

EUREKA   CA

Econo Lodge Downtown $-$$
1630 Fourth St., Eureka, CA
95501, Res. (800) 424-4777
Ph: (707) 443-8041 Fax: (707)
443-9275

Motel 6 $
1934 Broadway, Eureka, CA
95501, Res. (800) 466-8356
Ph: 707 445-9631 Fax: 707
444-3217

Super 8 Motel $-$$
1304 Fourth Street, Eureka,
CA 95501, Res. (800)
800-8000 Ph: (707) 443-3193

FAIRFIELD   CA

E-z 8 Motel $
3331 N. Texas Street,
Fairfield, CA 94533, Res.
800-326-6835 Ext. 65 Ph:
707-426-6161 Fax:
707-426-3608

Motel 6 $
1473 Holiday Ln, Fairfield,
CA 94533, Res. (800)
466-8356 Ph: 707 425-4565
Fax: 707 435-9232

Motel 6 $
2353 Magellan Rd, Fairfield,
CA 94533, Res. (800)
466-8356 Ph: 707 427-0800
Fax: 707 435-9209

FONTANA   CA

Econo Lodge $-$$
17133 Valley Blvd., Fontana,
CA 92335, Res. (800)
424-4777 Ph: (909) 822-5411

Motel 6 $
10195 Sierra Ave, Fontana,
CA 92335, Res. (800)
466-8356 Ph: 909 823-8686
Fax: 909 829-3150

FORTUNA   CA

Econo Lodge $-$$
275 12th St., Fortuna, CA
95540, Res. (800) 424-4777
Ph: (707) 725-6993 Fax: (707)
725-9681

Super 8 Motel $-$$
1805 Alamar Way, Fortuna,
CA 95540, Res. (800)
800-8000 Ph: (707) 725-2888
Fax: (707) 725-2888

FREMONT   CA

Econo Lodge $-$$
46101 Warm Springs Blvd.,
Fremont, CA 94539, Res.
(800) 424-4777 Ph: (510)
656-2800 Fax: (510) 659-0352

Motel 6 $
34047 Fremont Blvd,
Fremont, CA 94536, Res.
(800) 466-8356 Ph: 510
793-4848 Fax: 510 791-8170

Motel 6 $
46101 Research Ave,
Fremont, CA 94539, Res.
(800) 466-8356 Ph: 510
490-4528 Fax: 510 490-5937

FRESNO   CA

Economy Inns Of America $-$$
2570 South East St., Fresno,
CA 93706, Res. (800)
826-0778 Ph: (209) 486-1188

Economy Inns Of America $-$$
5021 N. Barcus Ave., Fresno,
CA 93722, Res. (800)
826-0778 Ph: (209) 276-1910

Motel 6 $
4245 N Blackstone Ave,
Fresno, CA 93726, Res. (800)
466-8356 Ph: 209 221-0800
Fax: 209 224-8298

Motel 6 $
4080 N Blackstone Ave,
Fresno, CA 93726, Res. (800)
466-8356 Ph: 209 222-2431
Fax: 209 229-8491

Motel 6 $
933 N Parkway Dr<EL>at Hwy
99, Fresno, CA 93728, Res.
(800) 466-8356 Ph: 209
233-3913 Fax: 209 498-8526

Motel 6 $
1240 Crystal Ave, Fresno,
CA 93728, Res. (800)
466-8356 Ph: 209 237-0855
Fax: 209 497-5869

Super 8 Motel $-$$
1087 North Parkway Drive,
Fresno, CA 93728, Res. (800)
800-8000 Ph: (209) 264-6248

FULLERTON   CA

Motel 6 $
1415 S Euclid St, Fullerton,
CA 92832, Res. (800)
466-8356 Ph: 714 992-0660
Fax: 714 992-0375

GARDEN GROVE   CA

Villager $-$$
8791 Garden Grove Blvd,
Garden Grove, CA 92641,
Res. (800) 328-7829 Ph: (714)
537-6752 Fax: (000) 000-0000

GILROY   CA

Super 8 Motel $-$$
8435 San Ysidro Avenue,
Gilroy, CA 95020, Res. (800)
800-8000 Ph: (408) 848-4108
Fax: (408) 848-2651

GLENDALE   CA

Econo Lodge $-$$
1437 E. Colorado St.,
Glendale, CA 91205, Res.
(800) 424-4777 Ph: (818)
246-8367 Fax: (818) 246-8374

GOLETA   CA

Motel 6 $
5897 Calle Real, Goleta, CA
93117, Res. (800) 466-8356
Ph: 805 964-3596 Fax: 805
683-0647

Super 8 Motel $-$$
6021 Hollister Avenue,
Goleta, CA 93117, Res. (800)
800-8000 Ph: (805) 967-5591
Fax: (805) 964-2461

HACIENDA HEIGHTS   CA

Motel 6 $
1154 S Seventh Ave,
Hacienda Heights, CA
91745, Res. (800) 466-8356
Ph: 818 968-9462 Fax: 818
968-8184

HARBOR CITY   CA

Motel 6 $
820 W Sepulveda Blvd,
Harbor City, CA 90710, Res.
(800) 466-8356 Ph: 310
549-9560 Fax: 310 835-2840

HAYWARD   CA

Motel 6 $
30155 Industrial Pkwy SW,
Hayward, CA 94544, Res.
(800) 466-8356 Ph: 510
489-8333 Fax: 510 489-1748

Super 8 Motel $-$$
2460 Whipple Road, Hayward,
CA 94544, Res. (800)
800-8000 Ph: (510) 489-3888

Super 8 Motel $-$$
21800 Foothill Boulevard,
Hayward, CA 94545, Res.
(800) 800-8000 Ph: (510)
733-5012 Fax: (510) 489-4070

Thriftlodge $-$$
21598 Foothill Blvd.,
Hayward, CA 94541, Res.
(800) 525-9055 Ph: (510)
538-4380 Fax: (510) 889-0728

HEMET   CA

Super 8 Motel $-$$
3510 West Florida Avenue,
Hemet, CA 92343, Res. (800)
800-8000 Ph: (714) 658-2281
Fax: (714) 925-6492

HESPERIA   CA

Super 8 Motel $-$$
12033 Oakwood Avenue,
Hesperia, CA 92345, Res.
(800) 800-8000 Ph: (619)
949-3231

HIGHLAND   CA

Super 8 Motel $-$$
26667 East Highland Avenue,
Highland, CA 92346, Res.
(800) 800-8000 Ph: (909)
864-0100 Fax: (909) 985-8388

HOLLYWOOD   CA

Motel 6 $
1738 N Whitley Ave,
Hollywood, CA 90028, Res.
(800) 466-8356 Ph: 213
464-6006 Fax: 213 464-4645

INDIO   CA

Motel 6 $
82195 Indio Blvd, Indio, CA
92201, Res. (800) 466-8356
Ph: 619 342-6311 Fax: 619
342-4157

Super 8 Motel $-$$
81753 Highway 111, Indio,
CA 92201, Res. (800)
800-8000 Ph: (619) 342-0264
Fax: (619) 342-6999

INGLEWOOD   CA

Econo Lodge $-$$
4123 W. Century Blvd.,
Inglewood, CA 90304, Res.
(800) 424-4777 Ph: (310)
672-7285 Fax: (310) 672-7295

Econo Lodge Airport $-$$
439 W. Manchester Blvd.,
Inglewood, CA 90301, Res.
(800) 424-4777 Ph: (310)
674-8596

Motel 6 $
5101 W Century Blvd,
Inglewood, CA 90304, Res.
(800) 466-8356 Ph: 310
419-1234 Fax: 310 677-7871

KING CITY   CA

Motel 6 $
3 Broadway Cir, King City,
CA 93930, Res. (800)
466-8356 Ph: 408 385-5000
Fax: 408 385-0943

LA MESA   CA

E-z 8 Motel $
7851 Fletcher Parkway, La
Mesa, CA 91942, Res.
800-326-6835 Ext. 58 Ph:
619-698-9444

Motel 6 $
7621 Alvarado Rd, La Mesa,
CA 91941, Res. (800)
466-8356 Ph: 619 464-7151
Fax: 619 466-3859

LANCASTER   CA

E-z 8 Motel $
43530 N. 17th Street West,
Lancaster, CA 93534, Res.
800-326-6835 Ext. 55 Ph:
805-945-9477 Fax:
805-726-9426

Motel 6 $
43540 17th St W, Lancaster,
CA 93534, Res. (800)
466-8356 Ph: 805 948-0435
Fax: 805 940-0657

LIVERMORE   CA

Motel 6 $
4673 Lassen Rd, Livermore,
CA 94550, Res. (800)
466-8356 Ph: 510 443-5300
Fax: 510 606-9347

LOMPOC   CA

Motel 6 $
1521 N iHi St, Lompoc, CA
93436, Res. (800) 466-8356
Ph: 805 735-7631 Fax: 805
736-0537

LONG BEACH   CA

Econo Lodge Convention $-$$
150 Alamitos Ave., Long
Beach, CA 90802, Res. (800)
424-4777 Ph: (310) 435-7621
Fax: (310) 436-4011

Motel 6 $
5665 E 7th St, Long Beach,
CA 90804, Res. (800)
466-8356 Ph: 310 597-1311
Fax: 310 597-2741

Super 8 Motel $-$$
4201 E. Pacific Coast Hwy.,
Long Beach, CA 90804, Res.
(800) 800-8000 Ph: (310)
597-7701 Fax: (310) 494-7373

LOS ANGELES   CA

Dragon Gate Inn $$
818 North Hill St., Los
Angeles, CA 90012, Res.
(800) 528-1234 Ph: (213)
617-3077 Fax: (213) 680-3653

Econo Lodge $-$$
777 N. Vine St., Los Angeles,
CA 90038, Res. (800)
424-4777 Ph: (213) 463-5671

Econo Lodge $-$$
11933 Washington Blvd. W.,
Los Angeles, CA 90066, Res.
(800) 424-4777 Ph: (310)
398-1651

Econo Lodge Wilshire $-$$
3400 W. 3rd St., Los Angeles,
CA 90020, Res. (800)
424-4777 Ph: (213) 385-0061
Fax: (213) 385-8517

Park Plaza Hotel $$
607 South Park View St., Los
Angeles, CA 90057, Ph: (213)
384-5281 Fax: (213) 480-1928

Super 8 Motel $-$$
4238 West Century
Boulevard, Los Angeles, CA
90303, Res. (800) 800-8000
Ph: (310) 672-0740 Fax: (310)
672-1904

LOST HILLS   CA

Economy Motels Of America
14684 Aloma St., P. O. Box
295, Lost Hills, CA 93249,
Res. (800) 826-0778 Ph: (805)
797-2371

Motel 6 $
14685 Warren St, Lost Hills,
CA 93249, Res. (800)
466-8356 Ph: 805 797-2346
Fax: 805 797-2976

MADERA   CA

Economy Motels Of America
1855 W. Cleveland Ave.,
Madera, CA 93637, Res.
(800) 826-0778 Ph: (209)
661-1131

MAMMOTH LAKES   CA

Econo Lodge $-$$
3626 Main St. (Hwy. 203),
Mammoth Lakes, CA 93546,
Res. (800) 424-4777 Ph: (619)
934-6855 Fax: (619) 934-5165

Motel 6 $
3372 Main St, Mammoth
Lakes, CA 93546, Res. (800)
466-8356 Ph: 760 934-6660
Fax: 706 934-6989

MARINA   CA

Motel 6 $
100 Reservation Rd, Marina,
CA 93933, Res. (800)
466-8356 Ph: 408 384-1000
Fax: 408 384-0314

Super 8 Motel $-$$
3280 Dunes Dr., Marina, CA
93933, Res. (800) 800-8000
Ph: (408) 384-1800

MARTINEZ   CA

Super 8 Motel $-$$
4015 Alhambra Ave.,
Martinez, CA 94553, Res.
(800) 800-8000 Ph: (510)
372-5500 Fax: (510) 228-8830

MARYSVILLE   CA

Econo Lodge $-$$
721 10th St., Marysville, CA
95901, Res. (800) 424-4777
Ph: (916) 742-8586 Fax: (916)
742-0132

Super 8 Motel $-$$
1078 N. Beale Rd., Marysville,
CA 95901, Res. (800)
800-8000 Ph: (916) 742-8238

M
O
T
E
L

MERCED   CA

Motel 6 $
1215 iRi St, Merced, CA
95340, Res. (800) 466-8356
Ph: 209 722-2737 Fax: 209
723-6672

Motel 6 $
1410 iVi St, Merced, CA
95340, Res. (800) 466-8356
Ph: 209 384-2181 Fax: 209
722-2152

MILPITAS   CA

Economy Inns Of America $-$$
270 South Abbott Ave.,
Milpitas, CA 95035, Res.
(800) 826-0778 Ph: (408)
946-8889

Super 8 Motel $-$$
485 South Main Street,
Milpitas, CA 95035, Res.
(800) 800-8000 Ph: (408)
946-1615 Fax: (408) 262-6128

MODESTO   CA

Motel 6 $
1920 W Orangeburg Ave,
Modesto, CA 95350, Res.
(800) 466-8356 Ph: 209
522-7271 Fax: 209 578-0188

Super 8 Motel $-$$
2025 W. Orangeburg Ave.,
Modesto, CA 95350-3741,
Res. (800) 800-8000 Ph: (209)
577-8008 Fax: (209) 575-4118

MOJAVE   CA

Econo Lodge $-$$
2145 SR 58, Mojave, CA
93501, Res. (800) 424-4777
Ph: (805) 824-2463 Fax: (805)
824-9508

Motel 6 $
16958 Hwy 58, Mojave, CA
93501, Res. (800) 466-8356
Ph: 805 824-4571 Fax: 805
824-8306

Scottish Inns $$
16352 Sierra Highway,
Mojave, CA 93501, Res. (800)
251-1962 Ph: (805) 824-9317
Fax: 805) 824-9393

MONTEREY   CA

Motel 6 $
2124 N Fremont St,
Monterey, CA 93940, Res.
(800) 466-8356 Ph: 408
646-8585 Fax: 408 372-7429

Super 8 Motel $-$$
2050 N. Fremont St.,
Monterey, CA 93940, Res.
(800) 800-8000 Ph: (408)
373-3081 Fax: (408) 646-1950

MORENO VALLEY   CA

Econo Lodge $-$$
24810 Sunnymead Blvd.,
Moreno Valley, CA 92388,
Res. (800) 424-4777 Ph: (909)
247-8582

Motel 6 $
24630 Sunnymead Blvd,
Moreno Valley, CA 92553,
Res. (800) 466-8356 Ph: 909
243-0075 Fax: 909 247-1349

Motel 6 $
23581 Alessandro Blvd,
Moreno Valley, CA 92553,
Res. (800) 466-8356 Ph: 909
656-4451 Fax: 909 653-0418

MORRO BAY   CA

Econo Lodge $-$$
1100 Main St., Morro Bay,
CA 93442, Res. (800)
424-4777 Ph: (805) 772-5609

Motel 6 $
298 Atascadero Rd, Morro
Bay, CA 93442, Res. (800)
466-8356 Ph: 805 772-5641
Fax: 805 772-3233

NATIONAL CITY   CA

Econo Lodge $-$$
1640 E. Plaza Blvd., National
City, CA 91950, Res. (800)
424-4777 Ph: (619) 474-9202
Fax: (619) 474-1685

NEEDLES   CA

Motel 6 $
1420 iJi St, Needles, CA
92363, Res. (800) 466-8356
Ph: 619 326-3399 Fax: 619
326-3857

Motel 6 $
1215 Hospitality Ln, Needles,
CA 92363, Res. (800)
466-8356 Ph: 619 326-5131
Fax: 619 326-3854

Super 8 Motel $-$$
1102 East Broadway,
Needles, CA 92363, Res.
(800) 800-8000 Ph: (619)
326-4501 Fax: (619) 326-2054

NEWARK   CA

E-z 8 Motel $
5555 Cedar Court, Newark,
CA 94560, Res. 800-326-6835
Ext. 56 Ph: 510-794-7775
Fax: 510-794-6909

Motel 6 $
5600 Cedar Ct, Newark, CA
94560, Res. (800) 466-8356
Ph: 510 791-5900 Fax: 510
793-6273

NEWBURY PARK   CA

E-z 8 Motel $
2434 W. Hillcrest Drive,
Newbury Park, CA 91320,
Res. 800-326-6835 Ext. 63
Ph: 805-499-0755 Fax:
805-499-2377

NORTH HIGHLANDS   CA

Motel 6 $
4600 Watt Ave, North
Highlands, CA 95660, Res.
(800) 466-8356 Ph: 916
973-8637 Fax: 916 971-9793

NORTH PALM SPRINGS   CA

Motel 6 $
63950 20th Ave, PO Box 942,
North Palm Springs, CA
92258, Res. (800) 466-8356
Ph: 619 251-1425 Fax: 619
251-0494

NORWALK   CA

Econo Lodge $-$$
12225 E. Firestone Blvd.,
Norwalk, CA 90650-4323,
Res. (800) 424-4777 Ph: (310)
868-0791 Fax: (310) 864-7373

Motel 6 $
10646 E Rosecrans Ave,
Norwalk, CA 90650, Res.
(800) 466-8356 Ph: 562
864-2567 Fax: 562 864-0531

OAKLAND   CA

E-z 8 Motel $
8471 Enterprise Way,
Oakland, CA 94621, Res.
800-326-6835 Ext. 61 Ph:
510-562-4888 Fax:
510-562-2077

Motel 6 $
8480 Edes Ave, Oakland, CA
94621, Res. (800) 466-8356
Ph: 510 638-1180 Fax: 510
568-7501

Motel 6 $
1801 Embarcadero, Oakland,
CA 94606, Res. (800)
466-8356 Ph: 510 436-0103
Fax: 510 436-7428

OCEANSIDE   CA

Motel 6 $
3708 Plaza Dr, Oceanside,
CA 92056, Res. (800)
466-8356 Ph: 619 941-1011
Fax: 619 941-5608

ONTARIO   CA

Motel 6 $
1560 E Fourth St, Ontario,
CA 91764-2636, Res. (800)
466-8356 Ph: 909 984-2424
Fax: 909 984-7326

Super 8 Motel $-$$
514 N. Vineyard, Ontario, CA
91764-4492, Res. (800)
800-8000 Ph: (714) 983-2886
Fax: (909) 988-2115

ORANGE   CA

Motel 6 $
2920 W Chapman Ave,
Orange, CA 92868, Res.
(800) 466-8356 Ph: 714
634-2441 Fax: 714 634-0127

OROVILLE   CA

Econo Lodge $-$$
1835 Feather River Blvd.,
Oroville, CA 95965, Res.
(800) 424-4777 Ph: (916)
533-8201 Fax: (916) 533-7515

Motel 6　　　　　　　　　$
505 Montgomery St, Oroville,
CA 95965, Res. (800)
466-8356 Ph: 916 532-9400
Fax: 916 534-7653

PALM DESERT	CA

Motel 6　　　　　　　　　$
78100 Varner Rd, Palm
Desert, CA 92211, Res. (800)
466-8356 Ph: 619 345-0550
Fax: 619 772-5027

PALM SPRINGS	CA

Budget Host Inn　　　$-$$
1277 S Palm Canyon Dr,
Palm Springs, CA 92262,
Res. (800) 283-4678 Ph: (619)
325-5574 Fax: (619) 327-2020

Motel 6　　　　　　　　　$
660 S Palm Canyon Dr, Palm
Springs, CA 92264, Res.
(800) 466-8356 Ph: 619
327-4200 Fax: 619 320-9827

Motel 6　　　　　　　　　$
595 E Palm Canyon Dr, Palm
Springs, CA 92264, Res.
(800) 466-8356 Ph: 619
325-6129 Fax: 619 320-9304

Super 8 Motel　　　　$-$$
1900 N. Palm Canyon Dr.,
Palm Springs, CA 92262,
Res. (800) 800-8000 Ph: (619)
322-3757

PALMDALE	CA

E-z 8 Motel　　　　　　　$
430 W. Palmdale Blvd.,
Palmdale, CA 93551, Res.
800-326-6835 Ext. 62 Ph:
805-273-6400 Fax:
805-273-4709

Motel 6　　　　　　　　　$
407 W Palmdale Blvd,
Palmdale, CA 93551, Res.
(800) 466-8356 Ph: 805
272-0660 Fax: 805 272-8935

Super 8 Motel　　　　$-$$
200 W Palmdale Blvd.,
Palmdale, CA 93550, Res.
(800) 800-8000 Ph: (805)
273-8000 Fax: (805) 266-4521

PALO ALTO	CA

Motel 6　　　　　　　　　$
4301 El Camino Real, Palo
Alto, CA 94306, Res. (800)
466-8356 Ph: 415 949-0833
Fax: 415 941-0782

Super 8 Motel　　　　$-$$
3200 El Camino Real, Palo
Alto, CA 94306, Res. (800)
800-8000 Ph: (415) 493-9085
Fax: (415) 493-8405

PASADENA	CA

Econo Lodge　　　　$-$$
2860 E. Colorado Blvd.,
Pasadena, CA 91107, Res.
(800) 424-4777 Ph: (818)
792-3700 Fax: (818) 792-0244

Econo Lodge Cal-tech　$-$$
1203 E. Colorado, Pasadena,
CA 91106, Res. (800)
424-4777 Ph: (818) 449-3170
Fax: (818) 577-8873

PASO ROBLES	CA

Motel 6　　　　　　　　　$
1134 Black Oak Dr, Paso
Robles, CA 93446, Res. (800)
466-8356 Ph: 805 239-9090
Fax: 805 238-6254

PETALUMA	CA

Motel 6　　　　　　　　　$
1368 N McDowell Blvd,
Petaluma, CA 94952, Res.
(800) 466-8356 Ph: 707
765-0333 Fax: 707 765-4577

PICO RIVERA	CA

Econo Lodge　　　　$-$$
8477 Telegraph Rd., Pico
Rivera, CA 90660, Res. (800)
424-4777 Ph: (310) 869-9588
Fax: (310) 861-4883

PINOLE	CA

Motel 6　　　　　　　　　$
1501 Fitzgerald Dr, Pinole,
CA 94564, Res. (800)
466-8356 Ph: 510 222-8174
Fax: 510 262-9435

PISMO BEACH	CA

Motel 6　　　　　　　　　$
860 4th St, Pismo Beach, CA
93449, Res. (800) 466-8356
Ph: 805 773-2665 Fax: 805
773-0723

PITTSBURG	CA

Motel 6　　　　　　　　　$
2101 Loveridge Rd, Pittsburg,
CA 94565, Res. (800)
466-8356 Ph: 510 427-1600
Fax: 510 432-0739

PLEASANTON	CA

Motel 6　　　　　　　　　$
5102 Hopyard Rd,
Pleasanton, CA 94588, Res.
(800) 466-8356 Ph: 510
463-2626 Fax: 510 225-0128

Super 8 Motel　　　　$-$$
5375 Owens Court,
Pleasanton, CA 94566-3336,
Res. (800) 800-8000 Ph: (510)
463-1300 Fax: (510) 734-8843

POMONA	CA

Motel 6　　　　　　　　　$
2470 S Garey Ave, Pomona,
CA 91766, Res. (800)
466-8356 Ph: 909 591-1871
Fax: 909 591-6674

PORTERVILLE	CA

Motel 6　　　　　　　　　$
935 W Morton Ave,
Porterville, CA 93257, Res.
(800) 466-8356 Ph: 209
781-7600 Fax: 209 782-9219

RANCHO CORDOVA	CA

Economy Inns Of America$-$$
12249 Folsom Blvd., Rancho
Cordova, CA 95670, Res.
(800) 826-0778 Ph: (916)
351-1213

Motel 6　　　　　　　　　$
10694 Olson Dr, Rancho
Cordova, CA 95670, Res.
(800) 466-8356 Ph: 916
635-8784 Fax: 916 852-1469

RANCHO MIRAGE	CA

Motel 6　　　　　　　　　$
69-570 Hwy 111, Rancho
Mirage, CA 92270, Res. (800)
466-8356 Ph: 619 324-8475
Fax: 619 328-0864

RED BLUFF	CA

Motel 6　　　　　　　　　$
20 Williams Ave, Red Bluff,
CA 96080, Res. (800)
466-8356 Ph: 916 527-9200
Fax: 916 528-1219

Super 8 Motel　　　　$-$$
203 Antelope Blvd., Red Bluff,
CA 96080-2901, Res. (800)
800-8000 Ph: (916) 527-8882
Fax: (916) 527-5078

REDDING	CA

Econo Lodge Downtown $-$$
2010 Pine St., Redding, CA
96001, Res. (800) 424-4777
Ph: (916) 243-3336 Fax: (916)
243-5730

Motel 6　　　　　　　　　$
1640 Hilltop Dr, Redding, CA
96002, Res. (800) 466-8356
Ph: 916 221-1800 Fax: 916
221-6175

Motel 6　　　　　　　　　$
1250 Twin View Blvd,
Redding, CA 96003, Res.
(800) 466-8356 Ph: 916
246-4470 Fax: 916 246-4268

Motel 6　　　　　　　　　$
2385 Bechelli Ln, Redding,
CA 96002, Res. (800)
466-8356 Ph: 916 221-0562
Fax: 916 222-0458

Super 8 Motel　　　　$-$$
5175 Churn Creek Rd.,
Redding, CA 96002, Res.
(800) 800-8000 Ph: (916)
221-8881 Fax: (916) 221-8881

Thriftlodge　　　　　　$-$$
413 N. Market St, Redding,
CA 96003, Res. (800)
525-9055 Ph: (916) 241-3010
Fax: (916) 241-9029

REDLANDS	CA

Super 8 Motel　　　　$-$$
1160 Arizona Street,
Redlands, CA 92374, Res.
(800) 800-8000 Ph: (909)
792-3175

M O T E L

REDWOOD CITY   CA

Super 8 Motel $-$$
2526 El Camino Real,
Redwood City, CA 94601,
Res. (800) 800-8000 Ph: (415)
366-0880 Fax: (415) 367-7958

RICHMOND   CA

Super 8 Motel $-$$
1598 Carlson Boulevard,
Richmond, CA 94804, Res.
(800) 800-8000 Ph: (510)
351-7304

RIDGECREST   CA

Econo Lodge $-$$
201 Inyo-Kern Rd.,
Ridgecrest, CA 93555, Res.
(800) 424-4777 Ph: (619)
446-2551 Fax: (619) 446-5740

Motel 6 $
535 S China Lake Blvd,
Ridgecrest, CA 93555, Res.
(800) 466-8356 Ph: 760
375-6866 Fax: 760 375-8784

RIVERSIDE   CA

Econo Lodge $-$$
9878 Magnolia Ave.,
Riverside, CA 92503, Res.
(800) 424-4777 Ph: (714)
687-3090 Fax: (714) 688-6606

Econo Lodge $-$$
1971 University Ave.,
Riverside, CA 92507, Res.
(800) 424-4777 Ph: (909)
684-6363 Fax: (909) 684-9228

Motel 6 $
1260 University Ave,
Riverside, CA 92507, Res.
(800) 466-8356 Ph: 909
784-2131 Fax: 909 784-1801

Motel 6 $
3663 La Sierra Ave,
Riverside, CA 92505, Res.
(800) 466-8356 Ph: 909
351-0764 Fax: 909 687-1430

Super 8 Motel $-$$
1199 University Avenue,
Riverside, CA 92507, Res.
(800) 800-8000 Ph: (909)
369-6645 Fax: (909) 369-6645

ROHNERT PARK   CA

Motel 6 $
6145 Commerce Blvd,
Rohnert Park, CA 94928,
Res. (800) 466-8356 Ph: 707
585-8888 Fax: 707 585-3443

ROSEMEAD   CA

Motel 6 $
1001 S San Gabriel Blvd,
Rosemead, CA 91770, Res.
(800) 466-8356 Ph: 818
572-6076 Fax: 818 280-6992

ROWLAND HEIGHTS   CA

Motel 6 $
18970 E Labin Ct, Rowland
Heights, CA 91748, Res.
(800) 466-8356 Ph: 818
964-5333 Fax: 818 912-2124

S. LAKE TAHOE   CA

Super 8 Motel $-$$
P.O. Box 18692, S. Lake
Tahoe, CA 96151, Res. (800)
800-8000 Ph: (916) 544-3476
Fax: (916) 542-4011

SACRAMENTO   CA

Econo Lodge $-$$
1319 30th St., Sacramento,
CA 95816, Res. (800)
424-4777 Ph: (916) 454-4400
Fax: (916) 736-2812

Inns Of America $
25 Howe Ave., Sacramento,
CA 95826, Res. (800)
826-0778 Ph: (916) 386-8404

Motel 6 $
7850 College Town Dr,
Sacramento, CA 95826,
Res. (800) 466-8356 Ph: 916
383-8110 Fax: 916 386-0971

Motel 6 $
1415 30th St, Sacramento,
CA 95816, Res. (800)
466-8356 Ph: 916 457-0777
Fax: 916 454-9814

Motel 6 $
5110 Interstate Ave,
Sacramento, CA 95842,
Res. (800) 466-8356 Ph: 916
331-8100 Fax: 916 339-2241

Motel 6 $
227 Jibboom St,
Sacramento, CA 95814,
Res. (800) 466-8356 Ph: 916
441-0733 Fax: 916 446-5941

Motel 6 $
7780 Stockton Blvd,
Sacramento, CA 95823,
Res. (800) 466-8356 Ph: 916
689-9141 Fax: 916 689-7340

Motel 6 $
7407 Elsie Ave, Sacramento,
CA 95828, Res. (800)
466-8356 Ph: 916 689-6555
Fax: 916 689-6495

Super 8 Motel $-$$
216 Bannon Street,
Sacramento, CA 95814,
Res. (800) 800-8000 Ph: (916)
447-5400 Fax: (916) 447-5153

Super 8 Motel $-$$
4317 Madison Avenue,
Sacramento, CA 95842,
Res. (800) 800-8000 Ph: (916)
334-7430 Fax: (916) 331-8916

Super 8 Motel $-$$
7216 55th Street,
Sacramento, CA 95823,
Res. (800) 800-8000 Ph: (916)
427-7925 Fax: (916) 424-9011

Super 8 Motel $-$$
9646 Micron Way,
Sacramento, CA 95827,
Res. (800) 800-8000 Ph: (916)
361-3131 Fax: (209) 473-0647

SALINAS   CA

Motel 6 $
140 Kern St, Salinas, CA
93901, Res. (800) 466-8356
Ph: 408 753-1711 Fax: 408
424-5187

Motel 6 $
1257 De La Torre Blvd,
Salinas, CA 93905, Res.
(800) 466-8356 Ph: 408
757-3077 Fax: 408 424-5185

Super 8 Motel $-$$
1030 Fairview Avenue,
Salinas, CA 93905, Res.
(800) 800-8000 Ph: (408)
422-6486

SAN BERNARDINO   CA

E-z 8 Motel $
1750 S. Waterman Avenue,
San Bernardino, CA 92408,
Res. 800-326-6835 Ext. 59
Ph: 909-888-4827 Fax:
909-888-4827 Ext. 152

Motel 6 $
1960 Ostrems Way, San
Bernardino, CA 92407, Res.
(800) 466-8356 Ph: 909
887-8191 Fax: 909 880-9231

Motel 6 $
111 Redlands Blvd, San
Bernardino, CA 92408, Res.
(800) 466-8356 Ph: 909
825-6666 Fax: 909 872-1104

Super 8 Motel $-$$
294 East Hospitality Lane,
San Bernardino, CA 92408,
Res. (800) 800-8000 Ph: (909)
381-1681 Fax: (909) 888-2150

Super 8 Motel $-$$
777 W. 6th Street, San
Bernardino, CA 92410, Res.
(800) 800-8000 Ph: (714)
889-3561 Fax: (909) 889-7127

SAN DIEGO   CA

E-z 8 Motel $
4747 Pacific Highway, San
Diego, CA 92110, Res.
800-326-6835 Ext. 50 Ph:
619-294-2512

E-z 8 Motel $
3333 Channel Way, San
Diego, CA 92110, Res.
800-326-6835 Ext. 53 Ph:
619-223-9500 Fax:
619-223-3168

E-z 8 Motel $
1010 Outer Road, San Diego,
CA 92154, Res. 800-326-6835
Ext.60 Ph: 619-575-8808

Econo Lodge By The Bay $-$$
1655 Pacific Hwy., San Diego,
CA 92101, Res. (800)
424-4777 Ph: (619) 232-6391
Fax: (619) 235-4622

Econo Lodge Sea World Area $$
3880 Greenwood St., San
Diego, CA 92110, Res. (800)
424-4777 Ph: (619) 543-9944
Fax: (619) 574-1347

Motel 6 $
2424 Hotel Circle North, San
Diego, CA 92108, Res. (800)
466-8356 Ph: 619 296-1612
Fax: 619 543-9305

Motel 6 $
5592 Clairemont Mesa Blvd,
San Diego, CA 92117, Res.
(800) 466-8356 Ph: 619
268-9758 Fax: 619 292-0832

Premier Inn $
2484 Hotel Circle Place, San
Diego, CA 92108, Res.
800-326-6835 Ext. 33 Ph:
619-292-8252 Fax:
619-291-6130

Super 8 Motel $-$$
4540 Mission Bay Drive, San
Diego, CA 92109, Res. (800)
800-8000 Ph: (619) 274-7888
Fax: (619) 274-7888

Super 8 Motel $-$$
1835 Columbia Street, San
Diego, CA 92101, Res. (800)
800-8000 Ph: (619) 237-9940
Fax: (619) 237-9940

Thriftlodge $-$$
1345 Tenth Avenue, San
Diego, CA 92101, Res. (800)
525-9055 Ph: (619) 234-6344
Fax: (619) 234-3433

Villager $-$$
660 G Street, San Diego,
CA 92101, Res. (800)
328-7829 Ph: (619) 238-4100
Fax: (619) 238-5310

SAN DIMAS   **CA**

Motel 6 $
502 W Arrow Hwy, San
Dimas, CA 91773, Res. (800)
466-8356 Ph: 909 592-5631
Fax: 909 394-5909

SAN FRANCISCO   **CA**

Allison Hotel $$
417 Stockton St., San
Francisco, CA 94108, Res.
(800) 628-6446 Ph: (415)
986-8737 Fax: (415) 392-0850

Amsterdam Hotel $$
749 Taylor St., San
Francisco, CA 94108, Res.
(800) 637-3444 Ph: (415)
673-3277 Fax: (415) 673-0453

Econo Lodge $-$$
825 Polk St., San Francisco,
CA 94109, Res. (800)
424-4777 Ph: (415) 673-0411
Fax: (415) 673-1212

Econo Lodge $-$$
2505 Lombard St., San
Francisco, CA 94123, Res.
(800) 424-4777 Ph: (415)
921-2505 Fax: (041) 592-1505

Golden Gate Hotel $$
775 Bush St., San Francisco,
CA 93108, Res. (800)
835-1118 Ph: (415) 392-3702
Fax: (415) 392-6202

San Remo Hotel $
2337 Mason St., San
Francisco, CA 94103, Res.
(800) 352-7366 Ph: (415)
776-8688 Fax: (415) 776-2811

Super 8 Motel $-$$
111 Mitchell Ave., San
Francisco, CA 94080, Res.
(800) 800-8000 Ph: (415)
877-0770 Fax: (415) 871-8377

Super 8 Motel $-$$
2440 Lombard Street, San
Francisco, CA 94123, Res.
(800) 800-8000 Ph: (415)
922-0244 Fax: (415) 922-0244

Super 8 Motel $-$$
1015 Geary Street, San
Francisco, CA 94102, Res.
(800) 800-8000 Ph: (415)
863-5018 Fax: (415) 885-2802

SAN JOSE   **CA**

E-z 8 Motel $
1550 N. First Street, San
Jose, CA 95112, Res.
800-326-6835 Ext. 22 Ph:
408-453-1830 Fax:
408-453-9822

E-z 8 Motel $
2050 N. First Street, San
Jose, CA 95131, Res.
800-326-6835 Ext. 25 Ph:
408-436-0636 Fax:
408-453-3410

Motel 6 $
2081 N First St, San Jose,
CA 95131, Res. (800)
466-8356 Ph: 408 436-8180
Fax: 408 441-1656

Motel 6 $
2560 Fontaine Rd, San Jose,
CA 95121, Res. (800)
466-8356 Ph: 408 270-3131
Fax: 408 270-6235

SAN LUIS OBISPO   **CA**

Motel 6 $
1625 Calle Joaquin, San Luis
Obispo, CA 93401, Res. (800)
466-8356 Ph: 805 541-6992
Fax: 805 547-1152

Motel 6 $
1433 Calle Joaquin, San Luis
Obispo, CA 93401, Res. (800)
466-8356 Ph: 805 549-9595
Fax: 805 544-2826

Super 8 Motel $-$$
1951 Monterey Street, San
Luis Obispo, CA 93401, Res.
(800) 800-8000 Ph: (805)
544-7895

SAN MATEO   **CA**

Super 8 Motel $-$$
140 North Bayshore
Boulevard, San Mateo, CA
94401, Res. (800) 800-8000
Ph: (415) 342-3273 Fax: (415)
342-4619

SAN SIMEON   **CA**

Motel 6 $
9070 Castillo Dr, San
Simeon, CA 93452, Res.
(800) 466-8356 Ph: 805
927-8691 Fax: 805 927-5341

SAN YSIDRO   **CA**

Economy Motels Of America $$
230 Via De San Ysidro, San
Ysidro, CA 92173, Res. (800)
826-0778 Ph: (619) 428-6191

Motel 6 $
160 E Calle Primera, San
Ysidro, CA 92173, Res. (800)
466-8356 Ph: 619 690-6663
Fax: 619 690-1949

SANTA ANA   **CA**

Motel 6 $
1717 E Dyer Rd, Santa Ana,
CA 92705, Res. (800)
466-8356 Ph: 714 261-1515
Fax: 714 261-1265

Motel 6 $
1623 E First St, Santa Ana,
CA 92701, Res. (800)
466-8356 Ph: 714 558-0500
Fax: 714 558-1574

Villager $-$$
1660 E 1st St, Santa Ana,
CA 92701, Res. (800)
328-7829 Ph: (714) 835-3311
Fax: (714) 973-1466

SANTA BARBARA   **CA**

Motel 6 $
443 Corona Del Mar, Santa
Barbara, CA 93103, Res.
(800) 466-8356 Ph: 805
564-1392 Fax: 805 963-4687

Motel 6 $
3505 State St, Santa
Barbara, CA 93105, Res.
(800) 466-8356 Ph: 805
687-5400 Fax: 805 569-5837

Thriftlodge $-$$
1816 State Street, Santa
Barbara, CA 93101, Res.
(800) 525-9055 Ph: (805)
569-2205 Fax: (805) 563-0758

SANTA CLARA   **CA**

E-z 8 Motel $
3550 El Camino Real, Santa
Clara, CA 95051, Res.
800-326-6835 Ext. 21 Ph:
408-246-3119 Fax:
408-246-2106

**M
O
T
E
L**

Econo Lodge Silicon Valley $-$$
2930 El Camino Real, Santa
Clara, CA 95051, Res. (800)
424-4777 Ph: (408) 241-3010
Fax: (408) 247-0623

Motel 6 $
3208 El Camino Real, Santa
Clara, CA 95051, Res. (800)
466-8356 Ph: 408 241-0200
Fax: 408 243-8237

Econo Lodge Boardwalk $-$$
550 Second St., Santa Cruz,
CA 95060, Res. (800)
424-4777 Ph: (408) 426-3626

Super 8 Motel $-$$
338 Riverside Ave., Santa
Cruz, CA 95060, Res. (800)
800-8000 Ph: (408) 426-3707

Super 8 Motel $-$$
321 Riverside Avenue, Santa
Cruz, CA 95060, Res. (800)
800-8000 Ph: (408) 423-9449

Villager $-$$
510 Liebrant Ave, Santa
Cruz, CA 95060, Res. (800)
328-7829 Ph: (408) 423-6020
Fax: (000) 000-0000

Motel 6 $
13412 Excelsior Dr, Santa Fe
Springs, CA 90670, Res.
(800) 466-8356 Ph: 310
921-0596 Fax: 310 926-2351

Motel 6 $
2040 N Preisker Ln, Santa
Maria, CA 93454, Res. (800)
466-8356 Ph: 805 928-8111
Fax: 805 349-1219

Motel 6 $
12733 S Hwy 33, Santa Nella,
CA 95322, Res. (800)
466-8356 Ph: 209 826-6644
Fax: 209 827-1524

Super 8 Motel $-$$
28821 W. Gonzaga Rd., Santa
Nella, CA 95322, Res. (800)
800-8000 Ph: (209) 827-8700

Econo Lodge $-$$
1800 Santa Rosa Ave., Santa
Rosa, CA 95407, Res. (800)
424-4777 Ph: (707) 523-3480
Fax: (707) 542-9243

Motel 6 $
3145 Cleveland Ave, Santa
Rosa, CA 95403, Res. (800)
466-8356 Ph: 707 525-9010
Fax: 707 528-2761

Motel 6 $
2760 Cleveland Ave, Santa
Rosa, CA 95403, Res. (800)
466-8356 Ph: 707 546-1500
Fax: 707 527-8070

Super 8 Motel $-$$
2632 N. Cleveland Ave.,
Santa Rosa, CA 95402, Res.
(800) 800-8000 Ph: (707)
542-5544 Fax: (707) 542-9738

Super 8 Motel $-$$
3142 S. Highland Ave.,
Selma, CA 93662, Res. (800)
800-8000 Ph: (209) 896-2800
Fax: (209) 896-7244

Motel 6 $
15711 Roscoe Blvd,
Sepulveda, CA 91343, Res.
(800) 466-8356 Ph: 818
894-9341 Fax: 818 894-2467

Motel 6 $
2566 N Erringer Rd, Simi
Valley, CA 93065, Res. (800)
466-8356 Ph: 805 526-3533
Fax: 805 579-1664

Econo Lodge $-$$
3536 Lake Tahoe Blvd, South
Lake Tahoe, CA 96150, Res.
(800) 424-4777 Ph: (916)
544-2036 Fax: (916) 544-3466

Motel 6 $
2375 Lake Tahoe Blvd, South
Lake Tahoe, CA 96150, Res.
(800) 466-8356 Ph: 916
542-1400 Fax: 916 542-2801

Econo Lodge Airport $-$$
222 S. Airport Blvd., South
San Francisco, CA 94080,
Res. (800) 424-4777 Ph: (415)
589-9055 Fax: (415) 871-1290

Super 8 Motel $-$$
9603 Campo Road, Spring
Valley, CA 91977, Res. (800)
800-8000 Ph: (619) 387-8660
Fax: (619) 460-7561

Motel 6 $
7450 Katella Ave, Stanton,
CA 90680, Res. (800)
466-8356 Ph: 714 891-0717
Fax: 714 373-6357

Econo Lodge $-$$
2210 Manthey Rd., Stockton,
CA 95206, Res. (800)
424-4777 Ph: (209) 466-5741
Fax: (209) 463-4631

Motel 6 $
1625 French Camp Turnpike
Rd, Stockton, CA 95206,
Res. (800) 466-8356 Ph: 209
467-3600 Fax: 209 464-2659

Motel 6 $
817 Navy Dr, Stockton, CA
95206, Res. (800) 466-8356
Ph: 209 946-0923 Fax: 209
464-3948

Motel 6 $
6717 Plymouth Rd, Stockton,
CA 95207, Res. (800)
466-8356 Ph: 209 951-8120
Fax: 209 474-3829

Super 8 Motel $-$$
2717 W. March Lane,
Stockton, CA 95209, Res.
(800) 800-8000 Ph: (209)
477-5576 Fax: (209) 473-0647

Economy Inns Of America $-$$
4376 Central Place, Suisun
City, CA 94585, Res. (800)
826-0778 Ph: (707) 864-1728

Scottish Inns $$
8365 Lehigh Avenue, Sun
Valley, CA 91352, Res. (800)
251-1962 Ph: (818) 504-2671
Fax: (805) 824-9393

Econo Lodge $-$$
385 Weddell Dr., Sunnyvale,
CA 94089, Res. (800)
424-4777 Ph: (408) 734-9700
Fax: (408) 745-1145

Motel 6 $
775 N Mathilda Ave,
Sunnyvale, CA 94086, Res.
(800) 466-8356 Ph: 408
736-4595 Fax: 408 738-2271

Motel 6 $
806 Ahwanee Ave,
Sunnyvale, CA 94086, Res.
(800) 466-8356 Ph: 408
720-1222 Fax: 408 720-0630

Super 8 Motel $-$$
1071 E. El Camino Real,
Sunnyvale, CA 94087, Res.
(800) 800-8000 Ph: (408)
244-9000 Fax: (408) 244-7354

Motel 6 $
12775 Encinitas Ave,
Sylmar, CA 91342, Res.
(800) 466-8356 Ph: 818
362-9491 Fax: 818 364-6914

Super 8 Motel $-$$
14955 Roxford Street,
Sylmar, CA 91342, Res.
(800) 800-8000 Ph: (818)
367-0141 Fax: (818) 367-2236

Motel 6 $
41900 Moreno Dr, Temecula,
CA 92590, Res. (800)
466-8356 Ph: 909 676-7199
Fax: 909 676-2619

THOUSAND OAKS   CA

Econo Lodge $-$$
1425 Thousand Oaks Blvd.,
Thousand Oaks, CA 91362,
Res. (800) 424-4777 Ph: (805)
496-0102 Fax: (805) 494-1295

Motel 6 $
1516 Newbury Rd, Thousand
Oaks, CA 91320, Res. (800)
466-8356 Ph: 805 499-0711
Fax: 805 375-0887

TRACY   CA

Motel 6 $
3810 Tracy Blvd, Tracy, CA
95376, Res. (800) 466-8356
Ph: 209 836-4900 Fax: 209
833-1949

TRUCKEE   CA

Super 8 Motel $-$$
11506 Deerfield Drive,
Truckee, CA 96161-0502,
Res. (800) 800-8000 Ph: (916)
587-8888

TULARE   CA

Inns Of America $
1183 N. Blackstone St.,
Tulare, CA 93274, Res. (800)
826-0778 Ph: (209) 686-0985

Motel 6 $
1111 N Blackstone Dr,
Tulare, CA 93274, Res. (800)
466-8356 Ph: 209 686-1611
Fax: 209 686-6374

TURLOCK   CA

Motel 6 $
250 S Walnut Ave, Turlock,
CA 95380, Res. (800)
466-8356 Ph: 209 667-4100
Fax: 209 667-8306

TWENTYNINE PALMS   CA

Motel 6 $
72562 Twentynine Palms
Hwy, Twentynine Palms, CA
92277, Res. (800) 466-8356
Ph: 619 367-2833 Fax: 619
367-4965

UKIAH   CA

Motel 6 $
1208 S State St, Ukiah, CA
95482, Res. (800) 466-8356
Ph: 707 468-5404 Fax: 707
462-8405

Super 8 Motel $-$$
1070 State St., Ukiah, CA
95482, Res. (800) 800-8000
Ph: (707) 462-6657 Fax: (707)
468-8665

UPPER LAKE   CA

Super 8 Motel $-$$
450 East Highway 20, Upper
Lake, CA 95485, Res. (800)
800-8000 Ph: (707) 275-0888

VACAVILLE   CA

Motel 6 $
107 Lawrence Dr, Vacaville,
CA 95687, Res. (800)
466-8356 Ph: 707 447-5550
Fax: 707 447-7625

Super 8 Motel $-$$
101 Allison Court, Vacaville,
CA 95688, Res. (800)
800-8000 Ph: (707) 449-8884

VALLEJO   CA

E-z 8 Motel $
4 Mariposa Street, Vallejo,
CA 94590, Res. 800-326-6835
Ext. 49 Ph: 707-554-1840
Fax: 707-647-0226

Motel 6 $
458 Fairgrounds Dr, Vallejo,
CA 94589, Res. (800)
466-8356 Ph: 707 642-7781
Fax: 707 647-7231

Motel 6 $
1455 Marine World Pkwy,
Vallejo, CA 94589-3103, Res.
(800) 466-8356 Ph: 707
643-7611 Fax: 707 554-0138

Motel 6 $
597 Sandy Beach Rd, Vallejo,
CA 94590, Res. (800)
466-8356 Ph: 707 552-2912
Fax: 707 645-9324

Thriftlodge $-$$
160 Lincoln Rd. East/I-80 at
Magazine, Vallejo, CA
94591, Res. (800) 525-9055
Ph: (707) 552-7220 Fax: (707)
644-3419

VENTURA   CA

Motel 6 $
2145 E Harbor Blvd, Ventura,
CA 93001, Res. (800)
466-8356 Ph: 805 643-5100
Fax: 805 643-4519

Motel 6 $
3075 Johnson Dr, Ventura,
CA 93003, Res. (800)
466-8356 Ph: 805 650-0080
Fax: 805 339-0926

VICTORVILLE   CA

E-z 8 Motel $
15401 Park Avenue East,
Victorville, CA 92392, Res.
800-326-6835 Ext. 48 Ph:
760-241-7516

Motel 6 $
16901 Stoddard Wells Rd,
Victorville, CA 92392, Res.
(800) 466-8356 Ph: 619
243-0666 Fax: 619 243-2554

VISALIA   CA

Econo Lodge $-$$
1400 S. Mooney Blvd.,
Visalia, CA 93277, Res. (800)
424-4777 Ph: (209) 732-6641
Fax: (209) 739-7520

Thriftlodge $-$$
4645 West Mineral King Ave.,
Visalia, CA 93277, Res. (800)
525-9055 Ph: (209) 732-5611
Fax: (209) 732-8039

WALNUT CREEK   CA

Motel 6 $
2389 N Main St, Walnut
Creek, CA 94596, Res. (800)
466-8356 Ph: 510 935-4010
Fax: 510 906-0860

WATSONVILLE   CA

Econo Lodge $-$$
970 Main St., Watsonville,
CA 95076, Res. (800)
424-4777 Ph: (408) 724-8881
Fax: (408) 724-2572

Motel 6 $
125 Silver Leaf Dr,
Watsonville, CA 95076, Res.
(800) 466-8356 Ph: 408
728-4144 Fax: 408 722-1173

WEED   CA

Motel 6 $
466 N Weed Blvd, Weed, CA
96094, Res. (800) 466-8356
Ph: 916 938-4101 Fax: 916
938-2436

WEST SACRAMENTO   CA

Motel 6 $
1254 Halyard Dr, West
Sacramento, CA 95691,
Res. (800) 466-8356 Ph: 916
372-3624 Fax: 916 372-0849

WESTMINSTER   CA

Motel 6 $
13100 Goldenwest,
Westminster, CA 92683,
Res. (800) 466-8356 Ph: 714
895-0042 Fax: 714 894-3423

Motel 6 $
6266 Westminster Ave,
Westminster, CA 92683,
Res. (800) 466-8356 Ph: 714
891-5366 Fax: 714 373-4287

Super 8 Motel $-$$
15559 Beach Blvd.,
Westminster, CA 92683,
Res. (800) 800-8000 Ph: (714)
895-5584

WHITTIER   CA

Motel 6 $
8221 S Pioneer Blvd,
Whittier, CA 90606, Res.
(800) 466-8356 Ph: 562
692-9101 Fax: 562 908-9561

WILLIAMS   CA

Motel 6 $
455 4th St, Williams, CA
95987, Res. (800) 466-8356
Ph: 916 473-5337 Fax: 916
473-5132

**M
O
T
E
L**

WILLOWS   **CA**

Super 8 Motel $-$$
457 Humboldt Ave., Willows,
CA 95988-2644, Res. (800)
800-8000 Ph: (916) 934-2871
Fax: (916) 934-5512

WOODLAND   **CA**

Motel 6 $
1564 Main St, Woodland, CA
95776, Res. (800) 466-8356
Ph: 916 666-6777 Fax: 916
668-4367

YREKA   **CA**

Motel 6 $
1785 S Main St, Yreka, CA
96097, Res. (800) 466-8356
Ph: 916 842-4111 Fax: 916
842-7864

YUCCA VALLEY   **CA**

Super 8 Motel $-$$
57096 29 Palms Hwy., Yucca
Valley, CA 92284, Res. (800)
800-8000 Ph: (619) 228-1773
Fax: (619) 365-7799

COLORADO

ALAMOSA   **CO**

Super 8 Motel $-$$
2505 West Main Street, Hwy.
160, Alamosa, CO 81101,
Res. (800) 800-8000 Ph: (719)
589-6447 Fax: (719) 589-4167

BOULDER   **CO**

Super 8 Motel $-$$
970 28th Street, Boulder,
CO 80303, Res. (800)
800-8000 Ph: (303) 443-7800

BRIGHTON   **CO**

Super 8 Motel $-$$
"1020 Old Brighton Rd,",
Brighton, CO 80601, Res.
(800) 800-8000 Ph: (303)
659-6063 Fax: (303) 659-9367

BRUSH   **CO**

Budget Host Empire Motel $-$$
1408 W Edison, Brush, CO
80723, Res. (800) 283-4678
Ph: (303) 842-2876

BUENA VISTA   **CO**

Super 8 Motel $-$$
530 N. US Highway 24,
Buena Vista, CO 81211,
Res. (800) 800-8000 Ph: (719)
395-8888

BURLINGTON   **CO**

Budget Host Chaparral Motel $-$$
405 S Lincoln, Burlington,
CO 80807, Res. (800)
283-4678 Ph: (719) 346-5361
Fax: (719) 346-8502

Super 8 Motel $-$$
2100 Fay, Burlington, CO
80807, Res. (800) 800-8000
Ph: (719) 346-5627 Fax: (719)
346-5627

CANON CITY   **CO**

Super 8 Motel $-$$
209 North 19th Street,
Canon City, CO 81212, Res.
(800) 800-8000 Ph: (719)
275-8687 Fax: (719) 275-8687

CASTLE ROCK   **CO**

Super 8 Motel $-$$
1020 Park St., Castle Rock,
CO 80104-1524, Res. (800)
800-8000 Ph: (303) 688-0880

COLORADO SPRGS   **CO**

Super 8 Motel $-$$
8135 N. Academy Blvd.,
Colorado Sprgs, CO
80918-3903, Res. (800)
800-8000 Ph: (719) 528-7100
Fax: (719) 528-2452

COLORADO SPRING   **CO**

Super 8 Motel $-$$
3270 N. Chestnut St.,
Colorado Spring, CO
80907-5014, Res. (800)
800-8000 Ph: (719) 632-2681
Fax: (719) 475-0606

Super 8 Motel $-$$
605 Peterson Rd., Colorado
Spring, CO 80915, Res. (800)
800-8000 Ph: (719) 597-4100
Fax: (719) 597-6885

Super 8 Motel $-$$
4604 Rusina Rd., Colorado
Spring, CO 80907, Res. (800)
800-8000 Ph: (719) 594-0964
Fax: (719) 475-0606

COLORADO SPRINGS   **CO**

Econo Lodge Downtown $-$$
714 N. Nevada Ave., Colorado
Springs, CO 80903, Res.
(800) 424-4777 Ph: (719)
636-3385 Fax: (719) 636-3924

Motel 6 $
3228 N Chestnut St,
Colorado Springs, CO
80907, Res. (800) 466-8356
Ph: 719 520-5400 Fax: 719
630-0377

CORTEZ   **CO**

Super 8 Motel $-$$
505 East Main Street, Cortez,
CO 81321, Res. (800)
800-8000 Ph: (303) 565-8888
Fax: (303) 565-6595

CRAIG   **CO**

Super 8 Motel $-$$
200 Hwy 13, Craig, CO
81625, Res. (800) 800-8000
Ph: (303) 824-3471

DENVER   **CO**

Motel 6 $
3050 W 49th Ave, Denver,
CO 80221, Res. (800)
466-8356 Ph: 303 455-8888
Fax: 303 433-2218

Motel 6 $
12020 E 39th Ave, Denver,
CO 80239, Res. (800)
466-8356 Ph: 303 371-1980
Fax: 303 375-7763

Super 8 Motel $-$$
2601 Zuni Street, Denver,
CO 80211, Res. (800)
800-8000 Ph: (303) 433-6677
Fax: (303) 455-1530

Super 8 Motel $-$$
5888 N. Broadway, Denver,
CO 80216, Res. (800)
800-8000 Ph: (303) 296-3100
Fax: (303) 296-0786

DILLON   **CO**

Super 8 Motel $-$$
P.O. Box B, Dillon, CO
80435, Res. (800) 800-8000
Ph: (303) 468-8888 Fax: (303)
468-2086

DURANGO   **CO**

Econo Lodge $-$$
2002 Main Ave., Durango,
CO 81301, Res. (800)
424-4777 Ph: (303) 247-4242

Super 8 Motel $-$$
20 Stewart Drive, Durango,
CO 81301, Res. (800)
800-8000 Ph: (303) 259-0590
Fax: (303) 247-5765

ENGLEWOOD   **CO**

Super 8 Motel $-$$
5150 S. Quebec St.,
Englewood, CO 80111, Res.
(800) 800-8000 Ph: (303)
771-8000 Fax: (303) 771-8000

EVANS   **CO**

Motel 6 $
3015 8th Ave, Evans, CO
80620, Res. (800) 466-8356
Ph: 970 351-6481 Fax: 970
353-3024

FORT COLLINS   **CO**

Budget Host Inn $-$$
1513 N College Ave, Fort
Collins, CO 80524, Res.
(800) 283-4678 Ph: (303)
484-0870 Fax: (303) 224-2998

Super 8 Motel $-$$
409 Centro Way, Fort Collins,
CO 80524, Res. (800)
800-8000 Ph: (303) 493-7701
Fax: (303) 493-7701

FORT LUPTON   **CO**

Motel 6 $
65 South Grand, Fort
Lupton, CO 80621, Res.
(800) 466-8356 Ph: 303
857-1800 Fax: 303 857-4600

FORT MORGAN   **CO**

Econo Lodge $-$$
1409 Barlow Rd., Fort
Morgan, CO 80701, Res.
(800) 424-4777 Fax: (000)
000-1000

Super 8 Motel $-$$
1220 N. Main Street, Fort Morgan, CO 80701, Res. (800) 800-8000 Ph: (303) 867-9443 Fax: (303) 867-8658

FRUITA   CO

Super 8 Motel $-$$
399 Crossroads Ave., Fruita, CO 81521, Res. (800) 800-8000 Ph: (303) 858-0808

FT. COLLINS   CO

Motel 6 $
3900 E Mulberry/State Hwy 14, Ft. Collins, CO 80524, Res. (800) 466-8356 Ph: 970 482-6466 Fax: 970 493-8189

GEORGETOWN   CO

Super 8 Motel $-$$
1600 Argentine Street, Georgetown, CO 80444, Res. (800) 800-8000 Ph: (303) 569-3211

GRAND JUNCTION   CO

Budget Host Inn $-$$
721 Horizon Dr, Grand Junction, CO 81506, Res. (800) 283-4678 Ph: (303) 243-6050 Fax: (303) 243-0310

Motel 6 $
776 Horizon Dr, Grand Junction, CO 81506, Res. (800) 466-8356 Ph: 970 243-2628 Fax: 970 243-0213

Super 8 Motel $-$$
728 Horizon Dr., Grand Junction, CO 81506, Res. (800) 800-8000 Ph: (303) 248-8080

GREELEY   CO

Super 8 Motel $-$$
2423 West 29th Street, Greeley, CO 80632, Res. (800) 800-8000 Ph: (303) 351-8880

GREENWOOD VILLAGE   CO

Motel 6 $
9201 E Arapahoe Rd, Greenwood Village, CO 80112, Res. (800) 466-8356 Ph: 303 790-8220 Fax: 303 799-3405

GUNNISON   CO

Super 8 Motel $-$$
411 E. Tomachi, Gunnison, CO 81230, Res. (800) 800-8000 Ph: (303) 641-3068

HENDERSON   CO

Super 8 Motel $-$$
9051 I-76, Henderson, CO 80640, Res. (800) 800-8000 Ph: (303) 287-8888 Fax: (303) 287-8881

LA JUNTA   CO

Super 8 Motel $-$$
27882 Frontage Road, La Junta, CO 81050, Res. (800) 800-8000 Ph: (719) 384-4408 Fax: (719) 384-2236

LAKEWOOD   CO

Econo Lodge West $-$$
715 Kipling St., Lakewood, CO 80215, Res. (800) 424-4777 Ph: (303) 232-5000 Fax: (303) 232-4814

Motel 6 $
480 Wadsworth Blvd, Lakewood, CO 80226, Res. (800) 466-8356 Ph: 303 232-4924 Fax: 303 274-4621

LAMAR   CO

Budget Host El Mar Motel $-$$
1210 S Main St, Lamar, CO 81052, Res. (800) 283-4678 Ph: (719) 336-4331 Fax: (719) 336-7931

Super 8 Motel $-$$
1202 N. Main Street, Lamar, CO 81052, Res. (800) 800-8000 Ph: (719) 336-3427 Fax: (719) 336-3427

LIMON   CO

Econo Lodge $-$$
I-70 & US 24, Limon, CO 80828, Res. (800) 424-4777 Ph: (719) 775-2867 Fax: (719) 775-2485

Super 8 Motel $-$$
P.O. Box 1202, I-70 & Hwy 24, Limon, CO 80828, Res. (800) 800-8000 Ph: (719) 775-2889

LONGMONT   CO

Budget Host Of Longmont $-$$
3815 Hwy 119 & I-25, Longmont, CO 80501, Res. (800) 283-4678 Ph: (303) 776-8700 Fax: (303) 776-8700

Super 8 Motel $-$$
10805 Turner Avenue, Longmont, CO 80504, Res. (800) 800-8000 Ph: (303) 772-0888 Fax: (303) 772-3717

Super 8 Motel $-$$
2446 North Main Street, Longmont, CO 80504, Res. (800) 800-8000 Ph: (303) 772-0888 Fax: (303) 772-8106

LOVELAND   CO

Budget Host Budget Eight $-$$
51429 Hwys 6 & 24, Loveland, CO 80537, Res. (800) 283-4678 Ph: (303) 945-5682

Budget Host Exit 254 Inn $-$$
2716 SE Frontage Rd, Loveland, CO 80537, Res. (800) 283-4678 Ph: (303) 667-5202

Super 8 Motel $-$$
1655 E. Eisenhower Blvd., Loveland, CO 80537, Res. (800) 800-8000 Ph: (303) 663-7000

MANITOU SPRINGS   CO

Super 8 Motel $-$$
229 Manitou Ave., Manitou Springs, CO 80829-2503, Res. (800) 800-8000 Ph: (719) 685-5898 Fax: (719) 685-5498

MONTROSE   CO

Super 8 Motel $-$$
1705 East Main Street, Montrose, CO 81401, Res. (800) 800-8000 Ph: (303) 249-9294 Fax: (303) 249-9294

PAGOSA SPRINGS   CO

Super 8 Motel $-$$
34 Piedra Road, Pagosa Springs, CO 81147, Res. (800) 800-8000 Ph: (303) 731-4005 Fax: (303) 731-4005

PARACHUTE   CO

Super 8 Motel $-$$
252 Green St., Parachute, CO 81635, Res. (800) 800-8000 Ph: (303) 285-7936 Fax: (303) 285-9538

PUEBLO   CO

Motel 6 $
960 Hwy 50 W, Pueblo, CO 81008, Res. (800) 466-8356 Ph: 719 543-8900 Fax: 719 543-5515

Motel 6 $
4103 N Elizabeth St, Pueblo, CO 81008, Res. (800) 466-8356 Ph: 719 543-6221 Fax: 719 546-9612

Super 8 Motel $-$$
1100 Hwy 50W, Pueblo, CO 81008, Res. (800) 800-8000 Ph: (719) 545-4104 Fax: (719) 545-4104

RIDGWAY   CO

Super 8 Motel $-$$
373 Palomino Trail, P.O. Box 608, Ridgway, CO 81432-0608, Res. (800) 800-8000 Ph: (303) 626-5444

SALIDA   CO

Super 8 Motel $-$$
525 W. Rainbow (Hwy 50), Salida, CO 81201, Res. (800) 800-8000 Ph: (719) 539-6689 Fax: (719) 539-7018

STEAMBOAT SPRNG   CO

Super 8 Motel $-$$
US Hwy 40 E., P.O. Box 147, Steamboat Sprng, CO 80477, Res. (800) 800-8000 Ph: (303) 879-5230

M O T E L

STERLING — CO

Super 8 Motel $-$$
12883 Hwy 61, Sterling, CO
80751, Res. (800) 800-8000
Ph: (970) 522-0300 Fax: (970)
522-8417

THORNTON — CO

Motel 6 $
6 W 83rd Pl, Thornton, CO
80221, Res. (800) 466-8356
Ph: 303 429-1550 Fax: 303
427-7513

TRINIDAD — CO

Budget Host Trinidad $-$$
10301 Santa Fe Trail Dr,
Trinidad, CO 81082, Res.
(800) 283-4678 Ph: (719)
846-3307

Super 8 Motel $-$$
1924 Freedom Road, Trinidad,
CO 81082, Res. (800)
800-8000 Ph: (719) 846-8280

WALSENBURG — CO

Budget Host Country Host $-$$
553 US 85-87 -- P.O. Box 190,
Walsenburg, CO 81089,
Res. (800) 283-4678 Ph: (719)
738-3800

WESTMINSTER — CO

Super 8 Motel $-$$
12055 Melody Drive,
Westminster, CO 80234,
Res. (800) 800-8000 Ph: (303)
451-7200 Fax: (303) 451-7200

WHEAT RIDGE — CO

Motel 6 $
9920 W 49th Ave, Wheat
Ridge, CO 80033, Res. (800)
466-8356 Ph: 303 424-0658
Fax: 303 431-2196

Motel 6 $
10300 S I-70 Frontage Rd,
Wheat Ridge, CO 80033,
Res. (800) 466-8356 Ph: 303
467-3172 Fax: 303 431-5896

WHEATRIDGE — CO

Super 8 Motel $-$$
10101 I-70 S. Frontage Road,
Wheatridge, CO 80033, Res.
(800) 800-8000 Ph: (303)
424-8300 Fax: (303) 424-8300

WINTER PARK — CO

Super 8 Motel $-$$
78641 U.S. Highway 40, P.O.
Box 35, Winter Park, CO
80482, Res. (800) 800-8000
Ph: (970) 726-8088 Fax: (970)
726-1101

CONNECTICUT

BRANFORD — CT

Motel 6 $
320 E Main St, Branford, CT
06405, Res. (800) 466-8356
Ph: 203 483-5828 Fax: 203
488-4579

CROMWELL — CT

Super 8 Motel $-$$
1 Industrial Park Dr.,
Cromwell, CT 06416, Res.
(800) 800-8000 Ph: (203)
632-8888

DANBURY — CT

Super 8 Motel $-$$
3 Lake Ave. Extension,
Danbury, CT 06811-5252,
Res. (800) 800-8000 Ph: (203)
743-0064 Fax: (203) 791-0049

EAST HARTFORD — CT

Econo Lodge $-$$
927 Main St., East Hartford,
CT 06108, Res. (800)
424-4777 Ph: (203) 289-7781
Fax: (203) 289-7966

ENFIELD — CT

Motel 6 $
11 Hazard Ave, Enfield, CT
06082, Res. (800) 466-8356
Ph: 860 741-3685 Fax: 860
741-5539

Super 8 Motel $-$$
1543 King Street, Enfield, CT
06082, Res. (800) 800-8000
Ph: (518) 427-2924

GROTON — CT

Econo Lodge $-$$
425 Bridge St., Groton, CT
06340, Res. (800) 424-4777
Ph: (203) 445-6550 Fax: (203)
445-5833

Super 8 Motel $-$$
173 Route 12, Groton, CT
06340, Res. (800) 800-8000
Ph: (203) 743-0064 Fax: (203)
446-0162

HARTFORD — CT

Super 8 Motel $-$$
57 W. Service Rd., Hartford,
CT 06120, Res. (800)
800-8000 Ph: (203) 246-8888
Fax: (203) 246-8888

NEW HAVEN — CT

Motel 6 $
270 Foxon Blvd, New Haven,
CT 06513, Res. (800)
466-8356 Ph: 203 469-0343
Fax: 203 468-0787

NIANTIC — CT

Motel 6 $
269 Flanders Rd, Niantic, CT
06357, Res. (800) 466-8356
Ph: 860 739-6991 Fax: 860
691-1828

SOUTHINGTON — CT

Motel 6 $
625 Queen St, Southington,
CT 06489, Res. (800)
466-8356 Ph: 860 621-7351
Fax: 860 620-0453

Red Carpet Inn $
30 Laning Street,
Southington, CT 06489,
Res. (800) 251-1962 Ph: (203)
628-0921 Fax: 203) 621-8545

STAMFORD — CT

Super 8 Motel $-$$
32 Grenhart Rd., Stamford,
CT 06902, Res. (800)
800-8000 Ph: (203) 324-8887
Fax: (203) 964-8465

TORRINGTON — CT

Super 8 Motel $-$$
492 E. Main St., Torrington,
CT 06790, Res. (800)
800-8000 Ph: (203) 496-0811
Fax: (203) 482-6796

WATERBURY — CT

Super 8 Motel $-$$
I-84 at Scott Road,
Waterbury, CT 06705, Res.
(800) 800-8000 Ph: (203)
757-0888 Fax: (203) 755-7671

WETHERSFIELD — CT

Motel 6 $
1341 Silas Deane Hwy,
Wethersfield, CT 06109,
Res. (800) 466-8356 Ph: 860
563-5900 Fax: 860 563-1213

WINDSOR LOCKS — CT

Motel 6 $
3 National Dr, Windsor
Locks, CT 06096, Res. (800)
466-8356 Ph: 860 292-6200
Fax: 860 623-1821

DELAWARE

NEW CASTLE — DE

Econo Lodge Airport $-$$
232 S. Dupont Hwy., New
Castle, DE 19720, Res. (800)
424-4777 Ph: (302) 322-4500
Fax: (302) 322-9612

Econo Lodge North $-$$
I-295 & SR 9, New Castle,
DE 19720, Res. (800)
424-4777 Ph: (302) 654-5400
Fax: (302) 654-5775

Motel 6 $
1200 W Ave/S Hwy 9, New
Castle, DE 19720, Res. (800)
466-8356 Ph: 302 571-1200
Fax: 302 571-1310

Super 8 Motel $-$$
215 South DuPont Highway,
New Castle, DE 19720, Res.
(800) 800-8000 Ph: (302)
322-9480 Fax: (302) 322-9480

REHOBOTH BEACH — DE

Econo Lodge Resort $-$$
4361 SR 1, Rehoboth Beach,
DE 19971, Res. (800)
424-4777 Ph: (302) 227-0500
Fax: (302) 227-2170

DISTRICT OF COLUMBIA

WASHINGTON · DC

Econo Lodge North East $-$$
1600 New York Ave. N.E.,
Washington, DC 20002,
Res. (800) 424-4777 Fax: (202)
832-3200 Fax: (202) 832-1791

Super 8 Motel $-$$
501 New York Avenue,
Washington, DC 20002,
Res. (800) 800-8000 Ph: (202)
543-7400 Fax: (202) 544-2327

FLORIDA

AVON PARK · FL

Econo Lodge Sebring $-$$
2511 US 27 S, Avon Park, FL
33825, Res. (800) 424-4777
Ph: (813) 453-2000 Fax: (813)
453-0820

BONIFAY · FL

Econo Lodge $-$$
2210 S. Waukesha St.,
Bonifay, FL 32425, Res. (800)
424-4777 Ph: (904) 547-9345
Fax: (904) 547-5023

BONITA SPRINGS · FL

Econo Lodge $-$$
28090 Quail's Nest Ln.,
Bonita Springs, FL 33923,
Res. (800) 424-4777 Ph: (813)
947-3366 Fax: (813) 947-6789

BRADENTON · FL

Econo Lodge Airport $-$$
6727-14th St. W., Bradenton,
FL 34207, Res. (800)
424-4777 Ph: (813) 758-7199
Fax: (813) 751-4947

Econo Lodge East $-$$
607-67th St. Cir. E.,
Bradenton, FL 34208, Res.
(800) 424-4777 Ph: (813)
745-1988

Motel 6 $
660 67 St Cir E, Bradenton,
FL 34208, Res. (800)
466-8356 Ph: 941 747-6005
Fax: 941 745-1388

CLEARWATER · FL

Econo Lodge Beachfront $-$$
625 S. Gulfview Blvd.,
Clearwater, FL 34630, Res.
(800) 424-4777 Ph: (813)
446-3400 Fax: (813) 446-4615

Econo Lodge Central $-$$
21252 US 19 N., Clearwater,
FL 34625, Res. (800)
424-4777 Ph: (813) 799-1569
Fax: (813) 796-3165

Super 8 Motel $-$$
13260 34th St., Clearwater,
FL 34622, Res. (800)
800-8000 Ph: (813) 572-8881
Fax: (813) 572-8881

Super 8 Motel $-$$
22950 US Hwy 19 N.,
Clearwater, FL 34625, Res.
(800) 800-8000 Ph: (813)
799-2678 Fax: (813) 726-7263

COCOA · FL

Econo Lodge Space Center $-$$
3220 N. Cocoa Blvd. (US 1),
Cocoa, FL 32926, Res. (800)
424-4777 Ph: (407) 632-4561
Fax: (407) 631-3756

COCOA BEACH · FL

Econo Lodge A1a $-$$
5500 N. Atlantic Ave., Cocoa
Beach, FL 32931, Res. (800)
424-4777 Ph: (407) 784-2550
Fax: (407) 868-7124

Motel 6 $
3701 N Atlantic Ave, Cocoa
Beach, FL 32931, Res. (800)
466-8356 Ph: 407 783-3103
Fax: 407 868-0875

CRESTVIEW · FL

Econo Lodge $-$$
3101 S. Ferdon Blvd.,
Crestview, FL 32536, Res.
(800) 424-4777 Ph: (904)
682-6255 Fax: (904) 682-7500

Super 8 Motel $-$$
3925 South Ferdon
Boulevard, Crestview, FL
32536, Res. (800) 800-8000
Ph: (904) 682-9649 Fax: (904)
682-9649

DANIA BEACH · FL

Motel 6 $
825 E Dania Beach Blvd,
Dania Beach, FL 33004,
Res. (800) 466-8356 Ph: 954
921-5505 Fax: 954 920-0591

DAVENPORT · FL

Motel 6 $
5620 US Hwy 27 N,
Davenport, FL 33837, Res.
(800) 466-8356 Ph: 941
424-2521 Fax: 941 424-0582

DAYTONA · FL

Villager $-$$
700 N. Atlantic Ave,
Daytona, FL 32118, Res.
(800) 328-7829 Ph: (904)
255-3411 Fax: (904) 257-7778

DAYTONA BEACH · FL

Budget Host Candlelight $-$$
1305 S. Ridgewood Ave,
Daytona Beach, FL 32114,
Res. (800) 283-4678 Ph: (904)
252-1142 Fax: (904) 252-1142

Econo Lodge Beachfront $-$$
301 S. Atlantic Ave.,
Daytona Beach, FL 32118,
Res. (800) 424-4777 Ph: (904)
255-6421 Fax: (904) 252-6195

Econo Lodge Racetracks $-$$
2250 Volusia Ave., Daytona
Beach, FL 32114, Res. (800)
424-4777 Ph: (904) 255-3661

Red Carpet Inn $$
1400 N. Atlantic Avenue,
Daytona Beach, FL 32118,
Res. (800) 251-1962 Ph: (904)
255-4588 Fax: (904) 253-6132

Red Carpet Inn $$
1855 South Ridgewood Ave,
Daytona Beach, FL 32119,
Res. (800) 251-1962 Ph: (904)
767-6681 Fax: (904) 767-6681

Scottish Inns $$
1515 South Ridgewood Ave,
Daytona Beach, FL 32114,
Res. (800) 251-1962 Ph: (904)
258-5742 Fax: (904) 253-7635

Super 8 Motel $-$$
2992 W. International
Speedway, Daytona Beach,
FL 32124, Res. (800)
800-8000 Ph: (904) 253-0643
Fax: (904) 238-5436

Super 8 Motel $-$$
930 N. Atlantic Ave.,
Daytona Beach, FL 32118,
Res. (800) 800-8000 Ph: (904)
255-6591 Fax: (904) 255-6647

DE FUNIAK SPRINGS · FL

Econo Lodge $-$$
1325 South Freeport Rd., De
Funiak Springs, FL 32433,
Res. (800) 424-4777 Ph: (904)
892-6115 Fax: (904) 892-0707

DEERFIELD BEACH · FL

Villager $-$$
1250 W. Hillsboro Blvd,
Deerfield Beach, FL 33442,
Res. (800) 328-7829 Ph: (954)
421-6555 Fax: (954) 360-0536

DUNEDIN · FL

Econo Lodge Waterfront $-$$
1414 Bayshore Blvd.,
Dunedin, FL 34698, Res.
(800) 424-4777 Ph: (813)
734-8851 Fax: (813) 736-1493

ELLISVILLE · FL

Red Carpet Inn $
I-75 & US Hwy 441 & 41 exit
80, Ellisville, FL 32056, Res.
(800) 251-1962 Ph: (904)
752-7582 Fax: (904) 752-7582

FLORIDA CITY · FL

Super 8 Motel $-$$
1202 North Krome Avenue,
Florida City, FL 33034, Res.
(800) 800-8000 Ph: (305)
245-0311 Fax: (305) 247-9136

FORT LAUDERDALE · FL

Motel 6 $
1801 SR 84, Fort Lauderdale,
FL 33315, Res (800)
466-8356 Ph: 954 760-7999
Fax: 954 832-0653

**M
O
T
E
L**

Red Carpet Inn $$
2440 State Road 84, Fort
Lauderdale, FL 33312, Res.
(800) 251-1962 Ph: (904)
792-8181 Fax: (954) 792-4202

FORT MYERS   **FL**

Econo Lodge North $-$$
13301 N. Cleveland, Fort
Myers, FL 33903, Res. (800)
424-4777 Ph: (813) 995-0571

Red Carpet Inn $$
4811 South Cleveland Ave,
Fort Myers, FL 33907, Res.
(800) 251-1962 Ph: (941)
936-3229 Fax: (941) 939-0424

FORT PIERCE   **FL**

Econo Lodge $-$$
7050 Okeechobee Rd., Fort
Pierce, FL 34945, Res. (800)
424-4777 Ph: (407) 465-8600

Super 8 Motel $-$$
612 S. 4th Street (US 1), Fort
Pierce, FL 34950, Res. (800)
800-8000 Ph: (407) 000-0000
Fax: (407) 466-8488

FORT WALTON BEACH   **FL**

Econo Lodge $-$$
1284 Marler Dr., Fort Walton
Beach, FL 32548, Res. (800)
424-4777 Ph: (904) 243-7123
Fax: (904) 243-7109

FT. MYERS   **FL**

Motel 6 $
3350 Marinatown Ln, Ft.
Myers, FL 33903, Res. (800)
466-8356 Ph: 941 656-5544
Fax: 941 656-6276

FT. PIERCE   **FL**

Motel 6 $
2500 Peters Rd, Ft. Pierce, FL
34945, Res. (800) 466-8356
Ph: 561 461-9937 Fax: 561
460-9472

FT WALTON BEACH   **FL**

Super 8 Motel $-$$
333 Miracle Strip Parkway
S.W., Ft Walton Beach, FL
32548, Res. (800) 800-8000
Ph: (904) 244-4999 Fax: (904)
243-5657

GAINESVILLE   **FL**

Econo Lodge University $-$$
2649 S.W. 13th St.,
Gainesville, FL 32608, Res.
(800) 424-4777 Ph: (904)
373-7816 Fax: (904) 373-7816

Econo Lodge West $-$$
700 N.W. 75th St.,
Gainesville, FL 32607, Res.
(800) 424-4777 Ph: (904)
332-2346 Fax: (904) 332-4426

Motel 6 $
4000 SW 40th Blvd,
Gainesville, FL 32608, Res.
(800) 466-8356 Ph: 352
373-1604 Fax: 352 335-8314

Scottish Inns $
4041 SW 13th St.,
Gainesville, FL 32608, Res.
(800) 251-1962 Ph: (352)
376-4423 Fax: (352) 335-2636

Scottish Inns $
4155 NW13th St.,
Gainesville, FL 32609, Res.
(800) 251-1962 Ph: (352)
376-2601 Fax: (352) 376-2601

Super 8 Motel $-$$
4202 SW 40th Blvd,
Gainesville, FL 32608, Res.
(800) 800-8000 Ph: (904)
378-3888 Fax: (904) 378-3888

HAINES CITY   **FL**

Econo Lodge $-$$
1504 US 27 S., Haines City,
FL 33844, Res. (800)
424-4777 Ph: (813) 422-8621
Fax: (813) 421-4745

HOBE SOUND   **FL**

Red Carpet Inn $$
8605 SE Federal Highway,
Hobe Sound, FL 33455, Res.
(800) 251-1962 Ph: (407)
546-3600 Fax: (407) 546-3610

HOMESTEAD   **FL**

Econo Lodge $-$$
27707 S. Dixie Hwy.,
Homestead, FL 33032, Res.
(800) 424-4777 Ph: (305)
245-4330 Fax: (305) 248-8518

JACKSONVILLE   **FL**

Econo Lodge Central $-$$
5221 University Blvd. W.,
Jacksonville, FL 32216, Res.
(800) 424-4777 Ph: (904)
737-1690 Fax: (904) 448-5638

Economy Inns Of America$-$$
4300 Salisbury Road,
Jacksonville, FL 32216, Res.
(800) 826-0778 Ph: (904)
281-0198

Economy Motels Of America$
5959 Youngerman Circle
East, Jacksonville, FL
32244, Res. (800) 826-0778
Ph: (904) 777-0160

Motel 6 $
8285 Dix Ellis Trail,
Jacksonville, FL 32256, Res.
(800) 466-8356 Ph: 904
731-8400 Fax: 904 730-0781

Motel 6 $
6107 Youngerman Cir,
Jacksonville, FL 32244, Res.
(800) 466-8356 Ph: 904
777-6100 Fax: 904 779-2223

Red Carpet Inn $$
5331 University Blvd. West,
Jacksonville, FL 32216, Res.
(800) 251-1962 Ph: (904)
733-8110 Fax: (904) 737-2505

Scottish Inns $$
2300 Phillips Highway,
Jacksonville, FL 32207, Res.
(800) 251-1962 Ph: (904)
396-2301 Fax: (904) 398-7839

Super 8 Motel $-$$
10901 Harts Rd,
Jacksonville, FL 32218, Res.
(800) 800-8000 Ph: (904)
751-3888 Fax: (904) 751-3888

Super 8 Motel $-$$
5929 Ramona Blvd.,
Jacksonville, FL 32205, Res.
(800) 800-8000 Ph: (904)
781-3878

JACKSONVILLE, FL   **FL**

Motel 6 $
10885 Harts Rd,
Jacksonville, Fl, FL 32218,
Res. (800) 466-8356 Ph: 904
757-8600 Fax: 904 757-2072

JASPER   **FL**

Scottish Inns $
I-75, exit 86, Jasper, FL
32052, Res. (800) 251-1962
Ph: (904) 792-1234 Fax: (904)
792-1118

JENNINGS   **FL**

Econo Lodge $-$$
I-75 & SR 143, Jennings, FL
32053, Res. (800) 424-4777
Ph: (904) 938-5500 Fax: (904)
938-5520

KEY WEST   **FL**

Econo Lodge $-$$
3820 N. Roosevelt Blvd., Key
West, FL 33040, Res. (800)
424-4777 Ph: (305) 294-5511
Fax: (305) 296-7939

KISSIMMEE   **FL**

Econo Lodge Maingate $-$$
4985 W. Irlo Bronson Hwy.,
Kissimmee, FL 34746, Res.
(800) 424-4777 Ph: (407)
396-4343 Fax: (407) 438-5883

Econo Lodge Maingate East$
4311 W. Irlo Bronson Hwy.,
Kissimmee, FL 34746, Res.
(800) 424-4777 Ph: (407)
396-7100 Fax: (407) 239-2636

Econo Lodge Maingate $-$$
7514 W. Irlo Bronson,
Kissimmee, FL 34746, Res.
(800) 424-4777 Ph: (407)
396-2000 Fax: (407) 396-1295

Econo Lodge Maingate West$
8620 W. Irlo Bronson Hwy.,
Kissimmee, FL 34747, Res.
(800) 424-4777 Ph: (407)
396-9300 Fax: (407) 396-8045

Economy Inns Of America$-$$
5367 W. Irlo Bronson Mem.
Highway, Kissimmee, FL
34746, Res. (800) 826-0778
Ph: (407) 396-4020

Inns Of America $
2945 Entry Point Blvd.,
Kissimmee, FL 34746, Res.
(800) 826-0778 Ph: (407)
396-7743

Motel 6 $
5731 W Irlo Bronson
Memorial Hwy, Kissimmee,
FL 34746, Res. (800)
466-8356 Ph: 407 396-6333
Fax: 407 396-7715

Motel 6 $
7455 W Bronson Hwy,
Kissimmee, FL 34747, Res.
(800) 466-8356 Ph: 407
396-6422 Fax: 407 396-0720

Red Carpet Inn $$
4700 W. Irlo Bronson
Highway, Kissimmee, FL
34746, Res. (800) 251-1962
Ph: (407) 396-0224 Fax: (407)
396-1133

Super 8 Motel $-$$
4880 W. Spacecoast Parkway,
Kissimmee, FL 34746, Res.
(800) 800-8000 Ph: (407)
396-1144 Fax: (407) 396-4389

Villager $-$$
4669 W. Irlo Bronson
Memorial, Kissimmee, FL
34746, Res. (800) 328-7829
Ph: (407) 396-1890 Fax: (407)
396-8336

LAKE CITY   FL

Econo Lodge $-$$
I-75 & US 90, Lake City, FL
32055, Res. (800) 424-4777
Ph: (904) 752-7891 Fax: (904)
755-9509

Econo Lodge South $-$$
Route 3, Box 173, Lake City,
FL 32055, Res. (800)
424-4777 Ph: (904) 755-9311
Fax: (904) 755-8864

Motel 6 $
US 90 W & Hall of Fame Dr,
Lake City, FL 32055, Res.
(800) 466-8356 Ph: 904
755-4664 Fax: 904 758-7753

Red Carpet Inn $
I-75 @ US 90, exit 82, Lake
City, FL 32055, Res. (800)
251-1962 Ph: (904) 755-1707
Fax: (904) 758-0028

Scottish Inns $
I-75, exit 82, Lake City, FL
32055, Res. (800) 251-1962
Ph: (904) 755-0230 Fax: (904)
755-5277

Super 8 Motel $-$$
I-75 & State Rd 47, PO Box
7094, Lake City, FL 32055,
Res. (800) 800-8000 Ph: (904)
752-6450 Fax: (904) 752-6450

Villager $-$$
Rt. 13, Lake City, FL 32055,
Res. (800) 328-7829 Ph: (904)
755-4308 Fax: (000) 000-0000

LAKE WALES   FL

Red Carpet Inn $
501 South Highway 27, Lake
Wales, FL 33853, Res. (800)
251-1962 Ph: (941) 676-7963
Fax: (941) 676-2569

Super 8 Motel $-$$
541 W. Central Ave, Lake
Wales, FL 33853, Res. (800)
800-8000 Ph: (813) 676-7925
Fax: (813) 676-6662

LAKELAND   FL

Econo Lodge Lake Parker$-$$
1817 E. Memorial Blvd.,
Lakeland, FL 33801, Res.
(800) 424-4777 Ph: (813)
688-9221 Fax: (813) 687-4797

Motel 6 $
3120 US Hwy 98 N, Lakeland,
FL 33809, Res. (800)
466-8356 Ph: 941 682-0643
Fax: 941 686-1701

Red Carpet Inn $$
1539 Memorial Blvd.,
Lakeland, FL 33801, Res.
(800) 251-1962 Ph: (941)
683-7821 Fax: (941) 683-3320

Scottish Inns $$
244 North Florida Ave,
Lakeland, FL 33801, Res.
(800) 251-1962 Ph: (941)
687-2530 Fax: (941) 688-1961

Villager $-$$
910 East Memorial Blvd,
Lakeland, FL 33801, Res.
(800) 328-7829 Ph: (941)
688-8926 Fax: (941) 683-0815

LANTANA   FL

Inns Of America
7051 Seacrest Blvd., Open
March 1996, Lantana, FL

Motel 6 $
1310 W Lantana Rd,
Lantana, FL 33462, Res.
(800) 466-8356 Ph: 561
585-5833 Fax: 561 547-9701

Super 8 Motel $-$$
1255 Hypoluso Road,
Lantana, FL 33462, Res.
(800) 800-8000 Ph: (407)
585-3970 Fax: (407) 586-3028

LEESBURG   FL

Budget Host Inn $-$$
1225 N 14th St, Leesburg, FL
34748, Res. (800) 283-4678
Ph: (904) 787-3534 Fax: (904)
787-0060

Econo Lodge $-$$
1115 W. North Blvd.,
Leesburg, FL 34748, Res.
(800) 424-4777 Ph: (904)
787-3131 Fax: (904) 365-1497

Scottish Inns $
1321 North 14th St.,
Leesburg, FL 34748, Res.
(800) 251-1962 Ph: (904)
787-3343 Fax: (904) 782-7312

Super 8 Motel $-$$
1392 North Blvd. West,
Leesburg, FL 34748, Res.
(800) 800-8000 Ph: (904)
787-6363 Fax: (904) 787-6363

LIVE OAK   FL

Econo Lodge $-$$
US 129 & I-10, Live Oak, FL
32060, Res. (800) 424-4777
Ph: (904) 362-7459 Fax: (904)
364-6598

Scottish Inns $
827 W. Howard St., Live Oak,
FL 32060, Res. (800)
251-1962 Ph: (904) 362-7828

MACCLENNY   FL

Econo Lodge $-$$
I-10 & SR 121, Macclenny,
FL 32063, Res. (800)
424-4777 Ph: (904) 259-3000
Fax: (904) 259-4418

MADISON   FL

Super 8 Motel $-$$
I-10 and SR 53, Madison, FL
32340, Res. (800) 800-8000
Ph: (904) 973-6267 Fax: (904)
973-6441

MELBOURNE   FL

Econo Lodge West $-$$
4505 W. New Haven Ave.,
Melbourne, FL 32904, Res.
(800) 424-4777 Ph: (407)
724-5450 Fax: (407) 984-7519

MICANOPY   FL

Scottish Inns $
I-75 & SR 234, Exit 73,
Micanopy, FL 32667, Res.
(800) 251-1962 Ph: (352)
466-3163 Fax: (352) 466-3069

MILTON   FL

Red Carpet Inn $
4905 Highway 87 So, Milton,
FL 32583, Res. (800)
251-1962 Ph: (904) 626-7931
Fax: (904) 623-4268

MONTICELLO   FL

Super 8 Motel $-$$
I-10 and US Hwy 19,
Monticello, FL 32344, Res.
(800) 800-8000 Ph: (904)
997-8888

MOUNT DORA   FL

Econo Lodge $-$$
300 N. New US 441, Mount
Dora, FL 32757, Res. (800)
424-4777 Ph: (904) 383-2181
Fax: (904) 383-4064

NAPLES   FL

Super 8 Motel $-$$
3880 Tollgate Blvd., Naples,
FL 33999, Res. (800)
800-8000 Ph: (813) 455-0808
Fax: (813) 455-7124

MOTEL

NEW PORT RICHEY   FL

Econo Lodge $-$$
7631 US 19, New Port Richey,
FL 34652, Res. (800)
424-4777 Ph: (813) 845-4990
Fax: (813) 845-4990

NORTH PALM BEACH   FL

Econo Lodge North $-$$
757 U.S. 1 North, North Palm
Beach, FL 33408, Res. (800)
424-4777 Ph: (407) 848-1424

OCALA   FL

Budget Host Western Motel $-$$
4013 NW Blitchton Rd,
Ocala, FL 32675, Res. (800)
283-4678 Ph: (904) 732-6940

Scottish Inns $
3520 W. Silver Springs Blvd.,
Ocala, FL 34470, Res. (800)
251-1962 Ph: (904) 629-7961

Super 8 Motel $-$$
3924 W. Silver Springs Blvd.,
Ocala, FL 32675, Res. (800)
800-8000 Ph: (904) 629-8794

OKEECHOBEE   FL

Scottish Inns $
3190 Highway 441 So.,
Okeechobee, FL 34974, Res.
(800) 251-1962 Ph: (941)
763-3293

ORANGE PARK   FL

Villager $-$$
141 Park Avenue, Orange
Park, FL 32073-0290, Res.
(800) 328-7829 Ph: (904)
264-5107 Fax: (904) 264-5107

ORLANDO   FL

Econo Lodge $-$$
5870 S. Orange Blossom
Trail, Orlando, FL 32809,
Res. (800) 424-4777 Ph: (407)
859-5410 Fax: (407) 857-4306

Econo Lodge Central $-$$
3300 W. Colonial Dr.,
Orlando, FL 32808, Res.
(800) 424-4777 Ph: (407)
293-7221 Fax: (407) 293-1166

Econo Lodge South $-$$
9401 Orange Blossom Trl.,
Orlando, FL 32821, Res.
(800) 424-4777 Ph: (407)
851-1050 Fax: (407) 438-9050

Inns Of America $
8222 Jamaican Court,
Orlando, FL 32819, Res.
(800) 826-0778 Ph: (407)
396-7743

Motel 6 $
5909 American Way,
Orlando, FL 32819, Res.
(800) 466-8356 Ph: 407
351-6500 Fax: 407 352-5481

Motel 6 $
5300 Adanson Rd, Orlando,
FL 32810, Res. (800)
466-8356 Ph: 407 647-1444
Fax: 407 647-1016

ORMOND BEACH   FL

Econo Lodge $-$$
1634 N. US 1, Ormond
Beach, FL 32174, Res. (800)
424-4777 Ph: (904) 672-6222

Econo Lodge On The Beach $-$$
295 S. Atlantic Ave., Ormond
Beach, FL 32176, Res. (800)
424-4777 Ph: (904) 672-2651
Fax: (000) 009-0472

Scottish Inns $
1608 North US 1 & I-95,
Ormond Beach, FL 32174,
Res. (800) 251-1962 Ph: (904)
677-8860 Fax: (904) 672-3717

Super 8 Motel $-$$
I-95 and US 1, Ormond
Beach, FL 32174, Res. (800)
800-8000 Ph: (904) 672-6222
Fax: (904) 677-2401

PALM BAY   FL

Motel 6 $
1170 Malabar Rd, SE, Palm
Bay, FL 32909, Res. (800)
466-8356 Ph: 407 951-8222
Fax: 407 723-0598

PALM HARBOR   FL

Econo Lodge $-$$
32000 US 19 N., Palm Harbor,
FL 34684, Res. (800)
424-4777 Ph: (813) 786-2529
Fax: (813) 786-7462

PANAMA CITY   FL

Econo Lodge $-$$
4411 W. US 98, Panama City,
FL 32401, Res. (800)
424-4777 Ph: (904) 785-2700
Fax: (904) 747-9168

Passport Inn $$
5003 West Highway 98,
Panama City, FL 32401, Res.
(800) 251-1962 Ph: (904)
769-2101 Fax: (904) 763-5875

Scottish Inns $$
4907 West US 98, Panama
City, FL 32401, Res. (800)
251-1962 Ph: (904) 769-2432
Fax: (904) 769-2432

Super 8 Motel $-$$
207 N. Highway 231, Panama
City, FL 32405-4701, Res.
(800) 800-8000 Ph: (904)
784-1988 Fax: (904) 784-1988

PANAMA CITY BEACH   FL

Red Carpet Inn $$
10811 Front Beach Rd.,
Panama City Beach, FL
32407, Res. (800) 251-1962
Ph: (904) 234-2811 Fax: (904)
233-6698

PENSACOLA   F

Econo Lodge $-$
7194 Pensacola Blvd.,
Pensacola, FL 32503, Res.
(800) 424-4777 Ph: (904)
479-8600

Motel 6
7226 Plantation Rd,
Pensacola, FL 32504, Res.
(800) 466-8356 Ph: 904
474-1060 Fax: 904 476-5104

Motel 6
7827 N Davis Hwy,
Pensacola, FL 32514, Res.
(800) 466-8356 Ph: 904
476-5386 Fax: 904 476-7458

Motel 6
5829 Pensacola Blvd,
Pensacola, FL 32505, Res.
(800) 466-8356 Ph: 904
477-7522 Fax: 904 476-7126

Red Carpet Inn $$
4448 Mobile Highway,
Pensacola, FL 32506, Res.
(800) 251-1962 Ph: (904)
456-7411 Fax: (904) 453-9645

Super 8 Motel $-$$
7220 Plantation Road,
Pensacola, FL 32504-6334,
Res. (800) 800-8000 Ph: (904)
476-8038 Fax: (904) 474-6284

POMPANO BEACH   F

Motel 6 $
1201 NW 31st Ave, Pompano
Beach, FL 33069, Res. (800)
466-8356 Ph: 954 977-8011
Fax: 954 972-0814

PORT CHARLOTTE   FL

Econo Lodge $-$$
4100 Tamiami Trail, Port
Charlotte, FL 33952, Res.
(800) 424-4777 Ph: (813)
743-2442 Fax: (813) 743-6376

PUNTA GORDA   FL

Motel 6 $
9300 Knights Dr, Punta
Gorda, FL 33950, Res. (800)
466-8356 Ph: 941 639-9585
Fax: 941 639-6820

RIVIERA BEACH   FL

Motel 6 $
3651 W Blue Heron Blvd,
Riviera Beach, FL 33404,
Res. (800) 466-8356 Ph: 561
863-1011 Fax: 561 842-1905

Super 8 Motel $-$$
4112 West Blue Heron
Boulevard, Riviera Beach, FL
33404, Res. (800) 800-8000
Ph: (407) 848-1188 Fax: (407)
848-4583

SAINT AUGUSTINE   FL

Econo Lodge $-$$
311 A1A Beach Blvd., Saint
Augustine, FL 32084, Res.
(800) 424-4777 Ph: (904)
471-2330 Fax: (904) 829-2090

Econo Lodge $-$$
2535 SR 16, Saint
Augustine, FL 32092, Res.
(800) 424-4777 Ph: (904)
829-5643 Fax: (904) 829-2090

SANFORD   **FL**

Super 8 Motel $-$$
4750 State Rd. 46 West,
Sanford, FL 32771-9220,
Res. (800) 800-8000 Ph: (407)
323-3445 Fax: (407) 323-3445

SARASOTA   **FL**

Thriftlodge $-$$
270 North Tamiami Trail,
Sarasota, FL 34236, Res.
(800) 525-9055 Ph: (813)
366-0414 Fax: (813) 954-3379

SILVER SPRINGS   **FL**

Econo Lodge $-$$
5331 NE Silver Springs Blvd.,
SILVER SPRINGS, FL 32688,
Res. (800) 424-4777 Ph: (904)
236-2383 Fax: (904) 236-5280

Villager $-$$
5131 E. Silver Springs Blvd,
Silver Springs, FL 34488,
Res. (800) 328-7829 Ph: (352)
236-2501 Fax: (352) 236-2046

ST. AUGUSTINE   **FL**

Red Carpet Inn $$
3101 Ponce de Leon Blvd., St.
Augustine, FL 32084, Res.
(800) 251-1962 Ph: (904)
829-3461 Fax: (904) 824-1509

Scottish Inns $$
2580 State Rd 16, St.
Augustine, FL 32092, Res.
(800) 251-1962 Ph: (904)
824-4436 Fax: (904) 823-9963

Scottish Inns $$
427 Anastasia Blvd., St.
Augustine, FL 32084, Res.
(800) 251-1962 Ph: (904)
824-5055 Fax: (904) 826-1794

Scottish Inns $$
110 San Marco Avenue, St.
Augustine, FL 32084, Res.
(800) 251-1962 Ph: (904)
824-2871 Fax: (904) 826-4149

Super 8 Motel $-$$
3552 N. Ponce de Leon Blvd.,
St. Augustine, FL 32084,
Res. (800) 800-8000 Ph: (904)
824-6399

TALLAHASSEE   **FL**

Econo Lodge North $-$$
2681 N. Monroe St.,
Tallahassee, FL 32303, Res.
(800) 424-4777 Ph: (904)
385-6155 Fax: (904) 385-6155

Motel 6 $
1027 Apalachee Pkwy,
Tallahassee, FL 32301, Res.
(800) 466-8356 Ph: 904
877-6171 Fax: 904 656-6120

Motel 6 $
1481 Timberlane Rd,
Tallahassee, FL 32312, Res.
(800) 466-8356 Ph: 904
668-2600 Fax: 904 894-3104

Motel 6 $
2738 N Monroe St,
Tallahassee, FL 32303, Res.
(800) 466-8356 Ph: 904
386-7878 Fax: 904 385-5616

Super 8 Motel $-$$
2702 N. Monroe St.,
Tallahassee, FL 32303, Res.
(800) 800-8000 Ph: (904)
386-8818 Fax: (904) 385-9583

TAMPA   **FL**

Budget Host Tampa Motel $-$$
3110 W Hillsboro Ave,
Tampa, FL 33614, Res. (800)
283-4678 Ph: (813) 786-8673
Fax: (813) 875-2928

Econo Lodge At Busch $-$$
1701 E. Busch Blvd., Tampa,
FL 33612, Res. (800)
424-4777 Ph: (813) 933-7681
Fax: (813) 935-3301

Econo Lodge East $-$$
2905 N. 50th St., Tampa, FL
33619, Res. (800) 424-4777
Ph: (813) 621-3541 Fax: (813)
626-9108

Econo Lodge Midtown $-$$
1020 S. Dale Mabry, Tampa,
FL 33629, Res. (800)
424-4777 Ph: (813) 254-3005
Fax: (813) 253-2909

Economy Inns Of America$-$$
6606 Dr. Martin Luther King
Blvd. E., Tampa, FL 33619,
Res. (800) 826-0778 Ph: (813)
623-6667

Motel 6 $
333 E Fowler Ave, Tampa, FL
33612, Res. (800) 466-8356
Ph: 813 932-4948 Fax: 813
931-4577

Motel 6 $
6510 N Hwy 301, Tampa, FL
33610, Res. (800) 466-8356
Ph: 813 628-0888 Fax: 813
620-4899

VENICE   **FL**

Motel 6 $
281 US Hwy 41 Bypass North,
Venice, FL 34292, Res. (800)
466-8356 Ph: 941 485-8255
Fax: 941 488-3005

VERO BEACH   **FL**

Super 8 Motel $-$$
8800 20th Street, Vero
Beach, FL 32966, Res. (800)
800-8000 Ph: (407) 562-9996
Fax: (407) 562-0716

WEST PALM BEACH   **FL**

Economy Inns Of America$$
4123 North Lake Blvd., West
Palm Beach, FL 33407, Res.
(800) 826-0778 Ph: (407)
626-4918

WILDWOOD   **FL**

Super 8 Motel $-$$
344 E. SR 44, Wildwood, FL
34785, Res. (800) 800-8000
Ph: (904) 748-3783 Fax: (904)
748-5401

WINTER GARDEN   **FL**

Super 8 Motel $-$$
13603 W. Colonial Drive,
Winter Garden, FL 34787,
Res. (800) 800-8000 Ph: (407)
654-2020 Fax: (407) 654-0140

WINTER HAVEN   **FL**

Budget Host Driftwood $-$$
970 Cypress Gardens Blvd,
Winter Haven, FL 33880,
Res. (800) 283-4678 Ph: (813)
294-4229 Fax: (813) 293-2089

GEORGIA

ACWORTH   **GA**

Super 8 Motel $-$$
4980 Cowan Rd., Acworth,
GA 30101, Res. (800)
800-8000 Ph: (404) 966-9700
Fax: (770) 974-7292

ADEL   **GA**

Econo Lodge $-$$
1102 W. 4th St. / I-75 Exit 10,
Adel, GA 31620, Res. (800)
424-4777 Ph: (912) 896-4523
Fax: (912) 896-4710

Scottish Inns $
911 West 4th Street, Adel,
GA 31620, Res. (800)
251-1962 Ph: (912) 896-2259
Fax: (912) 896-4032

Super 8 Motel $-$$
1102 W. 4th St., Adel, GA
31620, Res. (800) 800-8000
Ph: (912) 896-4523 Fax: (912)
896-4710

ALBANY   **GA**

Econo Lodge $-$$
1806 E. Oglethorpe Blvd.,
Albany, GA 31705, Res.
(800) 424-4777 Ph: (912)
883-5544

Motel 6 $
201 S Thornton Dr, Albany,
GA 31705, Res. (800)
466-8356 Ph: 912 439-0078
Fax: 912 439-1153

Super 8 Motel $-$$
2444 N. Slappey Blvd.,
Albany, GA 31702, Res.
(800) 800-8000 Ph: (912)
888-8388 Fax: (912) 888-8388

**M
O
T
E
L**

ASHBURN   GA

Super 8 Motel $-$$
332 E. Madison Ave.,
Ashburn, GA 31714, Res.
(800) 800-8000 Ph: (912)
567-4688 Fax: (912) 567-0248

ATHENS   GA

Downtowner Motor Inn $$
1198 South Milledge Avenue,
Athens, GA 30605, Res.
(800) 251-1962 Ph: (706)
549-2626 Fax: (706) 613-2520

Econo Lodge $-$$
2715 Atlanta Hwy., Athens,
GA 30606, Res. (800)
424-4777 Ph: (706) 549-1530
Fax: (706) 353-8114

Super 8 Motel $-$$
3425 Atlanta Highway,
Athens, GA 30606, Res.
(800) 800-8000 Ph: (706)
549-0251

ATLANTA   GA

Econo Lodge $-$$
1360 Virginia Ave., Atlanta,
GA 30344, Res. (800)
424-4777 Ph: (404) 761-5201
Fax: (404) 763-9534

Economy Inns Of America$-$$
3092 Presidential Parkway,
Atlanta, GA 30340, Res.
(800) 826-0778 Ph: (404)
454-8373

Motel 6 $
3585 Chamblee-Tucker Rd,
Atlanta, GA 30341, Res.
(800) 466-8356 Ph: 770
455-8000 Fax: 770 936-8479

Super 8 Motel $-$$
301 Fulton Industrial Circle,
Atlanta, GA 30336, Res.
(800) 800-8000 Ph: (404)
696-9713 Fax: (404) 696-9713

Villager $-$$
144 14th Street, Atlanta, GA
30318, Res. (800) 328-7829
Ph: (404) 873-4171 Fax: (404)
873-4176

AUGUSTA   GA

Econo Lodge Fort Gordon$-$$
2051 Gordon Hwy., Augusta,
GA 30909, Res. (800)
424-4777 Ph: (706) 738-6565
Fax: (706) 738-6565

Econo Lodge Martinez $-$$
4090 Belair Rd., Augusta,
GA 30909, Res. (800)
424-4777 Ph: (706) 863-0777
Fax: (706) 860-1562

Econo Lodge West $-$$
2852 Washington Rd.,
Augusta, GA 30909, Res.
(800) 424-4777 Ph: (706)
736-0707 Fax: (706) 737-5326

Motel 6 $
2650 Center W Pkwy,
Augusta, GA 30909, Res.
(800) 466-8356 Ph: 706
736-1934 Fax: 706 737-8628

Red Carpet Inn $$
1455 Walton Way, Augusta,
GA 30901, Res. (800)
251-1962 Ph: (706) 722-2224
Fax: (706) 722-4214

Scottish Inns $$
1636 Gordon Highway,
Augusta, GA 30906, Res.
(800) 251-1962 Ph: (706)
790-1380

Scottish Inns $$
1079 Stevens Creek Rd,
Augusta, GA 30907, Res.
(800) 251-1962 Ph: (706)
737-8121 Fax: (706) 737-8121

Super 8 Motel $-$$
2137 Gordon Hwy., Augusta,
GA 30906, Res. (800)
800-8000 Ph: (706) 738-5018
Fax: (706) 738-5018

Super 8 Motel $-$$
954 Fifth Street, Augusta,
GA 30901, Res. (800)
800-8000 Ph: (706) 724-0757
Fax: (706) 722-7233

BAXLEY   GA

Budget Host Western Motel$-$$
714 E Parker Rd--Rt 6, Box 4,
Baxley, GA 31513, Res. (800)
283-4678 Ph: (912) 367-2200
Fax: (912) 367-2200

Scottish Inns $
1179 Hatch Parkeway So,
Baxley, GA 31513, Res. (800)
251-1962 Ph: (912) 367-3652
Fax: (912) 367-3652

BRUNSWICK   GA

Motel 6 $
403 Butler Dr, Brunswick,
GA 31525, Res. (800)
466-8356 Ph: 912 264-8582
Fax: 912 264-6028

Super 8 Motel $-$$
472 Jesup Highway,
Brunswick, GA 31520-1216,
Res. (800) 800-8000 Ph: (912)
264-8800 Fax: (912) 265-0244

BRYON   GA

Passport Inn $
605 Chapman Rd., Bryon,
GA 31008, Res. (800)
251-1962 Ph: (912) 946-5200
Fax: (912) 956-2245

Red Carpet Inn $
I-75 & 247 Connector, exit 45,
Bryon, GA 31008, Res. (800)
251-1962 Ph: (912) 956-3800

BYRON   GA

Econo Lodge $-$$
I-75 Exit 46, Byron, GA
31008, Res. (800) 424-4777
Ph: (912) 956-5600 Fax: (000)
009-1256

Super 8 Motel $-$$
Exit 46 on GA State Route
49, Byron, GA 31008, Res.
(800) 800-8000 Ph: (912)
956-3311

CALHOUN   GA

Budget Host Shepherd Motel$$
P.O. Box 2407, Calhoun, GA
30701, Res. (800) 283-4678
Ph: (706) 629-8644

Econo Lodge $-$$
1438 US 41, Calhoun, GA
30701, Res. (800) 424-4777
Ph: (706) 625-5421 Fax: (706)
625-9309

Scottish Inns $
1510 Red Bud Rd., N.E.,
Calhoun, GA 30701, Res.
(800) 251-1962 Ph: (706)
629-8261 Fax: (706) 629-7693

Super 8 Motel $-$$
1446 U.S. Highway 41 North,
Calhoun, GA 30701, Res.
(800) 800-8000 Ph: (706)
602-1400 Fax: (706) 602-1906

CARTERSVILLE   GA

Budget Host Inn $-$$
851 Cass-White Rd,
Cartersville, GA 30120, Res.
(800) 283-4678 Ph: (404)
386-0350 Fax: (404) 386-0350

Econo Lodge $-$$
I-75 N. at Exit 125,
Cartersville, GA 30120, Res.
(800) 424-4777 Ph: (404)
386-3303

Econo Lodge $-$$
White-Cassville Rd.,
Cartersville, GA 30120, Res.
(800) 424-4777 Ph: (404)
386-0700

Motel 6 $
5657 Hwy 20 NE, Cartersville,
GA 30121, Res. (800)
466-8356 Ph: 770 386-1449
Fax: 770 387-0651

Red Carpet Inn $
851 Cass-White Rd.,
Cartersville, GA 30121, Res.
(800) 251-1962 Ph: (770)
382-8000 Fax: (770) 386-0350

Super 8 Motel $-$$
Route 294 & Route 20,
Cartersville, GA 30120, Res.
(800) 800-8000 Ph: (404)
382-8881 Fax: (404) 382-8881

CHATSWORTH   GA

Scottish Inns $
1279 Highway 411 South,
Chatsworth, GA 30705, Res.
(800) 251-1962 Ph: (706)
695-6894 Fax: (706) 517-5974

CHULA   GA

Red Carpet Inn $
I-75 & Chula Brookfield Rd.,
Chula, GA 31733, Res. (800)
251-1962 Ph: (912) 382-2686

COLLEGE PARK   GA

Super 8 Motel $-$$
2010 Sullivan Rd., College
Park, GA 30337, Res. (800)
800-8000 Ph: (404) 991-8985
Fax: (404) 991-8985

COLUMBUS   GA

Econo Lodge Ft. Benning$-$$
4483 Victory Dr., Columbus,
GA 31903, Res. (800)
424-4777 Ph: (706) 682-3803

Motel 6 $
3050 Victory Dr, Columbus,
GA 31903, Res. (800)
466-8356 Ph: 706 687-7214
Fax: 706 682-2362

Super 8 Motel $-$$
2935 Warm Springs Road,
Columbus, GA 31909-5248,
Res. (800) 800-8000 Ph: (706)
322-6580 Fax: (706) 324-2553

CORDELE   GA

Econo Lodge $-$$
1618 E. 16th Ave., Cordele,
GA 31015, Res. (800)
424-4777 Ph: (912) 273-2456
Fax: (912) 273-3151

Passport Inn $
1602 East 16th Avenue,
Cordele, GA 31015, Res.
(800) 251-1962 Ph: (912)
273-4088 Fax: (912) 273-8399

Super 8 Motel $-$$
I-75 and Farmers Market
Road, Cordele, GA 31015,
Res. (800) 800-8000 Ph: (912)
276-1008 Fax: (912) 276-0222

COVINGTON   GA

Econo Lodge $-$$
10101 Alcovy Jersey,
Covington, GA 30209, Res.
(800) 424-4777 Ph: (404)
786-4133 Fax: (404) 784-9307

DAHLONEGA   GA

Econo Lodge $-$$
801 N. Grove St., Dahlonega,
GA 30533, Res. (800)
424-4777 Ph: (706) 864-6191
Fax: (706) 864-6191

DALTON   GA

Motel 6 $
2200 Chattanooga Rd,
Dalton, GA 30720, Res.
(800) 466-8356 Ph: 706
278-5522 Fax: 706 278-9378

Super 8 Motel $-$$
"I-75, Exit 135", Dalton, GA
30720, Res. (800) 800-8000
Ph: (706) 277-9323 Fax: (706)
277-9323

DARIEN   GA

Super 8 Motel $-$$
I-95 at exit 10, Darien, GA
31533, Res. (800) 800-8000
Ph: (912) 437-6660 Fax: (912)
437-6660

DECATUR   GA

Econo Lodge $-$$
2574 Candler Rd., Decatur,
GA 30032, Res. (800)
424-4777 Ph: (404) 243-4422

Motel 6 $
2565 Wesley Chapel Rd,
Decatur, GA 30035, Res.
(800) 466-8356 Ph: 404
288-6911 Fax: 404 284-1068

Villager $-$$
2942 Ember Drive, Decatur,
GA 30034, Res. (800)
328-7829 Ph: (404) 241-8770
Fax: (000) 000-0000

DOUGLAS   GA

Super 8 Motel $-$$
1610 S. Peterson Ave.,
Douglas, GA 31533, Res.
(800) 800-8000 Ph: (912)
384-0886 Fax: (912) 384-0886

ELLIJAY   GA

Budget Host Top-o-ellijay$-$$
10 Jeff Davis Dr, Ellijay, GA
30540, Res. (800) 283-4678
Ph: (706) 635-5311 Fax: (706)
635-5313

FOREST PARK   GA

Super 8 Motel $-$$
410 Old Dixie Way, Forest
Park, GA 30050, Res. (800)
800-8000 Ph: (404) 363-8811
Fax: (404) 361-1789

FORSYTH   GA

Super 8 Motel $-$$
Interstate 75 and Highway
42, Forsyth, GA 31029, Res.
(800) 800-8000 Ph: (912)
994-9333

GRIFFIN   GA

Scottish Inns $
1709 North Expressway,
Griffin, GA 30223, Res. (800)
25101962 Ph: (770) 228-6000
Fax: (770) 412-7373

JONESBORO   GA

Scottish Inns $$
599 Battle Creek Rd,
Jonesboro, GA 30236, Res.
(800) 251-1962 Ph: (770)
603-7300 Fax: (770) 603-7300

KINGSLAND   GA

Super 8 Motel $-$$
PO Box 2247, I-95 & Hwy 40,
Kingsland, GA 31548, Res.
(800) 800-8000 Ph: (912)
729-6888 Fax: (912) 729-6888

LA GRANGE   GA

Super 8 Motel $-$$
29 Patillo Rd., La Grange, GA
30240, Res. (800) 800-8000
Ph: (706) 845-9093 Fax: (706)
845-9060

LOCUST GROVE   GA

Red Carpet Inn $
4829 Hampton Rd., Locust
Grove, GA 30248, Res. (800)
251-1962 Ph: (770) 957-2601
Fax: (770) 957-7014

Scottish Inns $
4679 Hampton Rd, Locust
Grove, GA 30248, Res. (800)
251-1962 Ph: (770) 957-9001
Fax: (770) 957-7857

Super 8 Motel $-$$
4605 Hampton Road, P.O.
Box 613, Locust Grove, GA
30248, Res. (800) 800-8000
Ph: (404) 957-2936 Fax: (404)
957-7014

MACON   GA

Econo Lodge $-$$
4951 Romeiser Dr. / at I-475
& US 80, Macon, GA 31206,
Res. (800) 424-4777 Ph: (912)
474-1661 Fax: (000) 912-7440

Motel 6 $
4991 Harrison Rd, Macon,
GA 31206, Res. (800)
466-8356 Ph: 912 474-2870
Fax: 912 477-4889

Passport Inn $
5022 Romeiser Dr, Macon,
GA 31206, Res. (800)
251-9162 Ph: (912) 474-2665
Fax: (912) 474-2402

Red Carpet Inn $
4604 Chambers Rd., Macon,
GA 31206, Res. (800)
25101962 Ph: (912) 781-2810
Fax: (912) 781-4782

Super 8 Motel $-$$
6007 Harrison Road, Macon,
GA 31206, Res. (800)
800-8000 Ph: (912) 788-8800

MADISON   GA

Econo Lodge $-$$
2080 Eatonton Rd., Madison,
GA 30650, Res. (800)
424-4777 Ph: (706) 342-3433

Super 8 Motel $-$$
2091 Eatonton Road,
Madison, GA 30650, Res.
(800) 800-8000 Ph: (706)
342-7800 Fax: (706) 342-3795

M O T E L

MARIETTA   GA

Economy Motels Of America
2682 Windy Hill Road,
Marietta, GA 30067, Res.
(800) 826-0778 Ph: (404)
951-2005

Motel 6 $
2360 Delk Rd, Marietta, GA
30067, Res. (800) 466-8356
Ph: 770 952-8161 Fax: 770
984-2307

Scottish Inns $$
2390 Delk Rd., Marietta, GA
30067, Res. (800) 251-1962
Ph: (404) 952-3365 Fax: (404)
952-7340

Super 8 Motel $-$$
2500 Delk Road, Marietta,
GA 30067, Res. (800)
800-8000 Ph: (404) 984-1570
Fax: (404) 933-9382

MCDONOUGH   GA

Red Carpet Inn $
1170 Hampton Rd.,
McDonough, GA 30253,
Res. (800) 251-1962 Ph: (770)
957-2458 Fax: (770) 957-8941

MILLEDGEVILLE   GA

Scottish Inns $
2474 North Columbia St.,
N.W. , Milledgeville, GA
31061, Res. (800) 251-1962
Ph: (912) 453-9491 Fax: (912)
453-1099

NORCROSS   GA

Motel 6 $
6015 Oakbrook Pkwy,
Norcross, GA 30093, Res.
(800) 466-8356 Ph: 770
446-2311 Fax: 770 246-1769

Villager $-$$
5122 Brook Hollow Pkwy,
Norcross, GA 30071, Res.
(800) 328-7829 Ph: (770)
446-5490 Fax: (770) 449-7676

PERRY   GA

Econo Lodge $-$$
624 Valley Dr., Perry, GA
31069, Res. (800) 424-4777
Ph: (912) 987-2585 Fax: (912)
987-4314

Red Carpet Inn $
105 Carrol Blvd., Perry, GA
31069, Res. (800) 251-1962
Ph: (912) 987-2200

Scottish Inns $
1519 Sam Nunn Blvd., Perry,
GA 31069, Res. (800)
251-1962 Ph: (912) 987-9709
Fax: (912) 987-5871

Scottish Inns $
106 General Couartney
Hodges Blvd., Perry, GA
31069, Res. (800) 251-1962
Ph: (912) 987-3622 Fax: (912)
987-0988

RICHMOND HILL   GA

Econo Lodge $-$$
I-95 & US 17 S., Exit 14,
Richmond Hill, GA 31324,
Res. (800) 424-4777 Ph: (912)
756-3312 Fax: (000) 009-1256

Motel 6 $
I-95 & US Hwy 17, Richmond
Hill, GA 31324, Res. (800)
466-8356 Ph: 912 756-3543
Fax: 912 756-3583

RICHMONG HILL   GA

Scottish Inns $$
I-95 @ US 17, Richmong Hill,
GA 31324, Res. (800)
251-1962 Ph: (912) 756-3861
Fax: (912) 756-5093

RINGGOLD   GA

Super 8 Motel $-$$
5400 Alabama Hwy, Ringgold,
GA 30736, Res. (800)
800-8000 Ph: (706) 965-7080
Fax: (706) 965-7130

RIVERDALE   GA

Red Carpet Inn $$
7618 Highway 85, Riverdale,
GA 30274, Res. (800)
251-1962 Ph: (770) 478-3600
Fax: (770) 603-9827

Scottish Inns $$
709 King Rd, Riverdale, GA
30274, Res. (800) 251-1962
Ph: (770) 907-3838 Fax: (770)
907-6114

ROME   GA

Scottish Inns $
1105 Martha Berry Blvd.,
Rome, GA 30165, Res. (800)
251-1962 Ph: (706) 295-5555
Fax: 706-234-3250

Super 8 Motel $-$$
1590 Dodd Blvd. SE, Rome,
GA 30161-6642, Res. (800)
800-8000 Ph: (706) 234-8182
Fax: (706) 290-0835

SAVANNAH   GA

Econo Lodge Gateway $-$$
7 Gateway Blvd. W.,
Savannah, GA 31419, Res.
(800) 424-4777 Ph: (912)
925-2280 Fax: (912) 925-1075

Econo Lodge Midtown $-$$
7500 Abercorn, Savannah,
GA 31406, Res. (800)
424-4777 Ph: (912) 352-1657
Fax: (009) 125-2157

Red Carpet Inn $$
1 Fort Argyle Rd., Savannah,
GA 31419, Res. (800)
251-1962 Ph: (912) 925-2640
Fax: (912) 925-7965

Scottish Inns $$
4005 Ogeechee Rd.,
Savannah, GA 31405, Res.
(800) 251-1962 Ph: (912)
236-8236 Fax: (912) 234-6733

Super 8 Motel $-$$
15 Fort Argyle Road,
Savannah, GA 31419, Res.
(800) 800-8000 Ph: (912)
927-8550

Villager $-$$
5711 Abercorn Street,
Savannah, GA 31405, Res.
(800) 328-7829 Ph: (912)
354-0434 Fax: (912) 351-0461

SPARKS   GA

Red Carpet Inn $
I-75, exit 12 at Barneyville Rd,
Sparks, GA 31647, Res.
(800) 251-1962 Ph: (912)
852-5200 Fax: (912) 852-5029

STOCKBRIDGE   GA

Motel 6 $
7233 Davidson Pkwy,
Stockbridge, GA 30281, Res.
(800) 466-8356 Ph: 770
389-1142 Fax: 770 507-8385

Super 8 Motel $-$$
1451 Hudson Bridge Road,
Stockbridge, GA 30281, Res.
(800) 800-8000 Ph: (404)
474-5758

THOMSON   GA

Econo Lodge $-$$
130 N. Seymour Dr.,
Thomson, GA 30824, Res.
(800) 424-4777 Ph: (706)
595-7144 Fax: (706) 595-1219

TIFTON   GA

Red Carpet Inn $
1025 West 2nd St., I-75, exit
19, Tifton, GA 31794, Res.
(800) 251-1962 Ph: (912)
382-0280 Fax: (912) 386-0316

Scottish Inns $
1409 Highway 82 West,
Tifton, GA 31794, Res. (800)
251-1962 Ph: (912) 386-2350
Fax: (912) 386-8673

Super 8 Motel $-$$
Interstate 75 & W. 2nd St.,
P.O. Box 47, Tifton, GA
31793, Res. (800) 800-8000
Ph: (912) 382-9500 Fax: (912)
382-6060

TUCKER   GA

Econo Lodge Stone $-$$
1820 Mountain Ind. Blvd.,
Tucker, GA 30084, Res.
(800) 424-4777 Ph: (404)
939-8440

Economy Inns Of America $-$$
1435 Montreal Road, Tucker,
GA 30084, Res. (800)
826-0778 Ph: (404) 938-3552

TYBEE ISLAND   GA

Econo Lodge $-$$
US 80 E., Tybee Island, GA
31328, Res. (800) 424-4777
Ph: (912) 786-4535 Fax: (912)
786-5657

UNADILLA   GA

Passport Inn $
I-75, exit 39, Unadilla, GA
31091, Res. (800) 251-1962
Ph: (912) 627-3258

Red Carpet Inn $
101 Robert St., I-75, exit 40,
Unadilla, GA 31091, Res.
(800) 251-1962 Ph: (912)
627-3261

Scottish Inns $
I-75, exit 39, Unadilla, GA
31091, Res. (800) 251-1962
Ph: (912) 627-3228 Fax: (912)
627-3594

UNION CITY   GA

Econo Lodge $-$$
7410 Oakley Rd., Union City,
GA 30291, Res. (800)
424-4777 Ph: (404) 964-9999

VALDOSTA   GA

Motel 6 $
2003 W Hill Ave., Valdosta,
GA 31601, Res. (800)
466-8356 Ph: 912 333-0047
Fax: 912 241-0998

Scottish Inns $
1114 St. Augustine Rd.,
Valdosta, GA 31601, Res.
(800) 251-1962 Ph: (912)
244-7900 Fax: (912) 247-9362

Villager $-$$
3570 Madison Highway,
Valdosta, GA 31601, Res.
(800) 328-7829 Ph: (912)
242-4664 Fax: (912) 242-0543

Villager $-$$
2110 West Hill Ave.,
Valdosta, GA 31603, Res.
(800) 328-7829 Ph: (912)
247-2440 Fax: (912) 244-7661

VIDALIA   GA

Scottish Inns $
705 Reese First St., Vidalia,
GA 30474, Res. (800)
251-1962 Ph: (912) 537-7611
Fax: (912) 538-0753

VILLA RICA   GA

Super 8 Motel $-$$
195 Highway 61 Connector,
Villa Rica, GA 30180, Res.
(800) 800-8000 Ph: (404)
459-8888 Fax: (404) 459-1211

WARNER ROBINS   GA

Super 8 Motel $-$$
105 Woodcrest Bovd.,
Warner Robins, GA
31093-8825, Res. (800)
800-8000 Ph: (912) 923-8600
Fax: (912) 922-3451

WAYCROSS   GA

Red Carpet Inn $
1740 Memorial Drive,
Waycross, GA 31501, Res.
(800) 251-1962 Ph: (912)
283-6134 Fax: (912) 283-8537

WHITE   GA

Scottish Inns $
2385 Highway 411, NE,
White, GA 30184, Res. (800)
251-1962 Ph: (770) 382-7011
Fax: (770) 382-4021

IDAHO

BOISE   ID

Motel 6 $
2323 Airport Way, Boise, ID
83705, Res. (800) 466-8356
Ph: 208 344-3506 Fax: 208
344-6264

Super 8 Motel $-$$
2773 Elder Street, Boise, ID
83705, Res. (800) 800-8000
Ph: (208) 344-8871 Fax: (208)
336-3237

COEUR D'ALENE   ID

Motel 6 $
416 Appleway, Coeur
D'Alene, ID 83814, Res.
(800) 466-8356 Ph: 208
664-6600 Fax: 208 667-9446

Super 8 Motel $-$$
505 West Appleway, Coeur
D'Alene, ID 83814, Res.
(800) 800-8000 Ph: (208)
765-8888 Fax: (208) 765-6156

DRIGGS   ID

Super 8 Motel $-$$
133 State Highway 33,
Driggs, ID 83422, Res. (800)
800-8000 Ph: (208) 354-8888
Fax: (208) 354-2962

IDAHO FALLS   ID

Motel 6 $
1448 W Broadway, Idaho
Falls, ID 83402, Res. (800)
466-8356 Ph: 208 522-0112
Fax: 208 522-7804

Super 8 Motel $-$$
705 Lindsay Blvd., Idaho
Falls, ID 83402-1821, Res.
(800) 800-8000 Ph: (208)
522-8880 Fax: (208) 522-0590

KELLOGG   ID

Super 8 Motel $-$$
611 Bunker Avenue, Kellogg,
ID 83837, Res. (800)
800-8000 Ph: (208) 783-1234
Fax: (208) 784-0461

LEWISTON   ID

Super 8 Motel $-$$
3120 North South Highway,
Lewiston, ID 83501, Res.
(800) 800-8000 Ph: (208)
743-8808 Fax: (208) 743-8808

MOSCOW   ID

Super 8 Motel $-$$
175 Peterson Dr., Moscow,
ID 83843, Res. (800)
800-8000 Ph: (208) 883-1503
Fax: (208) 883-4769

NAMPA   ID

Super 8 Motel $-$$
624 Nampa Blvd., Nampa, ID
83687, Res. (800) 800-8000
Ph: (208) 467-2888 Fax: (208)
467-2888

POCATELLO   ID

Motel 6 $
291 W Burnside Ave,
Pocatello, ID 83202, Res.
(800) 466-8356 Ph: 208
237-7880 Fax: 208 237-3115

Super 8 Motel $-$$
1330 Bench Rd., Pocatello, ID
83201, Res. (800) 800-8000
Ph: (208) 234-0888 Fax: (208)
232-0347

REXBURG   ID

Super 8 Motel $-$$
215 W. Main Street, Rexburg,
ID 83440, Res. (800)
800-8000 Ph: (208) 356-8888
Fax: (208) 356-8896

SANDPOINT   ID

Super 8 Motel $-$$
3245 Hwy. 95 North,
Sandpoint, ID 83864, Res.
(800) 800-8000 Ph: (208)
263-2210 Fax: (208) 263-2210

TWIN FALLS   ID

Econo Lodge $-$$
320 Main Ave. S., Twin Falls,
ID 83301, Res. (800)
424-4777 Ph: (208) 733-8770
Fax: (208) 734-7206

Motel 6 $
1472 Blue Lake Blvd N, Twin
Falls, ID 83301, Res. (800)
466-8356 Ph: 208 734-3993
Fax: 208 736-7368

Super 8 Motel $-$$
1260 Blue Lakes Blvd., Twin
Falls, ID 83301, Res. (800)
800-8000 Ph: (208) 734-5801
Fax: (208) 734-7556

ILLINOIS

ALTAMONT   IL

Super 8 Motel $-$$
RR 2 Box 296, Altamont, IL
62411, Res. (800) 800-8000
Ph: (618) 483-6300

ALTON   IL

Super 8 Motel $-$$
1800 Homer Adams Parkway,
Alton, IL 62002, Res. (800)
800-8000 Ph: (618) 465-8885
Fax: (618) 465-8964

ARCOLA   IL

Budget Host Arcola Inn $-$$
236 S Jacques St, Arcola, IL
61910, Res. (800) 283-4678
Ph: (217) 268-4971 Fax: (217)
268-3525

**M
O
T
E
L**

ARLINGTON HEIGHTS IL	**CHARLESTON** IL	**DWIGHT** IL
Motel 6 $	**Econo Lodge** $-$$	**Super 8 Motel** $-$$
441 W Algonquin Rd, Arlington Heights, IL 60005, Res. (800) 466-8356 Ph: 847 806-1230 Fax: 847 364-7413	810 W. Lincoln Hwy., Charleston, IL 61920, Res. (800) 424-4777 Ph: (217) 345-7689 Fax: (217) 345-7697	"I-55 & Highway 47, Exit #220", Dwight, IL 60420, Res. (800) 800-8000 Ph: (815) 584-1888 Fax: (815) 584-1888
AURORA IL	**CHICAGO** IL	**E HAZELCREST** IL
Motel 6 $	**Motel 6** $	**Motel 6** $
2380 N Farnsworth Ave<EL>& E-W Tlwy, Aurora, IL 60504, Res. (800) 466-8356 Ph: 630 851-3600 Fax: 630 978-1564	162 E Ontario St, Chicago, IL 60611, Res. (800) 466-8356 Ph: 312 787-3580 Fax: 312 787-1299	17214 Halsted St, E Hazelcrest, IL 60429, Res. (800) 466-8356 Ph: 708 957-9233 Fax: 708 922-0610
Super 8 Motel $-$$	**COLLINSVILLE** IL	**EAST MOLINE** IL
311 South Lincolnway, Aurora, IL 60542, Res. (800) 800-8000 Ph: (708) 896-0801 Fax: (708) 896-0801	**Motel 6** $ 295-A N Bluff Rd, Collinsville, IL 62234, Res. (800) 466-8356 Ph: 618 345-2100 Fax: 618 345-9160	**Super 8 Motel** $-$$ 2201 John Deere Expwy, "RR2, Box 286C", East Moline, IL 61244-9109, Res. (800) 800-8000 Ph: (309) 796-1999 Fax: (309) 796-1999
BEARDSTOWN IL		
Super 8 Motel $-$$	**Super 8 Motel** $-$$	**EAST PEORIA** IL
Hwy 678 & Hwy 100, Beardstown, IL 62618, Res. (800) 800-8000 Ph: (217) 323-5858	2 Gateway Drive, Collinsville, IL 62234, Res. (800) 800-8000 Ph: (618) 345-8008 Fax: (618) 344-7062	**Budget Host Inn** $-$$ 300 N Main St, East Peoria, IL 61611, Res. (800) 283-4678 Ph: (309) 694-4261 Fax: (309) 694-0309
BLOOMINGTON IL	**CRYSTAL LAKE** IL	
Super 8 Motel $-$$	**Super 8 Motel** $-$$	**Motel 6** $
818 IAA Drive, Bloomington, IL 61701, Res. (800) 800-8000 Ph: (309) 663-2388 Fax: (309) 663-2388	577 Crystal Point Drive, Crystal Lake, IL 60014, Res. (800) 800-8000 Ph: (815) 455-2388 Fax: (815) 455-2388	104 W Camp St, East Peoria, IL 61611, Res. (800) 466-8356 Ph: 309 699-7281 Fax: 309 694-7636
BOURBONNAIS IL	**DANVILLE** IL	**Super 8 Motel** $-$$
Motel 6 $	**Super 8 Motel** $-$$	725 Taylor Street, at E. Washington Street, East Peoria, IL 61611, Res. (800) 800-8000 Ph: (309) 698-8889 Fax: (309) 698-8885
IL Rt 50 and Armour Rd, Bourbonnais, IL 60914, Res. (800) 466-8356 Ph: 815 933-2300 Fax: 815 933-7485	377 Lynch Dr., Danville, IL 61832, Res. (800) 800-8000 Ph: (217) 443-4499 Fax: (217) 443-4499	
Super 8 Motel $-$$	**DECATUR** IL	**EFFINGHAM** IL
1390 Lock Drive, Bourbonnais, IL 60914, Res. (800) 800-8000 Ph: (815) 939-7888 Fax: (815) 939-7888	**Red Carpet Inn** $$ 3035 North Water St., Decatur, IL 62526, Res. (800) 251-1962 Ph: (217) 877-3380 Fax: (217) 877-3380	**Budget Host Lincoln Lodge** $-$$ I-57 & 70, Ext 162-Box 634, Effingham, IL 62401, Res. (800) 283-4678 Ph: (217) 342-4133 Fax: (217) 342-4133
BRIDGEVIEW IL		
Super 8 Motel $-$$	**Super 8 Motel** $-$$	**Econo Lodge** $-$$
7887 West 79th St., Bridgeview, IL 60455, Res. (800) 800-8000 Ph: (708) 458-8008 Fax: (708) 458-9248	3141 North Water Street, Decatur, IL 62526-2472, Res. (800) 800-8000 Ph: (217) 877-8888 Fax: (217) 877-8888	1205 N. Keller Dr., Effingham, IL 62401, Res. (800) 424-4777 Ph: (217) 347-7131 Fax: (217) 347-3363
CANTON IL	**DEKALB** IL	**Super 8 Motel** $-$$
Super 8 Motel $-$$	**Motel 6** $	1400 Thelma Keller Avenue, Effingham, IL 62401, Res. (800) 800-8000 Ph: (217) 342-6888 Fax: (217) 347-2863
2110 North Main Street, Canton, IL 61520, Res. (800) 800-8000 Ph: (309) 647-1888 Fax: (309) 647-1888	1116 W Lincoln Hwy, Dekalb, IL 60115, Res. (800) 466-8356 Ph: 815 756-3398 Fax: 815 756-1687	
CARBONDALE IL		**EL PASO** IL
Super 8 Motel $-$$	**Super 8 Motel** $-$$	**Super 8 Motel** $-$$
1180 East Main, Carbondale, IL 62901, Res. (800) 800-8000 Ph: (618) 457-8822 Fax: (618) 457-4186	800 West. Fairview Drive, DeKalb, IL 60115, Res. (800) 800-8000 Ph: (815) 748-4688 Fax: (815) 748-4688	880 West Main, El Paso, IL 61738, Res. (800) 800-8000 Ph: (309) 527-4949 Fax: (309) 527-7070
CHAMPAIGN IL	**DIXON** IL	**ELGIN** IL
Super 8 Motel $-$$	**Super 8 Motel** $-$$	**Super 8 Motel** $-$$
202 Marketview Drive, Champaign, IL 61820, Res. (800) 800-8000 Ph: (217) 359-2388 Fax: (217) 359-2388	1800 South Galena Avenue, Dixon, IL 61021, Res. (800) 800-8000 Ph: (815) 284-1800 Fax: (815) 284-1800	435 Airport Rd., Elgin, IL 60123, Res. (800) 800-8000 Ph: (708) 697-8828 Fax: (708) 697-8828

ELK GROVE VILLAGE   IL

Motel 6 $
1601 Oakton St, Elk Grove
Village, IL 60007, Res. (800)
466-8356 Ph: 847 981-9766
Fax: 847 364-6428

FAIRVIEW HTS.   IL

Super 8 Motel $-$$
45 Ludwig Drive, Fairview
Hts., IL 62208, Res. (800)
800-8000 Ph: (618) 398-8338
Fax: (618) 398-8158

FREEPORT   IL

Super 8 Motel $-$$
1649 Willard Dr., Freeport, IL
61032, Res. (800) 800-8000
Ph: (815) 232-8880 Fax: (815)
232-8907

GALESBURG   IL

Motel 6 $
1475 N Henderson St,
Galesburg, IL 61401, Res.
(800) 466-8356 Ph: 309
344-2401 Fax: 309 344-1960

Super 8 Motel $-$$
260 W. Main St., Galesburg,
IL 61401, Res. (800) 800-8000
Ph: (309) 342-5174 Fax: (309)
343-8237

GILMAN   IL

Budget Host Inn-gilman $-$$
723 S Crescent St, Gilman,
IL 60938, Res. (800) 283-4678
Ph: (815) 265-7261 Fax: 815)
265-7262

Super 8 Motel $-$$
1301 S. Crescent St.,
Gilman, IL 60938, Res. (800)
800-8000 Ph: (815) 265-7000
Fax: (815) 265-7000

GLENVIEW   IL

Motel 6 $
1535 Milwaukee Ave,
Glenview, IL 60025, Res.
(800) 466-8356 Ph: 847
390-7200 Fax: 847 390-0845

GREENVILLE   IL

Budget Host Inn $-$$
Rt 4 Box 183, Greenville, IL
62246, Res. (800) 283-4678
Ph: (618) 664-1950 Fax: (618)
664-1960

Super 8 Motel $-$$
I-70 & Rt 127, Greenville, IL
62246, Res. (800) 800-8000
Ph: (618) 664-0800

ILLINOIS   IL

Thriftlodge $-$$
7247 North Waukegan Rd.,
Illinois, IL 60648, Res. (800)
525-9055 Ph: (708) 647-9444
Fax: (708) 647-1913

JACKSONVILLE   IL

Motel 6 $
1716 W Morton Dr,
Jacksonville, IL 62650, Res.
(800) 466-8356 Ph: 217
243-7157 Fax: 217 243-1845

Super 8 Motel $-$$
1003 W. Morton Ave.,
Jacksonville, IL 62650, Res.
(800) 800-8000 Ph: (217)
479-0303

JOLIET   IL

Motel 6 $
3551 Mall Loop Dr, Joliet, IL
60431, Res. (800) 466-8356

Motel 6 $
1850 McDonough Rd, Joliet,
IL 60436, Res. (800) 466-8356
Ph: 815 729-2800 Fax: 815
729-9528

Super 8 Motel $-$$
1730 McDonough St, Joliet,
IL 60436, Res. (800) 800-8000
Ph: (815) 725-8855 Fax: (815)
725-8855

Super 8 Motel $-$$
3401 Mall Loop Drive, Joliet,
IL 60435, Res. (800) 800-8000
Ph: (815) 439-3838 Fax: (815)
439-3940

KEWANEE   IL

Super 8 Motel $-$$
US Hwy 34 and Route 78, 901
Tenney Street, Kewanee, IL
61443, Res. (800) 800-8000
Ph: (309) 853-8800 Fax: (309)
853-8800

LANSING   IL

Super 8 Motel $-$$
2151 Bernice Road, Lansing,
IL 60617, Res. (800) 800-8000
Ph: (708) 418-8884 Fax: (708)
418-8884

LE ROY   IL

Super 8 Motel $-$$
1 Demma Dr., Le Roy, IL
61752, Res. (800) 800-8000
Ph: (309) 962-4700 Fax: (309)
962-4700

LINCOLN   IL

Super 8 Motel $-$$
2800 Woodlawn Road,
Lincoln, IL 62656, Res. (800)
800-8000 Ph: (217) 287-7211
Fax: (217) 732-8886

LITCHFIELD   IL

Super 8 Motel $-$$
I-55 & IL Rte. 16, PO Box 281,
Litchfield, IL 62056, Res.
(800) 800-8000 Ph: (217)
324-7788 Fax: (217) 324-7789

LYONS   IL

Budget Host Chalet Motel $-$$
8640 W Ogden Ave, Lyons,
IL 60534, Res. (800) 283-4678
Ph: (708) 447-6363 Fax: (708)
447-8557

MACOMB   IL

Super 8 Motel $-$$
313 University Ave.,
Macomb, IL 61455, Res.
(800) 800-8000 Ph: (309)
836-8888 Fax: (309) 833-2646

MARION   IL

Motel 6 $
1008 Halfway Rd, Marion, IL
62959, Res. (800) 466-8356
Ph: 618 993-2631 Fax: 618
993-2719

Super 8 Motel $-$$
I-57 & Route 13, Marion, IL
62959, Res. (800) 800-8000
Ph: (618) 993-5577 Fax: (618)
997-6779

MARSHALL   IL

Super 8 Motel $-$$
Marshall Interstate Plaza,
Marshall, IL 62441, Res.
(800) 800-8000 Ph: (217)
826-6433

MATTOON   IL

Super 8 Motel $-$$
Rte. 16 East & I-57, Mattoon,
IL 61938, Res. (800) 800-8000
Ph: (217) 235-8808 Fax: (217)
258-8808

MCLEAN   IL

Super 8 Motel $-$$
"RR 1, Box 85", McLean, IL
61754, Res. (800) 800-8000
Ph: (309) 874-2366 Fax: (309)
874-2366

MENDOTA   IL

Super 8 Motel $-$$
508 E. US Hwy. 34, PO Box
526, Mendota, IL
61342-0526, Res. (800)
800-8000 Ph: (815) 539-7429
Fax: (815) 539-7429

MOKENA   IL

Super 8 Motel $-$$
9485 W 191st St, Mokena, IL
60448, Res. (800) 800-8000
Ph: (708) 479-7808 Fax: (708)
479-7808

MOLINE   IL

Motel 6 $
Quad City Airport Rd, Moline,
IL 61265, Res. (800) 466-8356
Ph: 309 764-8711 Fax: 309
762-4092

**M
O
T
E
L**

MONMOUTH   IL

Super 8 Motel $-$$
Near U.S. 34 & U.S. 67,
Monmouth, IL 61462, Res.
(800) 800-8000 Ph: (319)
358-6351 Fax: (319) 668-2097

MORRIS   IL

Super 8 Motel $-$$
70 Green Acres Drive,
Morris, IL 60450, Res. (800)
800-8000 Ph: (815) 942-3200
Fax: (815) 942-3325

MORTON   IL

Villager $-$$
128 Queenwood Road,
Morton, IL 61550, Res. (800)
328-7829 Ph: (309) 263-2511
Fax: (309) 266-7133

MT. VERNON   IL

Motel 6 $
333 S 44th St, Mt. Vernon,
IL 62864, Res. (800) 466-8356
Ph: 618 244-2383 Fax: 618
244-1697

Scottish Inns $
I-57, exit 103, Mt. Vernon, IL
62830, Res. (800) 251-1962
Ph: (618) 266-7254

Super 8 Motel $-$$
401 S. 44th St., Mt. Vernon,
IL 62864, Res. (800) 800-8000
Ph: (618) 242-8800 Fax: (618)
242-8247

MUNDELEIN   IL

Super 8 Motel $-$$
1950 S. Lake St., Mundelein,
IL 60060, Res. (800) 800-8000
Ph: (708) 949-8842 Fax: (708)
949-8842

MURPHYSBORO   IL

Super 8 Motel $-$$
Route 13 Box 429,
Murphysboro, IL 62966, Res.
(800) 800-8000 Ph: (618)
687-2244 Fax: (618) 687-2244

NORMAL   IL

Motel 6 $
1600 N Main St, Normal, IL
61761, Res. (800) 466-8356
Ph: 309 452-0422 Fax: 309
452-2639

Super 8 Motel $-$$
2 Traders Circle, Normal, IL
61761, Res. (800) 800-8000
Ph: (309) 454-5858 Fax: (309)
454-1172

NORTH CHICAGO   IL

Red Carpet Inn $$
3207 Buckley Rd., IL 137 & US
41, North Chicago, IL
60064, Res. (800) 251-1962
Ph: (847) 689-9400 Fax: (847)
689-0025

OKAWVILLE   IL

Super 8 Motel $-$$
I-64 & Route 177, P.O. Box
Drawer 515, Okawville, IL
62271-0515, Res. (800)
800-8000 Ph: (618) 243-6525

OLNEY   IL

Super 8 Motel $-$$
Hwy 130 & Hwy 50, Olney, IL
62450, Res. (800) 800-8000
Ph: (708) 893-7545

OTTAWA   IL

Super 8 Motel $-$$
500 East Etna Road, Ottawa,
IL 61350, Res. (800) 800-8000
Ph: (815) 434-2888 Fax: (815)
434-2891

PALATINE   IL

Motel 6 $
1450 E Dundee Rd, Palatine,
IL 60067, Res. (800) 466-8356
Ph: 847 359-0046 Fax: 847
358-5079

PARIS   IL

Scottish Inns $
Route 1 & 150 North, Paris,
IL 61944, Res. (800) 251-1962
Ph: (217) 465-6441 Fax: (217)
465-5507

Super 8 Motel $-$$
Hwy 150, Paris, IL 61944,
Res. (800) 800-8000 Ph: (217)
463-8888

PEKIN   IL

Super 8 Motel $-$$
3830 Kelly Street, Pekin, IL
61554, Res. (800) 800-8000
Ph: (309) 347-8888 Fax: (309)
347-8888

PEORIA   IL

Super 8 Motel $-$$
4025 W.War Memorial Drive,
Peoria, IL 61614, Res. (800)
800-8000 Ph: (309) 688-8074
Fax: (309) 688-8284

PERU   IL

Motel 6 $
1900 May Rd, Peru, IL
61354, Res. (800) 466-8356
Ph: 815 224-2785 Fax: 815
224-3074

Super 8 Motel $-$$
1851 May Road, Peru, IL
61354, Res. (800) 800-8000
Ph: (815) 223-1848 Fax: (815)
223-1848

PONTIAC   IL

Super 8 Motel $-$$
"Route 1, Box 198B", Pontiac,
IL 61764, Res. (800) 800-8000
Ph: (815) 844-6888 Fax: (815)
844-6888

PRINCETON   IL

Super 8 Motel $-$$
2929 N. Main Street,
Princeton, IL 61356, Res.
(800) 800-8000 Ph: (815)
872-8888 Fax: (815) 872-8888

QUINCY   IL

Super 8 Motel $-$$
224 N 36th St., Quincy, IL
62301, Res. (800) 800-8000
Ph: (217) 228-8808 Fax: (217)
228-8808

RANTOUL   IL

Super 8 Motel $-$$
207 S. Murray Road, Rantoul,
IL 61866, Res. (800) 800-8000
Ph: (217) 893-8888 Fax: (217)
893-9017

ROCHELLE   IL

Super 8 Motel $-$$
601 E. Hwy 38, Rochelle, IL
61068, Res. (800) 800-8000
Ph: (815) 562-2468 Fax: (815)
562-2468

ROCK FALLS   IL

Super 8 Motel $-$$
2100 1st Ave., Rock Falls, IL
61071, Res. (800) 800-8000
Ph: (815) 626-8880 Fax: (815)
626-9522

ROCKFORD   IL

Motel 6 $
3851 11th St, Rockford, IL
61109, Res. (800) 466-8356
Ph: 815 398-6080 Fax: 815
398-5816

Super 8 Motel $-$$
7646 Colosseum Dr.,
Rockford, IL 61107, Res.
(800) 800-8000 Ph: (815)
229-5522 Fax: (815) 229-5547

ROLLING MEADOWS   IL

Motel 6 $
1800 Winnetka Cir, Rolling
Meadows, IL 60008, Res.
(800) 466-8356 Ph: 847
818-8088 Fax: 847 392-2940

ROMEOVILLE   IL

Super 8 Motel $-$$
1301 Marquette Drive,
Romeoville, IL 60441, Res.
(800) 800-8000 Ph: (708)
759-8880 Fax: (708) 759-9391

SAINT CHARLES   IL

Econo Lodge $-$$
1600 E. Main St., Saint
Charles, IL 60174, Res. (800)
424-4777 Ph: (708) 584-5300
Fax: (708) 584-5395

SALEM   IL

Super 8 Motel $-$$
1704 W. Main St., Salem, IL
62881, Res. (800) 800-8000
Ph: (618) 548-5882 Fax: (618)
548-5882

SCHILLER PARK IL	**WASHINGTON** IL	**CENTERVILLE** IN

Motel 6 $
9408 W Lawrence Ave,
Schiller Park, IL 60176, Res.
(800) 466-8356 Ph: 847
671-4282 Fax: 847 928-1752

SPRINGFIELD IL

Motel 6 $
6010 S 6th St, Springfield, IL
62707, Res. (800) 466-8356
Ph: 217 529-1633 Fax: 217
585-1271

Super 8 Motel $-$$
1330 S. Dirksen Parkway,
Springfield, IL 62703, Res.
(800) 800-8000 Ph: (217)
528-8889 Fax: (217) 528-8809

Super 8 Motel $-$$
3675 S. 6th St., Springfield,
IL 62703, Res. (800) 800-8000
Ph: (217) 529-8898 Fax: (217)
529-4354

ST. CHARLES IL

Super 8 Motel $-$$
1520 E. Main St., St. Charles,
IL 60174, Res. (800) 800-8000
Ph: (708) 377-8388 Fax: (708)
377-1340

STAUNTON IL

Super 8 Motel $-$$
East Main Street, Staunton,
IL 62088, Res. (800) 800-8000
Ph: (618) 635-5353 Fax: (618)
635-8255

TROY IL

Scottish Inns $$
909 Edwardsville Rd., Troy, IL
62294, Res. (800) 251-1962
Ph: (618) 667-9916 Fax: (618)
667-9910

Super 8 Motel $-$$
Exit 18 of Hwy 55/70 & Hwy
162, Troy, IL 60435, Res.
(800) 800-8000 Ph: (618)
667-8888

TUSCOLA IL

Super 8 Motel $-$$
Route 36, P.O. Box 202,
Tuscola, IL 61953, Res. (800)
800-8000 Ph: (217) 253-5488
Fax: (217) 253-4337

URBANA IL

Motel 6 $
1906 N Cunningham Ave,
Urbana, IL 61801, Res. (800)
466-8356 Ph: 217 344-1082
Fax: 217 328-4108

VILLA PARK IL

Motel 6 $
10 W Roosevelt Rd, Villa
Park, IL 60181, Res. (800)
466-8356 Ph: 630 941-9100
Fax: 630 941-1167

Super 8 Motel $-$$
1884 Washington Road,
Washington, IL 61571, Res.
(800) 800-8000 Ph: (309)
444-8881 Fax: (309) 444-8881

WATSEKA IL

Super 8 Motel $-$$
710 W. Walnut Street,
Watseka, IL 60970, Res.
(800) 800-8000 Ph: (815)
432-6000 Fax: (815) 432-6000

WAUKEGAN IL

Super 8 Motel $-$$
630 N. Green Bay Road,
Waukegan, IL 60085, Res.
(800) 800-8000 Ph: (708)
249-2388 Fax: (708) 249-2388

Thriftlodge $-$$
222 West Grand Ave.,
Waukegan, IL 60085, Res.
(800) 525-9055 Ph: (708)
244-8950 Fax: (708) 244-0463

WOODSTOCK IL

Super 8 Motel $-$$
1220 Davis Road, Woodstock,
IL 60098, Res. (800) 800-8000
Ph: (815) 337-8808 Fax: (815)
337-8815

INDIANA

ANDERSON IN

Motel 6 $
5810 Scatterfield Rd,
Anderson, IN 46013, Res.
(800) 466-8356 Ph: 765
642-9023 Fax: 765 641-1186

BLOOMINGTON IN

Econo Lodge $-$$
4501 E. Third St.,
Bloomington, IN 47401, Res.
(800) 424-4777 Ph: (812)
332-2141 Fax: (812) 334-3957

Motel 6 $
126 S Franklin Rd,
Bloomington, IN 47401, Res.
(800) 466-8356 Ph: 812
332-0337 Fax: 812 332-1967

Motel 6 $
1800 N Walnut St,
Bloomington, IN 47402, Res.
(800) 466-8356 Ph: 812
332-0820 Fax: 812 337-1526

Super 8 Motel $-$$
1000 West State Road,
Bloomington, IN 47404, Res.
(800) 800-8000 Ph: (812)
323-8000 Fax: (812) 323-8000

CARLISLE IN

Super 8 Motel $-$$
Old Highway 41 South,
Carlisle, IN 47838, Res. (800)
800-8000 Ph: (812) 398-2500
Fax: (812) 398-2500

Super 8 Motel $-$$
2407 North Centerville Road,
Centerville, IN 47330, Res.
(800) 800-8000 Ph: (314)
855-5461

CHESTERTON IN

Econo Lodge $-$$
713 Plaza Dr., Chesterton, IN
46304, Res. (800) 424-4777
Ph: (219) 929-4416 Fax: (219)
926-8611

Super 8 Motel $-$$
418 Council Drive,
Chesterton, IN 46304, Res.
(800) 800-8000 Ph: (219)
929-5549 Fax: (219) 929-5549

CLARKSVILLE IN

Econo Lodge North $-$$
460 Auburn Ave., Clarksville,
IN 47129, Res. (800) 424-4777
Ph: (812) 288-6661 Fax: (812)
288-5923

COLUMBUS IN

Super 8 Motel $-$$
110 Brexpark Drive,
Columbus, IN 47201, Res.
(800) 800-8000 Ph: (812)
372-8828 Fax: (812) 372-8828

CRAWFORDSVILLE IN

Super 8 Motel $-$$
1025 Corey Blvd.,
Crawfordsville, IN 47933,
Res. (800) 800-8000 Ph: (317)
364-9999 Fax: (317) 364-9999

DALE IN

Budget Host Stone's Motel $-$$
410 S Washington St, Dale,
IN 47523, Res. (800) 283-4678
Ph: (812) 037-4448

Scottish Inns $$
I-65 & US 231, exit 57, Dale,
IN 47523, Res. (800) 251-1962
Ph: (812) 937-2816 Fax: (812)
937-4207

DALEVILLE IN

Super 8 Motel $-$$
I-69 & SR 67, Daleville, IN
47334, Res. (800) 800-8000
Ph: (317) 378-0888 Fax: (317)
378-0888

DECATUR IN

Super 8 Motel $-$$
US Highway 27 South,
Decatur, IN 46733, Res.
(800) 800-8000 Ph: (219)
724-8888 Fax: (219) 724-8888

ELKHART IN

Econo Lodge $-$$
52078 SR 19, Elkhart, IN
46514, Res. (800) 424-4777
Ph: (219) 262-0540

**M
O
T
E
L**

Super 8 Motel $-$$
345 Windsor Avenue,
Elkhart, IN 46514, Res. (800)
800-8000 Ph: (219) 264-4457
Fax: (219) 264-4457

EVANSVILLE **IN**

Motel 6 $
4321 Hwy 41 N, Evansville,
IN 47711, Res. (800) 466-8356
Ph: 812 424-6431 Fax: 812
424-7803

Super 8 Motel $-$$
4600 Morgan Avenue,
Evansville, IN 47715, Res.
(800) 800-8000 Ph: (812)
476-4008 Fax: (812) 476-4008

Thriftlodge $-$$
701 First Ave., Evansville, IN
47710, Res. (800) 525-9055
Ph: (812) 424-3886 Fax: (812)
424-0256

FORT WAYNE **IN**

Motel 6 $
3003 Coliseum Blvd W, Fort
Wayne, IN 46808, Res. (800)
466-8356 Ph: 219 482-3972
Fax: 219 471-7205

Super 8 Motel $-$$
522 Coliseum Blvd. East,
Fort Wayne, IN 46805, Res.
(800) 800-8000 Ph: (219)
484-8326 Fax: (219) 484-8326

FRANKLIN **IN**

Super 8 Motel $-$$
I-65 @ Exit 90, Franklin, IN
46131, Res. (800) 800-8000
Ph: (317) 738-0888 Fax: (708)
980-0177

GREENFIELD **IN**

Super 8 Motel $-$$
2100 North State Street,
Greenfield, IN 46140, Res.
(800) 800-8000 Ph: (317)
462-8899 Fax: (317) 462-8899

HAMMOND **IN**

Motel 6 $
3840 179th St, Hammond,
IN 46324, Res. (800) 466-8356
Ph: 219 845-0330 Fax: 219
845-7012

Super 8 Motel $-$$
3844 179th Street,
Hammond, IN 46323, Res.
(800) 800-8000 Ph: (219)
844-8888 Fax: (219) 844-5827

Super 8 Motel $-$$
4111 Calumet Ave.,
Hammond, IN 46327, Res.
(800) 800-8000 Ph: (219)
932-8888 Fax: (219) 932-1615

HOWE **IN**

Super 8 Motel $-$$
"7333 North State, Route 9",
Howe, IN 46746, Res. (800)
800-8000 Ph: (219) 562-2828
Fax: (219) 562-2815

INDIANAPOLIS **IN**

Econo Lodge East $-$$
4326 Sellers St.,
Indianapolis, IN 46226, Res.
(800) 424-4777 Ph: (317)
542-1031 Fax: (317) 542-9808

Econo Lodge South $-$$
4505 S. Harding St.,
Indianapolis, IN 46217, Res.
(800) 424-4777 Ph: (317)
788-9361 Fax: (317) 788-9361

Motel 6 $
5241 W Bradbury Ave<EL>at
Lynhurst Dr, Indianapolis,
IN 46241, Res. (800) 466-8356
Ph: 317 248-1231 Fax: 317
481-1728

Motel 6 $
2851 Shadeland Ave,
Indianapolis, IN 40921, Res.
(800) 466-8356 Ph: 317
546-5864 Fax: 317 568-0985

Super 8 Motel $-$$
4530 S. Emerson Ave.,
Indianapolis, IN 46203, Res.
(800) 800-8000 Ph: (317)
788-0955 Fax: (317) 788-0955

Super 8 Motel $-$$
4502 S. Harding St.,
Indianapolis, IN 46217, Res.
(800) 800-8000 Ph: (317)
788-4774 Fax: (317) 788-4774

JEFFERSONVILLE **IN**

Motel 6 $
2016 Old Hwy 31 E,
Jeffersonville, IN 47129,
Res. (800) 466-8356 Ph: 812
283-7703 Fax: 812 280-1695

Scottish Inns $
1560 East 10th S.,
Jeffersonville, IN 47130,
Res. (800) 251-1962 Ph: (812)
282-6694 Fax: (812) 288-4190

KOKOMO **IN**

Econo Lodge $-$$
2040 S. Reed Rd., Kokomo,
IN 46902, Res. (800) 424-4777
Ph: (317) 457-7561 Fax: (000)
003-1768

Motel 6 $
2808 S Reed Rd, Kokomo, IN
46902, Res. (800) 466-8356
Ph: 765 457-8211 Fax: 765
454-9774

LA PORTE **IN**

Super 8 Motel $-$$
438 Pine Lake Ave., La Porte,
IN 46350-2315, Res. (800)
800-8000 Ph: (219) 325-3808
Fax: (219) 324-6873

LEBANON **IN**

Super 8 Motel $-$$
I-65 North & SR 32, Lebanon,
IN 46852, Res. (800) 800-8000
Ph: (317) 482-9999 Fax: (317)
482-9999

LOGANSPORT **IN**

Super 8 Motel $-$$
3801 US 24 East, P.O. Box
813, Logansport, IN 46947,
Res. (800) 800-8000 Ph: (219)
753-6351 Fax: (219) 732-0111

MERRILLVILLE **IN**

Motel 6 $
8290 Louisianna St,
Merrillville, IN 46410, Res.
(800) 466-8356 Ph: 219
738-2701 Fax: 219 793-9237

Super 8 Motel $-$$
8300 Louisiana St.,
Merrillville, IN 46410-6312,
Res. (800) 800-8000 Ph: (219)
736-8383 Fax: (219) 736-8383

MICHIGAN CITY **IN**

Super 8 Motel $-$$
5724 S. Franklin, Michigan
City, IN 46360, Res. (800)
800-8000 Ph: (219) 879-0411
Fax: (219) 878-8909

MUNCIE **IN**

Super 8 Motel $-$$
3601 West Foxridge Lane,
Muncie, IN 47304, Res. (800)
800-8000 Ph: (317) 286-4333
Fax: (317) 286-4333

NOBELSVILLE **IN**

Super 8 Motel $-$$
I-69 & I-465 & US 32 & US 37,
Nobelsville, IN 46060, Res.
(800) 800-8000 Fax: (317)
788-4774

PLYMOUTH **IN**

Motel 6 $
2535 N Michigan Ave,
Plymouth, IN 46563, Res.
(800) 466-8356 Ph: 219
935-5911 Fax: 219 935-0630

Super 8 Motel $-$$
"2160 North Oak Road, #4",
Plymouth, IN 46563, Res.
(800) 800-8000 Ph: (219)
936-8856 Fax: (219) 936-2569

PORTAGE **IN**

Super 8 Motel $-$$
US 20, Portage, IN 46368,
Res. (800) 800-8000 Ph: (219)
762-8857

SEYMOUR **IN**

Econo Lodge $-$$
220 Commerce Dr.,
Seymour, IN 47274, Res.
(800) 424-4777 Ph: (812)
522-8000 Fax: (812) 378-3080

SHELBYVILLE **IN**

Super 8 Motel $-$$
20 Rampart Drive,
Shelbyville, IN 46176, Res.
(800) 800-8000 Ph: (317)
392-6239 Fax: (317) 392-6239

SOUTH BEND   IN

Motel 6 $
52624 US Hwy 31 N, South
Bend, IN 46637, Res. (800)
466-8356 Ph: 219 272-7072
Fax: 219 273-4475

Super 8 Motel $-$$
52825 U.S. 33 North, South
Bend, IN 46637, Res. (800)
800-8000 Ph: (219) 272-9000

SPEEDWAY   IN

Motel 6 $
6330 Debonair Ln, Speedway,
IN 46224, Res. (800) 466-8356
Ph: 317 293-3220 Fax: 317
329-7644

TERRE HAUTE   IN

Motel 6 $
1 W Honey Creek Dr, Terre
Haute, IN 47802, Res. (800)
466-8356 Ph: 812 238-1586
Fax: 812 238-1424

Super 8 Motel $-$$
3089 S. 1st Street, Terre
Haute, IN 47802, Res. (800)
800-8000 Ph: (812) 232-4890
Fax: (812) 232-4890

Thriftlodge $-$$
530 South 3rd St., Terre
Haute, IN 47807, Res. (800)
525-9055 Ph: (812) 232-7075
Fax: (812) 232-7079

VINCENNES   IN

Super 8 Motel $-$$
U.S. 41 at Hart Street,
Vincennes, IN 47591, Res.
(800) 800-8000 Ph: (812)
882-5101

IOWA

ALGONA   IA

Super 8 Motel $-$$
210 Norwood Dr., Algona, IA
50511-1134, Res. (800)
800-8000 Ph: (515) 295-7225
Fax: (515) 295-7225

AMES   IA

Super 8 Motel $-$$
1418 S. Dayton Rd., Ames,
IA 50010, Res. (800) 800-8000
Ph: (515) 232-6510 Fax: (515)
232-3922

ANAMOSA   IA

Super 8 Motel $-$$
100 Grant Wood Dr.,
Anamosa, IA 52205, Res.
(800) 800-8000 Ph: (319)
462-3888 Fax: (319) 462-3888

ANKENY   IA

Super 8 Motel $-$$
206 S.E. Delaware St.,
Ankeny, IA 50021, Res. (800)
800-8000 Ph: (515) 964-4503

ATLANTIC   IA

Econo Lodge $-$$
I-80 & US 71 Exit 60,
Atlantic, IA 50022, Res.
(800) 424-4777 Ph: (712)
243-4067

BOONE   IA

Super 8 Motel $-$$
1715 South Story Street,
Boone, IA 50036, Res. (800)
800-8000 Ph: (515) 432-8890
Fax: (515) 432-8890

BURLINGTON   IA

Super 8 Motel $-$$
3001 Kirkwood, Burlington,
IA 52601, Res. (800) 800-8000
Ph: (319) 752-9806 Fax: (319)
752-9806

Villager $-$$
2731 Mt. Pleasant St.,
Burlington, IA 52601, Res.
(800) 328-7829 Ph: (319)
752-7777 Fax: (000) 000-0000

CARROLL   IA

Econo Lodge $-$$
1225 Plaza Dr., Carroll, IA
51401, Res. (800) 424-4777
Ph: (712) 792-5156 Fax: (712)
792-6674

Super 8 Motel $-$$
N. Hwy. 71, Carroll, IA
51401-0713, Res. (800)
800-8000 Ph: (712) 792-4753
Fax: (712) 792-4753

CEDAR FALLS   IA

Econo Lodge $-$$
4117 University Ave., Cedar
Falls, IA 50613, Res. (800)
424-4777 Ph: (319) 277-6931

CEDAR RAPIDS   IA

Econo Lodge $-$$
622 33rd Ave. S.W., Cedar
Rapids, IA 52404, Res. (800)
424-4777 Ph: (319) 363-8888
Fax: (319) 363-8888

Super 8 Motel $-$$
400 SW 33rd. Ave., Cedar
Rapids, IA 52404-5407, Res.
(800) 800-8000 Ph: (319)
363-1755 Fax: (319) 363-1755

Super 8 Motel $-$$
720 33th Ave. SW (6th St.),
Cedar Rapids, IA 52404, Res.
(800) 800-8000 Ph: (319)
362-6002 Fax: (319) 362-6002

CENTERVILLE   IA

Super 8 Motel $-$$
"1021 N. 18th, Hwy 5N",
Centerville, IA 52544, Res.
(800) 800-8000 Ph: (515)
856-8888 Fax: (515) 856-8888

CHARITON   IA

Super 8 Motel $-$$
169 E. Grace Ave., Chariton,
IA 50049, Res. (800) 800-8000
Ph: (515) 774-8888 Fax: (515)
774-8888

CHEROKEE   IA

Super 8 Motel $-$$
1400 North Second Street,
Cherokee, IA 51021, Res.
(800) 800-8000 Ph: (712)
225-4278

CLEAR LAKE   IA

Super 8 Motel $-$$
PO Box 340, Clear Lake, IA
50428, Res. (800) 800-8000
Ph: (515) 357-7521 Fax: (515)
357-5999

CLINTON   IA

Super 8 Motel $-$$
1711 Lincoln Way, Clinton,
IA 52732, Res. (800) 800-8000
Ph: (319) 242-8870 Fax: (319)
242-8870

CORALVILLE   IA

Econo Lodge $-$$
815 1st. Ave., Coralville, IA
52241, Res. (800) 424-4777
Ph: (319) 354-6000

Motel 6 $
810 1st Ave, Coralville, IA
52241, Res. (800) 466-8356
Ph: 319 354-0030 Fax: 319
338-8751

Super 8 Motel $-$$
611 1st Ave., Coralville, IA
52241-2101, Res. (800)
800-8000 Ph: (319) 337-8388
Fax: (319) 337-4327

COUNCIL BLUFFS   IA

Motel 6 $
3032 S Expwy, Council
Bluffs, IA 51501, Res. (800)
466-8356 Ph: 712 366-2405
Fax: 712 366-8105

Super 8 Motel $-$$
2712 S. 24th Street, Council
Bluffs, IA 51501-6949, Res.
(800) 800-8000 Ph: (712)
322-2888

CRESTON   IA

Super 8 Motel $-$$
804 W. Taylor, P.O. Box 108,
Creston, IA 50801-3534,
Res. (800) 800-8000 Ph: (515)
782-6541 Fax: (515) 782-6541

DAVENPORT   IA

Motel 6 $
6111 N Brady St, Davenport,
IA 52806, Res. (800) 466-8356
Ph: 319 391-8997 Fax: 319
386-3167

**M
O
T
E
L**

Super 8 Motel $-$$
410 East 65th Street,
Davenport, IA 52807-3601,
Res. (800) 800-8000 Ph: (319)
388-9810 Fax: (319) 388-9810

DECORAH   **IA**

Super 8 Motel $-$$
P.O. Box 465, Decorah, IA
52101, Res. (800) 800-8000
Ph: (319) 382-8771 Fax: (319)
382-8771

Villager $-$$
Jct 9 & 52, Decorah, IA
52101, Res. (800) 328-7829
Ph: (319) 382-4241 Fax: (319)
382-4152

DES MOINES   **IA**

Budget Host Inn $-$$
7625 Hickman Rd, Des
Moines, IA 50322, Res. (800)
283-4678 Ph: (515) 276-5401

Econo Lodge Merele Hay M&H
5626 Douglas Ave., Des
Moines, IA 50310, Res. (800)
424-4777 Ph: (515) 278-1601
Fax: (515) 278-1601

Econo Lodge West $-$$
11000 Douglas Ave., Des
Moines, IA 50322, Res. (800)
424-4777 Ph: (515) 278-4601

Motel 6 $
4817 Fleur Dr, Des Moines,
IA 50321, Res. (800) 466-8356
Ph: 515 287-6364 Fax: 515
287-3909

Motel 6 $
4940 NE 14th St (50313), Des
Moines, IA 50313, Res. (800)
466-8356 Ph: 515 266-5456
Fax: 515 266-6954

Super 8 Motel $-$$
4755 Merle Hay Road, Des
Moines, IA 50323, Res. (800)
800-8000 Ph: (515) 278-8858
Fax: (515) 278-1287

DUBUQUE   **IA**

Motel 6 $
2670 Dodge St, Dubuque, IA
52003, Res. (800) 466-8356
Ph: 319 556-0880 Fax: 319
582-0190

Super 8 Motel $-$$
2730 Dodge Street,
Dubuque, IA 52003, Res.
(800) 800-8000 Ph: (319)
582-8898 Fax: (319) 582-8898

DYERSVILLE   **IA**

Super 8 Motel $-$$
"925 15th Avenue, S.E.",
Dyersville, IA 52040, Res.
(800) 800-8000 Ph: (319)
875-8885 Fax: (319) 875-8885

ESTHERVILLE   **IA**

Super 8 Motel $-$$
1919 Central Ave.,
Estherville, IA 51334, Res.
(800) 800-8000 Ph: (712)
362-2400 Fax: (712) 362-2800

FAIRFIELD   **IA**

Super 8 Motel $-$$
2901 W. Burlington Ave.,
Hwy 34 West, Fairfield, IA
52556, Res. (800) 800-8000
Ph: (515) 469-2000

FORT DODGE   **IA**

Budget Host Inn $-$$
116 Kenyon Rd, Fort Dodge,
IA 50501, Res. (800) 283-4678
Ph: (515) 955-8501 Fax: (515)
955-4968

Super 8 Motel $-$$
3040 S 5th Ave., Fort Dodge,
IA 50501-2928, Res. (800)
800-8000 Ph: (515) 576-8000
Fax: (515) 576-8000

FT. MADISON   **IA**

Super 8 Motel $-$$
Hwy 61, Ft. Madison, IA
52627, Res. (800) 800-8000
Ph: (319) 372-8500 Fax: (319)
372-8500

GRINNELL   **IA**

Super 8 Motel $-$$
"Hwy 146 & I-80, Exit 182",
Grinnell, IA 50112, Res.
(800) 800-8000 Ph: (515)
236-7888 Fax: (515) 236-7888

INDEPENDENCE   **IA**

Super 8 Motel $-$$
2000 1st West, PO Box 801,
Independence, IA 50644,
Res. (800) 800-8000 Ph: (319)
334-7041 Fax: (319) 334-4088

IOWA FALLS   **IA**

Super 8 Motel $-$$
839 S. Oak, Iowa Falls, IA
50126, Res. (800) 800-8000
Ph: (515) 648-4618 Fax: (515)
648-4610

KEOKUK   **IA**

Super 8 Motel $-$$
3511 Main Street, Keokuk,
IA 52632, Res. (800) 800-8000
Ph: (319) 524-3888 Fax: (319)
524-3888

KNOXVILLE   **IA**

Super 8 Motel $-$$
2205 North Lincoln,
Knoxville, IA 50138, Res.
(800) 800-8000 Ph: (515)
828-8808 Fax: (515) 828-8808

LAMONI   **IA**

Super 8 Motel $-$$
"Junction of I-35 & US Hwy
69,", Exit 4, Lamoni, IA
50140, Res. (800) 800-8000
Ph: (515) 784-7500 Fax: (515)
784-7500

LE MARS   **IA**

Super 8 Motel $-$$
"1201 Hawkeye Avenue,
S.W.", Le Mars, IA 51031,
Res. (800) 800-8000 Ph: (712)
546-8800 Fax: (712) 546-8800

MANCHESTER   **IA**

Super 8 Motel $-$$
1020 South Main Street,
Manchester, IA 52057, Res.
(800) 800-8000 Ph: (319)
927-2533

MAQUOKETA   **IA**

Super 8 Motel $-$$
10021 West Platt Street,
Maquoketa, IA 52060, Res.
(800) 800-8000 Ph: (319)
652-6888 Fax: (319) 652-6888

MARSHALLTOWN   **IA**

Super 8 Motel $-$$
Highway 14 South, P.O. Box
156, Marshalltown, IA
50158-0156, Res. (800)
800-8000 Ph: (515) 753-8181
Fax: (515) 753-8181

MASON CITY   **IA**

Thriftlodge $-$$
24 5th St. Southwest, Mason
City, IA 50401, Res. (800)
525-9055 Ph: (515) 424-2910
Fax: (515) 423-0274

MT. PLEASANT   **IA**

Super 8 Motel $-$$
U.S. Hwy 218 North, Mt.
Pleasant, IA 52641, Res.
(800) 800-8000 Ph: (319)
385-8888 Fax: (319) 385-8888

MUSCATINE   **IA**

Super 8 Motel $-$$
2900 North Hwy. 61,
Muscatine, IA 52761-5808,
Res. (800) 800-8000 Ph: (319)
263-9100 Fax: (319) 263-9100

NEW HAMPTON   **IA**

Super 8 Motel $-$$
825 South Linn Ave., New
Hampton, IA 50659, Res.
(800) 800-8000 Ph: (515)
394-3838 Fax: (515) 394-3838

NEWTON   **IA**

Super 8 Motel $-$$
1635 South 12th Avenue
West, Newton, IA 50208,
Res. (800) 800-8000 Ph: (515)
792-8868 Fax: (515) 792-8868

OSCEOLA   IA

Super 8 Motel $-$$
Jimmy Dean Ave.; Hwy. 34,
RR 3, Osceola, IA 50213,
Res. (800) 800-8000 Ph: (515)
342-6594 Fax: (515) 342-6594

OSKALOOSA   IA

Red Carpet Inn $$
2278 Highway 63, Oskaloosa,
IA 52577, Res. (800) 251-1962
Ph: (515) 673-8641 Fax: (515)
673-4111

Super 8 Motel $-$$
306 S. 17th Street,
Oskaloosa, IA 52577, Res.
(800) 800-8000 Ph: (515)
673-8481 Fax: (515) 673-8481

OTTUMWA   IA

Super 8 Motel $-$$
2823 N. Court, Ottumwa, IA
52501, Res. (800) 800-8000
Ph: (515) 684-5055 Fax: (515)
682-6622

PELLA   IA

Super 8 Motel $-$$
105 Oskaloosa, Pella, IA
50219, Res. (800) 800-8000
Ph: (515) 628-8181 Fax: (515)
628-8181

PERRY   IA

Super 8 Motel $-$$
701 26th St, Perry, IA
50220, Res. (800) 800-8000
Ph: (515) 465-5653 Fax: (515)
465-5653

ROCK VALLEY   IA

Super 8 Motel $-$$
2111 10th Street, Rock
Valley, IA 51247, Res. (800)
800-8000 Ph: (712) 476-9388

SIBLEY   IA

Super 8 Motel $-$$
1108 2nd Avenue, Sibley, IA
51249, Res. (800) 800-8000
Ph: (605) 335-1960 Fax: (712)
754-3479

SIOUX CENTER   IA

Econo Lodge $-$$
86 9th St. Cir., N.E., Sioux
Center, IA 51250, Res. (800)
424-4777 Ph: (712) 722-4000
Fax: (000) 007-1222

SIOUX CITY   IA

Motel 6 $
6166 Harbor Dr, Sioux City,
IA 51111, Res. (800) 466-8356
Ph: 712 277-3131 Fax: 712
255-4424

Super 8 Motel $-$$
4307 Stone Ave., Sioux City,
IA 51106-1912, Res. (800)
800-8000 Ph: (712) 274-1520
Fax: (712) 274-1520

SPENCER   IA

Super 8 Motel $-$$
"209 11th Street, S.W.",
Spencer, IA 51301, Res.
(800) 800-8000 Ph: (712)
262-8500 Fax: (712) 262-8500

SPIRIT LAKE   IA

Super 8 Motel $-$$
2501 Hwy 71, Spirit Lake, IA
51360, Res. (800) 800-8000
Ph: (712) 336-4901 Fax: (712)
336-4901

STORM LAKE   IA

Super 8 Motel $-$$
101 W. Milwaukee Ave.,
Storm Lake, IA 50588, Res.
(800) 800-8000 Ph: (712)
732-3063 Fax: (712) 732-3063

STORY CITY   IA

Super 8 Motel $-$$
515 Factory Outlet Dr., Story
City, IA 50248, Res. (800)
800-8000 Ph: (515) 733-5281

STUART   IA

Super 8 Motel $-$$
I-80 @ Exit 93, Stuart, IA
50250, Res. (800) 800-8000
Ph: (515) 523-2888

TOLEDO   IA

Super 8 Motel $-$$
207 Hwy 30 West, P.O. Box
81, Toledo, IA 52342, Res.
(800) 800-8000 Ph: (515)
484-5888

WALCOTT   IA

Super 8 Motel $-$$
I-80 Industrial Park, Walcott,
IA 52773, Res. (800) 800-8000
Ph: (319) 284-5083 Fax: (319)
284-5083

WALNUT   IA

Super 8 Motel $-$$
"Exit 46, I-80", Walnut, IA
51577, Res. (800) 800-8000
Ph: (712) 784-2221 Fax: (712)
243-2864

WASHINGTON   IA

Super 8 Motel $-$$
Highway 1 & Highway 92,
Washington, IA 52353, Res.
(800) 800-8000 Ph: (319)
354-2917 Fax: (319) 653-6621

WATERLOO   IA

Super 8 Motel $-$$
1825 LaPorte Rd., Waterloo,
IA 50707, Res. (800) 800-8000
Ph: (319) 233-1800 Fax: (319)
233-1800

WAVERLY   IA

Super 8 Motel $-$$
301 13th Avenue, Waverly,
IA 50677, Res. (800) 800-8000
Ph: (319) 352-0888 Fax: (319)
352-0888

WEBSTER CITY   IA

Super 8 Motel $-$$
305 Closz Dr., Webster City,
IA 50595, Res. (800) 800-8000
Ph: (319) 352-0888

WEST LIBERTY   IA

Econo Lodge $-$$
1943 Garfield Ave., West
Liberty, IA 52776, Res. (800)
424-4777 Ph: (319) 627-2171
Fax: (319) 627-2171

WILLIAMSBURG   IA

Super 8 Motel $-$$
Rural Route 2, Box 179H,
Williamsburg, IA 52361,
Res. (800) 800-8000 Ph: (319)
668-2800 Fax: (319) 668-2800

Super 8 Motel $-$$
1708 North Highland St,
(Hwy 149 N), Williamsburg,
IA 52361, Res. (800) 800-8000
Ph: (319) 668-9718 Fax: (319)
668-9770

WINTERSET   IA

Super 8 Motel $-$$
1312 N. 10th Street,
Winterset, IA 50208, Res.
(800) 800-8000 Ph: (515)
462-4888

KANSAS

ABILENE   KS

Super 8 Motel $-$$
"P.O. Box 723, 2207 N.
Buckeye", Abilene, KS
67410, Res. (800) 800-8000
Ph: (913) 263-4545 Fax: (913)
263-7448

COFFEYVILLE   KS

Super 8 Motel $-$$
104 W. 11th, Coffeyville, KS
67337, Res. (800) 800-8000
Ph: (316) 251-2250 Fax: (316)
251-3846

COLBY   KS

Budget Host Inn $-$$
1745 W 4th St, Colby, KS
67701, Res. (800) 283-4678
Ph: (913) 462-3338 Fax: (913)
462-6127

Econo Lodge $-$$
1985 S. Range, Colby, KS
67701, Res. (800) 424-4777
Ph: (913) 462-8201

Super 8 Motel $-$$
1040 Zelfer Ave., Colby, KS
67701-4107, Res. (800)
800-8000 Ph: (913) 462-8248

CONCORDIA   KS

Super 8 Motel $-$$
1320 Lincoln, Concordia, KS
66901, Res. (800) 800-8000
Ph: (913) 243-4200 Fax: (913)
243-1246

M O T E L

DODGE CITY   KS

Econo Lodge $-$$
1610 W. Wyatt Earp Blvd.,
Dodge City, KS 67801, Res.
(800) 424-4777 Ph: (316)
225-0231 Fax: (316) 225-8036

Super 8 Motel $-$$
1708 W. Wyatt Earp Blvd.,
Dodge City, KS 67801, Res.
(800) 800-8000 Ph: (316)
225-3924 Fax: (316) 225-5793

EL DORADO   KS

Super 8 Motel $-$$
2530 W. Central, El Dorado,
KS 67042, Res. (800)
800-8000 Ph: (316) 321-4888
Fax: (316) 321-4888

EMPORIA   KS

Budget Host Inn $-$$
1830 E Hwy 50, Emporia, KS
66801, Res. (800) 283-4678
Ph: (316) 343-6922

Motel 6 $
2630 W 18th Ave, Emporia,
KS 66801, Res. (800)
466-8356 Ph: 316 343-1240
Fax: 316 343-1923

Super 8 Motel $-$$
2913 West Hwy 50, Emporia,
KS 66801-5140, Res. (800)
800-8000 Ph: (316) 342-7567

GARDEN CITY   KS

Super 8 Motel $-$$
2808 N. Taylor, PO Box 1708,
Garden City, KS 67846, Res.
(800) 800-8000 Ph: (316)
275-9625 Fax: (316) 275-9625

GOODLAND   KS

Motel 6 $
2420 Commerce Rd,
Goodland, KS 67735-9753,
Res. (800) 466-8356 Ph: 913
899-5672 Fax: 913 899-2608

Super 8 Motel $-$$
2520 S. Hwy.27, Goodland,
KS 67735, Res. (800)
800-8000 Ph: (913) 899-7566
Fax: (913) 899-7566

GREAT BEND   KS

Super 8 Motel $-$$
3500 10th St., Great Bend,
KS 67530-3539, Res. (800)
800-8000 Ph: (316) 793-8486

HAYS   KS

Budget Host Villa Inn $-$$
810 E 8th St, Hays, KS
67601, Res. (800) 283-4678
Ph: (913) 625-2563 Fax: (913)
625-3967

Motel 6 $
3404 Vine St, Hays, KS
67601, Res. (800) 466-8356
Ph: 913 625-4282 Fax: 913
625-3430

Super 8 Motel $-$$
3730 Vine St., Hays, KS
67601, Res. (800) 800-8000
Ph: (913) 625-8048 Fax: (913)
625-4392

HUTCHINSON   KS

Super 8 Motel $-$$
1315 E. 11th Ave.,
Hutchinson, KS
67501-6129, Res. (800)
800-8000 Ph: (316) 662-6394

INDEPENDENCE   KS

Super 8 Motel $-$$
2400 West Main Street,
Independence, KS 67301,
Res. (800) 800-8000 Ph: (316)
331-8288 Fax: (316) 331-1730

JUNCTION CITY   KS

Budget Host Golden Wheat $-$$
820 S Washington, Junction
City, KS 66441, Res. (800)
283-4678 Ph: (913) 238-5106

Econo Lodge $-$$
211 W. Flinthills Blvd.,
Junction City, KS 66441,
Res. (800) 424-4777 Ph: (913)
238-8181 Fax: (913) 238-5092

KINGMAN   KS

Budget Host Copa Motel $-$$
1113 E Hwy 54, Kingman,
KS 67068, Res. (800)
283-4678 Ph: (316) 532-3118
Fax: (316) 532-5690

LANSING   KS

Econo Lodge $-$$
504 N. Main St., Lansing, KS
66043, Res. (800) 424-4777
Ph: (913) 727-2777 Fax: (913)
727-2862

LAWRENCE   KS

Super 8 Motel $-$$
515 McDonald Dr., Lawrence,
KS 66044, Res. (800)
800-8000 Ph: (913) 842-5721

LEAVENWORTH   KS

Super 8 Motel $-$$
303 Montana Court,
Leavenworth, KS 66048,
Res. (800) 800-8000 Ph: (913)
682-0744 Fax: (913) 682-0744

LENEXA   KS

Motel 6 $
9725 Lenexa Dr, Lenexa, KS
66215, Res. (800) 466-8356
Ph: 913 541-8558 Fax: 913
894-8726

Motel 6 $
9725 Lenexa Dr, Lenexa, KS
66215, Res. (800) 466-8356
Ph: 913 541-8558 Fax: 913
894-8726

Super 8 Motel $-$$
9601 Westgate, Lenexa, KS
66215, Res. (800) 800-8000
Ph: (913) 888-8899 Fax: (913)
888-9204

LIBERAL   K

Red Carpet Inn
488 East Pancake Blvd.,
Liberal, KS 67901, Res. (800
251-1962 Ph: (316) 624-5642

Super 8 Motel $-$$
747 E. Pancake Blvd, Liberal,
KS 67901, Res. (800)
800-8000 Ph: (316) 624-8880
Fax: (316) 624-6703

MANHATTAN   K

Motel 6
510 Tuttle Creek Blvd,
Manhattan, KS 66502, Res.
(800) 466-8356 Ph: 913
537-1022 Fax: 913 537-7307

Super 8 Motel $-$$
200 Tuttle Creek Blvd.,
Manhattan, KS 66502, Res.
(800) 800-8000 Ph: (913)
537-8468 Fax: (913) 537-8468

MARYSVILLE   KS

Super 8 Motel $-$$
East Highway 36, Marysville,
KS 66508, Res. (800)
800-8000 Ph: (913) 337-2378
Fax: (913) 562-5588

MCPHERSON   KS

Super 8 Motel $-$$
2110 E. Kansas, McPherson,
KS 67460-4008, Res. (800)
800-8000 Ph: (316) 241-8881

NEWTON   KS

Super 8 Motel $-$$
1620 E. 2nd Street, Newton,
KS 67114-5020, Res. (800)
800-8000 Ph: (316) 283-7611

NORTON   KS

Budget Host Hillcrest Motel $
W Hwy 36 -- P.O. Box 249,
Norton, KS 67654, Res. (800)
283-4678 Ph: (913) 877-3343

OLATHE   KS

Econo Lodge South $-$$
209 E. Flaming Rd., Olathe,
KS 66061, Res. (800)
424-4777 Ph: (913) 829-1312
Fax: (913) 829-1312

OTTAWA   KS

Econo Lodge $-$$
2331 South Cedar, Ottawa,
KS 66067, Res. (800)
424-4777 Ph: (913) 242-3400
Fax: (913) 242-1796

PARSONS   KS

Super 8 Motel $-$$
229 East Main Street,
Parsons, KS 67357, Res.
(800) 800-8000 Ph: (316)
421-8000 Fax: (417) 485-8868

PITTSBURG   KS

Super 8 Motel $-$$
3108 N. Broadway, Pittsburg,
KS 66762, Res. (800)
800-8000 Ph: (316) 232-1881
Fax: (316) 232-1881

PRATT   KS

Super 8 Motel $-$$
1906 E. 1st St., Pratt, KS
67124, Res. (800) 800-8000
Ph: (316) 672-5945 Fax: (316)
672-2969

QUINTER   KS

Budget Host Q Motel $-$$
Jct I-70 & Hwy 212, Quinter,
KS 67752, Res. (800)
283-4678 Ph: (913) 754-3337

RUSSELL   KS

Red Carpet Inn $$
I-70 & US 281, exit 184,
Russell, KS 67775, Res.
(800) 251-1962 Ph: (913)
483-2107 Fax: (913) 483-4447

Super 8 Motel $-$$
1405 South Fossil, Box 6,
Russell, KS 67665, Res.
(800) 800-8000 Ph: (913)
483-2488

SALINA   KS

Budget Host Vagabond II $-$$
217 S Broadway, Salina, KS
67401, Res. (800) 283-4678
Ph: (913) 825-7265 Fax: (913)
825-7003

Motel 6 $
635 W Diamond Dr, Salina,
KS 67401, Res. (800)
466-8356 Ph: 913 827-8397
Fax: 913 827-0213

Super 8 Motel $-$$
1640 West Crawford Street,
Salina, KS 67401, Res. (800)
800-8000 Ph: (913) 823-9215
Fax: (913) 823-9215

Super 8 Motel $-$$
120 East Diamond, Salina,
KS 67401, Res. (800)
800-8000 Ph: (913) 823-8808
Fax: (913) 823-8899

SHAWNEE MISSION   KS

Econo Lodge $-$$
7508 Shawnee Mission Pkwy.,
Shawnee Mission, KS
66202, Res. (800) 424-4777
Ph: (913) 262-9600 Fax: (913)
262-9600

TOPEKA   KS

Econo Lodge $-$$
1240 S. W. Wanamaker Rd.,
Topeka, KS 66604, Res. (800)
424-4777 Ph: (913) 273-6969
Fax: (000) 913-7336

Motel 6 $
709 Fairlawn Rd., Topeka, KS
66606, Res. (800) 466-8356
Ph: 913 272-8283 Fax: 913
271-1341

Motel 6 $
1224 Wanamaker Rd SW,
Topeka, KS 66604, Res. (800)
466-8356 Ph: 913 273-9888
Fax: 913 273-0665

Super 8 Motel $-$$
5968 S.W. 10th Street,
Topeka, KS 66604, Res. (800)
800-8000 Ph: (913) 273-5100
Fax: (913) 273-5100

WA KEENEY   KS

Budget Host Travel Inn $-$$
I-70 & Hwy 283 -- Box 2B, Wa
Keeney, KS 67672, Res.
(800) 283-4678 Ph: (913)
743-2121

WICHITA   KS

Econo Lodge Airport $-$$
6245 W. Kellogg, Wichita, KS
67209, Res. (800) 424-4777
Ph: (316) 945-5261 Fax: (316)
945-0077

Motel 6 $
5736 W Kellogg, Wichita, KS
67209, Res. (800) 466-8356
Ph: 316 945-8440 Fax: 316
945-9895

Super 8 Motel $-$$
527 S. Webb Rd., Wichita,
KS 67207, Res. (800)
800-8000 Ph: (316) 686-3888
Fax: (316) 686-1548

Super 8 Motel $-$$
6075 Air Cap Dr., Wichita,
KS 67219, Res. (800)
800-8000 Ph: (316) 744-2071

KENTUCKY

BARDSTOWN   KY

Red Carpet Inn $$
1714 New Haven Rd.,
Bardstown, KY 40004, Res.
(800) 251-1962 Ph: (502)
348-1112 Fax: (502) 348-1114

BEREA   KY

Econo Lodge $-$$
1010 Paint Lick Rd., Berea,
KY 40403-9501, Res. (800)
424-4777 Ph: (606) 986-9323

Super 8 Motel $-$$
196 Prince Royal Dr., Berea,
KY 40403, Res. (800)
800-8000 Ph: (606) 986-8426

BOWLING GREEN   KY

Motel 6 $
3139 Scottsville Rd, Bowling
Green, KY 42101, Res. (800)
466-8356 Ph: 502 843-0140
Fax: 502 782-6157

Scottish Inns $$
3140 Scottsville Rd., Bowling
Green, KY 42104, Res. (800)
251-1962 Ph: (502) 781-6550
Fax: (502) 781-9139

Super 8 Motel $-$$
250 Cumberland Trace Road,
Bowling Green, KY
42101-9646, Res. (800)
800-8000 Ph: (502) 781-9594
Fax: (502) 781-9599

Villager $-$$
802-31 W. Bypass, Bowling
Green, KY 42101, Res. (800)
328-7829 Ph: (502) 842-0321
Fax: (502) 746-6672

CAMPBELLSVILLE   KY

Super 8 Motel $-$$
100 Albion Road,
Campbellsville, KY 42718,
Res. (800) 800-8000 Ph: (502)
789-0808 Fax: (502) 789-0808

CARROLLTON   KY

Super 8 Motel $-$$
130 Slumber Lane,
Carrollton, KY 41008, Res.
(800) 800-8000 Ph: (502)
732-0252 Fax: (502) 732-0252

CAVE CITY   KY

Scottish Inns $
414 N. Dixie Hwy, Cave City,
KY 42127, Res. (800)
251-1962 Ph: (501) 773-3118
Fax: (502) 773-7151

CORBIN   KY

Red Carpet Inn $$
1891 Cumberland Rd.,
Corbin, KY 40701, Res. (800)
251-1962 Ph: (606) 528-7100
Fax: (606) 528-0255

Super 8 Motel $-$$
Rte. 11, Box 256-A1, Corbin,
KY 40701, Res. (800)
800-8000 Ph: (606) 528-8888
Fax: (606) 528-8888

COVINGTON   KY

Econo Lodge $-$$
633 Donaldson Rd.,
Covington, KY 41018, Res.
(800) 424-4777 Ph: (606)
342-5500

DANVILLE   KY

Super 8 Motel $-$$
3663 Hwy. 150/127 Bypass,
Danville, KY 40422, Res.
(800) 800-8000 Ph: (606)
236-8881 Fax: (606) 236-8881

DRY RIDGE   KY

Super 8 Motel $-$$
88 Blackburn Lane, Dry
Ridge, KY 41035, Res. (800)
800-8000 Ph: (606) 824-3700
Fax: (606) 824-3801

**M
O
T
E
L**

ELIZABETHTOWN   KY

Motel 6 $
Hwy 62 & I-65,
Elizabethtown, KY 42701,
Res. (800) 466-8356 Ph: 502
769-3102 Fax: 502 737-5873

Red Carpet Inn $
711 East Dixie Ave., I-65 & 31
W, Elizabethtown, KY
42701, Res. (800) 251-1962
Ph: (502) 765-2194 Fax: (502)
765-2194

Super 8 Motel $-$$
2028 North Mulberry St.,
Elizabethtown, KY 42701,
Res. (800) 800-8000 Ph: (502)
737-1088 Fax: (502) 737-1098

FLORENCE   KY

Budget Host Inn $-$$
8075 Steilen Dr., Florence,
KY 41042, Ph: (606) 371-0277
Fax: (606) 371-0286

Motel 6 $
7937 Dream St, Florence, KY
41042, Res. (800) 466-8356
Ph: 606 283-0909 Fax: 606
371-8837

Super 8 Motel $-$$
7928 Dream Street,
Florence, KY 41042, Res.
(800) 800-8000 Ph: (606)
283-1221 Fax: (619) 466-4725

FRANKFORT   KY

Red Carpet Inn $$
711 East Main St., I-64 to
US60 East, Frankfort, KY
40601, Res. (800) 251-1962
Ph: (502) 223-2041 Fax: (502)
223-2043

Super 8 Motel $-$$
1225 U. S. Highway 127
South, Frankfort, KY 40601,
Res. (800) 800-8000 Ph: (502)
875-3220 Fax: (502) 875-2342

FRANKLIN   KY

Super 8 Motel $-$$
2805 Scottsville Road,
Franklin, KY 42134, Res.
(800) 800-8000 Ph: (502)
586-8885 Fax: (502) 586-8885

GEORGETOWN   KY

Econo Lodge $-$$
3075 Paris Pike, Georgetown,
KY 40324, Res. (800)
424-4777 Ph: (502) 863-2240

Motel 6 $
401 Cherryblossom Way ,
Georgetown, KY 40324, Res.
(800) 466-8356 Ph: 502
863-1166 Fax: 502 868-5362

Super 8 Motel $-$$
I-75 & U.S. Hwy. 62,
Georgetown, KY 40324, Res.
(800) 800-8000 Ph: (502)
863-4888 Fax: (502) 868-0848

GRAYSON   KY

Econo Lodge $-$$
SR 1947, Grayson, KY
41143, Res. (800) 424-4777
Ph: (606) 474-7854 Fax: (606)
474-8425

HAZARD   KY

Super 8 Motel $-$$
125 Village Lane, Hazard, KY
41701, Res. (800) 800-8000
Ph: (606) 436-8888 Fax: (606)
439-0768

HENDERSON   KY

Scottish Inns $$
2820 US 41 North,
Henderson, KY 42420, Res.
(800) 251-1962 Fax: (502)
827-1806 Fax: (502) 827-8192

Super 8 Motel $-$$
2030 Highway 41 North,
Henderson, KY 42420, Res.
(800) 800-8000 Ph: (502)
827-5611 Fax: (502) 827-5615

HOPKINSVILLE   KY

Econo Lodge $-$$
2916 Ft. Campbell Blvd.,
Hopkinsville, KY 42240, Res.
(800) 424-4777 Ph: (502)
886-5242 Fax: (502) 886-4413

HORSE CAVE   KY

Budget Host Inn $-$$
I-65, Exit 58 -- Box 332,
Horse Cave, KY 42749, Res.
(800) 283-4678 Ph: (502)
786-2165 Fax: (502) 786-2168

INEZ   KY

Super 8 Motel $-$$
"Route 40, 645 & Blacklog
Road", Inez, KY 41224, Res.
(800) 800-8000 Ph: (606)
298-7800 Fax: (606) 298-3526

LEXINGTON   KY

Econo Lodge $-$$
5527 Athens-Boonesboro Rd.,
Lexington, KY 40509, Res.
(800) 424-4777 Ph: (606)
263-5101 Fax: (606) 263-5101

Econo Lodge North $-$$
925 Newtown Pike,
Lexington, KY 40511, Res.
(800) 424-4777 Ph: (606)
231-6300 Fax: (606) 231-6300

Master Hosts Inns $$
1375 Harrodsburg RD,
Lexington, KY 40504, Res.
(800) 251-1962 Ph:
800-354-9235 Fax: (606)
255-4281

Motel 6 $
2260 Elkhorn Rd, Lexington,
KY 40505, Res. (800)
466-8356 Ph: 606 293-1431
Fax: 606 293-8349

Super 8 Motel $-$$
2351 Buena Vista Road,
Lexington, KY 40505, Res.
(800) 800-8000 Ph: (606)
299-6241 Fax: (606) 299-6241

LONDON   KY

Budget Host Westgate Inn$$
West Daniel Boone Parkway,
London, KY 40741, Ph: (606)
878-7330

LOUISVILLE   KY

Red Carpet Inn $$
1640 So Hurstbourne Pkwy,
Louisville, KY 40220, Res.
(800) 251-1962 Ph: (502)
491-7320 Fax: (502) 499-7617

Super 8 Motel $-$$
4800 Preston Highway,
Louisville, KY 40213, Res.
(800) 800-8000 Ph: (502)
968-0088 Fax: (502) 968-0088

MADISONVILLE   KY

Econo Lodge $-$$
1117 E. Center St.,
Madisonville, KY 42431, Res
(800) 424-4777 Ph: (502)
821-0364 Fax: (502) 825-2008

MAYFIELD   KY

Super 8 Motel $-$$
Purchase Parkway Exit 24, at
State Hwy. 121, Mayfield, KY
42066, Res. (800) 800-8000
Ph: (502) 247-8899

MAYSVILLE   KY

Super 8 Motel $-$$
550 Tucker Drive, Maysville,
KY 41056, Res. (800)
800-8000 Ph: (606) 759-8888
Fax: (606) 759-8888

MOREHEAD   KY

Super 8 Motel $-$$
602 Fraley Drive, Morehead,
KY 40351, Res. (800)
800-8000 Ph: (606) 784-8882
Fax: (606) 784-9882

MOUNT VERNON   KY

Econo Lodge Renfro Valley$-$$
I-75 & US 25 (ex. 62), Mount
Vernon, KY 40456, Res.
(800) 424-4777 Ph: (606)
256-4621

MT. STERLING   KY

Scottish Inns $
517 Maysville Rd., I-64, exit
110, Mt. Sterling, KY 40353,
Res. (800) 251-1962 Ph: (606)
498-3424

MUNFORDVILLE   KY

Super 8 Motel $-$$
88 Stock Pen Rd.,
Munfordville, KY 42765, Res.
(800) 800-8000 Ph: (502)
524-4888 Fax: (502) 524-5888

NICHOLASVILLE — KY

Super 8 Motel $-$$
181 Imperial Way,
Nicholasville, KY 40356,
Res. (800) 800-8000 Ph: (606)
885-9889 Fax: (606) 885-1771

OWENSBORO — KY

Motel 6 $
4585 Frederica St,
Owensboro, KY 42301, Res.
(800) 466-8356 Ph: 502
686-8606 Fax: 502 683-2689

Super 8 Motel $-$$
1027 Goetz Dr, Owensboro,
KY 42301, Res. (800)
800-8000 Ph: (502) 685-3388
Fax: (502) 685-3388

PADUCAH — KY

Budget Host Inn $-$$
1234 Broadway, Paducah, KY
42001, Res. (800) 283-4678
Ph: (502) 443-8401

Motel 6 $
5120 Hinkleville Rd,
Paducah, KY 42001-9132,
Res. (800) 466-8356 Ph: 502
443-3672 Fax: 502 442-1412

Red Carpet Inn $$
2701 HC Mathis Dr., I-24, exit
2, Paducah, KY 42001, Res.
(800) 251-1962 Ph: (502)
443-5500

Super 8 Motel $-$$
"Old Caro Road at I-24, Exit
3", Paducah, KY 42001, Res.
(800) 800-8000 Ph: (502)
575-9605 Fax: (502) 575-9605

PRESTONSBURG — KY

Super 8 Motel $-$$
550 S. U.S. 23,
Prestonsburg, KY 41653,
Res. (800) 800-8000 Ph: (606)
886-3355 Fax: (606) 886-3399

RADCLIFF — KY

Econo Lodge $-$$
261 N. Dixie Hwy., Radcliff,
KY 40160, Res. (800)
424-4777 Ph: (502) 351-4488

Super 8 Motel $-$$
395 Redmar Blvd., Radcliff,
KY 40160, Res. (800)
800-8000 Ph: (502) 352-1888
Fax: (502) 352-1888

RICHMOND — KY

Econo Lodge $-$$
230 Eastern Bypass,
Richmond, KY 40475, Res.
(800) 424-4777 Ph: (606)
623-8813 Fax: (606) 624-3482

Motel 6 $
1698 Northgate Dr,
Richmond, KY 40475, Res.
(800) 466-8356 Ph: 606
623-0880 Fax: 606 623-8032

Super 8 Motel $-$$
107 N. Keeneland,
Richmond, KY 40475-8687,
Res. (800) 800-8000 Ph: (606)
624-1550 Fax: (606) 624-1553

S. WILLIAMSON — KY

Super 8 Motel $-$$
Southside Plaza #1, S.
Williamson, KY 41503, Res.
(800) 800-8000 Ph: (606)
237-5898 Fax: (606) 237-9863

SHEPHERDSVILLE — KY

Motel 6 $
144 Paroquet Springs Dr,
Shepherdsville, KY 40165,
Res. (800) 466-8356 Ph: 502
543-4400 Fax: 502 543-8972

SOMERSET — KY

Super 8 Motel $-$$
302 South Highway 27,
Somerset, KY 42501, Res.
(800) 800-8000 Ph: (606)
679-9279 Fax: (606) 679-9281

WHITESBURG — KY

Super 8 Motel $-$$
375 Hazard Road,
Whitesburg, KY 41858, Res.
(800) 800-8000 Ph: (606)
633-8888 Fax: (606) 633-3464

WILLIAMSTOWN — KY

Red Carpet Inn $$
401 So. Main St.,
Williamstown, KY 41097,
Res. (800) 251-1962 Ph: (606)
824-4305 Fax: (606) 824-6902

LOUISIANA

ALEXANDRIA — LA

Motel 6 $
546 MacArthur Dr,
Alexandria, LA 71301, Res.
(800) 466-8356 Ph: 318
445-2336 Fax: 318 448-3338

BATON ROUGE — LA

Motel 6 $
9901 Gwen Adele Ave, Baton
Rouge, LA 70816, Res. (800)
466-8356 Ph: 504 924-2130
Fax: 504 929-7150

Motel 6 $
10445 Rieger Rd, Baton
Rouge, LA 70809, Res. (800)
466-8356 Ph: 504 291-4912
Fax: 504 291-8554

BOSSIER CITY — LA

Motel 6 $
210 John Wesley Blvd,
Bossier City, LA 71112, Res.
(800) 466-8356 Ph: 318
742-3472 Fax: 318 746-9803

Red Carpet Inn $$
1968 Airline Dr., I-20, exit 22,
Bossier City, LA 71112, Res.
(800) 251-1962 Ph: (318)
746-9400 Fax: (318) 742-5266

DERIDDER — LA

Red Carpet Inn $$
806 No. Pine St., Hwy 171 No.,
DeRidder, LA 70634, Res.
(800) 251-1962 Ph: (318)
463-8605 Fax: (318) 462-8605

HAMMOND — LA

Super 8 Motel $-$$
Western Oaks Dr. & Hwy
190, Hammond, LA 70401,
Res. (800) 800-8000

HOUMA — LA

Red Carpet Inn $$
2115 Bayou Black Dr., US90
W., Houma, LA 70360, Res.
(800) 251-1962 Ph: (504)
876-4160 Fax: (504) 879-2352

LAFAYETTE — LA

Motel 6 $
2724 NE Evangeline Thruway,
Lafayette, LA 70507, Res.
(800) 466-8356 Ph: 318
233-2055 Fax: 318 269-9267

Super 8 Motel $-$$
2224 N.E. Evangeline Thwy.,
Lafayette, LA 70501, Res.
(800) 800-8000 Ph: (318)
232-8826 Fax: (318) 232-8826

LAKE CHARLES — LA

Motel 6 $
335 Hwy 171, Lake Charles,
LA 70601, Res. (800)
466-8356 Ph: 318 433-1773
Fax: 318 497-1884

MONROE — LA

Motel 6 $
1501 US Hwy 165 Bypass,
Monroe, LA 71202, Res.
(800) 466-8356 Ph: 318
322-5430 Fax: 318 388-6953

NATCHITOCHES — LA

Super 8 Motel $-$$
801 Hwy. 3110 Bypass,
Natchitoches, LA 71457,
Res. (800) 800-8000 Ph: (318)
352-1700 Fax: (318) 352-1700

NEW ORLEANS — LA

Econo Lodge $-$$
4940 Chef Menteur Hwy.,
New Orleans, LA 70126,
Res. (800) 424-4777

Old World Inn $$
1330 Prytania St., New
Orleans, LA 70130, Ph: (504)
566-1330

Scottish Inns $$
4200 Old Gentilly Rd., New
Orleans, LA 70128, Res.
(800) 251-1962 Ph: (504)
944-0151 Fax: (504) 945-3053

St. Vincent's Guest House $$
1500 Magazine St., New
Orleans, LA 70130, Ph: (504)
566-1515 Fax: (504) 566-1518

M O T E L

PORT ALLEN LA	**Scottish Inns** $$
Motel 6 $	1467 Hammond St., I-95, exit
2800 I-10 Frontage Rd, Port	45B, Bangor, ME 04401,
Allen, LA 70767, Res. (800)	Res. (800) 251-1962 Ph: (207)
466-8356 Ph: 504 343-5945	945-2934 Fax: (207) 945-3456
Fax: 504 389-5803	

PORT ALLEN LA

Motel 6 $
2800 I-10 Frontage Rd, Port Allen, LA 70767, Res. (800) 466-8356 Ph: 504 343-5945 Fax: 504 389-5803

RUSTON LA

Super 8 Motel $-$$
1101 Cooktown (Tech Dr.), Ruston, LA 71270, Res. (800) 800-8000 Fax: (318) 255-0588

SHREVEPORT LA

Econo Lodge Airport $-$$
4911 Monkhouse Dr., Shreveport, LA 71109, Res. (800) 424-4777 Ph: (318) 636-0771

Super 8 Motel $-$$
5204 Monkhouse Dr, Shreveport, LA 71109, Res. (800) 800-8000 Ph: (318) 635-8888

SLIDELL LA

Budget Host Slidell $-$$
1662 Gause Blvd, Slidell, LA 70458-2210, Res. (800) 283-4678 Ph: (504) 641-8800

Econo Lodge $-$$
I-10 & Gause Blvd., Slidell, LA 70459, Res. (800) 424-4777 Ph: (504) 641-2153

Motel 6 $
136 Taos St, Slidell, LA 70458, Res. (800) 466-8356 Ph: 504 649-7925 Fax: 504 643-3567

WEST MONROE LA

Super 8 Motel $-$$
1101 Glenwood Dr., West Monroe, LA 71291, Res. (800) 800-8000 Ph: (318) 325-6361 Fax: (318) 325-6361

MAINE

AUGUSTA ME

Motel 6 $
18 Edison Dr, Augusta, ME 04330, Res. (800) 466-8356 Ph: 207 622-0000 Fax: 207 622-1048

Super 8 Motel $-$$
395 Western Ave., Augusta, ME 04330, Res. (800) 800-8000 Ph: (207) 626-2888 Fax: (207) 623-8468

BANGOR ME

Econo Lodge $-$$
482 Odlin Rd., Bangor, ME 04401, Res. (800) 424-4777 Ph: (207) 942-6301 Fax: (207) 941-0949

Motel 6 $
1100 Hammond St, Bangor, ME 04401, Res. (800) 466-8356 Ph: 207 947-6921 Fax: 207 941-8543

Scottish Inns $$
1467 Hammond St., I-95, exit 45B, Bangor, ME 04401, Res. (800) 251-1962 Ph: (207) 945-2934 Fax: (207) 945-3456

Super 8 Motel $-$$
462 Odlin Road, Bangor, ME 04401, Res. (800) 800-8000 Ph: (207) 947-7289

BRUNSWICK ME

Econo Lodge $-$$
US 1 & I-95, Brunswick, ME 04011, Res. (800) 424-4777 Ph: (207) 729-9991

Super 8 Motel $-$$
224 Bath Road, Cooks Corner, Brunswick, ME 04011, Res. (800) 800-8000 Ph: (207) 725-8883 Fax: (207) 729-8766

FREEPORT ME

Super 8 Motel $-$$
218 Rte. 1 South, Freeport, ME 04032, Res. (800) 800-8000 Ph: (207) 865-1408 Fax: (207) 865-1417

HOULTON ME

Scottish Inns $$
I-95, exit 62, Bangor Rd., Houlton, ME 04730, Res. (800) 251-1962 Ph: (207) 532-2236 Fax: (207) 532-9893

KENNEBUNK ME

Econo Lodge $-$$
55 York St. US 1 S., Kennebunk, ME 04043, Res. (800) 424-4777 Ph: (207) 985-6100

KITTERY ME

Super 8 Motel $-$$
85 US Rt 1 I-95, Kittery, ME 03904, Res. (800) 800-8000 Ph: (207) 439-2000

LEWISTON ME

Motel 6 $
516 Pleasant St, Lewiston, ME 04240, Res. (800) 466-8356 Ph: 207 782-6558 Fax: 207 783-5270

Super 8 Motel $-$$
1440 Lisbon St., Lewiston, ME 04240, Res. (800) 800-8000 Ph: (207) 725-8883 Fax: (207) 784-1778

PORTLAND ME

Motel 6 $
One Riverside St, Portland, ME 04103, Res. (800) 466-8356 Ph: 207 775-0111 Fax: 207 775-0449

SANFORD ME

Super 8 Motel $-$$
"Rt. 109, Box 688", Sanford, ME 04073, Res. (800) 800-8000 Ph: (207) 324-8823 Fax: (207) 324-8782

WATERVILLE ME

Budget Host Airport Inn $-$$
400 Kennedy Memorial Dr, Waterville, ME 04901, Res. (800) 283-4678 Ph: (207) 873-3366 Fax: (207) 873-3366

Econo Lodge $-$$
455 Kennedy Memorial Dr., Waterville, ME 04901, Res. (800) 424-4777 Ph: (207) 872-5577

WESTBROOK ME

Super 8 Motel $-$$
"208 Larrabee Rd, Box 2", Westbrook, ME 04092-4751, Res. (800) 800-8000 Ph: (207) 854-1881 Fax: (207) 854-0078

MARYLAND

ABERDEEN MD

Econo Lodge $-$$
820 W. Bel Air Ave., Aberdeen, MD 21001, Res. (800) 424-4777 Ph: (410) 272-5500 Fax: (410) 272-7648

Super 8 Motel $-$$
1008 Beards Hill Rd., Aberdeen, MD 21001, Res. (800) 800-8000 Ph: (410) 272-5420 Fax: (410) 272-5420

ANNAPOLIS MD

Econo Lodge $-$$
2451 Riva Rd., Annapolis, MD 21401, Res. (800) 424-4777 Ph: (410) 224-4317 Fax: (410) 272-7648

Super 8 Motel $-$$
74 Old Mill Bottom Road North, Annapolis, MD 21401, Res. (800) 800-8000 Ph: (410) 757-2222 Fax: (410) 757-9838

BALTIMORE MD

Econo Lodge $-$$
5895 Bonnie View Ln., Baltimore, MD 21227, Res. (800) 424-4777 Ph: (410) 796-1020

Econo Lodge $-$$
407 Reisterstown Rd., Baltimore, MD 21208, Res. (800) 424-4777 Ph: (410) 484-1800 Fax: (410) 486-3882

Econo Lodge West $-$$
5801 Baltimore National Pike, Baltimore, MD 21228, Res. (800) 424-4777 Ph: (410) 744-5000 Fax: (410) 788-5197

Motel 6 $
1654 Whitehead Court, Baltimore, MD 21207, Res. (800) 466-8356 Ph: 410 265-7660 Fax: 410 944-0350

Super 8 Motel $-$$
3600 Pulaski Highway, Baltimore, MD 21224, Res. (800) 800-8000 Ph: (410) 327-7801 Fax: (410) 732-4318

BOWIE   MD

Econo Lodge $-$$
US 301 & 50 at SR 3, Bowie, MD 20718, Res. (800) 424-4777 Ph: (301) 464-2200 Fax: (301) 805-5563

CALIFORNIA   MD

Super 8 Motel $-$$
9290 Three Notch Road, California, MD 20619, Res. (800) 800-8000 Ph: (301) 862-9822 Fax: (301) 862-9822

CAMP SPRINGS   MD

Motel 6 $
5701 Allentown Rd, Camp Springs, MD 20746, Res. (800) 466-8356 Ph: 301 702-1061 Fax: 301 899-3478

Super 8 Motel $-$$
5151 Allentown Road, Camp Springs, MD 20746, Res. (800) 800-8000 Ph: (301) 899-7700 Fax: (301) 505-1195

CAPITOL HEIGHTS   MD

Motel 6 $
75 Hampton Park Blvd, Capitol Heights, MD 20743, Res. (800) 466-8356 Ph: 301 499-0800 Fax: 301 808-7253

CLINTON   MD

Econo Lodge Andrews Afb $-$$
7851 Malcolm Rd., Clinton, MD 20735, Res. (800) 424-4777 Ph: (301) 856-2800 Fax: (301) 856-0033

COCKEYSVILLE HUNT   MD

Econo Lodge $-$$
10100 York Rd., Cockeysville Hunt Valley, MD 21030, Res. (800) 424-4777 Ph: (410) 667-4900 Fax: (410) 667-1986

COLLEGE PARK   MD

Super 8 Motel $-$$
910 Baltimore Ave, College Park, MD 20740, Res. (800) 800-8000 Ph: (301) 474-0894 Fax: (301) 474-0894

EASTON   MD

Econo Lodge Intown $-$$
8175 Ocean Gateway, Easton, MD 21601, Res. (800) 424-4777 Ph: (410) 820-5555

ELKTON   MD

Econo Lodge $-$$
311 Belle Hill Rd., Elkton, MD 21921, Res. (800) 424-4777 Ph: (410) 392-5010

Motel 6 $
223 Belle Hill Rd, Elkton, MD 21921, Res. (800) 466-8356 Ph: 410 392-5020 Fax: 410 398-1143

ESSEX   MD

Super 8 Motel $-$$
98 Stemmers Run Rd., Essex, MD 21221, Res. (800) 800-8000 Ph: (410) 327-7801 Fax: (410) 780-0030

FREDERICK   MD

Super 8 Motel $-$$
5579 Spectrum Drive, Frederick, MD 21701, Res. (800) 800-8000 Ph: (301) 695-2881 Fax: (301) 695-7639

GAITHERSBURG   MD

Econo Lodge $-$$
18715 N. Frederick Ave., Gaithersburg, MD 20879, Res. (800) 424-4777 Ph: (301) 963-3840 Fax: (301) 948-7443

HAGERSTOWN   MD

Motel 6 $
11321 Massey Blvd, Hagerstown, MD 21740, Res. (800) 466-8356 Ph: 301 582-4445 Fax: 301 582-0942

Super 8 Motel $-$$
1220 Dual Hwy, Hagerstown, MD 21740, Res. (800) 800-8000 Ph: (301) 739-5800 Fax: (301) 739-5800

HAVRE DE GRACE   MD

Super 8 Motel $-$$
929 Pulaski Highway, Havre De Grace, MD 21078, Res. (800) 800-8000 Ph: (410) 939-1880 Fax: (410) 939-1880

JESSUP   MD

Super 8 Motel $-$$
8094 Washington Blvd., Jessup, MD 20794, Res. (800) 800-8000 Ph: (410) 796-0401 Fax: (410) 799-7736

JOPPA   MD

Super 8 Motel $-$$
1015 Pulaski Highway, Joppa, MD 21085, Res. (800) 800-8000 Ph: (410) 676-2700

LA PLATA   MD

Econo Lodge $-$$
US 301 & SR 6, La Plata, MD 20646, Res. (800) 424-4777 Ph: (301) 934-1400

Super 8 Motel $-$$
729 North Hwy 301, La Plata, MD 20646, Res. (800) 800-8000 Ph: (301) 934-3465 Fax: (301) 934-3709

LAUREL   MD

Budget Host Valencia Motel $-$$
10131 Washington Blvd, Laurel, MD 20723, Res. (800) 283-4678 Ph: (301) 725-4200

Econo Lodge Laurel $-$$
9700 Washington Blvd. / US 1, Laurel, MD 20723, Res. (800) 424-4777 Ph: (301) 776-8008 Fax: (301) 498-6661

Motel 6 $
3510 Old Annapolis Rd, Laurel, MD 20724, Res. (800) 466-8356 Ph: 301 497-1544 Fax: 301 317-8386

LAVALE   MD

Scottish Inns $$
1262 National Hwy, LaVale, MD 21502, Res. (800) 251-1962 Ph: (301) 729-2880 Fax: (301) 729-5275

Super 8 Motel $-$$
1301 National Hwy., LaVale, MD 21502, Res. (800) 800-8000 Ph: (301) 729-6265 Fax: (301) 729-6265

LINTHICUM HEIGHTS   MD

Motel 6 $
5179 Raynor Ave, Linthicum Heights, MD 21090, Res. (800) 466-8356 Ph: 410 636-9070 Fax: 410 789-0669

OCEAN CITY   MD

Econo Lodge $-$$
6007 Coastal Hwy., Ocean City, MD 21842, Res. (800) 424-4777 Ph: (410) 524-6100 Fax: (410) 524-1619

Econo Lodge Oceanblock $-$$
145th St. & Coastal Hwy., Ocean City, MD 21842, Res. (800) 424-4777 Ph: (410) 250-1155 Fax: (410) 250-1155

Econo Lodge Oceanfront $-$$
45th St. and Oceanfront, Ocean City, MD 21842, Res. (800) 424-4777 Ph: (410) 289-6424

PRINCESS ANNE   MD

Econo Lodge $-$$
US 13, Princess Anne, MD 21853, Res. (800) 424-4777 Ph: (410) 651-9400 Fax: (410) 651-2868

SALISBURY   MD

Budget Host Temple Hill $-$$
1510 S Salis Blvd, Salisbury, MD 21801, Res. (800) 283-4678 Ph: (410) 742-3284 Fax: (410) 742-5343

Econo Lodge Statesman $-$$
712 N. Salisbury Blvd., Salisbury, MD 21801, Res. (800) 424-4777 Ph: (410) 749-7155 Fax: (410) 749-6728

Super 8 Motel $-$$
2615 N. Salisbury Blvd., Salisbury, MD 21801, Res. (800) 800-8000 Ph: (410) 749-5131 Fax: (410) 749-5131

M O T E L

SILVER SPRING MD	**DUXBURY** MA	**MALDEN** MA

SILVER SPRING MD

Econo Lodge $-$$
7990 Georgia Ave., Silver
Spring, MD 20910, Res.
(800) 424-4777 Ph: (301)
565-3444 Fax: (301) 588-2207

THURMONT MD

Super 8 Motel $-$$
300 Tippin Drive, Thurmont,
MD 21788, Res. (800)
800-8000 Ph: (301) 271-7888
Fax: (301) 271-7888

WALDORF MD

Econo Lodge $-$$
US 301, Acton Lane, Waldorf,
MD 20601, Res. (800)
424-4777 Ph: (301) 645-0022
Fax: (301) 645-0058

Super 8 Motel $-$$
5050 Hwy 301 S., Waldorf,
MD 20601, Res. (800)
800-8000 Ph: (301) 932-8957
Fax: (301) 932-8957

MASSACHUSETTS

BOSTON MA

463 Beacon Street Guest $$
463 Beacon St., Boston, MA
02115, Ph: (617) 536-1302
Fax: (617) 247-8876

BRAINTREE MA

Motel 6 $
125 Union St, Braintree, MA
02184, Res. (800) 466-8356
Ph: 617 848-7890 Fax: 617
843-1929

BROOKLINE MA

Anthony's Town House $
1085 Beacon St., Brookline,
MA 02146, Ph: (617) 566-3972

CHICOPEE MA

Motel 6 $
Burnett Rd, Chicopee, MA
01020, Res. (800) 466-8356
Ph: 413 592-5141 Fax: 413
592-0564

DANVERS MA

Econo Lodge $-$$
50 Dayton St., Danvers, MA
01923, Res. (800) 424-4777
Ph: (508) 777-1700 Fax: (508)
777-4647

Motel 6 $
65 Newbury St/US 1,
Danvers, MA 01923-1072,
Res. (800) 466-8356 Ph: 508
774-8045 Fax: 508 774-0932

Super 8 Motel $-$$
225 Newbury Street,
Danvers, MA 01923, Res.
(800) 800-8000 Ph: (508)
774-6500

DUXBURY MA

Econo Lodge $-$$
2222 S. Military Hwy.,
Duxbury, MA 23320, Res.
(800) 424-4777 Ph: (804)
543-2200

FISKDALE MA

Econo Lodge $-$$
682 Main St., Fiskdale, MA
01518, Res. (800) 424-4777
Ph: (508) 347-2324

FRAMINGHAM MA

Econo Lodge $-$$
1186 Worcester Rd.,
Framingham, MA 01701,
Res. (800) 424-4777 Ph: (508)
879-1510 Fax: (508) 875-2686

Motel 6 $
1668 Worcester Rd,
Framingham, MA 01702,
Res. (800) 466-8356 Ph: 508
620-0500 Fax: 508 820-0868

GARDNER MA

Super 8 Motel $-$$
22 North Pearson Blvd,
Gardner, MA 01440, Res.
(800) 800-8000 Ph: (508)
630-2888 Fax: (508) 630-1716

GREENFIELD MA

Super 8 Motel $-$$
21 Colrain Rd, Greenfield,
MA 01301, Res. (800)
800-8000 Ph: (413) 774-5578
Fax: (413) 774-4383

HOLYOKE MA

Super 8 Motel $-$$
1515 Northampton St.,
Holyoke, MA 01040, Res.
(800) 800-8000 Ph: (413)
536-1980

HYANNIS MA

Budget Host Hyannis Motel $$
614 Rt. 132, Hyannis, MA
02601, Ph: (508) 775-8910
Fax: (508) 775-6476

LEE MA

Super 8 Motel $-$$
Route 20 & 128 Housatonic
St., Lee, MA 01238, Res.
(800) 800-8000 Ph: (413)
243-0143 Fax: (413) 243-3271

LEOMINSTER MA

Motel 6 $
Commercial St, Leominster,
MA 01453, Res. (800)
466-8356 Ph: 508 537-8161
Fax: 508 537-2082

Super 8 Motel $-$$
482 North Main Street,
Leominster, MA 01453, Res.
(800) 800-8000 Ph: (508)
537-2800 Fax: (508) 840-4367

MALDEN MA

Econo Lodge $-$$
321 Broadway, Malden, MA
02148, Res. (800) 424-4777
Ph: (617) 324-8500

MANSFIELD MA

Motel 6 $
60 Forbes Blvd, Mansfield,
MA 02048, Res. (800)
466-8356 Ph: 508 339-2323
Fax: 508 337-6733

MARLBOROUGH MA

Super 8 Motel $-$$
880 Donald J. Lynch Blvd.,
Marlborough, MA 01752,
Res. (800) 800-8000 Ph: (508)
460-1000 Fax: (508) 460-9103

N. ATTLEBORO MA

Super 8 Motel $-$$
787 S. Washington St., N.
Attleboro, MA 02760, Res.
(800) 800-8000 Ph: (508)
643-2900 Fax: (508) 643-2900

SEEKONK MA

Motel 6 $
821 Fall River Avenue,
Seekonk, MA 02771, Res.
(800) 466-8356 Ph: 508
336-7800 Fax: 508 336-0977

SHARON MA

Super 8 Motel $-$$
395 Old Post Rd. #1, Sharon,
MA 02067-1619, Res. (800)
800-8000 Ph: (617) 784-1000
Fax: (617) 784-1242

SOUTH DEERFIELD MA

Motel 6 $
Rt 5-10, South Deerfield, MA
01373, Res. (800) 466-8356
Ph: 413 665-7161 Fax: 413
665-7437

SOUTH YARMOUTH MA

Econo Lodge $-$$
37 Neptune Ln., South
Yarmouth, MA 02664, Res.
(800) 424-4777 Ph: (508)
394-9801

Motel 6 $
1314 Route 28, South
Yarmouth, MA 02664, Res.
(800) 466-8356 Ph: 508
394-4000 Fax: 508 394-4000

TEWKSBURY MA

Econo Lodge $-$$
95 Main St., Tewksbury, MA
01876, Res. (800) 424-4777
Ph: (508) 851-7301 Fax: (508)
851-9443

W SPRINGFIELD MA

Motel 6 $
106 Capital Dr, W Springfield,
MA 01089, Res. (800)
466-8356 Ph: 413 788-4000
Fax: 413 781-3168

W. YARMOUTH   MA

Super 8 Motel $-$$
36 East Main St., W.
Yarmouth, MA 02673, Res.
(800) 800-8000 Ph: (508)
775-3000

WEST SPRINGFIEL   MA

Super 8 Motel $-$$
1500 Riverdale St., West
Springfiel, MA 01089, Res.
(800) 800-8000 Ph: (413)
736-8080 Fax: (413) 747-9214

WEST SPRINGFIELD   MA

Econo Lodge $-$$
1533 Elm St., West
Springfield, MA 01089, Res.
(800) 424-4777 Ph: (413)
734-8278 Fax: (413) 736-7690

Red Carpet Inn $$
560 Rivedale St., West
Springfield, MA 01089, Res.
(800) 251-1962 Ph: (413)
733-6678 Fax: (413) 733-6678

WORCESTER   MA

Econo Lodge $-$$
531 Lincoln St., Worcester,
MA 01605, Res. (800)
424-4777 Ph: (508) 852-5800
Fax: (508) 852-4151

MICHIGAN

ADRIAN   MI

Super 8 Motel $-$$
1091 US 223, Adrian, MI
49221, Res. (800) 800-8000
Ph: (517) 265-8888 Fax: (517)
265-8888

ALLEGAN   MI

Budget Host Sunset Motel$-$$
1580 Lincoln Rd, Allegan, MI
49010, Res. (800) 283-4678
Ph: (616) 673-6622

ANN ARBOR   MI

Motel 6 $
3764 S State St, Ann Arbor,
MI 48108, Res. (800)
466-8356 Ph: 313 665-9900
Fax: 313 665-2202

AUBURN HILLS   MI

Motel 6 $
1471 Opdyke Rd, Auburn
Hills, MI 48326, Res. (800)
466-8356 Ph: 810 373-8440
Fax: 810 373-8642

BARAGA   MI

Super 8 Motel $-$$
790 Michigan Ave., P.O. Box
501, Baraga, MI 49908-0501,
Res. (800) 800-8000 Ph: (906)
353-6680 Fax: (906) 353-7246

BATTLE CREEK   MI

Motel 6 $
4775 Beckley Rd, Battle
Creek, MI 49015, Res. (800)
466-8356 Ph: 616 979-1141
Fax: 616 979-1733

Super 8 Motel $-$$
5395 Beckley Road, Battle
Creek, MI 49017, Res. (800)
800-8000 Ph: (616) 979-1828
Fax: (616) 979-1828

BELLEVILLE   MI

Super 8 Motel $-$$
45707 South I-94, Belleville,
MI 48111, Res. (800)
800-8000 Ph: (313) 699-1888
Fax: (313) 699-1888

BENTON HARBOR   MI

Motel 6 $
2063 Pipestone Rd, Benton
Harbor, MI 49022, Res. (800)
466-8356 Ph: 616 925-5100
Fax: 616 934-8404

Super 8 Motel $-$$
1950 East Napier Avenue,
Benton Harbor, MI 49022,
Res. (800) 800-8000 Ph: (616)
926-1371 Fax: (616) 926-1371

BIRCH RUN   MI

Super 8 Motel $-$$
9235 East Birch Run Road,
Birch Run, MI 48415, Res.
(800) 800-8000 Ph: (517)
624-4440 Fax: (517) 624-9439

BRIDGEPORT   MI

Motel 6 $
6361 Dixie Hwy, Bridgeport,
MI 48722, Res. (800)
466-8356 Ph: 517 777-2582
Fax: 517 777-9546

CADILLAC   MI

Super 8 Motel $-$$
211 West M-55, Cadillac, MI
49601, Res. (800) 800-8000
Ph: (616) 775-8561 Fax: (616)
775-9392

CANTON   MI

Super 8 Motel $-$$
3933 Lotz Rd, Canton, MI
48188, Res. (800) 800-8000
Ph: (313) 722-8880 Fax: (313)
722-8880

CANTON TOWNSHIP   MI

Motel 6 $
41216 Ford Rd, Canton
Township, MI 48187, Res.
(800) 466-8356 Ph: 313
981-5000 Fax: 313 981-5432

CHARLOTTE   MI

Super 8 Motel $-$$
740 E. Shepard, Charlotte,
MI 48813, Res. (800)
800-8000 Ph: (517) 543-8288
Fax: (517) 278-7899

CLARE   MI

Budget Host Clare Motel $-$$
1110 N Mcewan, Clare, MI
48617, Res. (800) 283-4678
Ph: (517) 386-7201 Fax: (517)
386-2362

CLAWSON   MI

Super 8 Motel $-$$
1145 W. Maple, Clawson, MI
48017, Res. (800) 800-8000
Ph: (810) 435-8881 Fax: (810)
435-8881

COLDWATER   MI

Econo Lodge $-$$
884 W. Chicago Rd.,
Coldwater, MI 49036, Res.
(800) 424-4777 Ph: (517)
278-4501

Super 8 Motel $-$$
600 Orleans Blvd., Coldwater,
MI 49036, Res. (800)
800-8000 Ph: (517) 278-8833
Fax: (517) 278-2347

ESCANABA   MI

Super 8 Motel $-$$
2415 North Lincoln,
Escanaba, MI 49829, Res.
(800) 800-8000 Ph: (906)
786-1000 Fax: (906) 786-7819

ESCANATA   MI

Budget Host Terrace Bay Inn$-$$
7146 P Road, Escanata, MI
49829, Ph: (906) 786-7554
Fax: (906) 786-7954

FARMINGTON HILLS   MI

Motel 6 $
38300 Grand River Ave,
Farmington Hills, MI 48335,
Res. (800) 466-8356 Ph: 810
471-0590 Fax: 810 471-2435

FLINT   MI

Econo Lodge $-$$
932 S. Center Rd., Flint, MI
48503, Res. (800) 424-4777
Ph: (810) 744-0200 Fax: (810)
744-2954

Motel 6 $
2324 Austin Pkwy, Flint, MI
48507, Res. (800) 466-8356
Ph: 810 767-7100 Fax: 810
767-5702

Super 8 Motel $-$$
3033 Claude Ave., Flint, MI
48507, Res. (800) 800-8000
Ph: (810) 230-7888 Fax: (810)
230-7888

Super 8 Motel $-$$
4178 W. Pierson Rd., Flint,
MI 48504, Res. (800)
800-8000 Ph: (810) 789-0400

GAYLORD   MI

Super 8 Motel $-$$
1042 W. Main St., Gaylord,
MI 49735, Res. (800)
800-8000 Ph: (517) 732-5193
Fax: (616) 436-7004

GRAND MARAIS   MI

Budget Host Welkers Lodge$-$$
Canal St- Box 277, Grand
Marais, MI 49839, Res. (800)
283-4678 Ph: (906) 494-2361
Fax: (906) 494-2371

M
O
T
E
L

GRAND RAPIDS	MI

Econo Lodge   S-SS
250 28th St., S.W., Grand
Rapids, MI 49548, Res. (800)
424-4777 Ph: (616) 452-2131
Fax: (616) 452-2929

Motel 6   S
3524 28th St SE, Grand
Rapids, MI 49508, Res. (800)
466-8356 Ph: 616 957-3511
Fax: 616 957-4369

GRAYLING	MI

Super 8 Motel   S-SS
5828 N.A. Miles Parkway,
Grayling, MI 49738, Res.
(800) 800-8000 Ph: (517)
348-8888 Fax: (517) 348-2030

HOLLAND	MI

Budget Host Wooden ShoeSS
US 31 Bypass at 16th,
Holland, MI 49423, Res.
(800) 283-4678 Ph: (616)
392-8521

Super 8 Motel   S-SS
680 E. 24th, Holland, MI
49423, Res. (800) 800-8000
Ph: (616) 396-8822 Fax: (616)
396-2050

HOUGHTON	MI

Super 8 Motel   S-SS
1200 E. Lakeshore Dr.,
Houghton, MI 49931, Res.
(800) 800-8000 Ph: (906)
482-2240 Fax: (906) 482-0686

IMLAY CITY	MI

Super 8 Motel   S-SS
6951 Newark Rd., Imlay City,
MI 48444, Res. (800)
800-8000 Ph: (313) 724-8700
Fax: (810) 724-4013

IONIA	MI

Super 8 Motel   S-SS
I-96 & 66, Ionia, MI 48846,
Res. (800) 800-8000 Ph: (616)
527-2828 Fax: (616) 527-0729

IRON MOUNTAIN	MI

Super 8 Motel   S-SS
2702 N Stephenson, Iron
Mountain, MI 49801, Res.
(800) 800-8000 Ph: (906)
774-3400 Fax: (906) 774-9903

IRONWOOD	MI

Budget Host Cloverland   S-SS
447 W Cloverland Dr,
Ironwood, MI 49938, Res.
(800) 283-4678 Ph: (906)
932-1260

Super 8 Motel   S-SS
160 East Cloverland Drive,
Ironwood, MI 49938, Res.
(800) 800-8000 Ph: (906)
932-3395 Fax: (906) 932-2507

JACKSON	MI

Motel 6   S
830 Royal Dr, Jackson, MI
49202, Res. (800) 466-8356
Ph: 517 789-7186 Fax: 517
789-5490

Super 8 Motel   S-SS
2001 Shirley Dr., Jackson,
MI 49202, Res. (800)
800-8000 Ph: (517) 788-8780
Fax: (517) 788-8780

KALAMAZOO	MI

Motel 6   S
3704 Van Rick Rd,
Kalamazoo, MI 49002, Res.
(800) 466-8356 Ph: 616
344-9255 Fax: 616 344-3014

Super 8 Motel   S-SS
618 Maple Hill Drive,
Kalamazoo, MI 49009-1032,
Res. (800) 800-8000 Ph: (616)
345-0146 Fax: (616) 345-0146

LANSING	MI

Motel 6   S
112 E Main St, Lansing, MI
48933, Res. (800) 466-8356
Ph: 517 484-8722 Fax: 517
484-9434

Motel 6   S
7326 W Saginaw Hwy,
Lansing, MI 48917, Res.
(800) 466-8356 Ph: 517
321-1444 Fax: 517 886-2024

Super 8 Motel   S-SS
910 American Rd, Lansing,
MI 48911, Res. (800)
800-8000 Ph: (517) 393-8008
Fax: (517) 393-8008

LIVONIA	MI

Super 8 Motel   S-SS
28512 Schoolcraft, Livonia,
MI 48150, Res. (800)
800-8000 Ph: (313) 425-5150
Fax: (313) 425-5150

MACKINAW CITY	MI

Budget Host Mackinaw CitySS
517 N Huron Ave-- Box 672,
Mackinaw City, MI 49701,
Res. (800) 283-4678 Ph: (616)
436-5543

Econo Lodge At The BridgeSS
412 Nicolet St., Mackinaw
City, MI 49701, Res. (800)
424-4777 Ph: (616) 436-5026
Fax: (616) 436-4172

Econo Lodge Lakeside   S-SS
519 S. Huron, Mackinaw
City, MI 49701, Res. (800)
424-4777 Ph: (616) 436-7111
Fax: (616) 436-5011

Motel 6   S
206 Nicolet St., Mackinaw
City, MI 49701, Res. (800)
466-8356 Ph: 616 436-8961
Fax: 616 436-7317

Super 8 Motel	S-SS

P.O. Box 98, 601 North
Huron, Mackinaw City, MI
49701, Res. (800) 800-8000
Ph: (616) 436-5252 Fax: (616)
436-7004

MADISON HEIGHTS	MI

Motel 6   S
32700 Barrington Rd,
Madison Heights, MI 48071,
Res. (800) 466-8356 Ph: 810
583-0500 Fax: 810 588-6945

MANISTIQUE	MI

Budget Host ManistiqueS-SS
US 2 E-- RT 1, Box 1505,
Manistique, MI 49854, Res.
(800) 283-4678 Ph: (906)
341-2552

Econo Lodge   S-SS
E. Lakeshore Dr., US 2,
Manistique, MI 49854, Res.
(800) 424-4777 Ph: (906)
341-6014 Fax: (000) 000-9060

MARQUETTE	MI

Budget Host Brentwood   S-SS
2603 US 41 W, Marquette, MI
49855, Res. (800) 283-4678
Ph: (906) 228-7494

Super 8 Motel   S-SS
1275 US Hwy 41 West,
Marquette, MI 49855, Res.
(800) 800-8000 Ph: (906)
228-8100 Fax: (906) 228-8100

MARYSVILLE	MI

Budget Host Inn   S-SS
1484 Gratiot Blvd, Marysville,
MI 48040, Res. (800)
283-4678 Ph: (810) 364-7500
Fax: (810) 364-4423

MOUNT PLEASANT	MI

Super 8 Motel   S-SS
2323 South Mission, Mount
Pleasant, MI 48804-0222,
Res. (800) 800-8000 Ph: (517)
773-8888 Fax: (517) 772-5371

MUSKEGON HEIGHT	MI

Super 8 Motel   S-SS
3380 Hoyt Street, Muskegon
Height, MI 49444-3165, Res.
(800) 800-8000 Ph: (616)
733-0088 Fax: (616) 733-0088

ONEKAMA	MI

Budget Host Alpine MotorS-SS
8127 US 31--box 366,
Onekama, MI 49675, Res.
(800) 283-4678 Ph: (616)
889-4281

PETOSKEY	MI

Econo Lodge   S-SS
1858 US 131 S., Petoskey, MI
49770, Res. (800) 424-4777
Ph: (616) 348-3324 Fax: (616)
348-3521

ROMULUS   MI

Super 8 Motel   S-$$
9863 Middlebelt Road,
Romulus, MI 48174, Res.
(800) 800-8000 Ph: (313)
946-8808 Fax: (313) 346-8808

ROSEVILLE   MI

Super 8 Motel   S-$$
20445 Erin St., Roseville, MI
48066, Res. (800) 800-8000
Ph: (810) 296-1730 Fax: (810)
296-1730

SAGINAW   MI

Super 8 Motel   S-$$
4848 Towne Centre Road,
Saginaw, MI 48603, Res.
(800) 800-8000 Ph: (517)
791-3003 Fax: (517) 791-3003

SAINT IGNACE   MI

Budget Host Inn   S-$$
700 N State St, Saint Ignace,
MI 49781, Res. (800)
283-4678 Ph: (906) 643-9666

Econo Lodge   S-$$
1030 N. State St., Saint
Ignace, MI 49781, Res. (800)
424-4777 Ph: (906) 643-8060
Fax: (906) 643-7923

SAULT ST. MARIE   MI

Super 8 Motel   S-$$
"3826 I-75, Business Spur",
Sault St. Marie, MI 49783,
Res. (800) 800-8000 Ph: (906)
632-8882 Fax: (906) 632-3766

SOUTHFIELD   MI

Econo Lodge   S-$$
23300 Telegraph Rd.,
Southfield, MI 48034, Res.
(800) 424-4777 Ph: (810)
358-1800 Fax: (810) 358-2008

STERLING HTS   MI

Super 8 Motel   S-$$
34550 Van Dyke, Sterling
Hts, MI 48312, Res. (800)
800-8000 Ph: (810) 795-8800
Fax: (810) 795-8800

STERLINGHEIGHTS   MI

Villager   S-$$
34858 Van Dyke Road,
SterlingHeights, MI 48312,
Res. (800) 328-7829 Ph: (810)
939-5555 Fax: (810) 939-7320

TAYLOR   MI

Super 8 Motel   S-$$
15101 Huron Street, Taylor,
MI 48180, Res. (800)
800-8000 Ph: (313) 283-8830
Fax: (313) 283-8830

TRAVERSE CITY   MI

Econo Lodge   S-$$
1065 SR 37 S. (M-37),
Traverse City, MI 49684,
Res. (800) 424-4777 Ph: (616)
943-3040 Fax: (616) 943-9559

Super 8 Motel   S-$$
1870 U.S. Hwy 31 North,
Traverse City, MI 49684,
Res. (800) 800-8000 Ph: (616)
938-1887 Fax: (616) 938-2451

WALKER   MI

Motel 6   S
777 Three Mile Rd, Walker,
MI 79504, Res. (800)
466-8356 Ph: 616 784-9375
Fax: 616 784-7721

WARREN   MI

Motel 6   S
8300 Chicago Rd, Warren, MI
48093, Res. (800) 466-8356
Ph: 810 826-9300 Fax: 810
979-4525

WEST BRANCH   MI

Super 8 Motel   S-$$
I-75 Exit 212 Cook Rd, West
Branch, MI 48661-0369,
Res. (800) 800-8000 Ph: (517)
345-8488

WETMORE   MI

Super 8 Motel   S-$$
M28 Federal Hwy 13,
Wetmore, MI 49895, Res.
(800) 800-8000 Ph: (906)
387-2466

WHITEHALL   MI

Super 8 Motel   S-$$
3080 Holton-Whitehall,
Whitehall, MI 49461, Res.
(800) 800-8000 Ph: (616)
894-4848 Fax: (616) 893-1705

WYOMING   MI

Super 8 Motel   S-$$
727 SW 44th Street,
Wyoming, MI 49509-4432,
Res. (800) 800-8000 Ph: (616)
530-8588 Fax: (616) 530-8588

MINNESOTA

ALBERT LEA   MN

Super 8 Motel   S-$$
2019 E. Main St., Albert Lea,
MN 56007, Res. (800)
800-8000 Ph: (507) 377-0591
Fax: (507) 377-0591

ALEXANDRIA   MN

Super 8 Motel   S-$$
4620 Hwy. 29 S., Alexandria,
MN 56308-2911, Res. (800)
800-8000 Ph: (612) 763-6552
Fax: (612) 763-6552

ANOKA   MN

Super 8 Motel   S-$$
1129 W. Main St., Anoka, MN
55303, Res. (800) 800-8000
Ph: (612) 422-8000 Fax: (612)
894-2771

APPLETON   MN

Super 8 Motel   S-$$
900 N. Munsterman,
Appleton, MN 56208, Res.
(800) 800-8000 Ph: (612)
289-2500

AUSTIN   MN

Super 8 Motel   S-$$
1401 14th St. N.W., Austin,
MN 55912, Res. (800)
800-8000 Ph: (507) 433-1801
Fax: (507) 433-1801

BAXTER   MN

Super 8 Motel   S-$$
P.O. Box 2505, Baxter, MN
56425-2505, Res. (800)
800-8000 Ph: (218) 828-4288
Fax: (218) 828-4288

BEMIDJI   MN

Super 8 Motel   S-$$
1815 Paul Bunyan Drive,
Bemidji, MN 56601-5602,
Res. (800) 800-8000 Ph: (218)
751-8481 Fax: (218) 751-8870

BLOOMINGTON   MN

Super 8 Motel   S-$$
7800 2nd Ave. South,
Bloomington, MN
55420-1206, Res. (800)
800-8000 Ph: (612) 888-8800
Fax: (612) 888-3469

BLUE EARTH   MN

Super 8 Motel   S-$$
1120 North Grove St., Box
394, Blue Earth, MN
56013-0394, Res. (800)
800-8000 Ph: (507) 526-7376
Fax: (507) 526-2246

BRAINERD   MN

Econo Lodge   S-$$
2655 US 371 S., Brainerd,
MN 56401, Res. (800)
424-4777 Ph: (218) 828-0027
Fax: (218) 828-0807

BROOKLYN CENTER   MN

Super 8 Motel   S-$$
6445 James Circle, Brooklyn
Center, MN 55430, Res.
(800) 800-8000 Ph: (612)
566-9810 Fax: (612) 566-8680

BROOKLYN PARK-   MN

Budget Host Inn   S-$$
6280 Lakeland Ave N,
Brooklyn Park- Minneapolis,
MN 55428, Res. (800)
283-4678 Ph: (612) 533-6455
Fax: (612) 533-1216

BUFFALO   MN

Super 8 Motel   S-$$
"303 10th Ave.,", Buffalo, MN
55313, Res. (800) 800-8000
Ph: (612) 682-5930 Fax: (612)
682-4431

M O T E L

BURNSVILLE   MN

Super 8 Motel $-$$
1101 Burnsville Pkwy.,
Burnsville, MN 55337-2343,
Res. (800) 800-8000 Ph: (612)
894-3400

CAMBRIDGE   MN

Budget Host Imperial Motel $-$$
643 N. Main, Cambridge, MN
55008, Ph: (612) 689-2200
Fax: (612) 689-1031

CHASKA   MN

Super 8 Motel $-$$
830 Yellow Brick Road,
Chaska, MN 55318, Res.
(800) 800-8000 Ph: (612)
448-7030 Fax: (612) 448-7030

CHISAGO CITY   MN

Super 8 Motel $-$$
11650 Lake Blvd(Hwy 8),
Chisago City, MN 55013,
Res. (800) 800-8000 Ph: (612)
257-8088 Fax: (612) 257-8088

CLOQUET   MN

Super 8 Motel $-$$
121 Big Lake Road, Cloquet,
MN 55720, Res. (800)
800-8000 Ph: (800) 800-8000

COTTAGE GROVE   MN

Super 8 Motel $-$$
7125 S. 80th St., Cottage
Grove, MN 55016, Res. (800)
800-8000 Ph: (612) 458-0313
Fax: (612) 458-0313

CRYSTAL   MN

Super 8 Motel $-$$
6000 Lakeland Ave. N,
Crystal, MN 55428, Res.
(800) 800-8000 Ph: (612)
537-8888 Fax: (612) 537-9629

DETROIT LAKES   MN

Budget Host Inn $-$$
895 Hwy 10 E, Detroit Lakes,
MN 56501, Res. (800)
283-4678 Ph: (218) 847-4454
Fax: (218) 847-3326

Super 8 Motel $-$$
400 Morrow Ave., Detroit
Lakes, MN 56501, Res. (800)
800-8000 Ph: (218) 847-1651
Fax: (218) 847-1651

DULUTH   MN

Motel 6 $
200 South 27th Ave. West,
Duluth, MN 55806, Res.
(800) 466-8356 Ph: 218
723-1123 Fax: 218 720-3084

Super 8 Motel $-$$
4100 West Superior Street,
Duluth, MN 55807-2725,
Res. (800) 800-8000 Ph: (218)
628-2241 Fax: (218) 628-2241

EAGAN   MN

Budget Host Inn $-$$
2745 Highway 55, Eagan, MN
55121, Ph: (612) 454-1211
Fax: (612) 686-7230

EDEN PRAIRIE   MN

Super 8 Motel $-$$
11500 West 78th Street,
Eden Prairie, MN
55344-4307, Res. (800)
800-8000 Ph: (612) 829-0888
Fax: (612) 829-0854

ELK RIVER   MN

Red Carpet Inn $$
17291 Highway 10, Elk River,
MN 55330, Res. (800)
251-1962 Ph: (612) 441-2424
Fax: (612) 241-9720

ELY   MN

Budget Host Motel Ely $-$$
1047 E Sheridan St, Ely, MN
55731, Res. (800) 283-4678
Ph: (218) 365-3227

Super 8 Motel $-$$
1605 East Sheridan St., Ely,
MN 55731, Res. (800)
800-8000 Ph: (218) 365-2873

EVELETH   MN

Super 8 Motel $-$$
1080 Industrial Park Drive,
Eveleth, MN 55734, Res.
(800) 800-8000 Ph: (218)
744-1661 Fax: (218) 744-4343

FAIRMONT   MN

Super 8 Motel $-$$
I-90 & MN 15, P.O. Box 922,
Fairmont, MN 56031-0422,
Res. (800) 800-8000 Ph: (507)
238-9444 Fax: (507) 238-9371

FARIBAULT   MN

Super 8 Motel $-$$
2509 N. Lyndale Ave.,
Faribault, MN 55021, Res.
(800) 800-8000 Ph: (507)
334-1634 Fax: (507) 332-8848

FERGUS FALLS   MN

Super 8 Motel $-$$
2454 College Way, Fergus
Falls, MN 56537, Res. (800)
800-8000 Ph: (218) 739-3261

FINLAYSON   MN

Super 8 Motel $-$$
2811 Hwy. 23 & I-35,
Finlayson, MN 55735, Res.
(800) 800-8000 Ph: (612)
245-5284 Fax: (612) 245-2233

FOSSTON   MN

Super 8 Motel $-$$
East Hwy 2 East, Fosston,
MN 56542, Res. (800)
800-8000 Ph: (218) 435-1088
Fax: (218) 435-6285

FRIDLEY- MINNEAPOL MN

Budget Host Inn $-$$
6881 Hwy 65, Fridley-
Minneapolis, MN 55432,
Res. (800) 283-4678 Ph: (612)
571-0420

GLENCOE   MN

Super 8 Motel $-$$
717 Morningside Dr.,
Glencoe, MN 55336, Res.
(800) 800-8000 Ph: (612)
864-6191

GOLDEN VALLEY   MN

Super 8 Motel $-$$
6300 Wayzata Blvd., Golden
Valley, MN 55416, Res. (800)
800-8000 Ph: (612) 546-6277
Fax: (612) 546-3431

GRAND MARAIS   MN

Econo Lodge $-$$
US 61 E., Grand Marais, MN
55604, Res. (800) 424-4777
Ph: (218) 387-2547 Fax: (218)
387-2381

Super 8 Motel $-$$
Hwy 61 W., Grand Marais,
MN 55604, Res. (800)
800-8000 Ph: (218) 387-2448
Fax: (218) 387-2448

GRAND RAPIDS   MN

Super 8 Motel $-$$
1902 S. Pokegama Ave., P.O.
Box 335, Grand Rapids, MN
55744-0335, Res. (800)
800-8000 Ph: (218) 327-1108
Fax: (218) 327-1108

GRANITE FALLS   MN

Super 8 Motel $-$$
845 W. Hwy 212, Granite
Falls, MN 56241, Res. (800)
800-8000 Ph: (612) 564-4075
Fax: (612) 564-4038

HASTINGS   MN

Super 8 Motel $-$$
2450 Vermillion St.,
Hastings, MN 55033, Res.
(800) 800-8000 Ph: (612)
438-8888 Fax: (612) 438-8888

HIBBING   MN

Super 8 Motel $-$$
1411 E. 40th St., Hibbing,
MN 55746, Res. (800)
800-8000 Ph: (218) 263-8982
Fax: (218) 263-8982

HUTCHINSON   MN

Super 8 Motel $-$$
1200 Hwy 15 S., P.O. Box 96,
Hutchinson, MN 55350,
Res. (800) 800-8000 Ph: (612)
587-9299 Fax: (612) 587-9299

INTERNATIONAL F　　MN	**MAPLEWOOD**　　MN	**Super 8 Motel**　　$-$$

INTERNATIONAL F　　MN

Super 8 Motel　　$-$$
2326 Hwy 53 Frontage Rd,
International F, MN 56649,
Res. (800) 800-8000 Ph: (218)
283-8811 Fax: (218) 283-8880

INTERNATIONAL FALLS　　MN

Budget Host International$-$$
10 Riverview Blvd.,
International Falls, MN
56649, Ph: (218) 283-2577
Fax: (218) 255-3688

JACKSON　　MN

Budget Host Prairie Winds$-$$
Hwys 16, 71 N-- Rr3, Box 17,
Jackson, MN 56143, Res.
(800) 283-4678 Ph: (507)
847-2020 Fax: (507) 847-2020

LAKEVILLE　　MN

Motel 6　　$
11274 210th St, Lakeville,
MN 55044, Res. (800)
466-8356 Ph: 612 469-1900
Fax: 612 469-5359

Super 8 Motel　　$-$$
20800 Kenrick Ave.,
Lakeville, MN 55044, Res.
(800) 800-8000 Ph: (612)
469-1134 Fax: (612) 469-1134

LITTLE FALLS　　MN

Super 8 Motel　　$-$$
300 12th Street NE, Little
Falls, MN 56345, Res. (800)
800-8000 Ph: (612) 632-2351
Fax: (612) 632-2351

LONG PRAIRIE　　MN

Budget Host Inn　　$-$$
417 Lake St. S., Long Prairie,
MN 56347, Ph: (612) 752-6118

Super 8 Motel　　$-$$
646 Lake St. South, Long
Prairie, MN 56347, Res. (800)
800-8000 Ph: (612) 732-4188
Fax: (612) 732-6159

LUVERNE　　MN

Super 8 Motel　　$-$$
I-90 & Highway 75, Luverne,
MN 56156, Res. (800)
800-8000 Ph: (507) 283-9541

MANKATO　　MN

Super 8 Motel　　$-$$
Hwy 169 N & Hwy 14 Jct,
Mankato, MN 56001, Res.
(800) 800-8000 Ph: (507)
387-4041 Fax: (507) 387-4107

MAPLE GROVE　　MN

Red Carpet Inn　　$$
7285 Forestview Ln, Maple
Grove, MN 55369, Res. (800)
251-1962 Ph: (612) 493-2277
Fax: (612) 493-4679

MAPLEWOOD　　MN

Super 8 Motel　　$-$$
285 N. Century Ave.,
Maplewood, MN 55119, Res.
(800) 800-8000 Ph: (612)
738-1600 Fax: (612) 738-9405

MARSHALL　　MN

Super 8 Motel　　$-$$
R.R. 1, Marshall, MN 56258,
Res. (800) 800-8000 Ph: (507)
537-1461 Fax: (507) 537-1461

MELROSE　　MN

Super 8 Motel　　$-$$
231 East County Rd 173,
Melrose, MN 56352, Res.
(800) 800-8000 Ph: (612)
256-4261 Fax: (701) 277-9237

MINNEAPOLIS　　MN

Econo Lodge　　$-$$
2500 University Ave. S.E.,
Minneapolis, MN 55414,
Res. (800) 424-4777 Ph: (612)
331-6000 Fax: (612) 331-6821

MOORHEAD　　MN

Super 8 Motel　　$-$$
3621 S. 8th St., Moorhead,
MN 56560, Res. (800)
800-8000 Ph: (218) 233-8880
Fax: (218) 233-8880

MORRIS　　MN

Super 8 Motel　　$-$$
US Hwy 59 & 28, Morris, MN
56267, Res. (800) 800-8000
Ph: (612) 589-8888 Fax: (612)
589-8888

NEW ULM　　MN

Super 8 Motel　　$-$$
1901 S. Broadway, New Ulm,
MN 56073, Res. (800)
800-8000 Ph: (507) 359-2400
Fax: (507) 359-1751

NORTHFIELD　　MN

Super 8 Motel　　$-$$
1420 Riverview Drive,
Northfield, MN 55057, Res.
(800) 800-8000 Ph: (507)
663-0371 Fax: (507) 526-2246

ONAMIA　　MN

Econo Lodge　　$-$$
40993 US 169, Onamia, MN
56359, Res. (800) 424-4777
Ph: (612) 532-3838 Fax: (612)
532-3812

ORTONVILLE　　MN

Econo Lodge　　$-$$
N. US 75, Ortonville, MN
56278, Res. (800) 424-4777
Ph: (612) 839-2414 Fax: (612)
839-2414

OWATONNA　　MN

Budget Host Inn　　$-$$
745 State Ave, Owatonna,
MN 55060, Res. (800)
283-4678 Ph: (507) 451-8712
Fax: (507) 451-4456

Super 8 Motel　　$-$$
P.O. Box 655, Owatonna, MN
55060, Res. (800) 800-8000
Ph: (507) 451-0380 Fax: (507)
451-0380

PARK RAPIDS　　MN

Super 8 Motel　　$-$$
PO Box 388, Hwy 34E, Park
Rapids, MN 56470, Res. (800)
800-8000 Ph: (218) 732-9704
Fax: (218) 732-9704

PERHAM　　MN

Super 8 Motel　　$-$$
106 Jake St. S.E., Perham,
MN 56573, Res. (800)
800-8000 Ph: (218) 346-7888
Fax: (218) 346-7880

PIPESTONE　　MN

Super 8 Motel　　$-$$
605 SE 8th Ave., Pipestone,
MN 56164, Res. (800)
800-8000 Ph: (507) 825-4217
Fax: (507) 825-4219

RED WING　　MN

Super 8 Motel　　$-$$
232 Withers Harbor Dr., Red
Wing, MN 55066, Res. (800)
800-8000 Ph: (612) 388-8590
Fax: (612) 388-1066

REDWOOD FALLS　　MN

Super 8 Motel　　$-$$
1305 East Bridge Street,
Redwood Falls, MN 56283,
Res. (800) 800-8000 Ph: (507)
637-3456 Fax: (507) 637-2507

RICHFIELD　　MN

Motel 6　　$
7640 Cedar Ave S, Richfield,
MN 55423, Res. (800)
466-8356 Ph: 612 861-4491
Fax: 612 798-4366

ROCHESTER　　MN

Econo Lodge Downtown　$-$$
519 Third Ave. S.W.,
Rochester, MN 55902, Res.
(800) 424-4777 Ph: (507)
288-1855 Fax: (507) 281-0668

Motel 6　　$
2107 W Frontage Rd,
Rochester, MN 55901, Res.
(800) 466-8356 Ph: 507
282-6625 Fax: 507 280-7987

Red Carpet Inn　　$$
2214 So. Broadway, Hwy 63,
Rochester, MN 55904, Res.
(800) 251-1962 Ph: (507)
282-7448 Fax: (507) 282-7448

Super 8 Motel　　$-$$
1230 South Broadway,
Rochester, MN 55901, Res.
(800) 800-8000 Ph: (507)
288-8288 Fax: (507) 288-4963

**M
O
T
E
L**

Super 8 Motel $-$$
1608 2nd St. S.W.,
Rochester, MN 55904, Res.
(800) 800-8000 Ph: (507)
282-9905 Fax: (507) 288-4335

Super 8 Motel $-$$
1850 S. Broadway Ave.,
Rochester, MN 55904, Res.
(800) 800-8000 Ph: (507)
282-9905 Fax: (507) 282-9905

Thriftlodge $-$$
1837 S. Broadway,
Rochester, MN 55904, Res.
(800) 525-9055 Ph: (507)
288-2031 Fax: (507) 288-2031
ext. 141

Villager $-$$
116 5th St, Rochester, MN
55902, Res. (800) 328-7829
Ph: (507) 289-1628 Fax: (507)
289-1628

ROGERS   MN

Super 8 Motel $-$$
21130 N. 134th Ave., Rogers,
MN 55374-9598, Res. (800)
800-8000 Ph: (612) 428-4000
Fax: (612) 428-4195

ROSEAU   MN

Super 8 Motel $-$$
318 Westside, Roseau, MN
56751-9797, Res. (800)
800-8000 Ph: (218) 463-2196
Fax: (218) 463-2196

ROSEVILLE   MN

Motel 6 $
2300 Cleveland Ave N,
Roseville, MN 55113, Res.
(800) 466-8356 Ph: 612
639-3988 Fax: 612 633-5748

Super 8 Motel $-$$
2401 Prior Ave. N., Roseville,
MN 55113-2714, Res. (800)
800-8000 Ph: (612) 636-8888
Fax: (612) 636-8854

SAUK CENTRE   MN

Econo Lodge $-$$
I-94 at Sauk Ctr. Exit, Sauk
Centre, MN 56378, Res.
(800) 424-4777 Ph: (612)
352-6581 Fax: (612) 352-6584

SHAKOPEE   MN

Budget Host Inn $-$$
1181 E 1st Ave, Shakopee,
MN 55379, Res. (800)
283-4678 Ph: (612) 445-9120
Fax: (612) 496-3546

Super 8 Motel $-$$
581 South Marschall Road,
Shakopee, MN 55379, Res.
(800) 800-8000 Ph: (612)
445-4221 Fax: (612) 445-4221

ST. CLOUD   MN

Motel 6 $
815 1st St S, St. Cloud, MN
56387, Res. (800) 466-8356
Ph: 320 253-7070 Fax: 320
253-0436

Super 8 Motel $-$$
50 Park Ave. South, P.O. Box
5176, St. Cloud, MN
56301-5176, Res. (800)
800-8000 Ph: (612) 253-5530
Fax: (612) 253-5530

ST. JAMES   MN

Super 8 Motel $-$$
Hwy 60 and Hickman Dr., St.
James, MN 56081, Res. (800)
800-8000 Ph: (507) 375-4708
Fax: (507) 375-3607

ST. JOSEPH   MN

Super 8 Motel $-$$
Minnesota St. and 15th Ave.
SE, St. Joseph, MN 56374,
Res. (800) 800-8000 Ph: (612)
363-7711 Fax: (612) 363-7711

STAPLES   MN

Super 8 Motel $-$$
"109 2nd Avenue, West",
Staples, MN 56479, Res.
(800) 800-8000 Ph: (602)
892-8889 Fax: (218) 894-3785

STILLWATER   MN

Super 8 Motel $-$$
2190 Frontage Road, Post
Office Box 2116, Stillwater,
MN 55082, Res. (800)
800-8000 Ph: (612) 430-3390
Fax: (612) 430-3990

THIEF RIVER FAL   MN

Super 8 Motel $-$$
Highway 59 South, Thief
River Fal, MN 56701, Res.
(800) 800-8000 Ph: (218)
681-6205 Fax: (218) 681-7519

WARROAD   MN

Super 8 Motel $-$$
Highway 11 West, Warroad,
MN 56763, Res. (800)
800-8000 Ph: (218) 386-3723
Fax: (218) 386-3725

WILLMAR   MN

Super 8 Motel $-$$
"2655 S. 1st, PO Box 286",
Willmar, MN 56201-0286,
Res. (800) 800-8000 Ph: (612)
235-7260 Fax: (612) 235-5580

WINDOM   MN

Super 8 Motel $-$$
222 3rd Ave. South, Windom,
MN 56101, Res. (800)
800-8000 Ph: (507) 831-1120

WINNEMUCCA   MN

Scottish Inns $
333 W. Winnemucca Blvd,
Winnemucca, MN 89445,
Res. (800) 251-1962 Ph: (702)
623-3703 Fax: (702) 625-2817

WINONA   MN

Super 8 Motel $-$$
1025 Sugar Loaf Rd., Winona,
MN 55987, Res. (800)
800-8000 Ph: (612) 235-7260
Fax: (507) 454-6066

WORTHINGTON   MN

Super 8 Motel $-$$
P.O. Box 98, Worthington,
MN 56187, Res. (800)
800-8000 Ph: (507) 372-7755
Fax: (507) 372-7755

ZUMBROTA   MN

Super 8 Motel $-$$
1439 N. Star Dr., Zumbrota,
MN 55992, Res. (800)
800-8000 Ph: (507) 732-7852
Fax: (507) 732-7885

MISSISSIPPI

BILOXI   MS

Econo Lodge Keesler Afb $-$$
1776 Beach Blvd., Biloxi, MS
39531, Res. (800) 424-4777
Ph: (601) 374-7644 Fax: (601)
374-7409

Motel 6 $
2476 Beach Blvd, Biloxi, MS
39531, Res. (800) 466-8356
Ph: 601 388-5130 Fax: 601
388-8819

Red Carpet Inn $$
2752 Beach Blvd., Biloxi, MS
39531, Res. (800) 251-1962
Ph: (601) 388-2610 Fax: (601)
388-7782

Super 8 Motel $-$$
1678 Beach Boulevard,
Biloxi, MS 39531, Res. (800)
800-8000 Ph: (601) 432-1984
Fax: (601) 435-0716

CANTON   MS

Econo Lodge $-$$
I-55 & Frontage Rd., Canton,
MS 39046, Res. (800)
424-4777 Ph: (601) 859-2643
Fax: (601) 859-7880

CARTHAGE   MS

Econo Lodge $-$$
SR 25 North, Carthage, MS
39051, Res. (800) 424-4777
Ph: (601) 267-7900

COLUMBUS   MS

Passport Inn $
2400 Hwy 182 East,
Columbus, MS 39701, Res.
(800) 251-1962 Ph: (601)
328-2551

CORINTH   MS

Econo Lodge $-$$
US 72 & 45, Corinth, MS
38834, Res. (800) 424-4777
Ph: (601) 287-4421 Fax: (601)
286-9535

DURANT · MS

Super 8 Motel $-$$
I-55 & Hwy 12, Durant, MS
39063, Res. (800) 800-8000
Ph: (601) 653-3881

GULFPORT · MS

Master Hosts Resorts $$
1410 Beach Dr., Gulfport,
MS 39507, Res. (800)
251-1962 Ph: (601) 896-1703
Fax: (601) 896-6934

Motel 6 $
9355 US Hwy 49, Gulfport,
MS 39503, Res. (800)
466-8356 Ph: 601 863-1890
Fax: 601 868-2445

HATTIESBURG · MS

Econo Lodge $-$$
3501 Hardy St., Hattiesburg,
MS 39401, Res. (800)
424-4777 Ph: (601) 264-0010
Fax: (601) 264-0010

Motel 6 $
6508 US Hwy 49,
Hattiesburg, MS 39401,
Res. (800) 466-8356 Ph: 601
544-6096 Fax: 601 582-7743

Scottish Inns $
6560 Hwy 49 No.,
Hattiesburg, MS 39401,
Res. (800) 251-1962 Ph: (601)
582-1211 Fax: (601) 582-1214

Super 8 Motel
Hwy 49 S. I-59, Hattiesburg,
MS 39401, Res. (800)
800-8000

JACKSON · MS

Econo Lodge $-$$
2450 US 80 W., Jackson, MS
39204, Res. (800) 424-4777
Ph: (601) 353-0340

Econo Lodge $-$$
232 S. Pearson Rd., Jackson,
MS 39208, Res. (800)
424-4777 Ph: (601) 932-4226

Econo Lodge $-$$
5925 I-55 N., Jackson, MS
39213, Res. (800) 424-4777
Ph: (601) 957-5500 Fax: (601)
978-1892

Motel 6 $
6145 I-55 N, Jackson, MS
39213, Res. (800) 466-8356
Ph: 601 956-8848 Fax: 601
956-1378

Red Carpet Inn $
2275 US Hwy 80 West,
Jackson, MS 39104, Res.
(800) 251-1962 Ph: (601)
948-5561 Fax: (601) 353-6658

Scottish Inns $
2263 US Hwy 80 West,
Jackson, MS 39204, Res.
(800) 251-1962 Ph: (601)
969-1144 Fax: (601) 353-6658

Super 8 Motel $-$$
2655 I-55 South, Jackson,
MS 39204, Res. (800)
800-8000 Ph: (601) 428-0511
Fax: (601) 372-1414

LAUREL · MS

Econo Lodge $-$$
123 Sixteenth Ave. N.,
Laurel, MS 39440, Res. (800)
424-4777 Ph: (601) 426-6585
Fax: (601) 426-6585

MAGEE · MS

Super 8 Motel $-$$
100 Hwy. 49 South, Magee,
MS 39111, Res. (800)
800-8000 Ph: (601) 849-2049

MERIDIAN · MS

Econo Lodge $-$$
2405 S. Frontage Rd.,
Meridian, MS 39301, Res.
(800) 424-4777 Ph: (601)
693-9393 Fax: (601) 693-9393

Motel 6 $
2309 S Frontage Rd ,
Meridian, MS 39301, Res.
(800) 466-8356 Ph: 601
482-1182 Fax: 601 483-9247

Scottish Inns $
1903 Frontage Rd., I-59 &
I-20, Meridian, MS 39301,
Res. (800) 251-1962 Ph: (601)
482-2487 Fax: (601) 485-7256

Super 8 Motel
605 Tom Bailey Drive,
Meridian, MS 39301, Res.
(800) 800-8000 Ph: (601)
482-8088 Fax: (601) 482-8088

NATCHEZ · MS

Scottish Inns $$
Sgt. Prentiss Dr., Hwy 61 So.,
Natchez, MS 39120, Res.
(800) 251-1962 Ph: (601)
442-9141 Fax: (601) 446-9945

PASCAGOULA · MS

Villager $-$$
6007 Hwy 90E, Pascagoula,
MS 39567, Res. (800)
328-7829 Ph: (601) 769-6200
Fax: (601) 762-6878

SARDIS · MS

Super 8 Motel $-$$
601 E. Lee Street, Sardis,
MS 38666, Res. (800)
800-8000 Ph: (601) 487-2311

TUNICA · MS

Super 8 Motel $-$$
3515 Hwy 61 North, Tunica,
MS 38676, Res. (800)
800-8000 Ph: (601) 363-1532

TUPELO · MS

Econo Lodge $-$$
1500 Mccullough Blvd.,
Tupelo, MS 38801, Res. (800)
424-4777 Ph: (601) 844-1904
Fax: (601) 844-0139

Scottish Inns $
401 North Gloster St.,
Tupelo, MS 38801, Res. (800)
251-1962 Ph: (601) 842-1961

VICKSBURG · MS

Scottish Inns $
3955 East Clay St.,
Vicksburg, MS 39180, Res.
(800) 251-1962 Ph: (601)
638-5511

Super 8 Motel $-$$
4127 I-20 Frontage Road,
Vicksburg, MS 39180, Res.
(800) 800-8000 Ph: (601)
638-5077 Fax: (601) 482-8088

MISSOURI

BETHANY · MO

Super 8 Motel $-$$
3600 Miller St., Bethany, MO
64424, Res. (800) 800-8000

BLUE SPRINGS · MO

Motel 6 $
901 W Jefferson St, Blue
Springs, MO 64015, Res.
(800) 466-8356 Ph: 816
228-9133 Fax: 816 228-1619

BOLIVAR · MO

Super 8 Motel $-$$
Hwy 13 & T, Bolivar, MO
65613, Res. (800) 800-8000
Ph: (417) 777-8888 Fax: (417)
326-8474

BOONVILLE · MO

Super 8 Motel $-$$
420 Americana, Boonville,
MO 65233, Res. (800)
800-8000 Ph: (816) 882-2900
Fax: (816) 882-7933

BRANSON · MO

Econo Lodge $-$$
230 S. Wildwood Dr.,
Branson, MO 65616, Res.
(800) 424-4777 Ph: (417)
336-4849 Fax: (417) 336-4862

Motel 6 $
2651 Shepherd of the Hills
Exp, Branson, MO 65616,
Res. (800) 466-8356 Ph: 417
336-6088 Fax: 417 334-5924

Super 8 Motel $-$$
2490 Green Mountain Drive,
Branson, MO 65616, Res.
(800) 800-8000 Ph: (417)
334-8880 Fax: (417) 335-3177

Villager $-$$
3524 Keeter St, Branson,
MO 65616, Res. (800)
328-7829 Ph: (417) 339-2197
Fax: (417) 334-2935

BRIDGETON · MO

Econo Lodge Airport $-$$
4575 N. Lindbergh Blvd.,
Bridgeton, MO 63044, Res.
(800) 424-4777 Ph: (314)
731-3000 Fax: (314) 731-3000

**M
O
T
E
L**

Motel 6 $
3655 Pennridge Dr,
Bridgeton, MO 63044, Res.
(800) 466-8356 Ph: 314
291-6100 Fax: 314 291-3797

Scottish Inns $$
4645 No. Lindberg, Bridgeton,
MO 63044, Res. (800)
251-1962 Ph: (314) 731-1010
Fax: (314) 731-0016

Super 8 Motel $-$$
12705 St. Charles Rock Road,
Bridgeton, MO 63044, Res.
(800) 800-8000 Ph: (314)
291-8845 Fax: (314) 291-8845

CABOOL	MO

Super 8 Motel $-$$
Hwy. 181, Cabool, MO
65867, Res. (800) 800-8000
Ph: (417) 962-5888 Fax: (417)
962-5602

CAMERON	MO

Budget Host Country Squire
501 Northland Dr., Cameron,
MO 64429, Ph: (816)
632-6623 Fax: (816) 632-5127

Super 8 Motel $-$$
Highways 36 & 69, Cameron,
MO 64229, Res. (800)
800-8000 Ph: (816) 632-8888
Fax: (816) 632-8888

CARTHAGE	MO

Econo Lodge $-$$
1441 W. Central, Carthage,
MO 64836, Res. (800)
424-4777 Ph: (417) 358-3900
Fax: (417) 358-6839

CASSVILLE	MO

Super 8 Motel $-$$
U.S. Highway 37, Cassville,
MO 65625, Res. (800)
800-8000 Ph: (417) 847-4888
Fax: (417) 847-4888

CHILLICOTHE	MO

Super 8 Motel $-$$
Highway 36, Chillicothe, MO
64601, Res. (800) 800-8000
Ph: (816) 646-7888

COLUMBIA	MO

Budget Host Inn $-$$
900 Vandiver Dr, Columbia,
MO 65202, Res. (800)
283-4678 Ph: (314) 449-1065
Fax: (314) 442-6266

Econo Lodge $-$$
900 I-70 Dr. S.W., Columbia,
MO 65203, Res. (800)
424-4777 Ph: (314) 442-1191
Fax: (314) 442-1191

Motel 6 $
1800 I-70 Dr SW, Columbia,
MO 65203, Res. (800)
466-8356 Ph: 573 445-8433
Fax: 573 446-1839

Motel 6 $
1718 N Providence Rd,
Columbia, MO 65202, Res.
(800) 466-8356 Ph: 573
442-9390 Fax: 573 875-5477

Scottish Inns $
2112 Business Loop 70 East,
Columbia, MO 65201, Res.
(800) 251-1962 Ph: (314)
449-3771

Super 8 Motel $-$$
3216 Clark Lane, Columbia,
MO 65202, Res. (800)
800-8000 Ph: (314) 474-8488
Fax: (314) 474-4180

CUBA	MO

Super 8 Motel $-$$
Highway 19 & I-44, Cuba,
MO 65453, Res. (800)
800-8000 Ph: (314) 885-2087
Fax: (314) 885-2089

DONIPHAN	MO

Econo Lodge $-$$
109 Smith Dr., Doniphan,
MO 63935, Res. (800)
424-4777 Ph: (314) 996-2101
Fax: (314) 996-4018

EUREKA	MO

Red Carpet Inn $$
1725 W. Fifth St., Eureka,
MO 63025, Res. (800)
251-1962 Ph: (314) 938-5348

FARMINGTON	MO

Super 8 Motel $-$$
930 Valley Creek Dr.,
Farmington, MO 63640,
Res. (800) 800-8000 Ph: (314)
760-0344 Fax: (314) 760-0846

FENTON	MO

Motel 6 $
1860 Bowles Ave, Fenton,
MO 63026, Res. (800)
466-8356 Ph: 314 349-1800
Fax: 314 326-3456

FULTON	MO

Budget Host Westwoods $-$$
422 Gaylord Dr, Fulton, MO
65251, Res. (800) 283-4678
Ph: (314) 642-5991

GRAIN VALLEY	MO

Scottish Inns $$
105 Sunny Lane Dr, Grain
Valley, MO 64029, Res. (800)
251-1962 Ph: (816) 224-3420
Fax: (816) 224-4438

GRANDVIEW	MO

Super 8 Motel $-$$
15201 South Highway 71,
Grandview, MO 64030, Res.
(800) 800-8000 Ph: (816)
331-0300 Fax: (816) 331-0300

HANNIBAL	MO

Econo Lodge $-$$
612 Mark Twain Ave.,
Hannibal, MO 63401, Res.
(800) 424-4777 Ph: (314)
221-1490

Super 8 Motel $-$$
120 Huckleberry Heights
Drive, Hannibal, MO 63401,
Res. (800) 800-8000 Ph: (314)
221-5863

HARRISONVILLE	MO

Super 8 Motel $-$$
2400 Rockhaven Road,
Harrisonville, MO 64701,
Res. (800) 800-8000 Ph: (816)
887-2999 Fax: (816) 887-5761

HIGGINSVILLE	MO

Super 8 Motel $-$$
P.O. Box 306, Higginsville,
MO 64037, Res. (800)
800-8000 Ph: (816) 584-7781
Fax: (816) 584-2601

HOLLISTER	MO

Econo Lodge $-$$
US 65, Hollister, MO 65672,
Res. (800) 424-4777 Ph: (417)
334-2770

INDEPENDENCE	MO

Super 8 Motel $-$$
4032 South Lynn Court
Drive, Independence, MO
64055-3360, Res. (800)
800-8000 Ph: (816) 833-1888
Fax: (816) 833-1888

JEFFERSON CITY	MO

Motel 6 $
1624 Jefferson St, Jefferson
City, MO 65109, Res. (800)
466-8356 Ph: 573 634-4220
Fax: 573 635-5284

Super 8 Motel $-$$
1710 Jefferson Street,
Jefferson City, MO 65110,
Res. (800) 800-8000 Ph: (314)
636-5456 Fax: (314) 636-0441

JOPLIN	MO

Motel 6 $
3031 S Range Line Rd,
Joplin, MO 64804, Res. (800)
466-8356 Ph: 417 781-6400
Fax: 417 781-5140

Super 8 Motel $-$$
2830 East 36th Street,
Joplin, MO 64804, Res. (800)
800-8000 Ph: (417) 782-8765
Fax: (417) 782-8765

KANSAS CITY	MO

Econo Lodge Airport $-$$
11300 N.W. Prairieview Rd.,
Kansas City, MO 64153,
Res. (800) 424-4777 Ph: (816)
464-5082

Econo Lodge Southeast $-$$
8500 E. SR 350, Kansas City,
MO 64133, Res. (800)
424-4777 Ph: (816) 353-3000
Fax: (816) 356-0048

Econo Lodge Stadium $-$$
5100 E. Linwood Blvd.,
Kansas City, MO 64128,
Res. (800) 424-4777 Ph: (816)
923-7777 Fax: (816) 923-6927

Motel 6 $
8230 NW Prairie View Rd,
Kansas City, MO 64152,
Res. (800) 466-8356 Ph: 816
741-6400 Fax: 816 746-5378

Motel 6 $
6400 E 87th St, Kansas City,
MO 64138, Res. (800)
466-8356 Ph: 816 333-4468
Fax: 816 333-7324

Super 8 Motel $-$$
6900 NW 83rd Terrace,
Kansas City, MO
64153-2043, Res. (800)
800-8000 Ph: (816) 587-0808
Fax: (816) 587-0808

KEARNEY   **M O**

Econo Lodge $-$$
505 Shanks Ave., Kearney,
MO 64060, Res. (800)
424-4777 Ph: (816) 635-6000
Fax: (816) 635-3860

Super 8 Motel $-$$
210 Platte Clay Way,
Kearney, MO 64060, Res.
(800) 800-8000 Ph: (816)
628-6800

KINGDOM CITY   **M O**

Super 8 Motel $-$$
I-70 & Highway 54, Kingdom
City, MO 65262, Res. (800)
800-8000 Ph: (314) 642-2888
Fax: (314) 642-2888

KIRKSVILLE   **M O**

Budget Host Village Inn $-$$
1304 S Baltimore, P.O. Box
673, Kirksville, MO 63501,
Res. (800) 283-4678 Ph: (816)
665-3722 Fax: (816) 665-6334

Super 8 Motel $-$$
1101 Country Club Drive,
Kirksville, MO 63501, Res.
(800) 800-8000 Ph: (816)
665-8826 Fax: (816) 665-8826

LAMAR   **M O**

Super 8 Motel $-$$
Highway 71 and Highway 160,
Lamar, MO 64759, Res. (800)
800-8000 Ph: (417) 682-2286
Fax: (417) 682-6688

LEBANON   **M O**

Econo Lodge $-$$
I-44 W. Bus. Loop, Lebanon,
MO 65536, Res. (800)
424-4777 Ph: (417) 588-3226

Scottish Inns $
1830 West Elm St., Lebanon,
MO 65536, Res. (800)
251-1962 Ph: (417) 532-3133
Fax: (417) 532-8659

Super 8 Motel $-$$
1831 W. Elm St., Lebanon,
MO 65536, Res. (800)
800-8000 Ph: (417) 588-2574
Fax: (417) 588-2580

LIBERTY   **M O**

Super 8 Motel $-$$
115 North Steward Road,
Liberty, MO 64068-1052,
Res. (800) 800-8000 Ph: (816)
781-9400 Fax: (816) 781-9400

MACON   **M O**

Super 8 Motel $-$$
"1420 N. Rutherford St., #2A",
Macon, MO 63552-1950,
Res. (800) 800-8000 Ph: (816)
385-5788 Fax: (816) 385-5788

MARSHALL   **M O**

Super 8 Motel $-$$
1355 W. College St.,
Marshall, MO 65340, Res.
(800) 800-8000 Ph: (816)
886-3359 Fax: (816) 886-3359

MARSTON   **M O**

Super 8 Motel $-$$
Box 277, Marston, MO
63866, Res. (800) 800-8000
Ph: (314) 643-9888

MARYVILLE   **M O**

Super 8 Motel $-$$
Hwy 71 South, Maryville,
MO 64468, Res. (800)
800-8000 Ph: (816) 582-8088

MEXICO   **M O**

Econo Lodge $-$$
US 54 S. & Hamilton Pkwy.,
Mexico, MO 65265, Res.
(800) 424-4777 Ph: (314)
581-1860

MOBERLY   **M O**

Super 8 Motel $-$$
300 Hwy 24 East, P.O. Box
176, Moberly, MO 65270,
Res. (800) 800-8000 Ph: (816)
263-8862 Fax: (816) 263-8862

MONROE CITY   **M O**

Econo Lodge $-$$
3 Gateway Sq., Monroe City,
MO 63456, Res. (800)
424-4777 Ph: (314) 735-4200
Fax: (314) 735-3493

MOUNT VERNON   **M O**

Budget Host Ranch Motel $-$$
Rt 1 Box 6b, Mount Vernon,
MO 65712, Res. (800)
283-4678 Ph: (417) 466-2125
Fax: (417) 466-4440

NEVADA   **M O**

Super 8 Motel $-$$
2301 E. Austin Blvd., P.O.
Box 529, Nevada, MO
64772-0529, Res. (800)
800-8000 Ph: (417) 667-8888

NIXA   **M O**

Super 8 Motel $-$$
418 N. Massey Blvd., Nixa,
MO 65714, Res. (800)
800-8000 Ph: (417) 725-0880
Fax: (417) 725-5046

O'FALLON   **M O**

Super 8 Motel $-$$
987 W. Terra Lane, O'Fallon,
MO 63353, Res. (800)
800-8000 Ph: (314) 272-7272
Fax: (314) 272-1633

OAK GROVE   **M O**

Econo Lodge $-$$
410 S.E. 1st. St., Oak Grove,
MO 64075, Res. (800)
424-4777 Ph: (816) 625-3681

OSAGE BEACH   **M O**

Scottish Inns $$
5404 Hwy 54, Osage Beach,
MO 65065, Res. (800)
251-1962 Ph: (314) 348-3123
Fax: (314) 348-3124

OZARK   **M O**

Super 8 Motel $-$$
299 North 20th Street,
Ozark, MO 65721, Res. (800)
800-8000 Ph: (417) 485-8800
Fax: (417) 485-8868

PERRYVILLE   **M O**

Budget Host Inn $-$$
221 S Kings Hwy, Perryville,
MO 63775, Res. (800)
283-4678 Ph: (314) 547-4516

POPLAR BLUFF   **M O**

Super 8 Motel $-$$
2831 N. Westwood Blvd.,
Poplar Bluff, MO 63901, Res.
(800) 800-8000 Ph: (314)
785-0176 Fax: (314) 785-2865

ROLLA   **M O**

Econo Lodge $-$$
1417 Martin Spring Dr.,
Rolla, MO 65401, Res. (800)
424-4777 Ph: (314) 341-3130
Fax: (314) 341-2129

Super 8 Motel $-$$
1201 Kings Highway, Rolla,
MO 65401, Res. (800)
800-8000 Ph: (314) 364-4156
Fax: (314) 341-2444

SAINT CHARLES   **M O**

Econo Lodge $-$$
3040 W. Clay, Saint Charles,
MO 63301, Res. (800)
424-4777 Ph: (314) 946-9992
Fax: (314) 724-7266

M
O
T
E
L

SAINT LOUIS MO	**Motel 6** $	**STRAFFORD** M(

Econco Lodge $-$$
1351 Dunn Rd., Saint Louis,
MO 63138, Res. (800)
424-4777 Ph: (314) 388-1500
Fax: (314) 388-0948

SAINTE GENEVIEVE MO

Econo Lodge $-$$
I-55 at Ozora Exit, Sainte
Genevieve, MO 63670, Res.
(800) 424-4777 Ph: (314)
543-2272 Fax: (314) 543-2272

SALEM MO

Scottish Inns $
1005 So. Main St., Salem,
MO 65560, Res. (800)
251-1962 Ph: (314) 729-4191
Fax: (314) 729-3126

SEDALIA MO

Super 8 Motel $-$$
3402 W. Broadway, Sedalia,
MO 65301, Res. (800)
800-8000 Ph: (816) 827-5890
Fax: (816) 827-5890

SIKESTON MO

Econo Lodge $-$$
110 S. Interstate / I-55 Ex.
67, Sikeston, MO 63801,
Res. (800) 424-4777 Ph: (314)
471-7400

Red Carpet Inn $
110 So Interstate Dr.,
Sikeston, MO 63801, Res.
(800) 251-1962 Ph: (573)
471-7400 Fax: (573) 472-3125

Super 8 Motel $-$$
2609 E. Malone Ave.,
Sikeston, MO 63801, Res.
(800) 800-8000 Ph: (314)
471-7944 Fax: (314) 471-7946

SMITHVILLE MO

Super 8 Motel $-$$
112 Cuttings Drive,
Smithville, MO 64089, Res.
(800) 800-8000 Ph: (816)
532-3088

SPRINGFIELD MO

Budget Host Loveland Inn $-$$
2601 N Glenstone,
Springfield, MO 65803, Res.
(800) 283-4678 Ph: (417)
865-6565 Fax: (417) 865-9008

Econo Lodge East $-$$
2611 N. Glenstone Ave.,
Springfield, MO 65803, Res.
(800) 424-4777 Ph: (417)
864-3565 Fax: (417) 865-0567

Econo Lodge West $-$$
2808 N. Kansas, Springfield,
MO 65803, Res. (800)
424-4777 Ph: (417) 869-5600
Fax: (417) 869-5600

Motel 6 $
3114 N Kentwood,
Springfield, MO 65803, Res.
(800) 466-8356 Ph: 417
833-0880 Fax: 417 833-5147

Motel 6 $
2455 N Glenstone Ave,
Springfield, MO 65803, Res.
(800) 466-8356 Ph: 417
869-4343 Fax: 417 869-5269

Scottish Inns $$
2933 N. Glenstone Ave.,
Springfield, MO 65803, Res.
(800) 251-1962 Ph: (417)
862-4301 Fax: (417) 862-2006

Super 8 Motel $-$$
3022 North Kentwood
Avenue, Springfield, MO
65803-4414, Res. (800)
800-8000 Ph: (417) 833-9218
Fax: (417) 833-9218

Super 8 Motel $-$$
3034 So. Moulder Ave.,
Springfield, MO 65804, Res.
(800) 800-8000 Ph: (417)
889-7313 Fax: (417) 886-3201

ST. CLAIR MO

Super 8 Motel $-$$
1010 S. Service Rd., St. Clair,
MO 63077, Res. (800)
800-8000 Ph: (314) 629-8080
Fax: (314) 629-1534

ST. JOSEPH MO

Motel 6 $
4021 Frederick Blvd., St.
Joseph, MO 64506, Res.
(800) 466-8356 Ph: 816
232-2311 Fax: 816 232-0254

Super 8 Motel $-$$
4024 Frederick Avenue, St.
Joseph, MO 64506-3157,
Res. (800) 800-8000 Ph: (816)
364-3031 Fax: (816) 364-3031

ST. LOUIS MO

Motel 6 $
4576 Woodson Rd at Airport,
St. Louis, MO 63134, Res.
(800) 466-8356 Ph: 314
427-1313 Fax: 314 427-0826

Motel 6 $
1405 Dunn Rd, St. Louis,
MO 63138, Res. (800)
466-8356 Ph: 314 869-9400
Fax: 314 869-8623

Motel 6 $
6500 S Lindbergh Blvd, St.
Louis, MO 63123, Res. (800)
466-8356 Ph: 314 892-3664
Fax: 314 892-1153

Super 8 Motel $-$$
2790 Target Dr, St Louis,
MO 63136, Res. (800)
800-8000 Ph: (314) 355-7808
Fax: (314) 355-0874

Super 8 Motel $-$$
501 Chestnut Street,
Strafford, MO 65757, Res.
(800) 800-8000 Ph: (417)
736-2817

SULLIVAN M(

Super 8 Motel $-$$
601 North Service Road, P.O.
Box 69, Sullivan, MO
63080, Res. (800) 800-8000
Ph: (314) 468-8076 Fax: (314)
468-8076

TRENTON M(

Super 8 Motel $-$$
28th St & US Hwy 65N,
Trenton, MO 64683, Res.
(800) 800-8000 Ph: (816)
359-2988 Fax: (816) 359-2988

WARRENSBURG MO

Econo Lodge $-$$
204 Cleveland St.,
Warrensburg, MO 64093,
Res. (800) 424-4777 Ph: (816)
429-2400 Fax: (816) 429-6426

Super 8 Motel $-$$
"440 Russell Ave.,", PO Box
780, Warrensburg, MO
64093-0231, Res. (800)
800-8000 Ph: (816) 429-2183
Fax: (314) 634-3373

WARRENTON MO

Econo Lodge $-$$
804 N. SR 47, Warrenton,
MO 63383, Res. (800)
424-4777 Ph: (314) 456-2522

Motel 6 $
804 N Hwy 47, Warrenton,
MO 63383, Res. (800)
466-8356 Ph: 314 456-2522
Fax: 314 456-2523

Super 8 Motel $-$$
N. Outer Service Rd. & Hwy
AA, Warrenton, MO 63383,
Res. (800) 800-8000 Ph: (314)
456-5157

WASHINGTON MO

Super 8 Motel $-$$
4050 Bieker Rd.,
Washington, MO 63090,
Res. (800) 800-8000 Ph: (314)
390-0088 Fax: (314) 390-0088

WAYNESVILLE MO

Econo Lodge $-$$
I-44 & Ft. Leonard Wood / Ex.
161A, Waynesville, MO
65583, Res. (800) 424-4777
Ph: (314) 336-7272 Fax: (314)
336-4307

Super 8 Motel $-$$
14175 Hwy. Z, Waynesville,
MO 65583, Res. (800)
800-8000 Ph: (314) 336-3036
Fax: (314) 336-3036

WENTZVILLE	MO

Super 8 Motel $-$$
4 Pantera Drive, Wentzville,
MO 63385, Res. (800)
800-8000 Ph: (314) 327-5300
Fax: (314) 639-1147

WEST PLAINS	MO

Super 8 Motel $-$$
1210 Porter Wagoner Blvd.,
West Plains, MO 65775,
Res. (800) 800-8000 Ph: (417)
256-8088 Fax: (417) 256-8088

MONTANA

BELGRADE	MT

Super 8 Motel $-$$
6450 Jackrabbit Lane,
Belgrade, MT 59714, Res.
(800) 800-8000 Ph: (406)
388-1493

BIG TIMBER	MT

Super 8 Motel $-$$
PO Box 1441, Big Timber, MT
59011, Res. (800) 800-8000
Ph: (406) 932-8888 Fax: (406)
932-4103

BILLINGS	MT

Econo Lodge Downtown $-$$
2601 4th Ave. N., Billings,
MT 59101, Res. (800)
424-4777 Ph: (406) 245-6646
Fax: (406) 245-9358

Motel 6 $
5353 Midland Rd, Billings,
MT 59102, Res. (800)
466-8356 Ph: 406 248-7551
Fax: 406 245-7032

Motel 6 $
5400 Midland Rd RR #9,
Billings, MT 59101, Res.
(800) 466-8356 Ph: 406
252-0093 Fax: 406 245-1121

Super 8 Motel $-$$
5400 Southgate Dr., Billings,
MT 59102-4631, Res. (800)
800-8000 Ph: (406) 248-8842

Villager $-$$
1709 1st Ave North, Billings,
MT 59101, Res. (800)
328-7829 Ph: (406) 252-4691
Fax: (406) 248-3170

BOZEMAN	MT

Econo Lodge Downtown $-$$
122 W. Main St., Bozeman,
MT 59715, Res. (800)
424-4777 Ph: (406) 587-4481
Fax: (406) 586-4053

Super 8 Motel $-$$
800 Wheat Dr., Bozeman,
MT 59715-2560, Res. (800)
800-8000 Ph: (406) 586-1521

BUTTE	MT

Super 8 Motel $-$$
2929 Harrison Ave., Butte,
MT 59701, Res. (800)
800-8000 Ph: (406) 494-6000
Fax: (406) 494-6000

COLSTRIP	MT

Super 8 Motel $-$$
Castle Rock Lake Dr. &, Main
Street, Colstrip, MT 59034,
Res. (800) 800-8000 Ph: (406)
748-3400

COLUMBIA HGTS	MT

Super 8 Motel $-$$
7440 Hwy 2 East, Columbia
Hgts, MT 59912, Res. (800)
800-8000 Ph: (406) 892-0888

COLUMBUS	MT

Super 8 Motel $-$$
602 8th Avenue North,
Columbus, MT 59019, Res.
(800) 800-8000 Ph: (406)
322-4101 Fax: (406) 322-4636

CONDON	MT

Super 8 Motel $-$$
Highway 83, P.O. Box 1278,
Condon, MT 59826, Res.
(800) 800-8000 Ph: (406)
754-2688

CONRAD	MT

Super 8 Motel $-$$
215 North Main Street,
Conrad, MT 59425, Res.
(800) 800-8000 Ph: (406)
278-7676 Fax: (406) 278-7971

DEER LODGE	MT

Super 8 Motel $-$$
1150 N. Main St., Deer Lodge,
MT 59722, Res. (800)
800-8000 Ph: (406) 846-2370
Fax: (406) 846-2373

DILLON	MT

Super 8 Motel $-$$
550 North Montana Street,
Dillon, MT 59725, Res. (800)
800-8000 Ph: (406) 683-4288
Fax: (406) 683-6251

GARDINER	MT

Super 8 Motel $-$$
Box 755, Gardiner, MT
59030, Res. (800) 800-8000
Ph: (406) 848-7401

GLENDIVE	MT

Budget Host Riverside Inn $$
Hc 44, Hwy 16, Glendive, MT
59330, Res. (800) 283-4678
Ph: (406) 365-2349

Super 8 Motel $-$$
1904 North Merrill Avenue,
Glendive, MT 59330, Res.
(800) 800-8000 Ph: (406)
365-5671 Fax: (406) 365-6157

GREAT FALLS	MT

Super 8 Motel $-$$
1214 13th S., Great Falls, MT
59405, Res. (800) 800-8000
Ph: (406) 727-7600 Fax: (406)
761-2291

HAMILTON	MT

Super 8 Motel $-$$
1325 N. First Street,
Hamilton, MT 59840, Res.
(800) 800-8000 Ph: (406)
363-2940

HARDIN	MT

Super 8 Motel $-$$
Intrsctn of I-90 & Hwy 47N,
Hardin, MT 59034, Res. (800)
800-8000 Ph: (406) 665-1700
Fax: (406) 665-1700

HAVRE	MT

Super 8 Motel $-$$
166 W. 19th Ave., Havre, MT
59501-6820, Res. (800)
800-8000 Ph: (406) 265-1411
Fax: (406) 265-1411

HELENA	MT

Econo Lodge Downtown $-$$
524 Last Chance Gulch,
Helena, MT 59601, Res.
(800) 424-4777 Ph: (406)
442-0600 Fax: (406) 443-1770

Motel 6 $
800 N Oregon St, Helena,
MT 59601, Res. (800)
466-8356 Ph: 406 442-9990
Fax: 406 449-7107

Super 8 Motel $-$$
2201 11th Avenue, Helena,
MT 59601-4843, Res. (800)
800-8000 Ph: (406) 443-2450
Fax: (406) 443-2450

KALISPELL	MT

Motel 6 $
1540 Hwy 93 S, Kalispell, MT
59901, Res. (800) 466-8356
Ph: 406 752-6355 Fax: 406
752-6358

Super 8 Motel $-$$
1341 East 1st Avenue,
Kalispell, MT 59901-5801,
Res. (800) 800-8000 Ph: (406)
755-1888 Fax: (407) 755-1887

LEWISTON	MT

Super 8 Motel $-$$
102 Wendell Avenue,
Lewiston, MT 59457, Res.
(800) 800-8000 Ph: (406)
538-2581 Fax: (406) 538-2581

LIBBY	MT

Budget Host Caboose Motel $$
Hwy 2 W, Box 792, Libby, MT
59923, Res. (800) 283-4678
Ph: (406) 293-6201 Fax: (406)
293-3621

Super 8 Motel $-$$
448 US Hwy 2W, Libby, MT
59923, Res. (800) 800-8000
Ph: (406) 293-2771 Fax: (406)
293-9871

**M
O
T
E
L**

LIVINGSTON	MT

Budget Host Parkway Motels
1124 West Park, Livingston, MT 59047, Res. (800) 283-4678 Ph: (406) 222-3840 Fax: (406) 222-7948

Super 8 Motel $-$$
7 Centennial Dr, PO Box 1385, Livingston, MT 59047-1385, Res. (800) 800-8000 Ph: (406) 222-7711 Fax: (406) 222-7711

MILES CITY	MT

Budget Host Custer's Inn $-$$
1209 S Haynes, Box 1235, Miles City, MT 59301, Res. (800) 283-4678 Ph: (406) 232-5170 Fax: (406) 232-5170

Motel 6 $
1314 Haynes Ave<EL>Rt 2, Box 3396, Miles City, MT 59301, Res. (800) 466-8356 Ph: 406 232-7040 Fax: 406 232-6540

Super 8 Motel $-$$
"RR 2, Highway 59 South", Miles City, MT 59301, Res. (800) 800-8000 Ph: (406) 232-5261 Fax: (406) 232-5262

MISSOULA	MT

Econo Lodge $-$$
1609 W. Broadway, Missoula, MT 59802, Res. (800) 424-4777 Ph: (406) 543-7231 Fax: (406) 728-1930

Super 8 Motel $-$$
3901 South Brooks St., Missoula, MT 59801, Res. (800) 800-8000 Ph: (406) 251-2255

Super 8 Motel $-$$
4703 North Reserve St., Missoula, MT 59802, Res. (800) 800-8000 Ph: (406) 549-1199 Fax: (406) 549-0677

POLSON	MT

Super 8 Motel $-$$
Jct Hwys 93 & 35, P.O. Box 318, Polson, MT 59860, Res. (800) 800-8000 Ph: (406) 883-6266

RED LODGE	MT

Super 8 Motel $-$$
1223 South Broadway, HC 49 Box 3375, Red Lodge, MT 59068, Res. (800) 800-8000 Ph: (406) 446-2288 Fax: (406) 446-3162

ST. REGIS	MT

Super 8 Motel $-$$
Old U.S. 10, P.O. Drawer L, St. Regis, MT 59866-0310, Res. (800) 800-8000 Ph: (406) 649-2422 Fax: (406) 649-2452

SUPERIOR	MT

Budget Host Big Sky Motel $$
103 4th Ave E, Box 458, Superior, MT 59872, Res. (800) 283-4678 Ph: (406) 822-4831

W YELLOWSTONE	MT

Super 8 Motel $-$$
1545 Targhee Pass Hwy., W Yellowstone, MT 59758-9618, Res. (800) 800-8000 Ph: (406) 646-9584 Fax: (406) 646-7404

WHITEFISH	MT

Super 8 Motel $-$$
800 Spokane Ave., Whitefish, MT 59937, Res. (800) 800-8000 Ph: (406) 862-8255

WHITEHALL	MT

Super 8 Motel $-$$
515 North Whitehall, Whitehall, MT 59759, Res. (800) 800-8000 Ph: (406) 287-5588

WIBAUX	MT

Super 8 Motel $
400 West 2nd Avenue North, Wibaux, MT 59353, Res. (800) 800-8000 Ph: (406) 652-1826

NEBRASKA

AINSWORTH	NE

Super 8 Motel $-$$
1025 E. 4th, Ainsworth, NE 69210, Res. (800) 800-8000 Ph: (402) 387-0700 Fax: (402) 387-2441

ALLIANCE	NE

Super 8 Motel $-$$
1419 W. 3rd Street, Alliance, NE 69301, Res. (800) 800-8000 Ph: (308) 762-8300

AURORA	NE

Budget Host Ken's Motel $-$$
1515 11th St, Aurora, NE 68818, Res. (800) 283-4678 Ph: (402) 694-3141

BEATRICE	NE

Super 8 Motel $-$$
3210 N. 6th. St., Beatrice, NE 68310, Res. (800) 800-8000 Ph: (402) 223-3536 Fax: (402) 223-3536

BELLEVUE	NE

Super 8 Motel $-$$
303 S. Fort Crook Road, Bellevue, NE 68005, Res. (800) 800-8000 Ph: (402) 291-1518 Fax: (402) 292-1726

BLAIR	NE

Super 8 Motel $-$$
558 South 13th Street, Blair, NE 68008, Res. (800) 800-8000 Ph: (402) 426-8888 Fax: (402) 426-8889

BROKEN BOW	N

Super 8 Motel $-$
215 E. S. 'E' Street, P.O. Box 66, Broken Bow, NE 68822-0066, Res. (800) 800-8000 Ph: (308) 872-6428 Fax: (308) 872-5031

CENTRAL CITY	N

Super 8 Motel $-$
1415 16th St., Central City, NE 68826, Res. (800) 800-8000 Ph: (308) 946-5055

CHADRON	N

Super 8 Motel $-$
Hwy. 20 West, Chadron, NE 69337, Res. (800) 800-8000 Ph: (308) 432-4471

COLUMBUS	N

Econo Lodge $-$
3803 23rd St., Columbus, NE 68601, Res. (800) 424-4777 Ph: (402) 564-9955 Fax: (402) 564-9436

Super 8 Motel $-$
3324 20th Street, Columbus, NE 68601, Res. (800) 800-8000 Ph: (402) 563-3456 Fax: (402) 563-3456

COZAD	N

Budget Host Circle S Motel $
440 S Meridian, Cozad, NE 69130, Res. (800) 283-4678 Ph: (308) 784-2290

FREMONT	N

Budget Host Relax Inn $-$
1435 E 23rd, Fremont, NE 68025, Res. (800) 283-4678 Ph: (402) 721-5656 Fax: (402) 721-5656

Super 8 Motel $-$
1250 East 23rd Street, Fremont, NE 68025-2411, Res. (800) 800-8000 Ph: (402) 727-4445 Fax: (402) 727-4445

GRAND ISLAND	N

Budget Host Island Inn $-$
2311 S Locust, Grand Island, NE 68801, Res. (800) 283-4678 Ph: (308) 382-1815

Motel 6 $
3021 S Locust St, Grand Island, NE 68801-8865, Res. (800) 466-8356 Ph: 308 384-4100 Fax: 308 384-7035

Super 8 Motel $-$
2603 South Locust, Grand Island, NE 68801-8227, Res. (800) 800-8000 Ph: (308) 384-4380 Fax: (308) 384-5015

HASTINGS	N

Super 8 Motel $-$
22nd St. Hwy.281, Hastings, NE 68901, Res. (800) 800-8000 Ph: (402) 463-8888

KEARNEY   NE

Budget Host Western Inn $-$$
P.O. Box 1903, Kearney, NE
68848, Res. (800) 283-4678
Ph: (308) 237-3153 Fax: (308)
234-6073

Super 8 Motel $-$$
15 W. 8th St., Kearney, NE
68847, Res. (800) 800-8000
Ph: (308) 234-5513

KIMBALL   NE

Super 8 Motel $-$$
I-80 & 71 Interchange, Box
117, Kimball, NE 69145,
Res. (800) 800-8000 Ph: (308)
235-4888 Fax: (308) 235-4888

LEXINGTON   NE

Budget Host Minute Man $-$$
301 S Bridge St., Lexington,
NE 68850, Res. (800)
283-4678 Ph: (308) 324-5544

Econo Lodge $-$$
I-80 at US 283, Lexington,
NE 68850, Res. (800)
424-4777 Ph: (308) 324-5601
Fax: (308) 324-4284

Super 8 Motel $-$$
R.R. 2, Box 149 U",
Lexington, NE 68850, Res.
(800) 800-8000 Ph: (308)
324-7434 Fax: (308) 324-7434

LINCOLN   NE

Budget Host Great Plains $-$$
2732 O Street, Lincoln, NE
68510, Res. (800) 283-4678
Ph: (402) 476-3253 Fax: (402)
476-7540

Econo Lodge Northeast $-$$
5600 Cornhusker Hwy.,
Lincoln, NE 68529, Res.
(800) 424-4777 Ph: (402)
464-5971

Motel 6 $
3001 NW 12th St, Lincoln,
NE 68521, Res. (800)
466-8356 Ph: 402 475-3211
Fax: 402 475-1632

Super 8 Motel $-$$
2635 West ""O"" Street",
Lincoln, NE 68528, Res.
(800) 800-8000 Ph: (402)
476-8887 Fax: (402) 476-8887

Super 8 Motel $-$$
2545 Cornhusker Highway,
Lincoln, NE 68521-1461,
Res. (800) 800-8000 Ph: (402)
467-4488 Fax: (402) 467-4488

MCCOOK   NE

Super 8 Motel $-$$
1103 E. B St., McCook, NE
69001, Res. (800) 800-8000
Ph: (308) 345-1141 Fax: (308)
345-1144

NORFOLK   NE

Super 8 Motel $-$$
1223 Omaha Ave., Norfolk,
NE 68701-5728, Res. (800)
800-8000 Ph: (402) 379-2220
Fax: (402) 379-3817

NORTH PLATTE   NE

Motel 6 $
1520 S Jeffers St, North
Platte, NE 69101, Res. (800)
466-8356 Ph: 308 534-6200
Fax: 308 532-5276

Super 8 Motel $-$$
220 Eugene Ave., North
Platte, NE 69101-9804, Res.
(800) 800-8000 Ph: (308)
532-4224 Fax: (308) 534-4317

O'NEILL   NE

Budget Host Carriage House $-$$
929 E Douglas St, P.O. Box
151, O'Neill, NE 68763, Res.
(800) 283-4678 Ph: (402)
336-3403 Fax: (402) 336-3409

Super 8 Motel $-$$
East Highway 20, O'Neill, NE
68763, Res. (800) 800-8000
Ph: (402) 336-3100 Fax: (402)
336-3100

OGALLALA   NE

Super 8 Motel $-$$
"500 East ""A"" S.", Ogallala,
NE 69153, Res. (800)
800-8000 Ph: (308) 284-2076
Fax: (308) 284-2590

OMAHA   NE

Econo Lodge West Central $-$$
3511 S. 84th St., Omaha, NE
68124, Res. (800) 424-4777
Ph: (402) 391-4321

Motel 6 $
10708 iMi St, Omaha, NE
68127, Res. (800) 466-8356
Ph: 402 331-3161 Fax: 402
597-0777

Super 8 Motel $-$$
10829 M Street, Omaha, NE
68137, Res. (800) 800-8000
Ph: (402) 339-2250 Fax: (402)
339-6622

Super 8 Motel $-$$
7111 Spring St., Omaha, NE
68106, Res. (800) 800-8000
Ph: (402) 390-0700 Fax: (402)
391-2063

Super 8 Motel $-$$
11610 West Dodge Road,
Omaha, NE 68154, Res.
(800) 800-8000 Ph: (402)
371-2520 Fax: (402) 492-8845

SCOTTSBLUFF   NE

Super 8 Motel $-$$
2202 Delta Drive,
Scottsbluff, NE 69361-2768,
Res. (800) 800-8000 Ph: (308)
635-1600 Fax: (308) 635-2483

SEWARD   NE

Super 8 Motel $-$$
S. Hwy. 15, Seward, NE
68434, Res. (800) 800-8000
Ph: (402) 643-3388 Fax: (402)
643-3980

SIDNEY   NE

Super 8 Motel $-$$
2115 W. Illinois St., Box 314,
Sidney, NE 69162, Res. (800)
800-8000 Ph: (308) 254-2081
Fax: (308) 254-2081

SOUTH SIOUX CITY   NE

Econo Lodge $-$$
4402 Dakota Ave., South
Sioux City, NE 68776, Res.
(800) 424-4777 Ph: (402)
494-4114 Fax: (402) 494-4114

VALENTINE   NE

Super 8 Motel $-$$
223 E. Hwy. 20, P.O. Box 653,
Valentine, NE 69201-0653,
Res. (800) 800-8000 Ph: (402)
376-1250 Fax: (402) 376-1211

WAYNE   NE

Super 8 Motel $-$$
610 Tomar Dr., Wayne, NE
68787, Res. (800) 800-8000
Ph: (402) 375-4898 Fax: (402)
375-4898

WEST POINT   NE

Super 8 Motel $-$$
1211 N. Lincoln St., West
Point, NE 68788, Res. (800)
800-8000 Ph: (402) 372-3998
Fax: (402) 372-3998

YORK   NE

Super 8 Motel $-$$
"I-80 & US 81, PO Box 532",
York, NE 68467-0532, Res.
(800) 800-8000 Ph: (402)
362-3388 Fax: (402) 362-3604

NEVADA

BOULDER CITY   NV

Super 8 Motel $-$$
704 Nevada Hwy, Boulder
City, NV 89005, Res. (800)
800-8000 Ph: (702) 294-8888
Fax: (702) 293-4344

CARSON CITY   NV

Motel 6 $
2749 S Carson St, Carson
City, NV 89701, Res. (800)
466-8356 Ph: 702 885-7710
Fax: 702 885-7671

Super 8 Motel $-$$
2829 South Carson St.,
Carson City, NV
89701-5514, Res. (800)
800-8000 Ph: (702) 883-7800
Fax: (702) 883-0376

M
O
T
E
L

ELKO   NV

Motel 6 $
3021 Idaho St, Elko, NV 89801, Res. (800) 466-8356 Ph: 702 738-4337 Fax: 702 753-8381

Super 8 Motel $-$$
1755 Idaho St, Elko, NV 89801, Res. (800) 800-8000 Ph: (702) 738-8488 Fax: (702) 738-4637

ELY   NV

Motel 6 $
7th St & Ave iOī, Ely, NV 89301, Res. (800) 466-8356 Ph: 702 289-6671 Fax: 702 289-4803

FALLON   NV

Econo Lodge $-$$
70 E. Williams Ave., Fallon, NV 89406, Res. (800) 424-4777 Ph: (702) 423-2194 Fax: (702) 423-7187

FERNLEY   NV

Super 8 Motel $-$$
1350 Newlands Dr, Fernley, NV 89408, Res. (800) 800-8000 Ph: (702) 575-5555 Fax: (702) 575-6546

LAS VEGAS   NV

Continental Hotel, Casino $$
4100 Paradise Road, Las Vegas, NV 89109, Res. (800) 777-4844 Ph: (702) 737-5555 Fax: (702) 369-8776

E-z 8 Motel $
5201 S. Industrial Road, Las Vegas, NV 89118, Res. 800-326-6835 Ext. 40 Ph: 702-739-9513 Fax: 702-739-7810

Econo Lodge $-$$
1150 Las Vegas Blvd. S., Las Vegas, NV 89104, Res. (800) 424-4777 Ph: (702) 382-6001 Fax: (702) 382-9180

Econo Lodge Downtown $-$$
520 S. Casino Center Blvd., Las Vegas, NV 89101, Res. (800) 424-4777 Ph: (702) 384-8211 Fax: (702) 384-8580

Motel 6 $
4125 Boulder Hwy, Las Vegas, NV 89121, Res. (800) 466-8356 Ph: 702 457-8051 Fax: 702 457-0265

Motel 6 $
5085 S Industrial Rd, Las Vegas, NV 89118, Res. (800) 466-8356 Ph: 702 739-6747 Fax: 702 736-5794

Motel 6 $
195 E Tropicana Ave, Las Vegas, NV 89109, Res. (800) 466-8356 Ph: 702 798-0728 Fax: 702 798-5657

Palace Station Hotel & $$
2411 West Sahara Ave., Las Vegas, NV 89102, Res. (800) 544-2411 Ph: (702) 367-2411 Fax: (702) 367-6138

Sam's Town Hotel & $$
5111 Boulder Highway, Las Vegas, NV 89122, Res. (800) 634-6371 Ph: (702) 456-777 Fax: (702) 454-8014

Super 8 Motel $-$$
5288 Boulder Hwy., Las Vegas, NV 89122-6003, Res. (800) 800-8000 Ph: (702) 435-8888 Fax: (702) 435-6953

Super 8 Motel $-$$
4250 S. Koval Lane, Las Vegas, NV 89109, Res. (800) 800-8000 Ph: (702) 794-0888 Fax: (702) 794-0888

Super 8 Motel $-$$
4435 Las Vegas Blvd. N., Las Vegas, NV 89115, Res. (800) 800-8000 Ph: (702) 644-5666 Fax: (310) 286-1544

MILL CITY   NV

Super 8 Motel $-$$
600 E. Frontage Rd., Mill City, NV 89418, Res. (800) 800-8000 Ph: (702) 538-7306 Fax: (702) 538-7319

RENO   NV

Motel 6 $
666 N Wells Ave, Reno, NV 89512, Res. (800) 466-8356 Ph: 702 329-8681 Fax: 702 329-2921

Motel 6 $
866 N Wells Ave, Reno, NV 89512, Res. (800) 466-8356 Ph: 702 786-9852 Fax: 702 786-3162

Motel 6 $
1400 Stardust St, Reno, NV 89503, Res. (800) 466-8356 Ph: 702 747-7390 Fax: 702 747-4527

SPARKS   NV

Motel 6 $
2405 Victorian Ave, Sparks, NV 89431, Res. (800) 466-8356 Ph: 702 358-1080 Fax: 702 358-4883

WELLS   NV

Motel 6 $
I-80/US Hwy 40 & US Hwy 93, Wells, NV 89835, Res. (800) 466-8356 Ph: 702 752-2116 Fax: 702 752-3192

Super 8 Motel $-$$
930 6th Street, Wells, NV 89835, Res. (800) 800-8000 Ph: (702) 752-3384 Fax: (702) 752-3384

WENDOVER   N

Super 8 Motel $-$
1325 Wendover Blvd., P.O. Box 2259, Wendover, NV 89883, Res. (800) 800-8000 Ph: (702) 664-2888 Fax: (702) 664-3051

WINNEMUCCA   N

Motel 6
1600 Winnemucca Blvd, Winnemucca, NV 89445, Res. (800) 466-8356 Ph: 702 623-1180 Fax: 702 623-4725

Super 8 Motel $-$
W. Winnemucca Blvd., Winnemucca, NV 89445, Res. (800) 800-8000 Ph: (702) 625-1818

NEW HAMPHSIRE

CONCORD   NI

Econo Lodge $-$
Gulf Street, Concord, NH 03301, Res. (800) 424-4777 Ph: (603) 224-4011 Fax: (603) 228-3353

KEENE   NI

Super 8 Motel $-$
3 Ashbrook Road, Keene, NI 03431, Res. (800) 800-8000 Ph: (603) 352-9780 Fax: (603) 357-5215

MANCHESTER   NI

Econo Lodge $-$
75 W. Hancock St., Manchester, NH 03102, Res. (800) 424-4777 Ph: (603) 624-0111 Fax: (603) 623-0268

Super 8 Motel $-$
2301 Brown Ave., Manchester, NH 03106, Res. (800) 800-8000 Ph: (603) 623-0883 Fax: (603) 624-9303

NASHUA   NH

Motel 6
2 Progress Ave, Nashua, NH 03062, Res. (800) 466-8356 Ph: 603 889-4151 Fax: 603 886-4721

TILTON   NH

Super 8 Motel $-$
RFD #1 Rte. 140, Tilton, NH 03276, Res. (800) 800-8000 Ph: (603) 286-8882 Fax: (603) 286-8788

NEW JERSEY

ABSECON   NJ

Econo Lodge $-$
328 White Horse Pike, Absecon, NJ 08201, Res. (800) 424-4777 Ph: (609) 652-3300 Fax: (609) 652-8885

Red Carpet Inn $$
206 E. White Horse Pike,
Absecon, NJ 08201, Res.
(800) 251-1962 Ph: (609)
652-3322 Fax: (609) 652-9647

Super 8 Motel $-$$
229 East Route 30, White
Horse Pike, Absecon, NJ
08201, Res. (800) 800-8000
Ph: (609) 652-1270 Fax: (609)
748-0666

ATLANTIC CITY   NJ

Econo Lodge Beach Block $-$$
3001 Pacific Ave., Atlantic
City, NJ 08401, Res. (800)
424-4777 Ph: (609) 344-2925
Fax: (609) 344-3270

Econo Lodge Boardwalk $-$$
117 S. Kentucky Ave.,
Atlantic City, NJ 08401,
Res. (800) 424-4777 Ph: (609)
344-9093 Fax: (609) 340-8065

Red Carpet Inn $$
1630 N. Albany Ave., Atlantic
City, NJ 08401, Res. (800)
251-1962 Ph: (609) 348-3171

BARRINGTON   NJ

Super 8 Motel $-$$
308 White Horse Pike,
Barrington, NJ 08007, Res.
(800) 800-8000 Ph: (609)
547-8000 Fax: (609) 573-9570

BELLMAWR   NJ

Econo Lodge $-$$
301 S. Black Horse Pk.,
Bellmawr, NJ 08031, Res.
(800) 424-4777 Ph: (609)
931-2800 Fax: (609) 931-6633

BORDENTOWN   NJ

Econo Lodge $-$$
US 130 & 206, Bordentown,
NJ 08505, Res. (800)
424-4777 Ph: (609) 298-5000
Fax: (609) 298-5009

BUENA   NJ

Econo Lodge $-$$
146 Old Tuckahoe Rd.,
Buena, NJ 08310, Res. (800)
424-4777 Ph: (609) 697-9000
Fax: (609) 697-9000

CARLSTADT   NJ

Econo Lodge $-$$
395 Washington Ave.,
Carlstadt, NJ 07072, Res.
(800) 424-4777 Ph: (201)
935-4600 Fax: (201) 935-0264

CHERRY HILL   NJ

Econo Lodge Nj State $-$$
SR 38 & Cuthbert Blvd.,
Cherry Hill, NJ 08002, Res.
(800) 424-4777 Ph: (609)
665-3630 Fax: (609) 662-7861

EAST BRUNSWICK   NJ

Motel 6 $
244 Rt 18, East Brunswick,
NJ 08816, Res. (800)
466-8356 Ph: 908 390-4545
Fax: 908 390-5414

ELIZABETH   NJ

Econo Lodge $-$$
853 Spring St., Elizabeth, NJ
07201, Res. (800) 424-4777
Ph: (908) 353-1365 Fax: (908)
353-2927

FARMINGDALE   NJ

Econo Lodge $-$$
5309 SR 33 & SR 34,
Farmingdale, NJ 07727, Res.
(800) 424-4777 Ph: (908)
938-3110

JERSEY CITY   NJ

Econo Lodge $-$$
750-762 Tonnelle Ave.,
Jersey City, NJ 07307, Res.
(800) 424-4777 Ph: (201)
420-9040

LAKEHURST   NJ

Econo Lodge $-$$
2016 SR 37 W., Lakehurst,
NJ 08733, Res. (800)
424-4777 Ph: (908) 657-7100
Fax: (908) 657-1672

MAPLE SHADE   NJ

Motel 6 $
Rt 73 North, Maple Shade,
NJ 08052, Res. (800)
466-8356 Ph: 609 235-3550
Fax: 609 439-9238

MOUNT LAUREL   NJ

Econo Lodge $-$$
611 Fellowship Rd., Mount
Laurel, NJ 08054, Res. (800)
424-4777 Ph: (609) 722-1919
Fax: (609) 722-0116

Red Carpet Inn $$
1104 Route 73, Mount
Laurel, NJ 08054, Res. (800)
251-1962 Ph: (908) 235-5610
Fax: (908) 235-6713

NEW BRUNSWICK   NJ

Econo Lodge University $-$$
26 US 1, New Brunswick, NJ
08901, Res. (800) 424-4777
Ph: (908) 828-8000 Fax: (908)
220-0314

PARAMUS   NJ

Red Carpet Inn $$
211 Route 17, Paramus, NJ
07652, Res. (800) 251-1962
Ph: (201) 261-8686 Fax: (201)
265-1195

PISCATAWAY   NJ

Motel 6 $
1012 Stelton Rd, Piscataway,
NJ 08854, Res. (800)
466-8356 Ph: 908 981-9200
Fax: 908 562-0550

PLEASANTVILLE   NJ

Econo Lodge Atlantic City $-$$
6641 Black Horse Pike / Egg
Harbor Township,
Pleasantville, NJ 08232,
Res. (800) 424-4777 Ph: (609)
484-8500 Fax: (609) 383-2068

SOMERS POINT   NJ

Econo Lodge $-$$
21 Mcarthur Blvd., Somers
Point, NJ 08244, Res. (800)
424-4777 Ph: (609) 927-3220
Fax: (609) 927-1751

Econo Lodge $-$$
119 US 9 S., Somers Point,
NJ 08244, Res. (800)
424-4777 Ph: (609) 390-3366
Fax: (000) 006-0990

WILLIAMSTOWN   NJ

Red Carpet Inn $$
105 No. Blackhorse Pike,
Williamstown, NJ 08094,
Res. (800) 251-1962 Ph: (609)
728-8000 Fax: (609) 875-6162

NEW MEXICO

ALAMOGORDO   NM

Motel 6 $
251 Panorama Blvd,
Alamogordo, NM 88310, Res.
(800) 466-8356 Ph: 505
434-5970 Fax: 505 437-5491

Super 8 Motel $-$$
3204 N. White Sands,
Alamogordo, NM 88310, Res.
(800) 800-8000 Ph: (505)
434-4205 Fax: (505) 434-4205

ALBUQUERQUE   NM

Econo Lodge $-$$
10331 Hotel Ave.,
Albuquerque, NM 87123,
Res. (800) 424-4777 Ph: (505)
271-8500 Fax: (505) 296-5984

Econo Lodge East $-$$
13211 Central Ave. N.E.,
Albuquerque, NM 87123,
Res. (800) 424-4777 Ph: (505)
292-7600 Fax: (505) 298-4536

Motel 6 $
3400 Prospect Ave NE,
Albuquerque, NM 87107,
Res. (800) 466-8356 Ph: 505
883-8813 Fax: 505 883-6056

Motel 6 $
13141 Central Ave NE,
Albuquerque, NM 87123,
Res. (800) 466-8356 Ph: 505
294-4600 Fax: 505 294-7564

Motel 6 $
1701 University Blvd NE,
Albuquerque, NM 87102,
Res. (800) 466-8356 Ph: 505
843-9228 Fax: 505 842-1757

Motel 6 $
6015 Iliff Rd NW,
Albuquerque, NM 87121,
Res. (800) 466-8356 Ph: 505
831-3400 Fax: 505 831-3609

MOTEL (vertical tab)

Motel 6 $
5701 Iliff Rd NW,
Albuquerque, NM 87105,
Res. (800) 466-8356 Ph: 505
831-8888 Fax: 505 831-6296

Motel 6 $
1000 Stadium Blvd SE,
Albuquerque, NM 87102,
Res. (800) 466-8356 Ph: 505
243-8017 Fax: 505 242-5137

Motel 6 $
8510 Pan American Freeway
NE, Albuquerque, NM
87109, Res. (800) 466-8356

Red Carpet Inn $$
75 Hotel Circle NE,
Albuquerque, NM 87123,
Res. (800) 251-1962 Ph: (505)
296-5465 Fax: (505) 237-1116

Super 8 Motel $-$$
"2500 University Blvd., NE",
Albuquerque, NM 87107,
Res. (800) 800-8000 Ph: (505)
888-4884 Fax: (505) 888-4884

Super 8 Motel $-$$
6030 Iliff N.W., Albuquerque,
NM 87121, Res. (800)
800-8000 Ph: (505) 836-5560
Fax: (505) 836-5560

BELEN   NM

Budget Host Rio $-$$
502 Rio Communities Blvd,
Belen, NM 87002, Res. (800)
283-4678 Ph: (505) 864-4451
Fax: (505) 864-7264

Super 8 Motel $-$$
428 S. M ain St., Belen, NM
87002, Res. (800) 800-8000
Ph: (505) 864-8188

BERNALILLO   NM

Super 8 Motel $-$$
165 Hwy. 44E, Bernalillo, NM
87004, Res. (800) 800-8000
Ph: (505) 867-0766

BLOOMFIELD   NM

Super 8 Motel $-$$
525 West Broadway,
Bloomfield, NM 87413, Res.
(800) 800-8000 Ph: (505)
632-8886

CARLSBAD   NM

Motel 6 $
3824 National Parks Hwy,
Carlsbad, NM 88220, Res.
(800) 466-8356 Ph: 505
885-0011 Fax: 505 887-7861

CLOVIS   NM

Motel 6 $
2620 Mabry Dr, Clovis, NM
88101, Res. (800) 466-8356
Ph: 505 762-2995 Fax: 505
762-6342

DEMING   NM

Motel 6 $
I-10 & Motel Dr., Mail
Address: PO Box 970,
Deming, NM 88031, Res.
(800) 466-8356 Ph: 505
546-2623 Fax: 505 546-0934

Super 8 Motel $-$$
1217 W. Pines, Deming, NM
88030, Res. (800) 800-8000
Ph: (505) 546-0481 Fax: (505)
546-0481

ESPANOLA   NM

Super 8 Motel $-$$
298 S. Riversider, Espanola,
NM 87532, Res. (800)
800-8000 Ph: (505) 753-5374
Fax: (505) 753-5339

FARMINGTON   NM

Motel 6 $
510 Scott Ave, Farmington,
NM 87401, Res. (800)
466-8356 Ph: 505 327-0242
Fax: 505 327-5617

Motel 6 $
1600 Bloomfield Hwy,
Farmington, NM 87401, Res.
(800) 466-8356 Ph: 505
326-4501 Fax: 505 326-3883

Super 8 Motel $-$$
1601 Bloomfield Hwy,
Farmington, NM 87401, Res.
(800) 800-8000 Ph: (505)
325-1813 Fax: (505) 325-1813

Villager $-$$
2530 Bloomfield Highway,
Farmington, NM 87401, Res.
(800) 328-7829 Ph: (505)
327-4433 Fax: (000) 000-0000

FORT SUMNER   NM

Super 8 Motel $-$$
1703 E. Sumner Avenue,
Fort Sumner, NM 88119,
Res. (800) 800-8000 Ph: (505)
355-7888

GALLUP   NM

Econo Lodge $-$$
3101 W. US 66, Gallup, NM
87301, Res. (800) 424-4777
Ph: (505) 722-3800

Motel 6 $
3306 W 66, Gallup, NM
87301, Res. (800) 466-8356
Ph: 505 863-4492 Fax: 505
863-5849

Super 8 Motel $-$$
1715 West Highway 66,
Gallup, NM 87301, Res. (800)
800-8000 Ph: (505) 722-5300
Fax: (505) 722-6200

GRANTS   NM

Motel 6 $
1505 E Santa Fe Ave,
Grants, NM 87020, Res.
(800) 466-8356 Ph: 505
285-4607 Fax: 505 285-6019

Super 8 Motel $-$$
1604 East Santa Fe Avenue,
Grants, NM 87020, Res.
(800) 800-8000 Ph: (505)
287-8811 Fax: (505) 876-4019

HOBBS   NM

Super 8 Motel $-$$
722 N. Marland, Hobbs, NM
88240, Res. (800) 800-8000
Ph: (505) 397-7511

LAS CRUCES   NM

Motel 6 $
235 La Posada Ln, Las
Cruces, NM 88001, Res.
(800) 466-8356 Ph: 505
525-1010 Fax: 505 525-0139

Super 8 Motel $-$$
245 La Posada Lane, Las
Cruces, NM 88001, Res.
(800) 800-8000 Ph: (505)
523-8695 Fax: (505) 523-8695

Super 8 Motel $-$$
4411 North Main Street, Las
Cruces, NM 88001, Res.
(800) 800-8000 Ph: (505)
382-1490 Fax: (505) 382-1849

LAS VEGAS   NM

Scottish Inns $$
1216 No. Grand Ave., Las
Vegas, NM 87701, Res. (800)
251-1962 Ph: (505) 425-9357
Fax: (505) 425-9357

Super 8 Motel $-$$
2029 N. Hwy. 85, Las Vegas,
NM 87701, Res. (800)
800-8000 Ph: (505) 425-5288
Fax: (505) 425-5288

LORDSBURG   NM

Super 8 Motel $-$$
110 E. Maple, Lordsburg, NM
88045, Res. (800) 800-8000
Ph: (505) 542-8882

MORIARTY   NM

Super 8 Motel $-$$
1611 West Old Route 66, P.O.
Box 1127, Moriarty, NM
87035-1127, Res. (800)
800-8000 Ph: (505) 832-6730
Fax: (505) 832-6730

PORTALES   NM

Super 8 Motel $-$$
1805 West 2nd Street,
Portales, NM 88130, Res.
(800) 800-8000 Ph: (505)
356-8518 Fax: (505) 359-0431

RATON   NM

Motel 6 $
1600 Cedar St, Raton, NM
87740, Res. (800) 466-8356
Ph: 505 445-2777 Fax: 505
445-5359

Super 8 Motel $-$$
1610 Cedar, Raton, NM
87740-2551, Res. (800)
800-8000 Ph: (505) 445-2355
Fax: (505) 445-2355

RIO RANCHO   NM

Super 8 Motel   S-SS
4100 Barbara Loop, Rio
Rancho, NM 87124, Res.
(800) 800-8000 Ph: (505)
896-8888

ROSWELL   NM

Super 8 Motel   S-SS
3575 N. MAin Street, Roswell,
NM 88201, Res. (800)
800-8000 Ph: (602) 443-8777

RUIDOSO   NM

Super 8 Motel   S-SS
100 Cliff Drive, Ruidoso, NM
88345-2600, Res. (800)
800-8000 Ph: (505) 378-8180
Fax: (505) 378-8372

SANTA FE   NM

Motel 6   S
3695 Cerrillos Rd, Santa Fe,
NM 87505, Res. (800)
466-8356 Ph: 505 471-4140
Fax: 505 474-4370

Motel 6   S
3007 Cerrillos Rd, Santa Fe,
NM 87505, Res. (800)
466-8356 Ph: 505 473-1380
Fax: 505 473-7784

Super 8 Motel   S-SS
3358 Cerrillos Rd., Santa Fe,
NM 87501, Res. (800)
800-8000 Ph: (505) 471-8811
Fax: (505) 471-3239

SANTA ROSA   NM

Motel 6   S
3400 Will Rogers Dr, Santa
Rosa, NM 88435, Res. (800)
466-8356 Ph: 505 472-3045
Fax: 505 472-5923

Super 8 Motel   S-SS
1201 Will Rogers Drive,
Santa Rosa, NM 88435, Res.
(800) 800-8000 Ph: (505)
472-5444 Fax: (505) 472-5388

SILVER CITY   NM

Super 8 Motel   S-SS
1040 East Highway 180,
Silver City, NM 88061, Res.
(800) 800-8000 Ph: (505)
388-1983 Fax: (505) 388-1983

SOCORRO   NM

Econo Lodge   S-SS
713 California St. N.W.,
Socorro, NM 87801, Res.
(800) 424-4777 Ph: (505)
835-1500 Fax: (505) 835-3261

Motel 6   S
807 S US Hwy 85, Socorro,
NM 87801, Res. (800)
466-8356 Ph: 505 835-4300
Fax: 505 835-3108

Super 8 Motel   S-SS
1121 Frontage Rd. NW,
Socorro, NM 87801, Res.
(800) 800-8000 Ph: (505)
835-4626 Fax: (505) 835-3988

TAOS   NM

Super 8 Motel   S-SS
Highway 68, Taos, NM
87581, Res. (800) 800-8000
Ph: (505) 758-1088

TRUTH CONSQ   NM

Super 8 Motel   S-SS
2701 North Date Street,
Truth Consq, NM 87901,
Res. (800) 800-8000 Ph: (505)
894-7888 Fax: (505) 894-7883

TUCUMCARI   NM

Budget Host Royal Palacio S-SS
1620 E Tucumcari Blvd,
Tucumcari, NM 88401, Res.
(800) 283-4678 Ph: (505)
461-1212

Econo Lodge   S-SS
3400 E. Tucumcari Blvd.,
Tucumcari, NM 88401, Res.
(800) 424-4777 Ph: (505)
461-4194 Fax: (505) 461-4911

Motel 6   S
2900 E Tucumcari Blvd,
Tucumcari, NM 88401, Res.
(800) 466-8356 Ph: 505
461-4791 Fax: 505 461-2283

Super 8 Motel   S-SS
4001 E. Tucumcari
Boulevard, Tucumcari, NM
88401, Res. (800) 800-8000
Ph: (605) 229-4848 Fax: (505)
461-4320

NEW YORK

ALBANY   NY

Econo Lodge Colonie Mall S-SS
1632 Central Ave., Albany,
NY 12205, Res. (800)
424-4777 Ph: (518) 456-8811
Fax: (518) 456-0811

Motel 6   S
100 Watervliet Ave, Albany,
NY 12206, Res. (800)
466-8356 Ph: 518 438-7447
Fax: 518 438-0594

Red Carpet Inn   SS
500 Northern Blvd., Albany,
NY 12204, Res. (800)
251-1962 Ph: (518) 462-5562

Super 8 Motel   S-SS
1579 Central Avenue,
Albany, NY 12205, Res. (800)
800-8000 Ph: (518) 869-8471
Fax: (518) 464-4010

AMHERST   NY

Motel 6   S
4400 Maple Rd, Amherst, NY
14226, Res. (800) 466-8356
Ph: 716 834-2231 Fax: 716
834-0872

Super 8 Motel   S-SS
#1 Flint Rd., Amherst, NY
14226-1047, Res. (800)
800-8000 Ph: (716) 688-0811
Fax: (716) 688-2365

AMSTERDAM   NY

Super 8 Motel   S-SS
Rte. 30 S., Amsterdam, NY
12010, Res. (800) 800-8000
Ph: (518) 843-5888 Fax: (518)
843-5888

AUBURN   NY

Super 8 Motel   S-SS
9 McMaster St., Auburn, NY
13021, Res. (800) 800-8000
Ph: (315) 253-8886 Fax: (315)
253-8329

BATH   NY

Super 8 Motel   S-SS
333 W. Morris, Bath, NY
14810-1030, Res. (800)
800-8000 Ph: (607) 776-2187
Fax: (607) 776-3206

BINGHAMTON   NY

Motel 6   S
1012 Front St, Binghamton,
NY 13905, Res. (800)
466-8356 Ph: 607 771-0400
Fax: 607 773-4781

Super 8 Motel   S-SS
650 Front St., Binghamton,
NY 13905-1536, Res. (800)
800-8000 Ph: (607) 773-8111
Fax: (607) 773-8111

Super 8 Motel   S-SS
P.O. Box 196 East Side
Station, Binghamton, NY
13904, Res. (800) 800-8000
Ph: (607) 775-3443

BROCKPORT   NY

Econo Lodge   S-SS
6575 4th Section Rd.,
Brockport, NY 14420, Res.
(800) 424-4777 Ph: (716)
637-3157 Fax: (716) 637-0434

BUFFALO   NY

Econo Lodge   S-SS
7200 Transit Rd., Buffalo, NY
14221, Res. (800) 424-4777
Ph: (716) 634-1500 Fax: (716)
634-1501

Econo Lodge South   S-SS
4344 Milestrip Rd., Buffalo,
NY 14219, Res. (800)
424-4777 Ph: (716) 825-7530
Fax: (716) 825-7530

CANANDAIGUA   NY

Econo Lodge Muar Lake S-SS
170 Eastern Blvd.,
Canandaigua, NY 14424,
Res. (800) 424-4777 Ph: (716)
394-9000 Fax: (716) 396-2560

CORFU   NY

Econo Lodge   S-SS
8493 SR 77, Corfu, NY
14036, Res. (800) 424-4777
Ph: (716) 599-4681 Fax: (716)
599-3730

M O T E L

CORTLAND NY	**GOVERNOR'S ISL.** NY	**KINGSTON** NY

Econo Lodge $-$$
3775 US 11, Cortland, NY
13045, Res. (800) 424-4777
Ph: (607) 753-7594 Fax: (607)
753-6508

Super 8 Motel $-$$
188 Clinton Ave. Extension,
Cortland, NY 13045-1321,
Res. (800) 800-8000 Ph: (607)
756-5622 Fax: (607) 753-6171

DUNKIRK NY

Econo Lodge $-$$
310 Lake Shore Dr., Dunkirk,
NY 14048, Res. (800)
424-4777 Ph: (716) 366-2200

EAST SYRACUSE NY

Motel 6 $
6577 Court St Rd, East
Syracuse, NY 13057-1225,
Res. (800) 466-8356 Ph: 315
433-1300 Fax: 315 437-2094

ELMIRA NY

Econo Lodge $-$$
1339 Cr 64, Elmira, NY
14903, Res. (800) 424-4777
Ph: (607) 739-2000 Fax: (607)
739-3552

ENDICOTT NY

Villager $-$$
214 Washington Ave,
Endicott, NY 13760, Res.
(800) 328-7829 Ph: (607)
754-6000 Fax: (000) 000-0000

FALCONER NY

Motel 6 $
1980 E Main St, Falconer, NY
14733, Res. (800) 466-8356
Ph: 716 665-3670 Fax: 716
664-7651

GATES NY

Motel 6 $
155 Buell Rd, Gates, NY
14624, Res. (800) 466-8356
Ph: 716 436-2170 Fax: 716
436-4814

GENEVA NY

Motel 6 $
485 Hamilton St, Geneva,
NY 14456, Res. (800)
466-8356 Ph: 315 789-4050
Fax: 315 781-2338

GLENS FALLS NY

Econo Lodge $-$$
29 Aviation Rd., Glens Falls,
NY 12801, Res. (800)
424-4777 Ph: (518) 793-3491
Fax: (518) 793-8678

Super 8 Motel $-$$
Corinth Road, "RD 4, Box
583", Glens Falls, NY 12801,
Res. (800) 800-8000 Ph: (518)
761-9780 Fax: (518) 761-1049

Super 8 Motel $-$$
Comfort Road, Governor's
Isl., NY 10004, Res. (800)
800-8000 Ph: (212) 269-8878
Fax: (212) 742-0926

HENRIETTA NY

Super 8 Motel $-$$
1000 Lehigh Station Rd,
Henrietta, NY 14467, Res.
(800) 800-8000 Ph: (716)
359-1630 Fax: (716) 359-1630

HICKSVILLE NY

Econo Lodge $-$$
429 Duffy Ave., Hicksville,
NY 11801, Res. (800)
424-4777 Ph: (516) 433-3900
Fax: (516) 433-3909

HOLBROOK NY

Red Carpet Inn $$
4444 Veterans Memorial Hwy,
Holbrook, NY 11741, Res.
(800) 251-1962 Ph: (516)
588-7700 Fax: (516) 588-9184

HORNELL NY

Super 8 Motel $-$$
Rt 36 & Webb Crossing,
Hornell, NY 14843, Res.
(800) 800-8000 Ph: (607)
324-6222 Fax: (607) 324-2990

HORSEHEADS NY

Motel 6 $
4133 Rt 17, Horseheads, NY
14845, Res. (800) 466-8356
Ph: 607 739-2525 Fax: 607
739-1051

Red Carpet Inn $$
3325 So Main St.,
Horseheads, NY 14845, Res.
(800) 251-1962 Ph: (607)
739-3831 Fax: (607) 739-7674

HYDE PARK NY

Super 8 Motel $-$$
528 Albany Post Rd, Hyde
Park, NY 12538, Res. (800)
800-8000 Ph: (914) 229-0088
Fax: (914) 229-8088

ITHACA NY

Econo Lodge $-$$
Cayuga Mall, Ithaca, NY
14850, Res. (800) 424-4777
Ph: (607) 257-1400 Fax: (607)
257-6359

Super 8 Motel $-$$
400 South Meadow St.,
Ithaca, NY 14850, Res. (800)
800-8000 Ph: (607) 273-8088
Fax: (607) 273-4832

JOHNSTOWN NY

Super 8 Motel $-$$
North Comrie Avenue,
Johnstown, NY 12095, Res.
(800) 800-8000 Ph: (518)
736-1838 Fax: (518) 736-1838

Super 8 Motel $-$$
487 Washington Ave.,
Kingston, NY 12401-2906,
Res. (800) 800-8000 Ph: (914)
338-3078 Fax: (914) 338-3078

LAKE GEORGE NY

Econo Lodge $-$$
431 Canada St., Lake George,
NY 12845, Res. (800)
424-4777 Ph: (518) 668-2689
Fax: (518) 798-3455

Super 8 Motel $-$$
"RD #2, Box 2541", Lake
George, NY 12845, Res. (800)
800-8000 Ph: (518) 623-2811
Fax: (518) 623-2874

LAKE PLACID NY

Econo Lodge $-$$
Cascade Rd. (SR 73), Lake
Placid, NY 12946, Res. (800)
424-4777 Ph: (518) 523-2817
Fax: (518) 523-2817

LATHAM NY

Super 8 Motel $-$$
681 Troy-Schenectady Rd.,
Latham, NY 12110, Res.
(800) 800-8000 Ph: (518)
783-8808 Fax: (518) 783-1002

LIVERPOOL NY

Econo Lodge $-$$
401 7th North St., Liverpool,
NY 13088, Res. (800)
424-4777 Ph: (315) 451-6000
Fax: (315) 451-0193

Super 8 Motel $-$$
421 7th N. St., Liverpool, NY
13088, Res. (800) 800-8000
Ph: (315) 451-8888

MALONE NY

Econo Lodge $-$$
227 W. Main St., Malone, NY
12953, Res. (800) 424-4777
Ph: (518) 483-0500 Fax: (518)
483-0500

Super 8 Motel $-$$
Finney Blvd., Malone, NY
12953, Res. (800) 800-8000
Ph: (518) 483-5700

MASSENA NY

Econo Lodge $-$$
Rd 1 Box 261, Massena, NY
13662, Res. (800) 424-4777
Ph: (315) 764-0246 Fax: (315)
764-9615

Super 8 Motel $-$$
Grove St. Extension,
Massena, NY 13662, Res.
(800) 800-8000 Ph: (315)
764-1065 Fax: (315) 764-9710

MIDDLETOWN NY

Super 8 Motel $-$$
563 Route 211 East,
Middletown, NY 10940, Res.
(800) 800-8000 Ph: (914)
692-5828 Fax: (914) 692-5828

MONTGOMERY   NY

Super 8 Motel $-$$
207 Montgomery Rd.,
Montgomery, NY 12549,
Res. (800) 800-8000 Ph: (914)
457-3143 Fax: (914) 457-3143

MONTICELLO   NY

Econo Lodge $-$$
190 Broadway, Monticello,
NY 12701, Res. (800)
424-4777 Ph: (914) 794-8800
Fax: (914) 794-8800

NEW PALTZ   NY

Econo Lodge $-$$
530 Main St., New Paltz, NY
12561, Res. (800) 424-4777
Ph: (914) 255-6200

Super 8 Motel $-$$
#7 Terwilliger Lane, New
Paltz, NY 12561-1619, Res.
(800) 800-8000 Ph: (914)
255-8865 Fax: (914) 255-1629

NEW YORK   NY

Broadway Bed & Breakfast$$-$
264 West 46th St., corner of
8th Ave., New York, NY
10036, Res. (800) 826-6300
Ph: (212) 768-2807 Fax: (212)
768-2807

Hotel Wolcott $65-$
4 West 31st St., New York,
NY 10001, Ph: (212) 563-2900
Fax: (212) 563-0096

The Excelsior $75-$
45 West 81st St., New York,
NY 10024, Res. (800)
368-4575 Ph: (212) 362-9200
Fax: (212) 721-2994

The Gershwin Hotel $20-$
7 East 27th St., New York,
NY 10016, Ph: (212) 545-8000
Fax: (212) 684-5546

The Larchmont Hotel $45-$
27 West 11th St., New York,
NY 10011, Ph: (212) 989-9333
Fax: (212) 989-9496

The Park Savoy $59-$
158 West 58th St., New York,
NY 10019, Ph: (212) 245-5755
Fax: (212) 765-0668

NEWBURGH   NY

Econo Lodge West Point $-$$
310 Windsor Hwy. / SR 32,
Newburgh, NY 12550, Res.
(800) 424-4777 Ph: (914)
561-6620 Fax: (914) 561-2739

Super 8 Motel $-$$
1058 B Union Avenue,
Newburgh, NY 12550, Res.
(800) 800-8000 Ph: (914)
564-5700 Fax: (914) 564-7338

NIAGARA FALLS   NY

Budget Host Ameri-cana$-$$
9401 Niagara Falls Blvd,
Niagara Falls, NY 14304,
Res. (800) 283-4678 Ph: (716)
297-2660 Fax: (716) 297-7675

Econo Lodge $-$$
7708 Niagara Falls Blvd.,
Niagara Falls, NY 14304,
Res. (800) 424-4777 Ph: (716)
283-0621 Fax: (007) 168-3221

Scottish Inns $$
5919 Niagara Falls Blvd.,
Niagara Falls, NY 14304,
Res. (800) 251-1962 Ph: (716)
283-1100 Fax: (716) 283-2150

Thriftlodge $-$$
200 Rainbow Blvd., Niagara
Falls, NY 14303, Res. (800)
525-9055 Ph: (716) 285-7316
Fax: (716) 285-8541

NORWICH   NY

Super 8 Motel $-$$
P.O. Box 1048, Route 12,
Norwich, NY 13815, Res.
(800) 800-8000 Ph: (607)
336-8880 Fax: (607) 336-2076

NYACK   NY

Super 8 Motel $-$$
47 West Main St., Nyack, NY
10960, Res. (800) 800-8000
Ph: (914) 353-3880 Fax: (914)
353-0271

ONEIDA   NY

Super 8 Motel $-$$
215 Genesse, Oneida, NY
13421, Res. (800) 800-8000
Ph: (315) 363-5168 Fax: (315)
363-4628

ONEONTA   NY

Master Hosts Inns $$
I-88, Exit 16(Emmons),
Oneonta, NY 13820, Res.
(800) 251-1962 Ph: (607)
432-1280 Fax: (607) 433-2972

OSWEGO   NY

Econo Lodge Riverfront $-$$
70 E. 1st St., Oswego, NY
13126, Res. (800) 424-4777
Ph: (315) 343-1600 Fax: (315)
343-1222

OWEGO   NY

Econo Lodge $-$$
20 Hickory Park Rd.(& SR 17),
Owego, NY 13827-1627, Res.
(800) 424-4777 Ph: (607)
687-9000 Fax: (607) 687-3034

PAINTED POST   NY

Econo Lodge $-$$
200 Robert Dann Dr.,
Painted Post, NY 14870, Res.
(800) 424-4777 Ph: (607)
962-4444 Fax: (607) 937-5397

Super 8 Motel $-$$
255 S. Hamilton, Painted
Post, NY 14870, Res. (800)
800-8000 Ph: (716) 688-0811
Fax: (607) 962-7115

PLATTSBURGH   NY

Econo Lodge $-$$
610 Upper Cornelia,
Plattsburgh, NY 12901, Res.
(800) 424-4777 Ph: (518)
561-1500 Fax: (518) 563-3144

Super 8 Motel $-$$
Route 9 North, Plattsburgh,
NY 12901, Res. (800)
800-8000 Ph: (518) 562-8888
Fax: (518) 562-8896

POUGHKEEPSIE   NY

Econo Lodge $-$$
426 South Rd.,
Poughkeepsie, NY 12601,
Res. (800) 424-4777 Ph: (914)
452-6600 Fax: (914) 454-2210

PULASKI   NY

Super 8 Motel $-$$
7611 Rome Road, Pulaski, NY
13142, Res. (800) 800-8000
Ph: (315) 298-4888 Fax: (315)
298-3293

RIPLEY   NY

Budget Host Colonial Sqms$-$$
Shortman Rd Exit 61 I-90,
Ripley, NY 14775, Res. (800)
283-4678 Ph: (716) 736-8000

ROCHESTER   NY

Econo Lodge $-$$
940 Jefferson Rd., Rochester,
NY 14623, Res. (800)
424-4777 Ph: (716) 427-2700
Fax: (716) 427-8504

RONKONKOMA   NY

Econo Lodge Macarthur $-$$
3055 Veterans Memorial Hwy.
/ SR454, Ronkonkoma, NY
11779, Res. (800) 424-4777
Ph: (516) 588-6800 Fax: (516)
588-6815

SAUGERTIES   NY

Super 8 Motel $-$$
2790 Rte 32N, Saugerties,
NY 12477, Res. (800)
800-8000 Ph: (914) 246-1565
Fax: (914) 246-1631

SCHENECTADY   NY

Super 8 Motel $-$$
3083 Carman Rd.,
Schenectady, NY 12303,
Res. (800) 800-8000 Ph: (518)
355-2190 Fax: (518) 356-3817

SIDNEY   NY

Super 8 Motel $-$$
4 Mang Dr., Sidney, NY
13838, Res. (800) 800-8000
Ph: (607) 563-8880 Fax: (607)
563-8889

**M
O
T
E
L**

SMITHTOWN NY

Econo Lodge $-$$
755 SR 347, Smithtown, NY
11787, Res. (800) 424-4777
Ph: (516) 724-9000 Fax: (516)
724-9000

SOUTHSIDE NY

Super 8 Motel $-$$
Route 23, "RD #2, Box 2116",
Southside, NY 13820-9802,
Res. (800) 800-8000 Ph: (607)
432-9505 Fax: (607) 432-9505

SPRING VALLEY NY

Econo Lodge $-$$
SR 59 East, Spring Valley,
NY 10977, Res. (800)
424-4777 Ph: (914) 623-3838
Fax: (914) 623-0190

SYRACUSE NY

Red Carpet Inn $$
2810 Brewton Rd., Syracuse,
NY 13212, Res. (800)
251-1962 Ph: (315) 454-3266

TICONDEROGA NY

Super 8 Motel $-$$
Rte 9N & 74, PO Box 567,
Ticonderoga, NY 12883, Res.
(800) 800-8000 Ph: (518)
585-2617 Fax: (518) 585-3521

TROY NY

Super 8 Motel $-$$
1 Fourth St., Troy, NY
12180, Res. (800) 800-8000
Ph: (518) 274-8800 Fax: (518)
274-0427

UTICA NY

Motel 6 $
150 N Genesee St, Utica, NY
13502, Res. (800) 466-8356
Ph: 315 797-8743 Fax: 315
797-1500

VERONA NY

Super 8 Motel $-$$
Route 365, Verona, NY
13478, Res. (800) 800-8000
Ph: (315) 363-0096 Fax: (315)
363-2797

WATERTOWN NY

Econo Lodge $-$$
1030 Arsenal St., Watertown,
NY 13601, Res. (800)
424-4777 Ph: (315) 782-5500
Fax: (315) 788-7608

Super 8 Motel $-$$
104 Breen Ave., Watertown,
NY 13601, Res. (800)
800-8000 Ph: (315) 786-6666
Fax: (315) 788-5676

WEBSTER NY

Super 8 Motel $-$$
2450 Empire Blvd., Webster,
NY 14580, Res. (800)
800-8000 Ph: (716) 454-2181

NORTH CAROLINA

ABERDEEN NC

Motel 6 $
1408 N Sandhills Blvd,
Aberdeen, NC 28315, Res.
(800) 466-8356 Ph: 910
944-5633 Fax: 910 944-1101

ASHEVILLE NC

Econo Lodge Biltmore $-$$
190 Tunnel Rd., Asheville,
NC 28805, Res. (800)
424-4777 Ph: (704) 254-9521

Econo Lodge Biltmore East $$
1430 Tunnel Rd., Asheville,
NC 28815, Res. (800)
424-4777 Ph: (704) 298-5519
Fax: (000) 007-0498

Motel 6 $
1415 Tunnel Rd, Asheville,
NC 28805, Res. (800)
466-8356 Ph: 704 299-3040
Fax: 704 298-3158

Super 8 Motel $-$$
8 Crowell Road, Asheville,
NC 28816-6164, Res. (800)
800-8000 Ph: (704) 667-8706
Fax: (704) 665-9119

BATTLEBORO NC

Motel 6 $
Rt 1, Box 162A, SR 48,
Battleboro, NC 27809, Res.
(800) 466-8356 Ph: 919
977-3505 Fax: 919 977-1770

Red Carpet Inn $$
I-95, exit 145, Battleboro, NC
27809, Res. (800) 251-1962
Ph: (919) 446-0771 Fax: (919)
446-6069

Scottish Inns $
I-95, exit 145, Battleboro, NC
287809, Res. (800) 251-1962
Ph: (919) 446-1831

BOONE NC

Red Carpet Inn $$
862 Blowing Rock Rd., Boone,
NC 28607, Res. (800)
251-1962 Ph: (704) 264-2457

Scottish Inns $$
782 Blowing Rock Rd., Boone,
NC 28607, Res. (800)
251-1962 Ph: (704) 264-2483

BURLINGTON NC

Motel 6 $
2155 Hanford Rd, Burlington,
NC 27215, Res. (800)
466-8356 Ph: 910 226-1325
Fax: 910 570-9158

Scottish Inns $$
2412 Maple Ave, Burlington,
NC 27215, Res. (800)
251-1962 Ph: (919) 227-2003

Super 8 Motel $-$$
802 Hoffman Mill Rd.,
Burlington, NC 27215, Res.
(800) 800-8000 Ph: (910)
584-8787 Fax: (910) 584-0594

CANTON N

Econo Lodge $-$
55 Buckeye Cove Rd.,
Canton, NC 28716, Res.
(800) 424-4777 Ph: (704)
648-0300

CHARLOTTE N

Econo Lodge $-$
I-85 & Little Rock Rd.,
Charlotte, NC 28214, Res.
(800) 424-4777 Ph: (704)
394-0172 Fax: (704) 394-0172

Econo Lodge North $-$
I-85, Sugar Creek Rd.,
Charlotte, NC 28213, Res.
(800) 424-4777 Ph: (704)
597-0470 Fax: (704) 597-0470

Motel 6
3430 St Vardell Ln,
Charlotte, NC 28210, Res.
(800) 466-8356 Ph: 704
527-0144 Fax: 704 522-9868

Super 8 Motel $-$
5125 N. I-85 Service Rd.,
Charlotte, NC 28269, Res.
(800) 800-8000 Ph: (704)
598-8820 Fax: (704) 525-6603

Super 8 Motel $-$
11300 Texland Blvd.,
Charlotte, NC 28273, Res.
(800) 800-8000 Ph: (704)
588-8488 Fax: (704) 588-8488

Super 8 Motel $-$
505 Clanton Road, Charlotte,
NC 28217, Res. (800)
800-8000 Ph: (704) 523-1404
Fax: (704) 525-6603

Villager $-$
7901 Nations Ford Road,
Charlotte, NC 28210, Res.
(800) 328-7829 Ph: (704)
522-0364 Fax: (704) 522-0364

Villager $-$
2403 Wilkinson Boulevard,
Charlotte, NC 28208, Res.
(800) 328-7829 Ph: (704)
375-8851 Fax: (000) 000-0000

Villager $-$
3433 Mulberry Church Rd.,
Charlotte, NC 28208, Res.
(800) 328-7829 Ph: (704)
394-1819 Fax: (704) 393-0207

CHEROKEE NC

Econo Lodge $-$$
Acquoni Road, Cherokee, NC
28719, Res. (800) 424-4777
Ph: (704) 497-2226 Fax: (704)
497-3427

CREEDMOOR NC

Econo Lodge $-$$
2574 Lyons Station Rd.,
Creedmoor, NC 27522, Res.
(800) 424-4777 Ph: (919)
575-6451

DUNN   NC

Econo Lodge $-$$
513 Spring Branch Rd.,
Dunn, NC 28334, Res. (800)
424-4777 Ph: (910) 892-6181

DURHAM   NC

Econo Lodge $-$$
2337 Guess Rd., Durham,
NC 27705, Res. (800)
424-4777 Ph: (919) 286-7746
Fax: (919) 383-5710

Scottish Inns $$
5303 Hwy 70 West, Durham,
NC 27705, Res. (919) 383-2561
251-1962 Fax: (919) 383-1087

Super 8 Motel $-$$
507 East Knox Street,
Durham, NC 27701, Res.
(800) 800-8000 Ph: (919)
683-1321 Fax: (919) 683-2498

FAYETTEVILLE   NC

Econo Lodge $-$$
I-95 & Exit 49, Fayetteville,
NC 28306, Res. (800)
424-4777 Ph: (910) 433-2100
Fax: (910) 433-2009

Motel 6 $
2076 Cedar Creek Rd,
Fayetteville, NC 28301, Res.
(800) 466-8356 Ph: 910
485-8122 Fax: 910 485-0701

FLETCHER   NC

Econo Lodge Airport $-$$
196 Underwood Rd., Fletcher,
NC 28732, Res. (800)
424-4777 Ph: (704) 684-1200
Fax: (000) 007-0487

GASTONIA   NC

Econo Lodge $-$$
I-85 at SR 274, Gastonia, NC
28052, Res. (800) 424-4777
Ph: (704) 867-1821

Motel 6 $
1721 Broadcast St, Gastonia,
NC 28052, Res. (800)
466-8356 Ph: 704 868-4900
Fax: 704 861-1603

GOLDSBORO   NC

Motel 6 $
701 Bypass 70 E, Goldsboro,
NC 27534, Res. (800)
466-8356 Ph: 919 734-4542
Fax: 919 734-3503

GRAHAM   NC

Econo Lodge $-$$
640 E. Harden St., Graham,
NC 27253, Res. (800)
424-4777 Ph: (910) 228-0231
Fax: (910) 229-5873

GREENSBORO   NC

Econo Lodge $-$$
3303 Isler St., Greensboro,
NC 27407, Res. (800)
424-4777 Ph: (910) 852-4080
Fax: (910) 855-5539

Motel 6 $
605 S Regional Rd,
Greensboro, NC 27409, Res.
(800) 466-8356 Ph: 910
668-2085 Fax: 910 454-6120

Motel 6 $
831 Greenhaven Dr,
Greensboro, NC 27406, Res.
(800) 466-8356 Ph: 910
854-0993 Fax: 910 854-2431

Super 8 Motel $-$$
2108 W. Meadowview Rd.,
Greensboro, NC 27403, Res.
(800) 800-8000 Ph: (910)
855-8888 Fax: (910) 855-8888

GREENVILLE   NC

Motel 6 $
3435 S Memorial Dr,
Greenville, NC 27834, Res.
(800) 466-8356 Ph: 919
355-5699 Fax: 919 355-5699

Super 8 Motel $-$$
1004 S. Memorial Drive,
Greenville, NC 27834, Res.
(800) 800-8000 Ph: (919)
758-8888 Fax: (919) 758-0523

HENDERSON   NC

Budget Host Inn $-$$
1727 N Garnett St,
Henderson, NC 27536, Res.
(800) 283-4678 Ph: (919)
492-2013 Fax: (919) 492-7908

Scottish Inns $$
1759 Garnett St.,
Henderson, NC 27536, Res.
(800) 251-1962 Ph: (919)
438-6172

HICKORY   NC

Econo Lodge $-$$
325 US 70 S.W., Hickory, NC
28603-1821, Res. (800)
424-4777 Ph: (704) 328-2111
Fax: (704) 328-2118

HIGH POINT   NC

Motel 6 $
200 Ardale Dr, High Point,
NC 27260, Res. (800)
466-8356 Ph: 910 841-7717
Fax: 910 841-7709

Super 8 Motel $-$$
400 S. Main St., High Point,
NC 27260, Res. (800)
800-8000 Ph: (919) 882-4103

JACKSONVILLE   NC

Super 8 Motel $-$$
2149 N. Marine Blvd.,
Jacksonville, NC 28546,
Res. (800) 800-8000 Ph: (919)
455-6888

KENLY   NC

Econo Lodge $-$$
US 301 & I-95, Kenly, NC
27542, Res. (800) 424-4777
Ph: (919) 284-1000

KILL DEVIL HILLS- NAG   NC

Budget Host Inn $-$$
P.O. Box 494, Kill Devil Hills-
Nags Head , NC 27959,
Res. (800) 283-4678 Ph: (919)
441-2503

KING   NC

Econo Lodge $-$$
US 52, Vesta St., King, NC
27021, Res. (800) 424-4777
Ph: (910) 983-5600 Fax: (910)
983-6989

LEXINGTON   NC

Super 8 Motel $-$$
1631 Cottongrove Road,
Lexington, NC 27292, Res.
(800) 800-8000 Ph: (704)
352-6444

LUMBERTON   NC

Econo Lodge $-$$
I-95 & SR 211, Lumberton,
NC 28359, Res. (800)
424-4777 Ph: (910) 738-7121
Fax: (910) 739-4351

Motel 6 $
2361 Lackey Rd, Lumberton,
NC 28358, Res. (800)
466-8356 Ph: 910 738-2410
Fax: 910 738-8562

Super 8 Motel $-$$
105 Jackson Square,
Fayetteville Rd, Lumberton,
NC 28358, Res. (800)
800-8000 Ph: (910) 671-4444
Fax: (910) 671-4444

MAGGIE VALLEY   NC

Scottish Inns $$
16 Soco Rd., Maggie Valley,
NC 28751, Res. (800)
251-1962 Ph: (704) 926-9137
Fax: :(704) 926-9139

MARION   NC

Econo Lodge $-$$
221 S. at I-40, Marion, NC
28752, Res. (800) 424-4777
Ph: (704) 659-7940 Fax: (704)
659-3713

MOCKSVILLE   NC

Scottish Inns $
1034 Yadkinville Rd.(Hwy 601
So), Mocksville, NC 27028,
Res. (800) 251-1962 Ph: (704)
634-2116 Fax: (704) 634-1413

MOORESVILLE   NC

Super 8 Motel $-$$
484 River Hwy., Mooresville,
NC 28115, Res. (800)
800-8000 Ph: (704) 662-6188
Fax: (704) 662-6188

MOREHEAD CITY   NC

Econo Lodge Crystal Coast-$$
3410 Bridges St., Morehead
City, NC 28557, Res. (800)
424-4777 Ph: (919) 247-2940
Fax: (919) 247-0746

**M
O
T
E
L**

MORGANTON   NC

Red Carpet Inn $$
2217 So Sterling St.,
Morganton, NC 28655, Res.
(800) 251-1962 Ph: (704)
437-6980

MURPHY   NC

Econo Lodge $-$$
100 Terrace St., Murphy, NC
28906, Res. (800) 424-4777
Ph: (704) 837-8880

RALEIGH   NC

Econo Lodge $-$$
3804 New Bern Ave., Raleigh,
NC 27610, Res. (800)
424-4777 Ph: (919) 231-8818
Fax: (919) 231-8007

Econo Lodge West $-$$
5110 Holly Ridge Dr.,
Raleigh, NC 27612, Res.
(800) 424-4777 Ph: (919)
782-3201

Motel 6 $
1401 Buck Jones Rd,
Raleigh, NC 27606, Res.
(800) 466-8356 Ph: 919
467-6171 Fax: 919 469-8259

Motel 6 $
3921 Arrow Dr, Raleigh, NC
27612, Res. (800) 466-8356
Ph: 919 782-7071 Fax: 919
783-6259

ROANOKE RAPIDS   NC

Motel 6 $
1911 Julian R. Allsbrook Hwy,
Roanoke Rapids, NC 27870,
Res. (800) 466-8356 Ph: 919
537-5252 Fax: 919 537-9469

ROCKINGHAM   NC

Super 8 Motel $-$$
416 South Hancock St. US 1,
Rockingham, NC 28379,
Res. (800) 800-8000 Ph: (910)
895-5231 Fax: (910) 895-3212

ROCKY MOUNT   NC

Super 8 Motel $-$$
307 Mosley Court, Rocky
Mount, NC 27801, Res. (800)
800-8000 Ph: (919) 977-2858
Fax: (919) 977-2858

SALISBURY   NC

Econo Lodge $-$$
1011 E. Innes St., Salisbury,
NC 28144, Res. (800)
424-4777 Ph: (704) 633-8850

SHELBY   NC

Super 8 Motel $-$$
1716 E. Dixon Blvd., Shelby,
NC 28150, Res. (800)
800-8000 Ph: (704) 484-2101

SPINDALE   NC

Super 8 Motel $-$$
210 Reservations Drive,
Spindale, NC 28160, Res.
(800) 800-8000 Ph: (704)
286-3681 Fax: (704) 286-8221

SPRING LAKE   NC

Super 8 Motel $-$$
256 South Main, Spring
Lake, NC 28390, Res. (800)
800-8000 Ph: (910) 436-8588
Fax: (910) 436-8588

STATESVILLE   NC

Econo Lodge North $-$$
725 Sullivan Rd., Statesville,
NC 28677, Res. (800)
424-4777 Ph: (704) 873-5236
Fax: (704) 872-0012

Econo Lodge South $-$$
I-77 at Exit 49b, Statesville,
NC 28687, Res. (800)
424-4777 Ph: (704) 872-5215
Fax: (704) 872-4936

Super 8 Motel $-$$
1125 Greenland Drive,
Statesville, NC 28677, Res.
(800) 800-8000 Ph: (704)
878-9888

WASHINGTON   NC

Econo Lodge North $-$$
1220 W. 15th St.,
Washington, NC 27889,
Res. (800) 424-4777 Ph: (919)
946-7781 Fax: (000) 009-1946

WAYNESVILLE   NC

Econo Lodge $-$$
1202 Russ Ave., Waynesville,
NC 28786, Res. (800)
424-4777 Ph: (704) 452-0353

WILMINGTON   NC

Motel 6 $
2828 Market on US 17/74
Bus, Wilmington, NC
28403, Res. (800) 466-8356
Ph: 910 762-0120 Fax: 910
762-0426

Super 8 Motel $-$$
3604 Market Street,
Wilmington, NC 28405, Res.
(800) 800-8000 Ph: (910)
343-9778 Fax: (910) 343-9778

WINSTON-SALEM   NC

Motel 6 $
3810 Patterson Ave,
Winston-Salem, NC 27105,
Res. (800) 466-8356 Ph: 910
661-1588 Fax: 910 767-8354

NORTH DAKOTA

BEULAH   ND

Super 8 Motel $-$$
720 Highway 49 North,
Beulah, ND 58523, Res.
(800) 800-8000 Ph: (701)
873-2850

BISMARCK   ND

Motel 6 $
2433 State St, Bismarck, ND
58501, Res. (800) 466-8356
Ph: 701 255-6878 Fax: 701
223-7534

Super 8 Motel $-$$
1125 East Capitol Avenue,
Bismarck, ND 58501, Res.
(800) 800-8000 Ph: (701)
255-1314 Fax: (701) 255-1314

BOWMAN   ND

Budget Host Four-u Motel $-$$
704 Hwy 12 W, Bowman, ND
58623, Res. (800) 283-4678
Ph: (701) 523-3243 Fax: (701)
523-3357

Super 8 Motel $-$$
614 S.W. 3rd Ave., Bowman,
ND 58623-0675, Res. (800)
800-8000 Ph: (701) 523-5613
Fax: (701) 523-5614

CARRINGTON   ND

Super 8 Motel $-$$
"Hwy. 281, 100 S. 4th Ave.",
Carrington, ND 58241, Res.
(800) 800-8000 Ph: (701)
652-3982 Fax: (701) 652-3984

DEVILS LAKE   ND

Super 8 Motel $-$$
RR #4, Devils Lake, ND
58301-9804, Res. (800)
800-8000 Ph: (701) 662-8656
Fax: (701) 662-8291

DICKINSON   ND

Super 8 Motel $-$$
637 West 12th St.,
Dickinson, ND 58601, Res.
(800) 800-8000 Ph: (701)
227-1215 Fax: (701) 227-1807

EDGELEY   ND

Super 8 Motel $-$$
US Hwy 281 & State Hwy 13,
PO Box 295 Industrial Park,
Edgeley, ND 58433, Res.
(800) 800-8000 Ph: (701)
493-2075 Fax: (701) 493-2075

FARGO   ND

Econo Lodge $-$$
1401 35th St. S., Fargo, ND
58103, Res. (800) 424-4777
Ph: (701) 232-3412 Fax: (701)
232-3412

Motel 6 $
1202 36th St S, Fargo, ND
58103, Res. (800) 466-8356
Ph: 701 232-9251 Fax: 701
239-4482

Super 8 Motel $-$$
3518 Interstate Blvd, Fargo,
ND 58103, Res. (800)
800-8000 Ph: (701) 232-9202
Fax: (701) 232-4543

GRAFTON　ND

Super 8 Motel　$-$$
948 W 12th St., Grafton, ND
58237-2122, Res. (800)
800-8000 Ph: (701) 352-0888
Fax: (612) 253-5530

GRAND FORKS　ND

Econo Lodge　$-$$
900 N. 43rd St., Grand Forks,
ND 58201, Res. (800)
424-4777 Ph: (701) 746-6666
Fax: (701) 746-6666

Super 8 Motel　$-$$
1122 North 43rd Street,
Grand Forks, ND 58203,
Res. (800) 800-8000 Ph: (701)
775-8138 Fax: (701) 775-8138

JAMESTOWN　ND

Super 8 Motel　$-$$
P.O. Box 1242, Jamestown,
ND 58402-1242, Res. (800)
800-8000 Ph: (701) 252-4715
Fax: (701) 251-1647

MAYVILLE　ND

Super 8 Motel　$-$$
34 Center Ave. S., Mayville,
ND 58257, Res. (800)
800-8000 Ph: (701) 786-9081

MINOT　ND

Super 8 Motel　$-$$
1315 North Broadway, Minot,
ND 58701-1366, Res. (800)
800-8000 Ph: (701) 852-1817
Fax: (701) 852-1817

TIOGA　ND

Super 8 Motel　$-$$
P.O. Box 760, 210 2nd St.
East, Tioga, ND 58852, Res.
(800) 800-8000 Ph: (701)
664-3395

VALLEY CITY　ND

Super 8 Motel　$-$$
822 11th ST. S.W., "Rte. 2,
Box 1", Valley City, ND
58702, Res. (800) 800-8000
Ph: (701) 845-1140 Fax: (701)
845-1140

WAHPETON　ND

Super 8 Motel　$-$$
995 21st Ave. N., Wahpeton,
ND 58075, Res. (800)
800-8000 Ph: (701) 642-8731
Fax: (701) 642-8731

WEST FARGO　ND

Super 8 Motel　$-$$
825 East Main Avenue, West
Fargo, ND 58078, Res. (800)
800-8000 Ph: (701) 282-7121
Fax: (701) 277-9237

WILLISTON　ND

Super 8 Motel　$-$$
2324 2nd Ave. W., P.O. Box
9073, Williston, ND
58801-0907, Res. (800)
800-8000 Ph: (701) 572-8371
Fax: (701) 774-8048

OHIO

AKRON　OH

Super 8 Motel　$-$$
79 Rothrock Road, Akron,
OH 44321-1330, Res. (800)
800-8000 Ph: (216) 666-8887
Fax: (216) 666-8887

ALLIANCE　OH

Super 8 Motel　$-$$
2330 W. State Street,
Alliance, OH 44601, Res.
(800) 800-8000 Ph: (216)
821-5688 Fax: (261) 821-5688

ALPHA　OH

Econo Lodge　$-$$
2220 US 35, Alpha, OH
45301, Res. (800) 424-4777
Ph: (513) 426-5822

AMHERST　OH

Motel 6　$
704 N Leavitt Rd, Amherst,
OH 44001, Res. (800)
466-8356 Ph: 216 988-3266
Fax: 216 988-3283

ATHENS　OH

Budget Host Coach Inn　$-$$
1000 Albany Rd (RT 50 W),
Athens, OH 45701, Res.
(800) 283-4678 Ph: (614)
594-2294

AUSTINTOWN　OH

Super 8 Motel　$-$$
5280 76 Drive, Austintown,
OH 44515, Res. (800)
800-8000 Ph: (216) 793-7788
Fax: (216) 793-7788

BOTKINS　OH

Budget Host Inn　$-$$
P.O. Box 478, Botkins, OH
45306, Res. (800) 283-4678
Ph: (513) 693-6911 Fax: (513)
693-8202

CANTON　OH

Super 8 Motel　$-$$
3950 Convenience Drive,
Canton, OH 44718, Res.
(800) 800-8000 Ph: (216)
492-5030 Fax: (216) 492-5030

CINCINNATI　OH

Budget Host Town Center　$-$$
3356 Central Pkwy,
Cincinnati, OH 45225, Res.
(800) 283-4678 Ph: (513)
559-1600 Fax: (513) 559-1616

Motel 6　$
3960 Nine Mile Rd,
Cincinnati, OH 45255, Res.
(800) 466-8356 Ph: 513
752-2262 Fax: 513 753-3190

Super 8 Motel　$-$$
11335 Chester Road,
Cincinnati, OH 45246, Res.
(800) 800-8000 Ph: (513)
772-3140 Fax: (513) 772-1931

CLEVELAND　OH

Super 8 Motel　$-$$
4751 Northfield Road,
Cleveland, OH 44128, Res.
(800) 800-8000 Ph: (216)
475-3100

COLUMBUS　OH

Econo Lodge　$-$$
920 Wilson Rd at I-70,
Columbus, OH 43204, Res.
(800) 424-4777 Ph: (614)
274-8581

Econo Lodge　$-$$
50 E. Wilson Bridge Rd.,
Columbus, OH 43085, Res.
(800) 424-4777 Ph: (614)
888-3666 Fax: (614) 888-3666

Motel 6　$
5910 Scarborough Blvd,
Columbus, OH 43232, Res.
(800) 466-8356 Ph: 614
755-2250 Fax: 614 860-9090

Motel 6　$
1289 E Dublin-Granville Rd,
Columbus, OH 43229, Res.
(800) 466-8356 Ph: 614
846-9860 Fax: 614 846-6563

Motel 6　$
5500 Renner Rd, Columbus,
OH 43228, Res. (800)
466-8356 Ph: 614 870-0993
Fax: 614 870-3548

Super 8 Motel　$-$$
1078 E. Dublin Granville Rd,
Columbus, OH 43229, Res.
(800) 800-8000 Ph: (614)
885-1601 Fax: (614) 885-1601

COSHOCTON　OH

Super 8 Motel　$-$$
70 S. Whitewoman Street,
Coshocton, OH 43812, Res.
(800) 800-8000 Ph: (614)
622-8899

CURTICE　OH

Econo Lodge Bay State Park　$-$$
10530 Corduroy Rd., Curtice,
OH 43412, Res. (800)
424-4777 Ph: (419) 836-2822
Fax: (419) 836-2823

DAYTON　OH

Econo Lodge　$-$$
2221 Wagoner Ford Rd.,
Dayton, OH 45414, Res.
(800) 424-4777 Ph: (513)
278-1500

Motel 6 $
7130 Miller Ln, Dayton, OH
45414, Res. (800) 466-8356
Ph: 937 898-3606 Fax: 937
890-3898

DELAWARE   OH

Super 8 Motel $-$$
US Highway 23 South,
Delaware, OH 43015, Res.
(800) 800-8000 Ph: (614)
363-8869 Fax: (614) 363-8869

EATON   OH

Econo Lodge $-$$
I-70 & US 127, Eaton, OH
45320, Res. (800) 424-4777
Ph: (513) 456-5959 Fax: (000)
513-5649

ENGLEWOOD   OH

Motel 6 $
1212 S Main St, Englewood,
OH 45322, Res. (800)
466-8356 Ph: 937 832-3770
Fax: 937 832-0128

FINDLAY   OH

Econo Lodge $-$$
316 Emma St., Findlay, OH
45840, Res. (800) 424-4777
Ph: (419) 422-0154 Fax: (419)
422-0154

Super 8 Motel $-$$
1600 Fox St., Findlay, OH
45839, Res. (800) 800-8000
Ph: (419) 422-8863 Fax: (419)
422-8863

FRANKLIN   OH

Econo Lodge $-$$
4385 E. 2nd St., Franklin,
OH 45005, Res. (800)
424-4777 Ph: (513) 746-3627

Super 8 Motel $-$$
3553 Commerce Dr.,
Franklin, OH 45005, Res.
(800) 800-8000 Ph: (513)
422-4888

GALLIPOLIS   OH

Econo Lodge Holzer Medical $-$$
260 Jackson Pike, Gallipolis,
OH 45631, Res. (800)
424-4777 Ph: (614) 446-7071
Fax: (614) 446-7071

Super 8 Motel $-$$
321 Upper River Rd.,
Gallipolis, OH 45631, Res.
(800) 800-8000 Ph: (614)
446-8080 Fax: (614) 446-8080

GIRARD   OH

Econo Lodge $-$$
1615 E. Liberty St., Girard,
OH 44420, Res. (800)
424-4777 Ph: (216) 759-9820

Motel 6 $
1600 Motor Inn Dr, Girard,
OH 44420, Res. (800)
466-8356 Ph: 330 759-7833
Fax: 330 759-0691

HILLIARD   OH

Motel 6 $
3950 Parkway Ln, Hilliard,
OH 43026, Res. (800)
466-8356 Ph: 614 771-1500
Fax: 614 529-8259

HUBER HEIGHTS   OH

Super 8 Motel $-$$
8110 Old Troy Pike, Huber
Heights, OH 45424, Res.
(800) 800-8000 Ph: (513)
237-1888 Fax: (513) 237-1888

KENT   OH

Super 8 Motel $-$$
4380 Edson Rd., Kent, OH
44240, Res. (800) 800-8000
Ph: (216) 678-8817 Fax: (216)
678-8817

LIMA   OH

Motel 6 $
1800 Harding Hwy, Lima,
OH 45804, Res. (800)
466-8356 Ph: 419 228-0456
Fax: 419 228-4630

Super 8 Motel $-$$
1430 Bellefontaine Avenue,
Lima, OH 45804, Res. (800)
800-8000 Ph: (419) 227-2221

Villager $-$$
418 W. Market St., Lima, OH
45801, Res. (800) 328-7829
Ph: (419) 228-2525 Fax: (419)
228-7790

MACEDONIA   OH

Motel 6 $
311 E Highland Rd,
Macedonia, OH 44056, Res.
(800) 466-8356 Ph: 216
468-1670 Fax: 216 467-9189

MANSFIELD   OH

Econo Lodge $-$$
1017 Koogle Rd., Mansfield,
OH 44903, Res. (800)
424-4777 Ph: (419) 589-3333
Fax: (000) 000-4190

Super 8 Motel $-$$
2425 Interstate Circle,
Mansfield, OH 44903, Res.
(800) 800-8000 Ph: (419)
756-8875 Fax: (419) 756-8875

MARIETTA   OH

Econo Lodge $-$$
702 Pike St., Marietta, OH
45750, Res. (800) 424-4777
Ph: (614) 374-8481 Fax: (000)
614-7481

Super 8 Motel $-$$
"46 Acme St., Washington
Center", Marietta, OH
45750, Res. (800) 800-8000
Ph: (614) 374-8888 Fax: (614)
374-8476

MARYSVILLE   OH

Super 8 Motel $-$$
10220 U.S. Hwy. 42,
Marysville, OH 43040, Res.
(800) 800-8000 Ph: (614)
873-4100 Fax: (614) 873-3314

MASSILLON   OH

Super 8 Motel $-$$
242 Lincolnway West,
Massillon, OH 44646, Res.
(800) 800-8000 Ph: (216)
837-8880 Fax: (216) 837-8880

MASSILON   OH

Red Carpet Inn $-$$
412 Lincoln Way E., Rte. 172
& 21, Massilon, OH 44646,
Res. (800) 251-1962 Ph: (330)
832-1538

MENTOR   OH

Super 8 Motel $-$$
7325 Palisades Parkway,
Mentor, OH 44060, Res.
(800) 800-8000 Ph: (216)
951-8558 Fax: (216) 951-8558

MIAMISBURG   OH

Motel 6 $
8101 Springboro Pike,
Miamisburg, OH 45342,
Res. (800) 466-8356 Ph: 937
434-8750 Fax: 937 434-6734

MIDDLEBURG HEIGHTS   OH

Motel 6 $
7219 Engle Rd, Middleburg
Heights, OH 44130, Res.
(800) 466-8356 Ph: 216
234-0990 Fax: 216 234-3475

MILAN   OH

Super 8 Motel $-$$
11313 Milan Road, Milan, OH
44846, Res. (800) 800-8000
Ph: (419) 499-4671 Fax: (419)
627-9770

MORAINE   OH

Super 8 Motel $-$$
2450 Dryden Rd., Moraine,
OH 45439, Res. (800)
800-8000 Ph: (513) 298-0380

MOUNT VERNON   OH

Super 8 Motel $-$$
1000 Coshocton Road,
Mount Vernon, OH 43050,
Res. (800) 800-8000 Ph: (614)
397-8885

N CANTON   OH

Motel 6 $
6880 Sunset Strip Ave NW, N
Canton, OH 44720, Res.
(800) 466-8356 Ph: 330
494-7611 Fax: 330 494-5366

N. JACKSON   OH

Red Carpet Inn $$
9694 Mahoning Ave., N.
Jackson, OH 44451, Res.
(800) 251-1962 Ph: (216)
538-2221

N. RIDGEVILLE OH

Super 8 Motel $-$$
32801 Lorain Road, N.
Ridgeville, OH 44039, Res.
(800) 800-8000 Ph: (216)
327-0500 Fax: (216) 327-0500

NEW PHILADELPHIA OH

Motel 6 $
181 Bluebell Dr SW, New
Philadelphia, OH 44663,
Res. (800) 466-8356 Ph: 330
339-6446 Fax: 330 339-7436

NORWALK OH

Econo Lodge $-$$
342 Milan Ave., Norwalk, OH
44857, Res. (800) 424-4777
Ph: (419) 668-5656 Fax: (419)
668-5656

OXFORD OH

Scottish Inns $$
5235 College Corner Pike,
Oxford, OH 45056, Res.
(800) 251-1962 Ph: (513)
523-6306 Fax: (513) 523-9693

PERRYSBURG OH

Red Carpet Inn $$
26054 N. Dixie Hwy.,
Perrysburg, OH 43551, Res.
(800) 251-1962 Ph: (419)
872-2902 Fax: (419) 872-0133

PORTSMOUTH OH

Super 8 Motel $-$$
4266 US Rte. 23 North,
Portsmouth, OH
45662-8801, Res. (800)
800-8000 Ph: (614) 353-8880

REYNOLDSBURG OH

Super 8 Motel $-$$
6201 Oaktree Lane,
Reynoldsburg, OH 43068,
Res. (800) 800-8000 Ph: (614)
575-1200 Fax: (614) 575-2837

RICHFIELD OH

Scottish Inns $
5175 Brecksville Rd.,
Richfield, OH 44286, Res.
(800) 251-1962 Ph: (216)
659-6661

ROSSFORD OH

Super 8 Motel $-$$
1135 Buck Rd, Rossford, OH
43460, Res. (800) 800-8000
Ph: (419) 666-4515

SANDUSKY OH

Econo Lodge Cedar Point $-$$
1904 Cleveland Rd.,
Sandusky, OH 44870, Res.
(800) 424-4777 Ph: (419)
627-9000

SHARONVILLE OH

Motel 6 $
3850 Hauck Rd, Sharonville,
OH 45241, Res. (800)
466-8356 Ph: 513 563-1123
Fax: 513 563-8242

Motel 6 $
2000 E Kemper Rd,
Sharonville, OH 45241, Res.
(800) 466-8356 Ph: 513
772-5944 Fax: 513 772-2680

SIDNEY OH

Econo Lodge $-$$
2009 W. Michigan St.,
Sidney, OH 45365, Res.
(800) 424-4777 Ph: (513)
492-9164 Fax: (513) 492-9164

ST. CLAIRSVILLE OH

Super 8 Motel $-$$
68400 Matthews Drive, St.
Clairsville, OH 43950-1733,
Res. (800) 800-8000 Ph: (614)
695-1994 Fax: (614) 695-1994

STEUBENVILLE OH

Super 8 Motel $-$$
1505 University Blvd.,
Steubenville, OH 43952,
Res. (800) 800-8000 Ph: (614)
282-4565 Fax: (614) 282-4565

STREETSBORO OH

Super 8 Motel $-$$
9420 S.R. 14, Streetsboro,
OH 44241, Res. (800)
800-8000 Ph: (800) 800-8000
Fax: (216) 678-0682

STRONGVILLE OH

Villager $-$$
9197 Pearl Rd, Strongville,
OH 44136, Res. (800)
328-7829 Ph: (216) 234-8801
Fax: (216) 234-6722

TOLEDO OH

Econo Lodge $-$$
1800 Miami St., Toledo, OH
43605, Res. (800) 424-4777
Ph: (419) 666-5120 Fax: (419)
666-4298

Motel 6 $
5335 Heatherdowns Blvd,
Toledo, OH 43614, Res. (800)
466-8356 Ph: 419 865-2308
Fax: 419 868-6180

TROY OH

Motel 6 $
1210 Brukner Drive, Troy,
OH 45373, Res. (800)
466-8356 Ph: 513 335-0013
Fax: 513 335-2011

Super 8 Motel $-$$
1330 Archer Drive, Troy, OH
45373, Res. (800) 800-8000
Ph: (513) 339-6564 Fax: (513)
339-6564

TWINSBURG OH

Super 8 Motel $-$$
8848 Twin Hills Dr,
Twinsburg, OH 44087, Res.
(800) 800-8000 Ph: (216)
425-2889 Fax: (216) 425-2889

WAPAKONETA OH

Super 8 Motel $-$$
511 Lunar Drive,
Wapakoneta, OH 45895,
Res. (800) 800-8000 Ph: (419)
738-8810 Fax: (419) 738-8810

WARREN OH

Scottish Inns $
4358 Youngstown Rd., SE,
Warren, OH 44484, Res.
(800) 251-1962 Ph: (216)
369-4100

WAUSEON OH

Super 8 Motel $-$$
8224 SH 108, Wauseon, OH
43567, Res. (800) 800-8000
Ph: (419) 335-9841

WINCHESTER OH

Budget Host Inn $-$$
18760 State Route 136,
Winchester, OH 45697,
Res. (800) 283-4678 Ph: (513)
695-0381

WOOSTER OH

Econo Lodge $-$$
2137 Lincoln Way E.,
Wooster, OH 44691, Res.
(800) 424-4777 Ph: (216)
264-8883 Fax: (216) 264-8883

YOUNGSTOWN OH

Super 8 Motel $-$$
4250 Belmont Avenue,
Youngstown, OH 44505,
Res. (800) 800-8000 Ph: (216)
759-0040

ZANESVILLE OH

Super 8 Motel $-$$
2440 National Rd, Zanesville,
OH 43701, Res. (800)
800-8000 Ph: (614) 455-3124
Fax: (614) 455-3124

Thriftlodge $-$$
58 North 6th St., Zanesville,
OH 43701, Res. (800)
525-9055 Ph: (614) 453-0611
Fax: (614) 453-9065

OKLAHOMA

ANADARKO OK

Red Carpet Inn $$
1415 East Central, Hwy 62,
Anadarko, OK 73005, Res.
(800) 251-1962 Ph: (405)
247-2491 Fax: (405) 247-2825

ARDMORE OK

Motel 6 $
120 Holiday Dr, Ardmore,
OK 73401, Res. (800)
466-8356 Ph: 405 226-7666
Fax: 405 223-5710

Super 8 Motel $-$$
2120 Hwy 142 W., Ardmore,
OK 73401, Res. (800)
800-8000 Ph: (405) 223-2201
Fax: (405) 223-2201

MOTEL

BARTLESVILLE   OK

Super 8 Motel $-$$
211 S.E. Washington Blvd.,
Bartlesville, OK 74006, Res.
(800) 800-8000 Ph: (918)
355-1122

BLACKWELL   OK

Super 8 Motel $-$$
1014 W. Doolin, Blackwell,
OK 74631, Res. (800)
800-8000 Ph: (405) 363-5945

BROKEN ARROW   OK

Econo Lodge $-$$
1401 N. Elm Pl., Broken
Arrow, OK 74012, Res. (800)
424-4777 Ph: (918) 258-6617
Fax: (918) 251-5660

CHANDLER   OK

Econo Lodge $-$$
600 N. Price, Chandler, OK
74834, Res. (800) 424-4777
Ph: (405) 258-2131 Fax: (405)
258-3090

CHECOTAH   OK

Budget Host I-40 Inn $-$$
P.O. Box 406, Checotah, OK
74426, Res. (800) 283-4678
Ph: (918) 473-2331

CHICKASHA   OK

Super 8 Motel $-$$
2728 South Fourth St.,
Chickasha, OK 73023, Res.
(800) 800-8000 Ph: (405)
942-7730 Fax: (405) 948-6238

CLINTON   OK

Super 8 Motel $-$$
1120 S. 10th St., Clinton,
OK 73601, Res. (800)
800-8000 Ph: (405) 323-4979

EL RENO   OK

Red Carpet Inn $$
2640 S. Country Club Rd., El
Reno, OK 73036, Res. (800)
251-1962 Ph: (405) 262-1526
Fax: (405) 262-2677

Super 8 Motel $-$$
2820 South Hwy 81, El Reno,
OK 73036, Res. (800)
800-8000 Ph: (405) 262-8246

ELK CITY   OK

Econo Lodge $-$$
108 Meadow Ridge, Elk City,
OK 73644, Res. (800)
424-4777 Ph: (405) 225-5120
Fax: (405) 225-0908

Motel 6 $
2500 E Hwy 66, Elk City, OK
73644, Res. (800) 466-8356
Ph: 405 225-6661 Fax: 405
243-4201

Super 8 Motel $-$$
2801 East Highway 66, Elk
City, OK 73644, Res. (800)
800-8000 Ph: (405) 225-9430
Fax: (405) 225-9430

ELK CITY SENTINEL   OK

Budget Host Inn $-$$
I-40 & Hwy 34, Elk City
Sentinel, OK 73664, Res.
(800) 283-4678 Ph: (405)
225-4020

ENID   OK

Econo Lodge $-$$
2523 Mercer Dr., Enid, OK
73701, Res. (800) 424-4777
Ph: (405) 237-3090

FREDERICK   OK

Scottish Inns $
1015 So. Main St., US183,
Frederick, OK 73542, Res.
(800) 251-1962 Ph: (405)
335-2129 Fax: (405) 335-7146

GUYMON   OK

Super 8 Motel $-$$
1201 Hwy 54 East, Guymon,
OK 73942, Res. (800)
800-8000 Ph: (405) 338-0507

HENRYETTA   OK

Super 8 Motel $-$$
I-40 & Dewey Bartlett Rd.,
Exit 237, Henryetta, OK
74437, Res. (800) 800-8000
Ph: (918) 652-2533

MCALESTER   OK

Super 8 Motel $-$$
2400 South Main, McAlester,
OK 74502, Res. (800)
800-8000 Ph: (918) 426-5400
Fax: (918) 426-5400

MIAMI   OK

Super 8 Motel $-$$
2120 E. Steve Owens Blvd.,
Miami, OK 74354-5321, Res.
(800) 800-8000 Ph: (918)
542-3382 Fax: (918) 542-3382

MIDWEST CITY   OK

Motel 6 $
6166 Tinker Diagonal,
Midwest City, OK 73110,
Res. (800) 466-8356 Ph: 405
737-6676 Fax: 405 737-2216

Super 8 Motel $-$$
6821 SE 29th, Midwest City,
OK 73110, Res. (800)
800-8000 Ph: (405) 732-0381
Fax: (405) 741-4614

MOORE   OK

Motel 6 $
1417 N Moore Ave, Moore,
OK 73160, Res. (800)
466-8356 Ph: 405 799-6616
Fax: 405 799-5053

Super 8 Motel $-$$
1520 N. Moore Rd., Moore,
OK 73160, Res. (800)
800-8000 Ph: (405) 794-4030
Fax: (405) 794-4030

MUSKOGEE   OK

Econo Lodge $-$$
2018 W. Shawnee Ave.,
Muskogee, OK 74401, Res.
(800) 424-4777 Ph: (918)
683-0101 Fax: (918) 687-7891

Motel 6 $
903 S 32nd St, Muskogee,
OK 74401, Res. (800)
466-8356 Ph: 918 683-8369
Fax: 918 683-9155

Super 8 Motel $-$$
2430 South 32nd Street,
Muskogee, OK 74401, Res.
(800) 800-8000 Ph: (918)
683-8888

OKLAHOMA CITY   OK

Econo Lodge $-$$
8200 W. I-40, Oklahoma City,
OK 73128, Res. (800)
424-4777 Ph: (405) 787-7051

Econo Lodge $-$$
7412 N. Bryant, Oklahoma
City, OK 73111, Res. (800)
424-4777 Ph: (405) 478-0205

Econo Lodge $-$$
1307 S.E. 44th St.,
Oklahoma City, OK 73129,
Res. (800) 424-4777 Ph: (405)
672-4533

Econo Lodge Airport $-$$
820 S. MaCarthur Blvd.,
Oklahoma City, OK 73128,
Res. (800) 424-4777 Ph: (405)
947-8651 Fax: (405) 942-6792

Motel 6 $
820 S Meridian Ave,
Oklahoma City, OK 73108,
Res. (800) 466-8356 Ph: 405
946-6662 Fax: 405 946-4058

Motel 6 $
12121 NE Expressway,
Oklahoma City, OK 73131,
Res. (800) 466-8356 Ph: 405
478-4030 Fax: 405 478-4158

Motel 6 $
11900 NE Expwy, Oklahoma
City, OK 73131, Res. (800)
466-8356 Ph: 405 478-8666
Fax: 405 478-7442

Motel 6 $
4200 W Interstate 40,
Oklahoma City, OK 73108,
Res. (800) 466-8356 Ph: 405
947-6550 Fax: 405 947-0970

Red Carpet Inn $$
11901 NE Expressway,
Oklahoma City, OK 73131,
Res. (800) 251-1962 Ph: (405)
478-0243

Red Carpet Inn $$
8217 So. I-35, exit 121A,
Oklahoma City, OK 73149,
Res. (800) 251-1962 Ph: (504)
632-0807 Fax: (405) 634-0390

Super 8 Motel $-$$
117 NE 13th St., Oklahoma
City, OK 73117, Res. (800)
800-8000 Ph: (405) 232-0404
Fax: (405) 235-2129

Super 8 Motel $-$$
3030 South I-35, Oklahoma
City, OK 73129, Res. (800)
800-8000 Ph: (405) 677-1000
Fax: (405) 947-7801

Super 8 Motel $-$$
811 South Meridian,
Oklahoma City, OK 73108,
Res. (800) 800-8000 Ph: (405)
947-7801 Fax: (405) 947-7801

Super 8 Motel $-$$
5000 North Bryant,
Oklahoma City, OK 73117,
Res. (800) 800-8000 Ph: (403)
785-8457 Fax: (405) 478-5403

PONCA CITY OK

Econo Lodge $-$$
212 S. 14th St., Ponca City,
OK 74601, Res. (800)
424-4777 Ph: (405) 762-3401
Fax: (405) 762-4550

Super 8 Motel $-$$
801 South 14th Street,
Ponca City, OK 74601, Res.
(800) 800-8000 Ph: (405)
762-1616 Fax: (405) 762-8777

PURCELL OK

Econo Lodge $-$$
500 US 74 S., Purcell, OK
73080, Res. (800) 424-4777
Ph: (405) 527-5603

SALLISAW OK

Econo Lodge $-$$
1403 E. Cherokee, Sallisaw,
OK 74955, Res. (800)
424-4777 Ph: (918) 775-7981
Fax: (918) 775-7981

Super 8 Motel $-$$
924 S. Kerr Blvd., Sallisaw,
OK 74955, Res. (800)
800-8000 Ph: (918) 775-8900

SAPULPA OK

Super 8 Motel $-$$
505 New Sapulpa Rd.,
Sapulpa, OK 74066, Res.
(800) 800-8000 Ph: (918)
227-3300 Fax: (918) 227-3300

SAVANNA OK

Budget Host Colonial Inn $-$$
US Hwy 69, Savanna, OK
74565, Res. (800) 283-4678
Ph: (918) 548-3506 Fax: (918)
423-7565

SHAWNEE OK

Budget Host Inn $-$$
4204 Hwy 177, Shawnee,
OK 74801, Res. (800)
283-4678 Ph: (405) 275-8430

Econo Lodge $-$$
5107 N. Harrison St.,
Shawnee, OK 74801, Res.
(800) 424-4777 Ph: (405)
275-6720

Motel 6 $
4981 N Harrison St,
Shawnee, OK 74801, Res.
(800) 466-8356 Ph: 405
275-5310 Fax: 405 275-6370

Super 8 Motel $-$$
4900 N. Harrison, Shawnee,
OK 74801, Res. (800)
800-8000 Ph: (800) 800-8000

STILLWATER OK

Motel 6 $
5122 W 6th Ave, Stillwater,
OK 74074, Res. (800)
466-8356 Ph: 405 624-0433
Fax: 405 624-0315

SULPHUR OK

Super 8 Motel $-$$
2110 W. Broadway, "Route 1,
Box 144", Sulphur, OK
73086, Res. (800) 800-8000
Ph: (405) 622-6500 Fax: (405)
947-7801

TULSA OK

Econo Lodge Airport $-$$
11620 E. Skelly Dr., Tulsa,
OK 74128, Res. (800)
424-4777 Ph: (918) 437-9200
Fax: (918) 437-2935

Motel 6 $
5828 W Skelly Dr, Tulsa, OK
74107, Res. (800) 466-8356
Ph: 918 445-0223 Fax: 918
445-2750

Motel 6 $
1011 S Garnett Rd, Tulsa,
OK 74128, Res. (800)
466-8356 Ph: 918 234-6200
Fax: 918 234-9421

Super 8 Motel $-$$
6616 East Archer Street,
Tulsa, OK 74115, Res. (800)
800-8000 Ph: (918) 836-1981
Fax: (918) 836-1981

Super 8 Motel $-$$
1347 E. Skelly Dr., Tulsa, OK
74105, Res. (800) 800-8000
Ph: (918) 743-4431

Super 8 Motel $-$$
11525 East Skelly Drive,
Tulsa, OK 74128, Res. (800)
800-8000 Ph: (800) 821-5526
Fax: (918) 438-7700

WAGONER OK

Super 8 Motel $-$$
805 S. Dewey, Wagoner, OK
74467, Res. (800) 800-8000
Ph: (918) 485-4818

WEATHERFORD OK

Econo Lodge $-$$
U.s. 54 & I-40, Weatherford,
OK 73096, Res. (800)
424-4777 Ph: (405) 772-7711
Fax: (405) 772-5450

Scottish Inns $
616 E. Main St., Weatherford,
OK 73096, Res. (800)
251-1962 Ph: (405) 772-3349

WEBBERS FALLS OK

Super 8 Motel $-$$
I-40 and Hwy. 100, Webbers
Falls, OK 74470, Res. (800)
800-8000 Ph: (918) 464-2272

OREGON

ASHLAND OR

Super 8 Motel $-$$
2350 Ashland St., Ashland,
OR 97520, Res. (800)
800-8000 Ph: (503) 482-8887
Fax: (503) 482-0914

BAKER CITY OR

Super 8 Motel $-$$
250 Campbell St., Baker City,
OR 97814, Res. (800)
800-8000 Ph: (503) 523-8282
Fax: (503) 523-9137

BEND OR

Super 8 Motel $-$$
1275 S. Hwy 97, Bend, OR
97702, Res. (800) 800-8000
Ph: (503) 388-6888 Fax: (503)
389-9056

COOS BAY OR

Motel 6 $
1445 Bayshore Dr, Coos Bay,
OR 97420, Res. (800)
466-8356 Ph: 541 267-7171
Fax: 541 267-4618

CORVALLIS OR

Econo Lodge $-$$
101 N.W. Van Buren,
Corvallis, OR 97330, Res.
(800) 424-4777 Ph: (503)
752-9601

Super 8 Motel $-$$
407 Northwest 2nd Street,
Corvallis, OR 97330, Res.
(800) 800-8000 Ph: (503)
758-8088

COTTAGE GROVE OR

Econo Lodge $-$$
1601 Gateway Blvd., Cottage
Grove, OR 97424, Res. (800)
424-4777 Ph: (503) 942-1000
Fax: (503) 942-1000

EUGENE OR

Econo Lodge $-$$
33100 Van Duyn Rd.,
Eugene, OR 97401, Res.
(800) 424-4777 Ph: (503)
484-2000 Fax: (503) 484-2431

M
O
T
E
L

Motel 6 $
3690 Glenwood Dr, Eugene,
OR 97403, Res. (800)
466-8356 Ph: 541 687-2395
Fax: 541 687-6828

GOLD BEACH   OR

Motel 6
94433 Jerry's Flat Rd, Gold
Beach, OR 97444, Res. (800)
466-8356 Ph: 541 247-4533
Fax: 541 247-0467

GRANTS PASS   OR

Motel 6 $
1800 Northeast 7th St,
Grants Pass, OR 97526,
Res. (800) 466-8356 Ph: 541
474-1331 Fax: 541 474-0136

Super 8 Motel $-$$
1949 NE 7th St., Grants
Pass, OR 97526, Res. (800)
800-8000 Ph: (503) 474-0888
Fax: (503) 474-0888

Thriftlodge $-$$
748 Southeast 7th Street,
(on US-199), Grants Pass,
OR 97526, Res. (800)
525-9055 Ph: (503) 476-7793
Fax: (503) 479-4812

KLAMATH   OR

Super 8 Motel $-$$
3805 Highway 97 North,
Klamath, OR 97601, Res.
(800) 800-8000 Ph: (503)
884-8880 Fax: (503) 884-0235

KLAMATH FALLS   OR

Econo Lodge $-$$
75 Main St., Klamath Falls,
OR 97601, Res. (800)
424-4777 Ph: (503) 884-7735
Fax: (050) 388-4865

Motel 6 $
5136 S 6th St, Klamath Falls,
OR 97603, Res. (800)
466-8356 Ph: 541 884-2110
Fax: 541 882-3384

LA GRANDE   OR

Super 8 Motel $-$$
"2407 E. ""R"" Ave.", La
Grande, OR 97850, Res.
(800) 800-8000 Ph: (503)
963-8080 Fax: (503) 963-2925

MEDFORD   OR

Motel 6 $
2400 Biddle Rd, Medford, OR
97504, Res. (800) 466-8356
Ph: 541 779-0550 Fax: 541
857-9573

Motel 6 $
950 Alba Dr, Medford, OR
97504, Res. (800) 466-8356
Ph: 541 773-4290 Fax: 541
857-9574

ONTARIO   OR

Motel 6 $
275 NE 12th St, Ontario, OR
97914, Res. (800) 466-8356
Ph: 541 889-6617 Fax: 541
889-8232

Super 8 Motel $-$$
266 Goodfellow St., Ontario,
OR 97914, Res. (800)
800-8000 Ph: (503) 889-8282
Fax: (503) 881-1400

PENDLETON   OR

Econo Lodge Downtown $-$$
201 S.W. Court Ave.,
Pendleton, OR 97801, Res.
(800) 424-4777 Ph: (503)
276-5252 Fax: (503) 278-1213

Motel 6 $
325 SE Nye Ave, Pendleton,
OR 97801, Res. (800)
466-8356 Ph: 541 276-3160
Fax: 541 276-7526

Super 8 Motel $-$$
601 S.E Nye Avenue,
Pendleton, OR 97801, Res.
(800) 800-8000 Ph: (503)
276-8881

PORTLAND   OR

Econo Lodge $-$$
518 N.E. Holladay St.,
Portland, OR 97232, Res.
(800) 424-4777 Ph: (503)
234-4391 Fax: (503) 236-8870

Econo Lodge $-$$
9520 N.E. Sandy Blvd.,
Portland, OR 97220, Res.
(800) 424-4777 Ph: (503)
252-6666 Fax: (503) 257-4848

Econo Lodge $-$$
17330 S.E. Mcloughlin Blvd.,
Portland, OR 97222, Res.
(800) 424-4777 Ph: (503)
654-2222 Fax: (503) 654-1300

Econo Lodge East Port $-$$
4512 S.E. 82nd Ave.,
Portland, OR 97266, Res.
(800) 424-4777 Ph: (503)
774-8876 Fax: (503) 788-9473

Motel 6 $
3104 SE Powell Blvd,
Portland, OR 97202, Res.
(800) 466-8356 Ph: 503
238-0600 Fax: 503 238-7167

Super 8 Motel $-$$
11011 NE Holman, Portland,
OR 97220, Res. (800)
800-8000 Ph: (503) 257-8988
Fax: (503) 253-1427

SALEM   OR

Motel 6 $
1401 Hawthorne Ave NE,
Salem, OR 97301, Res. (800)
466-8356 Ph: 503 371-8024
Fax: 503 371-7691

Motel 6
2250 Mission St, SE, Salem,
OR 97302, Res. (800)
466-8356 Ph: 503 588-7191
Fax: 503 588-0486

Super 8 Motel $-$$
1288 Hawthorne NE, Salem,
OR 97301, Res. (800)
800-8000 Ph: (503) 370-8888
Fax: (503) 370-8927

SPRINGFIELD   OR

Motel 6
3752 International Ct,
Springfield, OR 97477, Res.
(800) 466-8356 Ph: 541
741-1105 Fax: 541 741-6007

TIGARD   OR

Motel 6
17950 SW McEwan Rd,
Tigard, OR 97224, Res. (800)
466-8356 Ph: 503 620-2066
Fax: 503 639-7096

Motel 6
17959 SW McEwan Rd,
Tigard, OR 97224, Res. (800)
466-8356 Ph: 503 684-0760
Fax: 503 968-2539

TROUTDALE   OR

Motel 6
1610 NW Frontage Rd,
Troutdale, OR 97060, Res.
(800) 466-8356 Ph: 503
665-2254 Fax: 503 666-1849

WILSONVILLE   OR

Super 8 Motel $-$$
25438 SW Parkway Ave.,
Wilsonville, OR 97070, Res.
(800) 800-8000 Ph: (503)
682-2088 Fax: (503) 682-0453

PENNSYLVANIA

ALLENTOWN   PA

Econo Lodge $-$$
2115 Downyflake Ln.,
Allentown, PA 18103, Res.
(800) 424-4777 Ph: (215)
797-2200

ALTOONA   PA

Econo Lodge $-$$
2906 Pleasant Valley Blvd.,
Altoona, PA 16601, Res.
(800) 424-4777 Ph: (814)
944-3555 Fax: (814) 946-3258

Super 8 Motel $-$$
3535 Fairway Dr., Altoona,
PA 16602, Res. (800)
800-8000 Ph: (814) 942-5350
Fax: (814) 942-5350

BEDFORD   PA

Super 8 Motel $-$$
"Rd #2, Box 32A", Bedford,
PA 15522, Res. (800)
800-8000 Ph: (814) 623-5880
Fax: (814) 623-5880

BELLE VERNON   **PA**

Budget Host Cheeper Sleeper $
I-70 & RT 51, Belle Vernon,
PA 15012, Res. (800)
283-4678 Ph: (412) 929- 4501
Fax: (412) 929-8792

BETHLEHEM   **PA**

Econo Lodge Airport $-$$
US 22, Airport Rd. S.,
Bethlehem, PA 18018, Res.
(800) 424-4777 Ph: (610)
867-8681 Fax: (610) 867-6426

BLOOMSBURG   **PA**

Budget Host Patriot Inn $-$$
6305 New Berwick Hwy,
Bloomsburg, PA 17815, Res.
(800) 283-4678 Ph: (717)
387-1776 Fax: (717) 387-9611

Econo Lodge $-$$
189 Columbia Mall Dr.,
Bloomsburg, PA 17815, Res.
(800) 424-4777 Ph: (717)
387-0490 Fax: (717) 387-0893

BREEZEWOOD   **PA**

Econo Lodge $-$$
Rt. 1 Box 101-A, Breezewood,
PA 15533, Res. (800)
424-4777 Ph: (814) 735-4341
Fax: (814) 735-3958

BROOKVILLE   **PA**

Budget Host Gold Eagle Inn $-$$
250 W Main St, Brookville,
PA 15825-8413, Res. (800)
283-4678 Ph: (814) 849-7344
Fax: (814) 849-7345

Super 8 Motel $-$$
"Rd. 5, Box 149B", Brookville,
PA 15825, Res. (800)
800-8000 Ph: (814) 849-8840
Fax: (814) 849-8840

BURNHAM   **PA**

Super 8 Motel $-$$
9 Windmill Hill, Burnham,
PA 17009, Res. (800)
800-8000 Ph: (712) 242-8888
Fax: (717) 630-9124

BUTLER   **PA**

Super 8 Motel $-$$
228 Pittsburgh Rd., Butler,
PA 16001, Res. (800)
800-8000 Ph: (412) 287-8888
Fax: (412) 287-8888

CARLISLE   **PA**

Budget Host Coast To Coast $
1252 Harrisburg Pike,
Carlisle, PA 17013, Res.
(800) 283-4678 Ph: (717)
243-8585

Econo Lodge $-$$
1460 Harrisburg Pike,
Carlisle, PA 17013, Res.
(800) 424-4777 Ph: (717)
249-7775 Fax: (717) 249-7775

Motel 6 $
1153 Harrisburg Pike,
Carlisle, PA 17013, Res.
(800) 466-8356 Ph: 717
249-7622 Fax: 717 249-0597

Super 8 Motel $-$$
100 Alexander Spring Rd.,
Carlisle, PA 17013, Res.
(800) 800-8000 Ph: (717)
245-9898 Fax: (717) 245-9898

Super 8 Motel $-$$
1800 Harrisburg Pike,
Carlisle, PA 17013, Res.
(800) 800-8000 Ph: (717)
249-7000 Fax: (717) 249-9070

CHAMBERSBURG   **PA**

Econo Lodge $-$$
1110 Sheller Ave.,
Chambersburg, PA 17201,
Res. (800) 424-4777 Ph: (717)
264-8005 Fax: (717) 263-7720

CLARION   **PA**

Super 8 Motel $-$$
I-80 & SR 68 Exit 9, Clarion,
PA 16214, Res. (800)
800-8000 Ph: (814) 226-4550

CLEARFIELD   **PA**

Super 8 Motel $-$$
I-80 @ Clearfield Exit #19,
Clearfield, PA 16830, Res.
(800) 800-8000 Ph: (814)
768-7580

CORAOPOLIS   **PA**

Motel 6 $
1170 Thorn Run Road ,
Coraopolis, PA 15108, Res.
(800) 466-8356 Ph: 412
269-0990 Fax: 412 269-0462

Super 8 Motel $-$$
1455 Beers School Rd.,
Coraopolis, PA 15108, Res.
(800) 800-8000 Ph: (412)
264-7888 Fax: (412) 264-7888

DELMONT   **PA**

Super 8 Motel $-$$
180 Sheffield Drive,
Delmont, PA 15626, Res.
(800) 800-8000 Ph: (412)
468-4888

DENVER   **PA**

Econo Lodge $-$$
2015 N. Reading Rd., Denver,
PA 17517, Res. (800)
424-4777 Ph: (717) 336-4649
Fax: (717) 336-4649

Red Carpet Inn $$
2069 No. Reading Rd.,
Denver, PA 17517, Res.
(800) 251-1962 Ph: (717)
336-5254 Fax: (717) 336-0666

DOUGLASSVILLE   **PA**

Econo Lodge $-$$
387 Ben Franklin Hwy. / (US
422), Douglassville, PA
19518, Res. (800) 424-4777
Ph: (215) 385-3016 Fax: (000)
138-5016

DRUMS   **PA**

Econo Lodge $-$$
SR 309 & I-80, Drums, PA
18222, Res. (800) 424-4777
Ph: (717) 788-4121 Fax: (717)
788-3317

E. STROUDSBURG   **PA**

Super 8 Motel $-$$
340 Green Street Drive, E.
Stroudsburg, PA 18301,
Res. (800) 800-8000 Ph: (717)
424-7411 Fax: (717) 424-7411

ERIE   **PA**

Econo Lodge $-$$
8050 Peach St., Erie, PA
16509, Res. (800) 424-4777
Ph: (814) 866-5544 Fax: (000)
008-1466

Motel 6 $
7575 Peach St, Erie, PA
16509, Res. (800) 466-8356
Ph: 814 864-4811

ESSINGTON   **PA**

Econo Lodge Airport $-$$
600 SR 291, Essington, PA
19029, Res. (800) 424-4777
Ph: (215) 521-3900 Fax: (215)
521-3900

Motel 6 $
43 Industrial Hwy,
Essington, PA 19029, Res.
(800) 466-8356 Ph: 610
521-6650 Fax: 610 521-8846

ETTERS   **PA**

Super 8 Motel $-$$
70 Robinhood Dr., Etters, PA
17319, Res. (800) 800-8000
Ph: (717) 938-6200

FRACKVILLE   **PA**

Econo Lodge $-$$
501 S. Middle St., Frackville,
PA 17931, Res. (800)
424-4777 Ph: (717) 874-3838
Fax: (717) 874-3838

Motel 6 $
Rt 61 and I-81, Frackville, PA
17931, Res. (800) 466-8356
Ph: 717 874-1223 Fax: 717
874-1872

GETTYSBURG   **PA**

Budget Host Three Crowns $-$$
205 Steinwehr Ave,
Gettysburg, PA 17325, Res.
(800) 283-4678 Ph: (717)
334-3168

**M
O
T
E
L**

Econo Lodge $-$$
945 Baltimore Pike,
Gettysburg, PA 17325, Res.
(800) 424-4777 Ph: (717)
334-6715 Fax: (717) 334-6580

Red Carpet Inn $$
2450 Emmitsburg Rd., US
Bus. 15, Gettysburg, PA
17325, Res. (800) 251-1962
Ph: (717) 334-1345 Fax: (717)
334-5026

GRANTVILLE PA

Econo Lodge $-$$
Rt.1 Box 5005, Grantville, PA
17028, Res. (800) 424-4777
Ph: (717) 469-0631 Fax: (717)
469-0843

GREENCASTLE PA

Econo Lodge $-$$
735 Buchanan Trail E.,
Greencastle, PA 17225, Res.
(800) 424-4777 Ph: (717)
597-5255

GREENSBURG PA

Super 8 Motel $-$$
111 Sheraton Drive,
Greensburg, PA 15601, Res.
(800) 800-8000 Ph: (412)
838-8080

HANOVER PA

Super 8 Motel $-$$
Route 94 - Wentzel Drive,
Hanover, PA 17402, Res.
(800) 800-8000 Ph: (717)
630-8888 Fax: (717) 630-9124

HARMARVILLE PA

Super 8 Motel $-$$
8 Landings Drive,
Harmarville, PA 15238, Res.
(800) 800-8000 Ph: (412)
828-8900

HARRISBURG PA

Super 8 Motel $-$$
4131 Executive Park Drive,
Harrisburg, PA 17111, Res.
(800) 800-8000 Ph: (717)
564-7790 Fax: (717) 564-7790

Super 8 Motel $-$$
4125 North Front St.,
Harrisburg, PA 17110, Res.
(800) 800-8000 Ph: (717)
233-5891 Fax: (717) 233-5891

HERSHEY PA

Econo Lodge $-$$
115 Lucy Ave., Hershey, PA
17033, Res. (800) 424-4777
Ph: (717) 533-2515 Fax: (717)
533-2543

Red Carpet Inn $$
210 Hockersville Rd.,
Hershey, PA 17033, Res.
(800) 251-1962 Ph: (717)
534-1600 Fax: (717) 534-1381

INDIANA PA

Budget Host Inntowner $-$$
886 Wayne Ave Rear,
Indiana, PA 15701, Res.
(800) 283-4678 Ph: (412)
463-8726 Fax: (412) 463-9560

JOHNSTOWN PA

Motel 6 $
430 Napoleon Place,
Johnstown, PA 15901, Res.
(800) 466-8356 Ph: 814
536-1114 Fax: 814 536-0002

Super 8 Motel $-$$
1440 Scalp Avenue,
Johnstown, PA 15904, Res.
(800) 800-8000 Ph: (814)
266-8789 Fax: (814) 266-5285

KING OF PRUSSIA PA

Econo Lodge $-$$
815 W. Dekalb Pike, King Of
Prussia, PA 19406, Res.
(800) 424-4777 Ph: (610)
265-7200 Fax: (610) 265-7288

Motel 6 $
815 W. Dekalb Pike, King of
Prussia, PA 19406, Res.
(800) 466-8356 Ph: 610
265-7200 Fax: 610 265-7288

KUTZTOWN PA

Super 8 Motel $-$$
2160 Golden Key Rd.,
Kutztown, PA 19530, Res.
(800) 800-8000 Ph: (215)
385-4880 Fax: (610) 285-4452

LANCASTER PA

Econo Lodge North $-$$
2165 US 30 East, Lancaster,
PA 17602, Res. (800)
424-4777 Ph: (717) 299-6900
Fax: (717) 299-6900

Econo Lodge South $-$$
2140 US 30 East, Lancaster,
PA 17602, Res. (800)
424-4777 Ph: (717) 397-1900

Super 8 Motel $-$$
2129 East Lincoln Hwy.,
Lancaster, PA 17602, Res.
(800) 800-8000 Ph: (717)
939-8888 Fax: (717) 393-8888

LEVITTOWN PA

Econo Lodge $-$$
6201 Bristol Pike, Levittown,
PA 19057, Res. (800)
424-4777 Ph: (215) 946-1100
Fax: (215) 946-1180

LEWISBURG PA

Econo Lodge $-$$
US 15, Box 651, Lewisburg,
PA 17837, Res. (800)
424-4777 Ph: (717) 523-1106

MANHEIM PA

Red Carpet Inn $$
2845 Lebanon Rd., Manheim,
PA 17545, Res. (800)
251-1962 Ph: (717) 665-3118
Fax: (717) 665-5361

MEADVILLE P.

Super 8 Motel $-$
845 Conneaut Lake Road,
Meadville, PA 16335, Res.
(800) 800-8000 Ph: (814)
333-8883 Fax: (814) 333-8883

MIFFLINTOWN P.

Econo Lodge $-$$
US 322 at SR 35, Mifflintown,
PA 17059-0202, Res. (800)
424-4777 Ph: (717) 436-5981
Fax: (717) 436-5574

MIFFLINVILLE PA

Super 8 Motel $-$$
"I-80, Exit 37", Box E,
Mifflinville, PA 18631, Res.
(800) 800-8000 Ph: (717)
759-6778 Fax: (717) 759-6738

MILFORD P.

Red Carpet Inn $$
I-84, exit 10 on Rt. 6, Milford,
PA 18337, Res. (800)
251-1962 Ph: (717) 296-9444
Fax: (717) 296-4739

MONTOURSVILLE P.

Super 8 Motel $-$$
2815 Old Montoursville Rd.,
Montoursville, PA 17754,
Res. (800) 800-8000 Ph: (717)
368-8111 Fax: (717) 368-8555

MT. POCONO PA

Super 8 Motel $-$$
Rte. 611, Mt. Pocono, PA
18344, Res. (800) 800-8000
Ph: (717) 839-7728 Fax: (717)
839-7760

NEW CASTLE PA

Super 8 Motel $-$$
1699 New Butler Road
(Hwy.422), New Castle, PA
16101, Res. (800) 800-8000
Ph: (412) 658-8849 Fax: (412)
658-8849

NEW CUMBERLAND PA

Motel 6 $
200 Commerce Dr, New
Cumberland, PA 17070, Res
(800) 466-8356 Ph: 717
774-8910 Fax: 717 770-0433

NEW STANTON PA

Super 8 Motel $-$$
103 Bair Blvd., New Stanton,
PA 15672, Res. (800)
800-8000 Ph: (412) 925-8915
Fax: (412) 925-8915

NORTH EAST PA

Super 8 Motel $-$$
I-90 & Rt 89, North East, PA
16428, Res. (800) 800-8000
Ph: (814) 725-4567

NORTH EAST(ERIE)   PA

Red Carpet Inn $$
2264 East Main St., North
East(Erie), PA 16428, Res.
(800) 251-1962 Ph: (814)
725-4554 Fax: (814) 725-4426

PINE GROVE   PA

Econo Lodge $-$$
Rd 1, Box 581, Pine Grove,
PA 17963, Res. (800)
424-4777 Ph: (717) 345-4099
Fax: (717) 345-4984

PITTSBURGH   PA

Econo Lodge $-$$
4800 Steubenville Pike,
Pittsburgh, PA 15205, Res.
(800) 424-4777 Ph: (412)
922-6900 Fax: (412) 922-1474

Motel 6 $
211 Beecham Dr, Pittsburgh,
PA 15205, Res. (800)
466-8356 Ph: 412 922-9400
Fax: 412 921-1725

QUAKERTOWN   PA

Econo Lodge $-$$
1905 SR 663, PA Tpk., Ex. 32,
Quakertown, PA 18951, Res.
(800) 424-4777 Ph: (215)
538-3000 Fax: (215) 538-2311

READING   PA

Econo Lodge Northeast $-$$
2310 Fraver Dr., Reading, PA
19605, Res. (800) 424-4777
Ph: (610) 378-1145

Econo Lodge Northwest $-$$
635 Spring St., Reading, PA
19610, Res. (800) 424-4777
Ph: (610) 378-5105 Fax: (610)
373-3181

RONKS   PA

Red Carpet Inn $$
2884 Lincoln Hwy E., Ronks,
PA 17572, Res. (800)
251-1962 Ph: (717) 687-8020

SCRANTON   PA

Econo Lodge $-$$
1175 Kane St., Scranton, PA
18505, Res. (800) 424-4777
Ph: (717) 348-1000 Fax: (717)
348-0683

Econo Lodge $-$$
1027 O'neill Hwy., Scranton,
PA 18512, Res. (800)
424-4777 Ph: (717) 346-8782
Fax: (717) 346-7825

SHIPPENSBURG   PA

Budget Host Shippensburg$$
Hershey Rd, P.O. Box 349,
Shippensburg, PA 17257,
Res. (800) 283-4678 Ph: (717)
530-1234

Budget Host University $-$$
720 Walnut Bottom Rd, P.O.
Box 349, Shippensburg, PA
17257, Res. (800) 283-4678
Ph: (717) 532-7311 Fax: (717)
532-8872

SOMERSET   PA

Budget Host Inn $-$$
799 N Central Ave,
Somerset, PA 15501, Res.
(800) 283-4678 Ph: (814)
445-7988

Super 8 Motel $-$$
101 Miller Ave., Somerset,
PA 15501, Res. (800)
800-8000 Ph: (814) 445-8788
Fax: (814) 445-8788

WARREN   PA

Super 8 Motel $-$$
204 Struthers St., Warren,
PA 16365, Res. (800)
800-8000 Ph: (814) 723-8881
Fax: (814) 723-8881

WASHINGTON   PA

Motel 6 $
1283 Motel 6 Dr,
Washington, PA 15301, Res.
(800) 466-8356 Ph: 412
223-8040 Fax: 412 228-6445

WAYNESBURG   PA

Econo Lodge $-$$
350 Miller Ln., Waynesburg,
PA 15370, Res. (800)
424-4777 Ph: (412) 627-5544
Fax: (412) 627-5544

Super 8 Motel $-$$
800 Miller Lane,
Waynesburg, PA 15370,
Res. (800) 800-8000 Ph: (412)
627-8880 Fax: (412) 627-8880

WEXFORD   PA

Econo Lodge $-$$
107 V.i.p. Dr., Wexford, PA
15090, Res. (800) 424-4777
Ph: (412) 935-1000 Fax: (412)
935-6288

WILKES   PA

Red Carpet Inn $$
400 Kidder St., Wilkes, PA
18702, Res. (800) 251-1962
Ph: (717) 823-2171 Fax: (717)
825-4849

WILKES BARRE   PA

Econo Lodge $-$$
1075 Wilkes-Barre TWP. Blvd.
/ SR 309, Wilkes Barre, PA
18702, Res. (800) 424-4777
Ph: (717) 823-0600 Fax: (717)
823-3294

WILLIAMSPORT   PA

Econo Lodge $-$$
2401 E. Third St.,
Williamsport, PA 17701,
Res. (800) 424-4777 Ph: (717)
326-1501 Fax: (717) 326-9776

YORK   PA

Budget Host Spirit Of 76$-$$
1162 Haines Rd, York, PA
17402, Res. (800) 283-4678
Ph: (717) 755-1068 Fax: (717)
757-5571

Motel 6 $
125 Arsenal Rd, York, PA
17404, Res. (800) 466-8356
Ph: 717 846-6260 Fax: 717
845-5504

Super 8 Motel $-$$
40 Arsenal Road, York, PA
17404, Res. (800) 800-8000
Ph: (717) 852-8686 Fax: (717)
852-8686

RHODE ISLAND

MIDDLETOWN   RI

Budget Host Inn $-$$
1185 W. Main Road,
Middletown, RI 02842, Ph:
(401) 849-4700

NEWPORT   RI

Motel 6 $
249 JT Connell Hwy,
Newport, RI 02840, Res.
(800) 466-8356 Ph: 401
848-0600 Fax: 401 848-9966

WARWICK   RI

Master Hosts Inns $$
2138 Post Rd., Warwick, RI
02886, Res. (800) 251-1962
Ph: (401) 737-7400 Fax: (401)
739-6483

Motel 6 $
20 Jefferson Boulevard,
Warwick, RI 02888, Res.
(800) 466-8356 Ph: 401
467-9800 Fax: 401 467-6780

SOUTH CAROLINA

ALLENDALE   SC

Villager $-$$
671 N. Main St, Allendale,
SC 29810, Res. (800)
328-7829 Ph: (803) 584-2184
Fax: (000) 000-0000

ANDERSON   SC

Super 8 Motel $-$$
3302 Cinema Avenue,
Anderson, SC 29621-1346,
Res. (800) 800-8000 Ph: (803)
225-8384 Fax: (803) 261-9802

BEAUFORT   SC

Scottish Inns $
2221 Boundary St., Beaufort,
SC 29902, Res. (800)
251-1962 Ph: (803) 521-1555
Fax: (803) 521-1471

BENNETTSVILLE   SC

Master Hosts Inns $$
130 15-401 By-Pass West,
Bennettsville, SC 29512,
Res. (800) 251-1962 Ph: (803)
479-4051 Fax: (803) 479-2275

M
O
T
E
L

BISHOPVILLE   SC

Econo Lodge $-$$
1153 S. Main St., Bishopville,
SC 29010, Res. (800)
424-4777 Ph: (803) 428-3200
Fax: (803) 428-3200

CHARLESTON   SC

Econo Lodge $-$$
2237 Savannah Hwy.,
Charleston, SC 29414, Res.
(800) 424-4777 Ph: (803)
571-1880 Fax: (803) 766-9351

Motel 6 $
2551 Ashley Phosphate Rd,
Charleston, SC 29418, Res.
(800) 466-8356 Ph: 803
572-6590 Fax: 803 572-9026

Motel 6 $
2058 Savannah Hwy,
Charleston, SC 29407, Res.
(800) 466-8356 Ph: 803
556-5144 Fax: 803 556-2241

Super 8 Motel $-$$
2311 Ashley Phosphate,
Charleston, SC 29406, Res.
(800) 800-8000 Ph: (803)
572-2228 Fax: (803) 553-7849

COLUMBIA   SC

Econo Lodge $-$$
494 Piney Grove Rd.,
Columbia, SC 29210, Res.
(800) 424-4777 Ph: (803)
731-4060 Fax: (803) 798-6612

Econo Lodge Ft. Jackson $-$$
7700 Two Notch Rd.,
Columbia, SC 29223, Res.
(800) 424-4777 Ph: (803)
788-5544 Fax: (803) 788-5544

Economy Inns Of America $-$$
1776 Burning Tree Road,
Columbia, SC 29210, Res.
(800) 826-0778 Ph: (803)
798-9210

Motel 6 $
1776 Burning Tree Rd,
Columbia, SC 29210, Res.
(800) 466-8356 Ph: 803
798-9210 Fax: 803 772-6580

Scottish Inns $
127 Mornighill Dr., Columbia,
SC 29210, Res. (800)
251-1962 Ph: (803) 772-5833
Fax: (803) 772-6630

DILLON   SC

Econo Lodge $-$$
I-95 Exit 193, Dillon, SC
29536, Res. (800) 424-4777
Ph: (803) 774-4181

Super 8 Motel $-$$
Route 1-Box 75L, Dillon, SC
29536, Res. (800) 800-8000
Ph: (803) 774-4161 Fax: (803)
774-4461

FLORENCE   SC

Econo Lodge North $-$$
I-95 & US 52, Florence, SC
29502, Res. (800) 424-4777
Ph: (803) 665-8558 Fax: (803)
665-8558

Econo Lodge South $-$$
I-95 & US 76, Florence, SC
29501, Res. (800) 424-4777
Ph: (803) 662-7712

Motel 6 $
1834 W Lucas Rd, Florence,
SC 29501, Res. (800)
466-8356 Ph: 803 667-6100
Fax: 803 673-9555

Super 8 Motel $-$$
1832 W. Lucas St., Florence,
SC 29502, Res. (800)
800-8000 Ph: (803) 661-7267
Fax: (803) 661-7267

Villager $-$$
P.O. Box 3806, Florence, SC
29502, Res. (800) 328-7829
Ph: (803) 673-0070 Fax: (803)
661-6845

GOOSE CREEK   SC

Econo Lodge $-$$
401 Goose Creek Blvd. N.,
Goose Creek, SC 29445,
Res. (800) 424-4777 Ph: (803)
797-8200 Fax: (803) 797-6639

GREENVILLE   SC

Motel 6 $
224 Bruce Rd, Greenville,
SC 29605, Res. (800)
466-8356 Ph: 864 277-8630
Fax: 864 299-1239

Scottish Inns $
536 Wade Hampton Blvd.,
Greenville, SC 29609, Res.
(800) 251-1962 Ph: (803)
232-6416

GREENWOOD   SC

Econo Lodge $-$$
719 Bypass 25 NE,
Greenwood, SC 29646, Res.
(800) 424-4777 Ph: (803)
229-5329

Villager $-$$
230 Birchtree Drive,
Greenwood, SC 29649, Res.
(800) 328-7829 Ph: (864)
223-1818 Fax: (864) 223-1818

HARDEEVILLE   SC

Super 8 Motel $-$$
I-95 and US 17, Hardeeville,
SC 29927, Res. (800)
800-8000 Ph: (803) 784-2151
Fax: (803) 784-3026

HILTON HEAD   SC

Motel 6 $
830 William Hilton Pkwy,
Hilton Head, SC 29928, Res.
(800) 466-8356 Ph: 803
785-2700 Fax: 803 842-9543

MYRTLE BEACH   SC

Master Hosts Inns $$
2311 So Ocean Blvd., Myrtle
Beach, SC 29577, Res. (800)
251-1962 Ph: (803) 448-8373

Super 8 Motel $-$$
"3450 Hwy. 17, Bypass
South", Myrtle Beach, SC
29577, Res. (800) 800-8000
Ph: (803) 293-6100 Fax: (803)
293-6100

Super 8 Motel $-$$
1100 South Ocean Blvd.,
Myrtle Beach, SC 29577,
Res. (800) 800-8000 Ph: (803)
448-8414 Fax: (803) 448-8414

RICHBURG   SC

Econo Lodge $-$$
Rt. 1, Box 182, Richburg, SC
29729, Res. (800) 424-4777
Ph: (803) 789-3000 Fax: (803)
328-6288

Super 8 Motel $-$$
"I-77, exit 65 & US 9",
Richburg, SC 29729, Res.
(800) 800-8000 Ph: (803)
789-7888 Fax: (803) 789-5692

ROCK HILL   SC

Econo Lodge $-$$
962 Riverview Rd., Rock Hill,
SC 29730, Res. (800)
424-4777 Ph: (803) 329-3232
Fax: (803) 328-6288

SAINT GEORGE   SC

Econo Lodge $-$$
I-95 & US 78, Saint George,
SC 29477, Res. (800)
424-4777 Ph: (803) 563-4027
Fax: (803) 563-3558

SANTEE   SC

Super 8 Motel $-$$
9125 Old Hwy 60, Santee,
SC 29210, Res. (800)
800-8000 Ph: (803) 854-3456
Fax: (803) 854-4875

SPARTANBURG   SC

Econo Lodge $-$$
710 Sunbeam Rd,
Spartanburg, SC 29303,
Res. (800) 424-4777 Ph: (803)
578-9450 Fax: (803) 578-1458

Econo Lodge $-$$
6765 Pottery Rd.,
Spartanburg, SC 29301,
Res. (800) 424-4777 Ph: (803)
587-0129

Motel 6 $
105 Jones Rd, Spartanburg,
SC 29303, Res. (800)
466-8356 Ph: 864 573-6383
Fax: 864 582-7060

Super 8 Motel $-$$
1050 Chrisma Drive,
Spartanburg, SC 29303,
Res. (800) 800-8000 Ph: (803)
578-8880 Fax: (803) 000-0000

Villager $-$$
462 E Main St, Spartanburg,
SC 29302, Res. (800)
328-7829 Ph: (864) 585-3621
Fax: (864) 582-4544

SUMMERTON SC

Econo Lodge $-$$
I-95 & SR 102, Summerton,
SC 29148, Res. (800)
424-4777 Ph: (803) 485-2865
Fax: (803) 485-2865

SUMMERVILLE SC

Econo Lodge $-$$
110 Holiday Inn Dr.,
Summerville, SC 29483,
Res. (800) 424-4777 Ph: (803)
875-3022

TURBEVILLE SC

Super 8 Motel $-$$
I-95 @ Exit 135, Turbeville,
SC 29162, Res. (800)
800-8000 Ph: (803) 659-8060
Fax: (803) 659-8060

WALTERBORO SC

Super 8 Motel $-$$
"Rte.3, Box 760", Exit 57 &
I-95, Walterboro, SC 29488,
Res. (800) 800-8000 Ph: (803)
538-5383 Fax: (803) 538-5853

WEST COLUMBIA SC

Super 8 Motel $-$$
2516 Augusta Highway,
West Columbia, SC
29169-4546, Res. (800)
800-8000 Ph: (803) 796-4833
Fax: (803) 796-4833

YEMASSEE SC

Super 8 Motel $-$$
I-95 & Hwy 68, Yemassee,
SC 29945, Res. (800)
800-8000 Ph: (803) 589-2177
Fax: (803) 589-2008

SOUTH DAKOTA

ABERDEEN SD

Super 8 Motel $-$$
2405 S.E. 6th Avenue, P.O.
Box 1593, Aberdeen, SD
57401, Res. (800) 800-8000
Ph: (605) 229-5005 Fax: (605)
229-5005

Super 8 Motel $-$$
714 S. Hwy 281, PO Box 1593,
Aberdeen, SD 57401, Res.
(800) 800-8000 Ph: (605)
225-1711

Super 8 Motel $-$$
770 NW Hwy. 281, PO Box
1593, Aberdeen, SD
57402-1593, Res. (800)
800-8000 Ph: (605) 226-2288

ARLINGTON SD

Super 8 Motel $-$$
Box 230, Arlington, SD
57212, Res. (800) 800-8000
Ph: (605) 983-4609

BELLE FOURCHE SD

Super 8 Motel $-$$
501 National Street, Belle
Fourche, SD 57717, Res.
(800) 800-8000 Ph: (605)
892-3361

CHAMBERLAIN SD

Super 8 Motel $-$$
Lakeview Heights S. Main St,
Chamberlain, SD 57325,
Res. (800) 800-8000 Ph: (605)
734-6548

CUSTER SD

Super 8 Motel $-$$
415 W. Mt. Rushmore Rd.,
Custer, SD 57730, Res.
(800) 800-8000 Ph: (605)
673-2200

DEADWOOD SD

Super 8 Motel $-$$
196 Cliff Street, Deadwood,
SD 57732, Res. (800)
800-8000 Ph: (605) 578-2535
Fax: (605) 578-3604

EAGLE BUTTE SD

Super 8 Motel $-$$
Hwy 212 South, P.O. Box
180, Eagle Butte, SD
57625, Res. (800) 800-8000
Ph: (605) 964-8888

FAULKTON SD

Super 8 Motel $-$$
700 Main Street, P.O. Box
514, Faulkton, SD
57438-0514, Res. (800)
800-8000 Ph: (605) 598-4567

GETTYSBURG SD

Super 8 Motel $-$$
East Highway 212,
Gettysburg, SD 57442, Res.
(800) 800-8000 Ph: (605)
765-2373

HILL CITY SD

Super 8 Motel $-$$
209 Main Street, Hill City,
SD 57745-0184, Res. (800)
800-8000 Ph: (605) 574-4141
Fax: (605) 574-4755

HOT SPRINGS SD

Super 8 Motel $-$$
800 Mammoth St., Box 612,
Hot Springs, SD
57747-0612, Res. (800)
800-8000 Ph: (605) 745-3888

HURON SD

Super 8 Motel $-$$
2189 Dakota Ave. S, Huron,
SD 57350-4397, Res. (800)
800-8000 Ph: (605) 352-0740
Fax: (605) 352-0740

INTERIOR WALL SD

Badlands Budget Host $-$$
SR 2, Box 11B, Interior Wall,
SD 57790, Res. (800)
283-4678 Ph: (605) 433-5335

KADOKA SD

Super 8 Motel $-$$
"PO Box 334, Exit 150 E I-90",
Kadoka, SD 57543-0138,
Res. (800) 800-8000 Ph: (605)
837-2188 Fax: (800) 319-2409

KENNEBEC SD

Gerry's Budget Host Motel $-$$
HCR 81, Box 31, Kennebec,
SD 57544, Res. (800)
283-4678 Ph: (605) 869-2210

KIMBALL SD

Super 8 Motel $-$$
South Main Street, Kimball,
SD 57355, Res. (800)
800-8000 Ph: (605) 778-6088
Fax: (605) 778-6789

MADISON SD

Super 8 Motel $-$$
"Jct. Hwy. 34 & 81, PO Box 5",
Madison, SD 57042-0005,
Res. (800) 800-8000 Ph: (605)
256-6931

MILBANK SD

Super 8 Motel $-$$
E. Hwy. 12 PO Box 86,
Milbank, SD 57252-0086,
Res. (800) 800-8000 Ph: (605)
432-9288 Fax: (605) 432-6315

MILLER SD

Super 8 Motel $-$$
Hwy. 14 W & 15 N., Miller,
SD 57362-0141, Res. (800)
800-8000 Ph: (605) 853-2721
Fax: (605) 853-2721

MITCHELL SD

Motel 6 $
1309 S Ohlman St, Mitchell,
SD 57301, Res. (800)
466-8356 Ph: 605 996-0530
Fax: 605 995-2019

Super 8 Motel $-$$
I-90 at US Hwy. 37, PO Box
867, Mitchell, SD
57301-0867, Res. (800)
800-8000 Ph: (605) 996-9678
Fax: (605) 996-5339

MOBRIDGE SD

Super 8 Motel $-$$
P.O. Box 156, Mobridge, SD
57601, Res. (800) 800-8000
Ph: (605) 845-7215 Fax: (605)
845-3137

MURDO SD

Super 8 Motel $-$$
604 East 5th Street, Murdo,
SD 57559, Res. (800)
800-8000 Ph: (605) 669-2437

N. SIOUX CITY SD

Super 8 Motel $-$$
1300 River Drive, P.O. Box
266, N. Sioux City, SD
57049, Res. (800) 800-8000
Ph: (605) 232-4716 Fax: (605)
232-4718

MOTEL

PIERRE   SD

Budget Host State Motel $-$$
640 N. Euclid, Pierre, SD
57501, Ph: (605) 224-5896
Fax: (605) 224-1815

Super 8 Motel $-$$
320 West Sioux Avenue,
Pierre, SD 57501, Res. (800)
800-8000 Ph: (605) 224-1617
Fax: (605) 224-1617

PLANKINTON   SD

Super 8 Motel $-$$
801 S. Main St., "RR 3, P.O.
Box 1C", Plankinton, SD
57368, Res. (800) 800-8000
Ph: (605) 942-7722

RAPID CITY   SD

Budget Host Bel-air Motel $-$$
2101 Mt Rushmore Rd, Rapid
City, SD 57701, Res. (800)
283-4678 Ph: (605) 343-5126

Econo Lodge $-$$
625 E. Disk Dr., Rapid City,
SD 57701, Res. (800)
424-4777 Ph: (605) 342-6400
Fax: (605) 341-7908

Motel 6 $
620 E Latrobe St, Rapid City,
SD 57701, Res. (800)
466-8356 Ph: 605 343-3687
Fax: 605 343-7566

Super 8 Motel $-$$
2124 LaCrosse Street, Rapid
City, SD 57701-7859, Res.
(800) 800-8000 Ph: (605)
348-8070 Fax: (605) 348-0833

Super 8 Motel $-$$
2520 Tower Road, Rapid City,
SD 57701, Res. (800)
800-8000 Ph: (605) 342-4911
Fax: (605) 342-4911

REDFIELD   SD

Super 8 Motel $-$$
Highway 212 & 281 West,
Redfield, SD 57469, Res.
(800) 800-8000 Ph: (605)
472-0720

SELBY   SD

Super 8 Motel $-$$
5800 Lincoln Ave., Selby, SD
57472, Res. (800) 800-8000
Ph: (605) 649-7979

SIOUX FALLS   SD

Motel 6 $
3009 W Russell St, Sioux
Falls, SD 57107, Res. (800)
466-8356 Ph: 605 336-7800
Fax: 605 330-9273

Super 8 Motel $-$$
1508 West Russell Street,
Sioux Falls, SD 57104-1329,
Res. (800) 800-8000 Ph: (605)
339-9330 Fax: (605) 339-9330

Super 8 Motel $-$$
4808 North Cliff Avenue,
Sioux Falls, SD 57104, Res.
(800) 800-8000 Ph: (605)
339-9212

Super 8 Motel $-$$
4100 W. 41st St., Sioux Falls,
SD 57106-0717, Res. (800)
800-8000 Ph: (605) 361-9719

Thriftlodge $-$$
809 West Ave. North, Sioux
Falls, SD 57104, Res. (800)
525-9055 Ph: (605) 336-0230
Fax: (605) 331-4194

SPEARFISH   SD

Super 8 Motel $-$$
"I-90 at Exit 14, PO Box 316",
Spearfish, SD 57783-0316,
Res. (800) 800-8000 Ph: (605)
642-4721 Fax: (605) 348-9645

STURGIS   SD

Super 8 Motel $-$$
HC 55-Box 306, Sturgis, SD
57785, Res. (800) 800-8000
Ph: (605) 347-4447 Fax: (605)
347-2334

VERMILLION   SD

Budget Host Tomahawk $-$$
P.O. Box 363, Vermillion, SD
57069, Res. (800) 283-4678
Ph: (605) 624-2601

Super 8 Motel $-$$
1208 E. Cherry St,
Vermillion, SD 57069, Res.
(800) 800-8000 Ph: (605)
624-8005 Fax: (605) 624-8005

WAGNER   SD

Super 8 Motel $-$$
W. Hwy.46 & PO Box 881,
Wagner, SD 57380, Res.
(800) 800-8000 Ph: (605)
384-5464 Fax: (605) 384-3407

WALL   SD

Super 8 Motel $-$$
711 Glenn St., Wall, SD
57790, Res. (800) 800-8000
Ph: (605) 279-2688

WATERTOWN   SD

Budget Host Inn $-$$
309 8th Ave SE, Watertown,
SD 57201, Res. (800)
283-4678 Ph: (605) 886-8455
Fax: (605) 886-6248

Super 8 Motel $-$$
"503 14th Avenue, S.E.",
Watertown, SD 57201, Res.
(800) 800-8000 Ph: (605)
882-1900 Fax: (605) 882-1900

WEBSTER   SD

Super 8 Motel $-$$
P.O. Box 592, Webster, SD
57274, Res. (800) 800-8000
Ph: (605) 345-4701 Fax: (605)
345-4701

WINNER   SD

Super 8 Motel $-$$
902 East Highway 44,
Winner, SD 57580, Res.
(800) 800-8000 Ph: (605)
842-0991

YANKTON   SD

Super 8 Motel $-$$
Route 4, Box 36, Yankton,
SD 57078, Res. (800)
800-8000 Ph: (605) 665-6510
Fax: (605) 665-6510

TENNESSEE

ATHENS   TN

Scottish Inns $
712 Congress Pkwy, Athens,
TN 37303, Res. (800)
251-1962 Ph: (423) 745-4880

Super 8 Motel $-$$
2541 Decatur Pike, Athens,
TN 37303, Res. (800)
800-8000 Ph: (423) 745-4500

BRISTOL   TN

Econo Lodge Medical Center $-$$
I-81 & US 11 W., Ex. 74A,
Bristol, TN 37621, Res. (800)
424-4777 Ph: (615) 968-9119
Fax: (615) 968-9540

BRISTOLK   TN

Scottish Inns $
1403 Bluff City Hwy, Bristolk,
TN 37620, Res. (800)
251-1962 Ph: (423) 764-4145

CARYVILLE   TN

Budget Host Inn $-$$
101 Tennessee Dr Box 16,
Caryville, TN 37714, Res.
(800) 283-4678 Ph: (615)
562-9595

CHATTANOOGA   TN

Econo Lodge Airport $-$$
7421 Bonny Oaks Dr.,
Chattanooga, TN
37421-1084, Res. (800)
424-4777 Ph: (615) 499-9550
Fax: (615) 499-9550

Econo Lodge East Ridge $-$$
1417 St.thomas St.,
Chattanooga, TN 37412,
Res. (800) 424-4777 Ph: (615)
894-1417

Econo Lodge Lookout $-$$
3655 Cummings Hwy.,
Chattanooga, TN 37419,
Res. (800) 424-4777 Ph: (615)
821-2233 Fax: (615) 825-1964

Motel 6 $
7707 Lee Hwy., Chattanooga,
TN 37421, Res. (800)
466-8356 Ph: 423 892-7707
Fax: 423 899-3818

Super 8 Motel $-$$
20 Birmingham Road,
Chattanooga, TN
37419-2371, Res. (800)
800-8000 Ph: (615) 821-8880
Fax: (615) 821-5701

Super 8 Motel $-$$
1401 Mack Smith Road,
Chattanooga, TN 37412,
Res. (800) 800-8000 Ph: (615)
892-3888

CLARKSVILLE   TN

Econo Lodge $-$$
201 Holiday Rd., Clarksville,
TN 37040, Res. (800)
424-4777 Ph: (615) 645-6300
Fax: (615) 645-6300

Motel 6 $
881 Kraft St, Clarksville, TN
37040, Res. (800) 466-8356
Ph: 615 552-0045 Fax: 615
651-8516

Super 8 Motel $-$$
3065 Wilma Rudolph Blvd.,
intersection of I-24 & US 79,
Clarksville, TN 37040, Res.
(800) 800-8000 Ph: (615)
647-2002

CLEVELAND   TN

Econo Lodge $-$$
2650 Westside Dr. N.W.,
Cleveland, TN 37311, Res.
(800) 424-4777 Ph: (615)
472-3281 Fax: (615) 472-3281

Red Carpet Inn $
4501 25th St., Cleveland, TN
37311, Res. (800) 251-1962
Ph: (423) 476-6514 Fax: (423)
472-2019

Super 8 Motel $-$$
180 Bernham Drive,
Cleveland, TN 37312, Res.
(800) 800-8000 Ph: (615)
476-5555 Fax: (615) 476-4649

CLINTON   TN

Super 8 Motel $-$$
State Route 61 & I-75,
Clinton, TN 37716, Res.
(800) 800-8000 Ph: (615)
457-0565 Fax: (615) 457-0565

COLUMBIA   TN

Econo Lodge $-$$
SR 99 & I-65, Columbia, TN
38401, Res. (800) 424-4777
Ph: (615) 381-1410 Fax: (615)
380-1984

Scottish Inns $
1027 Nashville Hwy.,
Columbia, TN 38401, Res.
(800) 251-1962 Ph: (615)
388-6570 Fax: (615) 381-5001

COOKEVILLE   TN

Super 8 Motel $-$$
1330 Bunkerhill Road,
Cookeville, TN 38501, Res.
(800) 800-8000 Ph: (615)
528-5165 Fax: (615) 528-2020

CORNERSVILLE   TN

Econo Lodge $-$$
I-65 & SR 31 A, Cornersville,
TN 37047, Res. (800)
424-4777 Ph: (615) 293-2111

CROSSVILLE   TN

Scottish Inns $
2906 No Min St., Crossville,
TN 38555, Res. (800)
251-1962 Ph: (423) 745-4880
Fax: (423) 745-7369

Villager $-$$
714 N. Main St, Crossville,
TN 38555, Res. (800)
328-7829 Ph: (615) 484-7561
Fax: (615) 456-6381

DENMARK   TN

Econo Lodge West $-$$
196 Providence Rd.,
Denmark, TN 38391, Res.
(800) 424-4777 Ph: (901)
427-2778

DICKSON   TN

Econo Lodge $-$$
I-40 & SR 46, Dickson, TN
37055, Res. (800) 424-4777
Ph: (615) 446-0541 Fax: (615)
446-9950

EAST RIDGE   TN

Scottish Inns $$
6510 Ringgold Rd., East
Ridge, TN 37412, Res. (800)
251-1962 Ph: (423) 894-0911
Fax: (423) 894-0920

GATLINBURG   TN

Econo Lodge $-$$
248 Airport Rd., Gatlinburg,
TN 37738, Res. (800)
424-4777 Ph: (615) 436-5836
Fax: (615) 436-5043

Econo Lodge Downtown $-$$
247 Newton La., Gatlinburg,
TN 37738, Res. (800)
424-4777 Ph: (615) 436-6626
Fax: (000) 006-1536

Red Carpet Inn $
349 E. Parkway, Gatlinburg,
TN 37738, Res. (800)
251-1962 Ph: (615) 436-5179

Super 8 Motel $-$$
523 E. Parkway, Gatlinburg,
TN 37738, Res. (800)
800-8000 Ph: (615) 436-9750
Fax: (615) 436-3878

GOODLETTSVILLE   TN

Econo Lodge Rivergate $-$$
320 Long Hollow Pike,
Goodlettsville, TN 37072,
Res. (800) 424-4777 Ph: (615)
859-4988

Motel 6 $
323 Cartwright St,
Goodlettsville, TN 37072,
Res. (800) 466-8356 Ph: 615
859-9674 Fax: 615 851-6115

HARRIMAN   TN

Scottish Inns $
1867 So Roane St.,
Harriman, TN 37748, Res.
(800) 251-1962 Ph: (615)
882-6600

HURRICANE MILLS   TN

Super 8 Motel $-$$
"I-40 at Hwy 13, exit 143",
"Rte. 1, Box 79", Hurricane
Mills, TN 37078, Res. (800)
800-8000 Ph: (615) 296-2432
Fax: (615) 296-1135

JACKSON   TN

Super 8 Motel $-$$
2295 North Highland,
Jackson, TN 38305, Res.
(800) 800-8000 Ph: (901)
668-1145

JOHNSON CITY   TN

Super 8 Motel $-$$
108 Wesley Street, Johnson
City, TN 37601-1718, Res.
(800) 800-8000 Ph: (615)
282-8818 Fax: (615) 282-3265

KIMBALL   TN

Budget Host Inn $-$$
1850 Main St, Kimball, TN
37347, Res. (800) 283-4678
Ph: (615) 837-7185 Fax: (615)
837-7185

KINGSPORT   TN

Econo Lodge $-$$
1704 E. Stone Dr., Kingsport,
TN 37660, Res. (800)
424-4777 Ph: (615) 245-0286
Fax: (615) 245-2985

KINGSTON SPRINGS   TN

Scottish Inns $$
116 Luyben Hill Rd.,
Kingston Springs, TN
37082, Res. (800) 251-1962
Ph: (615) 952-3115 Fax: (615)
952-2530

KNOXVILLE   TN

Econo Lodge North $-$$
5505 Merchant Ctr. Blvd.,
Knoxville, TN 37912, Res.
(800) 424-4777 Ph: (615)
687-5680

Motel 6 $
402 Lovell Rd, Knoxville, TN
37922, Res. (800) 466-8356
Ph: 423 675-7200 Fax: 423
671-3339

Scottish Inns $$
9340 Park West Blvd.,
Knoxville, TN 37923, Res.
(800) 251-1962 Ph: (615)
693-6061 Fax: (615) 693-0702

Scottish Inns $$
2841 Alcoa Hwy, Knoxville,
TN 37920, Res. (800)
251-1962 Ph: (423) 577-6604
Fax: (423-577-4660

**M
O
T
E
L**

Scottish Inns $$
301 Callahan Dr., Knoxville,
TN 37912, Res. (800)
251-1962 Ph: (423) 689-777
Fax: (423) 688-7749

Super 8 Motel $-$$
6200 Paper Mill Road,
Knoxville, TN 37919, Res.
(800) 800-8000 Ph: (615)
584-8511 Fax: (615) 558-0991

Super 8 Motel $-$$
7585 Crosswood Blvd.,
Knoxville, TN 37914, Res.
(800) 800-8000 Ph: (615)
524-0855 Fax: (615) 558-0991

Super 8 Motel $-$$
503 Merchant Drive,
Knoxville, TN 37912, Res.
(800) 800-8000 Ph: (615)
689-7666 Fax: (615) 688-0099

KODAK TN

Econo Lodge $-$$
184 Dumplin Valley Rd,
Kodak, TN 37764, Res. (800)
424-4777 Ph: (615) 933-8141

LAKELAND TN

Super 8 Motel $-$$
9779 Huff N Puff, Lakeland,
TN 38002, Res. (800)
800-8000 Ph: (901) 372-4575

LEBANON TN

Budget Host Inn $-$$
903 Murfreesboro Rd,
Lebanon, TN 37087, Res.
(800) 283-4678 Ph: (615)
449-2900 Fax: (615) 449-5809

Scottish Inns $
638 So. Cumberland St.,
Lebanon, TN 37087, Res.
(800) 251-1962 Ph: (615)
444-5291 Fax: (615) 444-6556

Super 8 Motel $-$$
914 Murfreesboro Road,
Lebanon, TN 37087, Res.
(800) 800-8000 Ph: (615)
444-5636

LENOIR CITY TN

Econo Lodge $-$$
I-75, Ex. 81, Lenoir City, TN
37771, Res. (800) 424-4777
Ph: (615) 986-0295 Fax: (615)
986-0295

LOOKOUT MTN. TN

Scottish Inns $$
3210 Broad St., Lookout
Mtn., TN 37408, Res. (800)
251-1962 Ph: (423) 267-0414

MANCHESTER TN

Econo Lodge $-$$
Rt 8 Box 813, Manchester,
TN 37355, Res. (800)
424-4777 Ph: (615) 728-9530

Red Carpet Inn $$
I-24 & US Hwy 41,
Manchester, TN 37355, Res.
(800) 251-1962 Ph: (615)
728-9530 Fax: (615) 728-9539

Scottish Inns $$
2457 Hillsboro Blvd,
Manchester, TN 37355, Res.
(800) 251-1962 Ph: (615)
728-0506 Fax: (615) 728-0597

Super 8 Motel $-$$
2430 Hillsboro Blvd.,
Manchester, TN 37355, Res.
(800) 800-8000 Ph: (615)
728-9720 Fax: (615) 728-9720

MARTIN TN

Econo Lodge $-$$
853 University St., Martin,
TN 38237, Res. (800)
424-4777 Ph: (901) 587-4241
Fax: (901) 587-4649

MCMINNVILLE TN

Scottish Inns $
1105 Sparta Rd.,
McMinnville, TN 37110, Res.
(800) 251-1962 Ph: (615)
473-2181

MEMPHIS TN

Econo Lodge Airport $-$$
3456 Lamar Ave., Memphis,
TN 38118, Res. (800)
424-4777 Ph: (901) 365-7335

Motel 6 $
1321 Sycamore View Rd,
Memphis, TN 38134, Res.
(800) 466-8356 Ph: 901
382-8572 Fax: 901 385-0814

Motel 6 $
1117 E Brooks Rd, Memphis,
TN 38116, Res. (800)
466-8356 Ph: 901 346-0992
Fax: 901 396-3264

Super 8 Motel $-$$
6015 Macon Cove Road,
Memphis, TN 38134, Res.
(800) 800-8000 Ph: (901)
373-4888 Fax: (901) 373-4888

Super 8 Motel $-$$
1952 E. Shelby Dr.,
Memphis, TN 38116, Res.
(800) 800-8000 Ph: (901)
332-5777 Fax: (901) 332-5777

Villager $-$$
6790 Raleigh LaGrange Rd,
Memphis, TN 38134, Res.
(800) 328-7829 Ph: (901)
386-5500 Fax: (901) 752-4564

MILLINGTON TN

Econo Lodge Naval Support $$
8193 US 51 N., Millington, TN
38053, Res. (800) 424-4777
Ph: (901) 873-4400 Fax: (901)
873-4340

MONTEAGLE TI

Budget Host Country Inn $-$
I-24 Exit 134-po Box 188,
Monteagle, TN 37356, Res.
(800) 283-4678 Ph: (615)
924-2221

MORRISTOWN TI

Super 8 Motel $-$$
2430 E. Andrew Johnson
Hwy, Morristown, TN 37814
Res. (800) 800-8000 Ph: (615)
586-8880

MURFREESBORO TI

Motel 6 $
114 Chaffin Pl, Murfreesboro,
TN 37129, Res. (800)
466-8356 Ph: 615 890-8524
Fax: 615 896-2924

Scottish Inns $
2029 So. Church St.,
Murfreesboro, TN 37130,
Res. (800) 251-1962 Ph: (615)
896-3210 Fax: (615) 896-7936

NASHVILLE TI

Econo Lodge $-$$
2403 Brick Church Pike,
Nashville, TN 37207, Res.
(800) 424-4777 Ph: (615)
226-9805 Fax: (615) 227-2335

Econo Lodge Central $-$$
300 Interstate Dr., Nashville,
TN 37213, Res. (800)
424-4777 Ph: (615) 242-9621
Fax: (615) 255-1003

Econo Lodge North $-$$
110 Maplewood Ln.,
Nashville, TN 37207, Res.
(800) 424-4777 Ph: (615)
262-9193 Fax: (615) 228-8030

Econo Lodge Opryland Area $$
2460 Music Valley Dr.,
Nashville, TN 37214, Res.
(800) 424-4777 Ph: (615)
889-0090

Motel 6 $
420 Metroplex Dr, Nashville,
TN 37211, Res. (800)
466-8356 Ph: 615 833-8887
Fax: 615 831-2177

Motel 6 $
311 W Trinity Ln, Nashville,
TN 37207, Res. (800)
466-8356 Ph: 615 227-9696
Fax: 615 650-0935

Motel 6 $
95 Wallace Rd, Nashville, TN
37211, Res. (800) 466-8356
Ph: 615 333-9933 Fax: 615
832-7078

Scottish Inns $$
1501 Dickerson Rd.,
Nashville, TN 37207, Res.
(800) 251-1962 Ph: (615)
226-6940

Super 8 Motel $-$$
720 Royal Parkway, Nashville,
TN 37214, Res. (800)
800-8000 Ph: (615) 889-8887
Fax: (615) 889-8887

Super 8 Motel $-$$
412 Robertson Ave.,
Nashville, TN 37209, Res.
(800) 800-8000 Ph: (615)
356-0888 Fax: (615) 356-0888

Super 8 Motel $-$$
3320 Dickerson Pike,
Nashville, TN 37207, Res.
(800) 800-8000 Ph: (615)
226-1897 Fax: (615) 228-9068

Super 8 Motel $-$$
350 Harding Place, Nashville,
TN 37211, Res. (800)
800-8000 Ph: (615) 834-0620
Fax: (615) 781-2944

Villager $-$$
727 Briley Pkwy, Nashville,
TN 37217, Res. (800)
328-7829 Ph: (615) 367-9202
Fax: (615) 360-2488

OAK RIDGE   TN

Super 8 Motel $-$$
1590 Oak Ridge Turnpike,
Oak Ridge, TN 37830, Res.
(800) 800-8000 Ph: (615)
483-1200 Fax: (615) 482-9834

OOLTEWAH   TN

Super 8 Motel $-$$
5111 Hunter Road,
Ooltewah, TN 37363, Res.
(800) 800-8000 Ph: (615)
238-5951 Fax: (615) 238-5956

PARIS   TN

Super 8 Motel $-$$
1309 East Wood, Paris, TN
38242, Res. (800) 800-8000
Ph: (901) 644-7008

PIGEON FORGE   TN

Econo Lodge $-$$
2440 N. Parkway, Pigeon
Forge, TN 37868, Res. (800)
424-4777 Ph: (615) 428-1231
Fax: (615) 453-6879

Super 8 Motel $-$$
2613 Smoky Drive, Pigeon
Forge, TN 37863, Res. (800)
800-8000 Ph: (615) 429-4027
Fax: (615) 429-4472

Super 8 Motel $-$$
Emett Street, Pigeon Forge,
TN 37863, Res. (800)
800-8000

PORTLAND   TN

Budget Host Inn $-$$
5339 Long Rd, Portland, TN
37148, Res. (800) 283-4678
Ph: (615) 325-2005 Fax: (615)
325-7605

SEVIERVILLE   TN

Super 8 Motel $-$$
1400 Warfield Dunn Parkway,
Sevierville, TN 37876, Res.
(800) 800-8000 Ph: (615)
429-0887 Fax: (615) 429-3188

SWEETWATER   TN

Budget Host Inn $-$$
P.O. Box 587, Sweetwater,
TN 37874, Res. (800)
283-4678 Ph: (615) 337-9357
Fax: (615) 337-7436

Red Carpet Inn $
So. Main St., Sweetwater, TN
37874, Res. (800) 251-1962
Ph: (423) 337-3585

UNION CITY   TN

Super 8 Motel $-$$
1400 Vaden Avenue, Union
City, TN 38261, Res. (800)
800-8000 Ph: (901) 885-4444
Fax: (901) 885-4444

WHITES CREEK   TN

Super 8 Motel $-$$
7551 Old Hickory Blvd.,
Whites Creek, TN 37189,
Res. (800) 800-8000 Ph: (615)
876-3971 Fax: (615) 876-6710

TEXAS

ABILENE   TX

Econo Lodge $-$$
1633 W. Stamford, Abilene,
TX 79601, Res. (800)
424-4777 Ph: (915) 673-5424
Fax: (915) 673-0412

Motel 6 $
4951 W Stamford St, Abilene,
TX 79603, Res. (800)
466-8356 Ph: 915 672-8462
Fax: 915 672-3118

Super 8 Motel $-$$
I 20 and Hwy 351, Abilene,
TX 79601, Res. (800)
800-8000 Ph: (915) 673-5251
Fax: (915) 673-5314

AMARILLO   TX

Budget Host La Paloma Inn$-$$
2915 I-40 E, Amarillo, TX
79104, Res. (800) 283-4678
Ph: (806) 372-8101

Econo Lodge $-$$
I-40 & Lakeside Dr., Amarillo,
TX 79120, Res. (800)
424-4777 Ph: (806) 335-1561
Fax: (806) 335-1808

Motel 6 $
4301 I-40 E, Amarillo, TX
79104, Res. (800) 466-8356
Ph: 806 373-3045 Fax: 806
373-0546

Motel 6 $
2032 Paramount Blvd,
Amarillo, TX 79109, Res.
(800) 466-8356 Ph: 806
355-6554 Fax: 806 355-5317

Motel 6 $
3930 I-40 E, Amarillo, TX
79103, Res. (800) 466-8356
Ph: 806 374-6444 Fax: 806
371-0475

Motel 6 $
6030 I-40 W, Amarillo, TX
79106, Res. (800) 466-8356
Ph: 806 359-7651 Fax: 806
359-0236

Super 8 Motel $-$$
R.R. 2 - BOX 1045, Amarillo,
TX 79101, Res. (800)
800-8000 Ph: (806) 335-2836

ANTHONY   TX

Super 8 Motel $-$$
"100 N. Park Dr.,", Anthony,
TX 79821, Res. (800)
800-8000 Ph: (915) 886-2888
Fax: (915) 581-5056

ARLINGTON   TX

Motel 6 $
2626 E Randol Mill Rd,
Arlington, TX 76011, Res.
(800) 466-8356 Ph: 817
649-0147 Fax: 817 649-7130

AUSTIN   TX

Motel 6 $
5330 N Interregional Hwy,
Austin, TX 78751, Res. (800)
466-8356 Ph: 512 467-9111
Fax: 512 206-0573

Motel 6 $
8010 N Interstate 35, Austin,
TX 78753, Res. (800)
466-8356 Ph: 512 837-9890
Fax: 512 339-3045

Motel 6 $
9420 N Interstate 35, Austin,
TX 78753, Res. (800)
466-8356 Ph: 512 339-6161
Fax: 512 339-7852

Motel 6 $
2707 Interregional Hwy S,
Austin, TX 78741, Res. (800)
466-8356 Ph: 512 444-5882
Fax: 512 442-3759

Super 8 Motel $-$$
6000 Middle Fiskville Road,
Austin, TX 78752, Res. (800)
800-8000 Ph: (512) 467-8163
Fax: (512) 467-7644

BAY CITY   TX

Econo Lodge $-$$
3712 7th St., Bay City, TX
77414, Res. (800) 424-4777
Ph: (409) 245-5115 Fax: (409)
245-2173

BAYTOWN   TX

Motel 6 $
8911 Hwy 146, Baytown, TX
77520, Res. (800) 466-8356
Ph: 281 576-5777 Fax: 713
576-2351

M
O
T
E
L

BEAUMONT   TX

Econo Lodge $-$$
1155 I-10 S., Beaumont, TX
77701, Res. (800) 424-4777
Ph: (409) 835-5913 Fax: (409)
835-5913

Scottish Inns $$
2640 I-10 East, Beaumont,
TX 77703, Res. (800)
251-1962 Ph: (409) 895-0228
Fax: (409) 899-3152

Super 8 Motel $-$$
2850 I-10 East, Beaumont,
TX 77703, Res. (800)
800-8000 Ph: (409) 899-3040
Fax: (409) 899-3040

BELLMEAD   TX

Motel 6 $
1509 Hogan Ln, Bellmead,
TX 76705, Res. (800)
466-8356 Ph: 254 799-4957
Fax: 254 799-6183

BELTON   TX

Budget Host Inn $-$$
1520 S I-35, Belton, TX
76513, Res. (800) 283-4678
Ph: (817) 939-0744

BIG SPRING   TX

Econo Lodge $-$$
804 I-20 W., Big Spring, TX
79720, Res. (800) 424-4777
Ph: (915) 263-5200 Fax: (915)
263-5457

Motel 6 $
600 W I-20 Rt 2, Big Spring,
TX 79720, Res. (800)
466-8356 Ph: 915 267-1695
Fax: 915 267-4048

BROWNSVILLE   TX

Motel 6 $
2255 N Expwy, Brownsville,
TX 78520, Res. (800)
466-8356 Ph: 210 546-4699
Fax: 210 546-8982

CANTON   TX

Super 8 Motel $-$$
"Rt. 2, Box 8-A", Canton, TX
75103, Res. (800) 800-8000
Ph: (903) 567-6567

CHANNELVIEW   TX

Econo Lodge $-$$
17011 I-10 E., Channelview,
TX 77530, Res. (800)
424-4777 Ph: (713) 457-2966
Fax: (713) 457-6634

Super 8 Motel $-$$
15615 I-10 East,
Channelview, TX 77530,
Res. (800) 800-8000 Ph: (713)
452-0719

CHILDRESS   TX

Econo Lodge $-$$
1612 F N.W., US 287,
Childress, TX 79201, Res.
(800) 424-4777 Ph: (817)
937-3695 Fax: (817) 937-6956

CLEBURNE   TX

Budget Host Inn $-$$
2107 N Main, Cleburne, TX
76031, Res. (800) 283-4678
Ph: (817) 556-3631

CLUTE   TX

Motel 6 $
1000 SR 332, Clute, TX
77531, Res. (800) 466-8356
Ph: 409 265-4764 Fax: 409
265-4758

COLLEGE STATION   TX

Motel 6 $
2327 Texas Ave South,
College Station, TX 77840,
Res. (800) 466-8356 Ph: 409
696-3379 Fax: 409 693-6378

Super 8 Motel $-$$
301 Texas Avenue, College
Station, TX 77810, Res.
(800) 800-8000 Ph: (409)
846-8800

CONROE   TX

Motel 6 $
820 I-45 S, Conroe, TX
77304, Res. (800) 466-8356
Ph: 409 760-4003 Fax: 409
760-3159

CORPUS CHRISTI   TX

Motel 6 $
8202 S Padre Island Dr,
Corpus Christi, TX 78412,
Res. (800) 466-8356 Ph: 512
991-8858 Fax: 512 991-1698

Motel 6 $
845 Lantana St, Corpus
Christi, TX 78408, Res. (800)
466-8356 Ph: 512 289-9397
Fax: 512 289-0280

CORSICANA   TX

Econo Lodge $-$$
2021 Regal Dr., Corsicana,
TX 75110, Res. (800)
424-4777 Ph: (903) 874-4751
Fax: (903) 872-5990

Super 8 Motel $-$$
2021 Regal Dr., Corsicana,
TX 75110, Res. (800)
800-8000 Ph: (903) 874-4751
Fax: (903) 872-5990

DALHART   TX

Econo Lodge $-$$
123 Liberal St., Dalhart, TX
79022, Res. (800) 424-4777
Ph: (806) 249-6464

Super 8 Motel $-$$
East Highway 54, Dalhart,
TX 79022, Res. (800)
800-8000 Ph: (806) 249-8526
Fax: (806) 249-5119

DALLAS   TX

Econo Lodge Airport I-35 $-$$
2275 Valley View Lane,
Dallas, TX 75234, Res. (800)
424-4777 Ph: (214) 243-5500
Fax: (214) 243-8738

Motel 6 $
4325 Beltline Rd, Dallas, TX
75244, Res. (800) 466-8356
Ph: 972 386-4577 Fax: 972
386-4579

Motel 6 $
2660 Forest Ln, Dallas, TX
75234, Res. (800) 466-8356
Ph: 972 484-9111 Fax: 972
484-0214

Motel 6 $
2753 Forest Ln, Dallas, TX
75234, Res. (800) 466-8356
Ph: 972 620-2828 Fax: 972
620-9061

Motel 6 $
4220 Independence Dr,
Dallas, TX 75237, Res. (800)
466-8356 Ph: 972 296-3331
Fax: 972 709-9438

DEL RIO   TX

Motel 6 $
2115 Ave iFi, Del Rio, TX
78840, Res. (800) 466-8356
Ph: 210 774-2115 Fax: 210
774-4878

DENTON   TX

Motel 6 $
4125 Interstate 35 N,
Denton, TX 76207, Res.
(800) 466-8356 Ph: 940
566-4798 Fax: 940 591-0981

DUMAS   TX

Econo Lodge $-$$
1719 S. Dumas Ave.,
Dumas, TX 79029, Res.
(800) 424-4777 Ph: (806)
935-9098 Fax: (806) 935-7483

Super 8 Motel $-$$
119 W. 17th Street, Dumas,
TX 79029, Res. (800)
800-8000 Ph: (806) 935-6222

DUNCANVILLE   TX

Motel 6 $
202 Jellison Rd, Duncanville,
TX 75116, Res. (800)
466-8356 Ph: 972 296-0345
Fax: 972 296-7325

EASTLAND   TX

Econo Lodge $-$$
2001 I-20 W., Eastland, TX
76448, Res. (800) 424-4777
Ph: (817) 629-3324 Fax: (817)
629-8601

Super 8 Motel $-$$
3900 I-20 E., Eastland, TX
76448, Res. (800) 800-8000
Ph: (817) 629-3336

EL PASO   TX

Econo Lodge Ft. Bliss $-$$
6363 Montana Ave., El Paso,
TX 79925, Res. (800)
424-4777 Ph: (915) 778-3311
Fax: (915) 778-1097

Motel 6 $
4800 Gateway Blvd E, El Paso, TX 79905, Res. (800) 466-8356 Ph: 915 533-7521 Fax: 915 544-4904

Motel 6 $
11049 Gateway Blvd W, El Paso, TX 79935, Res. (800) 466-8356 Ph: 915 594-8533 Fax: 915 592-6603

Motel 6 $
1330 Lomaland Dr, El Paso, TX 79935, Res. (800) 466-8356 Ph: 915 592-6386 Fax: 915 592-4416

Motel 6 $
7840 N Mesa St, El Paso, TX 79932, Res. (800) 466-8356 Ph: 915 584-2129 Fax: 915 584-1643

EULESS TX

Motel 6 $
110 W Airport Frwy, Euless, TX 76039, Res. (800) 466-8356 Ph: 817 545-0141 Fax: 817 868-0584

FORT STOCKTON TX

Econo Lodge $-$$
800 E. Dickenson, Fort Stockton, TX 79735, Res. (800) 424-4777 Ph: (915) 336-9711 Fax: (915) 336-5815

FORT WORTH TX

Villager $-$$
3800 US Hwy 377 South, Fort Worth, TX 76116, Res. (800) 328-7829 Ph: (817) 560-2831 Fax: (000) 000-0000

FREDERICKSBURG TX

Budget Host Deluxe Motel $-$$
901 E Main, Fredericksburg, TX 78624, Res. (800) 283-4678 Ph: (210) 997-3344 Fax: (210) 997-4381

Econo Lodge $-$$
810 S. Adams, Fredericksburg, TX 78624, Res. (800) 424-4777 Ph: (210) 997-3437

FT. STOCKTON TX

Motel 6 $
3001 W Dickinson Blvd, Ft. Stockton, TX 79735, Res. (800) 466-8356 Ph: 915 336-9737 Fax: 915 336-8346

FT. WORTH TX

Motel 6 $
1236 Oakland Blvd, Ft. Worth, TX 76103, Res. (800) 466-8356 Ph: 817 834-7361 Fax: 817 834-1573

Motel 6 $
3271 Interstate 35 W, Ft. Worth, TX 76106, Res. (800) 466-8356 Ph: 817 625-4359 Fax: 817 625-8256

Motel 6 $
6600 S Frwy, Ft. Worth, TX 76134, Res. (800) 466-8356 Ph: 817 293-8595 Fax: 817 293-8577

Motel 6 $
4433 S Frwy, Ft. Worth, TX 76115, Res. (800) 466-8356 Ph: 817 921-4900 Fax: 817 921-2702

Motel 6 $
8701 Interstate 30 W, Ft. Worth, TX 76116, Res. (800) 466-8356 Ph: 817 244-9740 Fax: 817 244-1697

Super 8 Motel $-$$
7960 I-30 West, Ft. Worth, TX 76108, Res. (800) 800-8000 Ph: (817) 246-7168

GAINESVILLE TX

Budget Host Inn $-$$
N. I-35 Frontage Road Exit 499, Gainesville, TX 76240, Res. (800) 283-4678 Ph: (817) 665-2856

GALVESTON TX

Econo Lodge $-$$
2825 61st St., Galveston, TX 77551, Res. (800) 424-4777 Ph: (409) 744-7133 Fax: (409) 744-7133

Motel 6 $
7404 Ave J Broadway, Galveston, TX 77554, Res. (800) 466-8356 Ph: 409 740-3794 Fax: 409 740-4670

GARLAND TX

Motel 6 $
436 W I-30 and Beltline Rd, Garland, TX 75043, Res. (800) 466-8356 Ph: 972 226-7140 Fax: 972 226-2416

GIDDINGS TX

Econo Lodge $-$$
US 290 E., Giddings, TX 78942, Res. (800) 424-4777 Ph: (409) 542-9666 Fax: (409) 542-1245

GRAND PRAIRIE TX

Motel 6 $
406 E Safari Blvd, Grand Prairie, TX 75050, Res. (800) 466-8356 Ph: 972 642-9424 Fax: 972 262-3482

GREENVILLE TX

Motel 6 $
5109 Interstate 30, Greenville, TX 75401, Res. (800) 466-8356 Ph: 903 455-0515 Fax: 903 455-8314

GROOM TX

Budget Host Chalet Inn $-$$
I-408 & PM 2300, Groom, TX 79039, Ph: (806) 248-7524

GROVES TX

Motel 6 $
5201 E Pkwy<EL>Groves, TX, Groves, TX 77619, Res. (800) 466-8356 Ph: 409 962-6611 Fax: 409 962-8439

HARLINGEN TX

Motel 6 $
224 S US Expwy 77, Harlingen, TX 78550, Res. (800) 466-8356 Ph: 210 421-4200 Fax: 210 412-8159

Super 8 Motel $-$$
1115 S. Expressway 77/83, Harlingen, TX 78550, Res. (800) 800-8000 Ph: (210) 412-8873

HOUSTON TX

Econo Lodge Airport $-$$
7755 Airport Blvd., Houston, TX 77061, Res. (800) 424-4777 Ph: (713) 649-1123 Fax: (713) 644-1117

Econo Lodge Medical Center $-$$
7905 S. Main St., Houston, TX 77025, Res. (800) 424-4777 Ph: (713) 667-8200 Fax: (713) 665-6679

Econo Lodge West $-$$
9535 Katy Fwy., Houston, TX 77024, Res. (800) 424-4777 Ph: (713) 467-4411 Fax: (713) 467-3647

Motel 6 $
3223 S Loop W, Houston, TX 77025, Res. (800) 466-8356 Ph: 713 664-6425 Fax: 713 666-8514

Motel 6 $
16884 NW Frwy, Houston, TX 77040, Res. (800) 466-8356 Ph: 713 937-7056 Fax: 713 849-5240

Motel 6 $
5555 W 34th St, Houston, TX 77092, Res. (800) 466-8356 Ph: 713 682-8588 Fax: 713 681-8592

Motel 6 $
8800 Airport Blvd, Houston, TX 77061, Res. (800) 466-8356 Ph: 713 941-0990 Fax: 713 944-5147

Motel 6 $
9638 Plainfield Rd, Houston, TX 77036-8094, Res. (800) 466-8356 Ph: 713 778-0008 Fax: 713 771-2248

Motel 6 $
14833 Katy Frwy, Houston, TX 77094, Res. (800) 466-8356 Ph: 281 497-5000 Fax: 281 497-1472

M
O
T
E
L

Motel 6 $
2900 W Sam Houston
Prkway, Houston, TX
77042, Res. (800) 466-8356
Ph: 281 290-9188 Fax: 281
290-4470

Red Carpet Inn $$
6161 Gulf Freeway, Houston,
TX 77023, Res. (800)
251-1962 Ph: (713) 928-2871
Fax: (713) 928-3050

Red Carpet Inn $$
6868 Hornwood Dr.,
Houston, TX 77074, Res.
(800) 251-1962 Ph: (713)
981-8686

Scottish Inns $$
424 E. Tidwell Rd., Houston,
TX 77022, Res. (800)
251-1962 Ph: (713) 692-7300
Fax: :(713) 692-0126

Super 8 Motel $-$$
4020 SW Freeway, Houston,
TX 77027, Res. (800)
800-8000 Ph: (713) 623-4720
Fax: (713) 963-8526

Super 8 Motel $-$$
10015 S. Main, Houston, TX
77025, Res. (800) 800-8000
Ph: (713) 667-9173

Villager $-$$
4640 S. Main, Houston, TX
77002, Res. (800) 328-7829
Ph: (713) 523-3777 Fax: (713)
523-7501

Villager $-$$
7755 Airport Blvd., Houston,
TX 77061, Res. (800)
328-7829 Ph: (713) 649-1123
Fax: (713) 644-1117

HUNTSVILLE   TX

Econo Lodge $-$$
1501 I-45 N., Huntsville, TX
77340, Res. (800) 424-4777
Ph: (409) 295-6401 Fax: (409)
291-6007

Motel 6 $
1607 I-45, Huntsville, TX
77340, Res. (800) 466-8356
Ph: 409 291-6927 Fax: 409
291-8963

IRVING   TX

Motel 6 $
7800 Heathrow Dr, Irving,
TX 75063, Res. (800)
466-8356 Ph: 972 915-3993
Fax: 972 915-6843

Motel 6 $
510 S Loop 12, Irving, TX
75060, Res. (800) 466-8356
Ph: 972 438-4227 Fax: 972
554-0048

Super 8 Motel $-$$
4245 W. Airport Freeway,
Irving, TX 75014, Res. (800)
800-8000 Ph: (214) 257-1810

KATY   TX

Super 8 Motel $-$$
I-10 & Promenade, Katy, TX
77450, Res. (800) 800-8000
Ph: (713) 395-5757

KILLEEN   TX

Econo Lodge $-$$
606 E. Central Tx Expwy.,
Killeen, TX 76542, Res. (800)
424-4777 Ph: (817) 634-6868

Super 8 Motel $-$$
606 E. Central Texas Expy.,
Killeen, TX 76543, Res. (800)
800-8000 Ph: (817) 634-6868
Fax: (817) 634-6868

KINGSVILLE   TX

Econo Lodge $-$$
2502 E. Kennedy, Kingsville,
TX 78363, Res. (800)
424-4777 Ph: (512) 592-5251
Fax: (512) 592-6197

Motel 6 $
101 N US 77, Kingsville, TX
78363, Res. (800) 466-8356
Ph: 512 592-5106 Fax: 512
592-6947

LAREDO   TX

Motel 6 $
5920 San Bernardo Ave,
Laredo, TX 78041, Res. (800)
466-8356 Ph: 210 722-8133
Fax: 210 725-8212

Motel 6 $
5310 San Bernardo Ave,
Laredo, TX 78041, Res. (800)
466-8356 Ph: 210 725-8187
Fax: 210 725-0424

LEWISVILLE   TX

Motel 6 $
1705 Lakepointe Dr,
Lewisville, TX 75057, Res.
(800) 466-8356 Ph: 972
436-5008 Fax: 972 436-4862

LIVINGSTON   TX

Econo Lodge $-$$
117 US 59 Loop S.,
Livingston, TX 77351, Res.
(800) 424-4777 Ph: (409)
327-2451 Fax: (409) 327-2451

LONGVIEW   TX

Econo Lodge $-$$
3120 Estes Pkwy., Longview,
TX 75602, Res. (800)
424-4777 Ph: (903) 753-4884
Fax: (903) 753-8242

Motel 6 $
110 S Access Rd, Longview,
TX 75603, Res. (800)
466-8356 Ph: 903 758-5256
Fax: 903 758-6940

Super 8 Motel $-$$
3304 S. Eastman Rd.,
Longview, TX 75602, Res.
(800) 800-8000 Ph: (903)
758-0711

LUBBOCK   TX

Motel 6 $
909 66th St, Lubbock, TX
79412, Res. (800) 466-8356
Ph: 806 745-5541 Fax: 806
748-0889

Super 8 Motel $-$$
501 Avenue Q, Lubbock, TX
79401, Res. (800) 800-8000
Ph: (806) 762-8726

Super 8 Motel $-$$
5410 I-27, Lubbock, TX
79452, Res. (800) 800-8000
Ph: (806) 762-8400

LUFKIN   TX

Motel 6 $
1110 S Timberland Dr,
Lufkin, TX 75901, Res. (800)
466-8356 Ph: 409 637-7850
Fax: 409 637-7649

MARSHALL   TX

Motel 6 $
300 I-20 E, Marshall, TX
75670, Res. (800) 466-8356
Ph: 903 935-4393 Fax: 903
935-2380

MCALLEN   TX

Motel 6 $
700 W Expwy 83, Mcallen, TX
78501, Res. (800) 466-8356
Ph: 210 687-3700 Fax: 210
630-3180

Red Carpet Inn $$
US 83 @ Bus 83 & Jackson
Rd., McAllen, TX 78505,
Res. (800) 251-1962 Ph: (210)
787-5921 Fax: (210) 787-4250

MESQUITE   TX

Motel 6 $
3629 US Hwy 80, Mesquite,
TX 75150, Res. (800)
466-8356 Ph: 972 613-1662
Fax: 972 613-1248

MIDLAND   TX

Motel 6 $
1000 S Midkiff Rd, Midland,
TX 79701, Res. (800)
466-8356 Ph: 915 697-3197
Fax: 915 697-7631

Super 8 Motel $-$$
1000 West I-20, Midland, TX
79701, Res. (800) 800-8000
Ph: (915) 684-8888 Fax: (915)
686-0033

MINERAL WELLS   TX

Budget Host Mesa Motel $-$$
3601 E. Highway 180, Mineral
Wells, TX 76067, Ph: (817)
325-3377 Fax: (817) 325-3377

MT. VERNON   TX

Super 8 Motel $-$$
I-30 & Hwy 37, Mt. Vernon,
TX 75457, Res. (800)
800-8000 Fax: (903) 652-2433

N RICHLAND HILLS   TX

Motel 6 $
7804 Bedford Euless Rd, N
Richland Hills, TX 76180,
Res. (800) 466-8356 Ph: 817
485-3000 Fax: 817 485-8936

NACOGDOCHES   TX

Econo Lodge $-$$
2020 N.W. Loop 224,
Nacogdoches, TX 75961,
Res. (800) 424-4777 Ph: (409)
569-0880 Fax: (409) 560-0303

NEW BRAUFELS   TX

Budget Host Country Inn $-$$
210 Hwy. 180 E., New
Braufels, TX 78130, Ph: (210)
625-7373 Fax: (210) 629-2713

ODESSA   TX

Econo Lodge $-$$
1518 S. Grant, Odessa, TX
79761, Res. (800) 424-4777
Ph: (915) 333-1486

Motel 6 $
200 E I-20 Service Rd,
Odessa, TX 79766, Res.
(800) 466-8356 Ph: 915
333-4025 Fax: 915 333-2668

Super 8 Motel $-$$
6713 East Highway 80,
Odessa, TX 79761, Res.
(800) 800-8000 Ph: (915)
363-8281

ORANGE   TX

Motel 6 $
4407 27th St, Orange, TX
77632, Res. (800) 466-8356
Ph: 409 883-4891 Fax: 409
886-5211

PASADENA   TX

Econo Lodge $-$$
823 Pasadena Fwy.,
Pasadena, TX 77504, Res.
(800) 424-4777 Ph: (713)
747-0438

PECOS   TX

Motel 6 $
3002 S Cedar St, Pecos, TX
79772, Res. (800) 466-8356
Ph: 915 445-9034 Fax: 915
445-2005

PLANO   TX

Motel 6 $
2550 N Central Expwy, Plano,
TX 75074, Res. (800)
466-8356 Ph: 972 578-1626
Fax: 972 423-6994

Super 8 Motel $-$$
1704 North Central
Expressway, Plano, TX
75074, Res. (800) 800-8000
Ph: (214) 423-8300

ROBSTOWN   TX

Econo Lodge $-$$
2225 US 77 N., Robstown, TX
78380, Res. (800) 424-4777
Ph: (512) 387-9444 Fax: (517)
387-8869

SAN ANGELO   TX

Motel 6 $
311 N Bryant, San Angelo,
TX 76903, Res. (800)
466-8356 Ph: 915 658-8061
Fax: 915 653-3102

SAN ANTONIO   TX

Econo Lodge East $-$$
218 S. W.w. White Rd., San
Antonio, TX 78219, Res.
(800) 424-4777 Ph: (210)
333-3346 Fax: (210) 333-7564

Econo Lodge West $-$$
6735 US 90 W., San Antonio,
TX 78227, Res. (800)
424-4777 Ph: (210) 674-5711
Fax: (210) 674-5192

Motel 6 $
211 N Pecos St, San Antonio,
TX 78207, Res. (800)
466-8356 Ph: 210 225-1111
Fax: 210 222-1134

Motel 6 $
138 N WW White Rd, San
Antonio, TX 78219, Res.
(800) 466-8356 Ph: 210
333-1850 Fax: 210 333-1408

Motel 6 $
16500 IH-10 W, San Antonio,
TX 78257, Res. (800)
466-8356 Ph: 210 697-0731
Fax: 210 697-0383

Motel 6 $
4621 E Rittiman Rd, San
Antonio, TX 78218, Res.
(800) 466-8356 Ph: 210
653-8088 Fax: 210 653-9690

Motel 6 $
5522 N Pan Am Expwy, San
Antonio, TX 78218, Res.
(800) 466-8356 Ph: 210
661-8791 Fax: 210 666-5502

Motel 6 $
9503 Interstate Hwy 35 N,
San Antonio, TX 78233,
Res. (800) 466-8356 Ph: 210
650-4419 Fax: 210 650-0118

Motel 6 $
9400 Wurzbach Rd, San
Antonio, TX 78240, Res.
(800) 466-8356 Ph: 210
593-0013 Fax: 210 593-0268

Motel 6 $
2185 SW Loop 410, San
Antonio, TX 78227, Res.
(800) 466-8356 Ph: 210
673-9020 Fax: 210 673-1546

Super 8 Motel $-$$
11027 I-35 North, San
Antonio, TX 78233, Res.
(800) 800-8000 Ph: (210)
637-1033

Super 8 Motel $-$$
5336 Wurzbach Rd., San
Antonio, TX 78265, Res.
(800) 800-8000 Ph: (210)
520-0888 Fax: (210) 520-8852

Super 8 Motel $-$$
5319 Casa Bella, San
Antonio, TX 78249, Res.
(800) 800-8000 Ph: (210)
696-6916 Fax: (605) 225-3245

Super 8 Motel $-$$
3617 N. Pan Am Expwy, San
Antonio, TX 78219, Res.
(800) 800-8000 Ph: (210)
227-8888 Fax: (210) 224-2092

Villager $-$$
3911 I-35 North, San
Antonio, TX 78219, Res.
(800) 328-7829 Ph: (210)
224-4944 Fax: (210) 299-1969

SAN BENITO   TX

Budget Host Motel $-$$
2053 W Hwy 77 Busi, San
Benito, TX 78586, Res. (800)
283-4678 Ph: (210) 399-6148

SAN MARCOS   TX

Econo Lodge Marcos $-$$
811 S. Guadalupe St., San
Marcos, TX 78666, Res. (800)
424-4777 Ph: (512) 353-5300
Fax: (000) 512-5310

Motel 6 $
1321 I-35 N, San Marcos, TX
78666, Res. (800) 466-8356
Ph: 512 396-8705 Fax: 512
396-7162

SAN MARCUS   TX

Super 8 Motel $-$$
1429 I-35, San Marcus, TX
78666, Res. (800) 800-8000
Ph: (512) 396-0400

SEGUIN   TX

Econo Lodge $-$$
3013 N. SR 123 Bypass,
Seguin, TX 78155, Res. (800)
424-4777 Ph: (210) 372-3990
Fax: (210) 372-5382

SHAMROCK   TX

Econo Lodge $-$$
1006 E. 12th St., Shamrock,
TX 79079, Res. (800)
424-4777 Ph: (806) 256-2111

SHERMAN   TX

Super 8 Motel $-$$
111 East Highway 1417,
Sherman, TX 75090, Res.
(800) 800-8000 Ph: (903)
868-9325

SOUTH PADRE ISLAND   TX

Motel 6 $
4013 Padre Blvd, South Padre
Island, TX 78597, Res. (800)
466-8356 Ph: 210 761-7911
Fax: 210 761-6339

MOTEL

SPRING TX	**VAN HORN** TX	**UTAH**

Motel 6 $
19606 Cypresswood Ct,
Spring, TX 77388, Res. (800)
466-8356 Ph: 281 350-6400
Fax: 281 353-6927

STEPHENVILLE TX

Budget Host Texan Inn $-$$
P.O. Box 422, Stephenville,
TX 76401, Res. (800)
283-4678 Ph: (817) 968-5003
Fax: (817) 968-5060

SWEETWATER TX

Motel 6 $
510 NW Georgia, Sweetwater,
TX 79556, Res. (800)
466-8356 Ph: 915 235-4387
Fax: 915 235-8725

TEMPLE TX

Econo Lodge $-$$
1001 N. General Bruce Dr.,
Temple, TX 76504, Res. (800)
424-4777 Ph: (817) 771-1688
Fax: (817) 771-2283

Motel 6 $
1100 N General Bruce Dr,
Temple, TX 76504, Res. (800)
466-8356 Ph: 254 778-0272
Fax: 254 778-1839

Super 8 Motel $-$$
5505 S. General Bruce Dr.,
Temple, TX 76502, Res. (800)
800-8000 Ph: (817) 778-0962
Fax: (817) 778-1527

TEXARKANA TX

Econo Lodge $-$$
4505 N. Stateline Ave.,
Texarkana, TX 75501, Res.
(800) 424-4777 Ph: (903)
793-5546

Motel 6 $
1924 Hampton Rd,
Texarkana, TX 75503, Res.
(800) 466-8356 Ph: 903
793-1413 Fax: 903 793-5831

Motel 6 $
1924 Hampton Rd,
Texarkana, TX 75503, Res.
(800) 466-8356 Ph: 903
793-1413 Fax: 903 793-5831

TYLER TX

Econo Lodge $-$$
3209 W. Gentry Pkwy., Tyler,
TX 75702, Res. (800)
424-4777 Ph: (903) 593-0103
Fax: (903) 593-3184

Motel 6 $
3236 Brady Gentry Pkwy,
Tyler, TX 75702, Res. (800)
466-8356 Ph: 903 595-6691
Fax: 903 595-5367

Super 8 Motel $-$$
2616 N. Northwest Loop 323,
Tyler, TX 77502, Res. (800)
800-8000 Ph: (903) 593-8361
Fax: (903) 593-8756

Motel 6 $
1805 North Broadway, Van
Horn, TX 79855, Res. (800)
466-8356 Ph: 915 283-2992
Fax: 915 283-2111

Super 8 Motel $-$$
Golf Course Drive & I-10,
P.O. Box 9, Van Horn, TX
79855, Res. (800) 800-8000
Ph: (915) 283-2282

VERNON TX

Econo Lodge $-$$
4100 SR. 287 N.W., Vernon,
TX 76384, Res. (800)
424-4777 Ph: (817) 553-3384
Fax: (817) 553-3112

Super 8 Motel $-$$
"1829 Expressway, Highway
287", Vernon, TX 76384,
Res. (800) 800-8000 Ph: (817)
552-9321 Fax: (817) 552-9321

VICTORIA TX

Motel 6 $
3716 Houston Hwy, Victoria,
TX 77901, Res. (800)
466-8356 Ph: 512 573-1273
Fax: 512 573-1831

WACO TX

Motel 6 $
3120 Jack Kultgen Fwy,
Waco, TX 76706, Res. (800)
466-8356 Ph: 254 662-4622
Fax: 254 662-6407

Super 8 Motel $-$$
1320 S. Jack Kultgen Fwy,
Waco, TX 76706, Res. (800)
800-8000 Ph: (817) 754-1023
Fax: (817) 754-0127

WEATHERFORD TX

Super 8 Motel $-$$
111 W. I-20, Weatherford, TX
76087, Res. (800) 800-8000
Ph: (817) 594-8702 Fax: (817)
596-9766

WEBSTER TX

Motel 6 $
1001 W NASA Rd 1, Webster,
TX 77598, Res. (800)
466-8356 Ph: 281 332-4581
Fax: 281 332-0341

Super 8 Motel $-$$
Nasa Rd. # 1 & Kings Row Dr.,
Webster, TX 77598, Res.
(800) 800-8000 Fax: (903)
757-7031

WICHITA FALLS TX

Econo Lodge $-$$
1700 Fifth St., Wichita Falls,
TX 76301, Res. (800)
424-4777 Ph: (817) 761-1889

Motel 6 $
1812 Maurine St, Wichita
Falls, TX 76304, Res. (800)
466-8356 Ph: 940 322-8817
Fax: 940 322-5944

CEDAR CITY UT

Motel 6 $
1620 West 200 North, Cedar
City, UT 84720, Res. (800)
466-8356 Ph: 801 586-9200

Super 8 Motel $-$$
145 North 1550 West, Cedar
City, UT 84720, Res. (800)
800-8000 Ph: (801) 586-8880
Fax: (801) 586-8880

CLEARFIELD UT

Super 8 Motel $-$$
572 N. Main St., Clearfield,
UT 84015, Res. (800)
800-8000 Ph: (801) 825-8000

GREEN RIVER UT

Budget Host Book Cliff Lodge
P.O. Box 545, Green River,
UT 84525, Res. (800)
283-4678 Ph: (801) 564-3406
Fax: (801) 564-8359

Motel 6 $
946 E Main, Green River, UT
84525, Res. (800) 466-8356
Ph: 801 564-3436 Fax: 801
564-8272

Super 8 Motel $-$$
1248 East Main, Green River,
UT 84525, Res. (800)
800-8000 Ph: (801) 564-8888

HURRICANE UT

Motel 6 $
650 West State, Hurricane,
UT 84737, Res. (800)
466-8356 Ph: 801 635-4010
Fax: 801 635-4025

Super 8 Motel $-$$
700 West State Street,
Hurricane, UT 84737, Res.
(800) 800-8000 Ph: (801)
635-0808 Fax: (801) 635-0909

KANAB UT

Super 8 Motel $-$$
70 S. 200 West, Kanab, UT
84741, Res. (800) 800-8000
Ph: (801) 644-5500 Fax: (801)
644-5576

LOGAN UT

Super 8 Motel $-$$
865 Highway 89/91 South,
Logan, UT 84321, Res. (800)
800-8000 Ph: (801) 753-8883
Fax: (801) 753-2577

MIDVALE UT

Motel 6 $
496 N Catalpa St, Midvale,
UT 84047, Res. (800)
466-8356 Ph: 801 561-0058
Fax: 801 561-5753

MOAB   UT

Super 8 Motel $-$$
889 North Main Street, Moab,
UT 84532, Res. (800)
800-8000 Ph: (801) 259-8868
Fax: (801) 259-8968

NEPHI   UT

Motel 6 $
2195 South Main St, Nephi,
UT 84648, Res. (800)
466-8356 Ph: 801 623-0666

Super 8 Motel $-$$
1901 South Main, Nephi, UT
84648, Res. (800) 800-8000
Ph: (801) 623-0888

OGDEN   UT

Motel 6 $
1455 Washington Blvd,
Ogden, UT 84404, Res. (800)
466-8356 Ph: 801 627-4560
Fax: 801 392-1878

Motel 6 $
1500 W Riverdale Rd, Ogden,
UT 84405, Res. (800)
466-8356 Ph: 801 627-2880
Fax: 801 392-1713

Super 8 Motel $-$$
1508 West 2100 South,
Ogden, UT 84401-0214, Res.
(800) 800-8000 Ph: (801)
731-7100 Fax: (801) 731-2627

PRICE   UT

Budget Host Inn $-$$
145 N Carbonville Rd, Price,
UT 84501, Res. (800)
283-4678 Ph: (801) 637-2424
Fax: (801) 637-4551

PROVO   UT

Motel 6 $
1600 S University Ave, Provo,
UT 84601, Res. (800)
466-8356 Ph: 801 375-5064
Fax: 801 374-0266

Super 8 Motel $-$$
1288 S. University, Provo, UT
84601, Res. (800) 800-8000
Ph: (801) 375-8766 Fax: (801)
377-7569

RICHFIELD   UT

Budget Host Knights Inn $-$$
69 South Main Street,
Richfield, UT 84701, Res.
(800) 283-4678 Ph: (801)
896-8228 Fax: (801) 896-8228

Super 8 Motel $-$$
1575 N. Main St, Richfield,
UT 84701, Res. (800)
800-8000 Ph: (801) 896-9204

SALINA   UT

Budget Host Scenic Hills $-$$
75 E 1500 S, Salina, UT
84654, Res. (800) 283-4678
Ph: (801) 529-7483 Fax: (801)
529-3616

SALT LAKE CITY   UT

Econo Lodge $-$$
715 W. North Temple, Salt
Lake City, UT 84116, Res.
(800) 424-4777 Ph: (801)
363-0062 Fax: (801) 359-3926

Motel 6 $
176 W 6th S St, Salt Lake
City, UT 84101, Res. (800)
466-8356 Ph: 801 531-1252
Fax: 801 359-2859

Motel 6 $
1990 W N Temple St, Salt
Lake City, UT 84116, Res.
(800) 466-8356 Ph: 801
364-1053 Fax: 801 596-9152

Super 8 Motel $-$$
616 S. 200 W., Salt Lake City,
UT 84101-2705, Res. (800)
800-8000 Ph: (801) 534-0808
Fax: (801) 355-7735

SOUTH JORDAN   UT

Super 8 Motel $-$$
10722 South 300 West,
South Jordan, UT 84095,
Res. (800) 800-8000 Ph: (801)
553-8888 Fax: (801) 553-8888

ST GEORGE   UT

Econo Lodge $-$$
460 E. St. George Blvd., St
George, UT 84770, Res. (800)
424-4777 Ph: (801) 673-4861
Fax: (000) 008-0173

Motel 6 $
205 N 1000 E St, St. George,
UT 84770, Res. (800)
466-8356 Ph: 801 628-7979
Fax: 801 674-9907

Super 8 Motel $-$$
915 S. Bluff St., St. George,
UT 84770-5204, Res. (800)
800-8000 Ph: (801) 628-4251

VERNAL   UT

Econo Lodge Downtown $-$$
311 E. Main St., Vernal, UT
84078, Res. (800) 424-4777
Ph: (801) 789-2000 Fax: (801)
789-0947

WENDOVER   UT

Motel 6 $
561 E Wendover Blvd,
Wendover, UT 84083, Res.
(800) 466-8356 Ph: 801
665-2267 Fax: 801 665-2996

WOODS CROSS   UT

Motel 6 $
2433 S 800 W, Woods Cross,
UT 84087, Res. (800)
466-8356 Ph: 801 298-0289
Fax: 801 292-7423

VERMONT

BRATTLEBORO   VT

Econo Lodge $-$$
243 Canal St., Brattleboro,
VT 05301, Res. (800)
424-4777 Ph: (802) 254-2360

Motel 6 $
Putney Rd, Rt 5N,
Brattleboro, VT 05301, Res.
(800) 466-8356 Ph: 802
254-6007 Fax: 802 254-2508

Super 8 Motel $-$$
"Route 5, Box 137, Putney
Road", Brattleboro, VT
05301, Res. (800) 800-8000
Ph: (802) 254-8889 Fax: (802)
254-8323

MONTPELIER   VT

Econo Lodge $-$$
101 Northfield St.,
Montpelier, VT 05602, Res.
(800) 424-4777 Ph: (802)
223-5258 Fax: (802) 223-0716

NEWPORT   VT

Super 8 Motel $-$$
974 E. Main St., Newport, VT
05855, Res. (800) 800-8000
Ph: (802) 334-1775 Fax: (802)
334-1994

RUTLAND   VT

Econo Lodge Pico $-$$
US 4, Rutland, VT 05701,
Res. (800) 424-4777 Ph: (802)
773-6644 Fax: (802) 773-2193

S. BURLINGTON   VT

Super 8 Motel $-$$
1016 Shelburne Road, S.
Burlington, VT 05446, Res.
(800) 800-8000 Ph: (802)
863-2984

SAINT ALBANS   VT

Econo Lodge $-$$
287 S. Main St., Saint
Albans, VT 05478, Res. (800)
424-4777 Ph: (802) 524-5956
Fax: (802) 524-1735

SHELBURNE   VT

Econo Lodge $-$$
1961 Shelburne Rd.,
Shelburne, VT 05482, Res.
(800) 424-4777 Ph: (802)
985-3377 Fax: (802) 985-3377

SOUTH BURLINGTON   VT

Econo Lodge University $-$$
1076 Williston Rd., South
Burlington, VT 05403, Res.
(800) 424-4777 Ph: (802)
863-1125 Fax: (802) 658-1296

WHITE RIVER JUN   VT

Super 8 Motel $-$$
Rte 5 South, White River
Jun, VT 05001, Res. (800)
800-8000 Ph: (802) 295-7577

VIRGINIA

ABINGDON   VA

Super 8 Motel $-$$
298 Town Centre Dr., P.O.
Box 1746, Abingdon, VA
24210, Res. (800) 800-8000
Ph: (703) 676-3329 Fax: (703)
676-3329

M
O
T
E
L

ALEXANDRIA   VA

Econo Lodge Mt. Vernon $-$$
8849 Richmond Hwy.,
Alexandria, VA 22309, Res.
(800) 424-4777 Ph: (703)
780-0300 Fax: (703) 780-0842

Econo Lodge Old Town $-$$
700 N. Washington St.,
Alexandria, VA 22314, Res.
(800) 424-4777 Ph: (703)
836-5100 Fax: (703) 519-7015

APPOMATTOX   VA

Super 8 Motel $-$$
"Rte. 4, Box 100",
Appomattox, VA 24522, Res.
(800) 800-8000 Ph: (804)
352-2339 Fax: (804) 352-2339

ARLINGTON   VA

Econo Lodge National Airport $
2485 S. Glebe Rd., Arlington,
VA 22206, Res. (800)
424-4777 Ph: (703) 979-4100
Fax: (703) 979-6120

Econo Lodge North $-$$
3335 Lee Hwy., Arlington,
VA 22207, Res. (800)
424-4777 Ph: (703) 524-9800
Fax: (703) 522-7683

Econo Lodge West $-$$
6800 Lee Hwy., Arlington,
VA 22213, Res. (800)
424-4777 Ph: (703) 538-5300

ASHLAND   VA

Econo Lodge King's $-$$
I-95 & SR 54, Ashland, VA
23005, Res. (800) 424-4777
Ph: (804) 798-9221 Fax: (804)
790-2913

Super 8 Motel $-$$
806 England Street,
Ashland, VA 23005, Res.
(800) 800-8000 Ph: (804)
752-7000

BLACKSBURG   VA

Red Carpet Inn $$
1615 So. Main St.,
Blacksburg, VA 24060, Res.
(800) 251-1962 Ph: (540)
552-4011 Fax: (540) 951-2764

BRISTOL   VA

Budget Host Bristol Motor $-$$
1209 W State Street, Bristol,
VA 24201, Res. (800)
283-4678 Ph: (703) 669-5187

Econo Lodge $-$$
912 Commonwealth Ave.,
Bristol, VA 24201, Res. (800)
424-4777 Ph: (703) 466-2112
Fax: (703) 466-2112

Red Carpet Inn $
15589 Lee Highway, Bristol,
VA 24202, Res. (800)
251-1962 Ph: (703) 669-1151
Fax: (703) 669-1153

Scottish Inns $
15598 Lee Highway, Bristol,
VA 24202, Res. (800)
251-1962 Ph: (704) 669-4148
Fax: (703) 669-1193

Super 8 Motel $-$$
2139 Lee Hwy, Bristol, VA
24201-1627, Res. (800)
800-8000 Ph: (703) 466-8800
Fax: (703) 466-8800

CARROLLTON   VA

Econo Lodge Benns Church $-$$
SR 10 at SR 32, Carrollton,
VA 23314, Res. (800)
424-4777 Ph: (804) 357-9057

CHARLOTTESVILLE   VA

Econo Lodge North $-$$
2014 Holiday Dr.,
Charlottesville, VA 22901,
Res. (800) 424-4777 Ph: (804)
295-3185

Econo Lodge University $-$$
400 Emmet St.,
Charlottesville, VA 22903,
Res. (800) 424-4777 Ph: (804)
296-2104

Super 8 Motel $-$$
390 Greenbrier Dr.,
Charlottesville, VA 22906,
Res. (800) 800-8000 Ph: (804)
973-0888 Fax: (804) 973-2221

CHESAPEAKE   VA

Econo Lodge Bowers Hill $-$$
4725 W. Military Hwy.,
Chesapeake, VA 23321, Res.
(800) 424-4777 Ph: (804)
488-4963

Econo Lodge Churchland $-$$
3244 Western Branch,
Chesapeake, VA 23321, Res.
(800) 424-4777 Ph: (804)
484-6143

Motel 6 $
701 Woodlake Dr,
Chesapeake, VA 23320, Res.
(800) 466-8356 Ph: 757
420-2976 Fax: 757 366-9915

Super 8 Motel $-$$
100 Red Cedar Court,
Chesapeake, VA 23320, Res.
(800) 800-8000 Ph: (804)
547-8880

Super 8 Motel $-$$
3216 Churchland Blvd.,
Chesapeake, VA 23321, Res.
(800) 800-8000 Ph: (804)
686-8888 Fax: (804) 686-8888

CHESTER   VA

Super 8 Motel $-$$
2421 Southland Drive,
Chester, VA 23831, Res.
(800) 800-8000 Ph: (804)
748-0050 Fax: (804) 748-0050

CHRISTIANSBURG   VA

Econo Lodge $-$$
2430 Roanoke St.,
Christiansburg, VA 24073,
Res. (800) 424-4777 Ph: (703)
382-6161

Super 8 Motel $-$$
2780 Roanoke Rd.,
Christiansburg, VA 24073,
Res. (800) 800-8000 Ph: (703)
382-7421

Super 8 Motel $-$$
55 Laurel St. NE,
Christiansburg, VA 24073,
Res. (800) 800-8000 Ph: (703)
382-5813 Fax: (700) 382-5813

COLLINSVILLE   VA

Econo Lodge $-$$
800 S. Virginia Ave.,
Collinsville, VA 24078, Res.
(800) 424-4777 Ph: (703)
647-3941 Fax: (703) 647-1106

CULPEPER   VA

Super 8 Motel $-$$
889 Willis Lane, Culpeper,
VA 22701-3773, Res. (800)
800-8000 Ph: (703) 825-8088
Fax: (703) 825-8088

DANVILLE   VA

Super 8 Motel $-$$
2385 Riverside Drive,
Danville, VA 24541, Res.
(800) 800-8000 Ph: (804)
799-5845 Fax: (804) 799-5845

DOSWELL   VA

Econo Lodge $-$$
I-95 & SR 30, Doswell, VA
23047, Res. (800) 424-4777
Ph: (804) 876-3712 Fax: (804)
876-3741

DUMFRIES   VA

Econo Lodge $-$$
17005 Dumfries Rd.,
Dumfries, VA 22026, Res.
(800) 424-4777 Ph: (703)
221-4176 Fax: (703) 221-4176

Super 8 Motel $-$$
17336 Jefferson Davis
Highway, Dumfries, VA
22026, Res. (800) 800-8000
Ph: (703) 221-8838 Fax: (703)
221-0275

EMPORIA   VA

Econo Lodge $-$$
3173 Susset Dr., Emporia,
VA 23847, Res. (800)
424-4777 Ph: (804) 535-8535
Fax: (804) 535-8535

Red Carpet Inn $
1586 Skipper Rd., Emporia,
VA 23847, Res. (800)
251-1962 Ph: (804) 634-4181
Fax: (804) 34-0663

FAIRFAX   VA

Econo Lodge $-$$
9700 Lee Hwy., Fairfax, VA
22031, Res. (800) 424-4777
Ph: (703) 273-1160 Fax: (703)
273-1161

FALLS CHURCH   VA

Econo Lodge Pentagon $-$$
5666 Columbia Pike, Falls
Church, VA 22041, Res.
(800) 424-4777 Ph: (703)
820-5600 Fax: (703) 379-7482

FARMVILLE   VA

Scottish Inns $
Jct. Bus. 460 & 15N,
Farmville, VA 23901, Res.
(800) 251-1962 Ph: (804)
392-3929

Super 8 Motel $-$$
Hwy. 15 S., "HC 6, Box 1755",
Farmville, VA 23901, Res.
(800) 800-8000 Ph: (804)
392-8196 Fax: (804) 392-8196

FRANKLIN   VA

Super 8 Motel $-$$
1599 Armory Drive, Franklin,
VA 23581, Res. (800)
800-8000 Ph: (804) 562-2888
Fax: (804) 562-2888

FREDERICKSBURG   VA

Econo Lodge $-$$
5321 Jefferson Davis Hwy.,
Fredericksburg, VA 22408,
Res. (800) 424-4777 Ph: (703)
898-5440 Fax: (703) 898-6172

Econo Lodge Central $-$$
I-95, Exit 130b,
Fredericksburg, VA 22404,
Res. (800) 424-4777 Ph: (703)
786-8374 Fax: (703) 786-8811

Motel 6 $
401 Warrenton Rd,
Fredericksburg, VA 22405,
Res. (800) 466-8356 Ph: 540
371-5443 Fax: 540 371-7569

Super 8 Motel $-$$
3002 Mall Court,
Fredericksburg, VA 22401,
Res. (800) 800-8000 Ph: (703)
786-8881 Fax: (703) 786-8881

Super 8 Motel $-$$
5319 Jefferson Davis
Highway, Fredericksburg,
VA 22408, Res. (800)
800-8000 Ph: (703) 898-7100
Fax: (703) 786-8881

FRONT ROYAL   VA

Scottish Inns $$
533 So. Royal Ave., Front
Royal, VA 22630, Res. (800)
251-1962 Ph: (703) 636-6168
Fax: (703) 636-3120

Super 8 Motel $-$$
111 South St., Front Royal,
VA 22630, Res. (800)
800-8000 Ph: (703) 636-4888
Fax: (703) 636-4888

HAMPTON   VA

Econo Lodge Coliseum $-$$
2708 W. Mercury Blvd.,
Hampton, VA 23666, Res.
(800) 424-4777 Ph: (804)
826-8970 Fax: (804) 826-8970

Econo Lodge Langley Afb $-$$
1781 N. King St., Hampton,
VA 23669, Res. (800)
424-4777 Ph: (804) 723-0741

Super 8 Motel $-$$
1330 Thomas Street,
Hampton, VA 23669, Res.
(800) 800-8000 Ph: (804)
723-2888 Fax: (804) 723-2888

HARRISONBURG   VA

Econo Lodge $-$$
US 33 & I-81, Harrisonburg,
VA 22801, Res. (800)
424-4777 Ph: (703) 433-2576
Fax: (703) 433-2576

Motel 6 $
10 Linda Ln, Harrisonburg,
VA 22801, Res. (800)
466-8356 Ph: 540 433-6939
Fax: 540 564-0289

Red Carpet Inn $$
3210 So. Main St.,
Harrisonburg, VA 22801,
Res. (800) 251-1962 Ph: (703)
434-6704 Fax: (703) 434-9610

Scottish Inns $$
Route 11 North,
Harrisonburg, VA 22801,
Res. (800) 251-1962 Ph: (703)
434-5301 Fax: (703) 434-1950

Super 8 Motel $-$$
3330 South Main Street,
Harrisonburg, VA 22801,
Res. (800) 800-8000 Ph: (703)
433-8888 Fax: (703) 433-8888

HILLSVILLE   VA

Econo Lodge $-$$
I-77 & US 58, Hillsville, VA
24343, Res. (800) 424-4777
Ph: (703) 728-9118

LEXINGTON   VA

Econo Lodge $-$$
I-64 & U.S. 11, Lexington,
VA 24450, Res. (800)
424-4777 Ph: (703) 463-7371
Fax: (000) 007-0363

Super 8 Motel $-$$
"Route 7, Box 99", Lexington,
VA 24450, Res. (800)
800-8000 Ph: (703) 463-7858
Fax: (703) 463-7858

LYNCHBURG   VA

Econo Lodge $-$$
2400 Stadium Rd.,
Lynchburg, VA 24501, Res.
(800) 424-4777 Ph: (804)
847-1045

MADISON HEIGHTS   VA

Super 8 Motel $-$$
3410 Amherst Highway,
Madison Heights, VA 24572,
Res. (800) 800-8000 Ph: (804)
929-6506 Fax: (804) 929-6788

MANNASSAS   VA

Super 8 Motel $-$$
7249 New Market Court,
Mannassas, VA 22110, Res.
(800) 800-8000 Ph: (703)
369-1700 Fax: (703) 369-4451

MARION   VA

Budget Host Marion Motel $$
435 S Main St, Marion, VA
24354, Res. (800) 283-4678
Ph: (703) 783- 8511

MARTINSVILLE   VA

Super 8 Motel $-$$
960 North Memorial Blvd.,
Martinsville, VA 24112, Res.
(800) 800-8000 Ph: (703)
666-8888 Fax: (804) 666-8888

MCKENNEY   VA

Scottish Inns $
21723 Boydton Plan Rd.,
McKenney, VA 23872, Res.
(800) 251-1962 Ph: (804)
478-4481 Fax: (804) 478-4592

NEWPORT NEWS   VA

Econo Lodge Ft. Eustis $-$$
15237 Warwick Blvd.,
Newport News, VA 23602,
Res. (800) 424-4777 Ph: (804)
874-9244 Fax: (804) 872-6883

Econo Lodge Oyster Point $-$$
11845 Jefferson Ave.,
Newport News, VA 23606,
Res. (800) 424-4777 Ph: (804)
599-3237 Fax: (804) 599-0413

Motel 6 $
797 J Clyde-Morris Blvd,
Newport News, VA 23601,
Res. (800) 466-8356 Ph: 757
595-6336 Fax: 757 595-8124

Super 8 Motel $-$$
945 J. Clyde Morris Blvd.,
Newport News, VA 23601,
Res. (800) 800-8000 Ph: (804)
595-8888 Fax: (804) 595-8888

Super 8 Motel $-$$
6105 Jefferson Avenue,
Newport News, VA 23605,
Res. (800) 800-8000 Ph: (804)
825-1422 Fax: (804) 825-1422

NORFOLK   VA

Econo Lodge Airport $-$$
3343 N. Military Hwy.,
Norfolk, VA 23518, Res. (800)
424-4777 Ph: (804) 855-3116
Fax: (804) 857-6413

Econo Lodge Azalea Gardens $$
1850 E. Little Creek, Norfolk,
VA 23518, Res. (800)
424-4777 Ph: (804) 588-8888

M
O
T
E
L

Econo Lodge Military Circle $-$$
865 N. Military Hwy. / US 13,
Norfolk, VA 23502, Res. (800)
424-4777 Ph: (804) 461-4865

Econo Lodge Naval Base $-$$
8901 Hampton Blvd., Norfolk,
VA 23505, Res. (800)
424-4777 Ph: (804) 489-0801
Fax: (804) 489-3086

Econo Lodge Ocean View $-$$
1111 E. Ocean View Ave.,
Norfolk, VA 23503, Res. (800)
424-4777 Ph: (804) 480-1111

Econo Lodge Ocean View $-$$
9601 4th View St., Norfolk,
VA 23503, Res. (800)
424-4777 Ph: (804) 480-9611
Fax: (804) 480-1307

Motel 6 $
853 N Military Hwy, Norfolk,
VA 23502, Res. (800)
466-8356 Ph: 757 461-2380
Fax: 757 461-5639

Super 8 Motel $-$$
7940 Shore Drive, Norfolk,
VA 23518, Res. (800)
800-8000 Ph: (804) 588-7888
Fax: (804) 588-7888

NORTON   **VA**

Super 8 Motel $-$$
425 Wharton Lane, Route 58,
Norton, VA 24273, Res. (800)
800-8000 Ph: (703) 679-0893
Fax: (703) 679-0893

PETERSBURG   **VA**

Econo Lodge Fort Lee $-$$
25 S. Crater Rd., Petersburg,
VA 23803, Res. (800)
424-4777 Ph: (804) 861-4680
Fax: (804) 861-4680

Econo Lodge Interstate $-$$
12002 S. Crater Rd.,
Petersburg, VA 23805, Res.
(800) 424-4777 Ph: (804)
732-2000 Fax: (804) 732-2315

Econo Lodge South $-$$
16905 Parkdale Rd.,
Petersburg, VA 23805, Res.
(800) 424-4777 Ph: (804)
862-2717

Super 8 Motel $-$$
555 Wythe St. East,
Petersburg, VA 23803, Res.
(800) 800-8000 Ph: (804)
531-0793 Fax: (804) 861-0793

PORTSMOUTH   **VA**

Super 8 Motel $-$$
925 London Blvd.,
Portsmouth, VA 23704, Res.
(800) 800-8000 Ph: (804)
398-0612 Fax: (804) 398-0612

PULASKI   **VA**

Red Carpet Inn $$
I-85, exit 94, Pulaski, VA
24301, Res. (800) 251-1962
Ph: (703) 980-2230 Fax: (703)
980-0492

RADFORD   **VA**

Super 8 Motel $-$$
1600 Tyler Avenue, Radford,
VA 24141, Res. (800)
800-8000 Ph: (703) 731-9355
Fax: (703) 731-9355

RAVENSWOOD   **VA**

Scottish Inns $$
I-77. exit 146, Ravenswood,
VA 26164, Res. (800)
251-1962 Ph: (304) 273-2830
Fax: (304) 273-3445

RICHMOND   **VA**

Econo Lodge South $-$$
2125 Willis Rd., Richmond,
VA 23237, Res. (800)
424-4777 Ph: (804) 271-6031
Fax: (804) 271-6031

Econo Lodge West $-$$
6523 Midlothian Turnpike,
Richmond, VA 23225, Res.
(800) 424-4777 Ph: (804)
276-8241 Fax: (008) 047-6841

Super 8 Motel $-$$
7200 West Broad Street,
Richmond, VA 23294, Res.
(800) 800-8000 Ph: (804)
672-8128 Fax: (804) 672-8128

Super 8 Motel $-$$
5110 Williamsburg Road,
Richmond, VA 23231, Res.
(800) 800-8000 Ph: (804)
222-8008 Fax: (804) 222-8008

Super 8 Motel $-$$
8260 Midlothian Tpke,
Richmond, VA 23235, Res.
(800) 800-8000 Ph: (804)
320-2823 Fax: (804) 320-2823

Super 8 Motel $-$$
5615 ChamberLayne Road,
Richmond, VA 23227, Res.
(800) 800-8000 Ph: (804)
262-8880 Fax: (804) 262-8880

RIVERDALE   **VA**

Super 8 Motel $-$$
Route 360 and Route 58, Box
8, Riverdale, VA 24592, Res.
(800) 800-8000 Ph: (804)
572-8868 Fax: (804) 572-8868

ROANOKE   **VA**

Econo Lodge Downtown $-$$
308 Orange Ave., Roanoke,
VA 24016, Res. (800)
424-4777 Ph: (703) 343-2413

Super 8 Motel $-$$
6616 Thirlane Road,
Roanoke, VA 24019, Res.
(800) 800-8000 Ph: (703)
563-8888 Fax: (070) 356-3888

ROCKY MOUNT   **VA**

Budget Host Inn $-$$
Hwy 220 N, Rocky Mount,
VA 24151, Res. (800)
283-4678 Ph: (703) 483-9757
Fax: (703) 337-0821

SALEM   **VA**

Budget Host Blue Jay Motel $$
5399 W Main St, Salem, VA
24153, Res. (800) 283-4678
Ph: (703) 380-2080

Super 8 Motel $-$$
300 Wildwood Avenue,
Salem, VA 24153, Res. (800)
800-8000 Ph: (703) 389-0297
Fax: (703) 389-0297

SANDSTON   **VA**

Econo Lodge Airport $-$$
5408 Williamsburg Rd.,
Sandston, VA 23150, Res.
(800) 424-4777 Ph: (804)
222-1020

Motel 6 $
5704 Williamsburg Rd. (U.S.
Rt. 60), Sandston, VA
23150, Res. (800) 466-8356
Ph: 804 222-7600 Fax: 804
222-4153

SKIPPERS   **VA**

Econo Lodge $-$$
I-95 S. & SR 629, Skippers,
VA 23879-9704, Res. (800)
424-4777 Ph: (804) 634-6124

SOUTH HILL   **VA**

Econo Lodge $-$$
623 E. Atlantic St., South
Hill, VA 23970, Res. (800)
424-4777 Ph: (804) 447-7116
Fax: (804) 447-6985

Super 8 Motel $-$$
922 East Atlantic Street,
South Hill, VA 23970-3404,
Res. (800) 800-8000 Ph: (804)
447-7655 Fax: (804) 447-7655

SPRINGFIELD   **VA**

Motel 6 $
6868 Springfield Blvd,
Springfield, VA 22450, Res.
(800) 466-8356 Ph: 703
644-5311 Fax: 703 644-1077

STAUNTON   **VA**

Econo Lodge $-$$
I-81/64 Exit 213, Staunton,
VA 24401, Res. (800)
424-4777 Ph: (703) 337-1231
Fax: (703) 337-0821

Econo Lodge East $-$$
1031 Richmond Ave.,
Staunton, VA 24401, Res.
(800) 424-4777 Ph: (703)
885-5158 Fax: (703) 885-5281

Super 8 Motel $-$$
1015 Richmond Rd.,
Staunton, VA 24401, Res.
(800) 800-8000 Ph: (703)
886-2888 Fax: (703) 886-7432

SUFFOLK   **VA**

Econo Lodge $-$$
1017 N. Main St., Suffolk, VA
23434, Res. (800) 424-4777
Ph: (804) 539-3451 Fax: (804)
539-2094

Super 8 Motel $-$$
633 North Main St., Suffolk,
VA 23434, Res. (800)
800-8000 Ph: (804) 925-0992
Fax: (804) 925-0992

TAPPAHANNOCK VA

Super 8 Motel $-$$
Hwy. 17, P.O. Box 1748,
Tappahannock, VA 22560,
Res. (800) 800-8000 Ph: (804)
443-3888 Fax: (804) 443-3888

VERONA VA

Scottish Inns $
I-81, exit 227, Verona, VA
24482, Res. (800) 251-1962
Ph: (510) 248-8981 Fax: (510)
248-4312

VIRGINIA BEACH VA

Econo Lodge $-$$
5819 Northampton Blvd.,
Virginia Beach, VA 23455,
Res. (800) 424-4777 Ph: (804)
460-1000 Fax: (804) 464-3210

Econo Lodge Beach View $-$$
3108 Atlantic Ave., Virginia
Beach, VA 23451, Res. (800)
424-4777 Ph: (804) 425-7730

Econo Lodge Chesapeake $-$$
2968 Shore Dr., Virginia
Beach, VA 23451, Res. (800)
424-4777 Ph: (804) 481-0666
Fax: (804) 481-4756

Econo Lodge Expressway $-$$
3637 Bonney Rd., Virginia
Beach, VA 23452, Res. (800)
424-4777 Ph: (804) 486-5711
Fax: (000) 000-1486

Econo Lodge Oceanfront $-$$
1211 Atlantic Ave., Virginia
Beach, VA 23451, Res. (800)
424-4777 Ph: (804) 428-1183

WAYNESBORO VA

Super 8 Motel $-$$
2045 Rosser Avenue,
Waynesboro, VA 22980,
Res. (800) 800-8000 Ph: (703)
943-3888 Fax: (703) 943-3888

WILLIAMSBURG VA

Budget Host Governor $-$$
1508 Richmond Rd,
Williamsburg, VA 23185,
Res. (800) 283-4678 Ph: (804)
229-6444 Fax: (804) 253-2410

Econo Lodge Central $-$$
1900 Richmond Rd.,
Williamsburg, VA 23185,
Res. (800) 424-4777 Ph: (804)
229-6600 Fax: (804) 229-6600

Econo Lodge Historic Area $-$$
1402 Richmond Rd.,
Williamsburg, VA 23185,
Res. (800) 424-4777 Ph: (804)
220-2367 Fax: (804) 220-3527

Econo Lodge Parkway $-$$
442 Parkway Dr.,
Williamsburg, VA 23185,
Res. (800) 424-4777 Ph: (804)
229-7564 Fax: (000) 804-2916

Econo Lodge Pottery $-$$
7051 Richmond Rd.,
Williamsburg, VA 23188,
Res. (800) 424-4777 Ph: (804)
564-3341

Motel 6 $
3030 Richmond Rd,
Williamsburg, VA 23185,
Res. (800) 466-8356 Ph: 757
565-3433 Fax: 757 565-1013

Red Carpet Inn $$
7224 Merrimac Trail,
Williamsburg, VA 23185,
Res. (800) 251-1962 Ph: (757)
229-0400 Fax: (757) 220-3057

WINCHESTER VA

Econo Lodge North $-$$
1593 Martinsburg Pike,
Winchester, VA 22603, Res.
(800) 424-4777 Ph: (703)
662-4700 Fax: (703) 665-1762

Super 8 Motel $-$$
1077 Millwood Pike,
Winchester, VA 22602, Res.
(800) 800-8000 Ph: (703)
665-4450 Fax: (703) 665-4450

WOODBRIDGE VA

Econo Lodge $-$$
13317 Gordon Blvd.,
Woodbridge, VA 22191, Res.
(800) 424-4777 Ph: (703)
491-5196 Fax: (703) 491-5196

WOODSTOCK VA

Budget Host Inn $-$$
P.O. Box 483, Woodstock, VA
22664, Res. (800) 283-4678
Ph: (703) 459-4086 Fax: (703)
459-4043

WYTHEVILLE VA

Econo Lodge $-$$
1190 E. Main St., Wytheville,
VA 24382, Res. (800)
424-4777 Ph: (703) 228-5517

Motel 6 $
220 Lithia Rd, Wytheville,
VA 24382, Res. (800)
466-8356 Ph: 540 228-7988
Fax: 540 223-1860

Red Carpet Inn $$
280 Lithia Rd., Wytheville,
VA 24382, Res. (800)
251-1962 Ph: (540) 228-5525
Fax: (540) 228-5010

Super 8 Motel $-$$
130 Nye Circle, Wytheville,
VA 24382, Res. (800)
800-8000 Ph: (703) 228-6620
Fax: (703) 228-2600

WASHINGTON

BELLINGHAM WA

Motel 6 $
3701 Byron, Bellingham, WA
98225, Res. (800) 466-8356
Ph: 360 671-4494 Fax: 360
734-7367

BREMERTON WA

Super 8 Motel $-$$
5068 Kit Sap Way,
Bremerton, WA 98310, Res.
(800) 800-8000 Ph: (206)
377-8881 Fax: (206) 373-8755

CENTRALIA WA

Motel 6 $
1310 Belmont Ave, Centralia,
WA 98531, Res. (800)
466-8356 Ph: 360 330-2057
Fax: 360 330-2066

CLARKSTON WA

Motel 6 $
222 Bridge St, Clarkston,
WA 99403, Res. (800)
466-8356 Ph: 509 758-1631
Fax: 509 758-4942

ELLENSBURG WA

Super 8 Motel $-$$
1500 Canyon Rd.,
Ellensburg. WA 98926, Res.
(800) 800-8000 Ph: (509)
962-6888 Fax: (509) 962-6810

EVERETT WA

Motel 6 $
10006 Evergreen Way,
Everett, WA 98204, Res.
(800) 466-8356 Ph: 206
347-2060 Fax: 206 347-1529

Motel 6 $
224 128th St SW, Everett,
WA 98204, Res. (800)
466-8356 Ph: 206 353-8120
Fax: 206 347-2269

FEDERAL WAY WA

Super 8 Motel $-$$
1688 S. 348th St., Federal
Way, WA 98063, Res. (800)
800-8000 Ph: (206) 838-8808
Fax: (206) 874-6277

FIFE WA

Motel 6 $
5201 20th St E, Fife, WA
98424, Res. (800) 466-8356
Ph: 253 922-1270 Fax: 253
926-3662

ISSAQUAH WA

Motel 6 $
1885 15th Pl NW, Issaquah,
WA 98027, Res. (800)
466-8356 Ph: 206 392-8405
Fax: 206 557-6465

KELSO WA

Motel 6 $
106 Minor Rd, Kelso, WA
98626, Res. (800) 466-8356
Ph: 360 425-3229 Fax: 360
423-4650

M
O
T
E
L

Super 8 Motel $-$$
250 Kelso Dr., Kelso, WA
98626, Res. (800) 800-8000
Ph: (360) 423-8880 Fax: (206)
423-7956

KENNEWICK   WA

Super 8 Motel $-$$
626 N. Columbia Center Blvd.,
Kennewick, WA 99336, Res.
(800) 800-8000 Ph: (509)
736-6888 Fax: (509) 735-3878

KIRKLAND   WA

Motel 6 $
12010 120th Pl NE, Kirkland,
WA 98034, Res. (800)
466-8356 Ph: 206 821-5618
Fax: 206 821-7459

LACEY   WA

Super 8 Motel $-$$
P.O. Box 3802, 4615 Martin
Way, Lacey, WA 98503,
Res. (800) 800-8000 Ph: (206)
459-8888 Fax: (206) 438-0179

LONG BEACH   WA

Super 8 Motel $-$$
P.O. Box 220, 500 Ocean
Beach Blvd, Long Beach,
WA 98631, Res. (800)
800-8000 Ph: (206) 642-8988
Fax: (206) 642-8986

MOSES LAKE   WA

Motel 6 $
2822 Wapato Dr, Moses Lake,
WA 98837, Res. (800)
466-8356 Ph: 509 766-0250
Fax: 509 766-7762

Super 8 Motel $-$$
449 Melva Lane, Moses Lake,
WA 98837, Res. (800)
800-8000 Ph: (509) 765-8886
Fax: (509) 766-0779

PASCO   WA

Motel 6 $
1520 N Oregon St, Pasco,
WA 99301, Res. (800)
466-8356 Ph: 509 546-2010
Fax: 509 544-0279

PORT ANGELES   WA

Super 8 Motel $-$$
2104 E. 1st St., Port Angeles,
WA 98362, Res. (800)
800-8000 Ph: (206) 452-8401
Fax: (206) 452-4406

RICHLAND   WA

Econo Lodge Downtown $-$$
515 George Washington Way,
Richland, WA 99352, Res.
(800) 424-4777 Ph: (509)
946-6117 Fax: (509) 943-2463

SEATTLE   WA

Econo Lodge By The Space $-$$
325 Aurora Ave. N., Seattle,
WA 98109, Res. (800)
424-4777 Ph: (206) 441-0400
Fax: (206) 448-3353

Econo Lodge Sea-tac Airport $
13910 Pacific Hwy. S.,
Seattle, WA 98168, Res.
(800) 424-4777 Ph: (206)
244-0810 Fax: (206) 431-9503

Motel 6 $
16500 Pacific Hwy S, Seattle,
WA 98188, Res. (800)
466-8356 Ph: 206 246-4101
Fax: 206 244-3764

Motel 6 $
18900 47th Ave S, Seattle,
WA 98188, Res. (800)
466-8356 Ph: 206 241-1648
Fax: 206 244-3614

Motel 6 $
20651 Military Rd, Seattle,
WA 98198, Res. (800)
466-8356 Ph: 206 824-9902
Fax: 206 870-3842

Super 8 Motel $-$$
"3100 S. 192nd, P.O. Box
69153", Seattle, WA 98168,
Res. (800) 800-8000 Ph: (206)
433-8188 Fax: (206) 243-9103

SEQUIM   WA

Econo Lodge $-$$
801 E. Washington St.,
Sequim, WA 98382, Res.
(800) 424-4777 Ph: (206)
683-7113 Fax: (206) 683-7343

SHELTON   WA

Super 8 Motel $-$$
2943 Northview Circle, P.O.
Box 267, Shelton, WA
98584, Res. (800) 800-8000
Ph: (360) 426-1654 Fax: (360)
426-1847

SPOKANE   WA

Motel 6 $
1508 S Rustle St, Spokane,
WA 99224, Res. (800)
466-8356 Ph: 509 459-6120
Fax: 509 747-1857

Super 8 Motel $-$$
202 Argonne Rd., Spokane,
WA 99212-2448, Res. (800)
800-8000 Ph: (509) 928-4888
Fax: (509) 926-5511

Super 8 Motel $-$$
West 11102 Westbow Blvd.,
Spokane, WA 99204, Res.
(800) 800-8000 Ph: (509)
838-8800 Fax: (509) 624-3157

STEVENSON   WA

Econo Lodge $-$$
Mp 021 Frank Johns Rd. / SR
14, Stevenson, WA 98648,
Res. (800) 424-4777 Ph: (509)
427-5628 Fax: (509) 427-4995

TACOMA   WA

Econo Lodge North $-$$
3518 Pacific Hwy. E., Tacoma,
WA 98424, Res. (800)
424-4777 Ph: (206) 922-0550
Fax: (206) 922-3203

Econo Lodge South $-$$
9325 S. Tacoma Way,
Tacoma, WA 98499, Res.
(800) 424-4777 Ph: (206)
582-7550

Motel 6 $
1811 S 76th St, Tacoma, WA
98408, Res. (800) 466-8356
Ph: 253 473-7100 Fax: 253
472-7952

TUMWATER   WA

Motel 6 $
400 W Lee St, Tumwater,
WA 98501, Res. (800)
466-8356 Ph: 360 754-7320
Fax: 360 705-0655

UNION GAP   WA

Super 8 Motel $-$$
2605 Rudkin Road, P.O. Box
3108, Union Gap, WA
98903, Res. (800) 800-8000
Ph: (509) 248-8880 Fax: (509)
453-6997

WALLA WALLA   WA

Econo Lodge $-$$
305 N. 2nd Ave., Walla Walla,
WA 99362, Res. (800)
424-4777 Ph: (509) 529-4410
Fax: (509) 525-5777

Super 8 Motel $-$$
2315 Eastgate Street N,
Walla Walla, WA 99362, Res.
(800) 800-8000 Ph: (509)
525-8800 Fax: (509) 525-8832

WASHOUGAL   WA

Econo Lodge $-$$
544 6th St., Washougal, WA
98671, Res. (800) 424-4777
Ph: (206) 835-8591 Fax: (206)
835-2040

WENATCHEE   WA

Econo Lodge Downtown $-$$
700 N. Wenatchee Ave.,
Wenatchee, WA 98801, Res.
(800) 424-4777 Ph: (509)
663-8133 Fax: (509) 662-0826

YAKIMA   WA

Econo Lodge $-$$
510 N. First St., Yakima, WA
98901, Res. (800) 424-4777
Ph: (509) 457-6155 Fax: (509)
575-4653

Motel 6 $
1104 N 1st St, Yakima, WA
98901, Res. (800) 466-8356
Ph: 509 454-0080 Fax: 509
452-2241

WEST VIRGINIA

BECKLEY   WV

Super 8 Motel $-$$
2014 Harper Road, Beckley,
WV 25801, Res. (800)
800-8000 Ph: (304) 253-0802
Fax: (304) 253-0802

BLUEFIELD   WV

Econo Lodge $-$$
3400 Cumberland Rd.,
Bluefield, WV 24701, Res.
(800) 424-4777 Ph: (304)
327-8171

BRIDGEPORT   WV

Econo Lodge $-$$
SR 2, Box 168, Bridgeport,
WV 26330, Res. (800)
424-4777 Ph: (304) 842-7381
Fax: (304) 842-4809

CHARLESTON   WV

Budget Host Inn $-$$
3313 E. Kanawha Blvd.,
Charleston, WV 25306, Ph:
(304) 925-2592

Motel 6 $
6311 MacCorkle Ave SE,
Charleston, WV 25304, Res.
(800) 466-8356 Ph: 304
925-0471 Fax: 304 926-8489

CROSS LANES   WV

Motel 6 $
330 Goff Mountain Rd, Cross
Lanes, WV 25313, Res. (800)
466-8356 Ph: 304 776-5911
Fax: 304 776-7450

DAVIS   WV

Budget Host The Highlander $
P.O. Box 587, Davis, WV
26260, Res. (800) 283-4678
Ph: (304) 259-5551

DUNBAR   WV

Super 8 Motel $-$$
911 Dunbar Avenue,
Dunbar, WV 25064, Res.
(800) 800-8000 Ph: (304)
768-6888 Fax: (304) 768-6888

ELKINS   WV

Econo Lodge $-$$
Rt 1 Box 15, Elkins, WV
26241, Res. (800) 424-4777
Ph: (304) 636-5311 Fax: (304)
636-5311

Super 8 Motel $-$$
"Box 284, Route 3", Route
219 & 250 South, Elkins,
WV 26241, Res. (800)
800-8000 Ph: (304) 636-6500
Fax: (304) 636-6500

FAIRMONT   WV

Econo Lodge $-$$
SR 73 S., Fairmont, WV
26554, Res. (800) 424-4777
Ph: (304) 366-5995 Fax: (304)
366-6093

GHENT   WV

Econo Lodge At Winterplace $$
I-77 Exit 28 (Odd Rd.), Ghent,
WV 25843, Res. (800)
424-4777 Ph: (304) 787-3250

HUNTINGTON   WV

Econo Lodge $-$$
3325 US 60 E., Huntington,
WV 25705, Res. (800)
424-4777 Ph: (304) 529-1331
Fax: (304) 522-6011

KEYSER   WV

Econo Lodge $-$$
US 220 S., Keyser, WV
26726, Res. (800) 424-4777
Ph: (304) 788-0913 Fax: (304)
788-6219

LEWISBURG   WV

Budget Host Fort Savannah $$
204 N Jefferson St,
Lewisburg, WV 24901, Res.
(800) 283-4678 Ph: (304)
645-3055

Super 8 Motel $-$$
550 N. Jefferson St.,
Lewisburg, WV 24901, Res.
(800) 800-8000 Ph: (304)
647-3188 Fax: (304) 647-3188

LOGAN   WV

Super 8 Motel $-$$
316 Riverview Ave., Logan,
WV 25601, Res. (800)
800-8000 Ph: (304) 752-8787
Fax: (304) 752-8787

MARTINSBURG   WV

Econo Lodge $-$$
I-81, Spring Mills Rd.,
Martinsburg, WV 25401,
Res. (800) 424-4777 Ph: (304)
274-2181

Super 8 Motel $-$$
1600 Edwin Miller Blvd.,
Martinsburg, WV 25401,
Res. (800) 800-8000 Ph: (304)
263-0801 Fax: (304) 263-0801

MORGANTOWN   WV

Econo Lodge $-$$
15 Commerce Dr.,
Morgantown, WV 26505,
Res. (800) 424-4777 Ph: (304)
296-8774 Fax: (304) 299-8774

Econo Lodge Coliseum $-$$
3506 Monongahela Blvd.,
Morgantown, WV 26505,
Res. (800) 424-4777 Ph: (304)
599-8181 Fax: (304) 599-4866

PARKERSBURG   WV

Econo Lodge $-$$
I-77 at US 50, Parkersburg,
WV 26101, Res. (800)
424-4777 Ph: (304) 422-5401
Fax: (304) 422-5418

PHILIPPI   WV

Super 8 Motel $-$$
Rt 250 South, Philippi, WV
26416, Res. (800) 800-8000
Ph: (304) 457-5888

PRINCETON   WV

Super 8 Motel $-$$
901 Oakvale Rd., P.O. Box
5473, Princeton, WV 24740,
Res. (800) 800-8000 Ph: (304)
487-6161 Fax: (304) 487-9785

RIPLEY   WV

Econo Lodge $-$$
1 Hospitality Dr., Ripley, WV
25271, Res. (800) 424-4777
Ph: (304) 372-5000 Fax: (304)
372-5600

Super 8 Motel $-$$
102 Duke Dr., Ripley, WV
25271, Res. (800) 800-8000
Ph: (304) 372-8880 Fax: (304)
372-8880

S. MARTINSBURG   WV

Scottish Inns $$
1024 Winchester Ave., S.
Martinsburg, WV 25401,
Res. (800) 251-1962 Ph: (304)
267-2935 Fax: (304) 267-2935

SUMMERSVILLE   WV

Super 8 Motel $-$$
306 Merchants Walk,
Summersville, WV 26651,
Res. (800) 800-8000 Ph: (304)
872-4888 Fax: (304) 872-4888

WESTON   WV

Super 8 Motel $-$$
12 Market Place, Weston,
WV 26452, Res. (800)
800-8000 Ph: (304) 269-1086
Fax: (304) 269-1086

WISCONSIN

ANTIGO   WI

Super 8 Motel $-$$
535 Century Avenue, Antigo,
WI 54409, Res. (800)
800-8000 Ph: (715) 623-4188
Fax: (715) 623-5787

APPLETON   WI

Super 8 Motel $-$$
3624 W. College Ave.,
Appleton, WI 54914-3914,
Res. (800) 800-8000 Ph: (414)
731-0880 Fax: (414) 731-0880

ASHLAND   WI

Super 8 Motel $-$$
1610 W. Lakeshore Drive,
Ashland, WI 54806, Res.
(800) 800-8000 Ph: (715)
682-9377 Fax: (715) 682-5593

BEAVER DAM   WI

Super 8 Motel $-$$
711 Park Avenue, Beaver
Dam, WI 53711, Res. (800)
800-8000 Ph: (414) 887-8880
Fax: (414) 887-8880

BELOIT   WI

Econo Lodge $-$$
2956 Milwaukee Rd., Beloit,
WI 53511, Res. (800)
424-4777 Ph: (608) 364-4000
Fax: (608) 365-2611

Super 8 Motel $-$$
3002 Milwaukee Road, Beloit,
WI 53511, Res. (800)
800-8000 Ph: (608) 365-8680
Fax: (612) 631-0882

BROOKFIELD   WI

Motel 6 $
20300 W Bluemound Rd,
Brookfield, WI 53045, Res.
(800) 466-8356 Ph: 414
786-7337 Fax: 414 789-0510

CHETEK   WI

Super 8 Motel $-$$
115 2nd St., Chetek, WI
54728, Res. (800) 800-8000
Ph: (715) 924-4888

DELAVAN   WI

Super 8 Motel $-$$
518 Borg Road, Delavan, WI
53115, Res. (800) 800-8000
Ph: (414) 728-1700 Fax: (414)
728-1700

DODGEVILLE   WI

Super 8 Motel $-$$
1308 Johns St., Dodgeville,
WI 53533, Res. (800)
800-8000 Ph: (608) 935-3888
Fax: (608) 935-5259

EAU CLAIRE   WI

Super 8 Motel $-$$
6260 Texaco Drive, Eau
Claire, WI 54703, Res. (800)
800-8000 Ph: (715) 874-6888

FOND DU LAC   WI

Super 8 Motel $-$$
391 North Pioneer Road,
Fond Du Lac, WI 54935,
Res. (800) 800-8000 Ph: (414)
922-1088 Fax: (414) 922-1088

FRIENDSHIP   WI

Super 8 Motel $-$$
P.O. Box 72, 204 E.2nd
Street, Friendship, WI
53934, Res. (800) 800-8000
Ph: (609) 339-6869 Fax: (608)
339-3208

FT. ATKINSON   WI

Super 8 Motel $-$$
"205 South Water Street,
East", Ft. Atkinson, WI
53538, Res. (800) 800-8000
Ph: (414) 563-8444 Fax: (414)
563-8444

GERMANTOWN   WI

Super 8 Motel $-$$
N. 96 W. 17490 County Q,
Germantown, WI 53022,
Res. (800) 800-8000 Ph: (414)
255-0880 Fax: (414) 255-0880

GREEN BAY   WI

Motel 6 $
1614 Shawano Ave, Green
Bay, WI 54303, Res. (800)
466-8356 Ph: 414 494-6730
Fax: 414 494-0474

Super 8 Motel $-$$
2868 S. Oneida St., Green
Bay, WI 54304-0061, Res.
(800) 800-8000 Ph: (414)
494-2042 Fax: (414) 494-6959

Villager $-$$
119 N. Monroe Ave, Green
Bay, WI 54301, Res. (800)
328-7829 Ph: (414) 437-0525
Fax: (414) 437-6232

HARTFORD   WI

Super 8 Motel $-$$
1539 E. Sumner St.,
Hartford, WI 53027, Res.
(800) 800-8000 Ph: (414)
673-7431 Fax: (414) 673-3080

HAYWARD   WI

Super 8 Motel $-$$
317 S. Hwy. 27, Hayward, WI
54843, Res. (800) 800-8000
Ph: (715) 634-2646 Fax: (715)
634-2646

HUDSON   WI

Super 8 Motel $-$$
808 Dominion Dr., Hudson,
WI 54016, Res. (800)
800-8000 Ph: (715) 386-8800
Fax: (608) 654-5669

JANESVILLE   WI

Motel 6 $
3907 Milton Ave, Janesville,
WI 53546, Res. (800)
466-8356 Ph: 608 756-1742
Fax: 608 754-4493

Super 8 Motel $-$$
3430 Milton Avenue,
Janesville, WI 53545, Res.
(800) 800-8000 Ph: (608)
756-2040 Fax: (608) 756-2321

KENOSHA   WI

Super 8 Motel $-$$
7601 118th Avenue,
Kenosha, WI 53142-9299,
Res. (800) 800-8000 Ph: (414)
857-7963 Fax: (414) 857-7963

LA CROSSE   WI

Super 8 Motel $-$$
1625 Rose St., La Crosse, WI
54603-2205, Res. (800)
800-8000 Ph: (608) 756-2040
Fax: (608) 781-4366

LAKE DELTON   WI

Motel 6 $
PO Box 935, Fern Dell Rd,
Lake Delton, WI 53940, Res.
(800) 466-8356 Ph: 608
356-3984

LAKE GENEVA   WI

Budget Host Diplomat Motel $
1060 Wells St, Lake Geneva,
WI 53147, Res. (800)
283-4678 Ph: (414) 248-1809

MADISON   WI

Budget Host Aloha Inn $-$$
3177 E Washington,
Madison, WI 53704, Res.
(800) 283-4678 Ph: (608)
249-7667 Fax: (608) 249-7669

Motel 6 $
1754 Thierer Rd, Madison,
WI 53704, Res. (800)
466-8356 Ph: 608 241-8101
Fax: 608 241-0740

Motel 6 $
6402 E Broadway, Madison,
WI 53704, Res. (800)
466-8356 Ph: 608 221-0415
Fax: 608 221-0970

Super 8 Motel $-$$
1602 West Beltline Highway,
Madison, WI 53713, Res.
(800) 800-8000 Ph: (608)
258-8882 Fax: (608) 258-9578

MANITOWOC   WI

Super 8 Motel $-$$
4004 Calumet Ave.,
Manitowoc, WI 54220, Res.
(800) 800-8000 Ph: (414)
684-7841 Fax: (414) 684-8873

MARINETTE   WI

Super 8 Motel $-$$
1508 Marinette Ave.,
Marinette, WI 54143-3102,
Res. (800) 800-8000 Ph: (715)
735-7887 Fax: (715) 735-7455

MARSHFIELD   WI

Super 8 Motel $-$$
1651 N. Central Ave.,
Marshfield, WI 54449, Res.
(800) 800-8000 Ph: (715)
387-2233 Fax: (715) 384-8366

MENOMONIE   WI

Super 8 Motel $-$$
1622 North Broadway,
Menomonie, WI 54751, Res.
(800) 800-8000 Ph: (715)
235-8889 Fax: (715) 384-8366

MERRILL   WI

Super 8 Motel $-$$
3209 E. Main St., Merrill, WI
54452, Res. (800) 800-8000
Ph: (715) 536-6880 Fax: (715)
539-2602

MILWAUKEE   WI

Motel 6 $
5037 S Howell Ave,
Milwaukee, WI 53207, Res.
(800) 466-8356 Ph: 414
482-4414 Fax: 414 482-1089

Super 8 Motel $-$$
5253 South Howell Ave,
Milwaukee, WI 53207, Res.
(800) 800-8000 Ph: (414)
481-8488 Fax: (414) 481-8086

Super 8 Motel $-$$
8698 North Servite Dr.,
Milwaukee, WI 53223, Res.
(800) 800-8000 Ph: (414)
354-5354 Fax: (414) 354-4590

MINOCQUA   **WI**

Super 8 Motel $-$$
PO Box 325, Hwy 51 & 70W,
Minocqua, WI 54548, Res.
(800) 800-8000 Ph: (715)
356-9541 Fax: (715) 358-2152

MONROE   **WI**

Super 8 Motel $-$$
500 6th St., Monroe, WI
53566, Res. (800) 800-8000
Ph: (608) 325-1500 Fax: (608)
325-1500

OSHKOSH   **WI**

Super 8 Motel $-$$
PO Box 3168, Oshkosh, WI
54903-3168, Res. (800)
800-8000 Ph: (414) 426-2885
Fax: (414) 426-5488

OSSEO   **WI**

Budget Host Ten Seven Inn $-$$
1994 E 10th, Osseo, WI
54758, Res. (800) 283-4678
Ph: (715) 597-3114

PARK FALLS   **WI**

Super 8 Motel $-$$
1212 Hwy. 13S, Park Falls,
WI 54552, Res. (800)
800-8000 Ph: (715) 762-3383
Fax: (715) 762-2256

PLATTEVILLE   **WI**

Super 8 Motel $-$$
100 Hwy. 80-81 South,
Platteville, WI 53818, Res.
(800) 800-8000 Ph: (608)
348-8800 Fax: (608) 348-8800

PORTAGE   **WI**

Super 8 Motel $-$$
3000 Pinery Road, Portage,
WI 53818, Res. (800)
800-8000 Ph: (608) 348-8800
Fax: (608) 742-8330

PRAIRIE DU CHIE   **WI**

Super 8 Motel $-$$
"Hwys 18, 35 & 60 South",
Prairie du Chie, WI 53821,
Res. (800) 800-8000 Ph: (608)
326-8777 Fax: (608) 326-4787

RACINE   **WI**

Super 8 Motel $-$$
Highway 20, 7141 Kinzie
Avenue, Racine, WI 53406,
Res. (800) 800-8000 Ph: (414)
884-0486 Fax: (414) 884-0486

REEDSBURG   **WI**

Super 8 Motel $-$$
Highway 33, Reedsburg, WI
53959, Res. (800) 800-8000
Ph: (608) 524-2888 Fax: (608)
524-9658

RHINELANDER   **WI**

Super 8 Motel $-$$
667 West Kemp Street,
Rhinelander, WI 54501, Res.
(800) 800-8000 Ph: (715)
369-5880 Fax: (715) 369-2312

RICE LAKE   **WI**

Super 8 Motel $-$$
2401 South Main, Rice Lake,
WI 54868, Res. (800)
800-8000 Ph: (715) 234-6956
Fax: (715) 234-6956

RICHLAND CENTER   **WI**

Super 8 Motel $-$$
100 Foundry Drive, Richland
Center, WI 53581, Res. (800)
800-8000 Ph: (608) 647-8988

RIVER FALLS   **WI**

Super 8 Motel $-$$
1207 St. Croix St., River
Falls, WI 54022, Res. (800)
800-8000 Ph: (715) 425-8388
Fax: (715) 425-7103

SAUKVILLE   **WI**

Super 8 Motel $-$$
180 South Foster Road,
Saukville, WI 53080, Res.
(800) 800-8000 Ph: (414)
284-9399 Fax: (414) 284-9399

SHAWANO   **WI**

Super 8 Motel $-$$
211 Waukechon St.,
Shawano, WI 54166, Res.
(800) 800-8000 Ph: (715)
526-6688 Fax: (715) 526-6290

SHEBOYGAN   **WI**

Super 8 Motel $-$$
3402 Wilgus Rd., Sheboygan,
WI 53081-3408, Res. (800)
800-8000 Ph: (414) 458-8080

SPARTA   **WI**

Super 8 Motel $-$$
716 Avon Avenue, Sparta,
WI 54656, Res. (800)
800-8000 Ph: (608) 372-9030
Fax: (608) 269-8449

STEVENS PT   **WI**

Super 8 Motel $-$$
247 N. Division St, Stevens
Pt, WI 54481, Res. (800)
800-8000 Ph: (715) 341-8888

STURGEON BAY   **WI**

Super 8 Motel $-$$
409 Green Bay Rd, Sturgeon
Bay, WI 54235, Res. (800)
800-8000 Ph: (414) 743-9211
Fax: (414) 743-4143

SUN PRAIRIE   **WI**

Super 8 Motel $-$$
1033 Emerald Terrace, Sun
Prairie, WI 53590-2036, Res.
(800) 800-8000 Ph: (608)
837-8889

SUPERIOR   **WI**

Super 8 Motel $-$$
4901 E. 2nd, Superior, WI
54880, Res. (800) 800-8000
Ph: (715) 398-7686 Fax: (715)
398-7686

TOMAH   **WI**

Budget Host Daybreak Motel $-$$
Hwys 12 & 16E, Tomah, WI
54660, Res. (800) 283-4678
Ph: (608) 372-5946 Fax: (608)
372-5947

Econo Lodge $-$$
2005 N. Superior, Tomah, WI
54660, Res. (800) 424-4777
Ph: (608) 372-9100 Fax: (608)
372-6003

Super 8 Motel $-$$
P.O. Box 48, Tomah, WI
54660, Res. (800) 800-8000
Ph: (608) 372-3901 Fax: (608)
372-5792

VIROQUA   **WI**

Super 8 Motel $-$$
1325 North Main, Viroqua,
WI 54665, Res. (800)
800-8000 Ph: (608) 637-3100

WASHBURN   **WI**

Super 8 Motel $-$$
Harbor View Drive, Box 626,
Washburn, WI 54891, Res.
(800) 800-8000 Ph: (715)
373-5671 Fax: (715) 373-5674

WATERTOWN   **WI**

Super 8 Motel $-$$
1730 S. Church Street,
Watertown, WI 53094, Res.
(800) 800-8000 Ph: (414)
261-1188 Fax: (414) 261-1188

WAUKESHA   **WI**

Super 8 Motel $-$$
2501 Plaza Court, Waukesha,
WI 53186, Res. (800)
800-8000 Ph: (414) 785-1590
Fax: (414) 785-0281

WAUSAU   **WI**

Super 8 Motel $-$$
2006 West Stewart Avenue,
Wausau, WI 54401, Res.
(800) 800-8000 Ph: (715)
848-2888 Fax: (715) 842-9578

WAUTOMA   **WI**

Super 8 Motel $-$$
PO Box 578, Wautoma, WI
54982, Res. (800) 800-8000
Ph: (414) 787-4811 Fax: (414)
787-4305

M O T E L

WEST BEND   WI

Super 8 Motel $-$$
2433 W. Washington St.,
West Bend, WI 53095, Res.
(800) 800-8000 Ph: (414)
335-6788 Fax: (414) 335-6788

WHITEWATER   WI

Super 8 Motel $-$$
917 E. Milwaukee St.,
Whitewater, WI 53190, Res.
(800) 800-8000 Ph: (414)
473-8818

WINDSOR   WI

Super 8 Motel $-$$
I-90/94 & Highway 19, 4506
Lake Circle, Windsor, WI
53598, Res. (800) 800-8000
Ph: (608) 846-3971 Fax: (608)
846-9061

WISCONSIN DELLS   WI

Super 8 Motel $-$$
800 County Highway, P.O.
Box 467, Wisconsin Dells,
WI 53965, Res. (800)
800-8000 Ph: (608) 254-6464
Fax: (608) 254-2692

WISCONSIN RAPID   WI

Super 8 Motel $-$$
3410 8th St S, Wisconsin
Rapid, WI 54494, Res. (800)
800-8000 Ph: (715) 423-8080

WYOMING

BUFFALO   WY

Econo Lodge $-$$
333 Hart St., Buffalo, WY
82834, Res. (800) 424-4777
Ph: (307) 684-2219

Super 8 Motel $-$$
655 East Hart Street,
Buffalo, WY 82834, Res.
(800) 800-8000 Ph: (307)
684-2531

CASPER   WY

Motel 6 $
1150 Wilkins Cir, Casper, WY
82601, Res. (800) 466-8356
Ph: 307 234-3903 Fax: 307
234-8359

Super 8 Motel $-$$
3838 Cy Ave., Casper, WY
82604, Res. (800) 800-8000
Ph: (307) 266-3480

CHEYENNE   WY

Motel 6 $
1735 Westland Rd,
Cheyenne, WY 82001, Res.
(800) 466-8356 Ph: 307
635-6806 Fax: 307 638-3017

Super 8 Motel $-$$
1900 W. Lincolnway,
Cheyenne, WY 82001-3316,
Res. (800) 800-8000 Ph: (307)
635-8741 Fax: (307) 635-8741

CODY   WY

Super 8 Motel $-$$
730 Yellowstone Road, Cody,
WY 82414, Res. (800)
800-8000 Ph: (307) 527-6214
Fax: (305) 525-5127

DOUGLAS   WY

Super 8 Motel $-$$
314 Russell Ave., Douglas,
WY 82633-2306, Res. (800)
800-8000 Ph: (307) 358-6800
Fax: (307) 358-6800

DUBOIS   WY

Super 8 Motel $-$$
Hwy 287 Warm Springs
Addition, Dubois, WY
82513, Res. (800) 800-8000
Ph: (307) 455-3694

EVANSTON   WY

Motel 6 $
261 Bear River Drive,
Evanston, WY 82930, Res.
(800) 466-8356 Ph: 307
789-0791 Fax: 307 789-6156

Super 8 Motel $-$$
70 Bear River Drive,
Evanston, WY 82930, Res.
(800) 800-8000 Ph: (307)
789-7510 Fax: (307) 789-1200

GILLETTE   WY

Motel 6 $
2105 Rodgers Dr, Gillette,
WY 82716, Res. (800)
466-8356 Ph: 307 686-8600
Fax: 307 682-1938

Super 8 Motel $-$$
208 South Decker Court,
Gillette, WY 82716, Res.
(800) 800-8000 Ph: (307)
682-8078 Fax: (307) 682-8078

GREEN RIVER   WY

Super 8 Motel $-$$
280 West Flaming Gorge,
Green River, WY
82935-4105, Res. (800)
800-8000 Ph: (307) 875-9330

JACKSON   WY

Motel 6 $
600 S Hwy 89, Jackson, WY
83001, Res. (800) 466-8356
Ph: 307 733-1620 Fax: 307
734-9175

JACKSON HOLE   WY

Super 8 Motel $-$$
1520 Houth Hwy. 89, P.O.
Box 1382, Jackson Hole, WY
83001-1382, Res. (800)
800-8000 Ph: (307) 733-6833
Fax: (307) 739-1828

LANDER   WY

Budget Host Pronghorn $-$$
150 E Main St, Lander, WY
82520, Res. (800) 283-4678
Ph: (307) 332-3940 Fax: (307)
332-2651

LARAMIE   WY

Motel 6 $
621 Plaza Ln, Laramie, WY
82070, Res. (800) 466-8356
Ph: 307 742-2307 Fax: 307
742-3897

Super 8 Motel $-$$
I-80 & Curtis St., P.O. Box
1284, Laramie, WY 82070,
Res. (800) 800-8000 Ph: (307)
745-8901 Fax: (307) 742-0416

LOVELL   WY

Super 8 Motel $-$$
595 East Main Street, P.O.
Box 235, Lovell, WY 82431,
Res. (800) 800-8000 Ph: (307)
548-2725

POWELL   WY

Super 8 Motel $-$$
845 E. Coulter, Powell, WY
82435, Res. (800) 800-8000
Ph: (307) 754-7231

RAWLINS   WY

Super 8 Motel $-$$
2338 Wagon Circle Rd.,
Rawlins, WY 82301, Res.
(800) 800-8000 Ph: (307)
328-0630 Fax: (307) 328-1814

RIVERTON   WY

Super 8 Motel $-$$
1040 N. Federal Blvd.,
Riverton, WY 82501, Res.
(800) 800-8000 Ph: (307)
857-2400

ROCK SPRINGS   WY

Motel 6 $
2615 Commercial Way, Rock
Springs, WY 82901, Res.
(800) 466-8356 Ph: 307
362-1850 Fax: 307 362-5998

Super 8 Motel $-$$
88 Westland Way, Rock
Springs, WY 82901, Res.
(800) 800-8000 Ph: (307)
362-3800

SHERIDAN   WY

Super 8 Motel $-$$
2435 N. Main St., Sheridan,
WY 82801-9226, Res. (800)
800-8000 Ph: (307) 672-9725

SUNDANCE   WY

Budget Host Arrowhead $-$$
214 Cleveland Box 191,
Sundance, WY 82729, Res.
(800) 283-4678 Ph: (307)
283-3307

THERMOPOLIS   WY

Super 8 Motel $-$$
Us Hgwy 20 S. & Lane 5, P.O.
Box 569, Thermopolis, WY
82443, Res. (800) 800-8000
Ph: (307) 864-5515

REORDER EACH YEAR

Stay up-to-date with the latest edition of the Campus Lodging Guide. Each year, new locations are added and the information on price, availability and services provided is updated. To make your travel dollar go further, special features will focus on free services, deep-discounts, travel bargains, inexpensive alternative lodging, and opportunities for unique vacation experiences.

OUR COLLEGES & UNIVERSITIES

Our book and your use of it provides an important service to the colleges/universities listed. The additional revenues help reduce operational costs, thereby providing more funds for quantity education. Your support is greatly appreciated by each and every school listed herein.

GREAT GIFT IDEA FOR;

- ☞ **Christmas**
- ☞ **Birthday**
- ☞ **Graduation**
- ☞ **Retirement**
- ☞ **Parents**
- ☞ **Grandparents**
- ☞ **Children**
- ☞ **College Students**
- ☞ **Colleagues and Associates**
- ☞ **Friends**

Other Books Available through B&J Publications

The guide for those looking for clean, comfortable and affordable hotels in France.

- Listings for Paris and 20 other cities.
- 482 hotel listings
- Single, double, triple occupancies.
- Directions to hotels.
- What to pack.
- ...and more!

Paperback, 224 pages   Retail Price: $18.95

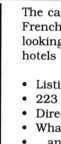

The campanion volume to An Insider's Guide to French Hotels... This is the guide for those looking. for clean, comfortable and affordable hotels in Italy.

- Listings for 33 cities.
- 223 hotel listings
- Directions to hotels.
- What to pack.
- ...and more!

Paperback, 184 pages   Retail Price: $18.95

The newest volume to the Insider's Guide series, for hotels in Spain...This is the guide for those looking for clean, comfortable and affordable hotels in Spain.

- Listings for 23 cities.
- 328 hotel lisings
- Directions to hotels.
- What to pack.
- ...and more!

Paperback, 224 pages   Retail Price: $18.95

A Visitors guide to companies that make some of your favorite products.

The information you need to find factory tours near your home or vacation destination.

Visit nearly 300 factories and company museums across the United States.

Paperback, 295 pages   Retail Price: $17.95

Order Form

Name .... _____

Address .... _____

City, State & Zip ...... _____

Country (if not USA) ...... _____

Phone, E-mail or Fax _____

To be used only if we have a problem with completing your order.

Prices and Quantity Discounts

When ordering more than one book you save $2.00 on each book.

                                                    Qty

Campus Lodging Guide .... $14.95 x _____ = $ _____

French Hotels .... $18.95 x _____ = $ _____

Italian Hotels .... $18.95 x _____ = $ _____

Spain Hotels .... $18.95 x _____ = $ _____

Watch It Made In The U.S.A. $17.95 x _____ = $ _____

Quantity Discount ** .... ($ 2.00) x _____ = $ (_____)

Shipping & Handling (See Chart Reverse Side) .... = $ _____

California Residents add Sales Tax .... = $ _____

Total for Order .... = $ _____

Payment Enclosed ❑ (U.S. Funds only, U.S. Bank Check, Postal money or U.S. Currency)

Charge to my: ❑ Visa ❑ Master Card ❑ Amex. ❑ Discover

Card # _____-_____-_____-_____ Exp. Date___/___

Cardholder's Signature_____

Make Check or Money Order Payable
to

Cut &
Paste ☞
Label

> **B & J Publications**
> **Post Office Box 5486**
> **Fullerton, CA 92838-0486 USA**

or

Call Toll Free (USA only) (800) 525-6633
(714) 525-6683, 8am-5pm PST M-F, Fax: 24 hrs. (714) 525-6625
Website: www.campus-lodging.com
E-mail: bjpubs@campus-lodging.com

Most orders are shipped within 48 hours of receipt

Shipped through U.S. Post Office	First Book	Additional Book	Delivery Time *
USA, Book Rate	$2.00	$.50	1-2 Weeks
USA, First Class	$3.25	$1.10	2-5 Days
Canada, Book Rate	$2.00	$1.00	2-4 Weeks
Canada, Air Mail	$4.00	$2.00	5-10 Days
Mexico, Book Rate	$3.00	$1.00	3-6 Weeks
All Overseas, Book Rate (Surface)	$3.00	$1.00	4-8 Weeks
Europe, Air Mail	$8.00	$6.00	10-15 Days
Asia/Africa, Air Mail	$10.00	$9.00	10-15 Days
Pacific Rim, Air Mail	$10.00	$9.00	10-15 Days

* Delivery time is approximated and will vary by method and final destination.
** To the same address at the same time.

Travel Notes

Travel Notes